Lecture Notes in Computer Science 16933

The series Lecture Notes in Computer Science (LNCS), including its subseries Lecture Notes in Artificial Intelligence (LNAI) and Lecture Notes in Bioinformatics (LNBI), has established itself as a medium for the publication of new developments in computer science and information technology research, teaching, and education.

LNCS enjoys close cooperation with the computer science R & D community, the series counts many renowned academics among its volume editors and paper authors, and collaborates with prestigious societies. Its mission is to serve this international community by providing an invaluable service, mainly focused on the publication of conference and workshop proceedings and postproceedings. LNCS commenced publication in 1973.

Gabriela Viale Pereira · Yannis Charalabidis ·
Evangelos Kalampokis · Ida Lindgren ·
Euripidis Loukis · Marijn Janssen ·
Panos Panagiotopoulos ·
Paula Rodriguez Müller · Efthimios Tambouris ·
Shefali Virkar · Anneke Zuiderwijk
Editors

Electronic Government

25th IFIP WG 8.5 International Conference, EGOV 2026
Athens, Greece, August 30 – September 3, 2026
Proceedings

Springer

Editors
Gabriela Viale Pereira
University for Continuing Education
Krems, Austria

Yannis Charalabidis
University of Aegean
Karlovassi, Greece

Evangelos Kalampokis
University of Macedonia
Thessaloniki, Greece

Ida Lindgren
Linköping University
Linköping, Sweden

Euripidis Loukis
University of Aegean
Karlovassi, Greece

Marijn Janssen
Delft University of Technology
Delft, The Netherlands

Panos Panagiotopoulos
Queen Mary University
London, UK

Paula Rodriguez Müller
Joint Research Center
Brussels, Belgium

Efthimios Tambouris
University of Macedonia
Thessaloniki, Greece

Shefali Virkar
Vienna University of Economics and Busi
Wien, Austria

Anneke Zuiderwijk
Delft University of Technology
Delft, The Netherlands

ISSN 0302-9743 ISSN 1611-3349 (electronic)
Lecture Notes in Computer Science
ISBN 978-3-032-35746-5 ISBN 978-3-032-35747-2 (eBook)
https://doi.org/10.1007/978-3-032-35747-2

This Springer imprint is published by the registered company Springer Nature Switzerland AG
The registered company address is: Gewerbestrasse 11, 6330 Cham, Switzerland

Preface

The EGOV-CeDEM-ePart 2026 conference, for short EGOV 2026, was organized by the IFIP WG 8.5 Information Systems in Public Administration. The conference was dedicated to digital or electronic government, open government, local government (smart cities), smart governance, artificial intelligence (AI), e-democracy, policy informatics, and electronic participation. With a long tradition along its various branches, the EGOV-CeDEM-ePart conference has earned its reputation of being the key and leading conference worldwide in the research domains of digital/electronic, open, and smart government, as well as electronic participation.

The call for papers attracted completed research papers, work-in-progress papers on ongoing research (including doctoral papers), posters, as well as workshops and practitioner papers. This volume contains only full research papers. All submissions were assessed through a double-blind peer-review process, with at least three reviewers per submission, and 27 papers were accepted from 84 submissions, giving an acceptance rate of 32%. The submitted papers were of high quality, and many reviewers indicated that the topics of the papers they reviewed were novel.

The review process was based on a double-blind reviewing process and conflicts of interest were actively avoided. Authors of papers submitted their papers to a track. The track chairs had access only to the papers within their own track and could assign reviewers and propose acceptance decisions. The lead track chairs were editors of the proceedings, in addition to the general chairs. Track chairs were not allowed to submit to their own track, nor were their close collaborators, to avoid any conflict of interest. Track chairs could either submit to another track or to the 'track chairs' track. The latter was handled by one of the general chairs, and these submissions were reviewed in the same way as all other submissions. The general chairs checked after the submission deadline whether there was any conflict of interest among the papers submitted to tracks, and if so, the respective paper was moved to another track. The track chairs checked that all papers were submitted anonymously. If not, the authors were asked to resubmit within a couple of days. Track chairs assigned the reviewers and selected the program committee members in such a way that experts in each area reviewed the papers and there were no conflicts of interest. After at least three reviews were received, the track chairs made a proposal for a decision per paper. The decisions were discussed in a meeting with the general and track chairs to ensure that the decisions were made in a consistent manner across tracks.

This volume includes papers distributed over the following tracks:

- General E-Government and E-Governance
- Emerging Issues and Innovations
- Smart Cities (Government, Districts, Communities and Regions)
- AI, Data Analytics and Automated Decision-Making
- Open Data: Social and Technical Aspects

As in previous years and per the recommendation of the Paper Awards Committee, the IFIP EGOV-CeDEM-ePart 2026 conference granted outstanding paper awards in three distinct categories:

- The most innovative research contribution
- The most compelling critical research reflection
- The most promising practical concept

The winners in each category were announced during the awards ceremony at the conference.

The IFIP EGOV 2026 conference was hosted by the Harokopio University of Athens and the University of the Aegean, Greece. The conference sessions took place at the Harokopio University of Athens.

As part of the conference, the PhD colloquium and the Junior Faculty School were hosted at Harokopio University of Athens. The PhD Colloquium was a full-day event on 30 August, open only to those who were admitted, and offered a limited number of PhD bursaries. The Junior Faculty School was a full-day event on 31 August, for sharing experiences to advance the career of young researchers interested in digitalization and government.

Many people behind the scenes make large events like this conference happen. We would like to thank the members of the Program Committee, the reviewers, and the track chairs for their great efforts in reviewing the submitted papers. We would also like to express our deep gratitude to Teta Stamati, Harokopio University of Athens, and Euripidis Loukis and Yannis Charalabidis, University of the Aegean, for hosting the conference. Last, but not least, we wish to thank Efthimios Tambouris, University of Macedonia, for supporting the local organization.

The papers in these proceedings range from societal to scientific, and from rigorous to innovative. We hope you enjoy reading them!

September 2026

Gabriela Viale Pereira
Yannis Charalabidis
Evangelos Kalampokis
Ida Lindgren
Euripidis Loukis
Marijn Janssen
Panos Panagiotopoulos
Paula Rodriguez Müller
Efthimios Tambouris
Shefali Virkar
Anneke Zuiderwijk

Organization

Conference Chairs

Yannis Charalabidis	University of the Aegean, Greece
Lieselot Danneels	Ghent University, Belgium
David Duenas-Cid	Kozminski University, Poland
Marijn Janssen	Delft University of Technology, The Netherlands
Ida Lindgren	Linköping University, Sweden
Euripidis Loukis	University of the Aegean, Greece
Peter Parycek	Fraunhofer FOKUS, Germany/University for Continuing Education Krems, Austria
Gabriela Viale Pereira	University for Continuing Education Krems, Austria
Gerhard Schwabe	University of Zurich, Switzerland
Teta Stamati	Harokopio University of Athens, Greece
Efthimios Tambouris	University of Macedonia, Greece

Program Committee Chairs

General eGovernment and E-Governance Track

Gabriela Viale Pereira	University for Continuing Education Krems, Austria
Marijn Janssen	Delft University of Technology, The Netherlands
Ida Lindgren	Linköping University, Sweden

General eDemocracy and eParticipation Track

David Duenas-Cid	Kozminski University, Poland
Noella Edelmann	University for Continuing Education Krems, Austria
Marius Rohde Johannessen	University of South-Eastern Norway
Sara Hofmann	University of Agder, Norway

Digital Technologies and Sustainable Development Track

Gianluca Misuraca	Universidad Politécnica de Madrid, Spain
Iryna Susha	Utrecht University, The Netherlands
René Reich	KU Leuven, Belgium
Jolien Ubacht	Delft University of Technology, The Netherlands

Digital Society Track

Leif Sundberg	Mid Sweden University, Sweden
Thomas Lampoltshammer	University for Continuing Education Krems, Austria
Lieselot Danneels	Ghent University, Belgium

Emerging Issues and Innovations Track

A. Paula Rodriguez Müller	Joint Research Centre, European Commission, Spain
Anastasija Nikiforova	Tartu University, Estonia
Francesco Mureddu	Lisbon Council, Belgium

AI, Data Analytics, and Automated Decision-Making Track

Evangelos Kalampokis	University of Macedonia, Greece
Habin Lee	Brunel University of London, UK
Euripidis Loukis	University of the Aegean, Greece

AI Governance and its Societal Challenges Track

Csaba Csáki	Corvinus University of Budapest, Hungary
Gregor Eibl	University for Continuing Education Krems, Austria
Aya Rizk	Linköping University, Sweden
Roel Dobbe	Technical University of Delft, The Netherlands

Smart Cities (Government, Districts, Communities and Regions) Track

Shefali Virkar	WU Vienna University of Economics and Business, Austria
Joep Crompvoets	KU Leuven, Belgium
Manuel Pedro Rodríguez Bolívar	University of Granada, Spain

Open Data: Social and Technical Aspects Track

Anneke Zuiderwijk	Delft University of Technology, The Netherlands
J. Ramon Gil-Garcia	University at Albany, State University of New York, USA
Efthimios Tambouris	University of Macedonia, Greece

Governance, Digital Legislation, and Policy Track

Edimara Mezzomo Luciano	Pontifical Catholic University of Rio Grande do Sul, Brazil
Peter Parycek	Fraunhofer FOKUS, Germany
Anna-Sophie Novak	University for Continuing Education Krems, Austria

Managing E-Government Track

Michael Koddebusch	ERCIS, University of Münster, Germany
Ulrik Bisgaard Ulsrod Røhl	Copenhagen Business School, Denmark
Maria A. Wimmer	University of Koblenz, Germany
Vera Spitzer	University of Koblenz, Germany

Practitioners - Researchers Collaboration Track

Lucy Temple	University for Continuing Education Krems, Austria
Ulf Melin	Linköping University, Sweden
Anthony Simonofski	University of Namur, Belgium

PhD Colloquium Chairs

Lieselot Danneels	Ghent University, Belgium
Michael Koddebusch	University of Münster, Germany
Gabriela Viale Pereira	University for Continuing Education Krems, Austria
Ramon Gil-Garcia	University at Albany, USA

Junior Faculty School Chairs

Lieselot Danneels	Ghent University, Belgium
Ramon Gil-Garcia	University at Albany, USA
Ida Lindgren	Linköping University, Sweden
Gabriela Viale Pereira	University for Continuing Education Krems, Austria

Workshops and Poster Chairs

Panos Panagiotopoulos	Queen Mary University of London, UK
Ida Lindgren	Linköping University, Sweden

Chair of Outstanding Papers Awards

Manuel Pedro Rodríguez Bolívar	University of Granada, Spain
Noella Edelmann	University for Continuing Education Krems, Austria

Program Committee

Valerie Albrecht	University for Continuing Education Krems, Austria
Cristina Alcaide Muñoz	University of Granada, Spain
Laura Alcaide-Muñoz	University of Granada, Spain
Charalampos Alexopoulos	University of the Aegean, Greece
Eric Andersson	Mid Sweden University, Sweden
Gunnar Auth	HSF Meissen University of Applied Sciences, Germany

Thiago Ávila	FGV's São Paulo School of Business Administration, Brazil
Cilia Baanstra	Delft University of Technology, Netherlands
Frank Bannister	Trinity College Dublin, Ireland
Ana Alice Baptista	University of Minho, Portugal
Lais Barbudo Carrasco	Mid Sweden University, Sweden
Luca Tom Bauer	Universität Bremen, Germany
Till Becker	University of Applied Sciences Emden/Leer, Germany
Iris Beerepoot	Utrecht University, Netherlands
Ramin Behbehani	Brunel University of London, UK
Peter Bellström	Karlstad University, Sweden
Flavia Bernardini	Universidade Federal Fluminense, Brazil
Lasse Berntzen	University of South-Eastern Norway, Norway
Nitesh Bharosa	Delft University of Technology, Netherlands
Ellinor Blom Lussi	Lund University, Sweden
Nicolas Bono Rossello	University of Namur, Belgium
Maria Booth	Linköping University, Sweden
Luzia Borgmann	RWTH Aachen University, Germany
Stylianos Bourmpoulias	University of Macedonia, Greece
Ida Bring Løberg	Norwegian Directorate of Labor and Welfare, Norway
Karin Brodén	Umeå University, Sweden
Peter André Busch	University of Agder, Norway
Eric Börner	TU Dresden, Germany
Luiz Paulo Carvalho	Federal University of Rio de Janeiro, Brazil
Cesar Casiano Flores	University of Twente, Netherlands
Seong Wook Chae	Hoseo University, South Korea
Letizia Chiappini	University of Twente, Netherlands
Antoine Clarinval	Umeå University, Sweden
Andreiwid Correa	Federal Institute of Sao Paulo, Brazil
Ilaria Crivellari	Norwegian University of Science and Technology, Norway
Joep Crompvoets	KU Leuven, Belgium
Matheus Cruz	Universidade Federal Fluminense, Brazil
Csaba Csaki	Corvinus University of Budapest, Hungary
Frank Danielsen	University of Agder, Norway
Lieselot Danneels	Ghent University/Vlerick Business School, Belgium
Lukas Daßler	Technische Universität München, Germany
Rosanna De Rosa	University of Naples Federico II, Italy
Simon Dechamps	University of Namur, Belgium

Roel Dobbe	Delft University of Technology, Netherlands
David Duenas-Cid	Kozminski University, Poland
Matthias Döring	University of Southern Denmark, Denmark
Noella Edelmann	Danube University Krems, Austria
Gregor Eibl	Danube University Krems, Austria
Eiri Elvestad	University of South-Eastern Norway, Norway
Maurus Enbergs	Delft University of Technology, Netherlands
Marie Eneman	University of Gothenburg, Sweden
Tove Engvall	Mid Sweden University, Sweden
Melanie Fink	University of Leiden, Netherlands
Fotios Fitsilis	Hellenic Parliament, Greece
Ana Mônica Fitz De Oliveira	Federal University of Rio Grande do Sul, Brazil
Steffen Fock	University of Bremen, Germany
Mary Francoli	Carleton University, Canada
Robin Fritzsche	Universität Bremen, Germany
Asbjørn Følstad	SINTEF, Norway
Alexandros Gerontas	University of Macedonia, Greece
J. Ramon Gil-Garcia	University at Albany, USA
Dimitris Gouscos	University of Athens, Greece
Kathleen Gregory	Leiden University, The Netherlands
Anushri Gupta	Indian Institute of Management, Ahmedabad, India
Stephan Haller	Bern University of Applied Sciences, Germany
Sofia Hamberg	Linköping University, Sweden
Shengnan Han	Stockholm University, Sweden
Ida Heggertveit	University of Agder, Norway
Andreas Hein	Technical University of Munich, Germany
Erica Hellmer	Mid Sweden University, Sweden
Sara Hofmann	University of Agder, Norway
Syed Sajid Hussain	Norwegian University of Science and Technology, Norway
Quan Huynh	Eindhoven University of Technology, Netherlands
Charlotte Högberg	Lund University, Sweden
Helena Iacobaeus	Linköping University, Sweden
Tupokigwe Isagah	UNU-EGOV, Portugal
Tomasz Janowski	Gdańsk University of Technology, Poland
Marijn Janssen	Delft University of Technology, Netherlands
Carlos E. Jimenez-Gomez	National Center for State Courts, USA
Marius Rohde Johannessen	University of South-Eastern Norway, Norway
Gideon Mekonnen Jonathan	Stockholm University, Sweden
Ina Jäger	Technical University of Munich, Germany
Evangelos Kalampokis	University of Macedonia, Greece

Niyazi Karabulut	Middle East Technical University, Türkiye
Nikos Karacapilidis	University of Patras, Greece
Evika Karamagioli	Paris 8 University, France
Areti Karamanou	University of Macedonia, Greece
Martin Karlsson	Mälardalen University, Sweden
Singara Rao Karna	Centre for Electronic Government and Open Democracy, Australia
Muhammad Irfan Khalid	University of Agder, Norway
Junchul Kim	Brunel University of London, UK
Sana Kiran	Maynooth University, Ireland
Fabian Kirstein	Fraunhofer FOKUS, Germany
Michael Koddebusch	University of Münster, Germany
Niklas Korte	University of Münster, Germany
Hun-Yeong Kwon	Korea University, South Korea
Thomas Lampoltshammer	University for Continuing Education Krems, Austria
Habin Lee	Brunel University of London, UK
Hong Joo Lee	Catholic University of Korea, South Korea
Kristina Lemmer	University of Siegen, Germany
Azi Lev-On	Ariel University, Israel
Yanliu Lin	Utrecht University, Netherlands
Ida Lindgren	Linköping University, Sweden
Johan Linåker	RISE Research Institutes of Sweden, Sweden
Martin Lnenicka	University of Hradec Králové, Czech Republic
Carolina Lopes	Pontifical Catholic University of Rio Grande do Sul, Brazil
Francisco J. Lopez-Pellicer	University of Zaragoza, Spain
Euripidis Loukis	University of the Aegean, Greece
Durval Lucas Jr.	Federal University of São Paulo, Brazil
Edimara Luciano	Pontifical Catholic University of Rio Grande do Sul, Brazil
Luis F. Luna-Reyes	University at Albany, SUNY, USA
Marie Anne Macadar	Federal University of Rio de Janeiro, Brazil
Christian Madsen	IT University of Copenhagen, Denmark
Maria Ioanna Maratsi	University of the Aegean, Greece/Stockholm University, Sweden
Amal Marzouki	Université du Québec à Rimouski, Canada
John McNutt	University of Delaware, USA
Ulf Melin	Linköping University, Sweden
Nimród Mike	Corvinus University of Budapest, Hungary
Petar Milić	University in Priština - Kosovska Mitrovica, Kosovo

Gianluca Carlo Misuraca	Politecnico di Milano, Italy
Catherine Mkude	Open University of Tanzania, Tanzania
Antonio Molin	University of Gothenburg, Sweden
José María Moreno-Jiménez	Universidad de Zaragoza, Spain
Daria Morozova	University of Leiden, The Netherlands
Francesca Morselli	Vrije University Amsterdam, The Netherlands
Solange Mukamurenzi	Linköping University, Sweden
Francesco Mureddu	Lisbon Council, Belgium
Binh An Patrick Nguyen	German University of Administrative Sciences Speyer/University of Münster, Germany
Matteo Nicolosi	Inspiring Futures Europe, Italy
Jeppe Agger Nielsen	Aalborg University, Denmark
Anastasija Nikiforova	University of Tartu, Estonia
Sem Nouws	Delft University of Technology, Netherlands
Anna-Sophie Novak	University for Continuing Education Krems, Austria
David Nowak	University of Münster, Germany
Vanessa Nunes	Inteli Leadership and Technology Institute, Brazil
Amizan Omar	University of Bradford, UK
Panos Panagiotopoulos	Queen Mary University of London, UK
Changwon Park	Brunel University of London, UK
Peter Parycek	University for Continuing Education Krems, Austria
Isabell Peters	TH Wildau Germany
Ismael Peña-López	Universitat Oberta de Catalunya, Spain
Willem Pieterson	Center for eGovernment Studies, The Netherlands
Gerti Pishtari	University for Continuing Education Krems, Austria
Celine Poppe	University of Münster, Germany
Andriana Prentza	University of Piraeus, Greece
Gyula Pál	Corvinus University of Budapest, Hungary
Barbara Re	University of Camerino, Italy
René Reich	KU Leuven, Belgium
Hajo A. Reijers	Utrecht University, Netherlands
Silvia Ribeiro	Federal University of Rio de Janeiro, Brazil
Aya Rizk	Linköping University, Sweden
Nina Rizun	Gdańsk University of Technology, Poland
A. Paula Rodriguez Müller	Joint Research Centre - European Commission, Spain
Manuel Pedro Rodríguez Bolívar	University of Granada, Spain
Ulrik B. U. Roehl	Copenhagen Business School, Denmark
Daniel Rudmark	Swedish National Road and Transport Research Institute, Sweden

Bruce Ryan	Edinburgh Napier University, UK
Michael Räckers	University of Münster, Germany
Igor Sampaio	Universidade Federal Fluminense, Brazil
Caterina Santoro	KU Leuven, Belgium
Dwi Sari	SUNY Albany, USA
Diogo Sasdelli	University for Continuing Education Krems, Austria
Antonia Sattlegger	Delft University of Technology, The Netherlands
Sven Schade	Joint Research Centre - European Commission, Italy
Michaela Schmidt	Norwegian University of Science and Technology, Norway
Johannes Schneider	University of Liechtenstein, Liechtenstein
Hendrik Scholta	Universität Speyer, Germany
Johannes Scholz	University of Salzburg Austria
Luiza Schuch de Azambuja	Tallinn University of Technology, Estonia
Gerhard Schwabe	Zurich University, Switzerland
Timon Sengewald	FAU Erlangen-Nürnberg, Germany
Uwe Serdült	Ritsumeikan University, Japan
Ashraf Shaharudin	Delft University of Technology, The Netherlands
Tobias Siebenlist	Rhine-Waal University of Applied Sciences, Germany
Anthony Simonofski	Université de Namur, Belgium
Emyana Sirait	Delft University of Technology, The Netherlands
Søren Skaarup	IT University of Copenhagen, Denmark
Erik Slingerland	HU University of Applied Sciences Utrecht, The Netherlands
Kari Smolander	Lappeenranta-Lahti University of Technology, Finland
Juliano Soares	Lappeenranta-Lahti University of Technology,Finland
Carl-Johan Sommar	Linköping University, Sweden
Vera Spitzer	Universität Koblenz, Germany
Janick Spycher	University of Fribourg, Switzerland
Per Steiner	Mid Sweden University, Sweden
Stefan Stepanovic	Université de Lausanne, Switzerland
Leif Sundberg	Mid Sweden University, Sweden
Anneli Sundqvist	Oslo Metropolitan University, Norway
Iryna Susha	Örebro University, Sweden
Dimitris Symeonidis	University of Tartu, Estonia
Iraklis Symeonidis	RISE Research Institutes of Sweden, Sweden
Øystein Sæbø	University of Agder, Norway
Efthimios Tambouris	University of Macedonia, Greece

Evrim Tan	KU Leuven, Belgium
Luca Tangi	Joint Research Centre - European Commission, Italy
Lucy Temple	University for Continuing Education Krems, Austria
Sara Thabit-Gonzalez	Joint Research Centre - European Commission, Estonia
Malin Tinjan	University of Gothenburg, Sweden
Hsien-Lee Tseng	National University of Tainan, Taiwan
Bernát Török	University of Public Service - Ludovika, Hungary
Jolien Ubacht	Delft University of Technology, The Netherlands
Louise van der Peet	Delft University of Technology, The Netherlands
Colin van Noordt	KU Leuven, Belgium
Gabriela Viale Pereira	Danube University Krems, Austria
Dulce Villegas	Universität Bremen,Germany
Shefali Virkar	WU Vienna University of Economics and Business, Austria
Gianluigi Viscusi	Linköping University, Sweden
Jose Viterbo	Universidade Federal Fluminense, Brazil
Jörn von Lucke	Zeppelin Universität Friedrichshafen, Germany
Craig Waltz	State University of New York at Albany, USA
Jan Westermann	University of Bremen, Germany
Guilherme Wiedenhöft	Federal University of Rio Grande, Brazil
Elin Wihlborg	Linköping University, Sweden
Moritz Wild	University for Continuing Education Krems, Austria
Maria A. Wimmer	University of Koblenz, Germany
Marc Wyszynski	Universität Bremen, Germany
Alexandros Xenakis	University of the Peloponnese, Greece
Xuan Xia	University of Lausanne, Switzerland
Dujuan Yang	Eindhoven University of Technology, The Netherlands
Liesanth Yde	NirmalarajanAalborg University, Denmark
Thomas Zefferer	A-SIT Plus GmbH, Austria
Dimitris Zeginis	University of Macedonia, Greece
Ying Zhang	Delft University of Technology, The Netherlands
Qinfeng Zhu	University of Groningen, The Netherlands
Anneke Zuiderwijk	Delft University of Technology, The Netherlands

Contents

Dynamic Purchasing Systems: Reference Architecture and Adoption Challenges in Germany

Ali AlMasri(✉), Andreas Schmitz, and Maria A. Wimmer

University of Koblenz, Universitätsstraße 1, 56070 Koblenz, Germany
{Almasriali,andreasschmitz,wimmer}@uni-koblenz.de

Abstract. Dynamic Purchasing Systems (DPS) are recognized within the European Union as flexible and efficient electronic procurement procedures capable of enhancing competition, transparency, and supplier participation. Despite these potentials, DPS adoption remains limited, particularly in Germany with its decentralized federal procurement structure. This paper first examines the current state of research and practice on DPS. Subsequently, it develops a federated DPS architecture tailored to the German public procurement context and identifies the key challenges that hinder DPS adoption. By systematically linking the existing body of knowledge to a concrete architectural design, the study provides both theoretical contributions to the DPS literature and practical guidance for policymakers and procurement practitioners seeking to advance digital public procurement in Germany.

Keywords: Dynamic Purchasing Systems · DPS · public sector e-procurement · challenges · DPS architecture · SMEs

1 Introduction

Public procurement represents a substantial share of governmental costs. It plays a critical role in the efficient and responsible delivery of public services [1, 2]. Consequently, public authorities are under increasing pressure to adopt procurement strategies that enhance efficiency, transparency, and value for money [3]. In response, procurement practices are progressively transitioning toward end-to-end digitalization, leveraging modern and flexible digital solutions [4, 5]. E-procurement systems have demonstrated their potential to streamline purchasing processes and improve collaboration between public buyers and private suppliers [2, 6].

While transformation is recognizable, existing e-procurement practices continue to face persistent challenges [2, 7–11]. Small and medium-sized enterprises (SMEs) often encounter structural and procedural barriers that limit their participation [2, 4, 8, 9] and decrease the level of competition [2, 12, 13]. Confrontational buyer-supplier relationships and narrowly defined award criteria, primarily centered on price, also limit

Published by Springer Nature Switzerland 2027
G. Viale Pereira et al. (Eds.): EGOV 2026, LNCS 16933, pp. 1–18, 2027.
https://doi.org/10.1007/978-3-032-35747-2_1

long-term efficiency and hinder innovation [6, 7]. These limitations highlight the need for more dynamic and inclusive public procurement.

Dynamic Purchasing Systems (DPS) have emerged as a promising approach to address these shortcomings by enabling continuous supplier participation and more flexible tendering processes [2, 6, 8, 9, 14–17]. However, despite successful adoption in several European countries, DPS implementation in Germany remains limited, particularly at the federal level [14].

This paper aims to analyze the current state of research and practice on DPSs and to investigate the potential of Dynamic Purchasing Systems within the German public procurement context. Furthermore, it develops a conceptual understanding of a DPS architecture tailored to the German federal context and systematically identifies the key challenges that hinder DPS adoption. The following research questions guide the study: **RQ1**: What is the current status of research and practice on DPS? **RQ2**: What would be a suitable DPS architecture in Germany? **RQ3**: What are the challenges that hinder DPS adoption in Germany? The main contributions of the study lie in offering a structured analysis of the current state on DPS and related adoption barriers, and in providing a federated reference architecture for DPS implementation in Germany. The paper delivers theoretical insights for researchers, and practical orientation for policymakers, procurement authorities, and system designers in public procurement.

The paper is structured as follows: Sect. 2 outlines the research design. Sections 3 and 4 introduce the regulatory and conceptual foundations of DPS, respectively, and thus answer RQ1. Section 5 presents the proposed DPS reference architecture that addresses RQ2. Section 6 summarizes the challenges that hinder DPS adoption in Germany, addressing RQ3. Section 7 discusses the findings and concludes the paper.

2 Research Methodology and Design

We adopt the Design Science Research (DSR) paradigm of Hevner et al. [18] and its operationalization through the six-step Design Science Research Methodology (DSRM) developed by Peffers et al. [19]. The DSR approach is appropriate because the primary objective of this research is to develop a federated DPS reference architecture as innovative IT artifact, while also contributing to theoretical knowledge regarding DPS adoption challenges. In line with DSR, the paper is structured around the three interdependent cycles of rigor, relevance, and design [18].

The rigor cycle is realized through a systematic literature review conducted in accordance with Kitchenham's guidelines [20], and the concept-centric synthesis of Webster and Watson [21]. Searches are performed in JSTOR and Google Scholar using DPS-related keywords and Boolean combinations as shown in Table 1. To ensure comprehensiveness, backward and forward citation tracking is applied [21]. The literature review includes academic publications, EU procurement directives, DPS guidelines, legislative texts, and authoritative reports. Only English-language sources published between 2001 and 2024 are considered. After a structured screening process (title, abstract, and full-text review), 31 sources are selected and assessed for methodological quality and relevance. The results of the rigor cycle synthesis are reflected in Sects. 3 and 4, answering RQ1. This ensures that the artifacts are grounded in established research and policy frameworks.

Table 1. Literature search stages and Keywords used from identification to inclusion

Database/Search Engine	Search Keywords Used	Initial Hits	After Duplicate Removal	After Title & Abstract Screening	Final Included Literature
JSTOR	("DPS" OR "Dynamic purchasing systems "AND "public procurement" OR "SME Challenges" OR "Central Purchasing bodies")	27	17	9	2
Google Scholar	"DPS" AND "e-procurement" AND "EU" OR "SME" AND "challenges" OR "public procurement" AND "DPS"	206	110	30	14
Manual addition via Google Scholar	Backward/forward citations, grey literature (guidelines, reports, laws)	–	–	–	15
Total		**233**	**127**	**39**	**31**

In the relevance cycle, insights are derived from institutional requirements, regulatory conditions, and stakeholder expectations specific to the German context. These are collected by studying relevant legal and institutional policies and regulations along desk research [22] and by conducting expert interviews with representatives of public procurement agencies. The legal constraints and organizational roles are then translated into functional and non-functional requirements, following [23, 24], which inform the system's structural design of the design cycle. These requirements are iteratively refined and aligned with EU procurement directives and Germany's decentralized governance structure to ensure contextual coherence and practical applicability.

Two semi-structured expert interviews were conducted on May 21, 2025, and June 5, 2025 to identify stakeholder-specific requirements and expectations for the implementation of a DPS in Germany, following a qualitative expert interview methodology [25]. These domain experts possess extensive experience in digital infrastructure, public procurement processes, and governmental procurement systems within the German context. The interviews focused on institutional, legal, organizational, and technical aspects relevant to DPS implementation. The collected insights contributed directly to the development and refinement of the proposed DPS architecture by identifying practical requirements, governance considerations, interoperability needs, and implementation challenges, thereby strengthening the practical relevance and contextual alignment of the research findings.

The design cycle is implemented by applying a structured architectural development approach across three interrelated layers: business, application, and technology [3, 26]. It integrates insights from the rigor and relevance cycles to iteratively refine the artifacts and derive structured analytical outputs. Requirements engineering principles [23, 24] are applied to formalize the stakeholder requirements and ensure traceability between identified needs and architectural components of the proposed architecture. The first result of the design cycle is the federated DPS reference architecture presented in Sect. 5, which addresses RQ2 and reflects both EU regulatory requirements and Germany's decentralized governance structures.

Through interaction between literature-based findings in the rigor cycle, practical insights into DPS barriers in Germany in the relevance cycle, and architectural design decisions in the design cycle of DSR, the paper also develops a comprehensive challenge matrix (Sect. 6, answering RQ3) to demonstrate how architectural design choices respond directly to empirically identified barriers to DPS adoption.

Evaluation of the DPS architecture is conducted through expert interviews and feedback sessions (2 interview and 3 feedback sessions), which validate the conceptual soundness and contextual feasibility of the proposed architecture. Overall, the paper integrates literature analysis, architectural development and evaluation, and the matrix design within a unified Design Science Research framework, ensuring theoretical foundation, methodological coherence and practical relevance.

3 Regulatory Environment of Dynamic Purchasing Systems

DPS is anchored in a clearly defined legal and regulatory framework that shapes its structure, operation, and implementation within the EU and its Member States. DPS was formally defined in Article 1(6) of Directive 2004/18/EC as a fully electronic procurement process for commonly used goods and services that are generally available on the market and meet the contracting authority's requirements [27]. The system remains open throughout its validity to any economic operator that satisfies the selection criteria and submits a compliant indicative tender [14, 27]. Importantly, this definition clarifies that DPS does not refer to a specific software solution but rather to an electronically supported procurement procedure [14, 27].

DPS was introduced into the EU procurement framework already in 2004 (see Table 2), recognizing its potential to increase competition and streamline public purchasing by reducing time and costs [14, 27, 28]. Under the 2004 directives, contracting authorities were required to establish DPS using the open procedure and to publish relevant notices in the Official Journal of the European Union [27, 28]. Yet, this procedural complexity and administrative burden limited widespread adoption.

A major reform occurred with the adoption of Directive 2014/24/EU and Directive 2014/25/EU, which substantially simplified and clarified the legal framework governing DPS [29, 31]. Article 34 of Directive 2014/24/EU redefined DPS as a procurement procedure based on the restricted procedure with no limitation on the number of suppliers

[31]. The revised framework expanded the scope of DPS to include works, services, and supplies, allowed for open-ended durations, enabled lot-based structuring, and simplified supplier admission through rolling entry mechanisms [14–16, 29, 30]. These changes significantly enhanced transparency, competition, and accessibility, particularly for SMEs [14–16, 30].

Table 2. Evolution of DPS from Directive 2004/18/EC to Directive 2014/24/EU

Feature	Directive 2004/18/EC	Directive 2014/24/EU	Implications
Introduction of DPS	First introduced as a procurement tool (Art. 1(6)) [27]	Retained and further detailed (Art. 34) [29]	DPS was created as a legitimate substitute for conventional procurement methods [14, 29]
Digital Requirement	Required to be fully electronic, but no technical guidance provided [27]	Strong emphasis on e-procurement; clarified digital procedures and interoperability [29]	Facilitated wider adoption by improving legal and technical clarity [14, 15]
Procedure	Open Procedure [27]	Restricted Procedure with no limitation of the number of suppliers [29]	Increase competition and transparency [14–16]
Scope of Use	Restricted to commonly used, off-the-shelf goods and services [27]	Extended to works, services, and supplies, including complex needs [29]	Enabling use in diverse sectors [14, 15]
Duration	No fixed time limits; in practice often short-term [27]	Explicitly allows open-ended duration [29]	Enables more strategic, long-term procurement planning [16, 30]
Admission of Suppliers	Open to new suppliers throughout, but process was hard and heavy [27]	Simplified admission with rolling entry; suppliers can join at any time if they meet criteria [29]	Increased competition and flexibility for SMEs [14–16, 30]
Use of Lots	Not explicitly addressed in DPS context [27]	DPS can be divided into lots [29]	Promotes participation of SMEs and specialization within DPS [14–16, 30]
Transparency & Reporting	Minimal provisions [27]	Increased transparency obligations and reporting requirements [29]	Enhances accountability and public trust [14, 16, 30]

Operationally, DPS is implemented through a two-stage process [14]. The first stage focuses on establishing the system and on pre-qualifying suppliers using standardized documentation such as the European Single Procurement Document (ESPD), allowing suppliers to join or reapply throughout the system's lifetime [14, 29]. The second stage involves the management of the DPS through mini competitions among qualified suppliers for specific contracts, ensuring equal treatment, flexibility in specifications, and rapid procurement cycles [6, 14, 16, 17, 32]. The regulatory evolution of DPS within the EU establishes its legal framework.

4 Conceptual Foundations of Dynamic Purchasing Systems

Public procurement has undergone a substantial transformation, shifting from traditional paper-based procedures toward increasingly digitalized systems [1, 33]. This evolution reflects a growing emphasis on efficiency, transparency, and innovation in procurement practices [33]. Within this context, e-procurement has emerged as a cornerstone of modern public procurement, particularly in the European Union, where regulatory frameworks mandate the use of electronic systems across procurement activities [34]. E-procurement encompasses the digital execution of key processes such as tendering, supplier registration, contract management, and communication, enabling automation, real-time transparency, and improved accessibility [34, 35].

The adoption of e-procurement delivers significant benefits, including reduced administrative costs, shorter procurement cycles, enhanced competition, and improved participation of small and medium-sized enterprises (SMEs) [34, 36]. Building on this digital foundation, advanced mechanisms such as DPS, e-catalogues, and e-auctions have gained prominence [4, 5]. In particular, DPS extends the capabilities of e-procurement by enabling continuous supplier participation, increasing market openness, fostering competition, reducing lead times, and further strengthening SME inclusion [2, 5, 6, 8, 9, 17, 30]. As such, DPS represents a natural progression of digital public procurement and a key instrument for achieving more flexible and inclusive procurement outcomes.

From a research perspective, the literature on DPS reflects growing scholarly interest, particularly in relation to legal interpretation, cost-effectiveness, and competitive dynamics. Yet, studies also highlight persistent legal ambiguities surrounding DPS procedural rules, including the reassessment of admitted suppliers, the transparency of award notices, and unclear timelines for supplier admission notifications [2, 3, 6, 8, 17]. These uncertainties are frequently cited as factors influencing contracting authorities' reluctance to adopt DPS, indicating that regulatory interpretation remains an active area of discussion in the academic discourse. Empirical research has also examined the economic implications of DPS implementation. Strand et al. report that, while DPS may entail higher administrative and setup costs for contracting authorities, participating firms often experience lower transaction costs [5]. This dual perspective suggests that DPS redistributes procedural burdens rather than uniformly reducing costs, an issue that continues to receive analytical attention. Özbilgin et al. position DPS as a strategic procurement instrument capable of improving spending management, enhancing forecasting accuracy, and supporting performance assessment through real-time information exchange among contracting authorities [6]. The publication demonstrates that research increasingly frames DPS not only as a procurement procedure but as a governance and performance management tool. Literature also consistently differentiates DPS from framework agreements, emphasizing its open and dynamic nature [6, 37]. Unlike framework agreements, DPS allows any economic operator meeting the qualification criteria to join the system at any time, thereby fostering ongoing competition and market openness [6, 37]. This distinction is central concerning competitive intensity and SME participation.

On the implementation and practices level, the growth in DPS adoption within the EU and associated countries is striking, with the total number of DPS implementations rising steadily from 145 in 2016 to 893 in 2020 [14]. This upward trend underscores an increasing recognition of DPS's value in enhancing procurement processes, especially in promoting competition and efficiency [2, 6, 8, 9, 14, 15, 17, 30]. Countries such as the Netherlands, Norway, Sweden, and the Czech Republic demonstrate extensive use, while others like Germany, Bulgaria, and Cyprus show limited adoption [14]. The adoption of DPS in the countries of extensive use led to reduced procurement time, increased competition, and measurable cost savings [14, 15, 30]. To add, successful DPS implementations have led to significant cost savings, such as a 10% reduction in costs [15].

The adoption and implementation of DPS is across different sectors within the EU. Estonia had established 19 DPSs by November 2020 in fields such as spare parts, software development, land surveying, vehicles, and solar panels. Hungary saw 14 DPSs in operation by 2020, mainly for food, healthcare, and IT products [14]. Slovenia also had eight DPSs by 2020, covering areas such as medical equipment, construction, design, geodetic and safety services, and medical waste management [14]. Contracting authorities using DPS in these countries include municipalities, medical centers, public law entities, and infrastructure-related entities. Norway, for instance, demonstrated extensive use through a transport company owned by the municipality of Oslo and Bergen municipality, illustrating how DPS has gained traction across a wide range of sectors in Europe [14].

The above analysis addresses RQ1 by examining current research and practice on DPS. While existing studies provide insights into legal interpretations, economic implications, and competitive effects of DPS, the amount of academic research remains limited. This highlights both the practical relevance of DPS across Europe and the need for more structured academic investigations. Building on the regulatory and conceptual foundations, the following section presents the proposed DPS reference architecture and discusses the resulting design outcomes, answering RQ2.

5 DPS Reference Architecture for Germany

The proposed DPS architecture, shown in Fig. 1 for the qualification of suppliers, and in Fig. 2 for the call for tenders, is grounded in a combination of systematic literature analysis, regulatory and policy review, and expert interviews conducted with practitioners in the fields of public procurement and e-procurement systems. Findings from the literature and interviews were translated into functional and non-functional requirements, which informed the architectural design decisions across the business, application, and technology layers. An overview of these decisions is given in Table 3. In particular, recurring challenges related to implementation complexity, interoperability, supplier participation, governance, and organizational readiness directly shaped the federated structure of the architecture and the allocation of responsibilities between federal services, Central Purchasing Bodies, contracting authorities, and economic operators. The reference architecture adopts a federated two-tier structure that balances centralized coordination with decentralized execution. At the federal level, a national DPS layer is responsible for defining common standards, shared services, and governance mechanisms that ensure interoperability, legal compliance, and consistency across the German procurement landscape. This national layer does not conduct procurement procedures itself; rather, it provides services that support decentralized DPS operations.

Table 3: Traceability Between Research Findings and Architectural Decisions

Architectural Element/Design Decision	Basis from Literature/Interviews	Supporting Sources
Federated DPS structure separating federal and state-level responsibilities	Reflects Germany's decentralized procurement structure and stakeholder requirements identified during expert interviews	Expert interviews
State-level DPS jointly managed by Central Purchasing Bodies (CPBs)	Inspired by the UK procurement marketplace model and DPS guidelines	DPS Guidelines [14]; UK DPS practices [15, 16, 32]
Centralized supplier qualification and validation service	Derived from DPS guidelines emphasizing reusable qualification and simplified supplier onboarding through ESPD	European Commission DPS Guidelines [14]; Directive 2014/24/EU [29]
Shared pool of qualified suppliers across DPS instances	Based on DPS principles of continuous supplier admission and reusable qualification mechanisms	Directive 2014/24/EU [29]; DPS Guidelines [14]; Expert interviews
State-level competition model for suppliers	Introduced to reduce excessive competition and improve SME participation	SME participation literature [2, 12, 38]; DPS Guidelines [14]; Expert interviews
Shared interoperable services and standardized interfaces	Motivated by interoperability and fragmentation challenges in German e-procurement systems	Expert interviews
CPBs acting as operational and competence centers	Derived from literature emphasizing professionalized procurement governance and support structures	DPS Guidelines [14]; UK procurement practices [15, 16, 30, 32, 39]

At the state level, individual DPSs are implemented and operated by Central Purchasing Bodies (CPBs). For modeling clarity, the architecture illustrates one or more CPB per federal state. Yet, CPBs are conceptualized as business actors rather than fixed organizational units. In practice, several German states operate multiple CPBs, often differentiated by sector (e.g., IT or healthcare) or by administrative hierarchy. In the proposed architecture, these CPBs do not operate separate DPS instances; instead, each federal state operates state-level DPS, which will be jointly managed or coordinated by one or more CPBs. Contracting Authorities (CAs) and Economic Operators (EOs) participate in this shared state-level DPS, ensuring a unified entry point per state while maintaining interoperability with federal-level validation and qualification services. This approach aligns with Germany's federal structure, where states retain autonomy over procurement while complying with EU directives governing CPBs.

A key architectural objective is to settle decentralized procurement autonomy with national-level coordination and oversight. This is achieved through shared federal services, most notably a centralized supplier validation and qualification service that qualifies suppliers into a joint pool of quailed suppliers. Suppliers are validated once at the federal level based on standardized criteria, ensuring consistent application of legal and procedural requirements. Once qualified, suppliers may participate in one or more state-level DPS instances without the need for repeated qualification. This design reduces administrative burden for both suppliers and contracting authorities while maintaining compliance with EU procurement laws. At the same time, state-level DPS instances retain control over tendering activities, procurement categories, and operational priorities, allowing adaptation to regional needs and sector-specific requirements.

From a market participation perspective, the proposed federated architecture directly addresses one of the major challenges identified in the literature: limited supplier motivation, particularly among SMEs, in overly competitive procurement environments. A fully centralized national DPS could result in excessively large supplier pools, intensifying competition and discouraging SME participation. The proposed architecture mitigates this risk by maintaining state-level supplier pools, even though suppliers are validated centrally. Suppliers may choose to join DPS instances selectively across states based on strategic relevance, capacity, or regional presence. This structure enhances the perceived attainability of tenders, strengthens SME participation, and preserves competition without compromising openness or transparency.

The DPS architecture is modeled using ArchiMate and structured across three interrelated layers: business, application, and technology. This layered approach ensures traceability from business roles and regulatory requirements down to application services and technical infrastructure. Together, these layers support the two core processes of a DPS: supplier qualification in Fig. 1, and dynamic tendering in Fig. 2. At the business layer, the Economic Operator initiates the process by registering and submitting qualification data, primarily the ESPD. This interaction is supported in the application layer by services such as the supplier profile service through the supplier interface and the qualification management service that qualifies the ESPD through the qualification engine, which orchestrates the validation workflow. At the technology layer, qualification data is processed by validation engines and stored in centralized registries and databases, supported by backup and archival mechanisms to ensure data persistence and

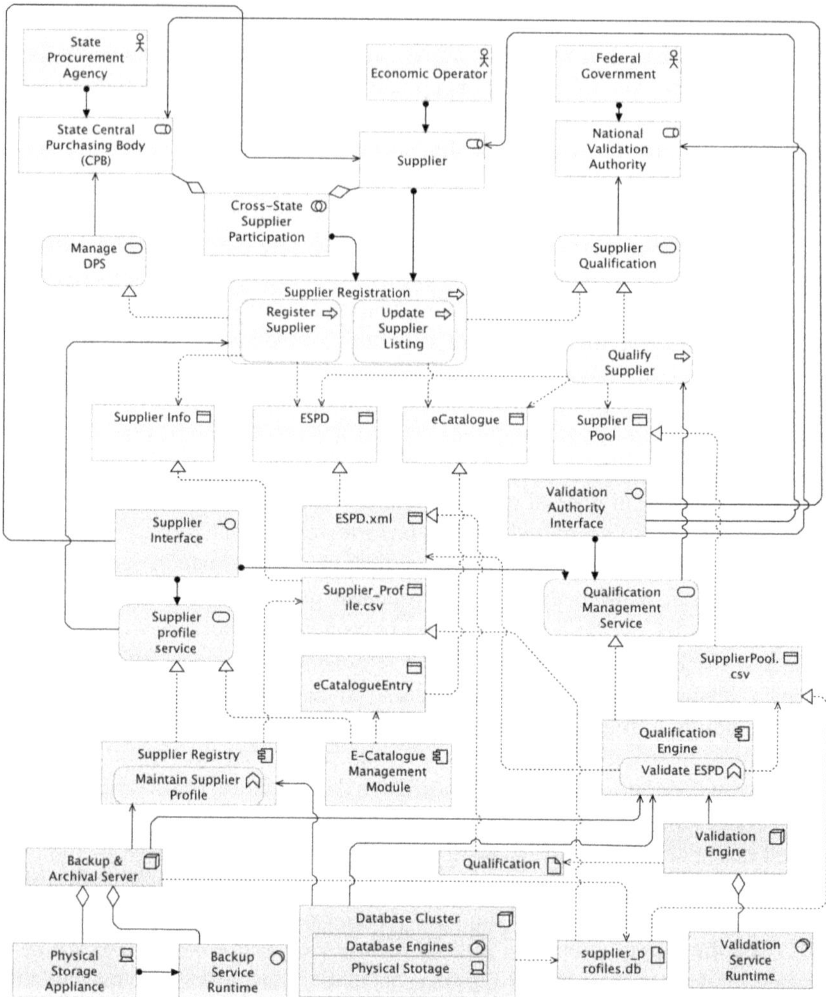

Fig. 1. DPS reference architecture for Supplier Qualification - Integration of layers

fault tolerance. The centralized validation service enables suppliers to be onboarded once and reused across multiple state-level DPS instances, reducing duplication and enhancing interoperability within the federated architecture.

The dynamic tendering stage becomes active once suppliers are successfully qualified and added to the joint pool of suppliers. CAs initiate mini competitions through the DPS portal, interacting with the system via secure authentication and access control mechanisms. Application services such as the tender lifecycle service coordinate core activities, including tender publication, evaluation, and award decisions. Qualified suppliers submit tenders through dedicated supplier interfaces, enabling parallel participation in different state-level DPS instances without requalification. The underlying technology infrastructure, such as authentication server, database cluster, load balancer, and application

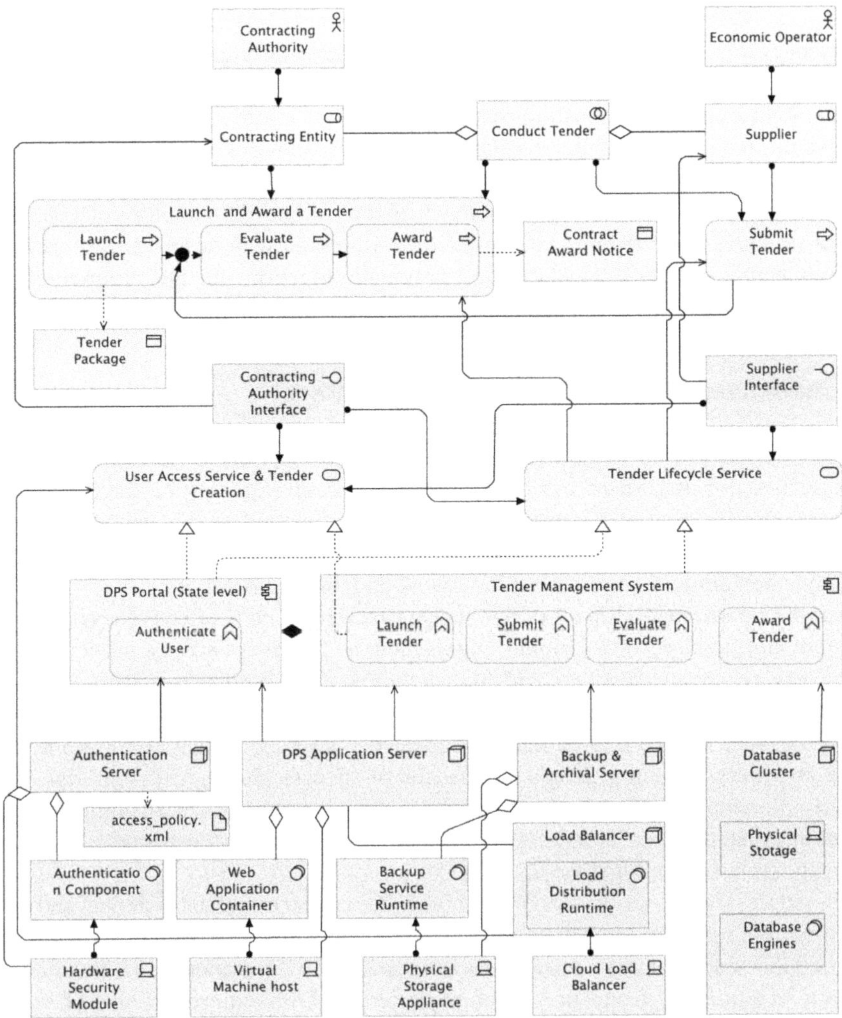

Fig. 2. DPS reference architecture for Call for Tenders - Integration of layers

server ensure scalability, security, and high availability throughout the tender lifecycle. This layered integration translates regulatory and procedural requirements into efficient, executable procurement workflows.

The federated nature of the architecture enhances scalability and resilience. Individual state-level DPS instances can be upgraded, extended, or maintained independently, reducing systemic risk and enabling gradual adoption across jurisdictions. Shared federal services further ensure economies of scale without imposing a uniform technical solution on heterogeneous stakeholders. To sustain these qualities in practice, the architecture supports systematic performance monitoring through key performance indicators (KPIs). Relevant KPIs include system availability and uptime, transaction response times under peak loads, supplier participation rates (particularly SME share), and average procurement cycle times. These indicators can be measured through a combination of automated system monitoring and administrative procurement data, supporting transparency, accountability, and continuous improvement.

Overall, the proposed federated DPS architecture demonstrates how Germany can implement a legally compliant, interoperable, and inclusive Dynamic Purchasing System that aligns with both EU procurement directives and the country's decentralized federal structure. By combining centralized coordination with decentralized execution, the architecture provides a scalable and pragmatic blueprint for DPS implementation and serves as a concrete architectural answer to RQ2.

6 Challenges Hindering Adoption of DPS

Despite the recognized benefits of DPS as outlined in Sects. 3 and 4, the adoption and effective use of DPS across the EU remain uneven. Existing research and policy guidance identify a set of interrelated challenges that extend market-related, technical, organizational, and institutional dimensions, which collectively hinder DPS adoption and implementation as summarized in Table 4 and discussed below.

Supplier participation is a critical success factor for DPS effectiveness. However, literature highlights several supplier engagement and market barriers, particularly perceived low success probability and high administrative burden for SMEs. Suppliers often hesitate to invest time and resources in DPS participation when competition is intense or when contracting authorities repeatedly award contracts to the same established providers, reducing perceived chances of success [2, 14, 15]. This risk is particularly pronounced in markets with many qualified suppliers, where competition can discourage sustained participation [14–16]. As a result, suppliers, especially SMEs, may disengage from DPS altogether [2, 14, 15].

The successful operation of a DPS is highly dependent on robust technical and digital infrastructure. Literature identifies several related challenges, including IT dependency, system failures and data inconsistencies, interoperability limitations, and insufficient IT support. As a fully electronic procurement procedure, DPS requires reliable IT systems, user-friendly interfaces, and continuous technical support [14, 15, 29, 31]. Where such infrastructure is lacking or inadequately maintained, procurement processes may be disrupted by system failures, data inconsistencies, or communication breakdowns [14–16].

Beyond technical infrastructure, knowledge and organizational readiness play a decisive role in DPS adoption. DPS is a relatively specialized procurement instrument, and both CAs and EOs may lack the expertise required to apply best practices effectively [14, 15]. Insufficient training and limited hands-on experience can result in procedural errors, inefficient tender management, and reduced supplier participation [16]. Authorities unfamiliar with DPS may fail to exploit its flexibility, while suppliers may withdraw if the system is perceived as overly complex or opaque [16]. Organizational rigidity further compounds these challenges. Public sector entities may be hesitant to transition from established procurement practices to DPS due to the learning curve associated with new systems and resistance to change in administrative structures [12, 40]. In Germany,

Table 4. Overview of challenges hindering DPS adoption summarized from literature

Category	Challenge	Description	References
Supplier Engagement & Market Barriers	Perceived low success probability	Intense competition discourages supplier participation	[2, 14–16]
	High administrative burden for SMEs	Qualification and compliance requirements push smaller firms and decrease participation	[2, 13, 38]
Technical & Digital Infrastructure	IT dependency	DPS requires fully electronic, reliable, and secure digital systems	[14, 15, 29, 31]
	System failures & data inconsistencies	Weak infrastructure can disrupt procurement workflows	[14–16]
	Interoperability limitations	Fragmented e-procurement platforms complicate integration	[12, 40]
	Insufficient IT support	Lack of technical maintenance and support reduces effectiveness	[6, 14–16]
Knowledge & Organizational Readiness	Limited DPS expertise	CAs and EOs may lack experience in managing DPS procedures	[14–16]
	Insufficient training	Limited hands-on support leads to procedural errors	[12, 14, 15]
	Resistance to change	Organizational rigid hinders transition from traditional procurement	[16, 40]
Implementation Complexity	Administrative burden & governance complexity	DPS setup and operation, managing qualifications, mini-competitions, compliance, and reporting require significant procedural effort and continuous system management that exceed CA capacities	[14–16, 32]
	Legal alignment effort	Alignment with evolving EU directives and national regulations requires expertise	[14, 41]

DPS adoption faces additional institutional and legal barriers. A strong emphasis on compliance, legal certainty, and procedural formalism often results in lengthy and rigid procurement processes that conflict with the flexibility inherent in DPS [40]. These legal and administrative complexities, implementation complexities, have been identified as key factors slowing DPS adoption, particularly at the federal and state levels [40].

Technological fragmentation further limits implementation. Although platforms such as eVergabe[1] have advanced digital procurement, interoperability between systems across administrative levels remains limited, complicating the integration of DPS into the broader e-procurement ecosystem [12, 40]. Market-related barriers disproportionately affect SMEs. In contrast to countries such as the United Kingdom, where DPS has facilitated broader SME inclusion [15, 16, 30, 32], the German procurement market remains dominated by large suppliers [2]. Strict pre-qualification requirements often exceed the administrative or financial capacities of smaller firms [2, 13, 41], while limited training opportunities and awareness further restrict SME participation [12, 14–16, 32]. Additionally, the costs associated with meeting technical, legal, and compliance requirements may discourage SMEs from engaging with DPS [2, 14–16]. Collectively, these barriers reduce competition, limit innovation, and undermine the transformative potential of DPS in public procurement [2, 3, 6, 14–16, 30, 32].

Lastly, the transition to fully digital procurement procedures entails significant technical and organizational adjustments. Establishing a DPS requires substantial administrative effort, investment in IT infrastructure, and alignment with evolving legal frameworks [14]. Studies in the UK consistently state that, despite overall adoption success, implementation complexity and limited supplier readiness, particularly among SMEs, remain persistent challenges [14–16, 30, 32].

Overall, the literature indicates that DPS adoption is hindered by several recurring challenges across European public procurement contexts as summarized in Table 4. These include supplier engagement and market barriers, such as perceived low success probability and high administrative burden for SMEs; technical and digital infrastructure challenges, including IT dependency, interoperability limitations, and insufficient technical support; knowledge and organizational readiness issues, such as limited DPS expertise, insufficient training, and resistance to change; and implementation complexity, which encompasses administrative burden, governance complexity, and legal alignment requirements [2, 12, 14–16, 32, 40].

7 Concluding Discussion and Outlook

This paper reviews research and practical implementation of Dynamic Purchasing Systems in the EU, extracts the challenges of DPS implementation in Germany and derives a structured, federated DPS reference architecture and measurable mitigation strategies, combining conceptual rigor with practical relevance along a DSR approach. By integrating literature synthesis, architectural design, and policy-oriented recommendations, the paper provides both an analytical framework and a practical blueprint for advancing DPS adoption in decentralized procurement environments.

[1] https://www.evergabe-online.info/e-Vergabe/DE/Home/homepage_node.html.

In doing so, the study addresses the research questions through a combination of literature analysis and design-oriented research. RQ1 is answered through a systematic analysis of academic literature, policy documents, and practical implementations to assess the current status of research and practice on DPS. RQ2 is addressed through the design and conceptual modeling of a federated DPS reference architecture tailored to the German federal procurement environment. RQ3 is answered by identifying and structuring the key challenges that hinder DPS adoption in Germany based on the reviewed literature, contextual analysis of the German procurement system, and the designed reference architecture. The reference architecture for the two main processes (qualification of suppliers and call for tender) integrates business processes, application services, and technological components into a coherent blueprint that reflects regulatory requirements and institutional complexity. While remaining conceptual, it advances academic understanding by providing a structured architectural perspective on DPS implementation and offers a practical blueprint for practitioners.

The architecture aligns with Germany's federal context by structuring supplier qualification and tender lifecycle management at the business layer, translating these processes into dedicated application components, and supporting them with modular and interoperable technological infrastructure. Beyond its structural design, the architecture directly addresses key adoption barriers identified in the literature. Implementation complexity is mitigated by assigning operational responsibility to state-level Central Purchasing Bodies, thereby reducing fragmentation and administrative burden on contracting authorities. Supplier engagement challenges, particularly for SMEs, are addressed through a federated competition model that balances inclusiveness and competition. Standardized services and centralized expertise further mitigate the technical issues, interoperability, and knowledge-related constraints. The architecture represents an integrated, context-sensitive response to the DPS adoption challenges.

The proposed DPS reference architecture is evaluated through qualitative expert assessment using semi-structured interviews and interactive feedback sessions with domain experts in public procurement and e-procurement systems. The evaluation aimed to assess the conceptual soundness, practical relevance, and alignment of the architecture with real-world procurement processes in the German federal context. Overall, the experts considered the architecture a promising and relevant approach for supporting DPS implementation. The evaluation confirmed the architectural structure and its alignment with stakeholder roles and procurement workflows, while also identifying areas for refinement, particularly regarding semantic clarity, structural coherence between architectural layers, and the visual organization of the models. Based on this feedback, improvements are incorporated, including clearer terminology, improved alignment between business, application, and technology layers, and the modularization of architectural diagrams. These refinements contributed to strengthening both the conceptual clarity and practical applicability of the proposed architecture.

This research has also limitations. First, the proposed DPS architecture remains at a conceptual level and has not been implemented or empirically tested in a live procurement environment. As a result, its performance and practical feasibility have not yet been validated through real-world deployments. Second, the analysis of challenges relies primarily on literature and selected European cases, which may not capture the full diversity of procurement practices across all administrative contexts. Additionally, the limited availability of academic studies on Dynamic Purchasing Systems necessitated the inclusion of a significant amount of grey literature in this study.

Future research should therefore focus on empirical evaluations of the proposed architecture, including pilot implementations, quantitative performance assessments, and longitudinal studies of supplier participation and procurement outcomes. Comparative analyses across different federal states or countries would provide deeper insights into institutional factors influencing DPS adoption. Also, future studies and analysis on the DPS are necessary to substantiate the current body of academic literature and fully capture the conceptual, technical, and institutional dimensions of DPS implementation.

Acknowledgments. This study was conducted in collaboration with the Kooperationsprojekt Digitale Beschaffung funded by FITKO.

Disclosure of Interests. The authors have no competing interests to declare.

References

1. Thai, K.V.: Public procurement re-examined. J. Public Procurement **1**(1), 9–50 (2001)
2. Schmitz, A., Wimmer, M.A.: Digital transformation in public procurement: a review of challenges for the participation of SMEs. In: Proceedings of the EGOV-CeDEM-ePart Conference, Ghent/Leuven, Belgium (2024)
3. Schmitz, A., Wimmer, M.A.: Framework for interoperable service architecture development. Gov. Inf. Q. **40**(4) (2023)
4. Becker, J., Niemann, M., Halsbenning, S.: Contribution to Growth: European Public Procurement Delivering Economic Benefits for Citizens and Businesses. European Parliament, Luxembourg (2018)
5. Strand, I., Ramada, P., Canton, E.: Public procurement in Europe. Publications Office of the European Union, Luxembourg (2011)
6. Özbilgin, I.G., Imamoğlu, M.Y.: The impact of dynamic purchasing systems in the electronic public procurement processes. Procedia Comput. Sci. **3**, 1571–1575 (2011)
7. Lloyd, R., McCue, C.: What is public procurement? Definitional problems and implications. In: International Public Procurement Conference Proceedings, vol. 3 (2004)
8. Siapera, M., Schmitz, A., Wimmer, M.A., Prentza, A.: Closing the gap: Leveraging data for seamless integration between pre-award and post-award in public procurement. In: Proceedings of the 57th Hawaii International Conference on System Sciences (2024)
9. Schmitz, A., Siapera, M., Prentza, A., Wimmer, M.A.: Harmonization in eProcurement: design of a holistic solution model for pre-award procedures. In: International Conference on Electronic Government (2023)
10. Ferk, P.: Can the implementation of full e-procurement into real life address the real challenges of EU public procurement? Eur. Procurement Public Private Partnership Law Rev. **11**(4), 327–339 (2016)
11. Moe, C., Päivärinta, T.: Challenges in information systems procurement in the Norwegian public sector. In: Electronic Government – EGOV 2011, pp. 404–417. Springer, Heidelberg (2011)
12. OECD: SMEs in Public Procurement: Practices and Strategies for Shared Benefits. OECD Publishing, Paris (2018)
13. Akenroye, T.O., Owens, J.D., Elbaz, J., Durowoju, O.A.: Dynamic capabilities for SME participation in public procurement. Bus. Process. Manag. J. **26**(4), 857–888 (2020)

14. European Commission: Dynamic Purchasing Systems Use Guidelines. Publications Office of the European Union, Luxembourg (2021
15. Eyo, A.: Evidence on use of dynamic purchasing systems in the United Kingdom. Public Procurem. Law Rev. **6**, 237–248 (2017)
16. Local Government Association: A Guide to Dynamic Purchasing Systems within the Public Sector. Local Government Association, London (2017)
17. Popa, I.G., Milandru, M.: The dynamic purchasing system – a modern public procurement solution. In: International Conference Knowledge-Based Organization, vol. 29, no. 2, pp. 127–132 (2023)
18. Bichler, M.: Design science in information systems research. Wirtschaftsinformatik **48**(2), 133–135 (2006). https://doi.org/10.1007/s11576-006-0028-8
19. Peffers, K., Tuunanen, T., Rothenberger, M.A., Chatterjee, S.: A design science research methodology for information systems research. J. Man Inf. Syst. **24**(3), 45–77 (2007)
20. Kitchenham, B.: Procedures for Performing Systematic Reviews. Keele University Technical Report (2004)
21. Webster, J., Watson, R.T.: Analyzing the past to prepare for the future: writing a literature review. MIS Q. **26**(2), xiii–xxiii (2002)
22. Mueller-Bloch, C., Kranz, J.: A framework for rigorously identifying research gaps in qualitative literature reviews (2015)
23. Hudaib, A., Masadeh, R., Haj Qasem, M., Alzaqebah, A.: Requirements prioritization techniques comparison. Mod. Appl. Sci. **12**(2) (2018)
24. Rehman, T., Khan, M.N.A., Riaz, N.: Analysis of requirement engineering processes, tools/techniques and methodologies. Int. J. Inf. Technol. Comput. Sci. **5**(3), 40–48 (2013)
25. Bogner, A., Littig, B., Menz, W.: Introduction: expert interviews—an introduction to a new methodological debate. In: Interviewing Experts, pp. 1–13. Palgrave Macmillan, London (2009)
26. The Open Group: The TOGAF® Standard, 10th edn. The Open Group (2022)
27. European Parliament: Directive 2004/18/EC on the coordination of procedures for the award of public works contracts, public supply contracts and public service contracts. Official Journal of the European Union (2004)
28. European Parliament: Directive 2004/17/EC coordinating procurement procedures of entities operating in water, energy, transport and postal services sectors. OJ of the EU (2004)
29. European Parliament: Directive 2014/24/EU on public procurement. OJ of the EU (2014)
30. Procurex England: Understanding the benefits of dynamic purchasing systems (DPS). https://www.procurexengland.co.uk/2025/03/17/understanding-the-benefits-of-dynamic-purchasing-systems-dps/. Accessed 15 Oct 2025
31. European Parliament: Directive 2014/25/EU on procurement by entities operating in the water, energy, transport and postal services sectors. Official J of the Europ Union (2014)
32. Crown Commercial Service: The Public Contracts Regulations 2015 and The Utilities Contract Regulations 2016 – Dynamic Purchasing Systems. Crown Commercial Service, London (2016)
33. Osborne, S.P.: Delivering public services: time for a new theory? Public Manag. Rev. **12**(1), 1–10 (2010)
34. Mohungoo, I., Brown, I., Kabanda, S.: A systematic review of implementation challenges in public e-procurement. In: Hattingh, M., et al. (eds.) Responsible Design, Implementation and Use of ICT, pp. 46–58. Springer, Cham (2020)
35. Mélon, L., Spruk, R.: The impact of e-procurement on institutional quality. J. Public Procurem. **20**(4), 333–375 (2020)
36. Vaidya, K., Sajeev, A.S.M., Callender, G.: Critical factors that influence e-procurement implementation success in the public sector. J. Public Procurem. **6**(1–2), 70–99 (2006)

37. Millett, T.: Modernising the public-private interface. Eur. Public Private Partnership Law Rev. **2**(4), 244–252 (2007)
38. Mahuwi, L., Israel, B.: A review on participation of SMEs in public procurement: opportunities, challenges, and policy implications (2023)
39. Crown Commercial Service: Dynamic Purchasing System Marketplace. https://supplierregistration.cabinetoffice.gov.uk/dps. Accessed 15 Mar 2026
40. OECD: Public Procurement in Germany: Strategic Dimensions for Well-being and Growth. OECD Publishing, Paris (2019)
41. Kidalov, M.V., Snider, K.F.: US and European public procurement policies for small and medium-sized enterprises (SME): a comparative perspective. Bus. Polit. **13**(4) (2011)

Public Procurement of Information Systems in Digital Government: A Scoping Review of Needs, Requirements, and Outcomes in Use

Mats Falkeman(✉)

Linköping University, 581 83 Linköping, Sweden
mats.falkeman@liu.se

Abstract. Public procurement is a central mechanism through which digital government is realized, yet research on how public organizations procure information systems remains fragmented within digital government scholarship. This scoping review maps research on public procurement of information systems within digital government and examines how prior studies conceptualize and analyze user needs, their translation into requirements, and their relation to later outcomes in use. Based on 14 studies identified through searches in Scopus, Web of Science Core Collection, and the Digital Government Reference Library, complemented by citation searching, the review shows that the literature provides comparatively strong insight into procurement processes, requirements work, and public–private relationships, but much weaker insight into how early procurement choices shape later implementation, use, and value-in-use. The review contributes a synthesis of a fragmented body of research on this topic and identifies a key research gap, deserving of more research interest: the limited traceability from needs and requirements to later outcomes in use.

Keywords: public procurement · information systems · digital government · user needs · value-in-use

1 Introduction

Digital government is realized not only through policy, strategy, and technological development, but also through the decisions by which public organizations define, specify, and acquire information systems. Public procurement is therefore a central mechanism through which organizational processes, service delivery, and digital infrastructures are shaped in practice [33]. At the same time, digital government research has emphasized that public-sector digitalization must be understood in relation to governance, organizational context, and public values rather than as a purely technical matter of implementation [3, 8, 16, 35].

When information systems are procured, an analytically important chain runs from user needs and organizational problem formulations to requirements, contractual arrangements, implementation, and later outcomes in use. This chain is not neutral.

Published by Springer Nature Switzerland 2027
G. Viale Pereira et al. (Eds.): EGOV 2026, LNCS 16933, pp. 19–35, 2027.
https://doi.org/10.1007/978-3-032-35747-2_2

Needs must be identified, prioritized, and translated into formal procurement artifacts such as specifications, evaluation criteria, and contracts while remaining aligned with legal and organizational conditions [22, 30]. From a sociotechnical perspective, system usability and value are therefore shaped not only during implementation and use, but also in the earlier stages in which needs are represented and stabilized [25, 26].

Prior research has identified recurring difficulties in the public acquisition of information systems, particularly in requirements work, uncertain needs assessment, and the translation of organizational needs into formal specifications that remain robust throughout the procurement process [12, 21, 22, 30].

Yet the knowledge base remains fragmented. Within digital government research, the public procurement of information systems remains a dispersed research topic, drawing on public procurement, information systems, and digital government perspectives [7, 15]. As a result, it remains unclear how this topic has been studied and how prior research conceptualizes and analyzes user needs, their translation into requirements, and their relation to implementation and later outcomes in use. In particular, the connection between early procurement stages and later outcomes in use, including value-in-use and public value, remains only partially developed despite its relevance to digital government research [19, 37]. Against this background, the aim of this study is to map research on public procurement of information systems within the digital government field and examine how this literature conceptualizes and analyzes user needs, their translation into requirements, and their relation to implementation and outcomes in use, including value-in-use. The study is guided by the following research questions:

RQ1: How has prior research studied the public procurement of information systems in digital government?

RQ2: How does literature conceptualize and analyze user needs, their translation into requirements, and their relation to implementation and outcomes in use, including value-in-use?

The review is geographically delimited to the EU/EEA in order to examine the topic within a comparatively coherent institutional and legal setting. The review contributes to research on public procurement of information systems in digital government in three ways. First, it maps and synthesizes a fragmented body of research on this topic. Second, it develops an analytical account of how the literature addresses the chain from user needs, through requirements and procurement-related formalization, to implementation and outcomes in use. Third, it identifies knowledge gaps concerning how user needs are translated, formalized, and followed across the procurement and implementation trajectory.

The remainder of the paper is structured as follows. Section 2 presents the conceptual framing of public procurement of information systems, with particular attention to user needs, the translation of needs into requirements, and outcomes in use. Section 3 describes the structured review design and the method for analyzing the included papers. Section 4 presents the findings of the review. Section 5 discusses the results and outlines implications for future research. Section 6 concludes the paper and gives direction for future research in this area.

2 Background and Conceptual Framing

This review approaches the public procurement of information systems as a sociotechnical and institutionally regulated process through which organizational needs are identified, translated into requirements, and formalized in procurement documents, contractual arrangements, and subsequent conditions of system use. In digital government, this process unfolds within governance structures and legal-regulatory arrangements shaped by accountability, legitimacy, transparency, and public oversight [31, 33]. Public procurement can therefore be understood not only as a procedure for selecting among available solutions, but also as a process through which requirements are defined, stakeholder needs are balanced, and conditions for later implementation, change, and benefits realization are shaped [21].

The conceptual framing of the study is organized around three linked analytical dimensions: user involvement and needs representation, the translation from needs to requirements, and outcomes in use, including value-in-use.

2.1 User Involvement and Needs Representation

User involvement has a long tradition in information systems research, particularly in sociotechnical approaches and participatory design, where information systems are understood in relation to the work practices, knowledge, and social contexts they are intended to support [4, 25]. In the Scandinavian tradition, this has also been linked to democratic influence in working life and to users' capacity to shape system design rather than merely serve as informants or recipients of finished solutions [5, 6].

In a procurement context, user involvement takes on a more specific role. The central issue is not only whether users participate, but how their needs are represented in the early stages where needs must be identified, prioritized, and aligned with procurement procedures, documents, and decision logics. In this study, users are therefore understood primarily as internal organizational actors, including end users, process owners, managers, IT functions, and other organizational representatives. The analytical focus is on which actors are included, when they are involved, how needs are articulated, and whether these needs influence the formal artifacts that later govern the procurement.

2.2 Translation from Needs to Requirements

To analyze the movement from needs to formal procurement artifacts, the study uses the concept of translation. Translation refers here to the processes through which organizational needs are transformed into formal requirements, evaluation criteria, contractual clauses, technical specifications, award criteria, and contract performance conditions [31].

This is not a neutral transfer of pre-existing needs, but a process of selection, prioritization, simplification, and formalization. In this process, assumptions are embedded regarding what counts as legitimate quality, acceptable risk, verifiable functionality, and desirable outcomes [21]. Procurement documents therefore function as key artifacts through which some needs are stabilized as binding, while others may be reduced, reformulated, or excluded. The tension between contextual relevance and formal precision is particularly important in public procurement of information systems, where requirements must be sufficiently precise for procurement purposes while remaining flexible enough to accommodate complex systems and changing organizational needs [21].

2.3 Outcomes in Use, Value-In-Use

A third analytical dimension concerns how the literature addresses outcomes once systems have been procured and put into use. In digital government research, public value and co-creation have become important for analyzing digitalization beyond narrow measures of efficiency, cost savings, or implementation success [27, 35]. To capture how such effects are realized in practice, the study also draws on the concept of value-in-use. The premise is that value does not arise at the point of acquisition or contract signing, but in actual use, when technology is integrated into organizational practices and enacted by different actors over time [13, 14, 26, 36].

In this study, outcomes are therefore defined broadly. They may include technical performance and stability, usability and user satisfaction, changes in work practices and processes, service quality and accessibility, as well as transparency, legality, and other public values. The analytical question is not only whether the literature reports such outcomes, but whether it connects them back to earlier decisions concerning needs representation, requirements formulation, and procurement logic.

2.4 Analytical Framework

Taken together, these three dimensions form the analytical framework used in this review. Figure 1 presents the public procurement of information systems in digital government as a sociotechnical arena linking: (1) user involvement and needs representation, (2) the translation of organizational needs into formal requirements, evaluation criteria, and contractual clauses, and (3) outcomes in use, including value-in-use and public values.

The framework is used as a heuristic for analyzing whether and how the included literature establishes traceable links between needs representation, requirements choices, and reported outcomes. It serves both as a guide for data charting and as an analytical lens for the findings and discussion sections. The purpose is not to assume that such links are always explicit, but to examine the extent to which the literature follows—or fails to follow—the chain from user needs to requirements and onward to use and value creation.

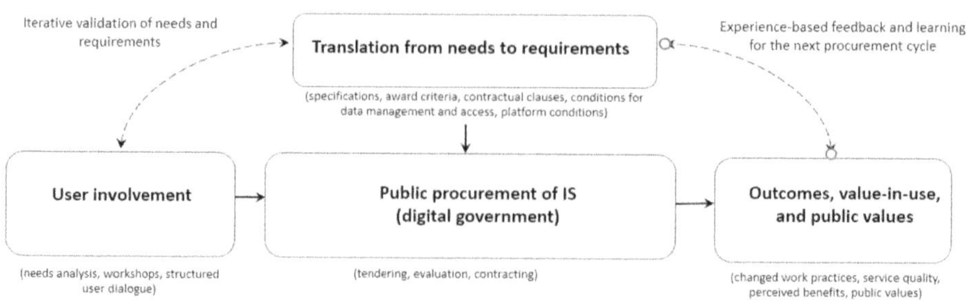

Fig. 1. Analytical framework for the public procurement of information systems in digital government as a sociotechnical arena

3 Research Method

To address the research questions, this study employed a scoping review. This approach was appropriate because public procurement of information systems is a fragmented research topic within digital government, with relevant contributions drawing on public procurement, information systems, and digital government scholarship [21]. Scoping reviews are particularly suitable when the aim is to map how a research topic has been studied, identify recurring themes and patterns, and make knowledge gaps visible, rather than synthesize effects in the manner of a systematic review [2, 18, 28]. The review was informed by established scoping review methodology, particularly Arksey and O'Malley [2], further developed by Levac et al. [18] and later advanced by Peters et al. [28]. Reporting was aligned with PRISMA-ScR [34], and PRISMA-S [29] informed the documentation of the search strategy.

3.1 Search Strategy and Sources

The final corpus comprises 14 studies identified through systematic searches in Scopus, Web of Science Core Collection, and the Digital Government Reference Library (DGRL), complemented by citation searching. The search strategy was structured around three concept blocks covering (1) the public sector, (2) public procurement or contracting, and (3) information systems, IT, or digital solutions. The keyword logic combined terms for public-sector context, such as public sector, government, municipality, and public administration; procurement and contracting, such as procurement, tender, contract, acquisition, and outsourcing; and information systems or digital technology, such as information system, information technology, ICT, digital system, software, and digital solution. Search strings were adapted to each source and applied to titles, abstracts, and keywords.

The DGRL search was conducted separately using DGRL Version 21.0, dated 1 December 2025. At the time of searching, the library contained 20,949 references, predominantly English-language and peer-reviewed, within the study domains of digital government, digital governance, and digital democracy. Because of the size and specific scope of the DGRL, records from this source were first processed in a separate screening file for practical and auditability reasons and were then imported into the main scoping review file. The main review file was established on 1 December 2025 and updated on 23 February 2026. The combined searches yielded 2,772 records before deduplication, screening, and eligibility assessment.

3.2 Selection Process and Eligibility Criteria

To ensure a clear and reproducible selection logic, inclusion and exclusion criteria were defined in relation to publication type, time period, language, phenomenon, object, context, geography, and the delimitation against e-procurement-only studies. The review included peer-reviewed journal articles, review articles, and conference papers published between 2000 and 2025. English-language publications were included, and records with unspecified language metadata were retained until their relevance could be clarified. The review was geographically delimited to the EU/EEA in order to examine public procurement of information systems within a comparatively coherent institutional and legal setting.

The selection process proceeded in several stages: deduplication, metadata-based pre-screening and screening, followed by full-text assessment. In the early stages, records were excluded when the metadata clearly indicated that they were outside the substantive or contextual scope of the review. Records with unclear geographic context or an ambiguous relation to the inclusion criteria were carried forward to full-text review for final assessment rather than being excluded prematurely.

Screening assessed whether a study (i) analyzed public procurement or contracting as a central phenomenon, (ii) addressed information systems or IT solutions as the object of procurement or as an analytically central artifact in the public sector, and (iii) had a clear contextual grounding in the EU/EEA. The geographic delimitation was applied cautiously during screening. Studies were excluded only when the metadata clearly showed that the empirical context was outside the EU/EEA and lacked relevant European connection. Records with unclear, mixed, or only partly specified geographic context were carried forward to full-text review for final assessment. Screening thus functioned as an initial delimitation stage, while full-text review was used to establish final geographic relevance.

As a complementary identification step, backward and forward citation chasing was conducted for a targeted set of conceptually central studies, in line with Wohlin [38]. Reports identified through citation searching were assessed according to the same principles as the other studies. The overall selection process is presented in Fig. 2.

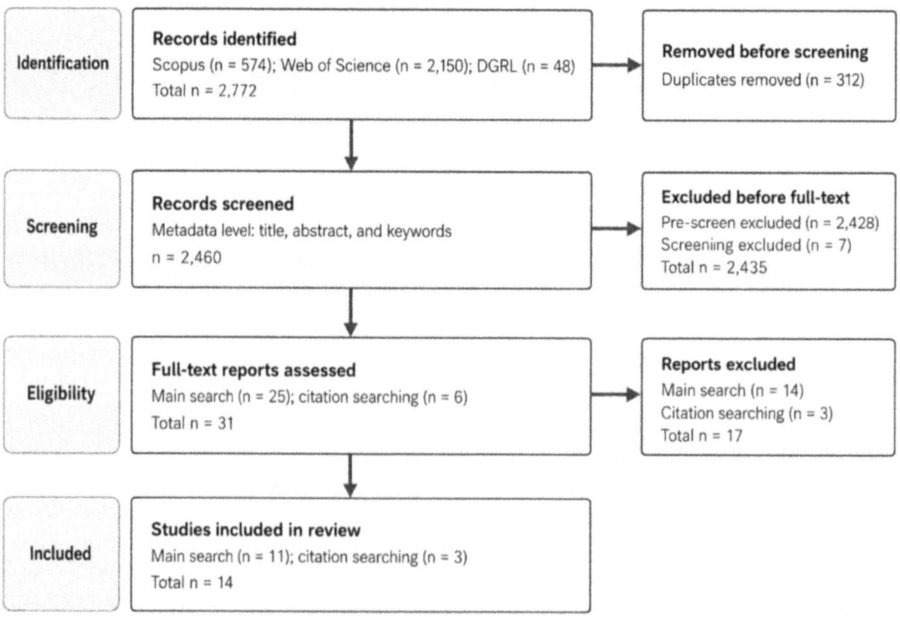

Fig. 2. PRISMA-ScR flow diagram

3.3 Data Charting and Analysis

All screening, full-text assessment, and data charting were conducted by the author. To support consistency and transparency, decisions were documented stepwise from identification and screening to full-text assessment and data charting. Studies that passed screening were then assessed in full text to determine final inclusion and to enable traceable data charting in line with the analytical framework. Data charting was conducted using a structured extraction scheme that captured both descriptive and analytical information. The descriptive charting covered core study characteristics such as publication type, empirical setting, and study design. The analytical charting focused on how each study conceptualized the procurement of information systems, how user needs were represented, how these needs were translated into requirements or other procurement-related formalizations, and whether the study addressed later implementation, use, or outcomes in use.

The charting process was iterative rather than purely mechanical. As studies were read in full, the extraction scheme was used to identify both recurring patterns across the corpus and important differences in how the chain from needs to requirements and later outcomes was conceptualized. The analytical framework was then used as a heuristic for synthesizing the material, with particular attention to whether the literature established traceable links between needs representation, requirements choices, and reported outcomes. In this sense, the analysis sought not to test causal effects, but to map how the literature itself described, conceptualized, and evidenced such relationships.

3.4 Rigor, Transparency, and Limitations

Several measures were taken to support rigor and transparency. First, the review followed an explicit and reproducible search and selection logic across all sources. Second, inclusion and exclusion decisions were tied to clearly defined criteria and applied stepwise from identification to full-text assessment. Third, the analytical framework provided a consistent basis for study selection, data charting, and synthesis, which supported traceability between the review questions and the reported findings.

At the same time, the review has important limitations. It is delimited to the EU/EEA and to peer-reviewed publications in English or with initially unspecified language metadata, which means that relevant work outside these boundaries may have been excluded. The corpus is also relatively small, reflecting both the narrow substantive focus and the fragmented state of the field. In line with scoping review methodology, the purpose of the study was to map and synthesize the field rather than to conduct a formal appraisal of evidence quality. The review therefore identifies how the literature has conceptualized and analyzed the phenomenon but does not rank the included studies according to evidential strength.

4 Findings

This section presents the main findings of the review. It first outlines the composition of the corpus and then analyzes how prior research has studied the public procurement of information systems in digital government. Across the reviewed literature, three recurring gaps structure the findings: limited attention to procurement as a process unfolding over time, limited knowledge of how organizational needs are translated into requirements, and weak traceability from requirements to later outcomes in use. Table 1 provides an overview of these gaps and their implications for future research.

The remainder of this section develops these findings in more detail. It begins with the composition of the reviewed corpus and then examines each of the three gaps in turn.

Table 1. Summary of research gaps identified in the literature

Research gap	What is missing in the current literature	Implications for future research
Process over time	Few process-oriented studies that follow critical incidents, turning points, and conflicts across multiple procurement phases	Longitudinal studies of the same procurement from early preparation to later use
Translation from needs to requirements	Limited knowledge of which mechanisms, intermediaries, and artifacts strengthen or weaken the translation	Studies of how concerns, dialogue, risk management, and requirements documents shape procurable requirements
Requirements to outcomes	Weak traceability between early requirements choices and later use, organizational consequences, value-in-use, and public value	Research designs that connect requirements work, contracts, implementation, monitoring, use, and public value outcomes across strategic, tactical, and operational levels

4.1 Characteristics of the Included Studies

The final corpus consists of 14 studies and shows clear methodological variation. The material is dominated by qualitative case studies, interpretive field studies, and document-based analyses, but also includes a Delphi study, a conceptually oriented study, and a legally oriented analysis. Overall, the field has developed primarily through qualitative and case-based research rather than through large-scale comparative or quantitative designs.

Geographically, the literature is concentrated in Nordic settings, especially Finland and Norway, with additional studies from Denmark, Estonia, and Belgium. The empirical contexts range from municipal and state procurements to outsourcing, innovation procurement, enterprise architecture, and digital infrastructure. Across these settings, the studies are concerned less with routine purchasing than with larger or more mission-critical information systems and digital solutions in the public sector (for an overview of the included studies, see Appendix A).

4.2 Public Procurement of Information Systems as a Process Over Time

Across the corpus, public procurement of information systems is studied primarily as a regulated process unfolding over time and across multiple stages, rather than as a single award decision. The analytical focus extends from requirements specification and choice of procedure to dialogue, evaluation, contracting, and, in some cases, implementation. Procurement therefore appears not merely as a legal or administrative procedure, but as an organizational process through which information systems are specified, negotiated, and made governable under conditions of transparency, equal treatment, and formal documentation [20, 30].

The reviewed studies are rarely concerned with routine acquisition. Instead, they focus on larger or more mission-critical systems, IT services, and digital infrastructures that are closely tied to core operations, coordination, or critical digital functions. A recurring feature is that the public–private relationship is treated as analytically central. Procurement emerges as an arena in which dependencies, competence asymmetries, and power relations between public organizations and private suppliers become consequential for how digitalization is organized and carried forward [11, 17, 24, 32].

The problems most often discussed concern requirements work under strong regulatory constraints, uneven competence among the actors involved, and tensions between formal legality and the need for learning, dialogue, and adaptation. Taken together, the literature suggests that the public procurement of information systems is mainly analyzed as an institutionally framed translation process through which organizational needs must be made legally, technically, and contractually manageable [21, 22].

4.3 From Needs to Requirements

The literature develops the front end of the analytical chain much more fully than its later phases. Most studies focus on how organizational goals, concerns, and problem definitions are incorporated into requirements specifications, calls for tenders, requests for proposals, and contracts. By contrast, it is much less common for studies to examine how those requirements are later related to actual use or organizational consequences. The material therefore reveals a clear asymmetry: it offers stronger insight into how needs are translated into requirements than into what procured systems later lead to in practice [20, 30].

On the needs side, organizational and operational problem formulations dominate. Needs are expressed mainly as goals, concerns, process requirements, and architectural or functional conditions rather than as ready-made individual user preferences. The actors articulating these needs are also primarily internal organizational roles, such as operational representatives, IT specialists, project managers, procurement specialists, and user representatives. The literature therefore suggests that needs largely appear as organizationally defined and institutionally filtered before they are formalized in procurement documents [1, 30].

In the more innovation-oriented studies, needs appear in a more open form. There, they are framed as challenges or need descriptions that are further developed through dialogue with suppliers rather than as detailed solution specifications from the outset. Even in these cases, however, needs are not treated as given. They are organized, interpreted, and delimited within the institutional conditions of the procuring organization [9, 10].

The translation from needs to requirements appears primarily as a document-based process in which organizational concerns and problem definitions are transformed into project plans, requirements specifications, procurement documents, and contractual terms. Procurement documents thus function as key intermediaries between organizational needs and what can later be procured, evaluated, and contracted [23, 30].

At the same time, this translation does not follow a single model. In some studies, it is described as a relatively sequential preparation phase; in others, it is more iterative and shaped by supplier dialogue, adaptation of existing requirements, or innovation-oriented forms of procurement. Several studies also show how fragile this translation can be. A recurring problem is how to formulate requirements that are precise enough for procurement purposes while remaining open enough to accommodate complex systems and changing needs. The findings therefore indicate that the translation from needs to requirements is decisive but unstable, shaped through documents, intermediaries, and regulatory conditions rather than through any simple transfer from needs to finalized requirements [21, 22].

4.4 From Requirements to Outcomes in Use

Compared with the link between needs and requirements, the connection between requirements and later outcomes in use is much less developed in the literature. Several studies remain focused on the early phases of procurement or on procurement documents and do not follow systems into actual use. When requirements are linked to later outcomes, this is usually done through implementation, acceptance, or post-implementation success rather than through an integrated analysis of outcomes in use or value-in-use over time [21, 30].

The clearest examples are studies that follow procurement beyond contract signing and show how ambitions for efficiency coexist with more mixed user experiences, or how ambiguities in requirements and data conversion continue to create problems after deployment. Even then, these links are usually indirect. The literature far more often analyzes how requirements are produced than how procured systems subsequently function in practice [20, 22].

5 Discussion

The review shows that the literature on public procurement of information systems has developed asymmetrically across the procurement trajectory. The strongest studies examine how needs and concerns are translated into requirements and procurement artefacts [22, 30]. By contrast, only a limited part of the corpus follows those formalizations into implementation, use, and outcomes in practice. In this respect, the review supports the conceptual framing in Sect. 2, which treats public procurement as an institutionally regulated part of digital government rather than as a narrow purchasing procedure [31, 33].

The geographical concentration of the corpus should be treated both as a limitation and as a contextual feature of the review. Although the search was delimited to the EU/EEA, the included studies are mainly situated in Nordic and Northern European public-sector contexts. This limits the transferability of the findings to other administrative and legal settings, but may also indicate that public procurement of information systems has been studied most visibly in contexts characterized by mature digital government, formalized procurement regimes, transparency requirements, and strong traditions of public-sector accountability. The findings should therefore be interpreted as contextually situated rather than universally generalizable.

5.1 Answering the Research Questions

Regarding how the literature has examined the public procurement of information systems (RQ1), the review shows that prior research mainly examines it as a regulated, multi-stage process rather than as a discrete award event [20, 22]. Process-oriented studies highlight requirements work, stakeholder management, negotiation, and continued coordination through implementation and acceptance [20, 22]. Public-private relations are also integral to this process. Innovation-oriented studies show that earlier and closer supplier interaction may support more exploratory and challenge-based specification [9], while also remaining constrained by formalized procedures that can make collaboration episodic and difficult [10]. Studies of outsourcing further show that buyer and provider motives may not align and may remain partly hidden [32]. Taken together, these studies suggest that public procurement of information systems is best understood as a governance arena in which innovation, formalization, supplier relations, and organizational interests must be balanced.

Regarding how needs are represented, translated into requirements, and connected to later outcomes (RQ2), the review shows that needs are conceptualized mainly as organizationally mediated concerns rather than as fixed individual preferences [30]. In the strongest studies of the early acquisition phases, needs are articulated by internal actors, including users, business owners and analysts, IT personnel, procurement specialists, and other organizational representatives, and are then translated into project plans, requirement specifications, calls for tenders, award criteria, and contracts [30]. This pattern is also visible in Alanne et al., where different internal actors carry different forms of knowledge and responsibility in the requirements work, yet the process still produces ambiguity and practical problems [1].

The review further shows that the literature is much more developed on the translation from needs to requirements than on the later translation from requirements to outcomes in use [22, 30]. This emphasis is consistent with Moe and Päivärinta, who identify clear and complete ex ante requirements as a major challenge in public IS procurement [21]. By contrast, only a limited part of the corpus follows procured systems closely enough in use to show how early formalizations shape later work practices and experienced outcomes [20, 39].

This weak traceability should be interpreted cautiously. It does not mean that early procurement choices are unimportant for later outcomes. Rather, it reflects a limitation in how the existing literature has been designed and what it has been able to observe. Many studies examine requirements work, procurement documents, or contracting decisions, but do not follow the same procurement into implementation, use, contract management, and benefit realization over time. The finding may also indicate weak organizational traceability between procurement decisions, follow-up mechanisms, and realized value-in-use. Outcome monitoring should therefore be treated as part of procurement governance rather than as a separate post-implementation concern. Without systematic follow-up of adoption, use, and organizational or public value outcomes, the link between needs, requirements, and value-in-use remains weak.

5.2 Framing a Research Agenda

The review points to three priorities for future research. First, more longitudinal studies are needed to follow the same procurement across preparation, specification, contracting, implementation, and use [20, 22]. Second, future research should examine which mechanisms, intermediaries, and organizational arrangements strengthen or weaken the translation from needs to requirements in practice [1, 30]. Third, the weakest point in the literature concerns traceability from requirements to outcomes in use, which calls for studies that connect requirements work, contracts, implementation, monitoring, use, and organizational consequences more explicitly over time [20, 21].

Future research should also examine how different system and delivery characteristics shape the procurement trajectory. The reviewed studies do not systematically distinguish between standard products, licensed solutions, tailored systems, or newly developed systems, nor between waterfall, agile, or DevOps-oriented delivery models. These distinctions may affect how user involvement, requirements work, testing, delivery, guarantee periods, and post-award follow-up are organized in public procurement of information systems. Future studies should also examine how value-in-use and public value can be evaluated after implementation, and how such outcomes can be related to earlier requirements and contractual arrangements across strategic, tactical, and operational levels.

6 Conclusion

The aim of this study was to map research on public procurement of information systems within digital government and to examine how the reviewed literature conceptualizes the links between needs, requirements, and outcomes in use. The review shows that this body of research provides comparatively strong insight into procurement processes, requirements work, and the formalization of organizational needs, but much weaker insight into how those early choices are connected to later implementation, use, and value-in-use.

The main conclusion is that public procurement of information systems can be understood as a sociotechnical translation chain in which needs representation, requirements formalization, and later use are closely connected, yet unevenly studied. By making this asymmetry visible, the review contributes an analytical vocabulary for studying public procurement of information systems as part of digital government. It also shifts attention from procurement as a bounded procedural event to procurement as a governing process through which future system use and value creation are partly shaped.

For practice, the findings suggest that public organizations should not treat procurement of information systems as a narrow compliance exercise focused only on procedure and award. Because needs are translated and stabilized through requirements, procurement documents, and contractual arrangements, early procurement choices shape the conditions for later implementation and use. The practical implication is therefore not simply that public organizations need "more user input," but that they need stronger capacity to represent, translate, and formalize organizational needs in ways that remain both operationally meaningful and legally manageable across the procurement process.

Acknowledgments. This article benefited from the use of ChatGPT (OpenAI) for language revision and editorial support in translating Swedish draft text into academic English. The tool was used only to improve clarity and readability. All conceptualization, study selection, analysis, interpretation, and final writing decisions were carried out by the author.

Disclosure of Interests. The author has no competing interests to declare that are relevant to the content of this article.

Appendix A Included Studies in the Review

This appendix provides a compact overview of the 14 studies included in the review.

Author (year)	Country/context	Study design	Procurement/IS focus
Alanne et al. (2015)	Finland, municipal social care	Qualitative interpretive single-case study	Requirements work, coordination problems, and negative outcomes in public IS procurement
De Coninck et al. (2018)	Belgium, Antwerp public ICT	Qualitative explanatory single-case study	Innovation procurement, startup participation, and exploratory ICT procurement
Farshchian et al. (2020)	Norway, municipalities and county office	Interpretive case study	Innovative public procurement of digital systems and collaboration challenges
Gjærum (2025)	Norway, small rural municipalities	Qualitative multiple-case study	Municipal IT/IS procurement, outsourcing, and buyer-provider relationships
Kalvet (2012)	Estonia, digital government	Conceptually oriented article with illustrative case	Public procurement for innovation in digital government
Lemmetti & Pekkola (2014)	Finland, public sector ICT	Content analysis of requests for proposals	Enterprise architecture in procurement documents

(continued)

(*continued*)

Author (year)	Country/context	Study design	Procurement/IS focus
Moe et al. (2006)	Norway, municipality	Interpretive multiple-case study	Tensions in public procurement of major information systems
Moe et al. (2017)	Norway, municipalities	Qualitative longitudinal multiple-case study	Dialectics in requirements specification in public IS procurement
Moe & Newman (2014)	Norway, municipalities	Interpretive field studies / multiple-case study	Procurement as an end-to-end process across multiple phases
Moe & Päivärinta (2011)	Norway, public sector	Delphi study	Key challenges in public procurement of information systems
Motzfeldt & Næsborg-Andersen (2018)	Denmark, digital public infrastructure	Conceptual and legal analysis	Legal limits to outsourcing critical digital infrastructure
Riihimäki & Pekkola (2021)	Finland, government agency	Qualitative single-case study	Buyer concerns in early acquisition and their effects on procurement artefacts
Seppälä et al. (2014)	Finland, national defense sector	Empirical case study	Hidden motives and buyer-supplier relations in public IT outsourcing
Ylinen & Pekkola (2018)	Finland, municipality	Interpretive qualitative single-case study	Contradictory outcomes in use after IS acquisition

References

1. Alanne, A., Hellsten, P., Pekkola, S., Saarenpää, I.: Three positives make one negative: public sector IS procurement. In: Tambouris, E., et al. (eds.) Electronic government: EGOV 2015. LNCS, vol. 9248, pp. 321–333. Springer, Heidelberg (2015). https://doi.org/10.1007/978-3-319-22479-4_24
2. Arksey, H., O'Malley, L.: Scoping studies: towards a methodological framework. Int. J. Soc. Res. Methodol. **8**(1), 19–32 (2005). https://doi.org/10.1080/1364557032000119616
3. Bannister, F., Connolly, R.: ICT, public values and transformative government: a framework and programme for research. Gov. Inf. Q. **31**(1), 119–128 (2014). https://doi.org/10.1016/j.giq.2013.07.005
4. Baxter, G., Sommerville, I.: Socio-technical systems: from design methods to systems engineering. Interact. Comput. **23**(1), 4–17 (2011). https://doi.org/10.1016/j.intcom.2010.07.003

5. Bjerknes, G., Bratteteig, T.: User participation and democracy: a discussion of scandinavian research on systems development. Scand. J. Inf. Syst. **7**(1), 75–100 (1995)
6. Bødker, S., Ehn, P., Sjögren, D., Sundblad, Y.: Co-operative design—perspectives on 20 years with “the Scandinavian IT Design Model”. In Proceedings of the First Nordic Conference on Human-Computer Interaction (NordiCHI 2000), pp. 22–24. Association for Computing Machinery (2000)
7. Boechat, G., Cunha, M.A., Gasser, U.: Public procurement and technology: a research agenda. Proceedings of the 16th International Conference on Theory and Practice of Electronic Governance, pp. 167–175 (2023). https://doi.org/10.1145/3614321.3614341
8. Cordella, A., Bonina, C.M.: A public value perspective for ICT-enabled public sector reforms: a theoretical reflection. Gov. Inf. Q. **29**(4), 512–520 (2012). https://doi.org/10.1016/j.giq.2012.03.004
9. De Coninck, B., Viaene, S., Leysen, J.: Public procurement of innovation through increased startup participation: the case of Digipolis (Research-in-progress). In: Bui, T.X. (ed.) Proceedings of the 51st Hawaii International Conference on System Sciences, pp. 2474–2483 (2018). https://doi.org/10.24251/HICSS.2018.312
10. Farshchian, B. A., Sætertrø, H., Stålaker, M.: Experiences from an interpretative case study of innovative public procurement of digital systems in the Norwegian public sector. In: Proceedings of the 24th International Conference on Evaluation and Assessment in Software Engineering (EASE ’20), pp. 373–374. Association for Computing Machinery (2020). https://doi.org/10.1145/3383219.3383271
11. Gjærum, A.: Digital transformation in local government – unpacking challenges in buyer-provider relations. Transforming Government: People, Process and Policy. Advance online publication (2025). https://doi.org/10.1108/TG-06-2025-0180
12. Goldfinch, S.: Pessimism, computer failure, and information systems development in the public sector. Public Adm. Rev. **67**(5), 917–929 (2007). https://doi.org/10.1111/j.1540-6210.2007.00778.x
13. Grönroos, C.: Value co-creation in service logic: a critical analysis. Mark. Theory **11**(3), 279–301 (2011). https://doi.org/10.1177/1470593111408177
14. Heeks, R.: Information systems and developing countries: failure, success, and local improvisations. Inf. Soc. **18**(2), 101–112 (2002). https://doi.org/10.1080/01972240290075039
15. Hudon, P.-A., Dumas, P., Garzón, C.: Recent research on public procurement: Should it become a subfield of public administration? Canadian Public Administrat./Administration publique du Canada, 64(2), 179–201 (2021). https://doi.org/10.1111/capa.12414
16. Janowski, T.: Digital government evolution: from transformation to contextualization. Gov. Inf. Q. **32**(3), 221–236 (2015). https://doi.org/10.1016/j.giq.2015.07.001
17. Lemmetti, J., Pekkola, S.: Enterprise architecture in public ICT procurement in Finland. In Electronic Government and Electronic Participation: Joint Proceedings of Ongoing Research, PhD Papers, Posters and Workshops of IFIP EGOV and IFIP ePart 2014. Innovation and the Public Sector, vol. 21, pp. 227–236. IOS Press (2014). https://doi.org/10.3233/978-1-61499-429-9-227
18. Levac, D., Colquhoun, H., O’Brien, K.K.: Scoping studies: advancing the methodology. Implement. Sci. **5**(1), 69 (2010). https://doi.org/10.1186/1748-5908-5-69
19. Malacina, I., Karttunen, E., Jääskeläinen, A., Lintukangas, K., Heikkilä, J., Kähkönen, A.-K.: Capturing the value creation in public procurement: a practice-based view. J. Purchas. Supply Manag. **28**(2), 100745 (2022). https://doi.org/10.1016/j.pursup.2021.100745
20. Moe, C.E., Newman, M.: The public procurement of IS: a process view. In Proceedings of the 47th Hawaii International Conference on System Sciences, pp. 2158–2167. IEEE (2014). https://doi.org/10.1109/HICSS.2014.272

21. Moe, C.E., Päivärinta, T.: Challenges in information systems procurement in the Norwegian public sector. In: Janssen, M., Scholl, H.J., Wimmer, M.A., Tan, Y.-H. (eds.) Electronic Government. LNCS, vol. 6846, pp. 404–417. Springer, Heidelberg (2011). https://doi.org/10.1007/978-3-642-22878-0_34
22. Moe, C.E., Newman, M., Sein, M.K.: The public procurement of information systems: dialectics in requirements specification. Eur. J. Inf. Syst. **26**(2), 143–163 (2017). https://doi.org/10.1057/s41303-017-0035-4
23. Moe, C.E., Risvand, A.C., Sein, M.K.: Limits of public procurement: Information systems acquisition. In: Wimmer, M.A., Scholl, H.J., Grönlund, Å., Andersen, K.V. (eds.) Electronic Government. LNCS, vol. 4084, pp. 281–292. Springer, Heidelberg (2006). https://doi.org/10.1007/11823100_25
24. Motzfeldt, H.M., Næsborg-Andersen, A.: Developing administrative law into handling the challenges of digital government in Denmark. Electron. J. e-Gov. **16**(2), 136–146 (2018)
25. Mumford, E.: A socio-technical approach to systems design. Requir. Eng. **5**(2), 125–133 (2000). https://doi.org/10.1007/PL00010345
26. Orlikowski, W.J.: Using technology and constituting structures: a practice lens for studying technology in organizations. Organ. Sci. **11**(4), 404–428 (2000). https://doi.org/10.1287/orsc.11.4.404.14600
27. Osborne, S.P., Radnor, Z., Strokosch, K.: Co-production and the co-creation of value in public services: a suitable case for treatment? Public Manag. Rev. **18**(5), 639–653 (2016). https://doi.org/10.1080/14719037.2015.1111927
28. Peters, M.D.J., et al.: Scoping reviews: reinforcing and advancing the methodology and application. Syst. Rev. **10**(1), 263 (2021). https://doi.org/10.1186/s13643-021-01821-3
29. Rethlefsen, M.L., et al.: PRISMA-S: An extension to the PRISMA statement for reporting literature searches in systematic reviews. Syst. Rev. **10**, 39 (2021). https://doi.org/10.1186/s13643-020-01542-z
30. Riihimäki, E., Pekkola, S.: Public buyer's concerns influencing the early phases of information system acquisition. Gov. Inf. Q. **38**(4), 101595 (2021). https://doi.org/10.1016/j.giq.2021.101595
31. Sanchez-Graells, A.: Digital Technologies and Public Procurement: Gatekeeping and Experimentation in Digital Public Governance. Oxford University Press (2024). https://doi.org/10.1093/oso/9780198866770.001.0001
32. Seppälä, J., Kyläheiko, K., Jantunen, A.: Revealing hidden motives behind outsourcing decisions: a case study relating to public information technology services. Int. J. Procurement Manag. **7**(5), 520–542 (2014). https://doi.org/10.1504/IJPM.2014.064617
33. Thai, K.V.: Public procurement re-examined. J. Public Procurement **1**(1), 9–50 (2001). https://doi.org/10.1108/JOPP-01-01-2001-B001
34. Tricco, A.C., et al.: PRISMA extension for scoping reviews (PRISMA-ScR): checklist and explanation. Ann. Int. Med. **169**(7), 467–473 (2018). https://doi.org/10.7326/M18-0850
35. Twizeyimana, J.D., Andersson, A.: The public value of e-government: a literature review. Gov. Inf. Q. **36**(2), 167–178 (2019). https://doi.org/10.1016/j.giq.2018.12.001
36. Vargo, S.L., Maglio, P.P., Akaka, M.A.: On value and value co-creation: a service systems and service logic perspective. Eur. Manag. J. **26**(3), 145–152 (2008). https://doi.org/10.1016/j.emj.2008.04.003
37. Weigl, L., Roth, T., Amard, A., Zavolokina, L.: When public values and user-centricity in e-government collide: a systematic review. Gov. Inf. Q. **41**(3), 101956 (2024). https://doi.org/10.1016/j.giq.2024.101956

38. Wohlin, C.: Guidelines for snowballing in systematic literature studies and a replication in software engineering. In: Proceedings of the 18th International Conference on Evaluation and Assessment in Software Engineering (EASE '14), pp. 1–10. Association for Computing Machinery (2014). https://doi.org/10.1145/2601248.2601268
39. Ylinen, M., Pekkola, S.: Searching success in a successful IS acquisition. In: Proceedings of the 51st Hawaii International Conference on System Sciences (HICSS), pp. 1–10 (2018). https://doi.org/10.24251/HICSS.2018.603

From Buzzword to Applicable Concept: A Taxonomy for the Personalisation of Public Services

Darius Farman(✉)

Swiss Graduate School of Public Administration (IDHEAP), University of Lausanne, Rue de la Mouline 28, 1022 Chavannes-près-Renens, Switzerland
darius.farman@unil.ch

Abstract. Personalised public services are viewed as a new frontier of digital government transformation, driven by advances in artificial intelligence and inspired by the success of personalisation in the private sector. Yet, directly replicating commercial models without accounting for public sector specificities risks undermining public values. Furthermore, the emerging literature on public service personalisation suffers from conceptual fuzziness, which hinders both service design and further research. This study makes a theoretical contribution by developing a taxonomy of personalisation comprising 9 dimensions and 25 characteristics. Its usefulness in enhancing conceptual clarity, untangling different forms of personalisation and accounting for public sector specificities is demonstrated through empirical cases, illustrating how the taxonomy can support both research and service design in the context of citizen-centric digital government. The taxonomy design process also identifies new directions for future research on a topic likely to gain relevance in the years ahead.

Keywords: Personalisation · Public service design · Citizen-centricity · Digital government transformation · Taxonomy design

1 Introduction

The belief that public services should be personalised, that is, adapted to their recipients' individual characteristics and situations, is today widely shared in the Western public sector [1]. Governments in the European Union aim for it [2], consulting firms advocate for it [3, 4] and so do international organisations [5–7].

Latest developments in artificial intelligence (AI) and big data analytics only amplify this trend, by enabling large-scale personalisation, such as "smart" services whose trigger, features and delivery are individually adapted to each citizen. Personalisation is considered part of the next maturity stage of digital government [8, 9]. It has been identified as a promising instrument to enhance citizen trust [10], efficiency [11], accessibility [12] and compliance [13].

Submission track: General e-government and e-governance track.

Published by Springer Nature Switzerland 2027
G. Viale Pereira et al. (Eds.): EGOV 2026, LNCS 16933, pp. 36–51, 2027.
https://doi.org/10.1007/978-3-032-35747-2_3

Before gaining traction in the public sector, personalisation has long been a topic of interest in business environments, such as marketing and e-commerce [14]. As a result, public service personalisation research could—and did—draw on a substantial literature on private sector contexts [15, 16]. This transfer is reinforced by policy narratives calling on the necessity for the public sector to catch up with the private sector [17]. While this replication across sectors is well acknowledged, the design of personalised public services is frequently assumed to mirror that of the private sector, without much differentiation. Until recently, it was not uncommon, for instance, to find blueprints for public service personalisation relying on the import of citizen data from social media [12]. The emerging research on personalisation in the public sector often uncritically models its approaches after those of the private sector. Often focused on implementation, it rarely interrogates whether, and in what ways, personalisation in the public sector may theoretically differ [e.g., 18].

It is easy to see how problematic the replication of commercial personalisation models can be in public services. Implemented without adaptation, private service personalisation risks undermine public values, by unfairly discriminating against citizens or businesses, violating privacy or producing opaque and unaccountable decisions. Even when setting these threats aside, the differences between the public and private sector in terms of end goals, legal constraints or organisational structure are likely to shape the scope and implementation of personalisation. For these reasons, defining personalisation and situating it within a public sector context is a timely and valuable endeavour, as the issue is expected to feature prominently in digital government transformation research [8, 19] and policy [1] of the coming years.

Given this complexity, the study seeks to address the following research questions: How can public service personalisation be conceptualised? And which aspects warrant particular attention in a public sector context? To answer these questions, it undertakes a theory-building investigation grounded in the nascent literature on public service personalisation. It does so by developing a taxonomy of personalisation from a public service design perspective. Taxonomy design is preferred over other approaches for its ability to differentiate various forms and properties of multifaceted phenomena. This approach proved fruitful, as the process identified no fewer than 9 dimensions and 25 characteristics relevant for the personalisation of public services.

The taxonomy is primarily aimed at digital government researchers and public service designers. Its theoretical contribution is threefold: (1) increase conceptual clarity of public service personalisation, (2) help distinguish different types of personalisation, with their respective challenges, constraints and merits, and (3) recognise characteristics of personalisation that may be absent or less common in the private sector.

2 Background

2.1 Definitional Challenges

Research on public service personalisation began in the 2000s. Its roots in the private sector are acknowledged from the outset [20] and underscored again in later studies [15, 16]. In the private sector, personalisation has a long history, with both practice and research gaining momentum in the 1960s through the emergence of direct marketing.

While personalisation predates information technologies (IT), IT diffusion and advances since the 1980s have been enabling new use cases at large scale [21].

Despite its enduring popularity in the private sector, personalisation has remained notoriously hard to define [22, 23]. One difficulty stems from the wide range of disciplines and contexts in which the concept is used [14]. Personalisation can take on different meanings, even within a single field such as digital marketing [22].

This conceptual lack of clarity is also evident in research on public service personalisation, where a focus on practical applications often motivates the use of context-specific definitions [e.g., 18] or the absence of definitions altogether [e.g., 12]. The fuzziness is further compounded by the rhetorical appeal of personalisation. Social policy research, in particular, has highlighted how personalisation has been used in government programs as a buzzword emptied of substantive meaning, semantically malleable and politically useful in neutralising conflict [24].

Growing scholarly interest in public service personalisation calls for more robust conceptualisations and definitional clarity [19]. Drawing on existing literature, this study defines service personalisation as *the process by which a service provider adapts a service based on the characteristics and situation of the service recipient, with or without their involvement*. In line with previous studies, active recipient contribution is seen as one subtype of personalisation, instead of a necessary condition of personalisation or an altogether different phenomenon, often labelled as customisation [14]. Besides, the definition excludes the personalisation of goods [23], as the focus on services is more relevant to the public sector. The definition is congruent with other specifications from both business [22] and government [13] contexts, suggesting the similarity of the process across sectors, besides variation in service type (commercial or public), provider type (firm or public authority) and recipient type (customer or citizen).

However, more than referential adaptations are needed to fully capture the specificities of public service personalisation. As argued earlier, the differences between the private and the public sector need to be considered, as they likely shape how personalisation is understood and applied.

2.2 Public Sector Specificities

How public service personalisation differs from its commercial counterpart has received limited scholarly attention. Pieterson et al. [13] and Homburg and Dijkshoorn [15] are the only identified contributors, both publishing over fifteen years ago. Drawing on their work, three public service specificities can be outlined.

The first, and arguably most important, is the principle of universalism. Unlike private services, many public services must ensure equality of access and equality of treatment for all citizens. For public service personalisation, this has two implications. First, digital types of personalisation should not worsen the digital divide or exclude individuals lacking the necessary devices or skills. Second, the adaptation of a service to individual circumstances should not exacerbate discrimination in access or treatment. While this rules out certain commercial practices (say, turning customers away), many forms of public service personalisation remain compatible with the universalism principle, for instance the dynamic adaptation of digital government portals [15].

The second specificity concerns privacy. Personalisation must comply with privacy regulations, such as the EU's General Data Protection Rules (GDPR). Although the GDPR grants public authorities somewhat greater flexibility than private actors in implementing service personalisation, governments are often subject to stronger public scrutiny and higher expectations [25]. Public service designers should therefore weigh the possible trade-offs between loss of privacy and gains in service quality resulting from personalisation [13, 15]. A point of particular relevance here is recipient modelling and profiling. In both the private and the public sector, digital personalisation relies on clustering personal data into profiles. Whereas personalisation has a nice ring to it, profiling on the other hand can have a negative connotation and evokes mass surveillance. Yet, both go hand in hand, as profiling is a prerequisite for personalisation [21]. The perceived risk is likely to depend on a many factors ranging from the sensitivity and the amount of data used to the controllability of the process [26].

The third specificity relates to the end goals of personalisation. Whereas the private sector seeks profit maximisation, public service personalisation is driven by public values within established legal mandates. As a result, it can serve a wider range of objectives, such as inclusiveness [12]. As is often the case in public policy, authorities can face goal conflicts and public value trade-offs [27]. Pieterson et al. [13], for example, view personalisation as a promising instrument to increase citizens' legal compliance, but do not address how to balance this with the privacy needs they themselves identify. Finally, differences in higher-order goals should not conceal similarities in lower-order goals. Both private and public service personalisation often aim at increasing recipient satisfaction, for example through personalised content [10].

3 Methodology

3.1 Method Selection

The scarce research on personalisation in the public sector suggests that a theory-building contribution is more valuable than a literature review, which is inherently limited to the existing literature. This study therefore develops a taxonomy of personalisation to answer the research questions. The choice of a taxonomy as a theory-building approach is motivated by three reasons. First, as noted earlier, personalisation has fuzzy conceptual boundaries, which increases the risk of confusion and impedes cumulative research by digital government scholars. Taxonomies help enhance conceptual clarity [28], which is one purpose of this study. Second, taxonomy design is well-suited to examine multidimensional phenomena such as personalisation, which appears in diverse forms. Third, the taxonomy as an end product is a practical tool useful for further work on personalisation, as it can support researchers and public service designers to better define public service personalisation, better distinguish its different types and, for the latter group, better assess their respective merits and limits in applied contexts.

3.2 Method Specifications

The taxonomy design follows Nickerson et al.'s seven-step approach, a method well-suited to studying digital transformation concepts [28]. It also takes into account the most recent taxonomy design recommendations of Kundisch et al. [29]. For example, their recommendation to specify the phenomenon, the target group and purpose of the taxonomy beforehand was addressed in the last section.

First, the perspective from which the taxonomy considers service personalisation ("meta-characteristic") is selected in accordance with its goals. In this study, the chosen meta-characteristic is personalisation *from a public service design perspective*, in line with the research questions and the target audience. Public service design encompasses a broad range of activities, from the design of symbols to that of entire systems, and differs from private sector design through its formal subordination to an overarching policy lifecycle and a legally constrained governance framework [30]—distinct from service policy and governance in a narrow sense. This study focuses on service characteristics and interactions with recipients, as these are what personalisation primarily transforms and where the risk of uncritically replicating commercial logics lies. Higher-order design aspects relevant for public service personalisation, such as the overarching public governance, are left for further research with a clear organisational focus.

Second, because taxonomy design is an iterative process, ending conditions must be defined to determine when the process is complete. Nickerson et al. distinguish subjective from objective ending conditions [28]. Subjective conditions ensure the taxonomy's usefulness, while objective conditions ensure that the final result complies with the definition of a taxonomy. In this study, the taxonomy design adheres to all ending conditions recommended by Nickerson et al. [28]. Subjective ending conditions require that the taxonomy is sufficiently (a) concise, (b) robust, (c) comprehensive, (d) extendible and (e) explanatory. Objective ending conditions are that (1) all objects are examined, (2) at least one object is classified under every characteristic of every dimension, (3) no object is merged with a similar object or split into multiple objects in the last iteration, (4–5) new dimensions or characteristics are neither added nor merged or split in the last iteration, (6) every characteristic is unique within its dimension, (7–8) each dimension and combination of characteristics is unique and not repeated. One caveat applies to condition (2): It is interpreted as satisfied by potential objects theoretically derived from existing ones. This aligns with Nickerson et al.'s recommendation to include future objects in order to increase the taxonomy's explanatory power [28].

The third step is the selection of a design approach. This study combines conceptual-to-empirical (C2E) and empirical-to-conceptual (E2C) approaches, in line with methodological recommendations [28, 29]. Given the limited literature on public service personalisation, C2E approaches alone would be insufficient. As a starting point, however, they allow for the incorporation of existing research as well as the review of adjacent domains—in this case, personalisation in the private sector. E2C approaches complement this by mitigating potential biases inherent in the existing literature, such as the disproportionate focus on a narrow set of applications (e.g., personalised recommendations). Steps four to seven, related to sampling procedures and taxonomy development, are presented next.

3.3 Sampling

Each design approach relies on distinct source material. C2E iterations draw on a review of the literature on public service personalisation. Following a screening of existing studies, the review was conducted on Web of Science using keyword search in titles and abstracts with: ("personali?ed" OR "personali?ation") AND ("public service*" OR "government* service*"). It included journal articles, conference papers, books and book chapters in English published between 2000 and 2025. The search yielded 238 results without duplicates. Excluding irrelevant items based on abstracts (-155), cross-checking with the 100 first results on Google Scholar (+8) and reaching result saturation through forward and backward snowballing search (+7) finally led to 98 results. In addition, 14 conceptual studies on private service personalisation found via snowballing were retained for one of the deductive iterations, as described below.

E2C iterations rely on an empirical collection of personalised public services. 110 objects were sampled from peer-reviewed literature, grey literature, online searches and the author's own knowledge. The sampling strategy was to encompass as many situations labelled as personalisation as possible, including various service types, policy areas and countries. Before the taxonomy design, all objects were verified to comply with the definition of personalisation. 26 objects were found to have no clear relation to personalisation and were excluded, leaving 84 objects. Finally, during the taxonomy design, similar objects were merged and service bundles were split [28].

3.4 Taxonomy Design

The strategy for identifying dimensions consisted in screening all characteristics associated with personalisation, following Podsakoff's guidelines [31]. Subsequently, concept characteristics varying within or across conceptualisations (E2C), or across objects (C2E), could be identified. The fact that personalisation targeted individuals in some cases and groups in others illustrates such variation. Each characteristic was then cross-checked against other source materials and other characteristics to ensure consistency.

The taxonomy design process required five iterations. As mentioned earlier, the first iteration was C2E to leverage existing insights from the public service personalisation literature as a baseline [29]. It was followed by an E2C iteration to complement the limited literature with empirical cases. For that purpose, 30 objects were non-randomly selected from the sample based on the meta-characteristic, with priority given to objects discussed in public service design documents (e.g., OECD reports). The third iteration reverted to the C2E approach. This time, commercial personalisation research sampled earlier was reviewed, so as to benefit from the more mature body of research in this domain. Crucially, each taxonomy operation was first evaluated in terms of its applicability to the public sector, accounting for the sector specificities described above, in order to avoid uncritical transfer from private sector settings. The fourth iteration was E2C and analysed 30 additional objects randomly selected, helping refine the taxonomy's stringency. The fifth iteration was again E2C and included all remaining objects from the sample. This iteration did not trigger any revision of the taxonomy.

At this point, all objective ending conditions were met, which triggered the review of the subjective ending conditions. These were also deemed fulfilled, formally concluding the design process. In total, the process required 23 taxonomy operations, all of which were documented in an appendix document. The resulting taxonomy, comprising 9 dimensions and 25 characteristics, is presented in the following section.

4 Results

4.1 Taxonomy Dimensions and Characteristics

The taxonomy is reported in Table 1. It relates its dimensions to three necessary conditions of personalisation—provider, recipient, process—while the fourth condition, public service, is the meta-characteristic of the taxonomy. This arrangement is meant as a structuring visual aid rather than a systematic and definitive categorisation.

The provider's ***motive*** refers to the benefits expected from personalisation. Since personalisation comes at a cost, the provider should expect prevailing benefits for itself, the recipient, society, or a combination of these. *Benefits for the provider* arise when personalisation decreases the public authority's workload, for example by reducing data processing costs through prefilled forms [32]. *Benefits for society* are a distinctive feature of the public sector and derive from governments' role in providing public goods. Personalisation may benefit third parties else than the service recipient, such as when it encourages compliance with rules [13]—for instance, reminding a driver to vacate a parking space shortly before the allotted time expires and a fine is incurred. Unlike in the private sector, public service personalisation can impose disadvantages on the recipient to advance some broader public interest.

Recipient type indicates whether the service targets a citizen or an organisation. The latter includes businesses, non-profits, or, conceivably, other government entities such as local municipalities, though no empirical example of the latter was found. This dimension matters for service design, as legal requirements (e.g., privacy) and recipient needs will differ accordingly.

Recipient granularity describes whether a service is personalised for an individual recipient or a segment of similar recipients, such as all citizens reaching legal adulthood within the current year. In the literature, this distinction is also labelled *individuated* or *one-to-one* personalisation, as opposed to *categorical*, *mass* or *one-to-N* personalisation [14, 23, 33]. In both the private and the public sector, more granularity is not always desirable and there is an "optimal degree of personalisation" for each case [15, 21]. One factor is effectiveness: What granularity is needed to achieve the personalisation goal? For instance, regional information based on recipient location can be implemented at the group level without individual adaptation. A second factor is cost or feasibility: Is the data and the technology available at an acceptable cost for this granularity level?

Recipient consent indicates whether recipients provided their consent to the personalisation process. While private providers often need recipient consent to implement personalisation, due to privacy rules such as the GDPR, public authorities might not need it, for instance when delivering universal public services and services of public interest [32]. Regardless of legal requirements, requesting consent may nonetheless be advisable in some situations, as perceived controllability was found to enhance user acceptance of public service personalisation [26].

Recipient role and ***data source*** are two sides of the same coin—viewed respectively from the recipient and process perspectives. As in the private sector, personalisation can be *explicit*, carried out with the *active* participation of the recipient, who either feeds data into the personalisation process or personalises (some say customises) the service

Table 1. Taxonomy of personalisation from a public service design perspective.

Condition	Dimension	Characteristics			
Provider	Motive° *D1*	Benefits for provider *C11*	Benefits for recipient *C12*	Benefits for society *C13*	
Recipient	Type° *D2*	Citizen *C21*	Private organisation *C22*	Public organisation *C23*	
	Granularity *D3*	Individual *C31*	Group *C32*		
	Consent *D4*	With *C41*	Without *C42*		
	Role°	Active	Passive		
Process	Data source *D5*	Explicit *C51*	Implicit *C52*		
	Data types° *D6*	Demographic *C61*	Situational *C62*	Behavioural *C63*	Environmental *C64*
	Techniques° *D7*	Human-driven *C71*	Static *C72*	Steered *C73*	Autonomous *C74*
	Visibility *D8*	Visible *C81*	Invisible *C82*		
	Purpose *D9*	Relevance-enhancing *C91*	Access-facilitating *C92*	Outcome-improving *C93*	
° means that characteristics are not mutually exclusive					

themselves. Conversely, *implicit* personalisation occurs while the recipient remains *passive*, relying on other sources such as data already held by public authorities or digital traces—data automatically captured from recipients' interactions with digital systems, including clickstreams, transaction logs or usage patterns. Digital government portals illustrate both approaches [26], depending on whether the interface is user-adaptable (*explicit*), self-adaptive based on data provided by the recipient at registration (*explicit*) or self-adaptive based on previous behaviour or known data (*implicit*).

Data types used for personalisation are grouped into four categories. *Demographic* data comprise recipient characteristics relevant to personalisation, such as age, gender, employment, and marital status. While some characteristics are stable or change little over time (e.g., date of birth, citizenship), many relevant to public services, such as income, change regularly, requiring frequent data updates to enable personalisation.

Situational data encompass changing circumstances experienced by service recipients, including current needs or goals. The main family of situational personalisation is life-event approaches. Life events are episodes in an individual's life associated with the need for public services, such as birth, marriage, moving or retirement. Life events can be the structuring criterion for the personalisation of digital government portals [18] or trigger related public services, for example after the birth of a child [32].

Behavioural data capture recipients' interests, preferences and habits. These are provided either directly (*D5*) or inferred from trace data. This category also includes data from recipients sharing similar characteristics to predict future behaviour, for example the observation of road use patterns to optimise traffic management in real time.

Environmental data include time and location. The main family of time-based personalisation is reminders, such as personal alerts for upcoming deadlines (e.g., the expiry of a passport). The traffic management example mentioned for behavioural data also relies on location and time data to operate.

Personalisation ***techniques*** are similar across the public and private sectors. The oldest form of personalisation, *human*, remains prevalent in person-to-person services such as education. Digitalisation enables three main families of algorithmic techniques. *Static* personalisation relies on predefined if-then rules, for example notifying students of scholarship availability if they meet eligibility requirements. *Steered* personalisation uses dynamic algorithms based on supervised machine learning. A much-publicised example is the Family Screening Tool deployed in Allegheny County, Pennsylvania, to assess child welfare risks using a predictive model trained on administrative data. *Autonomous* personalisation encompasses dynamic algorithms based on unsupervised machine learning, where humans determine the input data while algorithms independently infer patterns and define interpretive rules. Although no case of autonomous personalisation was found in the sample, its future adoption in public sector contexts is a possibility given its growing prevalence in the private sector. From a public service design perspective, distinguishing these techniques matters for several reasons, including cost, scalability, consistency, administrative discretion, accountability and interpretability.

Personalisation ***visibility*** refers to whether recipients are made aware of personalisation. This aspect is distinct from the transparency of the underlying code or algorithm. Austrian child benefits, cited by Scholta and Lindgren [32], illustrate *invisible* personalisation, as the life event "birth of a child" triggers the request, eligibility verification and delivery of family allowances to the parents without their awareness.

Process visibility interacts with *recipient involvement* (*D5*): implicit personalisation (*C52*) can occur either visibly or invisibly, whereas explicit personalisation (*C51*) is always visible. Making personalisation visible intuitively seems the better default, though this remains to be empirically verified. *Visibility* is also distinct from *recipient consent* (*D4*). Recipients may be informed that personalisation occurred without being able to oppose it; or they may have consented at an earlier stage yet remain unaware of ongoing personalisation—as in the self-adaptive digital government portal described above, where personalisation draws on data voluntarily provided during registration.

Public service personalisation can take many forms, yet ultimately serves three ***purposes***. A first purpose is to *enhance informational relevance*. This occurs when information is delivered selectively, showing only what is relevant to the recipient, or in a way that is most relevant to them. As in the private sector, this can be achieved by personalising any of three elements: content, layout (or interface) and communication channels [14]. Personalised city newsletters exemplify content personalisation. There is layout personalisation when a digital government portal dynamically adapts its interface, displaying first the services a given user is most likely to seek [12]. Finally, channel personalisation occurs when public documents are delivered through paper mail, email, or messaging platforms, according to recipient preferences [11]. The underlying goal of relevance enhancement is primarily to decrease information overload, though it can also improve conviviality, for instance when the communication references the recipient's name and personal situation. A second purpose is to *facilitate service access*, for example through prefilled forms, automated eligibility checks for means-tested benefits or public services triggered by a life event and delivered without the recipient's involvement. A last purpose of personalisation is to *improve service outcomes*. Current trends in personalised education and healthcare arguably offer the most illustrative examples. They also show that personalisation is not limited to service delivery, but can alter the nature of the service itself, beyond cases addressed by [16].

One last remark must be made regarding a specific class of objects in the sample: chatbots and digital assistants. The taxonomy may seem ill-suited to classify them, as they often bundle different personalised services, such as information provision or task assistance. However, such a tool can in fact help public service designers better distinguish and specify the various functions they wish to assign to their chatbot.

4.2 Taxonomy Demonstration Through Two Empirical Cases

This section demonstrates the applicability of the taxonomy through two examples: the Finnish e-Authorisations system [34] and the Maltese tax non-compliance detection tool [35]. Table 2 provides the classification of both cases according to the taxonomy.

The cases are drawn from the 2025 eGovernment Benchmark [36], which highlights tried-and-tested examples of digital transformation from EU member states, some of which involve personalisation. One limitation of this source is that it is skewed towards success stories. Such a bias however is present in other sources too and is unlikely to undermine the demonstration. Cases were selected based on variation in personalisation characteristics and from countries with different administrative traditions.

The Finnish e-Authorisations service is **a digital power-of-attorney register** enabling citizens and organisations to authorise another person or organisation to act on their behalf (*D2-D3*). The authorised representative may then access online services or complete physical transactions—such as withdrawing prescription-only medication at a pharmacy—with the digital register verifying the authorisation (*D7*). Beyond its convenience for users (*D9*), e-Authorisations is also reported to reduce administrative costs for Finnish authorities (*D1*). The service illustrates personalisation enabled by recipients themselves, who can choose their representative (*D4-D6, D8*). The service also relies on demographic data from public registries to perform the authorisation (*D6*). This example showcases a noteworthy case of personalisation, where service recipients are in full control and administrative costs are reduced for both citizens and public authorities. However, as evident from the case, such public service personalisation relies on a set of technological prerequisites that are typically met only by public authorities with a high level of digital government maturity (e.g., digital identification).

Table 2. Empirical demonstration of the taxonomy of personalisation.

Variables & dimensions	**Case details & characteristics**	
Case name and country	e-Authorisations (Finland)	SAS Viya (Malta)
Public service	Power of attorney	Tax compliance audit
Provider motive *D1*	Benefits for… ☑ Recipients ☑ Provider ☐ Society	Benefits for… ☐ Recipients ☐ Provider ☑ Society
Recipient type *D2*	☑ Citizen ☑ Private organisation ☐ Public organisation	☑ Citizen ☑ Private organisation ☐ Public organisation
Recipient granularity *D3*	☑ Individual ☐ Group	☑ Individual ☐ Group
Recipient consent *D4*	☑ With ☐ Without	☐ With ☑ Without
Recipient role	☑ Active ☐ Passive	☐ Active ☑ Passive
Process data source *D5*	☑ Explicit ☑ Implicit	☐ Explicit ☑ Implicit
Process data types *D6*	☑ Demographic ☑ Behavioural ☐ Situational ☐ Environmental	☑ Demographic ☑ Behavioural ☑ Situational ☐ Environmental
Process techniques *D7*	☐ Human-driven ☑ Static ☐ Steered ☐ Autonomous	☐ Human-driven ☐ Static ☑ Steered ☐ Autonomous
Process visibility *D8*	☑ Visible ☐ Invisible	☐ Visible ☑ Invisible
Process purpose *D9*	☐ Relevance-enhancing ☑ Access-facilitating ☐ Outcome-improving	☐ Relevance-enhancing ☐ Access-facilitating ☑ Outcome-improving

The Maltese Tax and Customs Administration (MTCA) contracted U.S. firm SAS to provide a non-compliance detection service covering both individual and organisational taxpayers (*D2-D3*). SAS software enables automated data analysis and visualisation of flagged cases based on selectable risk factors (*D7*). The MTCA feeds the system with data from fiscal registries, banks and third-party sources such as foreign tax authorities. Behavioural data, including a firm's customs activity, is also increasingly used (*D6*). The process operates without the recipients' knowledge (*D4-D5, D8*). While flagged cases are currently handled by staffers, interactions with the taxpayers could be automated in the future—to quote the head of the MTCA: "Proactively finding errors and noncompliance will allow us to promptly intervene to assist citizens and businesses in avoiding mistakes before they result in penalties" [35]. Although personalisation is framed as a benefit for taxpayers, it primarily serves the public good that is fiscal compliance rather than the direct interests of recipients (*D1*, *D9*). This case highlights the challenge of delineating, within data-intensive digital government, legitimate personalisation from practices that border on generalised surveillance or a presumption of guilt.

These examples illustrate the applicability of the taxonomy, as both cases can be described and categorised without major difficulty. Since not all characteristics are represented, readers interested in other types of personalisation can refer to the examples in the results section. What these cases teach us about public service personalisation, and the potential applications of the taxonomy, is discussed in the following section.

5 Discussion

5.1 Taxonomy Applications

The taxonomy equips both researchers and public service designers with a shared conceptual foundation for engaging with personalisation and supporting the next stages of digital government transformation. For digital government scholars, it helps *identify*, *describe*, *classify* and *distinguish* instances of public service personalisation [29]. Identification and description are particularly valuable given the fuzzy boundaries of the concept. For example, while service co-creation is certainly a phenomenon of interest, labelling it as service personalisation would stretch the concept too far. Classification and differentiation are equally useful given the wide variety of forms the phenomenon can take. Distinguishing between purposes (*D9*), for instance, helps understand the function personalisation serves across contexts as diverse as public administration, healthcare, social care, education, smart cities, policing and public communication.

Besides its theoretical applications, the taxonomy can support the work of public service designers across three phases of the design process [30]. In the definition phase, it facilitates a structured comparison between the existing service and the intended personalised version, helping designers identify necessary modifications, explore available personalisation options and assess the associated risks and costs—such as those related to the choice of personalisation algorithms (*D7*). Furthermore, it can support the comparison of alternative personalisation strategies, contributing to more comprehensive requirements specifications. This is useful given the clear design implications different approaches to personalisation can entail. For example, a service relying on implicit personalisation requires a markedly different data governance architecture than one based on explicit personalisation (*D5*). In the development phase, the taxonomy can serve as a checklist for critical aspects of personalisation—for instance, whether citizen consent is required or desirable (*D4*). Finally, in the evaluation phase, it provides a structuring framework for auditors to understand the type of personalisation implemented and to consider alternative configurations across one or more dimensions.

5.2 Insights from Taxonomy Design

Beyond its immediate applicability, the taxonomy also yields valuable insights that can benefit service design and further research. As previously mentioned, public service personalisation is often considered one of the upcoming innovations in digital government transformation, able to tackle a wide range of challenges crippling public services perceived as exclusionary, disempowering, inefficient and irresponsive [5].

The taxonomy suggests a more nuanced picture. Personalisation is not always the end game at the pinnacle of digital government maturity models. It can take very mundane, unimpressive forms, such as an email from your city warning you of public works in your street. In fact, the sheer diversity of personalisation cases raises the question of whether the concept is not too broad to be analytically useful, as questioned by social policy research [24]. This stems in part from the relational nature of personalisation, reflected in the definition: A personalised service is an enhanced version of a baseline service, which, once improved, shifts expectations and becomes the new standard. In many cases, a personalised service may not feel personal at all, as illustrated by the civil registry update after childbirth going unnoticed by parents. What is considered personalisation is likely to evolve over time, as is also observed in the case of automation [37].

The mundane nature of some personalised services should not, however, hide their potential value. The examples in the sample show that advanced algorithmic techniques are not always needed to achieve a positive impact. The Finnish e-Authorisations service, based on static if-then logic (*C72*), is a case in point.

Critically, personalisation does not necessarily translate into net public value. Take accessibility, which is expected to benefit from more personalisation [12]. Personalisation can enhance accessibility, for instance through the choice of communication channel [11], but can equally undermine it, for example when it imposes an excessive number of choices on recipients (*C51*) [33]. Personalisation thus carries potential trade-offs between target groups and between public values. Ultimately, personalisation's impact is contingent on the type of personalisation implemented, for whom, and how.

Regarding the universalism principle, no object in the sample revealed a clear breach. Some cases of outcome-improving personalisation (*C93*) remain ambiguous, however. In public services such as job counselling, differentiated treatment across recipients may arise. Providing more personalisation for easier cases is a well-studied problem ("cream-skimming"). Yet reserving personalisation for the most vulnerable recipients also constitutes a form of unequal treatment. Nonetheless, such approach is often justified as a means of ensuring fairness and achieving equitable outcomes for all. In some contexts, this may appear unproblematic, but in others, it may be controversial, such as using health data to personalise public insurance premiums. Thus, determining the extent to which a service can be personalised without violating the universalism principle is often a political question, reflecting the broader tension in liberal democracies between equality of opportunities and equality of outcomes.

5.3 Limitations and Areas for Further Research

While this work provides a conceptual step forward in the study of public service personalisation, it comes with certain limitations, which warrant further research.

One limitation is the absence of a dedicated ex post evaluation of the proposed taxonomy [29]. This absence motivates the search for preliminary expert validation at EGOV 2026, prior to a rigorous practitioner evaluation in future work.

Further research is also needed on the organisational and contextual dimensions of public service personalisation. As illustrated by the e-Authorisations and SAS Viya cases, personalisation is data-intensive and involves multiple actors, raising sensitive data governance issues. Organisational drivers and barriers, as well as contextual factors shaping service design across different political, administrative, and welfare traditions, likewise require further investigation.

The insights gained from the taxonomy also point to areas for further research. It highlighted the value of two currently missing tools: one to rank personalisation by implementation difficulty and another by risk to specific public values. While the taxonomy suggests that both vary depending on personalisation characteristics, it falls short of a systematic ranking approach. Developing such tools could help public service designers establish guidelines for prioritising personalisation projects and ensuring responsible implementation—echoing the responsible AI framework—while enabling researchers to better assess the maturity and merits of different approaches.

In addition, the taxonomy examines public service personalisation at high levels of aggregation, given its purposes and the state of prior research. However, *which* public service is transformed by *which* public organisation and for *which* recipient is likely to substantially influence personalisation approaches. More fine-grained analyses within specific taxonomy characteristics would yield valuable insights for service design.

The taxonomy also suggests a proximity between personalisation and other public service design approaches, such as *proactivity* [19, 32]. Clarifying their relationship would reduce conceptual ambiguity and facilitate further research, in particular on related public service innovations, such as *once-only* data provision or *digital nudges*.

Future contributions can be guided by the taxonomy designed in this study, which clarifies the concept of personalisation and maps its multifaceted nature—highlighting what can be personalised in public services, in which ways, and for what purposes.

6 Disclosure of Interests.

The author declares no competing interests.

References

1. Cerrillo-i-Martínez, A.: The personalization of digital services: how is it being driven by European Union Member States? Digit. Gov. Res. Pract. **6**(4), 1–19 (2025)
2. Council of the EU: Tallinn Declaration on eGovernment (2017). https://ec.europa.eu/newsroom/dae/redirection/document/47559. Accessed 10 Nov 2025
3. Deloitte Insights: Government Trends 2023 (2023). https://www.deloitte.com/uk/en/Industries/government-public/about/government-trends.html. Accessed 10 Nov 2025
4. Accenture: Social services: lead with impact (2021). https://www.accenture.com/content/dam/accenture/final/a-com-migration/pdf/pdf-149/accenture-social-services-lead-with-impact.pdf. Accessed 10 Nov 2025
5. OECD: Global Trends in Government Innovation 2024: Fostering Human-Centred Public Services. (2024). https://doi.org/10.1787/c1bc19c3-en. Accessed 8 Aug 2025
6. United Nations: UN e-Government Survey 2022: The Future of Digital Government. UN Publications (2022). https://doi.org/10.18356/9789210019446. Accessed 10 Nov 2025

7. World Bank: Indicators of citizen-centric public service delivery (2018). http://documents.worldbank.org/curated/en/775701527003544796. Accessed 10 Nov 2025
8. Dunleavy, P., Margetts, H.: Data science, artificial intelligence and the third wave of digital era governance. Public Policy Adm. **40**(2), 185–214 (2025)
9. Zuiderwijk, A., Chen, Y.-C., Salem, F.: Implications of the use of artificial intelligence in public governance: a systematic literature review and a research agenda. Gov. Inf. Q. **38**(3), 101577 (2021)
10. Chan, F., Thong, J., Brown, S., Venkatesh, V.: Design characteristics and service experience with e-government services: a public value perspective. Int. J. Inf. Manag. **80**, 102834 (2025)
11. Linders, D., Liao, C.Z.-P., Wang, C.-M.: Proactive e-Governance: flipping the service delivery model from pull to push in Taiwan. Gov. Inf. Q. **35**(4), S68–S76 (2018)
12. Ayachi, R., Boukhris, I., Mellouli, S., Ben Amor, N., Elouedi, Z.: Proactive and reactive e-government services recommendation. Univ. Access Inf. Soc. **15**(4), 681–697 (2016)
13. Pieterson, W., Ebbers, W., van Dijk, J.: Personalization in the public sector: an inventory of organizational and user obstacles towards personalization of electronic services in the public sector. Gov. Inf. Q. **24**(1), 148–164 (2007)
14. Fan, H., Poole, M.S.: What is Personalization? perspectives on the design and implementation of personalization in information systems. J. Organ. Comput. Electron. Commer. **16**(3–4), 179–202 (2006)
15. Homburg, V.M.F., Dijkshoorn, A.: Diffusion of personalized E-government services among dutch municipalities: an empirical investigation and explanation. Int. J. Electron. Gov. Res. **7**(3), 21–37 (2011)
16. Bertot, J., Estevez, E., Janowski, T.: Universal and contextualized public services: digital public service innovation framework. Gov. Inf. Q. **33**(2), 211–222 (2016)
17. Mettler, T., Miscione, G., Jacobs, C.D., Guenduez, A.A.: Same same but different: how policies frame societal-level digital transformation. Gov. Inf. Q. **41**(2), 101932 (2024)
18. Maksimova, M., Solvak, M., Krimmer, R.: Data-driven personalized E-government services: literature review and case study. In: Edelmann, N., et al. (eds.) EPART 2021, LNCS, vol. 12849, pp. 151–165. Springer, Cham (2021)
19. Nikiforova, A., Rodriguez Müller, A.P., Tangi, L., Martin-Bosch, J.: Proactive public services in the age of artificial intelligence: towards post-bureaucratic governance. In: Lindgren, I., et al. (eds.) EGOV 2025, LNCS, vol. 15944, pp. 395–413. Springer, Cham (2026)
20. O'Looney, J.: Personalization of government internet services. In: Proceedings of the 2nd National Conference on Digital Government Research (dg.o'01), Los Angeles (2001)
21. Tuzhilin, A.: Personalization: the state of the art and future directions. In: Adomavicius, G., Gupta, A. (eds.) Business Computing, pp. 3–44. Emerald Group Publishing (2009)
22. Chandra, S., Verma, S., Lim, W.M., Kumar, S., Donthu, N.: Personalization in personalized marketing: trends and ways forward. Psychol. Mark. **39**(8), 1529–1562 (2022)
23. Sunikka, A., Bragge, J.: Applying text-mining to personalization and customization research literature – who, what and where? Expert Syst. Appl. **39**(11), 10049–10058 (2012)
24. Needham, C.: Personalising Public Services: Understanding the Personalisation Narrative. Policy Press (2011)
25. Mikiver, M., Tupay, P.K.: Has the GDPR killed e-government? the "once-only" principle vs the principle of purpose limitation. Int. Data Priv. Law. **13**(3), 194–206 (2023)
26. van Velsen, L., van der Geest, T., van de Wijngaert, L., van den Berg, S., Steehouder, M.: Personalization has a price, controllability is the currency: predictors for the intention to use personalized egovernment websites. J. Organ. Comput. Electron. Commer. **25**(1) (2015)
27. Weigl, L., Roth, T., Amard, A., Zavolokina, L.: When public values and user-centricity in e-government collide – a systematic review. Gov. Inf. Q. **41**(3) (2024)
28. Nickerson, R.C., Varshney, U., Muntermann, J.: A method for taxonomy development and its application in information systems. Eur. J. Inf. Syst. **22**(3), 336–359 (2013)

29. Kundisch, D., et al.: An update for taxonomy designers. Bus. Inf. Syst. Eng. **64**(4), 421–439 (2022)
30. Junginger, S., Sangiorgi, D.: Public policy and public management: contextualizing service design in the public sector. In: Cooper, R., Junginger, S., Lockwood, T. (eds.) The Handbook of Design Management, pp. 480–494. Berg, Oxford (2011)
31. Podsakoff, P.M., MacKenzie, S.B., Podsakoff, N.P.: Recommendations for creating better concept definitions in the organizational, behavioral, and social sciences. Organ. Res. Methods **19**(2), 159–203 (2016)
32. Scholta, H., Lindgren, I.: Proactivity in digital public services: a conceptual analysis. Gov. Inf. Q. **40**(3), 101832 (2023)
33. Kwon, K., Kim, C.: How to design personalization in a context of customer retention: who personalizes what and to what extent? Electron. Commer. Res. Appl. **11**(2), 101–116 (2012)
34. Suomi.fi: Suomi.fi e-Authorizations. t.ly/PZsSM. Accessed 21 Oct 2025
35. SAS: Modernization initiative set to improve taxpayer compliance and morale. t.ly/FjqmA. Accessed 21 Oct 2025
36. European Commission: eGovernment Benchmark 2025: Background report. Publications Office of the European Union (2025). https://op.europa.eu/s/Ad7x. Accessed 21 Oct 2025
37. Lindgren, I., Scholta, H.: Untangling the relationship between public service automation and no-stop government. In: Lindgren, I., et al. (eds.) EGOV 2023, LNCS, vol. 14130, pp. 83–94. Springer, Cham (2023)

Digital Transformation and Corporate Governance in State-Owned Enterprises: An Analysis of the Mechanisms of Institutional Theory

Josiane Lima[1(✉)], Durval Lucas Junior[1(✉)], and Marcelo Henrique de Araujo[2(✉)]

[1] Federal University of Sao Paulo, Rua General Newton Estilac Leal, 932, Osasco, SP 06190-170, Brazil
durval.lucas@unifesp.br
[2] School of Economics, Business, Accounting and Actuarial Science, University of Sao Paulo, Av. Prof. Luciano Gualberto, 908, São Paulo, SP 05508-101, Brazil
marcelo.haraujo@usp.br

Abstract. This paper investigates the adoption of Digital Transformation (DT) to improve Corporate Governance (CG) processes in four Brazilian state-owned Information Technology enterprises (SERPRO, DATAPREV, CELEPAR, and PRODESP). Grounded in Institutional Theory (INT), this qualitative research employed a multiple-case study approach, combining document analysis and semi-structured interviews. The objective was to identify the driving institutional factors, the perceived benefits, and the barriers encountered in this process. The main findings reveal that coercive pressures from control bodies are the main driver for DT adoption in CG, followed by normative and mimetic pressures. It was observed that process restructuring precedes automation and that leadership sponsorship is crucial. The study concludes that federal state-owned enterprises reached a more advanced institutionalization stage (objectification, nearing sedimentation) than state-level ones (habitualization, nearing objectification). The research contributes by applying the INT lens to a specific public context, offering practical guidelines for managers.

Keywords: Corporate Governance · Digital Transformation · Brazilian State-Owned Enterprises · Institutional Theory

1 Introduction

Digital Transformation (DT) is a global, multidisciplinary phenomenon that re-shapes how organizations operate, interact with stakeholders, and deliver value through emergent technologies such as Artificial Intelligence (AI), Internet of Things (IoT), Big Data, Cloud Computing, and Blockchain [2, 31, 52, 53, 62, 63]. In the public sector, DT goes beyond optimizing internal processes toward improving service delivery to society,

Published by Springer Nature Switzerland 2027
G. Viale Pereira et al. (Eds.): EGOV 2026, LNCS 16933, pp. 52–67, 2027.
https://doi.org/10.1007/978-3-032-35747-2_4

with attention to transparency, agility, inclusion, and participation [4, 9, 41, 51, 64]. State-owned enterprises (SOE), private-law entities controlled by the government, have contributed to this technological development [48].

Corporate Governance (CG) in these companies tends to be more complex [60]. SOE are subject to political, social, economic, and regulatory influences that can generate conflicts over strategic direction and effectiveness [24], and their relationship with the government involves multiple simultaneous roles, as it acts as client, shareholder, creditor, and regulator [54, 60]. CG is therefore needed to coordinate technology adoption, reduce duplication and complexity, and guide internal DT [39, 65].

Although recent studies have investigated the DT-CG relationship in SOE abroad, such as Liu et al. [35], who studied two Chinese state-owned telecommunications enterprises (China Mobile and China Unicom) from an Institutional Theory (INT) perspective, the Brazilian context remains underexplored. Brazilian SOE possess specificities: they were created primarily to serve the public interest and national security [48], and they operate under a distinctive and recent governance framework, the SOE Law (Law 13,303/2016), enacted in response to governance failures. This differs from contexts such as China, where SOE act largely as instruments of industrial policy and compete at a larger commercial and international scale [35, 48]. This particularity justifies investigating IT SOE, which have played a pivotal role in advancing the technological development of the Brazilian public sector.

To understand the factors shaping DT adoption in this context, INT offers a suitable lens: by explaining how coercive, normative, and mimetic pressures shape organizational behavior [16, 42], it clarifies why SOE adopt certain practices and how these relate to their institutional environment. Institutional factors are central to the DT of IT SOE, though not in isolation from technological drivers [35], and INT is well suited to studying organizational change [28, 47].

This paper addresses the following research question: *What mechanisms of Institutional Theory explain the relationship between Digital Transformation and Corporate Governance in Brazilian IT SOE*? It examines how DT has been adopted to improve internal CG processes, identifying the institutional factors that influence adoption and the perceived benefits and barriers. A qualitative, multiple-case study was conducted across four Brazilian IT SOE of national and sub-national scope.

The paper contributes theoretically by applying the INT lens to the underexplored context of Brazilian IT SOE [28, 33]; in managerial terms, by identifying concrete benefits and barriers of adopting digital technologies within CG mechanisms [9, 22, 34]; and for public administration, by mapping the institutionalization stage of DT for CG across government domains, which may inform modernization policies [32, 60].

2 Literature Review

2.1 Corporate Governance in Brazilian State-Owned Enterprises

Corporate Governance (CG) in the public sector has been applied to combat corruption [13, 60] and is closely tied to public governance, since both address the agency-conflict problem [56, 58]. Its defining feature here is that citizens occupy the position of principal, seeking to maximize their interests, while politicians and public managers, as agents, tend to pursue electoral ones, generating a conflict of competing interests [5, 24]. CG in SOE therefore has a purpose beyond that of private firms, because the ultimate principal is the citizen [13, 56].

CG principles are objective recommendations that underpin good governance [29, 60], and in SOE they follow national and international references, such as the Federal Court of Accounts (FCA), the World Bank, and the OECD. The OECD Guidelines set ethical standards for public administration and recommend rules that prevent conflicts of interest among shareholders, the public administration, and third-party stakeholders, supporting open and well-functioning markets [59]. CG actions should thus align with society's interests [6] and optimize stakeholder outcomes [7], increasing the public value delivered to those who sustain the State; according to the FCA Framework [56], public organizations exist to execute public policies and provide services to society.

In 2016, Law 13,303 (the SOE Law) was enacted, incorporating most of the provisions the OECD deems necessary for good governance [19, 54, 59]. A reaction to corrupt acts within these companies [10], it guides them to prioritize the State's demands while remaining impartial toward political groups [24].

The reality of Brazilian SOE differs from that of other countries in three main respects. First, their mandate: under Article 173 of the Constitution, direct State economic activity is exceptional, admissible only on grounds of national security or relevant collective interest, so Brazilian SOE are oriented toward the public interest and public-service provision rather than acting as commercial or industrial-policy champions, unlike contexts such as China, where SOE are central instruments of industrial and strategic policy [35]. Second, scale and number: Brazil has a sizeable SOE sector (44 enterprises under direct federal control, besides subsidiaries and numerous state and municipal companies) with significant domestic influence across the social, economic, and political dimensions [24], yet few operate as large multinationals, whereas other countries concentrate SOE that compete at a larger international scale. Third, and most relevant here, the governance regime: a distinctive and recent statutory framework, the SOE Law (Law 13,303/2016), enacted in response to governance failures and complemented by a dense apparatus of control bodies (FCA, Brazilian Office of the Comptroller General (OCG), and Secretariat of Coordination and Governance of SOE(SEST)), subjects these companies to particularly intense compliance demands. Because the definition of a SOE also varies across countries, direct comparisons remain difficult [23, 48].

Governance in these companies is especially complex: beyond reconciling the interests of shareholders and administrators, it must account for citizens as the ultimate owners and users of the goods and services [13, 60]. This dualism can lead to decisions that, favoring the public interest, reduce immediate financial results. Accordingly, Brazilian governance policy has drawn on agency theory [30] to balance interests and curb principal-agent conflicts in the public sector [55].

Given this complexity, adhering to good governance practices is necessary for SOE to maintain focus and fulfill their social function [54]. SOE that adopted CG mechanisms strengthened their governance and increased net profits [13], and well-applied principles can build trust internally and with third parties [12].

2.2 Digital Transformation in Brazilian State-Owned Enterprises

In the private sector, Digital Transformation (DT) aims to provide technologies that improve organizational processes and impact on companies' value propositions [53]. In the public sector, DT helps modernize public management [17], making it more agile, participatory, and citizen-centered, considering aspects such as transparency, accessibility, and inclusion [4, 25, 41].

Brazilian SOE are allies in the Federal Government's DT mission [25], executing or enabling public policies that impact diverse social actors [24]. Government agencies have been rethinking entire processes and services, rather than merely digitizing individual documents [41]. This is evidenced by solutions such as "Gov.br platform", which enables data interoperability among agencies and entities and meets society's demands for simpler, less bureaucratic digital public services [14]. Information Technology (IT) SOE such as SERPRO, DATAPREV, PRODESP, and CELEPAR have contributed to DT in government, applying technologies to increase the efficiency of management and CG.

Benefits of DT for organizational performance and CG improvement have been discussed in the literature [18, 33, 67]. The use of digital technologies drives CG and the monitoring of organizational activities, potentially inducing changes in governance models. Companies must formulate DT strategies tailored to their realities, breaking away from traditional management systems and establishing a structure that supports transformation and organizational performance [67].

Studies conducted in the context of Chinese companies [18, 67] converge in affirming that DT has a positive impact on CG and business performance. However, they differ on which type of company benefits most: even the effects of DT tend to be more prominent in SOE [67], the benefits are more evident in non-SOE [18]. In the Brazilian context, the government has goals to make Public Administration more accessible to citizens through the DT [46], and these guidelines extend to SOE. CG can benefit from DT [9, 34, 45] because, by incorporating digital technologies, SOE strengthen the State's capacity to deliver more accessible and reliable services, increasing the perception of public value [36].

However, there must be administrative rationalization in adopting these technologies so that they deliver concrete benefits to the collectivity [36]. The adoption of digital technologies in the public sector is based on a citizen-centered approach, fostering governance practices such as accountability, control, monitoring, and transparency [25, 34, 38, 41, 45].

Alterations promoted by DT require legitimacy and are subject to changes in course that can lead to institutionalization, deinstitutionalization, and re-institutionalization [21]. In the case of SOE, this is a real possibility, given the influence of internal and external social actors [24, 56]. This connection between DT processes and institutionalization phenomena is explored in the following subsection, which presents Institutional Theory as a theoretical lens to understand these movements.

2.3 Institutional Theory

The rapid emergence of digital technologies pressures companies to align their strategies with a new digital landscape [57]. This is a greater challenge for SOE which, due to their public-sector linkage, face distinct pressures [24, 33, 56, 60]: their governance is influenced by the State, the market, and civil society, distinct sources of power, values, and norms that can generate conflicts over strategic direction.

To capture these relationships beyond governance theory, Filatotchev, Jackson and Nakajima [20] and, earlier, Greenwood and Meyer [27] stress the value of an institutional perspective, in which legal systems fundamentally affect the effectiveness of corporate governance [20]. This aligns with Meyer and Rowan's [42] Institutional Theory, rooted in Weberian principles of rationality and control [50]: the institutional environment of laws, regulations, and social norms shapes organizational behavior and gives practices a rule-like status. DiMaggio and Powell [16], however, note that the engine of organizational rationalization has since changed.

INT has evolved and been applied from different perspectives to explain organizational phenomena [44]. For Meyer and Rowan [42], such phenomena tend toward isomorphism, as organizations align with their institutional environment, through technical and exchange interdependencies, to survive and gain legitimacy.

Institutional isomorphism is a useful lens for much of modern organizational life [16]. Three diffusion mechanisms explain how practices and structures become institutionalized: *coercive isomorphism*, tied to political influence and legitimacy, arises from formal and informal pressures exerted by other organizations; *mimetic isomorphism* is a standard response to uncertainty, through the imitation of organizations perceived as successful or legitimate; and *normative isomorphism* stems from professionalization and the adoption of socially legitimized norms and standards.

These pressures drive organizational homogenization, which becomes evident once organizational fields are established [16]. In this respect, DiMaggio and Powell [16] and Meyer and Rowan [42] converge and complement each other in explaining institutionalization.

In a landscape of rapidly evolving technologies, the public sector must continuously monitor new trends. DT is distinctive in its speed, demanding agile, strategic responses [37], and Public Administration must address it collaboratively to produce public value [21]. As Santos Junior [50] observes, organizations that fail to reorganize in response to societal change risk performance problems and, ultimately, their own survival.

In Tolbert and Zucker's [61] model, environmental monitoring is a continuous and preceding process: the organization observes its field to adapt to change, including through DT-driven innovation. The model defines three institutionalization phases [61]: (i) *habitualization*, the development of new or experimental practices and behavioral patterns; (ii) *objectification*, a growing social consensus on the value of a structure and its increasing adoption; and (iii) *sedimentation*, the perpetuation of the structure over time.

INT has served as a foundational framework for understanding DT in public organizations, given its embeddedness in social, cultural, and political contexts [43, 47]. It is evolutionary and widely applied across domains such as IT, corporate governance, organizational strategy and change, and social responsibility [47], and several authors consider it timely for studying innovation and DT [28, 33, 40], as it foregrounds the sociocultural dimension of change [28]; Santos Junior [50] similarly found a direct link between Institutional Theory and the integration of Marketing and IT.

In this regard, Liu et al. [35] are a relevant reference: analyzing two leading Chinese state-owned telecommunications enterprises, they showed that coercive and normative institutional pressures, together with technological attraction, shaped the companies' DT paths, offering a basis for reflection and comparison with the present study despite the different context. This resonates with Amarante [1], for whom institutional differences are opportunities to better understand organizational complexity.

3 Methods

We adopted a qualitative approach with a descriptive-exploratory purpose, which supports interpreting the analyzed situation and gaining an in-depth understanding of the studied relationships [11] among DT, CG, and Institutional Theory (INT) [26].

We used a multiple-case design, whose comparative and replication logic allows patterns to be examined across cases and supports analytical generalization [66]. The initial universe comprised 18 Brazilian IT SOE operating at the national and subnational levels. After applying the criteria below, 14 companies (2 national and 12 subnational) were excluded for not meeting all of them, leaving four cases: two federal enterprises (SERPRO and DATAPREV) and two state enterprises (PRODESP and CELEPAR). The selection criteria were: (i) operation in the IT sector with a portfolio focused on public services, since these companies are simultaneously agents and subjects of DT, which makes them particularly suited to studying DT applied to CG; (ii) organizational and technological diversity, covering variations in structure, management models, and governance maturity; (iii) representativeness at their administrative level, prioritizing reference companies in each domain (SERPRO and DATAPREV are the main federal IT enterprises, and PRODESP and CELEPAR among the largest state ones); and (iv) availability of standardized, mandatory governance disclosures on transparency portals, ensuring a consistent comparative basis. Drawing cases from two administrative domains was deliberate: it enables the cross-domain comparison central to this study and supports both literal replication within a domain and theoretical replication between domains at different maturity levels [66]. Table 1 summarizes the profile of the selected companies.

We have conducted data collection through documentary research and semi-structured interviews. In the documentary research stage, we have selected the following documents for the year 2023, available in the companies' transparency portals: a) Sustainability Report and/or Integrated Report (Management), and b) Annual Letter on Public Policies and Corporate Governance. Such documents provide a consistent comparative basis, given that these companies, by legal and normative mandate, must make these instruments available annually, adhering to transparency and accountability standards to society. The complete list of documents used in this paper, including weblinks, is available on Appendix 1.

Semi-structured interviews served as a complementary source of evidence under an embedded design: while the documentary analysis covered all four companies and provided the comparative basis, the interviews explored one representative case in each administrative domain, SERPRO at the federal level and PRODESP at the subnational level, chosen for their representativeness and accessibility. The interviews aimed to complement and qualify the documentary evidence, not to generalize across cases. Limiting

Table 1. Profile of the enterprises analyzed

Characteristic	CELEPAR	DATAPREV	PRODESP	SERPRO
Control	State (Paraná)	Federal	State (São Paulo)	Federal
Founded	1964	1974	1969	1964
Legal Nature	Mixed-capital, privately held	Corporation (S.A.), privately held	Corporation (S.A.), privately held	Corporation (S.A.), privately held
Size	Large	Large	Large	Large
Headquarters	Curitiba (PR)	Brasília (DF)	Taboão da Serra (SP)	Brasília (DF)
Affiliation	Civil House Govt. of Paraná	Ministry of Management and Innovation	Secretary of Management and Digital Govt. (SP)	Ministry of Finance
Area of Operation	ICT for the public administration of PR	ICT for social public policies	ICT for the public administration of SP	ICT for the Federal Government

them to two companies restricts within-case analysis, a limitation partially offset by triangulation with documents from all four.

The interviews followed an 18-question script (Appendix 2), anchored in the study's theoretical constructs and organized into three thematic axes (DT, CG, and INT). Interviewees had to hold a management position, work directly in CG or related areas, and have experience with internal processes and practices. The number of interviewees differed between the companies because of each organization's internal policy on official disclosure, which determined the access granted rather than the research design: at PRODESP, access was authorized to a single key informant, the manager of the Governance Office, the role most directly responsible for CG; at SERPRO, to four managers from the Directorate responsible for governance. Although this asymmetry limits the depth achieved at PRODESP, the central position of its key informant and the corroboration from documentary sources mitigate it.

Data were analyzed through content analysis [3]. Coding criteria (Appendix 3) were defined from the subcategories of the three thematic axes established beforehand, and coding drew on interview fragments and institutional documents structured according to the theoretical constructs. Identifying the recording units allowed us to understand managers' perceptions of their organizational experiences in relation to the study's themes. Data processing was supported by electronic spreadsheets for organization and analysis, a transcription tool for the interviews, and XMind software to map concepts and the connections between categories.

4 Results and Discussion

4.1 Characterization of the Analyzed Enterprises

The four companies declare, in their 2023 management and sustainability reports, that they have been acting to promote the government's DT in their respective domains. Documentary analysis, based on institutional reports, Annual Letters of Public Policies and Corporate Governance, and transparency portals (reference year 2023), allowed for the identification of patterns among the groups. State-level companies (PRODESP and CELEPAR) underwent a restructuring of the CG area in 2023 and have been striving to formalize and standardize processes. Federal companies (SERPRO and DATAPREV) present, according to the indicators from the analyzed sources, a more consolidated level of governance maturity. Each case is presented in the following subsections.

4.2 PRODESP

PRODESP positions itself as an agent of digital transformation for the State of São Paulo, developing solutions for public management and the relationship with citizens. The company has a recently established CG structure and has sought to implement DT to support its internal governance processes. According to the Governance Office (GP) manager, the company is still in a development and testing phase, working to standardize its processes.

From an INT perspective, PRODESP is in the habitualization phase [61], with signs of transition to objectification, particularly in the control mechanism, where practices are becoming standardized and gaining internal and external acceptance. Its institutional pressures are predominantly coercive and mimetic, and the imitation of other organizations has been decisive in advancing through the phases. Regarding institutional pressures, coercive isomorphism and mimetic isomorphism were the most evident factors for PRODESP. Practices based on the imitation of other organizations have been decisive in driving the company's progress in transitioning through the phases of institutionalization.

A positive aspect identified is that PRODESP does not seem to face a lack of leadership sponsorship or low prioritization for meeting internal DT demands as a barrier. According to the literature, this is a favorable factor for the evolution of CG and advancement through the institutionalization phases, as leadership is a central aspect in DT processes [8, 15, 37, 39, 49]. The company also has internal manpower to develop tools and automation, which was not pointed out as a limiting factor. On the other hand, the main barrier identified for PRODESP is the need to restructure its internal processes before adopting DT for CG. This finding reinforces the indication that the company is in an initial stage of institutionalization regarding DT for CG [61].

4.3 CELEPAR

CELEPAR is a pioneer as the country's first public IT company and has used technologies such as IoT and artificial intelligence in health, education, and security in Paraná. According to the documentary analysis, the company carried out a restructuring of the

CG area in 2023, similar to PRODESP, and has sought to formalize and standardize its governance processes.

Institutional documents indicate that CELEPAR presents some new experimental practices for CG mechanisms, suggesting a predominant phase of habituation [61]. However, as observed in PRODESP, signs of transition to the objectification phase were identified, particularly in practices related to the control mechanism, which are in a stage of standardization and growing acceptance.

CELEPAR, under state control, shares with PRODESP an earlier pattern of institutionalization compared to the federal companies. Documentary results suggest that, although present, coercive pressures are complemented by mimetic pressures in the adoption of DT practices for CG.

4.4 SERPRO

SERPRO operates solutions that sustain State activities for governments, companies, and citizens, having driven the advancement of Digital Government. It was the company that most evidenced the adoption of digital technologies to support corporate governance among the analyzed cases. The interviews with the four managers of the Directorate responsible for the Governance area (GS1, GS2, GS3, GS4) provided a deeper understanding of how DT has been incorporated into CG processes across the company.

From the perspective of INT, SERPRO appears to be at a higher stage of institutionalization than PRODESP [61], with evidence of a transition to the sedimentation phase. This advancement has been accelerated by predominant coercive pressures, as well as by normative pressures that promote the consolidation of practices.

Coercive isomorphism proved to be the preponderant factor for the evolution of DT in SERPRO. The company is subject to controls carried out by supervisory, regulatory, and controlling bodies such as FCA, OCG, and Secretariat of Coordination and Governance of SOE (SEST), which monitor the legal compliance of federal SOE through indicators, acting to promote greater efficiency, transparency, and internal controls [24]. These pressures favor the adoption of digital technologies to support management and governance processes.

Furthermore, according to the central concept of Meyer and Rowan's [42] INT, large organizations exert influence on institutionalization processes, serving as a model for the field. In this sense, SERPRO, as a large IT company, seeks to legitimize itself in its field of action, somehow encouraging the evolution of other companies, such as PRODESP.

Regarding the perceived benefits, greater operational efficiency, transparency, agility, monitoring, data- and evidence-based decision-making, compliance, improvement of risk management, traceability, better communication, and accountability were highlighted. These elements help the company rationalize expenses and go beyond the organizational limit, bringing positive social impacts and increasing public value [34, 36, 46]. Gains in data security and the potential use of AI, applied safely, for organizational results were also highlighted [2, 31, 52].

Regarding barriers, SERPRO faces technological limitations with certain CG tools that do not always fully meet internal requirements. Other challenges include the lack of integration among tools and the internal capacity to meet specific DT CG demands.

The coercive factor, although preponderant as an accelerator, also proved to be a regulatory barrier. The number of norms and laws that the company must follow to maintain its institutional compliance is significant, and in areas such as the safe use of AI, there is still a lack of regulations. The speed of technological change and the resulting uncertainties were also identified as barriers, as they prevent the consolidation of practices, generating unpredictability and technological obsolescence. The company has been overcoming these challenges through modernization of its technological park, employee training, and partnerships, confirming its pursuit of a more advanced stage of institutionalization. However, barriers hinder the transition to the sedimentation phase [61].

4.5 DATAPREV

DATAPREV provides ICT solutions for the implementation of public policies, particularly in social areas related to Social Security, Labor, and Social Development. According to the documentary analysis, the company demonstrates a level of governance maturity comparable to that observed in SERPRO, which is expected, given that both operate in the federal domain and are subject to the same control and supervisory bodies.

Institutional documents indicate that DATAPREV has more consolidated CG structures than the state companies, with practices that suggest more advanced stages of institutionalization [61]. Coercive pressures, exerted by bodies such as FCA, OCG, and SEST, appear to be the predominant factor in the adoption of technologies to support CG, followed by normative pressures – a pattern similar to that observed in SERPRO. Thus, the homogeneity between the two federal companies in terms of governance maturity was one of the findings of the documentary research, as indicated by the indicators reported in the analyzed sources.

4.6 Comparative Analysis of the Cases

The comparison among the four cases reveals that the motivations for adopting technologies were not limited to a single factor, with multiple influences shaping the organizations [42]. SERPRO was the company that most clearly demonstrated the adoption of DT to support CG; however, the other companies have also utilized and developed DT to improve efficiency in their internal processes.

Coercive isomorphism was the predominant institutional pressure on the studied SOE. This finding is consistent with Liu et al. [35], who identified coercive pressures (policies and regulations) and normative pressures (social responsibility) as key forces shaping the DT path of two Chinese state-owned telecommunications enterprises. Fontes-Filho [24] notes that large public companies face greater pressure to adapt their practices, as they are expected to take a leadership role in adopting best practices disseminated in the market. In this sense, coercive and normative pressures are fostering factors for DT, as SOE, by seeking to align their practices with the institutional environment, comply with government determinations and good practices, thereby producing public value through DT [21].

The primacy of coercive pressure can be explained by the particular dependence of SOEs on the State, which simultaneously acts as shareholder, regulator, client, and creditor [54, 60]. Their legitimacy and continuity rest on legal compliance, and the SOE Law itself emerged as a response to governance failures; for this reason, the institutional field of these companies is primarily regulatory, unlike private companies, where competitive and mimetic pressures tend to prevail. This structural dependence makes coercive isomorphism the dominant mechanism [16]. Moreover, coercive pressure is distinctive in being sanction-backed and continuously monitored: bodies such as the FCA, OCG, and SEST translate it into specific demands, such as transparency portals, standardized data, traceability, and risk controls, that are most efficiently met through digital tools. Coercion therefore does not merely pressure these companies in general terms: it channels them toward DT for CG specifically, which is why it emerged as the most critical factor among the cases.

Regarding the institutionalization phases [61], the comparative analysis of the four companies revealed homogeneity in results across groups within the same domain. Subnational companies predominantly presented in the habitualization phase, with signs of a transition to objectification, especially in the control mechanism. The federal companies demonstrated a higher level of governance maturity, with evidence of a more advanced stage of institutionalization. The greater institutional maturity of the federal SOE can be attributed to three inter-related factors. First, they are embedded in a denser and more instrumented field of coercive oversight: at the federal level, bodies such as the FCA, OCG, and especially SEST monitor governance continuously through standardized indicators (e.g., IG-SEST), which translate compliance demands into concrete, measurable practices and thereby push them more rapidly from objectification toward sedimentation [61]. Subnational companies answer to state-level control structures whose pressure on CG digitalization is less standardized. Second, as large, nationally visible enterprises, the federal SOE face higher reputational stakes and are expected to serve as references in adopting good practices, intensifying the pressure to consolidate them [24, 60]. Third, the timing of formalization differs: the subnational companies only restructured their CG areas in 2023, placing them at an earlier point in the institutionalization process, whereas the federal SOE already exhibited consolidated governance structures, indicating earlier formalization and more time for practices to stabilize. This last point should be read with caution, since the evidence is cross-sectional: part of the observed gap may reflect time-since-adoption rather than the administrative domain as such.

The more in-depth comparison between SERPRO and PRODESP, made possible by the interviews, confirmed these patterns. SERPRO presents a more advanced stage of institutionalization, with evidence of transition to sedimentation, accelerated by coercive and normative pressures. PRODESP is in an initial phase, with a predominance of habitualization, driven by mimetic and coercive isomorphism. According to the central concept of Meyer and Rowan's [42] INT, large organizations exert influence on institutionalization processes, serving as a model for the field. SERPRO, as a large IT company, seeks to legitimize itself in its field of action, somehow encouraging the evolution of other companies, such as PRODESP.

Regarding benefits, the two interviewed SOE highlighted greater operational efficiency, transparency, agility, monitoring, data- and evidence-based decision-making, compliance, risk management, traceability, communication, accountability, and alignment with strategic planning. These elements help rationalize expenses and go beyond the organizational limit, bringing positive social impacts and increasing public value [34, 36, 46]. Gains with data security and the potential use of AI were also highlighted [2, 31, 52].

Regarding barriers, technological limitations of specific CG tools, a lack of integration between tools, and internal capacity to meet specific demands were identified for SERPRO. The coercive factor, although an accelerator, also proved to be a regulatory barrier, given the volume of norms to comply with and the lack of regulations for the use of AI. The speed of technological changes and the resulting uncertainties make it difficult to consolidate practices. For PRODESP, meeting internal demands was not pointed out as a limiting factor, as the company has internal manpower to develop tools. However, it faces organizational challenges stemming from internal process restructuring. Leadership was not identified as a barrier, which, according to the literature, is a favorable factor for leveraging CG and advancing in the institutionalization phases [8, 39, 49].

5 Conclusion

The findings show that coercive pressures from control bodies such as the FCA, OCG, and SEST are the predominant driver of DT for CG, especially in the control mechanism, followed by normative and then mimetic pressures, the latter more visible at earlier evolutionary stages. The two state enterprises, which restructured their CG areas in 2023, are predominantly in the habitualization phase with signs of transition to objectification, whereas the federal enterprises display greater governance maturity, with evidence of movement toward sedimentation.

This study makes three theoretical contributions. First, it extends the institutional reading of the DT-CG relationship to a scarcely explored context: Brazilian IT SOE. The institutional field here is shaped by the State-Owned Enterprises Law (Law 13,303/2016) and oversight of bodies such as the FCA, OCG, and SEST. This setting differs from those examined in prior work: Liu et al. [35] studied two Chinese telecommunications SOEs and found that coercive and normative pressures acted alongside technological attraction; in contrast, our cases show that DT for CG is driven mainly by regulatory and coercive forces, not by technological pull. This illustrates how the institutional environment shapes the mix of pressures. Second, the relative weight of coercive, normative, and mimetic pressures is not uniform. It varies across administrative domains and levels of governance maturity. This refines accounts that treat institutional pressure as monolithic. Third, and most distinctively, the study evidences a dual role of coercive pressure: it acts as an accelerator of DT adoption but also as a constraint. Regulatory rigidity, the volume of compliance norms, and gaps – such as the lack of regulation for safe AI use – create tension within the coercive mechanism. Prior accounts have tended to underemphasize this tension.

In terms of managerial implications, findings provide concrete guidance for SOE managers seeking to advance DT for CG. Three points stand out: 1) leadership sponsorship is an enabling condition for this advancement; 2) process restructuring should precede automation, since digitalizing an unstructured process tends to consolidate inefficiencies; and 3) the double-edged nature of coercive pressure means that compliance, while a powerful driver, can also slow adoption when norms are excessive or absent. Subnational SOE can accelerate their trajectory by learning mimetically from more mature federal SOE. These insights also extend to policymakers and control bodies: oversight indicators effectively induce DT, but greater regulatory clarity – notably for emerging technologies such as AI – would help coercive pressure enable rather than constrain modernization.

Future research could expand direct consultation with SOE representatives, diversify interviewee profiles to include IT and business managers, and extend the analysis to municipal-level technology companies, testing whether these institutionalization patterns recur. The framework integrating CG, DT, and INT can also be applied to other types of public organizations.

Appendix

To access the following content, please consult the supplementary file, available at https://drive.google.com/file/d/1P8VkIoGYLHgLv0pkQ5KTotg2Uj8b3ySY/view

APPENDIX 1: Corporate documents used as data source

APPENDIX 2: Interview Guide

APPENDIX 3: Coding scheme for content analysis

APPENDIX 4: Legislation consulted and mentioned in this paper

References

1. Amarante, J.M.: Institutional theory's past and future contributions to organization studies. Braz. Adm. Rev. **13**(3), 1 (2016)
2. Araujo, V.S., Zullo, B.A., Torres, M.: Big Data, algoritmos e inteligência artificial na Administração Pública: reflexões para a sua utilização em um ambiente democrático. A&C-Revista de Direito Administrativo & Constitucional **20**(80), 241–261 (2020)
3. Bardin, L. Análise de conteúdo. Edições 70 (2011)
4. Barros Júnior, J.M., Santa Rita, L.P., da Silva, W.V.: Digital transformation in Brazilian public administration: the systematic literature review. Revista FSA (Centro Universitário Santo Agostinho) **19**(5), 45–64 (2022)
5. Bevir, M.: Governança democrática: uma genealogia. Revista de Sociologia e Política **19**, 103–114 (2011)
6. Brazil. Casa Civil da Presidência da República. Guia da política de governança pública. Casa Civil (2018). Accessed 27 Aug 2024
7. Buta, B.O., Teixeira, M.A.C.: Governança pública em três dimensões: conceitual, mensural e democrática. Organizações Sociedade **27**, 370–395 (2020)
8. Chen, C.-L., et al.: Role of government to enhance digital transformation in small service business. Sustainability **13**(3), 1028 (2021)
9. Ciancarini, P., Giancarlo, R., Grimaudo, G.: Digital transformation in the public administrations: a guided tour for computer scientists. IEEE Access **12**, 22841–22865 (2024)
10. Coutinho, D.R., Mesquita, C.F.M., Nasser, M.V.N.A.M.: Empresas estatais entre serviços públicos e atividades econômicas. Revista Direito GV **15**, e1902 (2019)
11. Creswell, J.W., Creswell, J.D.: Projeto de pesquisa: Métodos qualitativo, quantitativo e misto. Penso Editora (2021)

12. Cristóvam, J.S., Bergamini, J.C.L.: Governança corporativa na Lei das Estatais: aspectos destacados sobre transparência, gestão de riscos e compliance. Revista de Direito Administrativo **278**(2), 179–210 (2019)
13. Cunha, T.N., Freitas, D.S.B., de Araújo, R.M.: Governança Corporativa e Lucro Estatal: Uma Análise a Partir da Lei das Estatais. Revista FSA (Centro Universitário Santo Agostinho) **17**(10), 52–79 (2020)
14. Dantas, C.F.: Governo digital: oferta de serviços digitais do Governo Federal disponibilizados no portal Gov. BR [Bachelor's thesis, Universidade Federal do Rio Grande do Norte] (2022)
15. Dillenburg, J., Froehlich, C., Bohnenberger, M.C.: A transformação digital e a liderança no contexto empresarial. Gestão e Desenvolvimento **20**(2), 5–27 (2023)
16. DiMaggio, P.J., Powell, W.W.: The iron cage revisited: Institutional isomorphism and collective rationality in organizational fields (American Sociological Review, 1983). Adv. Strateg. Manag. **17**, 143–166 (2000)
17. Fadwa, C., Mohamed, H.: The digital transformation of public administration: moving towards a digital revolution at the service of all users. Int. J. Prof. Bus. Rev. **15**(39) (2023)
18. Fang, Q., Yu, N., Xu, H.: Governance effects of digital transformation: from the perspective of accounting quality. China J. Account. Stud. **11**(1), 77–107 (2023)
19. Faria, A.P.R.O.: O processo legislativo da Lei das Estatais e a OCDE: um estudo sobre a convergência e a divergência dos modelos de regulação (2020). Accessed 28 Apr 2024. https://hdl.handle.net/10438/29308
20. Filatotchev, I., Jackson, G., Nakajima, C.: Corporate governance and national institutions: a review and emerging research agenda. Asia Pacific J. Manag. **30**, 965–986 (2013). Accessed 21 Apr 2024
21. Filgueiras, F., Flávio, C., Palotti, P.: Digital transformation and public service delivery in Brazil. Latin Am. Policy **10**(2), 195–219 (2019)
22. Fitzgerald, M., et al.: Embracing digital technology: a new strategic imperative. MIT Sloan Manag. Rev. **55**(2), 1 (2014)
23. Fontes Filho, J.R., Picolin, L.M.: Governança corporativa em empresas estatais: avanços, propostas e limitações. Revista de Administração Pública **42**, 1163–1188 (2008)
24. Fontes-Filho, J.R.: A governança corporativa em empresas estatais brasileiras frente à Lei de Responsabilidade das Estatais (Lei nº 13.303/2016) (2018)
25. Gomes, M.G.S., et al.: Transformação digital, governo digital e governança digital aplicados no âmbito público – uma revisão sistemática. Revista de Inovação e Tecnologia - RIT **12**(1), 17–34 (2022)
26. Graebner, M.E., Eisenhardt, K.M.: The seller's side of the story: acquisition as courtship and governance as syndicate in entrepreneurial firms. Adm. Sci. Q. **49**(3), 366–403 (2004)
27. Greenwood, R., Meyer, R.E.: Influencing ideas: a celebration of DiMaggio and Powell (1983). J. Manag. Inq. **17**(4), 258–264 (2008)
28. Hinings, B., Gegenhuber, T., Greenwood, R.: Digital innovation and transformation: an institutional perspective. Inf. Organ. **28**(1), 52–61 (2018)
29. IBGC. Código das Melhores Práticas de Governança Corporativa (IBGC 2023). Editora Foco (2023)
30. Jensen, M.C., Meckling, W.H.: Teoria da firma: comportamento dos administradores, custos de agência e estrutura de propriedade. Revista de Administração de Empresas **48**(2), 87–125 (2008)
31. Kim, S., Choi, B., Lew, Y.K.: Where is the age of digitalization heading? The meaning, characteristics, and implications of contemporary digital transformation. Sustainability **13**(16), 8909 (2021)
32. Kumar, V.: The Digital Transformation Journey: Emerging Practices and Trends. Springer, Heidelberg (2017)

33. Li, Z., et al.: Corporate digital transformation, governance shifts and executive pay-performance sensitivity. Int. Rev. Finan. Anal. **92**, 103060 (2024)
34. Lima, J.V.V., et al.: Transformação digital no setor público: resultados preliminares de um estudo terciário. In: Simpósio Brasileiro de Sistemas de Informação (SBSI), pp. 148–153. SBC (2023)
35. Liu, G., et al.: Understanding mechanisms of digital transformation in state-owned enterprises in China: an institutional perspective. Technol. Forecast. Soc. Chang. **202**, 123288 (2024)
36. Lopes, K.M.G., Luciano, E.M., Macadar, M.A.: Criando Valor Público em Serviços Digitais: uma proposta de conceito.Gestão.org **16**(7), 207–221 (2018)
37. Lopes, L. A. V. Papel da liderança como impulsionador da transformação digital e da eficiência organizacional [Doctoral dissertation] (2023). Accessed 4 May 2024. https://comum.rcaap.pt/handle/10400.26/50147
38. Luciano, E.M., Wiedenhoft, G.C., dos Santos, F.P.: Barreiras para a Ampliação de Transparência na Administração Pública Brasileira: Questões estruturais e culturais ou falta de estratégia e governança?. Administração Pública e Gestão Social (2018)
39. Matt, C., Hess, T., Benlian, A.: Digital transformation strategies. Bus. Inf. Syst. Eng. **57**, 339–343 (2015)
40. Melati, C., Janissek-Muniz, R.: A inteligência na gestão pública: uma análise sob a perspectiva institucional. Revista de Administração Pública **56**(6), 721–744 (2022)
41. Mergel, I., Edelmann, N., Haug, N.: Defining digital transformation: results from expert interviews. Gov. Inf. Q. **36**(4), 101385 (2019)
42. Meyer, J.W., Rowan, B.: Institutionalized organizations: formal structure as myth and ceremony. Am. J. Sociol. **83**(2), 340–363 (1977)
43. Morais, R., et al.: Diálogos Entre a Estratégia como Prática e a Teoria Institucional: Uma Revisão Integrativa. Revista FSA **19**(9) (2022)
44. Motke, F.D., Ravanello, F.S., Rodrigues, G.O.: Teoria institucional: um estudo bibliométrico da última década na Web of Science. Contextus: Revista Contemporânea de Economia e Gestão **14**(2), 63–86 (2016)
45. Mountasser, T., Abdellatif, M.: Digital transformation in public administration: a systematic literature review. Int. J. Prof. Bus. Rev. **8**(10), 1–27 (2023)
46. OECD. Digital government. OECD Publishing (2016). Accessed 7 May 2024. https://www.oecd-ilibrary.org/science-and-technology/broadband-policies-for-latin-america-and-the-caribbean/digital-government_9789264251823-15-en
47. de Pereira, F.A.M.: A evolução da teoria institucional nos estudos organizacionais: um campo de pesquisa a ser explorado. Revista Organizações em Contexto **8**(16), 275–295 (2012)
48. da Pereira, G. S.C.: Função socioeconômica das empresas estatais na era da tecnologia [Doctoral dissertation, Universidade Federal do Rio de Janeiro] (2020)
49. Porfírio, J.A., et al.: Leadership characteristics and digital transformation. J. Bus. Res. **124**, 610–619 (2021)
50. dos Santos Junior, D.L.: Mudanças ocorridas no marketing das organizações decorrentes do uso de plataformas de redes sociais: casos brasileiros [Doctoral dissertation] (2015). Accessed 27 July 2024. http://www.teses.usp.br/teses/disponiveis/12/12139/tde-22012016-110527/
51. Santos, A.V., Fonseca, P.G.: Transformação digital no serviço público brasileiro: uma revisão sistemática de literatura. Revista Formadores **15**(1) (2022)
52. Schiliro, D.: Digital economy and digital transformation. In: Digital Technologies for Entrepreneurship in Industry 4.0, pp. 26–42. IGI Global (2022)
53. Silva, A.C., da S. Freitas Junior, J.C.: Influência da Transformação Digital na Dinâmica da Proposta de Valor. Int. J. Prof. Bus. Rev. **8**(7), 129 (2023)
54. Silva, J.P.C.: Oportunidades de avanço institucional na governança das estatais brasileiras. Brasília/IPEA (2018). Accessed 18 Dec. https://ipea.gov.br/sites/images/mestrado/turma2/jean_paulo_castro_e_silva.pdf

55. Silva, M.S., de Schmidt, F.H., Kliass, P. (eds.): Empresas estatais: políticas públicas, governança e desempenho (2019). https://portalantigo.ipea.gov.br/portal/images/stories/PDFs/livros/livros/191125_livro_empresa_estatal_no_brasil.pdf
56. TCU. Referencial básico de governança aplicável a organizações públicas e outros entes jurisdicionados ao TCU (2020)
57. Teichert, R.: Digital transformation maturity: a systematic review of literature. Acta Universitatis Agriculturae et Silviculturae Mendelianae Brunensis (2019)
58. Teixeira, A.F., Gomes, R.C.: Governança pública: uma revisão conceitual. Revista do Serviço Público **70**(4), 519–550 (2019)
59. Thorstensen, V.H., Faria, A.P.: A OCDE e a governança corporativa de empresas estatais (2019). Accessed 28 Apr 2024. https://hdl.handle.net/10438/28451
60. Togni, G.L.: Governança Corporativa em Empresas Estatais: Reflexões a partir da ADI 7331/DF e do PL 28966/2022.Revista de Direito da ADVOCEF **20**(36), 29–48 (2024)
61. Tolbert, P.S., Zucker, L.G.: The institutionalization of institutional theory. In: Handbook of Organization Studies. Sage (1996)
62. Verhoef, P.C., et al.: Digital transformation: a multidisciplinary reflection and research agenda. J. Bus. Res. **122**, 889–901 (2021)
63. Vial, G.: Understanding digital transformation: a review and a research agenda. J. Strateg. Inf. Syst. **28**(2), 118–144 (2019)
64. Viana, A.C.A.: Transformação digital na administração pública: do governo eletrônico ao governo digital. Revista Eurolatinoamericana de Derecho Administrativo **8**(1), 115–136 (2021)
65. Wiedenhöft, G.C.: Relação entre a institucionalização dos mecanismos de governança de tecnologia da informação e o comportamento dos indivíduos: um estudo à luz da teoria institucional e do comportamento de cidadania organizacional [Doctoral dissertation] (2016)
66. Yin, R.K.: Estudo de Caso: Planejamento e métodos. Bookman Editora (2015)
67. Yu, Y.: Digital transformation, corporate governance and enterprise performance: empirical evidence from China. In: 2022 6th Annual International Conference on Data Science and Business Analytics (ICDSBA), pp. 362–369. IEEE (2022). Accessed 2 June 2024. https://ieeexplore.ieee.org/document/10129435/

How Open is Open: A Comparative Analysis of Infrastructural Openness in Digital Government

Josephine Lusi(✉), Eric Blake Jackson, and Ingrid Pappel

Tallinn University of Technology, Akadeemia tee 15A, Tallinn, Estonia
{josephine.lusi,eric.jackson,ingrid.pappel}@taltech.ee
https://taltech.ee/en/department-of-software-science

Abstract. Digital government maturity frameworks are widely used to compare national progress in public sector digital transformation. Yet their ability to capture infrastructural openness remains limited. Prominent indices such as the World Bank's GovTech Maturity Index often emphasise quantifiable and policy-facing indicators, such as the presence of digital portals, interoperability frameworks, and open data initiatives, while offering less direct evidence of the technical and institutional enablers of openness in practice. Our paper proposes a socio-technical framework that distinguishes among open resources, open processes, and open effects, and conceptualises an 'openness paradox', wherein, as openness becomes increasingly codified in maturity assessment, its deeper infrastructural conditions may remain only partially visible. Using a qualitative comparative case study of four high-maturity digital government cases; Estonia, Brazil, Japan, and the United Arab Emirates, the paper examines how openness is publicly evidenced across legal, institutional, and technical artefacts. The findings reveal that high digital maturity does not imply a uniform trajectory of infrastructural openness. Instead, similar maturity levels can coexist with different configurations of institutional and technical openness. The paper contributes to digital government literature by clarifying the limits of maturity-based openness assessment and by proposing a diagnostic approach for evaluating infrastructural openness beyond visible policy and service outputs.

Keywords: Digital government · Digital public infrastructure · Openness paradox · Infrastructural openness · Open government · General E-Government and E-Governance Track

1 Introduction

Global digital government indices, such as the United Nations E-Government Development Index [22] and the World Bank's GovTech Maturity Index [24], have become influential instruments for comparing public sector digital transformation across countries. These frameworks translate complex institutional,

Published by Springer Nature Switzerland 2027
G. Viale Pereira et al. (Eds.): EGOV 2026, LNCS 16933, pp. 68–82, 2027.
https://doi.org/10.1007/978-3-032-35747-2_5

administrative, and technological developments into comparable indicators [23,25] that inform reform priorities, investment decisions and international benchmarking. Yet the same act of comparison that gives these indices their policy influence also narrows what can be seen. National-level maturity assessments tend to privilege visible outputs, formal commitments, and broad socio-economic proxies [23,27], while paying less attention to the infrastructural choices that sustain digital government over time [7,13]. This limitation is especially consequential for digital public infrastructure (DPI) and digital public goods (DPGs), whose public value depends not only on adoption and scale, but also on the conditions under which their underlying components remain inspectable, reusable, interoperable, and governable [3,14,26].

This matters because openness is not only a public-facing attribute of digital government, rather, it is also an infrastructural condition. When maturity indices conflate visible policy-layer openness as proxies for infrastructural openness, they risk conflating symbolic accessibility with operational autonomy [1,13,17]. Policymakers may receive signals that reward visible compliance while leaving deeper vendor dependencies outside the frame of assessment [7,13]; benchmark designers may create equivalence among countries whose digital systems differ substantially in their inspectability, reuse, and auditability [17,23]; and citizens in turn, may lose meaningful oversight of systems that cannot be publicly challenged [1,9].

We conceptualise this tension as the *openness paradox.* As openness becomes increasingly codified within maturity frameworks, assessment practices may increasingly privilege those forms of openness that are easiest to observe, document, and score [1,17,27], while diverting attention from the technical and institutional arrangements that determine whether openness is operationally meaningful [7,13]. The paradox does not imply that maturity frameworks are without value nor that highly ranked digital governments are necessarily closed. Rather, it highlights a structural measurement limitation where the visible openness signals can coexist with infrastructural dependency, restricted reuse, or concentrated control. In such cases, openness becomes administratively legible without necessarily becoming infrastructurally embedded [7,13]. This paper argues that infrastructural openness must be conceptualised and compared as a socio-technical property of digital government systems [14], rather than as a residual indicator of digital maturity. It asks how infrastructural openness can be assessed across high-maturity digital government systems and what such an assessment reveals about the limits of maturity-based assessments. To address this paradox, we develop a socio-technical framework that distinguishes among open resources, open processes, and open effects, and apply it to four advanced but institutionally diverse cases [28]: Estonia, Brazil, Japan, and the United Arab Emirates.

The paper makes two contributions. First, it clarifies the distinction between visible, institutional, and infrastructural openness in digital government. Second, it offers a diagnostic framework for assessing how different forms of openness are represented or obscured in maturity indices. In doing so, the article offers scholars and policy practitioners a framework for assessing why public-facing openness should not be treated as a proxy for the openness of the digital foundations on which contemporary public administration increasingly depends.

2 Conceptual Framework

Openness in digital government can function both as a condition of digital transformation and as one of its outcomes [14,26]. In digital government, open phenomena and information technology are deeply intertwined. Nevertheless, the interpretation of openness is contingent on whether it adopts openness in its technical or governance arrangements [7,26]. Consequently, analysing openness necessitates asking what is opened, to whom, under which legal and technical conditions, and with what consequences for power, accountability, and public value. This conceptual framing adopts a socio-technical perspective that treats digital government infrastructure not as a neutral technical artefact, but as the product of interactions among technological architectures, institutional arrangements, administrative traditions, and societal values [7,14].

2.1 Openness in Digital Governments

In organisational and innovation research, openness is associated with knowledge sharing, distributed innovation, and value creation across institutional boundaries [7]. Open innovation describes the purposive inflow and outflow of knowledge to accelerate innovation beyond the boundaries of a single organisation, allowing innovation to emerge through external collaboration, reuse, and recombination. In the public sector, similar dynamics emerge when governments engage external actors through open data, collaborative service design, civic technology initiatives, and platform-based ecosystems [11,26]. Openness can therefore extend administrative capacity by broadening access to knowledge, capabilities, and participation in ways that closed bureaucratic systems often struggle to achieve [9,20].

Governments increasingly leverage openness as a language of transparency, participation, collaboration, and public value creation [9,14,26]. Open data portals, participatory platforms, and civic co-creation initiatives are often presented as evidence of a more open state [4,9]. These developments are significant, but they do not by themselves establish whether the government's infrastructure is open. For instance, a government may publish open data, encourage co-production, and maintain digital service portals while continuing to depend on closed architectures or proprietary software [7]. It is therefore essential to distinguish openness in governance from openness in infrastructure, a distinction that prevailing maturity frameworks have not yet systematically addressed [17,24].

2.2 From Open Government to Infrastructural Openness

Open principles have been institutionalised through government strategies, transparency reforms, action plans, and transnational policy agendas [26]. International organisations and transnational policy communities, such as the OECD, have played a central role in promoting openness as an administrative value [15,26]. Within this tradition, open government is commonly understood as a mode of governance in which state information becomes more transparent and public processes become more participatory and collaborative [7,9]. Open government data is a foundational component of this agenda [11], enabling access to public information in reusable formats [15,26] and supporting innovation, accountability, and participation.

Yet openness does not carry the same institutional meaning across political systems, and this variation matters for comparative assessment. Popper's concept of the open society [18] provides the normative baseline for this distinction. Openness, in this sense, is not exhausted by the publication of technical assets, the release of code, or the formal availability of standards. It refers to the institutional conditions under which knowledge can circulate, power can be scrutinised, risk can be made visible, and control can be contested, so that public institutions remain accountable to citizens rather than insulated by the very infrastructures through which they govern. A government that deploys the language of openness while limiting civil liberties or centralising control over digital infrastructure may satisfy the formal requirements of openness indicators while departing from the democratic logic that gives openness its normative force. This distinction shapes what 'high institutional openness' means when comparing a deliberative democracy with strong rights protections to a centralised governance system organised around different assumptions about participation, expression, and public accountability [1,18,19].

Hayek's argument that knowledge is inherently dispersed and that centralised systems struggle to harness dispersed knowledge effectively [10], provides a complementary institutional rationale for open infrastructure. Open technical systems are not only democratically preferable because they allow scrutiny. They are also epistemically productive because they enable distributed innovation, adaptation, and reuse across a wider range of actors. In this sense, infrastructural openness connects directly to questions of accountability, legitimacy, resilience, and public trust—dimensions that are central to public administration but underweighted in technical or maturity-based frameworks [1,9].

Historically, openness has also been central to the development of infrastructure itself [14]. The argument for open government infrastructures rests on the premise that public-sector data, software, standards, and systems developed with public resources should generate public value beyond the boundaries of the institution that produced them [9,26]. Open APIs, open standards, open-source components, shared reference architectures, and reusable digital building blocks create the technical and governance conditions for interoperability, modularity, reuse, and ecosystem participation [7,21], as reflected in the Government-as-a-Platform model [4]. In recent years, these concerns have been linked to digital sovereignty [8,24], understood as the collective capacity of states and communities to shape, govern, and safeguard the digital infrastructures, data, and standards on which they depend. Digital public infrastructure (DPI) and digital public goods (DPGs) [3,14] have therefore been framed as mechanisms through which states can retain meaningful control over critical digital systems and strengthen digital resilience [24]. Here, openness is not the opposite of control. It is one condition under which public control can remain accountable, adaptable, and collectively governed.

2.3 Open Resources, Open Processes, and Open Effects

To provide a more precise analysis of openness, this article distinguishes among open resources, open processes, and open effects. This distinction prevents treating openness as a singular, undifferentiated attribute of digital government [26]. It also makes visible the ways in which governments may be open in one dimension while remaining closed, opaque, or strategically controlled in another [7,13].

Open resources are technical artefacts that can be accessed, inspected, reused, modified, or shared under relatively permissive conditions [7,24]. These include open-source software, open standards, open APIs, open datasets, and reusable reference architectures. Open processes denote the degree to which participation, decision-making, design, implementation and governance are accessible to a broader range of actors [9,26], and include participatory policymaking, collaborative platform governance, multi-stakeholder co-design, and ecosystem-based innovation. Open effects refer to the intended outcomes associated with openness [9,11,26], such as transparency, accountability, competition, inclusion, innovation, interoperability, and democratic participation.

A socio-technical perspective reveals that these dimensions do not necessarily align. A government may promote open government values [26], such as transparency and civic participation, while relying on closed proprietary infrastructures [7]. Similarly, a government may publish open-source code without opening its decision-making processes or governance arrangements [19]. Furthermore, a government may enact participatory governance processes that broaden civic engagement without publishing openly reusable technical resources [9,19]. This is why openness cannot be treated as a binary condition. Rather, it is a socio-technical relationship that changes according to what is opened, to whom, under what conditions, and with what consequences [9,26]. Infrastructural openness is therefore shaped not only by technical choices but by the institutional environments, legal frameworks, and political traditions within which those choices are made, maintained and governed [7,18].

This three-dimensional perspective explains why maturity frameworks can misread openness. Frameworks that privilege visible policy commitments, public-facing services, and measurable outputs may register openness at the level of resources, processes, or effects while remaining blind to the closed technical components beneath them [13,17].

3 Study Design and Analytical Framework

This study examines infrastructural openness as a property that cannot be inferred directly from maturity scores, policy commitments, or the visible presence of digital government services. Openness becomes analytically meaningful only when traced through the legal, institutional, and technical arrangements that determine whether digital systems can be inspected, reused, audited, adapted, and governed over time [7,13]. For this reason, the study employs a comparative case study design [28], using the GTMI [24] as a maturity denominator rather than as a definitive measure of infrastructural openness. The GTMI provides a common reference point because it integrates diverse measures [5], including the UN E-Government Survey 2024, and includes openness-relevant indicators as described in our conceptual framework.

Cases are selected through purposive sampling using a maturity-held-high, openness-varied logic. The sampling frame is restricted to GTMI Group A countries [24], ensuring that variation in openness configurations, rather than variation in general digital maturity, drives the comparison. Four cases are selected to maximise variation across technical and institutional openness. Estonia represents a small EU member state with a rights-based constitutional order and a strong tradition of deliberative democracy [2], where digital infrastructure development has been closely aligned with transparency, judicial enforceability of data privacy, and individual accountability. Brazil represents a large federative democracy marked by significant socioeconomic inequality [15], where a strong federal commitment to open-source infrastructure coexists with uneven sub-national implementation capacity. Japan represents a technocratic administrative tradition with strong state coordination [17], where standardisation and efficiency take precedence over participatory openness. The United Arab Emirates represents a centralised, state-led governance model [24,26], where openness is primarily articulated through service delivery, economic competitiveness, and platform-enabled administrative performance. Together, these cases allow the study to examine whether similar maturity scores can conceal different infrastructural settlements around openness, authority, and control [17,28].

Data collection followed a structured protocol conducted between January and March 2026 and drew on four document types: national digital strategy documents and legislative texts; official technical documentation, including API catalogues, OSS licensing pages, and interoperability specifications; open data portal metadata and dataset inventories; and GTMI indicator reports and reproducibility data [5]. Documents were identified through official government portals, cross-referenced against GTMI indicator descriptions, and supplemented by targeted searches of national legislative repositories and technical documentation websites. The unit of analysis is the country case, represented through GTMI indicators triangulated with publicly verifiable artefacts such as legal instruments, official portals, software repositories, and interoperability frameworks. Where documents were not publicly accessible, or where licensing terms were absent from official sources, this was treated as evidence of limited verifiability rather than proof that openness was absent. This triangulation reduces the risk of mistaking missing index evidence for actual absence, or visible policy commitments for infrastructural openness [13,28].

3.1 Operationalizing Openness

Openness is operationalised through qualitative coding informed by the conceptual framework. The analysis is primarily deductive: the categories *open resources*, *open processes*, and *open effects* were derived from the framework before data examination [28]. These categories distinguish between the artefacts made open, the governance processes through which openness is enabled or constrained, and the effects openness produces for reuse, inspection, accountability, and adaptation. Within each category, evidence was coded at three levels: *asserted*, where openness is claimed in policy or institutional language without accompanying technical documentation; *indicated*, where supporting evidence exists but remains only partially verifiable; and *verified*, where openly accessible artefacts and documentation substantiate the claim.

For example, the GTMI indicator cluster for 'OSS policy present' was coded by examining whether a formal OSS policy or legislative mandate exists in accessible statutory text; whether specific OSS deployments or procurement guidelines are documented; and whether OSS-licensed components can be directly verified through accessible repositories or official licensing documentation. This procedure produced a differentiated coding profile across the three openness dimensions rather than reducing openness to a binary presence-or-absence score.

The coded evidence is mapped onto a four-quadrant analytical matrix, shown in Fig. 1. The matrix is used as a heuristic device rather than a formal scoring instrument [28]. It positions cases along two axes: Technical Openness, which captures the openness of infrastructural artefacts such as standards, code, APIs, data exchange layers, and documentation; and Institutional Openness, which captures the legal mandates, governance structures, rights protections, and participatory mechanisms that enable or require openness.

Quadrant 1, *Generative openness*, captures cases where strong technical openness is reinforced by strong institutional mandates. Quadrant 2, *Technocratic openness*, captures cases where technical capability and standardisation are comparatively strong, but institutional safeguards for citizen participation, accountability, or rights-based oversight are more limited. Quadrant 3, *Closed/Early-stage openness*, captures systems with limited openness across both axes, whether because infrastructures remain proprietary, documentation is sparse, or institutional mandates are weak. Quadrant 4, *Symbolic openness*, captures cases where openness is visible in policy commitments, portals, or institutional language, but is not matched by corresponding technical depth or verifiability.

4 Results and Discussion

This section presents the empirical findings in two steps. First, the case analyses examine how openness is configured in each country across open resources, open processes, and open effects. Second, the comparative summary brings these

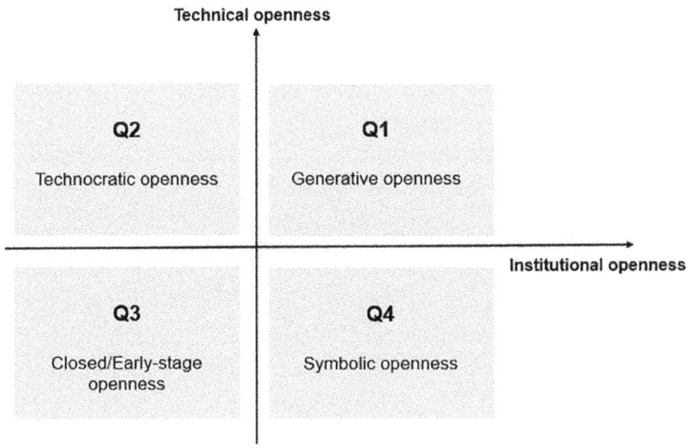

Fig. 1. Conceptual framework of openness indicators

findings together through Fig. 2 and Table 1, which show that the same GTMI maturity category can contain very different infrastructural openness arrangements.

4.1 Case Analysis

Estonia

Estonia represents the case in which the paradox is least pronounced, as the institutional and technical layers of the state have been deliberately aligned to make openness operational rather than merely declarative [24]. The Public Information Act[1] establishes an open-by-default principle that is not confined to policy rhetoric, and is enforced through architectural choices, i.e. the Once-Only Principle and the X-Road[2], which is a decentralised open-source interoperability backbone that enables cryptographically verifiable, auditable data exchange across public and private organisations [2]. The Keyless Signature Infrastructure (KSI) makes state data access inspectable at the citizen level through the Data Tracker,[3], while the national Open Data Portal,[4] structured through FAIR principles and DCAT-AP metadata standards under CC BY 4.0 licensing, reinforces the alignment between legal access rights and technical reusability.

Yet even generative openness carries residual concentrations of control. X-Road's institutional stewardship remains concentrated through the Nordic Institute for Interoperability Solutions, and the state's reliance on Guardtime for KSI implementation shows that open technical components can coexist with

[1] https://www.riigiteataja.ee/en/eli/514112013001/consolide.
[2] https://x-road.global/.
[3] https://www.ria.ee/en/state-information-system/people-centred-data-exchange/data-tracker.
[4] https://www.eesti.ee/eraisik/en/avaleht.

specialised vendor dependencies [12]. More fundamentally, Estonia's openness derives its normative force from the democratic governance tradition in which it is embedded, as citizens hold legally enforceable rights to audit state data access, and public information law is subject to judicial review [1,18]. Aggregate maturity scores do not capture this distinction, yet it is central to understanding why Estonia's openness differs from cases where similar public-facing instruments operate without comparable accountability structures.

Brazil
Brazil demonstrates the federative form of the paradox through its strong institutional mandates at the national level that coexist with uneven technical implementation across a highly decentralised state. Federal legal mandates, including the 2003 decree establishing free software guidelines (Decreto No. 4.553/2002 and subsequent OSS promotion decrees, publicly accessible), the Access to Information Law (Lei No. 12.527, 2011), and the Digital Government Law (Lei No. 14.129, 2021), establishes clear commitments to open-source licensing and proactive data disclosure [15], operationalised through the e-PING interoperability standards,[5] the Conecta gov.br API hub,[6] and the Software Público Brasileiro portal,[7] which enable code reuse and machine-to-machine integration across federal agencies. The gov.br[8] digital identity platform, built on RESTful APIs and open authentication standards, demonstrates how technical architecture can embed openness into the organisation of service delivery itself.

The paradox emerges when federal architecture is read against jurisdictional reality. Across 26 states and more than 5,500 municipalities, implementation capacity, technical staffing, procurement arrangements, and institutional incentives vary substantially. States such as Rio Grande do Sul and Minas Gerais have operationalised open data portals and interoperability standards, while others lack the resources to translate federal mandates into technical practice [15]. National-level maturity indicators treat federal policy as a proxy for openness across the entire state, a substitution the GTMI cannot correct for [17,24]. Brazil's configuration is therefore hybrid: generative at the centre, potentially symbolic at the periphery. Infrastructural openness in federative systems cannot be assessed through aggregate national scores alone [13,17].

Japan
Japan exemplifies technocratic openness as it is characterized by advanced technical standardization and interoperability maturity without equivalent generative institutional mandates. The establishment of the Digital Agency (2021)[9], Digital Procedures Act[10] and the Government Interoperability Framework

[5] https://eping.governoeletronico.gov.br/.
[6] https://gerenciador-conecta.readthedocs.io/.
[7] https://www.gov.br/governodigital/pt-br/plataformas-e-servicos-digitais/software-publico.
[8] https://www.gov.br/pt-br.
[9] https://www.digital.go.jp/en.
[10] https://www.japaneselawtranslation.go.jp/en/laws/view/4212/en.

(GIF)[11] establish strong legal baselines for transparency and digital-by-default services. However, participatory mechanisms remain limited, and the public participation system is widely criticised as one-way communication [17], reflecting a model of administrative transparency rather than deliberative openness, where efficiency and standardization take precedence over citizen co-creation.

Technically, the GIF and Core Vocabulary ensure cross-agency data compatibility and constrain proprietary divergence [7,20], while the Digital Marketplace[12] and the Open Contracting Data Standard (OCDS) aim to reduce vendor lock-in across more than 1,700 municipalities. Yet Japan lacks a comprehensive national OSS mandate and does not promote open-source adoption at scale, relying instead on localised initiatives (e.g., Tokyo Metropolitan Government) and civic tech movements like Code for Japan [6]. The result is a technically sophisticated digital government in which openness is a product of standardised coordination rather than publicly inspectable, community-governed infrastructure [17,24].

United Arab Emirates (UAE)
The UAE represents the performative form of the paradox in its clearest expression. Institutional commitments to openness are extensive and visible, through the UAE Centennial 2071,[13], the Personal Data Protection Law (2021),[14] the Bayanat.AE Open Data Portal[15] hosting over 3,000 datasets, the UAE API Marketplace,[16] and the UAE PASS[17] digital identity platform enabling access to over 15,000 services together constitute a substantial apparatus of public-facing digital state capacity.

The paradox lies beneath this visible layer. The backend technical infrastructure, including the Government Service Bus[18], FedNet cloud environment[19], and smart city platforms such as DubaiPulse[20], provide no accessible documentation on open-source adoption, source code availability, or licensing arrangements. Furthermore, no national open-source mandate, public code repository policy, or accessible licensing framework for core government infrastructure is identifiable through public channels. The UAE's high institutional openness score therefore reflects performance at the interface and policy layers rather than at the infrastructural layer. The UAE's framing of openness as an instrument of service

---

[11] https://www.digital.go.jp/en/policies/data_strategy_government_interoperability_framework.
[12] https://www.digital.go.jp/en/policies/dmp.
[13] https://u.ae/en/about-the-uae/strategies-initiatives-and-awards/strategies-plans-and-visions/innovation-and-future-shaping/uae-centennial-2071.
[14] https://uaelegislation.gov.ae/en/legislations/1972/download/.
[15] https://www.bayanat.ae.
[16] https://u.ae/en/about-the-uae/digital-uae/digital-transformation/platforms-and-apps/uae-api-marketplace.
[17] https://uaepass.ae/.
[18] https://u.ae/en/information-and-services/g2g-services/government-services-bus.
[19] https://u.ae/en/information-and-services/g2g-services/features-of-fednet.
[20] https://partnersportal.smartdubai.ae/Services/Details/c64fcb52-534f-4831-815f-ab5d4aed38b6.

excellence and economic competitiveness [8,26] reflects a governance model in which digital state capacity is consolidated through centralised administration rather than democratic accountability or judicially enforceable data governance rights [1,18]. This does not diminish the UAE's genuine achievements in digital service delivery; rather, it implies that cross-case comparisons require explicit acknowledgement of these normative differences.

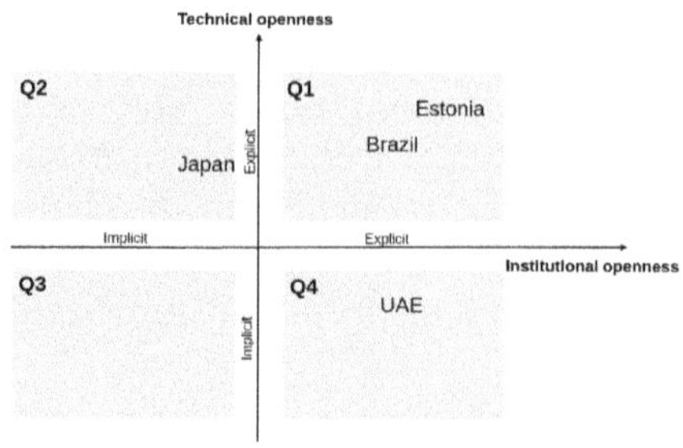

Fig. 2. Comparative positioning of country cases on the analytical matrix

4.2 Discussion

The four cases confirm the openness paradox not as a uniform failure of digital government maturity indices, but as a family of context-specific mismatches between institutional visibility and infrastructural verifiability, each shaped by the governance logic and accountability arrangements of its political context. Figure 2 maps the conceptual positioning of the four cases, while Table 1 presents the empirical evidence behind those positions.

Estonia shows the weakest form of the paradox because legal rights, open-source infrastructure, auditability, and democratic accountability are closely aligned, even though vendor dependencies and institutional stewardship complicate claims of full community-governed openness. Brazil shows a federative paradox, where national-level generativity coexists with uneven sub-national implementation. Japan shows a technocratic paradox, where standardisation and administrative coordination are strong, but open-source generativity and participatory openness remain limited. The UAE shows a performative paradox, where highly visible openness at the policy and service layers is not matched by comparable transparency at the infrastructural layer.

These configurations demonstrate that openness is not a scalar property that increases with digital maturity. It is a socio-technical configuration shaped by legal mandates, technical architecture, procurement structures, licensing regimes, and regime context [7,13,26]. A government may be open in its datasets but closed in its source code; open in its API strategy but opaque in its cloud dependencies [1,7]; open in its interoperability standards but closed in its participatory governance. Maturity indices can detect some of these signals, but they

Table 1. Comparative configurations of infrastructural openness across four high-maturity digital governments.

Case	Open Resources	Open Processes	Open Effects	Evidence Status	Configuration
Estonia	Strong: X-Road (open-source); open data portal; CC BY 4.0 datasets; DCAT-AP and FAIR-aligned metadata.	Strong: open-by-default legal framework; Once-Only Principle; decentralised data exchange; citizen Data Tracker; judicially reviewable public information rights.	Strong: reusable infrastructure; cross-border data exchange; citizen auditability; high alignment between legal rights and technical enforceability.	Publicly documented, with residual questions concerning vendor dependence and institutional stewardship.	Generative openness: high institutional and high infrastructural openness.
Brazil	Strong federally: e-PING; Software Público Brasileiro; Conecta gov.br API environment; gov.br identity platform using open authentication standards.	Strong nationally, uneven sub-nationally: Access to Information Law; Digital Government Law; national interoperability and reuse policies; variable implementation across states and municipalities.	Mixed: federal openness supports reuse and integration; sub-national variation limits uniform infrastructural openness across the nation.	Publicly documented federally; partially documented and uneven at the sub-national level.	Federative openness: generative at the centre, uneven across the federation.
Japan	Moderate: GIF; Core Vocabulary; Digital Marketplace; open contracting initiatives; no national OSS mandate.	Moderate: strong standardisation governance; limited co-design mechanisms; openness mediated through technocratic coordination.	Moderate: improved interoperability, limited open-source generativity.	Partially documented; several technical and procurement claims require stronger official citation.	Technocratic openness: high standardisation, limited generativity.
UAE	Limited to moderate: Bayanat.AE open data portal; UAE API Marketplace; UAE PASS; limited public documentation on backend infrastructure, OSS licensing, or code accessibility.	Limited: state-led and service-oriented model; limited evidence of multi-stakeholder governance, public code reuse, or civic co-design for core infrastructure.	Mixed: strong digital service delivery, limited public auditability, and rights-based accountability.	Public-facing artefacts documented; core infrastructural openness not publicly verifiable.	Symbolic openness: high interface visibility, limited infrastructural inspectability.

are structurally ill-equipped to distinguish among their political and technical meanings.

Regime context explains much of this variation. Estonia's openness is rights-backed and embedded in democratic accountability structures. The UAE's openness is state-directed, service-facing, and organised through technocratic administration. Brazil's openness is mediated by federalism, while Japan's is mediated by administrative standardisation. Treating these cases as equivalent because they occupy the same maturity conflates different governance philosophies and different accountability relations [17,18]. The framework developed here supports configurational comparison rather than linear ranking. Its purpose is not to establish causal explanations for why countries adopt particular openness models, but to identify how different forms of openness are represented, simplified, or obscured by maturity-based assessment.

This analysis clarifies both the value and the limits of maturity frameworks. Instruments such as the GTMI are useful for comparing visible socio-technical outputs, policy commitments, and service delivery capabilities [13,17,24]. However, they are less equipped to assess whether government software is openly licensed, whether code is accessible, whether documentation enables reuse, whether technical components are independently auditable, whether procurement produces lock-in, or whether infrastructure is governed through accountable institutional arrangements. Countries can therefore appear similarly mature while differing substantially in the degree to which openness is embedded in their digital foundations. For scholars and policy practitioners, the implication is direct. Public-facing openness should not be treated as a proxy for the openness of the digital foundations on which contemporary public administration increasingly depends. Comparative frameworks should therefore distinguish between institutional visibility and infrastructural openness, and they should interpret both in relation to regime context, governance design, and technical verifiability. Without that distinction, maturity indices risk scoring openness where they can see it, while overlooking where it actually resides.

5 Conclusion

Digital governments do not become open simply by declaring it. They become open, or fail to, through the legal frameworks that enforce access rights, the technical architectures that make reuse and inspection possible, and the governance arrangements that determine whether those conditions are maintained over time. The openness paradox names what happens when assessment frameworks lose sight of this distinction. As openness becomes increasingly valued and codified in maturity indices, institutional actors are incentivised to signal it through visible artefacts rather than embed it within core technical infrastructure [24].

Through a comparative analysis of Estonia, Brazil, Japan, and the United Arab Emirates, four states that score similarly on the GTMI yet differ substantially in how openness is technically constituted, this paper demonstrates that the paradox is empirically observable and takes context-specific forms: federative fragmentation in Brazil, technocratic standardisation in Japan, performative signalling in the UAE, and a rights-backed but imperfect generativity in Estonia. Conceptually, the analysis disaggregates openness into open resources, open processes, and open effects, showing that these dimensions need not co-occur and that their configuration is shaped as much by regime context as by technical choice. High institutional openness in a rights-based democracy carries different accountability implications than the same score in a centralised technocratic state [1,18], a distinction that aggregate maturity indices cannot register, and comparative research cannot safely ignore [13,17].

These findings carry clear implications for both research and assessment design. The study focuses on high-maturity GTMI Group A countries [24] and relies on publicly available documentation, meaning that what is visible determines what can be assessed, a limitation that itself reflects the paradox. Future research should test whether the paradox also appears in lower-maturity contexts, develop verifiable indicators of technical openness [13], and address subnational variation in federative systems [15]. Combining documentation analysis with expert interviews and technical repository analysis would allow researchers to distinguish performative from substantive openness in ambiguous cases [28]. For policymakers, the central implication is that openness assessments must look beyond strategies and public-facing platforms to assess whether the digital foundations of the state are open and democratically accountable. Without that shift, maturity indices will continue to measure the openness states declare rather than the openness their infrastructures permit.

Disclosure of Interests. The authors have no competing interests to declare that are relevant to the content of this article.

References

1. Bannister, F., Connolly, R.: The trouble with transparency: a critical review of openness in e-government. Policy Internet **3**(1), 1–30 (2011)
2. Blake Jackson, E., Dreyling, R., Pappel, I.: A historical analysis on interoperability in Estonian data exchange architecture: perspectives from the past and for the future. In: Proceedings of the 14th International Conference on Theory and Practice of Electronic Governance (ICEGOV 2021), pp. 111–116. ACM, New York (2021)
3. Clark, J., Marin, G., Ardic Alper, O.P., Galicia Rabadan, G.A.: Digital Public Infrastructure and Development: A World Bank Group Approach. Digital Transformation White Paper, vol. 1. World Bank, Washington, D.C. (2025). http://hdl.handle.net/10986/42935, License: CC BY-NC 3.0 IGO
4. Cordella, A., Paletti, A.: Government as a platform, orchestration, and public value creation: the Italian case. Gov. Inf. Q. **36**(4), 101409 (2019). https://doi.org/10.1016/j.giq.2019.101409
5. Dener, C., et al.: Reproducibility package for GovTech Maturity Index (GTMI) 2025 Update, World Bank (2025). https://doi.org/10.60572/50TK-0S28
6. European Commission: OSS Country Intelligence Report Japan. Interoperable Europe, Brussels (2024). https://interoperable-europe.ec.europa.eu/sites/default/files/inline-files/OSS%20Country%20Intelligence%20Report%20Japan.pdf. Accessed 16 Mar 2026
7. Fishenden, J., Thompson, M.: Digital government, open architecture, and innovation: why public sector IT will never be the same again. J. Public Adm. Res. Theory **23**(4), 977–1004 (2013)
8. Floridi, L.: The fight for digital sovereignty: what it is, and why it matters, especially for the EU. Philosophy Technol. **33**(3), 369 (2020)
9. Harrison, T.M., et al.: Open government and e-government: Democratic challenges from a public value perspective. In: Bertot, J.C., Nahon, K., Chun, S.A., Luna-Reyes, L.F., Atluri, V. (eds.) Proceedings of the 12th Annual International Conference on Digital Government Research (DG.O 2011): Digital Government Innovation in Challenging Times, pp. 245–253. ACM, New York (2011)

10. Hayek, F.A.: The use of knowledge in society. Am. Econ. Rev. **35**(4), 519–530 (1945)
11. Janssen, M., Charalabidis, Y., Zuiderwijk, A.: Benefits, adoption barriers and myths of open data and open government. Inf. Syst. Manag. **29**(4), 258–268 (2012)
12. Kitsing, M.: An evaluation of e-government in Estonia. In: Proceedings of Internet, Politics and Policy, pp. 16–17 (2010)
13. Linåker, J., Muto, S.: Advancing Digital Government: Integrating Open Source Software Enablement Indicators in Maturity Indexes. arXiv preprint arXiv:2510.04603 (2025). https://arxiv.org/abs/2510.04603. Accessed 16 Mar 2026
14. Lusi, J., Lorenz, B., Pappel, I.: Innovation or reinvention? A systematic and bibliometric review of public sector digital infrastructure. J. Open Innovation Technol. Market Complex. **11**(3), 100593 (2025)
15. OECD: Digital Government Review of Brazil: Towards the Digital Transformation of the Public Sector. OECD Digital Government Studies, OECD Publishing, Paris (2018). https://doi.org/10.1787/9789264307636-en
16. Panagiotopoulos, P., Klievink, B., Cordella, A.: Public value creation in digital government. Gov. Inf. Q. **36**(4), 101421 (2019). https://doi.org/10.1016/j.giq.2019.101421
17. Pirannejad, A., Ingrams, A.: Open government maturity models: a global comparison. Soc. Sci. Comput. Rev. **41**(4), 1140–1165 (2023)
18. Popper, K.R.: The Open Society and Its Enemies. Vol. 1–2. Routledge, London (1945)
19. Shkabatur, J.: Transparency with (out) accountability: open government in the United States. Yale L. Pol'y Rev. **31**, 79 (2012)
20. Simon, K.D.: The value of open standards and open-source software in government environments. IBM Syst. J. **44**(2), 227–238 (2005)
21. Tiwana, A.: Platform Ecosystems: Aligning Architecture. Governance and Strategy. Morgan Kaufmann, Waltham, MA (2014)
22. United Nations: UN E-Government Survey 2024: Accelerating digital transformation for sustainable development. United Nations, New York, NY (2024). https://publicadministration.un.org/egovkb/en-us/Reports/UN-E-Government-Survey-2024. Accessed 15 Mar 2026
23. Valdés, G., Solar, M., Astudillo, H., Iribarren, M., Concha, G., Visconti, M.: Conception, development and implementation of an e-Government maturity model in public agencies. Gov. Inf. Q. **28**(2), 176–187 (2011)
24. Vasconcelos, J.R., et al.: GovTech Maturity Index 2025: Tracking Public Sector Digital Transformation Worldwide. Prosperity Insight Series. World Bank, Washington, D.C. (2025). http://documents.worldbank.org/curated/en/099121725193511608. Accessed 15 Mar 2026
25. Veljković, N., Bogdanović-Dinić, S., Stoimenov, L.: Benchmarking open government: an open data perspective. Gov. Inf. Q. **31**(2), 278–290 (2014)
26. Wilkinson, R., Krasodomski, A., Wilkinson, I.: The case for expanding digital public infrastructure: How open, scalable technology can serve citizens, preserve sovereignty and save money. Research Paper. Royal Institute of International Affairs, London (2025). https://doi.org/10.55317/9781784136604
27. Wirtz, B.W., Birkmeyer, S.: Open government: origin, development, and conceptual perspectives. Int. J. Public Adm. **38**(5), 381–396 (2015)
28. Yin, R.K.: Case study research: Design and methods, vol. 5. Sage, Thousand Oaks (2009)

Digital Government and Discretion in Street-Level Bureaucracy: A Policy Analysis from The Netherlands

Guido Ongena(✉), Carolijn Schrijver, Erik Slingerland, Jeroen van Grondelle, and Wouter Bronsgeest

University of Applied Sciences Utrecht, Utrecht, The Netherlands
guido.ongena@hu.nl

Abstract. Discretion is a central concept in street-level bureaucracy, yet its role is evolving in the context of digital transformation in public administration. This paper examines how discretion is reflected in policy discourse and organizational practices within Dutch public service organizations. The study draws on focus group discussions with public employees from municipalities and national government agencies involved in policy development and digital transformation initiatives. The data were analyzed using qualitative text analysis supported by large language models. The findings show that discretion is shaped by the interaction between external mandates, organizational visions, and implementation practices. Legal frameworks, accountability mechanisms, and political priorities continue to define the boundaries within which discretion can be exercised. At the same time, organizations increasingly emphasize citizen-centered service delivery and the importance of professional judgment. However, translating these ambitions into practice remains challenging due to digital infrastructures, standardized procedures, and organizational silos. The study highlights how discretion in digitally transforming public administrations emerges from the interaction between legal, technological, and organizational factors.

Keywords: Digital Government · Discretion · Street-Level Bureaucracy

1 Introduction

The concept of street-level bureaucracy lies at the heart of public administration research concerned with how policies are translated into practice. Originally developed by Michael Lipsky [1, 2], the theory emphasizes that public policies are not simply implemented top-down; rather, they are lived, interpreted, and often reshaped by frontline public officials who interact directly with citizens (e.g., municipal clerks, social workers, police officers, and teachers) in everyday service encounters. These frontline workers—street-level bureaucrats—operate under conditions of uncertainty, limited resources, and divergent citizen needs, making professional discretion central to their work. Discretion here refers to the judgment and choice that these employees exercise when interpreting and applying general policy rules to specific cases, especially where rules are incomplete or ambiguous.

Published by Springer Nature Switzerland 2027
G. Viale Pereira et al. (Eds.): EGOV 2026, LNCS 16933, pp. 83–97, 2027.
https://doi.org/10.1007/978-3-032-35747-2_6

In recent years, public administrations have undergone digital transformation, integrating information systems into their daily operations. This digital transformation encompasses not only the adoption of new tools (e.g., e-service portals, automated workflows) but also systemic changes in how services are organized, delivered, and managed. Proponents argue that such a transformation can improve efficiency, accessibility, and transparency in public service delivery. Yet digitalization also raises important questions about how it interacts with human discretion at the street level [3]. Buffat [4] explored this interaction, identifying two contrasting perspectives on how digital technologies affect street-level discretion. The curtailment thesis posits that ICT systems can reduce or eliminate discretionary space by embedding decisions in standardized algorithms and workflows that leave little room for individual judgment [5, 6]. Conversely, the enablement thesis suggests that digital tools can augment discretion by providing frontline workers and citizens with richer information resources, enhanced decision support, and new modes of interaction that extend the capacity for responsive, context-sensitive judgment.

Empirical research increasingly complicates this binary. For example, studies show that automation can influence the perception of discretionary power and enforcement styles even when formal roles remain unchanged. Although literature also shows that these roles also change due to digital transformation [7]. These findings suggest that digital systems do not uniformly diminish or expand discretion but rather reshape the conditions under which discretion is exercised [8]. Further, literature emphasizes that digital transformation in public sectors involves strategic decisions about design, implementation, and governance of technology—all of which have implications for frontline work and policy execution. For instance, Vervaenen and Danneels [9] review digital strategy frameworks in public organizations, showing that strategic choices in digitalization influence how services are delivered and how human and digital elements interact.

While current discretion studies are mainly focused on discretion as used and thus examined street-level bureaucrats (e.g., [10–13]) or have a narrow focus on digital technology [14], this paper aims to examine how the digital transformation is reflected in public policy with regard to discretion in street-level bureaucracy. By drawing on classic street-level bureaucracy theory and contemporary digital government literature, the study analyses how policy conceptualizes, structures, and addresses discretionary space amid digital transformation.

We analyzed governmental agencies in the Netherlands that administer public services and operate as street-level bureaucracies. In the Dutch context, the concept of discretion has gained renewed prominence following several high-profile administrative scandals, most notably the childcare benefits affair, in which bias, ignored warning signals, and a lack of proportionality had severe consequences for large numbers of citizens. These events triggered intense political and societal debate about the functioning of public administration and the position of civil servants within it. In response, Dutch political discourse has increasingly emphasized the responsible use of discretionary authority as a means to better account for individual circumstances, recognize early signals, and prevent disproportionate governmental action. Civil servants are no longer viewed solely as implementers of legislation, but also as actors with a responsibility to safeguard citizens and uphold principles of good governance [15]. This renewed attention reflects a broader tension within public administration between vertical governance, which is rooted in hierarchy, legal compliance, and rule-based implementation, and horizontal governance, in which rules and practices evolve through interaction between government, society, and frontline professionals [16]. The contemporary debate on discretion thus illustrates the ongoing search for balance between legal certainty, accountability, and responsiveness to citizens' lived realities.

2 Theoretical Background

2.1 Street-Level Bureaucracy and Discretion in Policy Implementation

The concept of street-level bureaucracy provides a foundational framework for understanding how public policies are implemented in practice. Lipsky [1, 2] defines street-level bureaucrats as public service workers who interact directly with citizens and possess substantial discretion in the execution of their work. These actors operate at the interface between the state and citizens, where abstract policy goals are translated into concrete decisions affecting individuals' rights and access to public services.

Lipsky [2] argues that street-level bureaucrats effectively become de facto policymakers, as their routine decisions cumulatively shape policy outcomes. This is particularly the case in contexts characterized by high caseloads, limited resources, ambiguous rules, and conflicting policy objectives. Rather than being anomalies, discretionary practices are thus a structural feature of public service delivery. In addition, street bureaucrats see the first developments within society that could give rise to new impetus for enforcement, regulations, and possibly amended or new legislation [17].

Discretion is a central concept in Street-Level Bureaucracy and refers to the latitude of judgment available to frontline officials when applying policy rules [1]. Because laws and regulations cannot fully anticipate the complexity and variability of real-world situations, policy implementation necessarily involves interpretation and choice. Subsequent scholarship has refined this concept by distinguishing between discretion-as-granted—the formal decision space defined by legal and organizational frameworks—and discretion-as-used, which captures how street-level bureaucrats exercise judgment in practice [18, 19]. This distinction highlights that discretion is not merely an individual attribute or preference but is shaped by institutional arrangements, organizational cultures, professional norms, and the nature of the public service task itself. While discretion-as-used is often associated with bottom-up dynamics [19], this study focuses on discretion-as-granted, emphasizing the top-down structures and institutional conditions that shape frontline decision-making [19].

Discretion plays a dual role in public administration. On the one hand, it enables responsiveness, equity, and professional judgment; on the other, it raises concerns about consistency, accountability, and potential arbitrariness. Understanding how discretion is structured and exercised is, therefore, essential for evaluating the democratic and administrative quality of public service delivery.

2.2 Digital Transformation and Discretion

Digital transformation has become a defining feature of contemporary public administration. It refers not only to the adoption of information and communication technologies but also to broader organizational and institutional changes in how public services are designed, delivered, and governed [9, 20]. Digital tools such as e-government platforms, automated workflows, and decision-support systems increasingly mediate interactions between citizens and public authorities.

From a theoretical perspective, digital transformation challenges traditional assumptions about bureaucratic work. By encoding rules into software systems and standardizing procedures, digital technologies can redistribute decision-making authority within organizations and alter the relationship between human judgment and formal rules.

The interaction between digitalization and street-level discretion has received growing scholarly attention. Bovens and Zouridis [21] argue that ICT can contribute to a shift from street-level to system-level bureaucracy, where decision-making logic is increasingly embedded in technological systems rather than exercised by frontline workers.

Building on this literature, Buffat [4] conceptualizes the effects of e-government on street-level discretion through two competing theses. The curtailment thesis suggests that digital systems constrain discretion by limiting choice and standardizing decisions. In contrast, the enablement thesis emphasizes that digital tools can support discretion by providing better information, enhancing transparency, and facilitating more informed judgment.

Recognizing that the effects of digital transformation on discretion can vary across contexts and are shaped by system design, organizational settings, and service characteristics, this paper adopts a nuanced perspective and employs discretion as an analytical lens to examine its implications for frontline policy implementation.

2.3 An Institutional Lens on Street- Level Bureaucracy

Street-Level Bureaucracy has traditionally focused on the discretionary practices of frontline public servants and their interactions with citizens. Lipsky's seminal work conceptualizes street-level bureaucrats as policy actors who interpret and implement rules under conditions of limited resources, ambiguity, and competing demands [2]. This perspective has been particularly influential in explaining micro-level implementation processes, especially the role of discretion in everyday encounters between public officials and service users [22]. However, scholars have noted that SLB theory provides more limited analytical leverage for explaining how broader organizational and institutional structures shape frontline practices [23].

An institutional lens extends SLB theory by situating frontline discretion within wider systems of rules, norms, and governance arrangements. Institutional Theory emphasizes that organizational behavior is shaped not only by formal regulations and policy mandates but also by legitimacy pressures, professional norms, and culturally embedded expectations [24, 25]. From this perspective, discretion is institutionally embedded rather than solely individually enacted. Organizational routines, managerial systems, accountability structures, and interorganizational pressures shape both the scope of discretion-as-granted and the ways in which discretion is exercised in practice [26].

Combining SLB with an institutional perspective, therefore, enables a multi-level understanding of policy implementation. At the micro level, frontline actors interpret and apply policy in concrete interactions, while at meso and macro levels, institutional arrangements structure the organizational conditions under which these interactions occur [27]. This integrated framework allows street-level practices to be understood not only as individual coping strategies but also as outcomes shaped by broader organizational and institutional environments.

3 Research Method

This study adopts a qualitative policy analysis [28] to examine how digitalization is reflected in public policy concerning discretion in street-level bureaucracy. The analysis focuses on how policy conceptualizes, frames, and regulates discretionary space in the context of digital transformation.

3.1 Data Collection and Sample

We conducted 5 focus group discussions with informants from 4 municipalities and 1 national governmental agency. These organizations were selected because they were already engaged in and had gained experience implementing discretion in street-level bureaucracy. This was done while also ensuring the selection included organizations of diverse sizes and were located across multiple provinces across the Netherlands, both within and outside the Randstad, in order to capture a diverse range of perspectives.

40 participants involved in policy-making within their respective organizations were selected. Table 1 presents an overview of respondents' gender, years of experience, and professional roles. Participants were purposively selected based on their responsibility for strategic direction, coordination, governance, and oversight of policy development and digital transformation initiatives within their organizations.

The focus groups were guided by a semi-structured topic guide designed to explore how discretion and the human dimension are framed in the context of digital transformation. The guide was organized into three thematic blocks. The first block addressed the broader institutional environment in which the organization operates. It aimed to identify external pressures, formal obligations, and structural conditions that shape how discretion and digitalization are articulated at the policy level. The second block examined the organization's internal logic, core values, and strategic ambitions. This section sought to understand how discretion and digitalization are normatively framed within

Table 1. Participant Characteristics.

Factor	Characteristic	N	Proportion (%)
Organizational level	National	9	23%
	Municipal	31	78%
Gender	Male	16	40%
	Female	24	60%
Years of experience	≤5 years	12	30%
	6–15 years	20	50%
	16–25 years	5	13%
	26+ years	3	8%
Professional role	Advisory and Policy	11	28%
	Strategic and Program Management	18	45%
	Service Design and Citizen Interaction	3	8%
	Operational Management	8	20%

the organization and how these ambitions are expressed in strategic discourse. The third block focused on the translation of policy ambitions into organizational structures and processes. It explored how abstract policy principles, particularly those concerning discretion and the human dimension, are embedded in governance arrangements and digital infrastructures. As shown in Table 2, each thematic block was operationalized into a set of guiding topics.

Table 2. Focus group topic guide.

Block	Topics
Organizational context and external mandates	• Legal and regulatory frameworks (e.g., legislation, policy mandates, supervisory frameworks) • Ministerial or political directives and strategic goals • Accountability and performance requirements (e.g., KPIs, monitoring, reporting obligations) • Digitalization mandates and frameworks (e.g., national digital government strategies, Common Ground)

(continued)

Table 2. (*continued*)

Block	Topics
Organizational vision and ambitions	• The organization's understanding of the "human dimension" in public service delivery • Internal interpretations of citizen-centeredness and organizational culture • Strategic ambitions regarding discretion and tailored service provision • The relationship between digital transformation and the safeguarding of the human dimension • The extent to which principles such as "human-centered service for all" are embedded in organizational discourse
Translation into organizational practice	• Governance and organizational design choices (e.g., responsibilities, decision-making structures) • The development of internal guidelines, protocols, and implementation frameworks • Capacity-related decisions (e.g., staffing, training, use of technology) • Process design and digital systems, including their influence on work processes and citizen interactions • Monitoring and evaluation mechanisms related to tailored service provision and discretionary space

3.2 Data Analysis

We analyzed the focus group transcripts using topic classification with the KWALLM application, an open-source tool developed by Kennispunt Twente for qualitative text analysis with large language models (LLMs) [29]. The transcripts were manually preprocessed, yielding a dataset of 1,093 participant quotes that was loaded into KWALLM. As the interviews were conducted in Dutch, the Ministral 3:14B model was used to analyze the texts due to its strong performance on multilingual tasks and its ability to run locally. The quotes were classified by the LLM according to the themes defined in the focus group topic guide. An additional reject option was included to handle quotes with low classification certainty [30, 31]. The research team subsequently reviewed and interpreted the classifications to ensure alignment with the study's conceptual framework on discretion and digital transformation.

Based on this classification, subsets of quotes were created for each thematic category. These subsets were further examined to identify participants' perspectives and to detect emerging topics not explicitly captured in the topic guide. The interpretations were discussed among the researchers involved in the focus groups in order to reach agreement on the findings. For each thematic category, the LLM was prompted to generate a short English summary describing the perspectives reflected in the classified quotes. This summary served as the basis for the discussion between researchers on what findings emerged for each thematic category. This was done by providing the research summary and discussing, based on the quotes, what elements they agreed with, disagreed with, and missed in the summary. This discussion formed the basis for the findings. By situating the automated classifications within an interpretive qualitative analysis, the approach combines the analytical capabilities of LLM-supported topic classification with established qualitative research practices, enabling a systematic exploration of themes related to discretion, digital governance, and the human dimension. The LLM prompts and dataset are accessible through the open science framework (OSF) repository [32].

4 Findings

Below, we present the findings from our analysis, organized according to the three main thematic blocks used in the topic guide. These blocks are further elaborated in the following (Sects. 4.1–4.3), where we also illustrate the findings with quotations from participants representing the different public organizations included in the study.

4.1 Organizational Context and External Mandates

The organizational context and external institutional mandates shaping digital transformation and discretion focus on external governance conditions, including legal and regulatory frameworks, ministerial and political directives, accountability and performance requirements such as KPIs and reporting obligations, and national digitalization policies and strategies. The aim was to explore the formal institutional pressures and boundary conditions within which public organizations operate, and how these conditions structure policy implementation, organizational decision-making, and the framing of discretion in the context of digital transformation.

A recurring theme concerns the dominant role of legal frameworks as both drivers and constraints in public service delivery. Participants referred to legislation such as the Participation Act, the General Data Protection Regulation, and the Environmental Act as defining the operational boundaries within which organizations operate. Recent developments in the Participation Act, for example, require municipalities to take a more proactive role in informing citizens about their rights. At the same time, detailed legal requirements and concerns about legal robustness were described as limiting the room for discretionary decision-making and encouraging cautious policy implementation.

Political steering also shapes the context in which policies are implemented. Participants noted that differences in local political priorities can influence how policies are interpreted and applied across municipalities, for example, in the balance between enforcement-oriented approaches and more proactive, citizen-centered service provision: *"[...] In my estimation, that has a lot to do with the political color. We have a board of mayor and aldermen here consisting of GroenLinks and D66... They simply consider this very important. [...] [... has a] truly right-wing political color, so they are focused on enforcement"*. In addition, national policy agendas and ministerial priorities, such as the Hervormingsagenda Jeugd (Youth Reform Agenda), were described as influencing local policy directions.

Participants also referred to national definitions, mandates and initiatives around the human dimension in public service delivery as abstract and open for interpretation. This is also the case within digitalization initiatives, like the Nederlandse Digitaliseringsstrategie (Dutch Digitalization Strategy), which provide strategic guidance but are perceived as offering limited concrete direction on integrating discretion into digital services: *"The latest one is that Dutch digitalization strategy that came out. [...] What I find typical is that the whole concept of the "human dimension" isn't mentioned there. [...] It says a lot and it says very little at the same time"*.

Digitalization was described as having a dual role in public service delivery. On the one hand, digital systems support standardization and efficiency, for example, through platforms and digital data exchange infrastructures. On the other hand, participants indicated that digital systems could introduce rigid structures that make it difficult to adapt services to individual situations. Several participants identified limitations in existing ICT infrastructures that can impede changes in work processes, even when organizational decisions have already been made: *"[Digital systems] impede the adaptation of work processes at a very basic level. Whichever work process you want to adapt, you are dealing with ICT components these days. And if I make a change... If I decide now, today, as the Management Team, that we want to change this in our work processes, then we have to go through such a cycle that we might be able to start in June next year. But then everything has to go along with it, and all ideas have to be at the top of everyone's priority list."*. In addition, participants noted that data-driven automation or limited system integration may fail to adequately account for individual circumstances when early warning signals are not identified in time. Respondents emphasized the importance of detecting the need for tailored service provision at an early stage in order to prevent problems from escalating rather than addressing issues retrospectively. Finally, participants indicated that performance indicators related to discretion are generally not prescribed through formal national frameworks. Participants noted that this results in a level of ambiguity provides flexibility for organizations to develop indicators within organizations.

4.2 Organizational Vision and Ambitions

The organization's vision and strategic ambitions concerning discretion and the human dimension in public service delivery are reflected in how discretion is conceptualized internally, including interpretations of citizen-centeredness, public values, and organizational culture. Strategic ambitions related to tailored service provision and the role of professional judgment are articulated in programmatic and project documentation. Digital transformation is framed in relation to safeguarding the human dimension, and particular attention is given to the extent to which principles such as human-centered service for all are embedded in organizational discourse and strategic narratives.

While the discretion is widely adopted as a guiding principle, participants indicated that its practical meaning often remains ambiguous. Several participants noted that the concept is broadly supported but rarely operationalized in concrete terms, which leads to varying interpretations across organizations. In some cases, it is framed as context-sensitive and trust-based service delivery, where employees are encouraged to exercise professional judgment and consider citizens' individual situations. Others describe it primarily as a cultural shift that requires internal motivation and organizational learning, while also acknowledging that political priorities and managerial objectives may limit its application. Some participants also pointed to small-scale initiatives aimed at facilitating tailored support and early detection of problems.

A further theme concerns the importance of organizational culture and employee empowerment in enabling the human dimension in service delivery. Participants highlighted the need to foster trust in frontline professionals and to provide sufficient space for employees to exercise professional judgment when addressing individual cases. *"It is very easy to tell the workforce to be flexible and to offer customized solutions. But there is a manager above them. And yes, they think: as long as I don't have to commit or phase things, it will be easy"*. Creating clear expectations and boundaries, and initiatives such as internal consultation structures and case-based discussions were mentioned as mechanisms to support tailored solutions. At the same time, participants noted that cultural change requires time and sustained organizational effort: Longstanding administrative routines and established working methods can make it difficult to shift toward more flexible and responsive approaches, emphasizing the need for training, organizational support, and a supportive work environment.

A recurring theme concerns the tension between digitalization and human-centered service delivery. Digital tools, such as self-service portals and chatbots, are seen as enablers of efficiency: *"For example, we have now started chatting, and then you reach a different group that you shouldn't always call. That helps too"* but also risk depersonalizing interactions. Hybrid models that combine digital-first approaches with human fallback have been implemented in some organizations. Yet, limitations in IT infrastructure, slow system adaptation, and privacy regulations often hinder their effectiveness. In other cases, organizations adopt a more cautious approach, prioritizing direct human interaction through phone or face-to-face support to ensure accessibility for all citizens. Overall, digitalization is viewed as a tool to support, rather than replace, the human dimension in public services.

4.3 Translation into Organizational Practice

Strategic ambitions in organizational practice relate to governance and organizational design choices, including the allocation of responsibilities and decision-making structures. Attention was given to the development of internal guidelines, protocols, and implementation frameworks that operationalize policy objectives. This also addressed capacity-related decisions, such as staffing, training, and the use of technology, as well as the design of processes and digital systems and their influence on work practices and citizen interactions. Finally, it considered monitoring and evaluation mechanisms aimed at assessing tailored service provision and the exercise of discretionary space.

A key theme concerns the role of middle management in translating discretion into practice. Participants indicated that middle managers occupy a pivotal position between strategic ambitions and operational implementation. In this role, they must balance legal requirements with the need for flexibility in responding to individual cases. At the same time, middle managers face constraints such as limited resources, shortages of specialized staff, and competing organizational priorities: *"We very often have to work with the business case here. [tailored services]"*. Consequently, they are often required to make practical decisions about how policy objectives can be implemented within existing organizational and legal boundaries.

Another theme concerns the interaction between frontline discretion and organizational structures. Participants described how professionals in social services, enforcement, and citizen support frequently adapted standardized procedures to respond to individual circumstances. Rather than applying rules rigidly, practitioners often relied on consultation and collaboration within and across organizations to find workable solutions in cases where formal procedures were perceived as insufficient. This flexibility enabled faster responses and more tailored support, although such actions still depended on approval from higher levels within the organization. However, structural constraints limit their flexibility. Standardized processes designed for the majority of cases, limited cross-departmental collaboration, privacy and legal restrictions, and workload pressures all restrict discretionary action. To navigate these constraints, employees frequently rely on informal networks and professional judgment, although such practices are not systematically embedded within organizational structures, resulting in inconsistent application of discretion: *"and you have to know the social, the front-line field. That's it. Because I hear that very often from new people who have just joined the organization. Where is it all located? What is our social work field? Where can I turn for help? And that isn't documented"*.

Digital transformation was described as both enabling and constraining the realization of discretion. Legislative frameworks such as the Act on the Modernization of Electronic Administrative Communication require governments to provide digital services while also offering alternative channels for citizens who cannot use digital means. In practice, however, participants noted that legacy systems and existing IT infrastructures can limit flexibility. Even relatively small adjustments to work processes may require lengthy technical development cycles. As a result, digitalization can create a paradox: while intended to simplify citizen interaction, system constraints and slow adaptation may reduce the ability to respond to individual needs: *"For the entire ICT side, or in automation or digitization, you are talking about limited resources and manpower there, and they are already very busy keeping existing systems running. Let alone being able to discuss a change in work processes with each other at all. And this is in the direction of a human scale, but even if we had wanted to develop in a different direction, you have the same problem"*.

5 Discussion

This study examined how discretion is reflected in organizational discourse and policy contexts in Dutch public service organizations undergoing digital transformation by taking an institutional lens on street-level bureaucracy. The findings highlight how discretion is shaped by three interrelated dimensions: external institutional mandates, organizational visions and ambitions, and the translation of these ambitions into organizational practice. Together, these dimensions illustrate how discretion is embedded in broader governance arrangements rather than solely located at the frontline of service delivery.

First, the results show that external institutional mandates strongly structure the scope of discretion. Legal frameworks, accountability mechanisms, and political priorities define the boundaries within which public organizations operate. Although recent political discourse in the Netherlands emphasizes the need for more context-sensitive public administration following administrative failures, organizations remain strongly oriented toward legal compliance and risk avoidance. This finding aligns with classic work on street-level bureaucracy, which emphasizes that discretion is exercised within institutional constraints rather than in complete autonomy [1]. More recent research similarly highlights that governments increasingly attempt to manage and structure discretion through governance frameworks and performance regimes [4, 18].

Second, the findings regarding organizational visions and ambitions illustrate the normative framing of discretion in contemporary public administration. The human dimension and citizen-centered service delivery are widely promoted in strategic narratives, yet participants reported that these concepts often remain ambiguous and open to interpretation. This observation resonates with research showing that policy narratives around responsiveness and personalization frequently coexist with managerial and accountability pressures that limit practical flexibility [8]. The ambiguity surrounding such concepts may lead to different interpretations across organizations and actors, highlighting the importance of organizational culture and internal governance structures in shaping how discretion is understood and applied.

Third, the results demonstrate how discretion is translated into practice through organizational arrangements, digital infrastructures, and managerial processes. Participants described how digital systems, standardized procedures, and siloed organizational structures can constrain discretionary action, even when strategic ambitions emphasize flexibility. At the same time, frontline professionals often rely on professional judgment and informal collaboration networks to address individual situations. These findings reflect broader debates on digital era governance, which suggest that digital technologies can both constrain and reshape discretion by embedding rules and procedures in technical systems [21]. Recent studies similarly show that automation and digital decision-support systems may influence the exercise of discretion rather than eliminating it [8, 23].

Finally, the analysis highlights the critical role of middle management in mediating between policy ambitions and frontline practice. Middle managers operate at the intersection of legal requirements, organizational priorities, and operational constraints, translating abstract policy goals into workable practices. Previous research has emphasized that discretion is exercised not only by frontline professionals but also shaped by managerial decisions and organizational governance structures [18, 33]. The findings of this study reinforce this perspective by showing how middle managers play a key role in balancing accountability, efficiency, and responsiveness.

Taken together, the findings suggest that discretion in digitally transforming public administrations emerges from the interaction between legal frameworks, digital infrastructures, and organizational practices. Understanding these interactions is essential for designing governance arrangements that enable professional judgment while maintaining accountability and consistency in public service delivery.

6 Conclusion

This study explored how discretion is reflected in organizational discourse and practices within Dutch public service organizations undergoing digital transformation. The findings show that discretion is shaped by the interaction between external mandates, organizational visions, and the translation of these ambitions into everyday practices. Legal frameworks, accountability mechanisms, and political priorities continue to define the boundaries within which discretion can be exercised. At the same time, organizations increasingly emphasize citizen-centered service delivery and the importance of professional judgment. However, translating these ambitions into practice remains challenging. Digital infrastructures, standardized procedures, and organizational silos may limit the flexibility required to address individual circumstances. In this context, middle managers play a crucial role in balancing legal requirements, organizational priorities, and the need for responsive service delivery. Overall, the study shows that enabling discretion in the digital era requires aligning legal, technological, and organizational arrangements to support professional judgment while maintaining accountability.

This study is subject to several limitations. First, the relatively small sample size limits the generalizability of the findings, resulting in a primarily descriptive analysis. Priority was given to capturing a broad range of perspectives and phenomena; consequently, further research is needed to draw more definitive conclusions regarding the specific mechanisms and strategies that can support flexible digital service delivery while preserving human street-level discretion. Follow-up studies should also examine how differences in organizational level (municipal, regional, or national), organizational size, and other characteristics shape the findings presented in this paper. Second, this study focused primarily on the perspectives of policymakers. Research involving citizens and frontline employees is necessary to validate and enrich the findings, as well as to identify potential policymaker blind spots. Third, this study was conducted in the Netherlands. The Dutch legal, cultural, and political context—for example, the childcare benefits scandal and Dutch terminology— may limit the transferability of the findings to other national contexts.

References

1. Lipsky, M.: Street-Level Bureaucracy: Dilemmas of the Individual in Public Services. Russell Sage Foundation, New York (1980)
2. Lipsky, M.: Street-Level Bureaucracy: Dilemmas of the Individual in Public Services. Russell Sage Foundation, New York (2010)
3. Larsen, F., Møller, M.Ø., Raaphorst, N.: Public management and street-level bureaucrats. Public Manag. Rev. **27**, 1857–1867 (2025). https://doi.org/10.1080/14719037.2025.2493875
4. Buffat, A.: Street-level bureaucracy and e-government. Public Manag. Rev. **17**, 149–161 (2015). https://doi.org/10.1080/14719037.2013.771699

5. Marienfeldt, J.: Does digital government hollow out the essence of street-level bureaucracy? A systematic literature review of how digital tools' foster curtailment, enablement and continuation of street-level decision-making. Soc. Policy Adm. **58**, 831–855 (2024). https://doi.org/10.1111/spol.12991
6. Schou, J., Pors, A.S.: Digital by default? A qualitative study of exclusion in digitalised welfare. Soc. Policy Adm. **53**, 464–477 (2019). https://doi.org/10.1111/spol.12470
7. Melin, U., Madsen, C.Ø., Larsson, K.K.: Five bureaucratic roles in the age of digital transformation – Insights from scandinavian public organizations. In: Janssen, M., et al. (eds.) Electronic Government, pp. 99–115. Springer Nature Switzerland, Cham (2024). https://doi.org/10.1007/978-3-031-70274-7_7
8. De Boer, N., Raaphorst, N.: Automation and discretion: explaining the effect of automation on how street-level bureaucrats enforce. Public Manag. Rev. **25**, 42–62 (2023). https://doi.org/10.1080/14719037.2021.1937684
9. Vervaenen, V., Danneels, L.: Digital strategy in the public sector: an exploratory literature review. In: CEUR Workshop Proceedings (2024)
10. Breit, E., Egeland, C., Løberg, I.B., Røhnebæk, M.T.: Digital coping: how frontline workers cope with digital service encounters. Soc. Policy Adm. **55**, 833–847 (2021). https://doi.org/10.1111/spol.12664
11. Hansen, H., Lundberg, K., Syltevik, L.J.: Digitalization, street-level bureaucracy and welfare users' experiences. Soc. Policy Adm. **52**, 67–90 (2018). https://doi.org/10.1111/spol.12283
12. Løberg, I.B.: Efficiency through digitalization? How electronic communication between frontline workers and clients can spur a demand for services. Gov. Inf. Q. **38**, 101551 (2021). https://doi.org/10.1016/j.giq.2020.101551
13. Pors, A., Schou, J.: Street-level morality at the digital frontlines: an ethnographic study of moral mediation in welfare work. Adm. Theory Praxis. **43**, 154–171 (2021). https://doi.org/10.1080/10841806.2020.1782137
14. Busch, P.A., Henriksen, H.Z.: Digital discretion: a systematic literature review of ICT and street-level discretion. Inf. Polity **23**, 3–28 (2018). https://doi.org/10.3233/IP-170050
15. Rijksoverheid: Brochure: Nederlandse code voor goed openbaar bestuur (2009). https://www.rijksoverheid.nl/onderwerpen/kwaliteit-en-integriteit-overheidsinstanties/documenten/brochures/2009/06/23/brochure-nederlandse-code-voor-goed-openbaar-bestuur
16. Koppenjan, J., Kars, M., van der Voort, H.: Verticale politiek in horizontale beleidsnetwerken: kaderstelling als koppelingsarrangement. Beleid en Maatschappij **34** (2007)
17. Steinbacher, C.: The voice of implementation: exploring the link between street-level integration and sectoral policy outcomes. Regul. Governance **19**, 540–557 (2025). https://doi.org/10.1111/rego.12605
18. Tummers, L., Bekkers, V.: Policy implementation, street-level bureaucracy, and the importance of discretion. Public Manag. Rev. **16**, 527–547 (2014). https://doi.org/10.1080/14719037.2013.841978
19. Taylor, I., Kelly, J.: Professionals, discretion and public sector reform in the UK: re-visiting Lipsky. Int. J. Public Sect. Manag. **19**, 629–642 (2006). https://doi.org/10.1108/09513550610704662
20. Snellen, I.: Electronic governance: implications for citizens, politicians and public servants. Int. Rev. Adm. Sci. **68**, 183–198 (2002). https://doi.org/10.1177/0020852302682002
21. Bovens, M., Zouridis, S.: From street-level to system-level bureaucracies: how information and communication technology is transforming administrative discretion and constitutional control. Public Adm. Rev. **62**, 174–184 (2002). https://doi.org/10.1111/0033-3352.00168
22. Brodkin, E.Z.: Policy work: street-level organizations under new managerialism. J. Public Adm. Res. Theory. **21**, i253–i277 (2011). https://doi.org/10.1093/jopart/muq093
23. Hupe, P., Hill, M.: Street-level bureaucracy and public accountability. Public Adm. **85**, 279–299 (2007). https://doi.org/10.1111/j.1467-9299.2007.00650.x

24. Meyer, J.W., Rowan, B.: Institutionalized organizations: formal structure as myth and ceremony. Am. J. Sociol. **83**, 340–363 (1977). https://doi.org/10.1086/226550
25. DiMaggio, P.J., Powell, W.W.: The iron cage revisited institutional isomorphism and collective rationality in organizational fields. In: Advances in Strategic Management, pp. 143–166. Emerald (MCB UP), Bingley (2000). https://doi.org/10.1016/S0742-3322(00)17011-1
26. Maynard-Moody, S., Musheno, M.: Cops, Teachers, Counselors: Stories from the Front Lines of Public Service. University of Michigan Press, Ann Arbor, MI (2022). https://doi.org/10.3998/mpub.12247078
27. Scott, W.R.: Institutions and Organizations: Ideas, Interests, and Identities. SAGE, Los Angeles, California (2014)
28. Weimer, D.L., Vining, A.R.: Policy Analysis: Concepts and Practice. Routledge, 6 Edition. | New York : Routledge, 2017. | Revised edition of Policy analysis, 2011 (2017). https://doi.org/10.4324/9781315442129
29. Kennispunt Twente: KWALLM: An app for qualitative text analysis with large language models (LLMs) (2024). https://github.com/KennispuntTwente/KWALLM
30. Tax, D.M.J., Duin, R.P.W.: Growing a multi-class classifier with a reject option. Pattern Recogn. Lett. **29**, 1565–1570 (2008). https://doi.org/10.1016/j.patrec.2008.03.010
31. Jiang, H., Kim, B., Guan, M.Y., Gupta, M.: To trust or not to trust a classifier. https://arxiv.org/abs/1805.11783 (2018)
32. Ongena, G., Slingerland, E.: Digital government and discretion in street-level bureaucracy: a policy analysis from the Netherlands: Dataset (2026). https://osf.io/73pux/overview?view_only=c9cb41c3afdb491091e475caca39e04b
33. Van Berkel, R.: Making welfare conditional: a street-level perspective. Soc. Policy Adm. **54**, 191–204 (2020). https://doi.org/10.1111/spol.12564

Gendered Digital Inequality in Online Public Service Use: Evidence from Brazil

Julia Veneziani(✉), Raquel Guimarães, and Maria Alexandra Cunha

Fundação Getulio Vargas EAESP, São Paulo, SP, Brazil
juliaveneziani01@gmail.com

Abstract. Research on digital government often treats the use of online public services as a uniform phenomenon, overlooking how patterns of engagement may vary across service domains and levels of digital completion. This paper examines how gender, conditioned by race, education and income shape the use of digital public services in Brazil. Drawing on nationally representative microdata from the ICT Households Survey 2025, it uses weighted statistical models to analyze both broader forms of digital public service use and fully online service completion. The study distinguishes between two groups of services: care-related services (health, education, and transportation/urban services) and financial/administrative services (personal documents, labor/social security, taxes/fees, and justice). The findings suggest that gender inequalities in digital government are domain-specific and sensitive to how digital engagement is measured. Women are more likely to use care-related digital services, while men are more likely to use financial-administrative services. Across models, education and income remain the strongest predictors of digital public service use. The paper contributes to the digital government literature by providing evidence from Brazil that digital inequality is shaped not only by material resources, but also by gendered patterns of interaction with the state, and that these inequalities may vary according to both policy domain and level of digital engagement.

Keywords: digital government · digital inequality · gender · public services

1 Introduction

Digitalization has been widely associated with the promise of making processes faster, more efficient, and more accessible by reducing execution time, minimizing physical storage requirements, integrating data and eliminating the need for physical displacement. However, the mere transfer of physical processes to the digital environment does not necessarily guarantee deep social or cultural transformations (Mergel et al., 2019).

This research was supported by the Brazilian National Council for Scientific and Technological Development (CNPq) and by the São Paulo Research Foundation (FAPESP) - The Effect of Digital Leadership Training on Digital Transformation in Government: Field Experimental Evidence from Brazil.

Published by Springer Nature Switzerland 2027
G. Viale Pereira et al. (Eds.): EGOV 2026, LNCS 16933, pp. 98–112, 2027.
https://doi.org/10.1007/978-3-032-35747-2_7

According to Perez (2010), digital transformation may represent a paradigm shift, but its effects depend on institutional, political, and social structures that shape how technologies are appropriated and distributed within society. Recent changes in government driven by digital transformation have increasingly become the subject of scholarly inquiry, bringing into debate how digitalization reshapes the relationship between citizens and the state (Dutil et al., 2008). This scenario becomes even more complex in the context of electronic government, particularly when considering deeply rooted social dynamics such as gender and race relations that have been historically constructed over centuries.

While the state seeks to expand access to gain efficiency of public policies, it may also reproduce or intensify pre-existing inequalities (Cameron, 2019; Hirata, 2016; Gonzales, 1984). In this sense, understanding who benefits and who is excluded from digital public services becomes essential to assessing the effects of digital transformation on social equity.

This article draws on sociological perspectives on gender, particularly theories of the sexual division of labor, to analyze how gender relations between men and women are reflected in the use of online public services. Drawing on authors who examine reproductive labor (Federici, 2019; Hirata, 2016), the impact of these dynamics on welfare models (Naldini, 2003; Little, 1994), and inequalities in digital access (Macaya et al., 2021; Melchiori, 2025), this research seeks to analyze gendered patterns in the use of digital public services in Brazil. Rather than treating gender in isolation, the study considers how these patterns are conditioned by race, education and family income. The central research question guiding this study is: To what extent does gender, conditioned by race, education and income influence the use of digital public services in Brazil? Accordingly, gender is treated as the central analytical dimension of the article, while the remaining independent variables are included as complementary that capture multidimensional socioeconomic and generational inequalities.

The study uses data from the ICT Households Survey 2024, conducted by the Regional Center for Studies on the Development of the Information Society (Cetic.br), linked to the Brazilian Network Information Center (NIC.br). The survey measures ownership and use of information and communication technologies among the Brazilian population. Demographic, social, and digital service usage variables related to government services and e-commerce were selected for analysis. Data processing and statistical analyses were conducted using RStudio, applying descriptive analyses, predictive analyses, and weighted regression models that respect the complex sampling design of the survey.

This study makes three main contributions to the literature. First, it offers empirical insights to the literature on digital government and inequality by examining gendered patterns of digital public service use in a Global South context. Second, it provides empirical evidence from Brazil, a large middle-income country, where digital government expansion occurs alongside persistent structural inequalities (Ribeiro et al., 2021). Third, it contributes methodologically by applying weighted statistical models to nationally representative survey data, offering a replicable framework for analyzing digital service use in other contexts.

In addition to this introduction, the article is organized as follows. Section 2 presents the theoretical framework, discussing the sexual division of labor, welfare models, care responsibilities, and digital inequality. Section 3 describes the data, variables, and methodological procedures used in the empirical analysis. Section 4 presents the descriptive and multivariate results. Section 5 discusses the findings in light of the theoretical framework and the literature on gender and digital government. Section 6 concludes by revisiting the research question, summarizing the main findings, acknowledging the study's limitations, and suggesting avenues for future research.

2 Theoretical Background

2.1 Sexual Division of Labor and Care Work

From the 1970s onward, feminist scholars increasingly examined what came to be known as the sexual division of labor. This concept refers to a socially and historically constructed division of labor organized around relations between men and women (Hirata & Kergoat, 2007). According to this perspective, the sexual division of labor is structured by two main principles: the principle of separation, which assigns distinct tasks to men and women according to socially constructed gender roles, and the hierarchical principle, which attributes greater value, prestige, and legitimacy to men's work.

This division was institutionalized by the family wage (Fraser, 1994), which consolidated a sharper distinction of "work" at home and at the workplace (Cameron, 2019). In this configuration, men were increasingly expected to perform paid labor in the productive sphere, while women were assigned responsibility for unpaid labor in the domestic and reproductive sphere. From a materialist feminist perspective, this distinction is fundamental: productive labor refers to activities directly linked to economic production, whereas reproductive labor sustains the conditions necessary for the reproduction of labor power and of the economic system itself (Federici, 2019).

In this sense, domestic labor encompasses the set of activities involved in maintaining daily life and reproducing the labor force. It includes cooking, cleaning, caring for children, older adults, and sick family members, as well as managing the material and emotional conditions of household survival (Federici, 2020). Although these arrangements are historically constituted, their effects remain central to contemporary gender inequalities. Care work continues to be disproportionately assigned to women and is still frequently performed in unpaid or poorly remunerated forms (Hirata, 2016; Bourdieu, 2001). In Brazil, this asymmetry remains particularly visible: according to data from the Institute for Applied Economic Research, women spend on average 27 h per week on unpaid domestic and care work, while men spend around 13 h (Pinheiro et al., 2023). This dimension of labor division for care work goes beyond education and health in child and elder care (Folbre, 1994), and goes as far as public transport use, in what the literature calls "mobility of care" (Sánchez de Madariaga, 2013), as women's double and sometimes triple journeys as caretakers lead to multiple short trips a day. These trips are commonly undertaken whilst carrying shopping and/or accompanied by small children, and usually rely on walking or public transportation services, thus making women the major users of public transport (Peters, 1998; Little, 1994).

Within this framework, it is also essential to consider how class and race shape the organization of domestic and care labor. Hirata (2016), revisiting the historical development of care work in Brazil, argues that the country's pattern of reproductive labor is deeply marked by the legacy of slavery, which contributed to the consolidation of domestic service as a socially devalued and racialized occupation. This racial dimension is central to the work of Gonzales (1984) and Carneiro (2011), who show how care labor in Brazil has historically been naturalized through the figure of Black women. The sexual division of labor, therefore, cannot be understood in isolation from racial and class hierarchies. Rather, it operates through a transversal structure in which women occupy unequal positions, and Black and poor women bear a disproportionate share of reproductive and care responsibilities.

2.2 Welfare Policies and Digitalization

The arrangements produced by the sexual division of labor have important implications for welfare policies. Naldini (2003) classifies family models within welfare states, describing the male breadwinner model, in which the nuclear family is organized around the assumption that women and children are financially dependent on a male provider. In this model, women's unpaid work within the household is treated as a private resource rather than as a social need requiring public support. As a result, welfare systems structured around this arrangement tend to invest less in public care services such as childcare, long-term care, and other forms of social support, since care is assumed to be provided within the family, mainly by women (Saraceno & Naldini, 2011).

Within the breadwinner arrangements, it is also important to stress the implications for men's and women's relations to the state. As it is men who carry most formal relations with the market, women's "dependent" status in relation to men also applies to social security entitlements and tax (Lewis, 1992). This dynamic empowers men not only financially but also symbolically when navigating bureaucratic services (Bourdieu, 2014). As a consequence, women's access to many aspects of citizenship (documentation, tax regularity, pensions) can be conditioned by men.

By contrast to this model, feminist critiques of welfare regimes have long emphasized the need for greater state involvement in the provision and redistribution of care. Ferrera (1996), also working from a gender-sensitive perspective, describes the dual-earner model, in which both men and women are expected to participate in paid work and in which care responsibilities are less strictly tied to the traditional family structure. This model has important implications for fiscal priorities and social policy design, as it requires greater public investment in care-related services and infrastructure. In this sense, welfare arrangements are not neutral: they reflect and reinforce assumptions about family, dependency, labor, and citizenship.

Considering the extent and multiplicity of care work division, the debate on public services and gender has become especially relevant in contemporary processes of digitalization. In Melchiori (2025), gender is discussed in the context of digital welfare, with particular attention to the new roles citizens assume in their interactions with public services. On the one hand, digital tools can expand access, reduce administrative burdens, and create new opportunities for autonomy and participation – for example, by enabling small-scale entrepreneurship and facilitating greater economic autonomy. On the other hand, they may shift responsibilities previously held by public institutions onto individuals and families, thereby intensifying existing inequalities (Cao and Ma, 2025) – as the digitalization of welfare and social assistance can impose new burdens on women, particularly older and poorer women, who are often responsible for navigating complex bureaucratic systems with reduced digital literacy while also carrying out unpaid care work (Madsen et al., 2022; Melchiori, 2025).

The literature on digital inequality in Brazil has increasingly emphasized that unequal access to technologies cannot be reduced to simple issues of connectivity. What matters is also the capacity to use digital tools effectively, autonomously, and under favorable social conditions (Macaya et al., 2021; Mota, Santos & Silva, 2025). In a country marked by deep socioeconomic and territorial disparities, digitalization can intensify barriers associated with class, age, gender, and race, thereby excluding already vulnerable groups from the benefits of online interaction. This issue becomes particularly significant in the field of digital government, where online public services are increasingly central to citizens' relationships with the state. Given that, policy digitalization is not a mere technological tool change, but a social and political process that may reproduce unequal patterns of state access and administrative burden. If women and men interact differently with public services because of their distinct social roles, and if these interactions are mediated by unequal digital resources and capabilities, then digital public service use is likely to reflect both the social organization of care and broader structures of inequality.

3 Methodology

This research adopts a quantitative, descriptive, and deductive approach to examine gendered patterns in the use of digital public services in Brazil [19, 20], considering how these patterns are conditioned by race, education and income. Gender is the central analytical dimension of the study, while the other variables are included to account for broader socioeconomic and racial inequalities that may shape digital public service use (Wooldridge, 2016; Chen et al., 2021). This choice is justified by the nature of the research question, which focuses on measurable relationships between variables, as well as by the availability of a nationally representative dataset. The deductive character of the study derives from the application of theoretical assumptions related to the sexual division of labor and digital exclusion to an empirical dataset, with the aim of identifying patterns of digital inequality. The explanatory dimension of the research emerges from the inferential statistical analyses conducted.

The analysis is based on secondary microdata from the ICT Households Survey 2025, conducted by the Regional Center for Studies on the Development of the Information Society (Cetic.br), affiliated with the Brazilian Network Information Center (NIC.br). The ICT Households questionnaire is organized into different thematic modules, covering multiple dimensions of technology access and use, including computer use, internet use, electronic government, e-commerce, digital skills, mobile phone use, selected applications, artificial intelligence, and cultural activities.

This article focuses specifically on the digital government model. This module was selected because it contains the questions directly related to citizens' interactions with public services through the internet. Within it, the G1 variables capture whether respondents used the internet in relation to specific public service domains, while the G2 variables capture whether these services were completed entirely online. Therefore, the terms G1 and G2 refer to question blocks from the ICT Households questionnaire, rather than to analytical categories created independently by the authors.

Based on the digital government module, the empirical strategy distinguishes between two levels of digital engagement. The first concerns broader digital public service use, based on the G1 variables. These indicators capture whether the respondent used the internet in relation to a given public service domain, regardless of whether the interaction involved information-seeking, a partially digital process, or full online completion. The second concerns fully online service completion, based on the G2 variables, which identify whether the respondent completed the service entirely online rather than combining digital and in-person steps or using the internet only for information. This distinction is analytically important because accessing a digital channel and completing a service end-to-end online may reflect different barriers, capabilities, and forms of administrative burden.

In addition to an overall indicator of digital government use, the study constructs two analytically defined groups of public services. The first group encompasses services connected to care-work as discussed in our literature review (Sect. 2), including health, education, and transportation/urban services – that is, services associated with the care of the household. (Fraser, 1994; Hirata, 2016; Folbre, 1994; Sánchez de Madariga, 2013; Peters, 1998; Little, 1994). The second group, financial-administrative services, includes personal documents, labor and social security, taxes and fees, and justice-related services (Fraser, 1994; Naldini, 2003; Lewis, 1992; Bourdieu, 2014; Madsen et al., 2025). The distinction is grounded in the article's theoretical argument that patterns of interaction with the state are partly shaped by the social organization of care, household maintenance, and administrative responsibilities.

For each service group, the article constructs three dependent variables. First, a binary indicator identifies whether the respondent used at least one service in that group. Second, a binary indicator captures whether the respondent completed at least one service in that group fully online. Third, a count variable measures the number of service domains used within the group. Together, these indicators make it possible to compare broader patterns of digital engagement with more demanding forms of digital completion, while also capturing variation in the breadth of service use across domains.

The main independent variables are gender, race, education and family income. Gender is the central analytical dimension of the study, as the article examines whether gendered social roles, as established in the literature, are reflected in different patterns of digital public service use. The other independent variables are included to account for intersecting forms of inequality that may condition these gendered patterns. Race is included because digital inequality may reproduce racial hierarchies; education and family income capture socioeconomic resources associated with digital access and use.

Data processing and statistical analysis were conducted in RStudio. The analysis begins with weighted descriptive statistics to characterize the sample and estimate the prevalence of digital public service use across social groups. Design-based mean comparison tests are then used to examine bivariate differences. To estimate adjusted associations between the independent variables and the outcomes of interest, the study employs survey-weighted generalized linear models using the sampling design and weights provided by the dataset. Binary outcomes are estimated with logistic models using a quasi-binomial family, while count outcomes are estimated with quasi-Poisson models. This modeling strategy is intended to produce estimates that are consistent with the complex survey design and suitable for the distribution of the dependent variables analyzed here. Based on this analytical strategy, the article evaluates the following expectations:

H1: *Women are more likely than men to use care-related digital public services.*

H2: *Men are more likely than women to use financial-administrative digital public services.*

H3: *Socioeconomic and racial inequalities remain strong predictors of digital public service use across service domains and levels of digital engagement.*

These expectations are tested through models that compare both aggregated and disaggregated outcomes. Rather than assuming that digital public service use is uniform, the analysis examines whether the relevance of gender varies across service domains and whether it changes when the outcome shifts from broader use to full online completion.

Because the study relies on secondary survey data, it cannot directly measure subjective dimensions such as perceived barriers, trust in government platforms, or user experience. In addition, the observational nature of the analysis does not allow for causal inference, but only for the identification of statistically significant associations. Even so, the use of nationally representative data, survey-weighted models, and differentiated measures of digital engagement provides a robust basis for examining how social inequalities shape digital public service use in Brazil.

4 Results and Discussion

4.1 Descriptive Statistics

The weighted sample is slightly majority female, with women representing 52% of respondents. It is also racially diverse: respondents who self-identify as Brown/Mixed-race constitute the largest racial group, followed by White and Black respondents. The sample is concentrated in lower income brackets, with a substantial proportion of respondents living in households earning up to two minimum wages. In educational terms, most respondents are concentrated in the elementary and secondary education categories, although a relevant share report higher education.

At the aggregate level, 55.99% of respondents reported having used at least one digital public service in the reference period. When disaggregated by gender, women report a slightly higher rate of use than men: 57.91% of female respondents reported using digital public services, compared to 53.96% of male respondents. The design-based mean comparison test indicates that this difference is statistically significant, although substantively modest, with a mean difference of approximately 3.95 percentage points ($t = 1.963$, $df = 24{,}533$, $p = 0.0496$). Descriptively, women therefore appear somewhat more engaged with digital public services overall.

However, the sociodemographic profile of respondents suggests that this difference should not be interpreted as a simple sign of greater digital inclusion among women. Table 1 presents the weighted distribution of race, household income, and educational attainment by gender. The table shows that women are more concentrated in the lowest income categories and among respondents with no income, while men are more represented in the highest income bracket. At the same time, women are more represented among respondents with higher education. These patterns indicate that gendered digital public service use is embedded in intersecting socioeconomic conditions: women report slightly higher overall use despite occupying a more vulnerable income position, while also showing higher levels of formal education.

In racial terms, the largest groups among both men and women are Brown/Mixed-race and White respondents. Among men, 23% identify as Brown/Mixed-race and 16% as White, while among women these proportions are 25% and 17%, respectively. Black respondents represent 7.2% of men and 7.4% of women.

Asian/Yellow respondents are slightly more represented among women than men, while Indigenous respondents are slightly more represented among men. These distributions indicate that racial composition varies only moderately by gender, but race remains part of the broader social structure within which digital government is accessed.

Income differences are more pronounced. Women are more concentrated in the lowest income category: 15% of women are in households earning up to one minimum wage, compared to 12% of men. Women are also more represented among respondents with no income, 0.7% compared to 0.4% among men. By contrast, men are more represented in the highest income group, especially above ten minimum wages, where they account for 2.3% compared to 1.4% among women. Educational attainment also differs by gender. Women are more represented among respondents with higher education, 13% compared to 8.4% among men, and slightly more represented among those with secondary education, 21% compared to 20%. Men, in turn, are more concentrated in the elementary education category, 18% compared to 16% among women.

Taken together, these descriptive results suggest that gender differences in digital public service use cannot be interpreted in isolation. Women's slightly higher overall use coexists with greater income vulnerability and higher levels of formal education. This supports the expectation that socioeconomic inequalities remain important for understanding digital government use, but also indicates that these inequalities operate in complex ways across gender groups rather than through a simple linear pattern of advantage or disadvantage.

4.2 Digital Public Service Use by Gender and Service Domain

The descriptive results by service domain reveal a clear gendered segmentation in broader forms of digital use. Figure 1 shows the weighted proportion of digital public service use by gender and service domain.

The pattern is domain-specific rather than uniform. Men report higher levels of use in personal documents, taxes and fees, justice, security, and labor/social security. Women, in turn, report higher levels of use in health and education, while transportation and urban services display near parity. Specifically, men report higher use of personal documents (38.6% versus 30.3%), taxes and fees (34.8% versus 24.5%), justice (18.6% versus 13.6%), security (11.9% versus 8.1%), and labor/social security services (30.8% versus 27.0%). Women report higher use of health services (41.6% versus 30.1%) and

Table 1. Sociodemographic characteristics of respondents who used digital government services.

Variables	Male N = 89,740,166	Female N = 95,668,469
Race/Color		
White	29,495,293 (16%)	31,795,148 (17%)
Black	13,097,929 (7.2%)	13,501,038 (7.4%)
Brown/Mixed-race	42,719,637 (23%)	45,715,930 (25%)
Asian/Yellow	1,309,924 (0.7%)	1,929,191 (1.1%)
Indigenous	1,311,124 (0.7%)	1,072,584 (0.6%)
Household income		
Up to 1 minimum wage	20,630,850 (12%)	26,116,236 (15%)
More than 1 to 2 minimum wages	23,734,307 (14%)	25,335,822 (15%)
More than 2 to 3 minimum wages	15,502,872 (9.2%)	14,489,802 (8.6%)
More than 3 to 5 minimum wages	11,792,499 (7.0%)	9,865,039 (5.8%)
More than 5 to 10 minimum wages	5,720,923 (3.4%)	7,389,002 (4.4%)
More than 10 minimum wages	3,932,453 (2.3%)	2,360,072 (1.4%)
No income	728,185 (0.4%)	1,208,975 (0.7%)
Educational attainment		
Illiterate/Early childhood education	3,035,687 (1.6%)	2,803,200 (1.5%)
Elementary education	33,066,043 (18%)	29,725,176 (16%)
Secondary education	38,008,578 (20%)	39,668,763 (21%)
Higher education	15,629,859 (8.4%)	23,471,330 (13%)

Note. Values are presented as weighted population estimates, with percentages in parentheses. Percentages refer to the total weighted sample

education services (19.8% versus 16.3%). Transportation and urban services are similar across gender groups, with 17.0% among women and 16.4% among men.

These differences become clearer when services are aggregated into the two analytical groups proposed in this article. In the aggregated statistics, women are more likely than men to report using at least one care-related service, with **53.7%** of women reporting use compared to **45.0%** of men. By contrast, men are more likely to report using at least one financial-administrative service, with 61.5% of men reporting use compared to 50.9% of women. Descriptively, these results support H1 and H2: women are more engaged in domains associated with care responsibilities, while men are more present in domains related to documentation, taxation, justice, security, and labor-market administration. By contrast, the descriptive results for fully online completion are more mixed. In health, women show slightly lower rates of full online completion than men, 22.4% compared to 23.5%. The same occurs in transportation and urban services, 37.8%

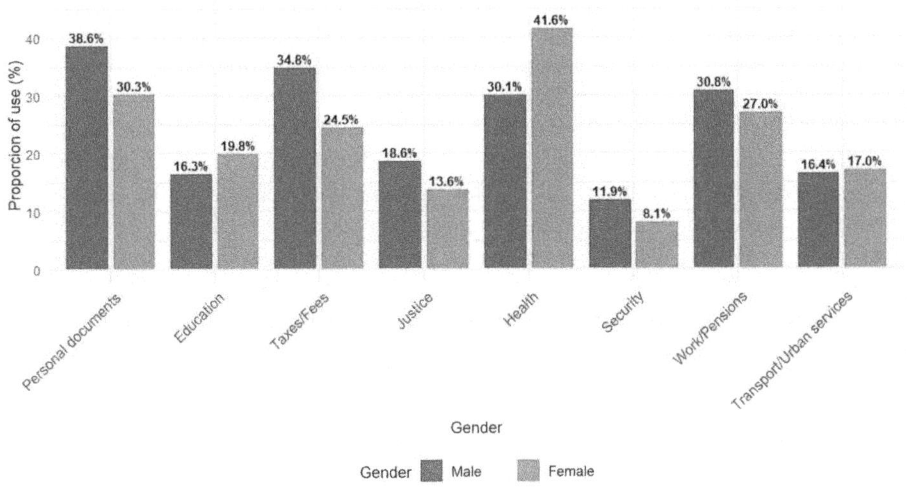

Fig. 1. Weighted proportion of digital public service use by gender and service domain (ICT Households Survey 2025)

compared to 39.2%, and in justice, 36.5% compared to 46.8%. In taxes and fees, however, women show a higher rate of full online completion, 64.0% compared to 57.8%. Taken together, these descriptive results suggest that gender differences are more visible in broader forms of digital use than in the narrower outcome of end-to-end online completion.

4.3 Multivariate Results

The overall weighted logistic model indicates that gender is not a statistically significant predictor of digital public service use once controls are introduced (= 0.026, $p = 0.789$; OR = 1.03). This means that, when digital public service use is treated as a single aggregate outcome, women and men do not differ significantly after accounting for race, education, income, and age. In this model, education and income emerge as the strongest and most consistent determinants of overall use. Compared to the lowest educational category, the odds of using digital public services are substantially higher among respondents in the elementary (OR = 3.76), secondary (OR = 16.47), and higher education (OR = 45.38) categories. Income also follows a positive gradient up to the 5–10 minimum-wage bracket.

The framework-grouped logistic models provide clearer evidence of gendered patterns. In the model for care-related services, women are significantly more likely than men to report using at least one service in the group (= 0.362, $p < 0.001$; OR = 1.44). In the model for financial-administrative services, the coefficient for women is negative and highly significant (= -0.490, $p < 0.001$; OR = 0.61), indicating lower odds of use than men. These results confirm that gender becomes analytically relevant once digital public service use is disaggregated by substantive domain rather than treated as a single aggregate outcome. The models restricted to fully online completion present a different pattern. Unlike the previous models, which capture whether respondents used at least one service within each domain, these models focus on the more restrictive outcome of completing the service entirely online. This distinction is important because broader use and full online completion may reflect different forms of digital engagement and different barriers. Once the dependent variable is limited to full online completion, the gender coefficient is no longer statistically significant in either domain. This indicates that the social responsibilities that bring citizens into contact with specific public services are not necessarily the same as the resources required to complete a service entirely online.

In these models, education remains relevant, especially in the financial-administrative domain, and income is also more strongly associated with financial-administrative services than with care-related services. This suggests that broader digital service use and full online completion capture different dimensions of inequality. Gender is more strongly associated with the type of service domain accessed, while end-to-end online completion appears to depend more heavily on educational and material resources.

The count models reinforce this interpretation. Women use a larger number of care-related services and a smaller number of financial - administrative services. In both domains, educational attainment increases the number of services used. Income shows relatively limited effects on the intensity of care-related service use, but a stronger positive gradient in the financial-administrative domain. These findings indicate that gender differences are not limited to whether citizens use digital public services at all; they also shape the breadth of engagement across different domains of state interaction.

4.4 Main Findings

The findings provide evidence from the Brazilian case that digital public service use is shaped by the intersection between gendered social roles, socioeconomic resources, and the domains through which citizens interact with the state. The results support H1 and H2. Women are more likely to use care-related digital public services, while men are more likely to use financial-administrative services. This pattern is consistent with the literature on the sexual division of labor, which argues that women remain disproportionately responsible for reproductive labor, household maintenance, and care work (Federici, 2019, 2020; Hirata, 2016; Hirata & Kergoat, 2007). As Hirata and Kergoat (2007) suggest, gendered labor arrangements are structured both by separation, which assigns different types of work to men and women, and by hierarchy, which attributes greater social and economic value to men's work. The results indicate that these offline arrangements are reflected in digital interactions with the state. Women's greater use of health, education, and transportation or urban services can be interpreted as an extension of their continued responsibility for care, family management, and everyday social reproduction. In this sense, digital government does not suspend the sexual division of labor; rather, it translates it into new forms of digital service use.

Men's greater use of financial-administrative services also dialogues with the welfare literature reviewed in the article. In male breadwinner arrangements, men have historically occupied a stronger position in relation to formal labor markets, taxation, documentation, pensions, and bureaucratic recognition (Fraser, 1994; Lewis, 1992; Naldini, 2003). As discussed by Lewis (1992), Naldini (2003), and Saraceno and Naldini (2011), welfare systems are not neutral: they define who is recognized as a worker, dependent, taxpayer, beneficiary, or rights-holder. The greater male engagement with documents, taxes and fees, justice, labor, and social security services suggests that digital government reproduces these differentiated institutional pathways.

The literature on digital transformation emphasizes that technological change does not automatically produce social transformation. Instead, its effects depend on the institutional and social structures through which technologies are implemented and appropriated (Mergel et al., 2019; Perez, 2010). The results of this article reinforce this point: when public services are aggregated into a single indicator, gender is not a significant predictor once controls are introduced. However, when services are disaggregated by substantive domain, gender becomes analytically relevant. Therefore, the gendered inequality identified here is not simply about whether men or women use digital government more, but about which parts of the state they access digitally and what social responsibilities lead them to do so.

The distinction between aggregate use and domain-specific use also helps clarify the relationship between digital inequality and administrative burden.

The literature on digital welfare shows that digitalization may transfer responsibilities from public institutions to individuals and families, requiring citizens to assume new roles in navigating services, information, and bureaucratic procedures (Melchiori, 2025). This is especially relevant for women, who often manage not only their own interactions with the state, but also those related to children, older adults, sick family members, and household needs. In this sense, women's higher use of care-related services should not be interpreted simply as greater digital empowerment. It may also indicate greater exposure to digitally mediated care responsibilities and to the burden of navigating public services on behalf of others.

H3 receives partial support. The descriptive table shows that women report slightly higher overall use of digital government services than men, and the design-based t-test indicates that this difference is statistically significant, although modest. However, the socioeconomic profile of users reveals a more complex pattern. Women are more concentrated in the lowest income categories and among respondents with no income, while men are more represented in the highest income brackets. At the same time, women show higher levels of formal education, especially higher education. These findings suggest that women's greater digital public service use emerges from the combination of greater care-related responsibilities, higher educational attainment, and persistent income vulnerability.

Race also remains an important dimension of the social context in which digital government is accessed, although the descriptive results do not allow claims about its independent effect. This does not mean that racial inequality is absent. On the contrary, the theoretical framework suggests that race operates together with gender and class in structuring care work, domestic labor, and access to citizenship. As Gonzales (1984), Carneiro (2011), and Hirata (2016) argue, reproductive labor in Brazil is historically racialized, particularly through the association between Black and poor women and devalued care and domestic work. Therefore, race should be understood as part of the broader social structure within which digital government is accessed, even when its effect is not uniformly visible in descriptive comparisons by gender.

Taken together, the findings suggest that digital government in Brazil reorganizes existing inequalities through digital interfaces, making some social divisions visible in the type of services accessed and others in the socioeconomic conditions under which access occurs. Women's slightly higher overall use of digital public services does not necessarily indicate greater inclusion or autonomy. It may reflect their greater exposure to care-related demands, their role in managing household interactions with the state, and the transfer of administrative responsibilities to citizens under digital welfare arrangements.

5 Final Considerations

This article examined how gender, conditioned by race, education, and income, shapes the use of digital public services in Brazil. Using nationally representative data from the ICT Households Survey 2025, it argued that digital government should not be analyzed as a socially neutral or homogeneous field of interaction. The findings show that inequalities in digital public service use vary according to the substantive domain of the service and the social profile of users. Digital engagement with the state is therefore not only a technical question of access, but also a social process embedded in unequal distributions of care, income, education, and bureaucratic responsibility.

The main contribution of the article is to show that gendered patterns become clearer when public services are disaggregated. Women are more likely to use care-related services, while men are more likely to use financial-administrative services. These differences are not fully visible in aggregate models, where gender is not significant once controls are introduced. This suggests that digital inequality is not only about whether citizens access digital government, but also about which domains of state action they access and how these domains correspond to socially distributed responsibilities. In this sense, digital government may reproduce differentiated pathways of citizenship, with women more connected to services associated with care and everyday social reproduction, and men more connected to administrative, financial, and formal labor-market relations with the state.

The results also show that gender does not replace other structural determinants of inequality. Education and income remain central to understanding digital public service use. The descriptive evidence for H3 reinforces this point: women report slightly higher overall use of digital government services than men, and this difference is statistically significant, although modest. However, this higher use occurs despite women being more concentrated in the lowest income categories and among respondents with no income. Women also show higher levels of formal education, which may help explain their greater reported use under conditions of greater income vulnerability. These findings indicate that women's digital engagement should not be interpreted simply as greater digital inclusion, but as the result of intersecting social positions involving care responsibilities, education, and economic disadvantage.

Race remains an important dimension of the social context in which digital government is accessed, although the descriptive results do not allow claims about its independent effect. The racial composition of respondents shows moderate differences across gender groups, suggesting that racial inequality should be understood in relation to other social markers, especially income, education, and gendered responsibilities.

These findings have implications for research and policy. For research, they suggest that studies of digital government should move beyond aggregate indicators of online service use and pay greater attention to differences across policy domains, social groups, and stages of the service journey. For policy, they indicate that expanding digital channels is not enough to ensure equitable access. Governments must also address the unequal conditions under which citizens search for information, navigate procedures, and complete transactions, including differences in education, material resources, territorial infrastructure, and responsibilities of care and administration. This is particularly important to ensure that digitalization does not create additional burdens for populations already facing socioeconomic vulnerability.

Some limitations should be noted. Because the article relies on secondary survey data, it cannot directly assess user experience, perceived barriers, trust in digital platforms, or the quality of service interactions. The observational design also allows only the identification of associations, not causal effects. In addition, the grouping of services into care-related and financial-administrative domains is a theoretical-analytical choice that future research may refine. Even so, the use of nationally representative data and differentiated measures of service use offers a robust basis for advancing the study of digital inequality in public service access.

Future research could deepen this agenda by incorporating qualitative evidence on digital public service journeys, testing interaction effects between gender, race, education, and income, and comparing whether similar domain-specific patterns appear in other national contexts. More broadly, the article suggests that the digitalization of the state does not dissolve preexisting inequalities. Rather, it reorganizes them through new interfaces, procedures, and expectations of citizen self-service. Understanding digital government in unequal societies therefore requires attention not only to access and connectivity, but also to the social organization of everyday interactions with the state.

References

Bourdieu, P.: Masculine Domination. Stanford University Press, Stanford (2001)

Bourdieu, P.: On the State: Lectures at the Collège de France, 1989–1992. Polity Press, Cambridge (2014)

Cao, J., Ma, L.: Digital transformation, administrative burden, and citizen–state interactions: a case of the old age allowance policy in China. Rev. Policy Res. (2025). https://doi.org/10.1111/ropr.70063

Cameron, D.: Feminism: A Brief Introduction to the Ideas, Debates, and Politics of the Movement. University of Chicago Press, Chicago (2019)

Carneiro, S.: Racism, Sexism, and Inequality in Brazil. Selo Negro, São Paulo (2011)

Chen, J.C., Rubin, E.A., Cornwall, G.J.: Data Science for Public Policy. Springer, Cham (2021). https://doi.org/10.1007/978-3-030-71352-2

Dutil, P., Howard, C., Langford, J., Roy, J.: Rethinking government–public relationships in a digital world. J. Inform. Tech. Polit. **4**(1), 77–90 (2008). https://doi.org/10.1300/J516v04n01_06

Federici, S.: Social reproduction theory: history, issues and present challenges. Radic. Philos. **204**, 55–57 (2019)

Federici, S.: Caliban and the Witch: Women, the Body and Primitive Accumulation. Autonomedia, Brooklyn (2020)

Ferrera, M.: The southern model of welfare in social Europe. J. Eur. Soc. Policy **6**(1), 17–37 (1996). https://doi.org/10.1177/095892879600600102

Folbre, N.: Who Pays for the Kids? Gender and the Structures of Constraint. Routledge, London (1994)

Fraser, N.: After the family wage: gender equity and the welfare state. Polit. Theory **22**(4), 591–618 (1994)

Gonzalez, L.: Racism and sexism in Brazilian culture. Revista Ciências Sociais Hoje, 223–244 (1984)

Hirata, H.: Care work. SUR – Int. J. Hum. Rights **13**(24), 53–64 (2016)

Hirata, H., Kergoat, D.: New configurations of the sexual division of labor. Cad. Pesqui. **37**(132), 595–609 (2007). https://doi.org/10.1590/S0100-15742007000300005

Lewis, J.: Gender and the development of welfare regimes. J. Eur. Soc. Policy **2**(3), 159–173 (1992). https://doi.org/10.1177/095892879200200301

Macaya, J.F.M., Ribeiro, M.M., Jereissati, T., dos Reis Lima, C., Cunha, M.A.: Gendering the digital divide: the use of electronic government services and implications for the digital gender gap. Inf. Polity **26**(2), 131–146 (2021). https://doi.org/10.3233/IP-200307

Madsen, C.Ø., Lindgren, I., Melin, U.: The accidental caseworker: how digital self-service influences citizens' administrative burden. Gov. Inf. Q. **39**(1) (2022). https://doi.org/10.1016/j.giq.2021.101653

Melchiori, C.E.: Digital welfare and women's ambivalent lived experiences: an interpretative phenomenological analysis. In: Smith, J.M. (ed.) Succeeding in Digital Self-Service: Knowledge-Sharing in Citizen-Caseworker Interactions, pp. 306–324. Springer (2025). https://doi.org/10.1007/978-3-032-02515-9

Mergel, I., Edelmann, N., Haug, N.: Defining digital transformation: results from expert interviews. Gov. Inf. Q. **36**(4), 101385 (2019). https://doi.org/10.1016/j.giq.2019.06.002

Mota, F., Santos, J., Silva, M.: E-gov for whom? Profile and challenges for non-users in the Brazilian context. Inf. Dev. (2025). https://doi.org/10.1177/02666669251327184

Naldini, M.: The Family in the Mediterranean Welfare States. Frank Cass, London (2003)

NIC.br: Survey on the Use of Information and Communication Technologies in Brazilian Households: TIC Households Survey, 2024 Edition. NIC.br, São Paulo (2024)

Perez, C.: Technological revolutions and techno-economic paradigms. Camb. J. Econ. **34**(1), 185–202 (2010)

Peters, D.: Breadwinners, homemakers and beasts of burden: a gender perspective on transport and mobility. Sustain. Dev. Int. **1**, 33–36 (1998)

Pinheiro, L., Medeiros, M., Costa, J., Barbosa, A.H.: Gender is what matters: determinants of unpaid domestic work in Brazil. Discussion Paper No. 2920. Ipea, Brasília (2023)

Ribeiro, M.M., Macaya, J.F.M., Storino, F., Portilho, L., Barbosa, A.F., Cunha, M.A.V.C.: Capacidades estatais em tecnologias de informação e comunicação dos estados e exclusão digital no Brasil. Boletim de Análise Político-Institucional **30**, 87–100 (2021). https://doi.org/10.38116/bapi30art8

Sánchez de Madariaga, I.: Mobility of care: introducing new concepts in urban transport. In: Sánchez de Madariaga, I., Roberts, M. (eds.) Fair Shared Cities: The Impact of Gender Planning in Europe, pp. 33–48. Ashgate, Aldershot (2013)

Saraceno, C., Naldini, M.: Reconciling Family and Work: Old and New Pacts Between the Sexes and Generations. Il Mulino, Bologna (2011)

Wooldridge, J.M.: Introductory Econometrics: A Modern Approach, 6th edn. Cengage Learning, Boston (2016)

From Legal Mandate to Everyday Work: A Survey of Open Data Coordinators in German Public Administration

Isabell von Falkenhausen(✉) and Merle Heider

Fraunhofer Institute for Open Communication Systems, Kaiserin-Augusta-Allee 31, 10589 Berlin, Germany
isabell.von.falkenhausen@fokus.fraunhofer.de

Abstract. Roles that facilitate the provision of Open Government Data (OGD) are increasingly found in German public administration. Formal role descriptions and guidance documents provide insight into responsibilities and strategic placement of these functions, but there is little empirical knowledge about what Open Data Coordinators (ODCs) do in practice, how they are embedded in organisational structures, and what challenges they face. We address this gap with an anonymous online survey of 44 ODCs or comparable contact persons in German public authorities. The questionnaire captured organisational location, allocation of working time, models for distributing open data tasks, key responsibilities and priorities, and perceived barriers and effects on data management. Our findings show that open data coordination is a cross-cutting function that spans the entire authority but accounts for only a small share of coordinators' formal task profiles. Responsibility for OGD is mostly decentralised or hybrid: specialist departments retain data ownership, while coordinators advise them and/or handle publication. Coordinators prioritise supporting publication and acting as central internal contact points, but report persistent shortages of human and financial resources and limited management guidance as key impediments, even though many observe incremental improvements in data management. The paper offers an empirical mapping of these roles and outlines implications for their design, resourcing and institutionalisation in public administration.

Keywords: Open Data · Open Government Data · Data Governance · Open Data Roles · Public Administration

1 Introduction

Open Government Data (OGD) refers to data produced by public organisations that is freely available for anyone to use, reuse, and redistribute [1], based on the principle that information created with public resources should be publicly accessible. Prior research highlights multiple potential benefits, including greater

Published by Springer Nature Switzerland 2027
G. Viale Pereira et al. (Eds.): EGOV 2026, LNCS 16933, pp. 113–129, 2027.
https://doi.org/10.1007/978-3-032-35747-2_8

transparency, economic innovation, citizen participation, new public services and more efficient administration [2,3]. In response, governments have introduced legal frameworks, strategies and technical infrastructures to support the systematic publication of public sector information [2]. In Germany, the national GovData portal, established in 2013, aggregates datasets from federal, state and municipal administrations and provides access to over 147,000 datasets (March 2026), complemented by numerous regional and local open data portals.

Despite these institutional developments, the practical implementation of open data policies remains uneven. International comparisons place Germany only in the middle range of open data maturity, and the publication of datasets often progresses slowly [4]. Publishing OGD poses significant organisational challenges. Authorities must balance legal requirements (such as data protection and licensing), ensure appropriate technical infrastructures and data quality, and coordinate activities across departments [5]. At the same time, many administrations are only beginning to establish systematic processes for data management and publication, while being asked to move from a custodial to a publishing role that introduces new expectations and uncertainties regarding responsibilities and institutional roles [6]. These developments highlight that the implementation of OGD policies depends not only on technological infrastructures and legal frameworks, but also on organisational capabilities and data governance. Recent debates on data stewardship and information management emphasise that publishing datasets alone is not sufficient: data must be embedded in technical and organisational infrastructures that keep them meaningful, usable and sustainable over time [7]. Similar arguments arise in discussions on AI governance, which stress that trustworthy and accountable AI systems rely on mature data governance practices ensuring data quality, provenance and appropriate use [8].

Implementing open data initiatives often entails organisational change within public administrations, as data-related activities must be coordinated across departments and administrative levels, requiring a professional human infrastructure to manage these processes [9–11]. Analogous to digital transformation, where internal change agents guide colleagues in adopting new digital practices and bridge the gap between strategic initiatives and everyday work [12], coordination roles in OGD can support organisational actors in navigating the practical challenges of data publication and management. Yet institutional structures for coordinating open data are often weak: a survey among German municipalities found that only 6% of municipalities with fewer than 50,000 inhabitants and 12% of medium-sized municipalities were able to identify a person formally responsible for open data [13]. Moreover, comparatively little attention has been paid to the practical roles and responsibilities of the staff within administrations who actually enable authorities to provide open data [7].

Despite this growing relevance, little is known about how such coordination roles are implemented in practice. In Germany, the legally mandated Open Data Coordinator (ODC) has become a blueprint for open data coordination in many public organisations, yet its practical enactment remains poorly understood. Moreover, Novais et al. [14] emphasize the need to broaden the geographic coverage of OGD research beyond a small number of frequently studied countries. Analysing the German case contributes insights from a federal administrative system with relatively recent open data legislation.

Against this background, the paper addresses the following research questions: (1) How are open data coordination roles organisationally embedded and resourced in German public authorities? (2) Which tasks and priorities define these roles in practice? (3) Which organisational models and perceived barriers shape the implementation of open data coordination, and what effects do coordinators observe on broader data management? To answer these questions, we draw on an anonymous online survey among 44 employees who act as ODCs or comparable contact persons in German public authorities and analyse the organisational positioning, task profiles, responsibility models and perceived impediments associated with the ODC function. The paper thereby advances understanding of how formally defined roles are interpreted and enacted in OGD governance and discusses implications for further institutionalising and professionalising open data governance structures.

2 Background

OGD forms part of broader data governance arrangements in public organisations. Data governance refers to the structures, responsibilities, standards and processes through which organisations manage and use data, embedding data-related responsibilities in organisational structures and everyday administrative work rather than treating them as a purely technical issue [15,16]. In the public sector, data governance links strategic objectives with the operational management of data by defining responsibilities, coordination mechanisms and procedures across organisational units [15].

Within such arrangements, open data publication is an organisational task that requires clearly allocated responsibilities and coordination across multiple actors. A central element of data governance is therefore the establishment of roles that coordinate data-related activities across organisational units. The German IT Planning Council explicitly identifies roles and data competencies as a key field of action for data governance in the public sector [15]. Dedicated coordination and stewardship functions are seen as crucial for managing these cross-cutting processes and implementing open data policies [7,10].

In Germany, the ODC exemplifies a formalised coordination role for OGD. The First Open Data Act (2017) amended the E-Government Act and created a legal basis for publishing federal administrative data as open data. The Second Open Data Act (2021) introduced §12a E-Government Act, requiring federal authorities to designate an ODC as a central contact point for open data. The ODC is tasked with promoting the identification, publication and reuse of open data within the authority (§12a para. 9). Several federal states have adopted similar open data laws, some of which also require the appointment of ODCs.

Building on this legal framework, guidelines from the Federal Competence Center for Open Data specify that ODCs act as internal and external contact points, advise on data publication, support staff (for instance through training and consultation) and contribute to developing organisational open data guidelines [17]. The role thus combines data management, coordination and communication tasks at the intersection of strategic and operational activities within public organisations [5].

To better understand the emergence and functioning of such positions, sociological role theory provides a useful analytical perspective. It understands roles as patterns of expected behaviour associated with a social position [18]. In organisational and institutional contexts, such roles are shaped by formal rules and informal norms; individuals often face multiple and partly conflicting expectations, which can lead to tensions and role conflicts that must be negotiated in everyday practice [19]. In this paper, we use the term "role" to denote the bundle of tasks, responsibilities and expectations attached to positions coordinating open data activities within public organisations. Public institutions comprise many such roles, which structure interactions but always leave room for interpretation by role holders. Examining how ODCs enact their roles in practice is therefore central to understanding OGD governance in public administration, particularly in cross-cutting policy areas where responsibilities span organisational boundaries [10,20].

3 Method

Survey Design. The results presented in this paper stem from a larger online survey on open data roles in Germany. We only report the parts of the questionnaire that are relevant for this study. The survey was implemented in LimeSurvey, administered in German, and participation was fully anonymous. All questions were optional to minimise re-identification risks, particularly for respondents from small organisations or with unique role profiles. We use English translations of the original German items in this paper.

The questionnaire combined single- and multiple-choice items, matrix questions with Likert-type answer scales, and free-text fields. In the section analysed here, we asked about:

- characteristics of the authority (level of administration, size),
- the ODC's role (role title, organisational location, area of responsibility, share of working time devoted to open data),
- the organisational distribution of open data responsibilities (central, decentral, hybrid, ad-hoc, other),
- tasks associated with the ODC role (extent of responsibility for 13 task areas, prioritisation of the three most important tasks, perceived appropriateness of the overall task scope),
- factors hindering the implementation of open data (11 potential impediments rated on a five-point Likert scale, plus free-text additions),
- perceived improvements through open data implementation for general data handling (closed question plus free-text examples),

- and any further comments on aspects not covered by the questionnaire (free text).

In developing the questionnaire, the response options were derived from prior work and practice-based insights. The five response options on how open data provision is organised within an authority (e.g. central, decentral, hybrid) were constructed based on the authors' experience and observations from working closely with public sector organisations on open data. Furthermore, the list of 13 tasks associated with the ODC role was taken from responsibilities identified in an earlier study on open data stewardship [10]. Lastly, the eleven factors used to capture impediments to open data implementation were derived from a mini-survey conducted during a workshop at the Public Data Conference 2025 at the Fraunhofer FOKUS Institute, in which public sector employees working on open data identified central barriers from their practice.

User Testing and Verification. To validate the survey questionnaire and gather feedback, two user tests were conducted using the think-aloud method with ODCs from the federal and municipal level. The pre-tests focused on the clarity and unambiguity of wording, the ease of access and use of the online survey, and the perceived relevance and completeness of the questions.

Dissemination. The survey was disseminated via newsletters, mailing lists and an interactive workshop format to reach practitioners in the German open data community. Specifically, the survey was shared from the beginning to mid-December 2025 through the open data newsletter of the Bertelsmann Stiftung, the eGov-News newsletter of the Fraunhofer FOKUS Institute, and the mailing list of the Competence Center for Open Data in Germany. In addition, the survey was presented in a barcamp session organised by the Bertelsmann Stiftung. The survey was active until beginning of February 2026.

Data Cleaning. After collecting the data, basic data cleaning was necessary to create usable results. Submissions with no answers (cases where participants only opened the survey link but did not respond) were fully removed. Free-text responses were harmonised where necessary (e.g. consolidation of gendered terms such as *Datenkoordinatorin* and *Datenkoordinator*, or in cases where an entry posed a re-identification risk) in order to enable consistent analysis.

4 Findings

In total, 44 public administration employees participated in the survey, although not all respondents completed every question.

4.1 Institutional Characteristics

For the description of institutional characteristics presented in this section, we draw on up to 43 responses per item.

With regard to administrative level, the sample is dominated by federal authorities: 28 respondents (around 65%) work at the federal level. Nine respondents (21%) come from the municipal level, and four (9%) from the state (Länder) level. One respondent each reports working at the district level and in another type of organisation (2% each). The results should therefore be interpreted primarily as reflecting experiences from the federal and, to a lesser extent, municipal context.

The participating authorities are mostly medium-sized to large organisations. Only two respondents (5%) report working in very small authorities with up to 50 employees. Fourteen respondents (33%) are based in authorities with 251–1,000 employees, while the largest group, 27 respondents (63%), comes from authorities with more than 1,000 employees. Overall, the survey thus mainly captures open data coordination roles in larger public institutions.

4.2 Organisation of the ODC Role

Organisational Location. ODCs are most frequently situated in specialist departments (*Fachbereich*, 28%) or central administrative units (*Z-Abteilung*, 26%), which together account for just over half of all respondents. Around one fifth (19%) are located in IT departments, while smaller shares work in executive staff units (*Stabsstellen*, 7%) or policy/strategy departments (*Grundsatz-Abteilungen*, 5%), and 16% report other forms of organisational placement. Overall, this pattern points to a dispersed institutional anchoring of the role rather than a single dominant organisational home (N = 43).

Area of Responsibility. The vast majority of respondents (about 88%) report that their area of responsibility covers the entire authority. Only a small number indicate that their function is limited to a specific department or section, or describe other, more narrowly defined scopes. This suggests that, regardless of their organisational location, ODCs typically have a cross-cutting mandate that spans the whole organisation (N = 43). However, this finding should be interpreted in light of the strong representation of federal and large authorities in the sample.

Proportion of Task Profile. The survey also captured the share of each respondent's overall task profile accounted for by the ODC role. The role is often assigned to staff who already have other responsibilities, so it usually represents only part of their official duties and, in some cases, is not even formally reflected in their task profile. For around two fifths of respondents (38%), open data coordination makes up none or up to a quarter of their official task profile; a further 24% report a share between one quarter and one half. Only about two fifths in total (19% each for a share of half to three quarters and a share of three quarters to 100%) state that the role occupies more than half of their official profile. This confirms that open data coordination is frequently added on to other responsibilities and is not accounted for in the official task profile, possibly leading to resource conflicts in the employee's working time. It is only rarely established as a full-time position (N = 37). Given that the sample is dominated by large federal institutions, which typically have more resources than smaller municipal or state-level institutions, the share of the task profile allocated to the ODC role would likely be even lower in those smaller institutions.

Role Titles. The distribution of job titles among the 32 respondents shows substantial heterogeneity in how the open data coordination function is labelled across authorities. While explicitly open-data-related titles such as Open Data Coordinator (*Open Data Koordinator:in*, 10 respondents) and Open Data Commissioner (*Open Data Beauftragte:r*, 7 respondents) are most common, a number of respondents hold more general or differently framed roles. These include Leadership role (*Leitungsfunktion*, 3; this category aggregates three entries to minimize identification risks), General Data Management (*Allg. Datenmanagement*, 2), Open Data Manager (2), Open Data Clerk (*Sachbearbeiter Open Data*, 2), Head Clerk for Innovation (*Dezernent für Innovation*, 1), IT Engineer Open Data (*IT Ingenieur:in Open Data*, 1), Liaison Officer (1), Open Data contact partner (*Open Data Ansprechpartner*, 1), Project Manager (*Projektmanager:in*, 1), and Open Data Consultant (*Referent:in Open Data*, 1). This indicates that open data responsibilities are sometimes institutionalised in dedicated positions, but are also embedded in broader or more generic roles.

4.3 Open Data Implementation

Organisational Model of Open Data Provision. As shown in Table 1, there is no single dominant organisational model for open data coordination, but a clear tendency towards decentralised arrangements. The most common setup is a decentralised model with an advisory ODC: in 36% of cases, the specialist departments handle the tasks up to publication themselves, while the ODC mainly advises and supports them. Another 19% report a model in which data responsibility lies with departments, but the ODC handles publication, and 17% describe a hybrid model where some departments manage parts of the process themselves while others delegate more to the coordinator.

By contrast, only 10% work in a fully centralised model, where tasks from data monitoring through to publication lie primarily with the ODC. A smaller group (7%) indicate ad-hoc responsibilities without a fixed role distribution, and 12% report other models. Overall, the findings suggest that the ODC role is more often embedded as a supporting or shared function within a decentralised structure than as a single central unit that owns the entire open data process. Given that the sample is dominated by large federal authorities, these patterns may partly reflect the organisational complexity of larger administrations. The free-text responses indicate that in some authorities the organisational model for open data is still in flux: processes and responsibilities are only being developed, clarified, or determined.

Table 1. Organisational distribution models of open data responsibilities (N = 42)

Organisational model	n	%
Central ODC: Tasks ranging from data monitoring to publication are primarily the responsibility of the ODC.	4	10%
Dept-owned data, ODC publishes: Data responsibility lies with the specialist departments. They send the data to be published to the ODC, who is solely responsible for publication.	8	19%
Decentralised, ODC advisory: The tasks up to publication are carried out decentrally in the specialist departments; the ODC primarily acts in an advisory and supportive capacity.	15	36%
Hybrid: dept & ODC: Some specialist departments take on parts of the process themselves, while others mainly delegate the tasks to the ODC.	7	17%
Ad-hoc responsibilities: There is no fixed distribution of roles; open data tasks are taken on an ad hoc basis.	3	7%
Other	5	12%

Tasks of the ODC Role. Figure 1 shows how respondents (N = 39) position different activities in relation to their role as ODC. The role is most clearly associated with supporting and publishing open data, ensuring compliance with open data regulations, acting as a central internal contact point, exchanging with other authorities, and contributing to cultural change and community engagement: for each of these activities, more than half of respondents describe them as core responsibilities. A second group of tasks, consisting of gaining an overview of existing data, identifying and evaluating datasets, coordinating with other departments, and providing training or internal knowledge transfer, is less firmly anchored, with around 40–50% seeing them as core tasks and many others reporting that they are only sometimes part of their responsibilities or shared with other roles.

Other activities are even less consistently located within the ODC role. Ensuring data quality, process management and acting as a central external contact person are each reported as core responsibilities by fewer than 40% and are often carried out by other units. For many of these activities, including data overview and identification, data quality, coordination with other departments, process management, training, external communication and community engagement, over 30% of respondents state that they are only sometimes part of their role, and for some (notably data overview, data quality and process management) more than 20% indicate that they are mainly handled by other roles.

In addition, respondents used the free-text field to describe a range of further tasks linked to the ODC role. These include preparing and visualising data, managing the open data portal or platform, drafting internal directives and coordinating software implementation processes. Some coordinators also report responsibilities for "data excellence" in the sense of broader data governance and data management, including the conception, implementation and maintenance of an internal metadata catalogue. Others emphasise more strategic functions, such as embedding open data within organisational data strategies and implementing and monitoring the EU implementing act on high-value datasets, as well as taking on responsibilities for data ethics at the municipal level.

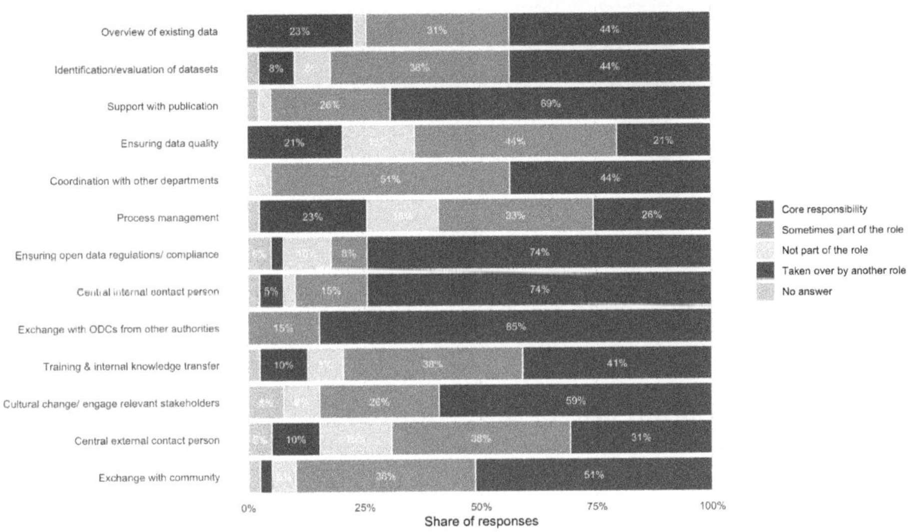

Fig. 1. Likert items for the question: Do the following tasks fall within the scope of your role as ODC? If not, are these tasks carried out by other roles? (N = 39).

Most Important Tasks of the ODC Role. Figure 2 summarises which tasks respondents (N = 40) consider most important for open data coordination. Participants could select up to three tasks, resulting in 115 votes in total. The top priority is support with the publication of open data, accounting for around 22% of all votes. Acting as a central internal contact person (about 15%) and contributing to cultural change or stakeholder engagement (about 13%) also rank highly, followed by gaining an overview of existing data and identifying or evaluating datasets for publication (each about 10%). In contrast, more operational, specialised, and external-facing activities collectively receive much lower shares, indicating that respondents primarily view open data coordination as centred on supporting publication and serving as an internal hub.

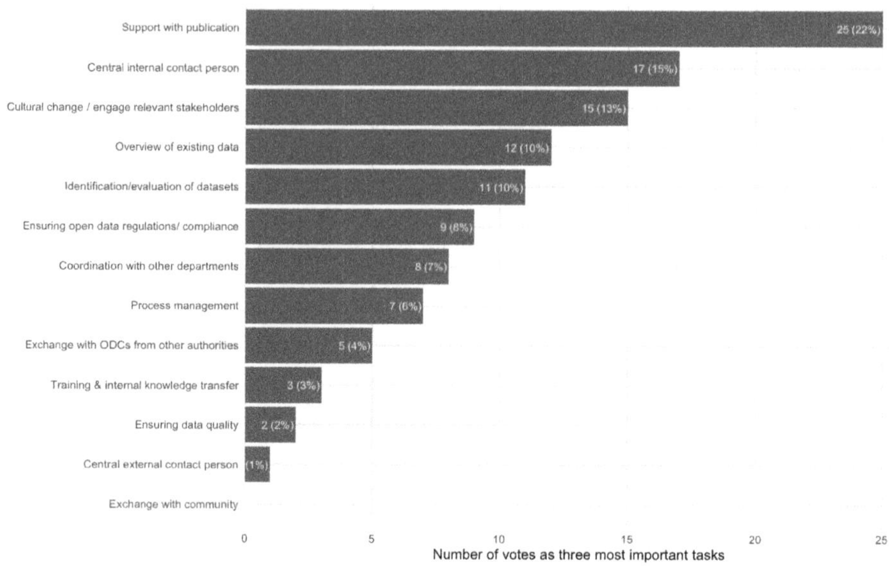

Fig. 2. Most important tasks of an open data coordinator. Total votes across all items, with a maximum of three votes per participant: 115.

Perceived Appropriateness of the Scope of the Tasks of the ODC Role. Among the 38 respondents, a clear majority perceived the scope of the tasks of the ODC role as appropriate: 58% indicated that the role covers about the right number of areas of responsibility. Views that the role covers too many or too few areas were evenly split and less common, with 21% judging the scope as rather or far too broad and 21% as rather or far too narrow. Overall, these results suggest that the current scope of the ODC role is broadly seen as adequate, with only small groups at each end of the spectrum.

Barriers to the Implementation of Open Data. Figure 3 shows how 40 respondents rate eleven potential factors that impede efforts to implement open data in their authority, on a five-point Likert scale from "not at all" to "very strongly." Several barriers are very widespread: more than half of respondents say that lack of data skills among staff, insufficient human or financial resources, lack of openness to open data and data culture, no overview of existing data, no clear guidance from management, and unclear benefits of open data for staff or management impair implementation "quite strongly" or "very strongly." Among these, insufficient human or financial resources and no clear guidance from management stand out, with over 30% of respondents rating each as a "very strong" impediment. Since the sample mainly consists of larger authorities, these findings indicate that such challenges persist even in comparatively resource-rich administrative settings.

By contrast, some factors are less commonly seen as obstacles. For lack of data skills among staff and uncertainty regarding data protection, more than a quarter of respondents indicate that these factors impair open data implementation "rather little" or "not at all." This suggests that, although coordinators may actively work to reduce these barriers, they still perceive resource constraints and strategic direction from management as the most pressing issues for open data implementation in their authorities.

Across the free-text responses, participants highlighted several additional factors hindering open data implementation. They pointed to legal and regulatory uncertainties, including unclear definitions in the Open Data Act (e.g. "raw data"), a lack of concrete guidance on handling sensitive or security-relevant information, unclear responsibilities when multiple authorities are involved, incomplete legal expertise, and confusion around licensing choices. Respondents also emphasized structural and resource-related barriers: open data coordination roles that are heavily under-resourced, missing binding directives from higher-level authorities, limited or temporary staffing, a lack of national infrastructure for publishing large data volumes, and procurement practices that neither prioritise open data nor build internal capacities, but instead rely on external contractors. In addition, cultural and organizational factors were described as obstacles: low willingness to innovate and limited awareness of data and open data issues at both management and staff levels, the absence of a data strategy, data governance and compliance structures, siloed thinking across departments, risk aversion, and the perception among staff that open data primarily creates extra work without obvious personal benefit. Technical challenges were also mentioned, particularly the difficulty of complying with legal requirements for very large research datasets (tens to hundreds of terabytes) that are expected to be made available via web interfaces or APIs.

Improvements in General Data Management. Lastly, we asked respondents whether measures to implement open data had already led to concrete improvements in their authority's general handling of data (e.g., efficiency, transparency, innovation). A majority reported positive effects: 20% indicated significant improvements and 53% minor improvements, while 27% stated that they had not observed any improvements so far.

The free-text responses mainly point to organisational and process-related changes. Respondents report that data infrastructure is being built up and open data processes are gradually being established, with some initiatives still at an early stage. They also highlight the creation of dedicated roles or units, the introduction of internal guidelines and standardised publication workflows, as well as awareness-raising activities and faster publication of relevant datasets as concrete positive effects of open data implementation.

Further Comments. The open-ended comments highlight several broader concerns that go beyond the structured questions in the survey. Respondents note a lack of overarching strategies and concrete guidelines to build data literacy and

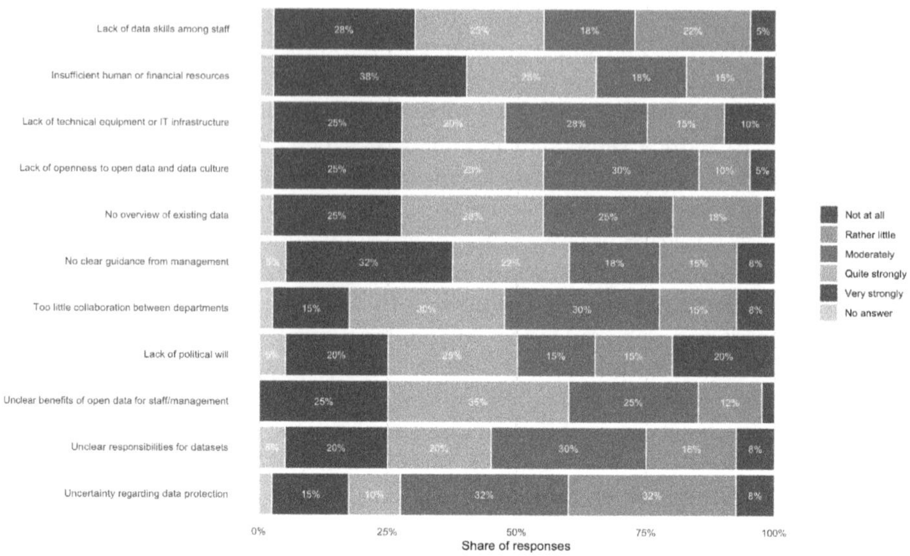

Fig. 3. Likert items for the question: How strongly do the following factors impair the work on implementing open data in your authority? (N = 40).

ensure data quality as a prerequisite for the introduction of AI across government data holdings. They also criticise the absence of sanctions for non-compliance with §12a EGovG, which means that progress on open data often depends heavily on the mindset and commitment of senior leadership. In addition, participants call for central, reusable materials (e.g. example lists, slide decks on the benefits of open data and best-practice cases) to complement training offers for coordinators. Finally, one respondent points out that indirectly federal, privately organised bodies are excluded from existing ODC trainings and meetings, which limits their access to capacity-building and peer exchange.

5 Discussion and Conclusion

This section discusses the main findings of the survey and reflects on implications for the organisation of open data coordination roles in German public administration. It concludes with limitations and avenues for future research.

The scope and context of the findings are shaped by the composition of the sample, which is dominated by federal and other large authorities. As a result, the results primarily reflect conditions in comparatively resource-rich and early-moving parts of the public sector. Small municipalities and districts are only weakly represented, so the findings should be generalised to other administrative levels with caution.

The findings indicate that open data coordination roles are only partially institutionalised within public administration. While legal frameworks such as the Second Open Data Act formally require federal authorities to designate ODCs, the organisational implementation of this role varies substantially across authorities. In most cases, coordinators hold a *cross-cutting mandate* that often covers the entire organisation, but the role is weakly anchored in formal task profiles and is *rarely a full-time position*; for many respondents, open data coordination accounts for a quarter or less of their official duties. This suggests that the legal requirement to appoint ODCs has often been implemented by assigning responsibilities to existing positions rather than by creating dedicated posts. From the perspective of role theory, this corresponds to a formally defined expectation that is integrated into pre-existing roles, leaving considerable room for interpretation and negotiation in everyday practice.

The survey reveals considerable heterogeneity in role titles and organisational locations. In some organisations, open data responsibilities are assigned to dedicated positions explicitly labelled as ODCs or commissioners, whereas in others they are embedded in broader roles related to data management, project management or innovation. Coordinators can be found in specialist departments, central administrative units, IT departments, and staff or strategy units, without a single dominant organisational home. This diversity suggests that the role is still evolving and has not yet stabilised as a clearly defined organisational function. Rather than representing a uniform position with a standardised mandate, open data coordination is being *fitted into existing structures* and adapted to local administrative contexts. Our findings mirror those reported by Shepherd et al. [7], who found substantial variation in organisational responsibilities, job titles and organisational arrangements for open government data across different public-sector organisations in England. Similar forms of variation are also visible in our data. At the same time, respondents in our survey share a common institutional reference point in the formally established ODC role, which may contribute to greater consistency in responsibilities and expectations than observed in the more heterogeneous organisational settings examined by Shepherd et al.

The findings indicate that responsibility for open data provision is predominantly organised through decentralised or hybrid models. Specialist departments generally retain ownership of data and carry out substantive work on datasets, while ODCs advise them and/or take over publication. Fully centralised models, in which coordinators manage the entire process from data monitoring to publication, are the exception. In several authorities, organisational models and processes are still evolving, with responsibilities being clarified or adjusted over time.

The task profiles reported by respondents are consistent with this picture. Coordinators most commonly regard supporting and publishing open data, ensuring compliance with open data regulations, acting as central internal contact points and exchanging with other authorities as core responsibilities. They also frequently report contributions to cultural change and stakeholder engagement. Other tasks, such as gaining an overview of existing data, identifying and evaluating datasets, coordinating with other departments, and providing training or internal knowledge transfer are less uniformly anchored. Many coordinators regard these activities as core elements of their role, but they are also frequently shared with other functions or taken on only in specific cases. Activities such as ensuring data quality, process management, acting as central external contact points and community engagement are even less consistently located within the open data coordination role and are often carried out by other units. Overall, this suggests that open data coordination in its current form concentrates on internal coordination and publication support rather than on comprehensive data governance, for example systematic quality assurance, process design or external ecosystem building. Elements of these broader tasks are included in many cases, but typically not as top priorities. In this sense, the role currently aligns more with a *change agent* as mentioned by Fischer & Breaugh [12] or a *facilitator who supports* other actors in publishing data than with a fully fledged data steward with end-to-end responsibility.

Despite the breadth of tasks associated with the role, a majority of respondents consider the overall scope of responsibilities to be appropriate. This indicates that the definition of the role itself is not generally seen as problematic by those who occupy it. At the same time, respondents report pronounced resource and governance constraints. Insufficient human and financial resources and a lack of clear guidance from management are perceived as particularly strong impediments to open data implementation. Additional cultural and organisational barriers include limited openness to open data within organisations, a lack of overview of existing data, unclear benefits for staff and management, siloed working practices, risk aversion and the perception of open data as additional work. Structural factors such as legal and regulatory uncertainties, limited infrastructure and procurement practices that do not build internal capacities further shape the context in which coordinators operate.

This combination of broadly accepted role scope and reported resource shortages points to a *mismatch between expectations and enabling conditions*. From a role-theoretical perspective, this mismatch can be understood as a tension between role expectations and organisational capacities [19]. Coordinators are tasked with facilitating open data across entire authorities, often on top of other responsibilities and with limited formal authority, while *key structural and cultural preconditions for open data are not yet fully established*. This may contribute to the perception that institutional arrangements for coordinating open data are still underdeveloped, despite the existence of formal role descriptions and legal mandates.

Nevertheless, many respondents report that open data initiatives have already led to at least minor improvements in data management. These include the development of data infrastructures and open data processes, the creation of dedicated roles or units, the introduction of internal guidelines and standardised publication workflows, and increased awareness of data-related issues. Open data coordination can thus function as a *driver for more systematic data handling*, even if progress is uneven and dependent on local conditions.

The findings point to several implications for the further development of open data coordination roles. First, *the institutional anchoring and resourcing of coordinators should be strengthened* through clearer mandates, adequate allocation of staff time and, where appropriate, permanent dedicated roles. Second, the *distribution of responsibilities* between coordinators, specialist departments, IT and legal units needs to be clarified so that processes for data preparation, quality assurance and publication are transparent and understood by all actors. Third, *management engagement, internal communication and data culture should be enhanced*, for example through explicit leadership support, internal strategies and awareness-raising measures. Central support offers such as training, reusable communication materials and peer exchange formats can complement these efforts across authorities.

6 Limitations and Future Research

This study has several limitations. The sample is relatively small and dominated by federal and large authorities, which restricts the generalisability of the findings, particularly to smaller municipalities and districts. Participation was voluntary and may over-represent organisations and individuals already more engaged with open data. The analysis is based on self-reported assessments by coordinators and does not include the perspectives of other stakeholders. Finally, the cross-sectional design provides only a snapshot and cannot capture how roles and organisational arrangements develop over time.

Future research could address these limitations by conducting qualitative case studies in selected authorities to examine how open data coordination is enacted in everyday practice and how coordinators interact with other organisational units. Comparative studies across federal states, administrative levels and countries could shed light on how different legal and institutional contexts shape these roles. Further work could also link role configurations and organisational models to outcomes.

Acknowledgments. The authors used the generative AI tool ChatGPT (OpenAI, version GPT-5) for AI assisted copy editing, including language refinement and text shortening and as a tool to support debugging in R. The tool was not used to generate original content, research questions, data, results, or interpretations. All content, arguments, and conclusions remain the sole responsibility of the authors.

Disclosure of Interests. The authors have no competing interests to declare that are relevant to the content of this article.

References

1. Foundation, O.K.: What is Open Data?
2. Kraus, S., Basanta, E.P.T.: Open Data in der Berliner Verwaltung. Verwaltung und Manag. **3**, 118–128 (2021)
3. Safarov, I., Meijer, A., Grimmelikhuijsen, S.: Utilization of open government data: a systematic literature review of types, conditions, effects and users. Inf. Polity **22**, 1–24 (2017)
4. Union, E.: Explore 2025 Open Data Maturity Report|EDP (2025)
5. Klessmann, J., Staab, T.: Strategische Bereitstellung offener Verwaltungsdaten (2018). Section: publikationen
6. Commission, E.: Digital Decade 2024: eGovernment Benchmark - Insight Report (2024)
7. Shepherd, E., et al.: Open government data: critical information management perspectives. Rec. Manag. J. **29**, 152–167 (2019)
8. Verhulst, S.G., Schüür, F.: Toward AI Governance That Works: Examining the Building Blocks of AI and the Impacts (2025)
9. Verhulst, S.G.: Reimagining data responsibility: 10 new approaches toward a culture of trust in re-using data to address critical public needs. Data Policy **3**, e6 (2021)
10. von Falkenhausen, I., Plomin, J., Heider, M.: Stewarding of open government data - a versatile task requiring a versatile role. In: Lindgren, I. et al. (eds.) Electronic Government, Cham, pp. 101–114, Springer Nature Switzerland (2025)
11. Seibel, B.: Open Data in der Berliner Verwaltung (2018)
12. Fischer, C., Breaugh, J.: Navigating Digital Transformation? The Guiding Role and Socialization Processes of Change Agents. Public Administration, vol. n/a (2025). _eprint: https://onlinelibrary.wiley.com/doi/pdf/10.1111/padm.70024
13. Bürger, T., Hoch, A.: Open Data in Kommunen (2020)
14. Novais, T., De Albuquerque, J.P., Craveiro, G.S.: An Account of Research On Open Government Data (2007- 2012): A Systematic Literature Review (2013). Conference Name: Electronic Government and Electronic Participation - Joint Proceedings of Ongoing Research of IFIP EGOV and IFIP ePart 2013 ISBN: 9783885796152 ISSN: 1617-5468 Meeting Name: Electronic Government and Electronic Participation - Joint Proceedings of Ongoing Research of IFIP EGOV and IFIP ePart 2013 Pages: 76-83 Volume: P-221
15. Planungsrat, I.: Handlungsleitfaden Data Governance (2025)
16. Bollweg, L.M.: Was ist Data Governance? In: Bollweg, L.M. (ed.) Data Governance für Manager : Datengetriebene Prozess- und Systemoptimierung als Taktgeber der digitalen Transformation, pp. 11–50, Berlin, Heidelberg: Springer (2021)
17. Bundesverwaltungsamt: Leitfaden Open-Data-Koordination (2022)

18. Banton, M.: Role. In: The Social Science Encyclopedia, London and New Yorg: Routledge Taylor & Francis Group, 2nd edition ed. (1996)
19. Biddle, B.J.: Recent development in role theory. Ann. Rev. Sociol. **12**, 67–92 (1986)
20. Poulsen, B.: The Question of Roles and Identities in Public Administration. Scandinavian Political Studies, vol. 30, no. 4, pp. 469–490 (2007). _eprint: https://onlinelibrary.wiley.com/doi/pdf/10.1111/j.1467-9477.2007.00189.x

SCPDM: A Linked Data Model for the Documentation and Replication of Smart City Projects

Michael Gysel[1](✉), Lukas Koch-Ruchay[2,3], and Luis Moßburger[3]

[1] Fraunhofer FOKUS, Berlin, Germany
michael.gysel@fokus.fraunhofer.de
[2] Data Competence Center for Cities and Region, Berlin, Germany
lukas.koch-ruchay@dksr.city
[3] Sparkup, Neumarkt, Germany
luis.mossburger@spark-up.de

Abstract. Smart city initiatives across European municipalities frequently suffer from "pilotitis": successful projects remain isolated pilots whose organizational knowledge, technical workflows, and resource configurations are not systematically transferred to other cities. While semantic standards exist for individual components, including DCAT for datasets, SSN/SOSA for sensor hardware, and P-PLAN for workflow modeling, no unified data model connects these layers to represent a smart city project as a whole. This paper presents the Smart City Project Data Model (SCPDM), a Linked Data model that treats the smart city project, rather than the smart city asset, as its central organizing concept. The SCPDM formalizes relationships between organizational governance phases, technical process steps, and the hardware, software, and datasets required for implementation, producing a structured "project blueprint" that municipalities can discover, compare, and adapt to local contexts. The model was developed through the analysis of 17 municipal digital twin projects in Bavaria, expert workshops, ontology reuse, and iterative validation with municipal stakeholders, and implemented as the semantic backbone of twin.bydata. A case study from Haar demonstrates its practical applicability for documenting real-world smart city projects using Linked Data.

Keywords: Smart City · Linked Data · Digital Twin · Knowledge Transfer · DCAT-AP

1 Introduction

The proliferation of smart city initiatives across European municipalities over the last decade has not translated into widespread knowledge transfer. The domain instead suffers from "pilotitis": successful initiatives remain isolated pilot projects

Published by Springer Nature Switzerland 2027
G. Viale Pereira et al. (Eds.): EGOV 2026, LNCS 16933, pp. 130–146, 2027.
https://doi.org/10.1007/978-3-032-35747-2_9

that fail to replicate in other municipal contexts. While urban data platforms have improved the sharing of *data* between cities, the sharing of *project knowledge*, including the organizational decisions, technical workflows, and specific resources behind a successful implementation, remains manual, unstructured, and largely tacit.

This paper presents the SCPDM, a Linked Data model that addresses this gap by modeling smart city projects as replicable "blueprints." The SCPDM treats the smart city project, rather than the smart city asset, as its central organizing concept, and formalizes the relationships between organizational governance phases, technical process steps, and the concrete hardware, software, and datasets required for implementation. By integrating rather than replacing existing semantic standards such as DCAT [19], SSN/SOSA [9], P-PLAN [6], and PROV-O [14], the SCPDM enables municipalities to publish structured descriptions of their initiatives and allows others to discover, compare, and replicate them.

The contributions of this paper are threefold. First, we present the SCPDM itself, which unifies organizational governance modeling and technical workflow specification within a single semantic data model grounded in established W3C and industry ontologies. Second, we describe the implementation of the SCPDM as the semantic backbone of twin.bydata, a production platform built on the open-source piveau ecosystem for documenting, discovering, and comparing smart city projects across Bavarian municipalities. Third, we validate the model through its application to real-world municipal digital twin projects, demonstrating its practical expressiveness and applicability.

The remainder of this paper is structured as follows. Section 2 provides background and motivation. Section 3 reviews related work across smart city data models, asset-centric ontologies, and benchmarking frameworks. Section 4 presents the methodology. Section 5 details the data model. Section 6 describes the platform implementation and a case study from the municipality of Haar. Section 7 discusses implications, Sect. 8 addresses limitations and future work, and Sect. 9 concludes.

2 Background and Motivation

German federal and state governments have made substantial investments in municipal smart city development. The federal Modellprojekte Smart Cities (MPSC) programme has allocated €820 million across 73 municipalities since 2019, aiming to create transferable solutions for Germany's roughly 11,000 municipalities [2]. State programmes such as Bavaria's "TwinBy" initiative have supported municipalities in developing domain-specific digital twins [1]. Yet despite this investment, many smart city pilots fade out after the pilot stage and fail to generate scalable solutions [20]. Research on smart city governance emphasizes that such initiatives depend not only on technical infrastructure, but also on people, institutions, administrative processes, and cross-organizational collaboration [15,16]. The SCPDM is therefore positioned as a technical artifact for representing socio-technical project knowledge: it does not claim to resolve governance, procurement, or capacity constraints, but documents how organizational decisions, technical workflows, and resource configurations are combined in existing initiatives so municipalities can discover comparable projects and assess which elements may be reused or adapted to local conditions [17].

Current dissemination formats remain limited: workshops reach only direct attendees, while PDF reports are difficult to search, compare, or harvest programmatically. A municipal project manager asking, for example, "Which Bavarian cities have deployed traffic sensors, at what cost, and through which procurement model?" has no structured way to retrieve this information without extensive manual research.

The work presented in this paper was developed within the twin.bydata project, funded by the Bavarian State Ministry for Digital Affairs and coordinated by Bayern Innovativ [1]. The programme supported 17 municipal digital twin projects across Bavaria, including Haar, Kempten, Schwabach, and the NordAllianz, in domains such as mobility, energy, and environmental monitoring. With funding of up to €50,000 for individual municipalities and €75,000 for intermunicipal projects, participating municipalities worked with a consortium of service providers to build digital twins within one year. The heterogeneity of these 17 projects provided both the empirical foundation and the practical testbed for the data model presented in this paper.

This setting motivated the core design requirement of the SCPDM: a semantic model that captures not only what resources a project uses, but also the organizational and technical processes through which those resources are orchestrated, in a format that is both human-readable and machine-queryable.

3 Related Work

The landscape of smart city data modeling is characterized by a significant dichotomy: while robust standards exist for high-level strategic benchmarking and low-level technical components, there remains no unified data model that links these layers to facilitate smart city project replication.

Well-established standards exist to describe individual components of a smart city project: DCAT [19] for publishing and discovering data catalogs, SSN/SOSA [9] for modeling sensors, actuators, and their observations, and P-PLAN [6] and PROV-O [14] for representing workflow plans and their executions. While these ontologies effectively model isolated components, they lack the unifying semantic data model required to represent a holistic smart city project, thereby preventing municipalities from easily sharing and replicating successful initiatives.

Holistic smart city frameworks such as the Six Dimensions model [7], Smart City Wheel [4], and ISO 37120 [11] provide taxonomies for benchmarking city performance, while the Triple Helix [5] and Quadruple Helix [3] models analyze stakeholder interrelations. However, these frameworks are tailored for assessment rather than replication, and they lack the operational data models required to document the actual execution of a smart city initiative.

A closely related line of work is the Smart District Data Infrastructure (SDDI), which served as the documentation framework for the 17 Bavarian digital twin projects used in Phase 1 of our methodology [8,13]. SDDI is an important conceptual foundation for the SCPDM, particularly its structured approach to linking sensors, data, and 3D urban context through a metadata catalogue and a CityGML-based Virtual District Model (VDM). Our approach differs in two respects: first, we move beyond a strictly urban digital twin perspective towards a more abstract representation of smart city projects that does not require a VDM or 3D city model; second, we implement the SCPDM as a fully semantic ontology for constructing knowledge graphs, enabling graph traversal, semantic search, and cross-project reasoning that go beyond SDDI's catalogue-centric orientation.

4 Methodology

The ontology design process was driven by two main principles: ontology reuse and co-creation involving domain experts, users in public administration, and knowledge engineers. Our approach follows the NeOn Methodology [18], which systematically supports the reuse, merging, and re-engineering of existing ontologies, while embedding these activities into an agile, user-driven development process with wireframe-based testing involving end-users. In total, four phases produced three successive ontology versions, evaluated using competency questions (see Sect. 4.2 and Fig. 1). The phases map to established NeOn scenarios: Phase 1 applies *reuse and re-engineering of non-ontological resources*; Phases 2 and 3 combine *from specification to implementation*, *reuse of ontology design patterns*, and *reuse, merging, and re-engineering of ontological resources*; and Phase 4 applies *restructuring* and *localisation of ontological resources*.

4.1 Ontology Design Process

Phase 1: Analysis of Existing Digital Twin Descriptions. A total of 17 digital twin model descriptions from Bavarian municipalities, covering the complete set of projects documented according to the SDDI framework [8,13] during the twin.bydata project, were collected and systematically analyzed. The descriptions were qualitatively coded by the modeling team to extract recurring entities, relationships, and components, which were then consolidated through systematic comparison across municipalities into a shared set of candidate abstractions that informed the domain model developed in Phase 2.

Phase 2: Expert Workshops and Domain Model Development. Building on the identified patterns, the second phase employed expert workshops to develop and iteratively refine the initial ontology structure. The workshops involved three Smart City domain experts and two Linked Data engineers, who

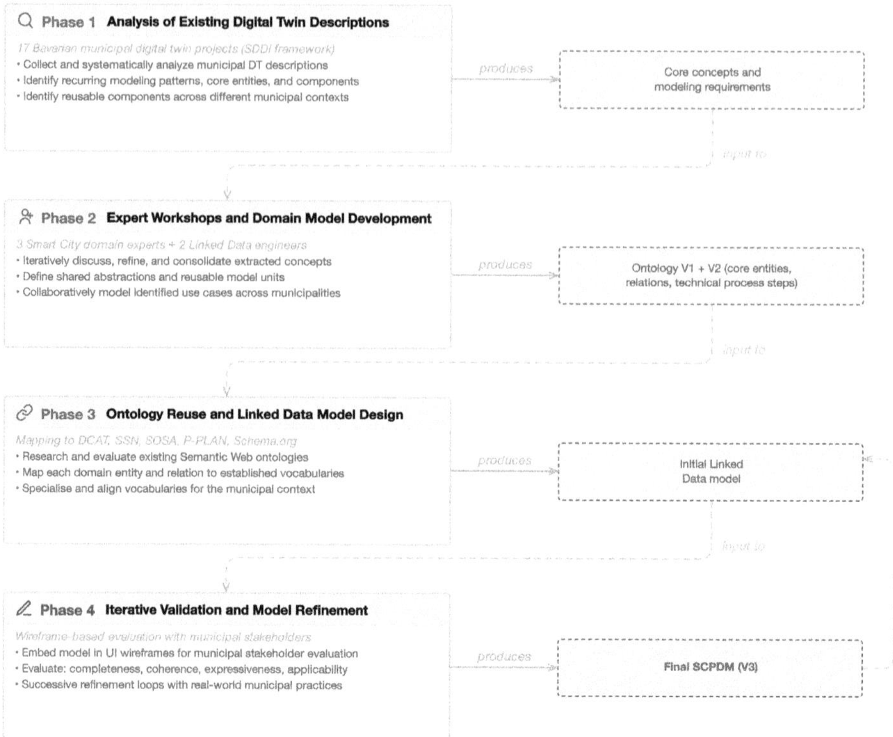

Fig. 1. Overview of the four-phase SCPDM ontology design methodology.

collaboratively modeled the identified municipal use cases with the goal of defining shared abstractions and reusable model units applicable across all municipalities. The resulting ontology versions 1 and 2 capture core project, data, software, and hardware entities and introduce explicit technical process steps.

Phase 3: Ontology Reuse and Linked Data Model Design. In Phase 3, the domain model was translated into a formal Linked Data model by mapping each domain entity to an established ontology. Following the NeOn reuse scenarios outlined above, candidate ontologies were assessed for domain coverage, standardization status, and mutual compatibility. For data resources, `dcat:Dataset` [19] was selected given its status as the foundation of the DCAT-AP standard adopted across European data portals. For hardware modeling, `ssn:System` and its SOSA module [9] were chosen as W3C Recommendations with fine-grained sensor/actuator distinctions that closely matched the hardware entities from Phase 2. For technical workflow modeling, `p-plan:Step` [6] was adopted as it extends PROV-O [14] with explicit plan-level abstractions suited to the process steps identified in the domain model. For the central project entity and software assets, `schema:Project` and `schema:SoftwareApplication` were adopted due to Schema.org's broad adoption and built-in support for organizational metadata. Where domain requirements exceeded the scope of a single vocabulary, classes were composed through property-level alignment rather than subclassing, preserving the original semantics of each reused ontology.

Phase 4: Iterative Validation and Model Refinement. In the final phase, the model was adapted, clarified, and extended based on user feedback and concrete municipal requirements, leading to ontology version 3. To enable real-world evaluation, the Linked Data model was embedded into a user interface using wireframes, allowing municipal stakeholders to apply the model directly. Stakeholder feedback identified two key gaps in Version 2: the absence of organizational governance phases to capture administrative decisions and lessons learned, and the inability to trace shared hardware or software components across projects. Addressing these gaps produced Version 3, which introduced the Project Phase (`schema:QAPage`) and Manufacturer (`foaf:Organization`) classes described in Sect. 5.

4.2 Method Evaluation

To assess how well the evolving ontology supports the information needs of municipal stakeholders, we evaluated the model using Competency Questions (CQs), an established artifact-evaluation method within the design science paradigm [10]. The evaluation was explicitly aligned with the three main iterations of the ontology that emerged along the four-phase methodology:

- **Version 1 (V1)** – initial domain model after a Smart City expert workshop
- **Version 2 (V2)** – refined model with explicit technical process steps after a governance-focused evaluation workshop
- **Version 3 (V3)** – final model including organizational project phases and cross-project manufacturer relations after wireframe-based user testing

Rather than counting classes or properties, the evaluation focuses on whether the ontology can answer questions that are meaningful for practitioners in municipalities, thereby demonstrating the progressive maturation of the SCPDM.

Evaluation Design: Tiers of Competency Questions. The CQs were grouped into four tiers that reflect increasing levels of expressiveness and integration:

1. **Tier 1 – Project Discovery**
   High-level questions that support basic discovery and comparison of Smart City projects (e.g. domain, technology focus, budget, funding, and resource requirements). These questions reflect what municipal users expect from a registry of Smart City projects.

2. **Tier 2 – Technical Workflow and Resources**
   Questions that capture the technical stack of a project, including software, hardware, datasets, and analytical methods, as well as their interrelations in technical process steps. This tier reflects typical needs of technical staff when planning or replicating smart city solutions.
3. **Tier 3 – Organisational Governance**
   Questions that connect technical activities to the organisational lifecycle of a project. These questions require explicit modeling of project phases (Initiation, Planning, Implementation, Reflection) and the association of technical steps and reflections (e.g. interview material, references) with these phases.
4. **Tier 4 – Cross-layer Federation and Reuse**
   Questions that cut across multiple projects by leveraging shared provenance anchors, specifically manufacturers of software and hardware components. These questions are crucial for identifying reuse opportunities and assessing vendor dependencies across municipalities.

Competency Questions and Ontology Versions. Table 1 summarises the final set of CQs used for evaluation, grouped by tier and indicating for each ontology version whether the question can be answered.

Interpretation. The CQ-based evaluation highlights a stepwise increase in expressiveness and usefulness of the SCPDM:

- **Version 1** already supports a rich set of Tier 1 and Tier 2 questions, enabling project discovery and basic technical analysis.
- **Version 2** introduces explicit technical process steps with ordered sequences and typed inputs/outputs, enabling detailed workflow queries (CQ15, CQ16, CQ17).
- **Version 3** adds organisational project phases and manufacturer relations, which unlock Tier 3 and Tier 4 questions on governance and cross-project reuse (CQ18–CQ22).

This progression shows that the SCPDM goes beyond a DCAT-only catalogue by integrating project, process, and provenance information relevant to planning, governance, and the assessment of potential reuse across Smart City digital twin projects.

5 Data Model

The SCPDM is a semantic data model designed to transform isolated smart city pilot projects into replicable "blueprints" that other municipalities can learn from. Per Fig. 2, the SCPDM models the project lifecycle, treating the smart city project as a graph connecting the organizational decision-making processes, the technical workflows, and the specific technological resources required for implementation. The model is organized into three layers: Project Metadata (Sect. 5.2), Process Modeling (Sect. 5.3), and the Resource Layer (Sect. 5.4).

5.1 Ontology Reuse

To ensure interoperability with the broader European data ecosystem, the SCPDM adheres to the principles of ontology reuse. Rather than defining a data schema from scratch, the SCPDM extends well-established W3C and industry

Table 1. Competency questions and answerability by ontology version.

CQ	Tier	Question (short description)	V1	V2	V3
Tier 1 – Project Discovery					
CQ1	1	Which Smart City projects address domain X (e.g. mobility, energy, environment)?	✓	✓	✓
CQ2	1	Which projects have technological focus Y (e.g. IoT, AI, data platforms)?	✓	✓	✓
CQ3	1	Which projects have a total cost below threshold Z?	✓	✓	✓
CQ4	1	Which projects use funding programme or funding type F?	✓	✓	✓
CQ5	1	Which projects require at least N FTE or a duration longer than T months?	✓	✓	✓
Tier 2 – Technical Workflow and Resources					
CQ6	2	Which software is used in project P and which license model applies to this software?	✓	✓	✓
CQ7	2	Which process steps in project P perform data processing, storage, or visualisation, and which software is used in these steps?	~	✓	✓
CQ8	2	Which analytical methods (e.g. regression, time-series analysis, clustering, anomaly detection) are used in project P?	✓	✓	✓
CQ9	2	For method M in project P, which datasets are used and what are their properties (license, format, frequency, origin)?	✓	✓	✓
CQ10	2	Which hardware (sensors) generates the data used in project P, and what are their sensor types and power supply characteristics?	✓	✓	✓
CQ11	2	Which projects use datasets with restrictive licenses?	✓	✓	✓
CQ12	2	Which projects use real-time or near real-time data as opposed to static data?	✓	✓	✓
CQ13	2	Which methods are typically applied for application area A (e.g. traffic analysis, environmental monitoring)?	✓	✓	✓
CQ14	2	In which projects are machine-learning methods used, and which data sources and software products are involved?	✓	✓	✓
CQ15	2	What is the ordered sequence of technical process steps that defines the workflow in project P?	–	✓	✓
CQ16	2	Which inputs (software, hardware, datasets) and outputs (software, datasets) are associated with each technical process step in project P?	–	✓	✓
CQ17	2	Which technical process steps in project P belong to the activity types *data processing*, *data modeling*, *data visualisation*, or *user defined*?	–	✓	✓
Tier 3 – Organisational Governance					
CQ18	3	Which organisational project phases (Initiation, Planning, Implementation, Reflection) has project P already completed, and which phases are still pending?	–	–	✓
CQ19	3	Which challenges, decisions, or information needs have been documented for each project phase of project P (e.g. via interview Q&A or references)?	–	–	✓
CQ20	3	In which project phase are which technical process steps executed (e.g. data collection in *Implementation*, evaluation activities in *Reflection*)?	–	–	✓
Tier 4 – Cross-layer Federation and Reuse					
CQ21	4	Which manufacturers supply hardware or software that is used in more than one project?	–	–	✓
CQ22	4	Which projects share the same hardware or software from a given manufacturer, and which datasets are processed with these components in each project?	–	–	✓

Legend: ✓ = fully answerable; – = not answerable; ~ = partially answerable (capabilities existed but were not yet modeled as explicit, ordered process steps).

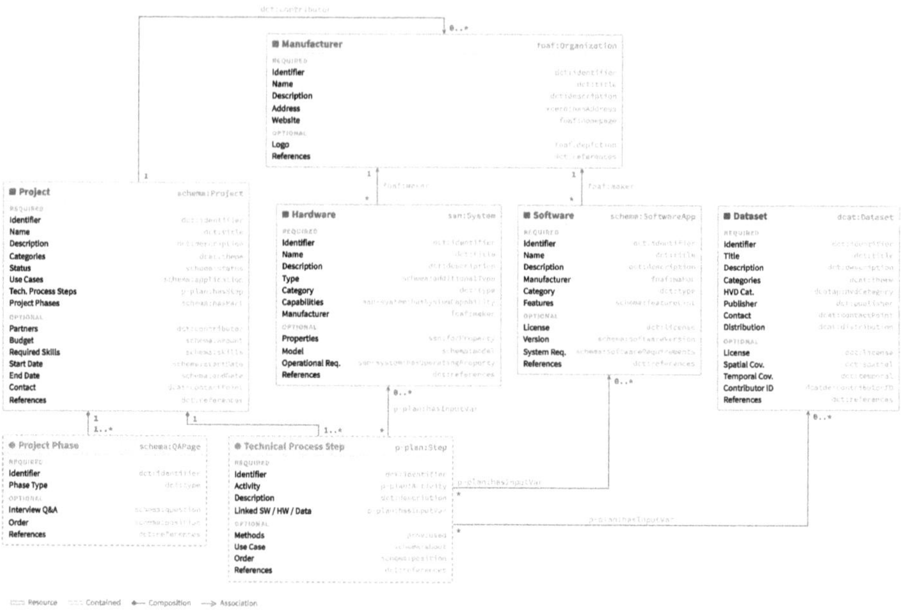

Fig. 2. Smart City Project Data Model.

standards: DCAT-AP for dataset cataloguing, SSN/SOSA for hardware and sensor modeling, P-PLAN for workflow representation, and Schema.org for project and software metadata. The rationale for each vocabulary selection is detailed in the methodology (Sect. 4.1, Phase 3). The resulting semantic architecture is depicted in Fig. 2. The SHACL shapes and an example instantiation are available in an accompanying repository.[1]

5.2 Project Metadata

The central entity of the SCPDM is the Project class (`schema:Project`), which serves as the root node of the knowledge graph and aggregates three categories of information. First, it captures discovery metadata: a multilingual title, description, status, thematic classification (e.g., Mobility or Environment), and fine-grained Application Areas (e.g., Air Quality Monitoring or Traffic Flow Analysis), enabling projects to be searched and compared within a catalogue. Second, it documents the operational requirements for replication, including budget, required expertise, contributing partners, and project contacts, allowing a municipality to assess its own institutional readiness before committing to adoption. Third, the Project class anchors the two process layers that constitute the core of the SCPDM: the Organizational Phases, which capture governance decisions and

[1] https://doi.org/10.5281/zenodo.20720092.

administrative learnings, and the Technical Process Steps, which define the engineering workflow and its resource dependencies. This structural linkage ensures that high-level project metadata remains connected to the granular steps and resources required to reproduce the project's outcomes.

5.3 Process Modeling

The SCPDM bifurcates the project lifecycle into two distinct workflows: the *Organizational Project Phases*, which capture the governance and strategic decision-making, and the *Technical Process Steps*, which model the engineering workflow and resource orchestration. This dual-structure approach acknowledges that smart city failure points can be both administrative and technological.

Organizational Project Phases. The Organizational Phases layer is designed to capture the "tacit knowledge" of a project, including the strategic rationale, hurdles, and administrative learnings that are rarely documented in technical specifications. The SCPDM structures this lifecycle into four standardized phases: *Initiation*, *Planning*, *Implementation*, and *Reflection*.

To formalize the capture of qualitative experiences within the knowledge graph, each organizational phase is treated as a container for a structured dialogue, represented as a series of questions and accepted answers. This approach transforms unstructured "lessons learned" documents into queryable semantic data.

For example, rather than simply recording that a procurement phase occurred, the model prompts the project owner to answer specific decision-support questions, such as "Which tender format was chosen and why?" or "What legal hurdles delayed the sensor deployment?" By embedding these Q&A structures directly into the SCPDM, the model establishes a governance audit trail. This extends the system's utility beyond technical specifications, enabling municipalities to query for administrative strategies and preemptively identify bureaucratic bottlenecks.

Technical Process Steps. While the organizational layer handles the "who" and "why," the Technical Process Steps define the "what" and "how," modeling the concrete engineering workflow required to deploy the solution. The SCPDM adopts the P-PLAN ontology to represent this workflow as a structured series of execution steps.

Each step in this workflow is categorized into one of four controlled activity types: *Data Acquisition*, *Data Processing*, *Data Simulation*, or *Data Visualization*. Each step is further linked to its overarching project use case and to the specific technical methodologies or frameworks employed during execution. Crucially, these steps act as semantic nodes that link an abstract activity to the concrete assets required to execute it. Each step declares the resources it consumes as inputs, where each input can be a hardware system, a software application, or a dataset from the Resource Layer. An explicit ordering property defines the execution sequence, so that the full set of steps forms a directed workflow connecting raw data acquisition through processing and simulation to final visualization.

5.4 The Resource Layer

The Resource Layer catalogs the concrete technological resources required to execute the workflows defined in the Technical Process Steps. Rather than creating new vocabularies for these components, this layer relies strictly on ontology reuse to ensure semantic interoperability with existing data ecosystems. It is organized around four classes: Manufacturer, Hardware, Software, and Data.

The Manufacturer class (`foaf:Organization`) serves as the shared provenance anchor: both the Hardware class (`ssn:System`) and the Software class (`schema:SoftwareApplication`) reference their manufacturer via `foaf:maker`, enabling cross-project queries by vendor. The Hardware class models physical devices using three SOSA subtypes (Sensor, Actuator, and Platform), capturing general device information, system capabilities, observed properties, and operational constraints such as power supply and connectivity. The Software class documents general application information, features, license, and system requirements. When either resource is linked to a Technical Process Step, only the specific capabilities or features utilized in that step are referenced, and hardware linkages additionally capture deployment-specific context such as installation location and host platform.

The Data class (`dcat:Dataset`) follows the DCAT-AP standard to ensure seamless integration with European data portals, capturing general dataset information including thematic, spatial, and temporal coverage, distribution mechanisms, and licensing terms. Compliance with European directives is tracked through High Value Dataset categorization and applicable legislation references.

6 Implementation and Case Study

6.1 Implementation

To validate the SCPDM in a real-world setting, the ontology was implemented as the semantic backbone of twin.bydata, a centralized platform for documenting, discovering, and comparing smart city projects across Bavarian municipalities.

The twin.bydata platform was built on piveau [12], an open-source data management ecosystem developed for the public sector. The selection of piveau was motivated by its native support for DCAT-AP and its extensible SHACL-based schema system. To operationalize the SCPDM classes beyond piveau's native `dcat:Catalog` and `dcat:Dataset` scope, dedicated SHACL shapes were defined for the core Project (`schema:Project`), Technical Process Step (`p-plan:Step`), Organizational Phase (`schema:QAPage`), Hardware (`ssn:System`), Software (`schema:SoftwareApplication`), Manufacturer (`foaf:Organization`), and Dataset (`dcat:Dataset`) classes.

The catalog aggregates metadata from three provider types, each populating a different layer of the SCPDM. Municipal project teams contribute Project metadata, Organizational Phases, and Technical Process Steps through the web interface, documenting the project "recipe" that forms the model's core value proposition. Hardware and software manufacturers provide Resource Layer metadata on technical specifications, capabilities, and operational requirements. Dataset metadata is harvested from external open data portals via piveau's DCAT-AP capabilities and linked to the Technical Process Steps that use them. This decoupled ingestion model validates a key design principle of the SCPDM: independently contributed semantic components can form coherent, queryable project blueprints.

6.2 Case Study

To evaluate the practical applicability of the SCPDM, the model was applied to real-world municipal projects. The modeling process is demonstrated using the municipality of Haar as an example.

Haar is a municipality in the district of Munich (Landkreis München) in Upper Bavaria. The municipality implemented a digital twin in the domain of smart mobility, capturing traffic flows consisting of pedestrians, bicycles, and cars using camera-based sensor systems. The collected data are processed and visualized using a 3D model to support monitoring and analytical use cases.

The modeling of the Haar digital twin is illustrated in Fig. 3; the corresponding RDF instance data is included in the accompanying repository (see Footnote 4). The project "Ganzheitlicher Digitaler Zwilling Haar" is modeled

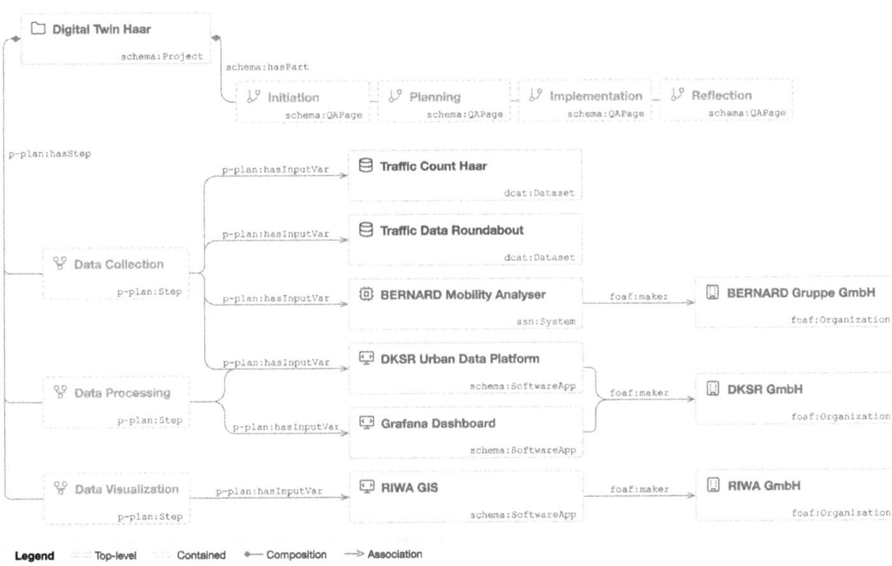

Fig. 3. SCPDM instantiation for the Haar digital twin project.

according to the three main layers of the SCPDM: Project Metadata, Process Modeling, and the Resource Layer.

Project Metadata. At the project level, the initiative is represented as an instance of `schema:Project`, capturing its title, description, thematic classification in the smart mobility domain, relevant application areas (e.g. traffic flow analysis), project status, budget, contributing partners, required skills, and links to further documentation. Together, these fields support both project discovery and assessment of replication feasibility.

Process Modeling. The four organizational phases (Initiation, Planning, Implementation, Reflection) are each annotated with Q&A structures that capture qualitative insights such as procurement decisions and legal hurdles encountered during the project. The technical workflow consists of three process steps modeled as instances of `p-plan:Step`. The Data Collection step captures sensor data using the BERNARD Mobility Analyser hardware system, the DKSR Urban Data Platform, and two traffic datasets (Traffic Count Haar and Traffic Data Roundabout). The Data Processing step integrates and enriches the collected data using the DKSR Urban Data Platform and a Grafana Dashboard. The Data Visualization step presents the processed results using RIWA GIS.

Resource Layer. The concrete technological assets used in Haar are captured in the Resource Layer. The BERNARD Mobility Analyser is modeled as an `ssn:System` consisting of multiple sensor platforms, each deployed at a specific intersection such as Kreisverkehr Leibstraße and Leibstraße/Wasserburger Straße. Their locations, observed properties, and system capabilities are captured at the deployment level, supporting queries such as which intersections are monitored and by which sensor types. The real-time traffic dataset is represented as a `dcat:Dataset` with DCAT-AP metadata describing its thematic, spatial, and temporal coverage, distribution format, and licensing conditions.

Finally, the project's contributing organizations, including RIWA GmbH, BERNARD Gruppe ZT GmbH, and DKSR GmbH, are modeled as manufacturers and project contributors, enabling cross-project queries about vendor involvement and demonstrating how the SCPDM connects governance structures with concrete technical resources in a real-world deployment.

7 Discussion

The implications of the SCPDM can be structured into two vertical layers following the logic of a federal nation like Germany: the layer of municipalities cooperating with each other, and the layer of the regional federal government coordinating such projects.

At the municipal level, the SCPDM provides a structured channel for knowledge transfer between smart city practitioners. Because the model is both machine-readable and human-readable, it supports programmatic discovery and comparison alongside manual browsing, enabling a municipality to assess whether an existing project matches its own requirements before committing resources.

At the regional level, each project documented using the SCPDM contributes to an interconnected, machine-readable knowledge graph of smart city initiatives. Although the twin.bydata platform focuses on digital twins, the data model itself can represent other smart city project types. Applied region- or nation-wide, such a knowledge graph could provide an overview of deployed hardware, licensed software, budget allocations, and other operational metadata across participating municipalities. For a federal state, this could support digital strategy coordination, including the identification of recurring vendor dependencies, opportunities for shared software procurement, and potential interregional projects that leverage existing sensor infrastructure. In essence, the knowledge graph can complement fragmented reporting with a single queryable resource for coordinating digital strategy at the regional level.

Finally, the need for such a model extends beyond the smart city domain. Open data use cases, for example, are typically documented in unstructured blog posts that cannot be harvested or compared programmatically. The SCPDM could be applied to enable standardized, machine-readable representation of such use cases across national and European data portals.

8 Limitations and Future Work

Three limitations of the current work should be acknowledged.

First, the SCPDM captures a snapshot of a project at the time of documentation, but does not currently model project versioning or temporal evolution. A municipality that iterates on its sensor infrastructure after initial documentation would need to manually update catalog entries, and the history of such changes is not preserved. Future work should investigate temporal versioning mechanisms, potentially leveraging PROV-O's existing support for entity revision and derivation.

Second, the SCPDM was developed and validated within a single Bavarian funding programme comprising 17 digital twin projects, and the twin.bydata catalog has not yet been extended to other federal states or national contexts. While this corpus was sufficient to identify recurring modeling patterns, it does not establish generalizability across different administrative systems, regulatory contexts, or levels of municipal capacity. Broader deployment across additional federal states, regulatory contexts, and structurally different project types would provide a more rigorous test of the model's expressiveness and interoperability.

Third, the practical utility of the SCPDM is currently limited by the effort required to populate and query the knowledge graph. Project documentation must be entered manually through the catalog interface, and querying the resulting knowledge graph requires either the platform UI or SPARQL expertise. Future work could address both barriers simultaneously: NLP or LLM-based methods could be used to extract SCPDM-compatible metadata from existing unstructured project reports, accelerating catalog population, while natural language query interfaces could allow municipal project managers to interrogate the knowledge graph conversationally without requiring technical expertise in semantic web technologies.

9 Conclusion

This paper presented the SCPDM, a Linked Data model that supports the structured documentation, discovery, comparison, and reuse of smart city projects across municipalities. By treating the smart city project, rather than the smart city asset, as its central organizing concept, the SCPDM addresses a persistent gap in the existing standards landscape: the absence of a semantic data model that connects organizational governance decisions, technical implementation workflows, and the specific hardware, software, and datasets required for deployment. The result is a "project blueprint" that turns isolated pilot projects into transferable, queryable project knowledge.

The model was validated through its implementation as the semantic backbone of twin.bydata, a production platform built on the open-source piveau ecosystem. The catalog's decoupled architecture, in which municipalities, manufacturers, and open data portals independently populate different semantic layers, demonstrated that the SCPDM can integrate heterogeneous contributions into coherent project blueprints. The application of the model to real-world digital twin projects across Bavarian municipalities, including the case study of Haar, confirmed its practical applicability in diverse municipal contexts.

While the current deployment is limited to Bavaria, the model's reliance on established W3C and European vocabularies positions it for adoption beyond a single federal state or project type. Future work will focus on extending the catalog to additional German federal states, integrating automated metadata extraction from existing project documentation, and publishing the ontology as a reusable open artifact to support broader community adoption.

Acknowledgments. This work was developed within the twin.bydata project, funded by the Bayerisches Staatsministerium für Digitales and coordinated by Bayern Innovativ.

Disclosure of Interests. The authors are affiliated with organizations that contributed to the development of the twin.bydata platform and the piveau ecosystem described in this paper.

References

1. Bayern Innovativ: TwinBy – Digitale Zwillinge für Bayern (2024). https://twinby.bayern/. funded by the Bayerisches Staatsministerium für Digitales. Accessed 2025
2. BMWSB: Modellprojekte smart cities (2024). https://www.smart-city-dialog.de/en/about-us/model-projects-smart-cities, Accessed 2025

3. Carayannis, E.G., Campbell, D.F.: "mode 3" and "quadruple helix": Toward a 21st century fractal innovation ecosystem. Int. J. Technol. Manag. **46**(3–4), 201–234 (2009)
4. Cohen, B.: The smartest cities in the world 2015: Methodology (2014). https://www.fastcompany.com/3038818/the-smartest-cities-in-the-world-2015-methodology
5. Etzkowitz, H., Leydesdorff, L.: The dynamics of innovation: from national systems and "mode 2" to a triple helix of university-industry-government relations. Res. Policy **29**(2), 109–123 (2000)
6. Garijo, D., Gil, Y.: The P-Plan Ontology for Representing Workflows. In: Proceedings of the 1st International Workshop on Workflow Approaches to New Data-centric Science (WANDS) (2012)
7. Giffinger, R., Fertner, C., Kramar, H., Kalasek, R., Pichler-Milanovi, N., Meijers, E.: Smart Cities: Ranking of European Medium-Sized Cities. Tech. rep., Vienna University of Technology (2007). http://www.smart-cities.eu/download/smart_cities_final_report.pdf
8. Gitahi, J., Knezevic, M., Kolbe, T.H.: IoT sensors management in urban digital twin catalog. In: Urban Digital Twins for a Sustainable Transformation of Cities Conference (2025)
9. Haller, A., Janowicz, K., Cox, S., Lefrançois, M.: Semantic Sensor Network Ontology. W3C Recommendation (2017). https://www.w3.org/TR/vocab-ssn/
10. Hevner, A.R., March, S.T., Park, J., Ram, S.: Design science in information systems research. MIS Q. **28**(1), 75–105 (2004). https://doi.org/10.2307/25148625
11. International Organization for Standardization: ISO 37120:2018 Sustainable cities and communities – Indicators for city services and quality of life (2018). https://www.iso.org/standard/68498.html
12. Kirstein, F., Stefanidis, K., Dittwald, B., Dutkowski, S., Urbanek, S., Hauswirth, M.: Piveau: A Large-Scale Open Data Management Platform Based on Semantic Web Technologies. In: Harth, A., Kirrane, S., Ngonga Ngomo, A.-C., Paulheim, H., Rula, A., Gentile, A.L., Haase, P., Cochez, M. (eds.) ESWC 2020. LNCS, vol. 12123, pp. 648–664. Springer, Cham (2020). https://doi.org/10.1007/978-3-030-49461-2_38
13. Knezevic, M., Donaubauer, A., Kolbe, T.H.: SDDI-minimal ecosystem for the establishment of urban digital twins. Publikationen der DGPF **32**, 151–168 (2024)
14. Lebo, T., Sahoo, S., McGuinness, D.: PROV-O: The PROV ontology. W3C Recommendation (2013). https://www.w3.org/TR/prov-o/
15. Meijer, A., Rodríguez Bolívar, M.P.: Governing the smart city: A review of the literature on smart urban governance. Int. Rev. Adm. Sci. **82**(2), 392–408 (2016). https://doi.org/10.1177/0020852314564308
16. Nam, T., Pardo, T.A.: Conceptualizing smart city with dimensions of technology, people, and institutions. In: Proceedings of the 12th Annual International Digital Government Research Conference: Digital Government Innovation in Challenging Times, pp. 282–291. dg.o '11, Association for Computing Machinery, New York, NY, USA (2011). https://doi.org/10.1145/2037556.2037602
17. Pfefferle, M.: Scaling Germany's smart cities and smart regions (2023). https://cities-today.com/industry/scaling-germanys-smart-cities-and-smart-regions/, originally published in KommunalPraxis 2/2022

18. Suárez-Figueroa, M.C., Gómez-Pérez, A., Fernández-López, M.: The NeOn Methodology for Ontology Engineering. In: Suárez-Figueroa, M.C., Gómez-Pérez, A., Motta, E., Gangemi, A. (eds.) Ontology Engineering in a Networked World, pp. 9–34. Springer, Heidelberg (2012). https://doi.org/10.1007/978-3-642-24794-1_2
19. W3C: Data Catalog Vocabulary (DCAT) - Version 2. W3C Recommendation (2020). https://www.w3.org/TR/vocab-dcat-2/
20. van Winden, W., van den Buuse, D.: Smart city pilot projects: Exploring the dimensions and conditions of scaling up. J. Urban Technol. **24**(4), 51–72 (2017). https://doi.org/10.1080/10630732.2017.1348884

Why Do Some Cities Become Smart Faster? A Panel Data Analysis of Smart City Performance Across 81 Cities

Niyazi Karabulut[1](✉), Hemalata Vasudavan[2], and Ayşegül Saylam[3]

[1] Necmettin Erbakan University, Konya, Türkiye
karabulutnyz@gmail.com
[2] Asia Pacific University of Technology and Innovation, Bukit Jalil, Kuala Lumpur, Malaysia
[3] Hacettepe University, Ankara, Türkiye
aysegulk@hacettepe.edu.tr

Abstract. This study examines why some cities become smart faster than others. To do this, it analyzes the determinants and dynamics of smart city development. It uses a panel dataset covering 81 cities in Türkiye and the period 2020–2024, along with data on access to telecommunication infrastructure, city size (population), and economic capacity for the same years. Random effects panel regression models are estimated to examine the impact of these variables on smart city maturity levels. Beyond the basic model, the study incorporates two additional analytical approaches to capture the dynamic and multidimensional nature of smart city development. First, it estimates a convergence model to examine whether cities with lower initial smart city maturity levels develop faster over time. Second, it performs component-level regression analyses for 16 sub-dimensions of the smart city index to investigate heterogeneous effects across different domains. The findings reveal that city size is the most consistent and statistically significant determinant of smart city performance, thus highlighting the role of scale effects in urban digital transformation. In contrast, the variables of access to telecommunications infrastructure and economic capacity did not show statistically significant effects in the aggregate model. This suggests that the effects of these variables may be indirect. Convergence analysis showed that smart city development follows non-uniform trajectories among cities. The results at the component level revealed both heterogeneity and homogeneity at certain points in different dimensions. In short, the study offers a dynamic and multidimensional perspective on smart city analysis and contributes to the literature by providing empirical evidence from a broad national dataset.

Keywords: Smart Cities · smart city maturity assessment · panel data

1 Introduction

The concept of smart cities has occupied a key position in discussions on urban governance, digital transformation, and sustainable development in recent years. With the proliferation of information and communication technologies (ICT), data analytics, and

Published by Springer Nature Switzerland 2027
G. Viale Pereira et al. (Eds.): EGOV 2026, LNCS 16933, pp. 147–164, 2027.
https://doi.org/10.1007/978-3-032-35747-2_10

digital platforms, cities have begun to transform their infrastructure, services, and governance processes through digital technologies. Significant investments are being made by various governments and cities in terms of digital platforms, telecommunications infrastructure, and other innovative tools [1, 2]. Therefore, smart city development has become an integral part of a country's policy agenda to promote economic growth and governance.

Despite the increasing global momentum toward smart city development, cities are experiencing different levels of progress in their transformation journeys. While some cities rapidly advance toward higher levels of smart city maturity, others are progressing more slowly despite having similar policy goals and strategic initiatives [3, 4].

These disparities raise questions regarding the dynamics of smart city development and the factors that influence the speed at which cities transition toward becoming smart cities [5]. Various international standards and evaluation models developed within the framework of the smart city approach aim to measure and compare the smart city maturity levels of cities [6]. Such measurement studies help cities assess their current status, make strategic decisions, and use their resources more effectively [7, 8].

Furthermore, regular measurements make the development of cities over time visible, serving as an important decision support tool for policymakers [9]. However, a significant portion of the smart city literature focuses on examining the smart city capacity or rankings of cities at a specific time. Most existing studies focus on defining the components of the smart city concept, developing measurement frameworks, or comparing the current performance of cities [7, 8]. However, the question of how cities develop their smart city transformation over time and why some cities progress faster than others has been addressed relatively limitedly in the literature. Yet, smart city transformation is a dynamic process, and significant differences in development are observed among cities. This study aims to explain the changes in the smart city maturity levels of cities by focusing on the research questions:

"Why do some cities become smart faster?"

"Which factors explain differences in smart city maturity levels across cities over time?"

To answer these questions, the study performs panel data analysis using National Smart City Maturity Index of Türkiye data from 81 provinces in Türkiye between 2020 and 2024 [10, 11]. This study measures and analyzes the factors influencing the dynamics and changes of smart city development in cities. Specifically, it examines the effects of the access to telecommunication infrastructure, city population, and economic capacity both on the smart city development and on its 16 components. Also, by including lagged index data in the analysis, it analyzes the dynamics of change in the index.

This research contributes to the literature in several ways. Firstly, it provides a dynamic perspective to the smart city literature by examining the smart city development processes of cities through panel data analysis. Secondly, the study provides empirical evidence on the determinants of smart city performance by examining the roles of digital infrastructure, urban population, and economic capacity. Thirdly, by using a national smart city maturity index covering all 81 cities in Türkiye, it offers a comprehensive empirical analysis in the context of a developing country where large-scale empirical research on smart city development is relatively limited. Finally, unlike many existing smart city indices that reflect cumulative or long-term structural capacities, the index used in this study is recalculated annually based on annual data, thus enabling the analysis of improvements and declines in smart city performance over time. This dynamic structure allows the study to capture the fluctuating and nonlinear nature of smart city transformation processes and provide new insights into why some cities progress faster than others.

The remainder of the paper is organized as follows. The next section presents the conceptual and theoretical background and reviews the relevant literature. The methodology and empirical models are then introduced, followed by the presentation of findings. The paper concludes with a discussion of the results and their policy implications.

2 Conceptual and Theoretical Background

The increasing urban population and the widespread adoption of digital technologies have necessitated a comprehensive transformation in the field of urban management [4]. With smart cities, digital technologies and local governments have become intertwined, and the understanding of digitalization has expanded to include local elements. Digital technologies are utilized in many different areas of urban management, from city planning to how public services are delivered. For this reason, smart cities and many digital applications related to them have become frequently studied in the literature [12].

There is no consensus in the literature regarding the definition of the smart city concept [13]. Approaches, policies, and designs for smart cities differ according to the political, administrative, technological, and cultural characteristics of countries or regions [14]. This difference has been shaped by different perspectives in the literature, parallel to the different characteristics of the smart city concept and the expectations towards it [15]. It is possible to classify the basic approaches to the smart city concept as the administrative, environmental, technological, economic, and data-based approaches [13]. However, it is generally accepted in all definitions that smart cities will provide benefits in terms of improving the quality of urban life and utilizing digital technologies in solving urban problems [4].

The Smart City Wheel, proposed by Cohen [16], conceptualizes smart city development through six core dimensions: smart economy, smart people, smart governance, smart mobility, smart environment, and smart living. These dimensions represent key areas in which cities integrate technological innovation, human capital, and governance to improve urban sustainability and quality of life. The European Smart Cities framework, developed by Giffinger et al. [17], introduced a hierarchical model consisting of six characteristics and 74 indicators based on Cohen's model. The framework allows cities to measure their performance through multiple assessment methods while enabling them to compare their urban development progress with other cities.

Contemporary research on smart cities has emerged from the earlier research on smart cities, as they focus on the ways in which cities develop based on their technological resources and their economic resources, as well as the characteristics of the population. Recent frameworks describe smart city transformation as a multi-stage process involving goal definition, technology innovation, strategy development, implementation, and evaluation [3]. These stages highlight the interaction between technological infrastructure, governance mechanisms, and stakeholder participation in shaping the urban digital transformation process. In addition to these six basic dimensions of smart cities, there are also sub-dimensions that differ among sectors. The management of many sectoral dimensions such as smart health, transportation, and education is included in the content of the concept. Therefore, a smart city aims both at the increased use of digital technology and the maximum benefit derived from it, and at the development of social elements to the same extent. In fact, the literature states that smart cities will become smart along with the development of social and public elements within them [14, 18].

3 Literature

Researchers employ many different approaches to capture the multifaceted nature of smart cities since smart city development encompasses multidimensional elements. Among these approaches, researchers often prefer indices that combine multiple indicators into a single composite measure, as this allows for comparisons between cities and over time. One of the central methodological challenges in measuring smart city development is the selection and combination of indicators. Indeed, smart city indices need to combine indicators reflecting both technological capacity and socioeconomic capabilities [18]. Researchers use different approaches to combine indicators, including statistical methods such as weighted summation, normalization techniques, and principal component analysis (PCA). Weighted index models are common because they allow for the assignment of relative importance to different dimensions of smart city development [19].

Smart city indices serve several important analytical purposes beyond methodological considerations [18]. They allow policymakers to identify strengths and weaknesses in different urban systems by enabling benchmarking and comparative analysis between cities. They also make it possible to track how cities evolve over time by facilitating the monitoring of urban transformation processes, Moreover, composite indices can be used in empirical research to analyze the determinants and outcomes of smart city development and correlate smart city performance with many key factors such as economic growth, innovation capacity, governance structures, and digital infrastructure [19].

3.1 Measuring Smart City Maturity

Several international standards have been developed to provide standardized metrics for evaluating smart city performance. Among the most important of these are the PAS 181 and ISO 37120 and 37122 standards. Developed by the British Standards Institute, PAS 181 offers a strategic framework for smart city development and emphasizes integrated urban governance, data-driven decision-making, and cross-sectoral collaboration [20]. Also, the ISO 37120 standard allows cities to compare their performance in key areas such as infrastructure, transportation, public safety, and environmental management by creating indicators for city services and quality of life [21]. Complementing this standard, ISO 37122 focuses specifically on indicators for smart cities [22].

In academic studies, Caragliu et al. [23], analyzing European cities, show that investments in human capital, social infrastructure, and ICT are strongly associated with higher smart city performance. Similarly, Neirotti et al. [14] and Giffinger et al. [17] examined the spread of smart city initiatives in European cities by analyzing different areas of smart city applications such as mobility, energy, environment and governance. Nam and Pardo [9] emphasized that smart city development should be understood as a dynamic process shaped by technological innovation, policy frameworks and urban governance structures. Kourtit and Nijkamp [24] investigated the link between smart city features and urban competitiveness and found that cities with stronger knowledge economies and innovation ecosystems tend to perform better in smart city rankings. Furthermore, Bibri and Krogstie [19] assessed the digital transformation performance of cities using smart sustainable city indicators and showed that smart city development is closely related to digital infrastructure investments, data management capacity and innovation ecosystems.

Numerous international frameworks have also been developed to assess and guide smart city development. Firstly, United Nation's UN-Habitat Smart Cities Framework [5] assesses smart city transformation by focusing on digital infrastructure, governance, sustainability, inclusiveness. Secondly, a widely recognized initiative is the Smart Sustainable Cities developed by the International Telecommunication Union (ITU) [26]. This framework focuses on the role of ICTs in improving urban sustainability, efficiency, and quality of life. Another example is The Cities in Motion Index, which consists of nine dimensions and 101 indicators, including human capital, social cohesion, economy, governance, environment, city planning, international projection, and technology [27]. Another influential framework is the Morgenstadt Framework [28], developed by the Fraunhofer Institute as part of the Morgenstadt City Insights initiative. It assesses smart city development across multiple urban systems, including governance structures, infrastructure, energy, mobility, and innovation ecosystems [28].

In addition, the Smart City Index, developed by the International Institute for Management Development (IMD), focuses on assessing cities' readiness to implement smart technologies and digital solutions. By evaluating factors such as infrastructure, mobility, health, governance, and citizen perceptions, the model helps cities identify gaps in their readiness for smart city initiatives [29]. Finally, at the European level, the Digital Economy and Society Index (DESI) developed by the European Commission measures digital readiness and smart transformation capacity of European cities by using connectivity, digital skills, digital services, and technology integration [30].

3.2 Smart City Transformation as a Dynamic Process

Recent research considers smart city development as a dynamic transformation process rather than a static state. Cities are gradually adopting digital technologies as they improve their technological capabilities, governance capacities, and economic resources [2, 7]. However, much of the existing literature focuses on conceptual models or cross-sectional comparisons of cities [8]. The temporal dynamics of smart city transformation have not been sufficiently investigated. Based on the frameworks described, this study analyzes smart city development as a dynamic process.

A key question in the literature is whether cities tend to converge in their development patterns over time. The concept of convergence refers to the tendency of regions with lower initial development levels to grow faster than more developed regions, thus reducing inequalities over time [31, 32]. A similar question can be raised in the context of smart city maturity. The tendency of cities with lower initial smart city maturity levels to develop faster than more developed cities indicates the existence of a convergence process in smart city transformation. In such a scenario, less developed cities can gradually catch up with developed cities. However, as more developed cities continue to evolve faster, divergences in smart city development and widening gaps between cities are occurring. Despite its importance, empirical research examining the convergence dynamics in smart city development remains limited. Therefore, this study also investigates whether cities with lower initial smart city maturity levels experience faster improvements in smart city performance over time.

The smart city maturity index analyzed in this study is derived from the national smart city maturity assessment model developed by the Ministry of Environment, Urbanization, and Climate Change within the framework of Türkiye's National Smart Cities Strategy [10, 11]. This model is primarily based on the Morgenstadt Framework [28] and integrates indicator structures compatible with ISO 37120 and 37122 [21, 22] standards. By combining internationally recognized standards with nationally relevant indicators, the framework enables both systematic monitoring of smart city development within the country and comparability with global smart city assessment approaches. In this study, using this model as the basis for the smart city index provides a comprehensive measurement of the smart transformation processes of cities and allows the analysis to capture the differences in smart city development between cities and over time. Indeed, the index, prepared since 2020, evaluates cities under 16 subheadings (Fig. 1): "*governance, environment, economy, energy, people, transportation, buildings, health, disaster, security, information security, information technologies, communication technologies, space, GIS, infrastructure*". Each of these subheadings is based on data collected from national and reliable data sources according to the criteria defined for each component. To create the index, data on 77 different criteria related to the 16 subheadings were collected, normalized from 0–100, weighted according to its importance, and finally, the overall score is calculated using a weighted average [11]. Also, each subheading is a whole in itself and can be analyzed separately in the assessments. This can be considered one of the most important features of the index. Indeed, evaluating the components that make up a whole using independent databases and evaluation methods increases the strength of that index.

The most important feature of the index is that, unlike many international smart city indices, it is recalculated annually using the same methodological framework and based on data from that year. Therefore, the index values do not show a monotonic upward trend between years but may increase or decrease depending on the performance of cities within the relevant year. Consequently, this study analyzes not only increases but also possible declines in the smart city maturity levels of cities, revealing the dynamic structure of smart city transformation more realistically. This feature offers a significant analytical advantage by demonstrating that smart city transformation is not a linear and unidirectional process. While many international studies use indices that mostly reflect the position of cities at a specific point in time or their long-term cumulative development, the index used in this study can more accurately capture the annual performance changes of cities. Therefore, this study also analyzes the fluctuations that occur in the smart city

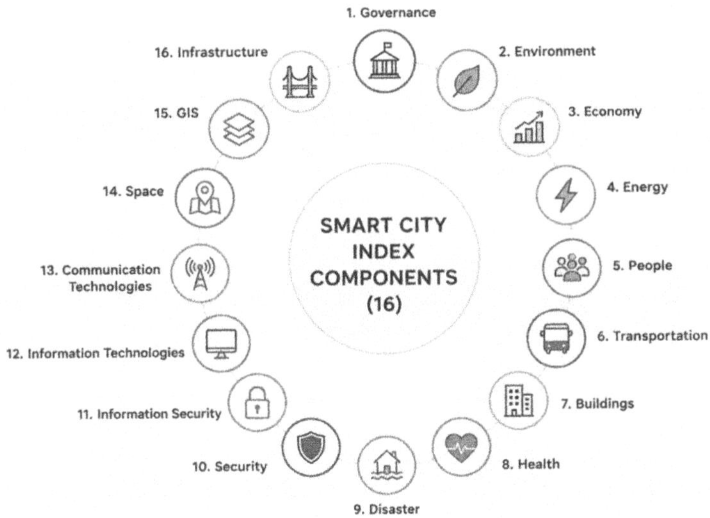

Fig. 1. Smart City Index Components

transformation processes of cities. This makes a significant contribution to the literature by showing that the smart city transformation is a dynamic process that is constantly changing and influenced by different factors, rather than a static outcome.

Although the Smart City Maturity Index reflects the overall smart city performance of cities, it is possible for cities to have different development dynamics in different areas. Therefore, as an additional analysis in this study, each of the 16 sub-components of the index was treated as a dependent variable, and separate regression models were estimated using the same independent variables. This analysis revealed in which areas cities are developing faster in smart city transformation and which areas are more affected by factors such as telecommunication infrastructure, city size, or economic capacity. Previous studies have highlighted broadband access, internet connectivity, and digital communications infrastructure as critical elements of digital transformation and smart urban services [4, 14, 23]. While governance capacity, human capital, and innovation ecosystems, together with many other factors, also contribute to smart city development, telecommunications infrastructure was chosen because it forms the core technological platform upon which many smart city functions are connected.

As a result, in this study, smart city development is analyzed with the roll-out of telecommunication and broadband networks [4], the city size (population) [8] and economic capacity [17, 23, 28], which are the key drivers of the smart city transformation not included in the index's evaluation criteria.

4 Methodology

This section presents the dataset, variables, research hypotheses, and empirical strategy of the study. The analysis relies on panel data covering all 81 cities in Türkiye between 2020 and 2024 and employs both random effects regression and convergence models.

4.1 Data

The dataset of the study combines information from multiple sources, including the national smart city maturity assessment framework and national statistical institute database. Therefore, the main dependent variable in the analysis is the smart city maturity index score, which measures the level of smart city maturity in various areas based on international standards. To examine the dynamics of smart city development, the study also focuses on the changes in the smart city index over time. Moreover, the 16 components of the index were treated as dependent variables in the study, and analysis was also performed at the component level.

The independent variable of this study is access to telecommunications infrastructure, calculated as a composite index of fiber infrastructure length, mobile broadband subscriptions, and fixed broadband subscriptions; and the control variables are log(population), obtained by taking the natural logarithm of the population; and GDP per capita at the city level. The city population variable was included in logarithmic form to control for differences at the urban scale. The per capita GDP variable at the city level was added to the model to control for the economic capacity of the cities. The selection of these variables was influenced by their theoretical potential to influence the smart city maturity level, as well as the fact that they were not used when constructing the index score. Indeed, the infrastructure, a subcomponent of the index, is measured using the quantity and quality of projects municipal infrastructure projects; the people variable is measured using education-based variables; and the economy variable is measured using the budgets of city municipalities [11]. The inclusion of these independent variables in the model aimed to provide a more citizen-centric assessment rather than one based solely on municipality data. Telecommunications data was collected from the Information Technologies and Communications Authority of Türkiye (BTK) [33], population and GDP values are obtained from the official national statistical sources [34].

In the literature, in addition to these variables, human capital and innovation ecosystem variables are also frequently preferred in smart city evaluations. In this study, data for these two variables were not included in the research model because they are already included in the smart city index measurement [11]. Within this framework, the study aims to explain the digital transformation processes of cities by examining the key factors affecting their smart city performance through panel data analysis.

4.2 Research Hypotheses

The literature emphasizes that smart city transformation emerges as a result of the interaction of various factors such as the economic capacity of cities, the level of digital infrastructure, institutional capacity, and city scale [14, 23]. Therefore, the smart city performance of cities is shaped under different structural conditions, and significant performance differences can emerge between cities. This study focuses on three key groups of variables to examine the fundamental factors explaining the smart city performance of cities: citizens' access to digital infrastructure capacity, city size, and economic capacity.

The literature emphasizes that telecommunication infrastructure plays a decisive role in the digital transformation capacity of cities [4, 23, 28]. Therefore, a wide access to telecommunication infrastructure is expected to positively influence the smart city performance of cities. The literature frequently emphasizes that city size plays a significant role in digital transformation and innovation activities [8, 14]. Therefore, cities with larger populations are expected to have higher smart city performance. Economic capacity also plays a significant role in the development of innovation activities and technology ecosystems [17, 23]. Economically more developed cities are expected to have higher smart city performance. This study also investigates whether cities converge or diverge in their smart city development trajectories, as it examines the dynamic models of smart city development over time. According to theoretical expectations [31], cities with lower smart city maturity will develop faster than more developed cities, reducing disparities over time. Furthermore, given the multidimensional nature of smart city development, it is important to examine whether the effects of key explanatory variables differ among the various components of the smart city index. Digital infrastructure may be more strongly associated with technology-focused components, while city size and economic capacity may play a more prominent role in governance-related and service-oriented dimensions. Therefore, analysing only the overall index may obscure significant differences in different areas of smart city development. Treating each sub-dimension of the smart city index as a dependent variable provides a more nuanced understanding of how different factors influence specific aspects of smart city transformation.

The effects of these factors on smart city performance are discussed theoretically above, and research hypotheses are developed accordingly.

H1: High access to telecommunication infrastructure positively affects the smart city performance of cities
H2: As city size increases, the smart city performance of cities increases.
H3: As the economic capacity of cities increases, their smart city performance increases.
H4: Cities with lower initial smart city maturity levels experience faster improvements in smart city performance over time.
H5: The effects of digital infrastructure, city size, and economic capacity on smart city performance differ among the different components of the smart city index.

4.3 Empirical Model

To account for unobserved heterogeneity across cities, panel data techniques are employed in the analysis. In particular, city-specific effects are incorporated into the model to control for unobservable factors that may influence smart city performance, such as geographical characteristics, historical development patterns, and institutional structures. In panel data analysis, the choice between fixed effects and random effects models depends on whether the unobservable heterogeneity between cities is related to the independent variables. The Hausman test was applied to determine the appropriate model selection. According to the Hausman test results, the difference between fixed effects and random effects models was not statistically significant ($p > 0.05$). This result shows that the unobservable effects between cities are not systematically related to the independent variables. Within this framework, the following random effects panel regression model was estimated in the study. Robust standard errors are used to address potential heteroskedasticity. The empirical specification is as follows (first model):

$$SmartIndex_{!"} = \beta_{\#} + \beta_{\$}TelecomIndex_{!"} + \beta_{\%}logPopulation_{!"} + \beta_{\&}GDPpc_{!"} + \mu_{!} + \epsilon_{!"}$$

where *SmartIndex*$_{!''}$ represents the smart city maturity index for city i in year t, *TelecomIndex*$_{!''}$ represents the access to telecommunications infrastructure index, *log-Population*$_{!''}$ is the logarithm of population, *GDPpc*$_{!''}$ represents GDP per capita, $\mu_{!}$ captures unobserved city-specific random effects, and $\epsilon_{!''}$ is the idiosyncratic error term.

An additional regression model was estimated in this study to examine whether smart city development follows a convergence pattern. In this model, the change in the smart city index is used as the dependent variable, while the lagged value of the index is included as the explanatory variable. This specification allows for the analysis of whether cities with lower initial smart city maturity levels show faster improvement over time. The second model of the study is:

$$\Delta SmartIndex_{!"} = \alpha + \beta SmartIndexd_{!,"(\$} + \gamma TelecomIndex_{!"} + \delta logPopulation_{!"} + \theta GDPpc_{!"} + \epsilon_{!"}$$

Finally, this study further explores the multidimensional nature of smart city development by conducting component-level analyses. To investigate whether the effects of the explanatory variables differ across these domains, separate panel data models are estimated for each component. In these models, each component score is treated as a dependent variable, while the same set of explanatory variables is retained. This approach allows for identifying heterogeneous effects of digital infrastructure, city size, and economic capacity across different dimensions of smart city development. The econometric specification for component-level analysis is as follows (Third model):

$$Component_{),!"} = \alpha_{)} + \beta_{\$)}Telecom_{!"} + \beta_{\%)}logPopulation_{!"} + \beta_{\&)}GDPpc_{!"} + \mu_{!} + \lambda_{"} + \varepsilon_{!"}$$

where *Component*$_{),!''}$ represents the score of the component k(k = 1, 2,…, 16) for city i in year t. The coefficients $\beta_{\$)}$, $\beta_{\%)}$, $\beta_{\&)}$capture the component-specific effects of explanatory variables. Data processing, cleaning, and analysis were performed using RStudio software with the tidyverse and plm, as well as the R standard packages.

5 Findings and Discussion

Table 1 presents descriptive statistics for the first model. The dataset consists of a total of 405 observations. According to the Smart City Index variable values, cities generally have a low-to-medium level of smart city development, but there are significant differences between cities. Some cities are completely undeveloped, while others are quite advanced (Min–Max (0 – 73.30)). Skewness is right-skewed, meaning most cities have low values, while a few have very high values. Kurtosis shows a slightly sharper-than-normal distribution, meaning extreme values exist. In short, smart city development is not homogeneous; a few advanced cities push the average upwards. Access to telecommunications infrastructure values are quite balanced and homogeneously distributed among cities. The population variable shows that there are a few very large cities in the dataset and that the distribution is distorted. Therefore, it is seen that the log transformation normalizes the population distribution and makes it more suitable for analysis. Finally, the per capita income variable shows that there are a few high-income cities, but these cities raise the average and make the distribution more unequal.

Table 1. Descriptive statistics

Variable	Mean	Std.Dev	Min	Max	Skew	Kurtosis
Smartcityindex	18.74	14.36	0.00	73.30	1.38	1.59
Telecomindex	0.58	0.07	0.39	0.83	0.13	0.51
Pop	1048423	1895487	81910	15907951	5.99	41.92
Log(pop)	13.29	0.97	11.31	16.58	0.59	0.63
GDP_pc	8746.76	3598.18	2809	24452	1.19	2.21

According to the correlation analysis results in Fig. 2, there are positive relationships between the smart city index and all independent variables. The strongest relationship was observed with the log population variable. There are moderately positive relationships between telecommunications infrastructure and per capita income level and the smart city index. Correlations show that as the population increases, the level of smart cities tends to increase. They also indicate that as access to telecommunications infrastructure and GDP per capita increase, the level of smart cities tends to increase as well, although these effects are not as strong as population size. The fact that the correlation coefficients between the independent variables are below 0.70 shows that there is no serious multicollinearity problem in the model.

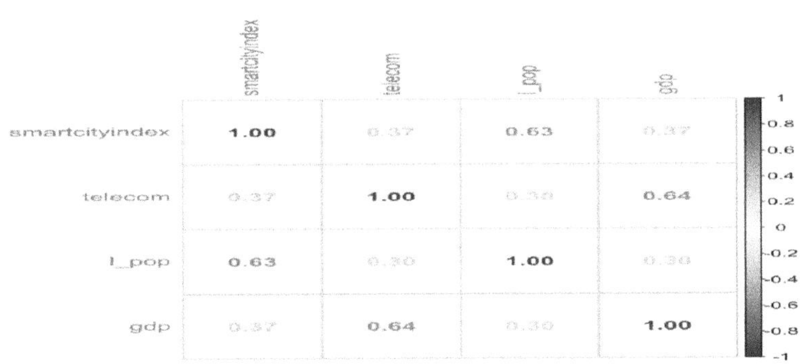

Fig. 2. Correlation Analysis

When examining the regression results in Table 2 below, it is observed that the only statistically significant variable in the model is log(pop). Accordingly, an increase in city size is associated with a significant increase in the smart city index. The variable of access to telecommunications infrastructure is not statistically significant; the fact that the confidence interval includes zero indicates that the effect of this variable is uncertain. This suggests that the effect of access to telecommunications infrastructure on smart city development is not direct or that this effect is not at a distinctive level for cities. In other words, while digital infrastructure forms a necessary foundation for the development of smart city applications, access to this infrastructure does not have the capacity to significantly impact the performance. The per capita income variable was also not found to be statistically significant, indicating that economic well-being alone is not sufficient to explain the level of smart cities. Although a positive relationship was detected between these variables in the correlation analysis, it was observed that these effects disappeared in the multivariate model. This indicates that the effects of these variables are not independent but rather act in conjunction with other variables, and that they lose their explanatory power, especially when the population variable is controlled. However, according to the model results, the explanatory power is limited.

Table 2. Panel regression results for the first model

	Smart city index		
Predictors	Estimates	CI	p
(Intercept)	−106.36	−135.57 – -77.15	**<0.001**
telecomindex	11.67	−15.13 – 38.48	0.392
Log(pop)	8.72	6.61 – 10.83	**<0.001**
GDP_pc	0.00	−0.00 – 0.00	0.222
Observations	405		
R^2 / R^2 adjusted	0.200 / 0.194		

The model using the change in the smart city index as the dependent variable in Table 3 indicates that the average annual change is positive and statistically significant.

To account for potential heteroskedasticity, serial correlation, and cross-sectional dependence in the panel data, Driscoll–Kraay robust standard errors were applied in this model. Among the explanatory variables, log population has a negative and statistically significant effect, suggesting that larger cities experience slower changes in smart city performance over time. Changes in the other variables are not statistically significant. The overall model explains approximately 4% of the variation in the index changes, which is typical for difference-based models. The results of the change model, which aims to analyze which factors are related to increases or decreases in the smart city performance of cities, show that the smart city transformation processes of cities are not a linear development process, but when evaluated in the context of the effects of independent variables, it reveals that the annual change in index scores shows similar characteristics as the index. The most important finding here is that cities with lower maturity levels tend to develop faster, especially due to the population effect.

Finally, Table 4 below shows the random effects panel regression results estimated separately for the 16 subcomponents of the smart city index. Subcomponent analyses also reveal that smart city transformation is a multidimensional process that cannot be

Table 3. Panel regression results for the second model

change index			
Predictors	Estimates	CI	p
(Intercept)	18.49	4.61 – 32.37	**0.009**
Telecomindex	−5.76	−22.11 – 10.58	0.489
Log(pop)	−1.25	−2.25 – -0.25	**0.015**
GDP_pc	0.00	−0.00 – 0.00	0.138
Observations	324		
R^2 / R^2 adjusted	0.043 / 0.044		

reduced to a single policy area. However, the significant impact of the population variable on all components is an important finding showing that the factors constituting the smart city maturity level converge on a common denominator and can be activated in response to similar triggers.

The most important finding is that the population variable is positive and statistically significant in all 16 models. It is the strongest and most consistent determinant of all smart city components. This finding shows that city size triggers positive developments in many smart city components. The strongest effects of population were particularly seen on the GIS, Infrastructure, Governance, and Disaster Management scores.

The access to telecommunications infrastructure variable, as in the main model, is mostly statistically insignificant, but it has a positive and significant effect on the environment score and a negative and borderline significant effect on the infrastructure score. Contrary to expectations, the effect of access to telecommunications infrastructure is not general and systematic but only appears in the environmental dimension. Interestingly, its negative correlation with the infrastructure component score can be simply explained by the fact that as citizens' access to telecommunications infrastructure increases, the municipalities' focus on infrastructure projects decreases.

Although GDP per capita has low coefficients in general, it is seen to have an effect in some models. However, its positive effect on some components and its negative effect on others indicate an inconsistency. Economic development alone supports development in some areas, while in others it may show a negative relationship due to structural/institutional differences. It has positive and significant effects on environment, economy, people, transportation, security, and GIS scores; but it has negative and significant effects on governance, disaster management, information technology, space management, infrastructure, and information security scores. However, there is no pattern was found among these effects.

In terms of the explanatory power of the models, the best explained dimensions (high R2) are environment, transportation, economy, and people; on the other hand, the least explained dimensions are buildings, health, and energy.

In Table 5, the hypotheses (H1–H5) and their corresponding test results are presented based on the findings of the study.

Table 4. Panel regression results for all 16 components (third model)

	Governance		Environment		Economy		Energy	
Pred	Est	p	Est	p	Est	p	Est	p
(Intercept)	−108.57	**<0.001**	−82.10	**<0.001**	−104.25	**<0.001**	−112.90	**<0.001**
telecom	−16.42	0.453	33.27	**0.021**	26.31	0.134	28.72	0.135
Log(pop)	11.97	**<0.001**	4.56	**<0.001**	7.07	**<0.001**	8.53	**<0.001**
GDP_pc	−0.00	**0.030**	0.00	**<0.001**	0.00	**<0.001**	−0.00	0.559
R^2 / R^2adj	0.141 / 0.134		0.357 / 0.352		0.213 / 0.207		0.099 / 0.092	
	People		Transportation		Buildings		Health	
Pred	*Est*	*p*	*Est*	*p*	*Est*	*p*	*Est*	*p*
(Intercept)	−109.59	**<0.001**	−105.86	**<0.001**	−54.24	**<0.001**	−23.42	**0.042**
telecom	26.31	0.191	6.90	0.653	−6.12	0.603	16.12	0.212
Log(pop)	7.99	**<0.001**	8.03	**<0.001**	4.78	**<0.001**	3.63	**<0.001**
GDP_pc	0.00	**<0.001**	0.00	**<0.001**	−0.00	0.988	0.00	0.279
R^2 / R^2adj	0.212 / 0.206		0.255 / 0.249		0.074 / 0.067		0.086 / 0.079	
	Infrastructure		Commtech		Infotech		Space	
Pred	*Est*	*p*	*Est*	*p*	*Est*	*p*	*Est*	*p*
(Intercept)	−141.25	**<0.001**	−114.57	**0.001**	−110.44	**<0.001**	−122.19	**<0.001**
telecom	2.44	**0.043**	35.66	0.155	15.80	0.390	−2.53	0.900
Log(pop)	12.30	**<0.001**	7.66	**<0.001**	8.91	**<0.001**	11.00	**<0.001**
GDP_pc	−0.00	**0.002**	0.00	**<0.001**	−0.00	**0.007**	−0.00	**0.007**
R^2 / R^2adj	0.160 / 0.154		0.173 / 0.166		0.123 / 0.117		0.173 / 0.166	
	GIS		Security		Disaster		Infosec	
Pred	*Est*	*p*	*Est*	*p*	*Est*	*p*	*Est*	*p*
(Intercept)	−139.74	**<0.001**	−60.07	**<0.001**	−133.59	**<0.001**	−125.50	**<0.001**
Telecom	−44.72	0.059	13.95	0.468	18.12	0.386	17.67	0.401
Log(pop)	14.39	**<0.001**	3.80	**<0.001**	11.65	**<0.001**	11.00	**<0.001**
GDP_pc	−0.00	0.394	0.00	**<0.001**	−0.00	**0.006**	−0.00	**<0.001**
R^2 / R^2adj	0.166 / 0.160		0.143 / 0.137		0.160 / 0.154		0.175 / 0.169	

Table 5. Hypotheses Results

Hypotheses	Results
H1	Telecommunications infrastructure has no significant direct effect on smart city performance

(continued)

Table 5. *(continued)*

Hypotheses	Results
H2	City size have a significant impact on the development and dissemination of smart city applications
H3	Economic capacity has no significant direct effect on smart city performance
H4	Smart City Maturity Levels has a significant impact on smart city performance
H5	The effects of the explanatory variables vary significantly among the 16 sub-components

6 Conclusion

The main aim of this study is to explain the differences in the smart city transformation processes of cities and why some cities become smart cities faster than others. To this end, the study provides a comprehensive empirical assessment of the structural determinants and dynamics of smart city development. The findings are consistent with studies in the literature that emphasize the impact of city size on innovation capacity, knowledge production, and technological adaptation [14, 23, 35].

At the same time, it was found that telecommunications infrastructure and per capita income do not have a significant direct impact on overall smart city performance. This shows that smart city transformation is not an economic or technology-focused process, it includes a managerial and societal transformation [36]. Convergence analysis revealed that cities do not follow a simple development pattern. Some less mature cities are developing faster, further emphasizing that smart city development is not a linear process and can vary from city to city. Finally, component-level analyses, which provide a deeper look at index-level findings, revealed that while development patterns differ from policy domain to policy domain, they are generally driven by similar structural factors. Component-level regression results reveal both heterogeneity and homogeneity at certain points across different dimensions of smart city development.

This study concludes that differences in the development process of smart cities cannot be explained by the influence of a single factor. It highlights the need for a broader perspective, including structural characteristics, local and temporal features. The findings offer several important implications for policymakers and urban decision-makers. First, city size has a strong and consistent influence. This influence has shown that smaller cities may face structural disadvantages in smart city transformation. However, the change analysis also revealed that cities with lower smart city maturity levels have the potential for faster change. Therefore, policymakers should design separately targeted mechanisms for smaller and larger cities. Second, while digital infrastructure remains necessary, it needs to be complemented by smart city projects. In this context, policymakers should focus on integrating infrastructure investments into broader urban innovation strategies. Third, there is a lack of a strong correlation between economic capacity and smart city performance. This relationship demonstrates the need for effectively translating financial resources into policy outcomes.

Despite its contributions, this study has some limitations that open new avenues for future research. First, the options for explanatory variables in the empirical analysis is limited by the availability of city-level data. The limited availability of comparable sub-national data is a common challenge in urban and regional empirical research [4, 17, 24, 32]. Second, the dataset used in this study covers a relatively short time span (2020–2024). Third, although the study examines the determinants of smart city development using a comprehensive national index, the analysis does not fully reflect qualitative factors such as governance practices, corporate collaboration, or local innovation ecosystems that could significantly impact smart city initiatives.

Finally, while the component-level analysis provides valuable insights into the multidimensional nature of smart city development, it addresses each component independently. Future research could utilize more advanced techniques, such as multi-level modelling or structural equation modelling, to better capture the interdependencies between components. Further research could also expand the set of explanatory variables by incorporating indicators related to governance quality, digital governance capacity, innovation ecosystems, and local policy initiatives. In addition, comparative studies covering cities from different countries could provide further insights into how national institutional contexts shape the dynamics of smart city development.

Acknowledgments. During the preparation of this work, the authors used Grammarly tool for grammar and spelling check. After using this tool, the authors reviewed and edited the content as needed and take full responsibility for the publication's content.

References

1. Ngo, H.V., Le, Q.: Smart city: An approach from the view of smart urban governance. Int. J. Sustain. Constr. Eng. Technol. **12**(1), 314–322 (2021). https://doi.org/10.30880/ijscet.2021.12.01.029
2. Ulya, A., Susanto, T.D., Dharmawan, Y.S., Subriadi, A.P.: Major dimensions of smart city: a systematic literature review. Procedia Comput. Sci. **234**, 996–1003 (2024). https://doi.org/10.1016/j.procs.2024.03.089
3. Dai, Y., Hasanefendic, S., Bossink, B.: A systematic literature review of the smart city transformation process: the role and interaction of stakeholders and technology. Sustain. Cities Soc. **101** (2024). https://doi.org/10.1016/j.scs.2023.105112
4. Glasmeier, A., Christopherson, S.: Thinking about smart cities. Camb. J. Reg. Econ. Soc. **8**(3), 3–12 (2015)
5. UN-Habitat: People-centered smart cities: Smart cities flagship programme. United Nations Human Settlements Programme (2020)
6. Lai, C.M.T., Cole, A.: Measuring progress of smart cities: indexing the smart city indices. Urban Governance **3**(1), 45–57 (2023). https://doi.org/10.1016/j.ugj.2022.11.004
7. Sharifi, A.: A critical review of selected smart city assessment tools and indicator sets. J. Clean. Prod. **233**, 1269–1283 (2019)
8. Patrão, C., Moura, P., Almeida, A.T.D.: Review of smart city assessment tools. Smart Cities **3**(4), 1117–1132 (2020)
9. Nam, T., Pardo, T.A.: Conceptualizing smart city with dimensions of technology, people, and institutions. In: Bertot, J., et al. (eds.) Proceedings of the 12th Annual International Digital Government Research Conference (d.go11), pp. 282–291. Maryland, USA (2011)

10. Türkiye Ministry of Environment: Urbanization and climate change, national smart cities strategy and action plan 2020–2023. Government of Türkiye. https://www.akillisehirler.gov.tr/wp-content/uploads/EylemPlani.pdf. Accessed 15 Mar 2026
11. Türkiye Ministry of Environment: Urbanization and climate change, national smart city maturity evaluation model. https://akillisehirler.csb.gov.tr/olgunluk-degerlendirme-modeli/. Accessed 15 Mar 2026
12. Tamer, H.Y.: Akilli Şehirlerde Veri Yönetimi Yaklaşimlari. Abant Sosyal Bilimler Dergisi **22**(2), 519–534 (2022)
13. Al Nuaimi, E., Al-Neyadi, H., Mohamed, N., Al-Jaroodi, J.: Applications of big data to smart cities. J. Internet Serv. Appl. **6**(25), 1–15 (2015)
14. Neirotti, P., De Marco, A., Cagliano, A.C., Mangano, G., Scorrano, F.: Current trends in smart city initiatives: some stylised facts. Cities **38**, 25–36 (2014)
15. Wu, S.M., Chen, T.C., Wu, Y.J., Lytras, M.: Smart cities in Taiwan: a perspective on big data applications. Sustainability **10**(1), 106 (2018)
16. Cohen, B.: What exactly is a smart city (2012). https://www.fastcompany.com/1680538/what-exactly-is-a-smart-city. Accessed 15 Mar 2026
17. Giffinger, R., Fertner, C., Kramar, H., Kalasek, R., Pichler-Milanović, N., Meijers, E.: Smart Cities: Ranking of European Medium-Sized Cities. Vienna University of Technology, Centre of Regional Science (2007)
18. Albino, V., Berardi, U., Dangelico, R.M.: Smart cities: definitions, dimensions, performance, and initiatives. J. Urban Technol. **22**(1), 3–21 (2015). https://doi.org/10.1080/10630732.2014.942092
19. Bibri, S.E., Krogstie, J.: Smart sustainable cities of the future: an extensive interdisciplinary literature review. Sustain. Cities Soc. **31**, 183–212 (2017). https://doi.org/10.1016/j.scs.2017.02.016
20. BSI: PAS 181: Smart City Framework – Guide to establishing strategies for smart cities (2014)
21. ISO: ISO 37120: Sustainable Cities and Communities – Indicators for city services and quality of life (2018). https://www.iso.org/standard/68498.html. Accessed 10 Mar 2026
22. ISO: ISO 37122: Indicators for smart cities (2019). https://www.iso.org/standard/69050.html. Accessed 10 Mar 2026
23. Caragliu, A., Del Bo, C., Nijkamp, P.: Smart cities in Europe. J. Urban Technol. **18**(2), 65–82 (2011). https://doi.org/10.1080/10630732.2011.601117
24. Kourtit, K., Nijkamp, P.: Smart cities in the innovation age. Innov. Eur. J. Soc. Sci. Res. **25**(2), 93–95 (2012)
25. Yigitcanlar, T., et al.: Understanding 'smart cities': intertwining development drivers with desired outcomes in a multidimensional framework. Cities **81**, 145–160 (2018)
26. ITU, Smart Sustainable Cities. https://www.itu.int/en/mediacentre/backgrounders/Pages/smart-sustainable-cities.aspx. Accessed 05 Mar 2026
27. Berrone, P., Ricart, J.E., Duch, A., Carrasco, C.: IESE cities in motion index 2019. IESE, ST-509-E. https://blog.iese.edu/cities-challenges-and-management/2019/05/10/iese-citiesin-motion-index-2019. Accessed 05 Mar 2026
28. Fraunhofer Institute: Morgenstadt City Insights Framework (2014). https://www.morgenstadt.de/content/dam/morgenstadt/en/documents/Executive_Summary_mci_Phase%201_digital%20(2).pdf. Accessed 06 Mar 2026
29. IMD: IMD smart city index 2025. https://www.imd.org/smart-city-observatory/home/. Accessed 10 Mar 2026
30. European Commission: Digital economy and society index (DESI) report. https://digitalstrategy.ec.europa.eu/en/policies/desi. Accessed 10 Mar 2026
31. Barro, R.J., Sala-i-Martin, X.: Convergence. J. Polit. Econ. **100**(2), 223–251 (1992). https://doi.org/10.1086/261816

32. Rodríguez-Pose, A.: Do institutions matter for regional development? Reg. Stud. **47**(7), 1034–1047 (2013). https://doi.org/10.1080/00343404.2012.748978
33. BTK: Yıllık İl İstatistikleri. http://btk.gov.tr/yillik-il-istatistikleri. Accessed 16 Mar 2026
34. Turkstat: Geographical Statistical Portal. https://cip.tuik.gov.tr. Accessed 16 Mar 2026
35. Chourabi, H., et al.: Understanding smart cities: an integrative framework. In: Proceedings of the 45th Hawaii International Conference on System Science (HICSS), pp. 2289–2297. Hawai (2012)
36. Puron-Cid, G., Gil-Garcia, J.R.: Are smart cities too expensive in the long term? Analyzing the effects of ICT infrastructure on municipal financial sustainability. Sustainability **14**(10), 6055 (2022). https://doi.org/10.3390/su14106055

Conceptualizing a Digital Civic Innovation Platform

Timon Sengewald[1,2](✉)

[1] Rosenheim Technical University of Applied Sciences, Stadtplatz 32, 83278 Traunstein, Germany
timon.sengewald@th-rosenheim.de

[2] Friedrich-Alexander-Universität Erlangen-Nürnberg, Lange Gasse 20, 90403 Nürnberg, Germany

Abstract. Municipalities face increasing polycrises—interconnected environmental, social, and economic challenges—that demand collaborative and innovative solutions. While digital platforms and open innovation initiatives in many municipalities have gained traction, they often overlooking citizen self-organization. This study promotes a digital civic innovation platform designed to empower citizens and grassroots groups by providing access to funding, knowledge, tools, and collaborators. Using the e-Government Work System Framework as a theoretical foundation, the research employs an iterative Design Science Research process to develop and evaluate a platform that bridges these gaps. This research contributes to the discourse on digital platforms as catalysts for citizen-driven innovation by offering insights into the core functions that a digital platform needs to support civic innovators. The conceptualized platform presents opportunities for practitioners to address the unmet needs of civic innovators, enabling more effective and sustainable urban transformation.

Keywords: Citizen-driven innovation · Urban open innovation · Digital civic innovation platform

1 Introduction

Cities are at the center of many of the most pressing challenges of the 21st century [1–3]. As of 2020, about 80 percent of the global population lives in urban areas. Projections indicate that this figure will continue to rise, with future population growth concentrated in cities and megacities [4]. This rapid urban growth, accompanied by rural depopulation, aging infrastructure, and escalating demands for sustainable and inclusive services, places an unprecedented strain on municipal governments. Local authorities must manage these complexities and ensure their responses are equitable, adaptive, and aligned with the needs of diverse communities. However, traditional governance models, which are often top-down and bureaucratic, struggle to keep pace with the dynamic and multifaceted nature of urban life.

This article is part of the author's dissertation project at Friedrich-Alexander-Universität Erlangen-Nürnberg. Substantial parts of this article will be reprinted in the author's doctoral thesis.

Published by Springer Nature Switzerland 2027
G. Viale Pereira et al. (Eds.): EGOV 2026, LNCS 16933, pp. 165–181, 2027.
https://doi.org/10.1007/978-3-032-35747-2_11

Over the past two decades, municipalities worldwide have adopted the concept of smart cities, leveraging interconnected IT systems, big data, and digital platforms to improve quality of life and well-being [2, 5–8]. However, the concept of a 'smart city' is more than just technological deployment. It represents an ongoing transformation in how local governments engage with their residents, design services, and address collective challenges [9]. Active citizen involvement is central to this transformation—not as passive recipients of services, but as co-creators of solutions [10]. Citizen participation is widely recognized as a cornerstone of smart governance, ensuring that urban development reflects the priorities and aspirations of the entire community.

Despite this ideal, a persistent gap exists between rhetoric and reality. Although citizen engagement is deeply rooted in public administration through mechanisms such as polls, town halls, and consultative committees, these traditional forms often fail to foster meaningful and sustained collaboration [6, 11, 12]. Open innovation tools, such as hackathons, digital platforms, and participatory budgeting, have introduced new avenues for problem-solving [e.g., 13, 14]. These tools promise to unlock residents' creative potential, generate novel ideas, increase public engagement, and ultimately boost satisfaction with municipal governance. However, their implementation has revealed a paradox: even as cities invest in participatory initiatives, many still grapple with the 'absent citizen' phenomenon [12]. Nevertheless, citizens are not disengaged; they are often dissatisfied with the processes themselves, frustrated by perceived tokenism, opaque decision-making, and the misalignment between their contributions and municipal priorities [15].

Open innovation approaches recognize the value of engaging diverse stakeholders and can serve as a response. For example, citizen-driven innovation has proven its ability to mobilize resources and ideas [16–18]. Initiatives like the "*Wir vs. Virus*" hackathon engaged over 28,000 participants who developed 1,500 solutions during the pandemic [19, 20]. Global efforts like the "*EU vs. Virus*" hackathon [13, 18] also demonstrate how crises can catalyze public sector innovation [21]. For example, *Amsterdam Smart City* has introduced a digital platform [22], to engage citizens in collaborative problem-solving. The literature on e-participation also notes an expansion of digital tools from mere participation to supporting for citizens as co-creators [23]. Digital tools can help support different stages and activities of the innovation process. For example, the exploration of and the ability to learn from previously implemented solutions or defined problems is an important activity to support the creative process [24]. However, these platforms often focus on top-down engagement rather than enabling citizens to self-organize and drive innovation independently [17, 25].

Although cities are encouraged to empower citizens to actively shape innovation processes [27], current platforms rarely provide the necessary tools to connect innovators with the right collaborators, such as advocates, funders, or experts, or to provide access to essential resources, such as knowledge, spaces, and testing opportunities. Therefore, this study aims to answer the following research question:

RQ: *How should a digital platform for civil society be designed to promote citizen-driven innovation?*

This study introduces a novel IS artifact developed over two years through a design science research (DSR) project [28]. The project aimed to design a digital platform that would enable self-organization within civil society and address the aforementioned research question. The artifact represents the architecture for a digital platform that comprises different functionalities identified during the study. For example, it could help civic innovators share current problems identified in a municipality and find previous projects within a digital archive that could serve as inspiration. It could also provide an overview of and recommendations for locally available resources that could be used for the project. In the remaining part of this article, the context of the research study as well as the *eGovernment Work Systems Framework (eGovWSF)* will be outlined. Following an outline of the *DSR* approach using design echelons [29], the data collection and analysis process that was used to build this artifact.

2 Theoretical Background

2.1 The Context of Citizen-Driven Innovation in Municipalities

Open innovation, in the sense of collaborative problem solving within cities, is often hailed as a cornerstone of smart city transformation. It promises to democratize urban development and foster inclusive and adaptive solutions [30]. The scientific literature widely agrees that overcoming such crises requires joint efforts from scientists, businesses, public administrators, and civil society members [31, 32]. In particular, civil society can play a central role in addressing these issues when the public sector is under-resourced [33–35]. Citizen-driven innovation thereby refers mainly to projects that are initiated – often characterized as grassroot innovation, mainly driven or led by citizens [17, 36]. Thus, citizen-driven innovation represents a second, complementary approach

Table 1. Overview of digital platform types used of open innovation.

Digital Platform Type/Example	Description
Open Feedback/*FixMyStreet*	Platforms enabling citizens to report local issues (e.g., potholes, graffiti) to authorities through a digital interface, with tracking of resolution status. Typically initiated by governments to improve service efficiency and transparency [38]
Open Problem Solving/*Challenge.gov*	Government-led platforms where citizens help to solve predefined public challenges (e.g., technology, health, energy) with monetary or non-monetary rewards. Solutions are evaluated by experts or public voting, with transparent processes [39]
Open Ideation/*My Linz*	Bottom-up platforms where citizens freely propose ideas for policies, services, or urban projects. Features include collaborative refinement through comments and votes, with no pre-set agenda, fostering grassroots initiatives [40]
Open Governance/*Decidim Barcelona*	Top-down digital platforms for structured public input on pre-selected policy options or budget allocations. Includes digital polls/surveys with transparent results and implementation tracking [41]
Open Discussion and Collaboration/*Amsterdam Smart City*	Community-driven forums for open-ended debate on urban issues (e.g., mobility, sustainability). Enables self-organized projects, resource-sharing, and collaboration without central authority control [22]

to government-driven innovation, which can help municipalities solve problems with the support of civil society [37].

2.2 The e-Government Work System Framework

The *eGovWSF* [42] is based on the *Work Systems Theory (WST)* [43, 44]. *WST* provides a generic model for analyzing the interaction between human participants, technologies, information and processes within organizational systems to produce services or products for customers. The *WST* has also been used to conceptualize digital open innovation platforms [e.g., 45], as is the focus of this study. Although Alter's *WST* provides a general foundation for understanding work systems [43], the *eGovWSF* adapts this framework to the specific context of public sector digitization, where the objectives, constraints, and stakeholder dynamics differ considerably from those in the private sector [42].

The *eGovWSF* framework breaks down e-government systems into twelve interconnected elements, categorized into three distinct layers [42]: elements that are largely outside the system, elements that are partially inside and partially outside, and elements that are fully embedded within it. Externally, the framework highlights the influence of the social, economic and political environment, including public values, legal regulations and digital infrastructure—factors that shape the operational logic and effectiveness of e-government initiatives. For example, compliance with data protection laws (e.g., GDPR) or political directives can enable or constrain digital transformation efforts. Additionally, policies and strategies, often formulated by external government bodies, guide the development and implementation of e-government systems. However, these may sometimes conflict with internal organizational priorities.

The framework emphasizes value for society (e.g., transparency, efficiency and democratic participation), external stakeholders (e.g., citizens, businesses and other public entities) and public e-services (e.g., online portals and automated administrative processes) at the interface between internal and external domains.

The operational core of the system comprises processes and activities (such as case handling and workflow automation), internal stakeholders (public employees, IT specialists and managers), information (citizen records and administrative data) and digital technologies (software, hardware and platforms). A key distinction from Alter's original *WST* is the explicit inclusion of internal policies and strategies, which transform broader political mandates into actionable guidelines for public service delivery.

3 Research Design

This research project falls within the *DSR* research paradigm [28, 46, 47]. The *DSR* with design echelons (^{e}DSR) methodology, as presented by Tuunanen et al. [29], was used more specifically. The methodology was introduced as a way to address complexity within projects that involve sociotechnical phenomena and could not fully be covered by the previous process-based approaches. Echelons are smaller units that are performed within five central activities: 1) Problem analysis, 2) Objectives and requirements definition, 3) Design and development, 4) Demonstration, and 5) Evaluation [29].

For each of the five ^{e}*DSR* phases (1) Problem analysis, 2) Objectives and requirements definition, 3) Design and development, 4) Demonstration, and 5) Evaluation).

Table 2 provides an overview of the data collection activities and participants for each of the five ^{e}*DSR* phases.

Table 2. Overview of the data collection activities.

eDSR Phase	Description	Duration/ Total
Problem Analysis	A workshop with fourteen participants was conducted to identify problems and determine requirements for the artifact. To gain a comprehensive understanding of the challenges in citizen-driven innovation, the participants consisted of diverse stakeholders, including citizens, municipal staff, and consultants. The workshop consisted of two rounds of parallel focus groups, with three groups per round	24–35 min./ 206 min
Objectives and Requirements Definition	A secondary analysis of a previous interview study with 15 participants involved in six different citizen-driven projects was conducted to derive design requirements	23–80 min./ 696 min
Design and development	Two workshops were conducted during the design phase with two seasoned consultants from an urban social innovation incubator	82–120 min./ 202 min
Demonstration	Five demonstrations were conducted with two seasoned innovation consultants, three civic innovators, and three staff members of a municipality's civic engagement department to validate the artifact's proof of concept	38–103 min./ 246 min
Evaluation	Five demonstrations were conducted with four civic innovators and one seasoned innovation consultant to validate the artifact's proof of value	32–58 min./ 241 min

As shown in Table 2 all participants involved in the data collection activities received financial compensation if they did not participate in relation to their main job (e.g., municipal employees). Despite the ethical and data quality implications of providing false information [48–50], appropriate compensation acknowledges also contributions and may improve data quality [51]. Since citizen-driven innovation projects pursue public value and already require substantial unpaid time from participants. Participants received financial compensation at the rate of Germany's minimum wage, which aligns with recommendations that compensation should approximate market labor value [51].

Deductive Thematic Analysis was used to analyze stakeholder feedback using the *eGovWSF* as a predefined coding schema. This approach aligns with the integration of qualitative methods and DSR [52]. They highlight how qualitative designs can enhance the rigor and relevance of artifact development. Interview transcripts were systematically coded, focus group discussions, and expert feedback according to the twelve *eGovWSF* elements (e.g., value for society, public e-services, digital technologies) to identify patterns and validate the alignment with stakeholder needs. This method ensured a structured, theory-driven analysis that bridges qualitative insights with the practical goals of DSR and supports the iterative refinement of the platform's design.

Thematic analysis is a structured, six-step process used to systematically identify and interpret patterns in qualitative data. First, the researcher familiarizes themselves with the data by repeatedly reading transcripts or notes. Second, initial codes are generated by applying the predefined *eGovWSF* as a coding schema to ensure alignment with elements such as 'Value for Society' or 'Public e-Services.' Examples of the coding process for each of the *eGovWSF* elements can be found in Table 3.

Third, codes are grouped into potential themes that capture broader patterns, such as 'Supporting funding search.' Fourth, the themes are reviewed and refined to ensure they accurately reflect the data and address the research questions. The fifth step is to clearly define and name each theme, using illustrative quotes to highlight its significance. Finally, the results were compiled into a coherent report that links the themes to the *eGovWSF* and provides actionable insights for the iterative design and development of the digital open innovation platform.

4 Conceptualizing a Civic Innovation Platform

4.1 Problem Analysis

The first problem analysis echelon began with an exploratory workshop with 14 participants, during which three parallel focus groups were conducted in two rounds. The first round focused on identifying problem domains within the city. The second round focused on brainstorming solutions that could resolve these problems. Throughout the discussions, participants repeatedly noted that civic innovators face significant challenges in securing support and initiating engagement. Specifically, gaining access to project funding was identified as a primary barrier.

These findings align with prior research indicating that the most successful projects often rely on robust personal networks from which innovators can recruit collaborators and resources [36]. Robert D. Putnam [53] conceptualizes the advantages derived from such connections as social capital, identifying it as a critical determinant of success.

Table 3. Examples of the coding process using *eGovWSF* elements.

Exemplary *eGovWSF* element	Exemplary Coding Fragment
Social, economic and political environment	*"... in the end, the topic of self-realization is often a major driver in all this innovative civic innovation. And that often means that I just want to do it now, and I want to experience it myself and see how it works. And I don't necessarily want to hear about all the things that might not work."*
Value for society	*"I understand that support is sometimes necessary because not everyone goes into counseling. Even with us, only a very small number of people who want to do something for the greater good end up here."*
External Stakeholders	*"Once it's on the market, it will also be used a lot by advisory organizations, because they are also a kind of gatekeeper or filter. If someone is completely new to the field ... that person will in most cases be less creative. They can't handle the terms in this table, where I think, you can write an application somehow. And they'll probably say that's not what I do. So, of course, that will remain the task of the advisors...."*
Public e-services	*"I can see the use case for both, but especially for me. I would use the tool immediately. Normally, I can't name any relevant foundations, or maybe two or three from the region. And the rest? I don't know if they're a good fit. But if I have an overview like this, it's a huge advantage for me and I can give people 3 to 5 recommendations."*
Processes and activities	*"Both a list of contacts and a list of funding opportunities. These need to be kept up to date somehow, otherwise they quickly become irrelevant."*

Consequently, effective innovation appears to depend not only on individual initiative but also on the initiator's ability to mobilize social capital and engage actors who fulfill distinct functional roles. While networking is similarly recognized as a key mechanism in other open innovation formats—such as hackathons—for connecting innovators with collaborators or sponsors [e.g., 14, 54], these formats present their own limitations. Specifically, constraints related to time and physical location can act as significant barriers to participation in civic hackathons and similar events [55], potentially excluding those without the necessary flexibility or proximity. This well-known challenge in the academic literature was explicitly confirmed during our focus group discussions, where participants reported that securing time to attend such events is a significant hurdle.

The central issue was determining the optimal design of a digital platform to promote citizen-driven innovation by helping project initiators find potential collaborators such as co-creators, sponsors, and advisors.

4.2 Objectives and Requirements Definition

This echelon involved a secondary focused analysis [56, 57] of interviews from a previous study [36]. Since the interviews were conducted by the same researcher in a similar context, problems with epistemological boundaries can be considered minimal [58]. The coding focused on extracting actionable objectives and requirements for the platform. Because the interviewees were citizen innovators who had successfully launched projects, the analysis revealed essential activities and resource types for an effective matchmaking platform.

The first requirement formulated was that the system should list relevant funding opportunities, as this was also identified during the problem analysis. However, finding sponsors was also often mentioned as a problem in the interview analysis.

The second requirement that was formulated was the ability to list local available resources other the funding. The rationale behind this requirement was that funding can be difficult to obtain, and the amount that can be applied for is sometimes limited. However, local organizations such as Fab Labs and other open workshops often provide access to equipment and machinery at low or no cost.

A third requirement was the ability to list current projects in order to find potential collaborators. As mentioned, people often have the same or similar ideas at the same time, and some people want to support existing projects without having their own ideas. In both cases, listing existing initiatives would be a good solution.

4.3 Design and Development

Two workshops were conducted with a local social innovation incubator and a social entrepreneurship accelerator. The current requirements and ideas for the platform were presented and discussed in the interviews. Since both have worked extensively with citizen innovators, the interviews aimed to draw on their expertise and knowledge about a potential support structure. Additionally, since both organizations perform similar networking activities and provide recommendations to their clients (e.g., funding opportunities), the second objective was to formalize these activities and translate them into design requirements for the platform.

During these workshops, a fourth requirement was identified: the ability to explore previous projects, both successful and unsuccessful, to give project initiators the chance to learn from past experiences. Furthermore, the second requirement was expanded to include knowledge resources, as documentation that describes in detail what to do for many concepts, such as urban gardens, already exists.

The following paragraph presents the synthesized results of the workshops on designing a platform to empower individuals and grassroots groups to develop and carry out local civic projects. The platform addresses the need for inclusive, accessible, and locally grounded innovation by providing personalized recommendations for funding, coaching, tools, and knowledge. The **Fehler! Verweisquelle konnte nicht gefunden werden.** Below provides an overview of the digital civic innovation platform as a snapshot according to the *eGovWSF*. This high-level overview captures the platform's core elements, including its societal value, stakeholders, services, processes, information, technologies, and internal strategies.

<table>
<tr><th colspan="3">Value for Society [V]</th></tr>
<tr><td colspan="3">[V1] Democratizing innovation and participation in smart city development.
[V2] Increasing problem-solving capability by fosters collaboration among citizens and other stakeholder groups within the city.</td></tr>
<tr><th>External Stakeholders [ES]</th><th colspan="2">Public e-Services [Serv]</th></tr>
<tr><td>[ES1] Citizen/ Organizations as resource provider
[ES2] Citizen Innovators as resource users
[ES3] Intermediaries like innovation consultants</td><td colspan="2">[Serv1] Funding search: Identifying and recommending suitable funding sources.
[Serv2] Tool and material search: Locating available resources and equipment locally.
[Serv3] Collaborator search: Finding complementary skills and partnership opportunities.
[Serv4] Project search: Enabling systematic learning from past projects to enhance creativity.</td></tr>
<tr><th colspan="3">Processes and Activities [P]</th></tr>
<tr><td colspan="3">[P1] Reposting funding opportunities: Curating and updating available grants from public/private sources
[P2] Supporting project exploration: Enabling discovery of past projects and lessons learned
[P3] Recommendation generation: Algorithmically suggesting relevant funding, collaborators, and past projects</td></tr>
<tr><th>Internal Stakeholders [IS]</th><th>Information [I]</th><th>Digital Technologies [DT]</th></tr>
<tr><td>[IS1] Administrators (Either from public or civic institutions)
[IS2] Municipality as system provider</td><td>[I1] Local challenges or problems
[I2] Project idea descriptions
[I3] Documentation of past projects
[I4] Local knowledge resources, tools and materials
[I5] Funding opportunities</td><td>[DT1] Matchmaking algorithms
[DT2] Web-based platform</td></tr>
<tr><th colspan="3">Internal Strategies and Policies [ISP]</th></tr>
<tr><td colspan="3">[ISP1] Open data principles</td></tr>
</table>

Fig. 1. An eGovWSF snapshot of the civic innovation platform.

4.4 Demonstration

The demonstration echelon aimed to prove the feasibility and usability as a proof of concept through prototype testing. Two user types were addressed: 1) citizen innovators and 2) social innovation consultants. A functional prototype with the following key features was developed: 1) Funding Search, 2) Tools/Materials Search, 3) Projects Search, 4) Challenges, and 5) Ideas Repository and conducted five demonstrations to validate and further refine the design. The goal of the demonstration was to evaluate the comprehensiveness of the architecture, not the interface design or effectiveness of the matchmaking algorithm. Figure 2 shows a screenshot of the prototype that was used during the demonstrations and evaluations. For example, the interface for the funding search focuses on three key input parameters: project description, applicant description, and required funding amount. These parameters were identified as essential for achieving an effective yet minimal funding match.

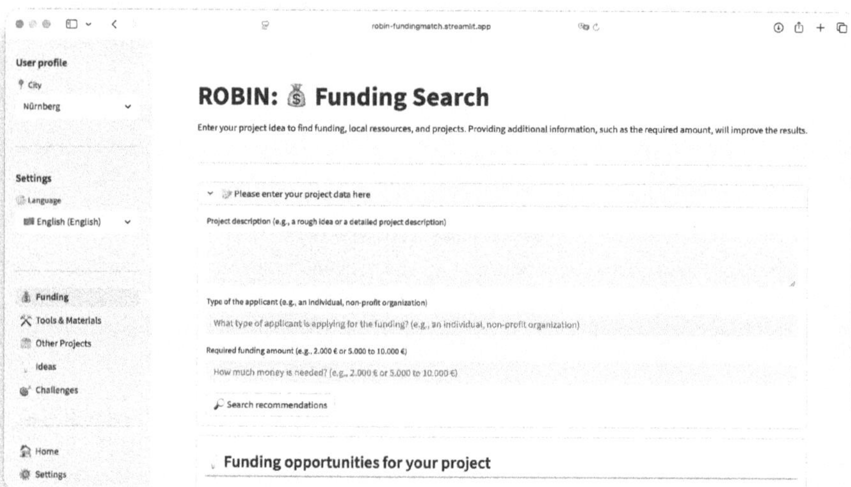

Fig. 2. Screenshot of the artifact instantiation used in the demonstrations

4.5 Evaluation

The evaluation echelon consisted of five demonstrations with four civic innovators and one seasoned innovation consultant. The goal of the evaluation was the comprehensiveness of the architecture, not the interface design or effectiveness of the matchmaking algorithm. For example, one of the innovator teams stated the following regarding the funding search [Serv1]:

> *"If we had had such a tool, finding funding would have been much easier for us."*

The recommendation mechanism ([P3] and [DT1]) was particularly highlighted as valuable for funding searches because a large number of funding opportunities would otherwise need to be evaluated manually, especially regarding funding.

"... there are already many of these support programs from a wide variety of sources. Of course, it would be cool to find out right away whether something is a good fit for me or not."

During these final demonstrations, the comprehensiveness of the functions was confirmed, as no additional requirements or missing functions were identified. For example, one of the participants stated:

"Yes, overall, I have to say you did a really great job. When I think about how much it would have helped us if we'd had this during the project, it would have been a huge help. Because it just makes networking possible. Especially since you basically have the right links and contact information right there."

5 Discussion

5.1 Theoretical Implications

Digital platforms designed to support civic innovation and open governance typically fall into two categories: top-down and bottom-up. Top-down platforms, such as public participation platforms (e.g., Consul and Decidim) and citizen feedback systems, are structured to facilitate consultation, transparency, and decision-making processes led by municipal or government authorities. While these platforms enhance democratic engagement by enabling citizens to voice their opinions, vote on proposals, and participate in deliberative processes, they often lack the mechanisms necessary to support the implementation of citizen-driven initiatives. They focus on gathering input rather than providing the support necessary for citizens to act as autonomous innovators.

On the other hand, bottom-up platforms, such as idea-sharing platforms (e.g., Amsterdam InChange) and hackathon-based systems, prioritize generating and discussing ideas. However, these platforms often neglect to address the practical implementation challenges of innovation, such as securing funding, accessing materials and equipment, and finding collaborators. Consequently, citizens are often left with promising concepts but no clear pathway to execution, which is a critical gap given that the primary challenge in innovation is implementation, not ideation [59]. This study introduces a Digital Civic Innovation Platform (CIP), a new class of information systems that systematize grassroots innovation. CRM operate similarly to Enterprise Resource Planning (ERP) systems, which standardize organizational workflows, and Customer Relationship Management (CRM) systems, which streamline customer interactions. This design addresses a fundamental limitation of current civic technology: the absence of structured support for self-organized, citizen-driven innovation.

The *eGovWSF* mapping shows a multi-sided work system where citizens, municipalities, and advisory organizations interact through structured information flows. Unlike other e-government systems presented before that focus on service delivery, the presented artifact emphasizes self-organization capabilities of civic innovators.

5.2 Practical Implications

In an era when municipalities are faced with mounting challenges, from climate adaptation to social inequality, yet operate with limited resources, citizen-driven innovation provides an opportunity to develop context-specific, community-led solutions. A digital matchmaking platform provides the necessary infrastructure for self-organization, transforming ad hoc civic efforts into a structured, scalable channel for open innovation. By co-creating and co-governing these platforms with civil society, municipalities can reduce implementation costs for the necessary transformation. Existing systems often neglect the needs of grassroots innovators, focusing instead on top-down or bottom-up engagement without adequately supporting citizen-led initiatives. Implementing this model empowers communities and positions municipalities as leaders in participatory governance, transforming collective challenges into opportunities for sustainable problem-solving.

5.3 Limitations

The main limitation is that the artifact underwent iterative evaluation through demonstrations with stakeholders. This study lacks a naturalistic evaluation in a real-world setting [60]. The demonstrations were conducted in controlled or semi-controlled environments, which may not have fully captured the complexities and dynamics of the artifact's intended use context. Naturalistic evaluations require long-term engagement with users in their authentic environments. Due to the scope and timeline of this study, embedding the artifact in ongoing projects or organizations for an extended period was not feasible. Collecting longitudinal data, such as tracking projects over months or years, would have required significant resources, including sustained access to participants, funding for fieldwork, and coordination with multiple stakeholders.

A second limitation relates to the fact that the artifact was primarily designed and evaluated in urban contexts, with participants drawn from large cities and their surrounding metropolitan areas. While these settings provided a rich ecosystem of stakeholders and projects for testing, the findings may not fully apply to rural or less-resourced regions, where challenges, stakeholder dynamics, and infrastructure differ significantly.

5.4 Future Research Outlook

To address the limitations of the current study, particularly the lack of naturalistic evaluation, future research could focus on deploying the artifact in real-world settings, such as ongoing citizen-led projects or municipal initiatives. Longitudinal field studies could assess the artifact's long-term usability, impact, and adaptability while capturing emergent challenges and unintended consequences in authentic contexts.

This study provides valuable insights into the design and implementation. However, several *eGovWSF* elements remain under-explored. The *eGovWSF* offers a valuable theoretical framework for advancing research on digital civic innovation platforms. As these systems evolve from conceptual designs into real-world implementations, the framework can guide future research to address gaps, refine functionalities, and develop evidence-based recommendations for successful deployment. Below, key areas of further research organized by theoretical, empirical, and practical dimensions are outlined.

6 Conclusion

This study has conceptualized a digital civic innovation platform as a novel IS artifact. The platform developed through this research offers a concrete way to bridge the gap between top-down participation mechanisms and genuine citizen self-organization.

In closing, it is hoped that this research will contribute meaningfully to the ongoing conversation about digital support for citizen-driven innovation. This vibrant and evolving field has much yet to be discovered. May this work inspire further exploration and collaboration to ultimately create more resilient urban futures.

Acknowledgments. This research project is funded by the Bavarian Research Institute for Digital Transformation (bidt), an institute of the Bavarian Academy of Sciences and Humanities (Grant no: KON-23-039). The authors are responsible for the content of this publication.

Disclosure of Interests. The author has no competing interests to declare that are relevant to the content of this article.

References

1. Posselt, T., Riemer, M., Sa'd, R., Walsh, B.: Breaking the walls of complex systems change in cities: a service ecosystems and psychological perspective. JCCPE **1**, 32–60 (2022). https://doi.org/10.3138/jccpe-2022.1.1.0009
2. Rosemann, M., Becker, J., Chasin, F.: City 5.0. Bus. Inf. Syst. Eng. **63**, 71–77 (2021). https://doi.org/10.1007/s12599-020-00674-9
3. Selby, J.D., Desouza, K.C.: Fragile cities in the developed world: a conceptual framework. Cities **91**, 180–192 (2019). https://doi.org/10.1016/j.cities.2018.11.018
4. Publications Office of the European Union: Atlas of the Human Planet 2024 (2024)
5. Ahad, M.A., Paiva, S., Tripathi, G., Feroz, N.: Enabling technologies and sustainable smart cities. Sustain. Cities Soc. **61**, 102301 (2020). https://doi.org/10.1016/j.scs.2020.102301
6. Hollands, R.G.: Will the real smart city please stand up?: Intelligent, progressive or entrepreneurial? City **12**, 303–320 (2008). https://doi.org/10.1080/13604810802479126
7. Hosseini, S., Frank, L., Fridgen, G., Heger, S.: Do not forget about smart towns: how to bring customized digital innovation to rural areas. Bus. Inf. Syst. Eng. **60**, 243–257 (2018). https://doi.org/10.1007/s12599-018-0536-2
8. Janssen, M., Charalabidis, Y., Zuiderwijk, A.: Benefits, adoption barriers and myths of open data and open government. Inf. Syst. Manag. **29**, 258–268 (2012). https://doi.org/10.1080/10580530.2012.716740
9. Nam, T.: Suggesting frameworks of citizen-sourcing via Government 2.0. Gov. Inf. Q. **29**, 12–20 (2012). https://doi.org/10.1016/j.giq.2011.07.005

10. Van Waart, P., Mulder, I., De Bont, C.: A participatory approach for envisioning a smart city. Soc. Sci. Comput. Rev. **34**, 708–723 (2016). https://doi.org/10.1177/0894439315611099
11. Arnstein, S.R.: A ladder of citizen participation. J. Am. Inst. Plann. **35**, 216–224 (1969). https://doi.org/10.1080/01944366908977225
12. Shelton, T., Lodato, T.: Actually existing smart citizens: expertise and (non)participation in the making of the smart city. City **23**, 35–52 (2019). https://doi.org/10.1080/13604813.2019.1575115
13. Bertello, A., Bogers, M.L.A.M., De Bernardi, P.: Open innovation in the face of the COVID-19 grand challenge: insights from the Pan-European hackathon 'EUvsVirus.' R & D Manag. **52**, 178–192 (2022). https://doi.org/10.1111/radm.12456
14. Yuan, Q., Gasco-Hernandez, M.: Open innovation in the public sector: creating public value through civic hackathons. Public Manag. Rev. **23**, 523–544 (2021). https://doi.org/10.1080/14719037.2019.1695884
15. Van Twist, A., Melenhorst, M., Veenstra, M., Ruijer, E., Kolk, M., Meijer, A.: Designing Guidelines for Smart City Collaboration Tools. In: Proceedings of the 55th Hawaii International Conference on System Sciences (2022). https://doi.org/10.24251/HICSS.2022.334
16. Baccarne, B., Mechant, P., Schuurman, D., Colpaert, P., Marez, L.D.: Urban socio-technical innovations with and by citizens. Interdisc. Stud. J. **3**, 143–156 (2014)
17. Eskelinen, J., Garcia Robles, A., Lindy, I., Marsh, J., Muente-Kunigami, A.: Citizen-driven innovation: A guidebook for city mayors and public administrators (2015)
18. Gama, K.: Successful models of hackathons and innovation contests to crowdsource rapid responses to COVID-19. Digit. Gov.: Res. Pract. **2**, 1–7 (2021). https://doi.org/10.1145/3431806
19. Gegenhuber, T., Mair, J., Lührsen, R., Thäter, L.: Open Social Innovation in Deutschland verstetigen (2021)
20. Gegenhuber, T., Mair, J., Lührsen, R., Thäter, L.: Orchestrating distributed data governance in open social innovation. Inf. Organ. **33**, 100453 (2023). https://doi.org/10.1016/j.infoandorg.2023.100453
21. Korte, N., Püchel, L., Brandt, T.: Crises as drivers for digital innovation in the public sector: insights from COVID-19. In: ECIS 2023 Research-in-Progress Papers, p. 69, Kristiansand, Norway (2023)
22. Putra, Z.D.W., Van der Knaap, W.G.: Urban innovation system and the role of an open web-based platform: the case of Amsterdam smart city. J. Reg. City Plann. **29**, 234 (2018). https://doi.org/10.5614/jrcp.2018.29.3.4
23. Shin, B., et al.: A systematic analysis of digital tools for citizen participation. Gov. Inf. Q. **41**, 101954 (2024). https://doi.org/10.1016/j.giq.2024.101954
24. Shneiderman, B.: Creativity support tools: accelerating discovery and innovation. Commun. ACM **50**, 20–32 (2007). https://doi.org/10.1145/1323688.1323689
25. von Hippel, E.: Democratizing innovation: the evolving phenomenon of user innovation. Int. J. Innovation Sci. **1**, 12 (2009)

26. Capdevila, I., Zarlenga, M.I.: Smart city or smart citizens? The Barcelona case. J. Strateg. Manag. **8**, 266–282 (2015). https://doi.org/10.1108/JSMA-03-2015-0030
27. Ahdekivi, V., Ghanbari, H., Rossi, M.: Building Climate Resilience in Smart Cities Using Open Data Services. Presented at the Hawaii International Conference on System Sciences (2023). https://doi.org/10.24251/HICSS.2023.248
28. Hevner, A.R., March, S.T., Park, J., Ram, S.: Design science in information systems research. MISQ. **28**, 75–105 (2004). https://doi.org/10.2307/25148625
29. Tuunanen, T., Winter, R., Vom Brocke, J.: Dealing with complexity in design science research: a methodology using design echelons. MISQ. **48**, 427–458 (2024). https://doi.org/10.25300/MISQ/2023/16700
30. Hernández-Muñoz, J.M., et al.: Smart cities at the forefront of the future internet. In: Domingue, J., et al. (eds.) The Future Internet, pp. 447–462. Springer Berlin Heidelberg, Berlin, Heidelberg (2011). https://doi.org/10.1007/978-3-642-20898-0_32
31. Bhatia, R., Pihlajamaa, M., Hyytinen, K., Jäntti, A.: Capabilities for transformative sustainability management in cities. Public Manag. Rev. 1–25 (2024). https://doi.org/10.1080/14719037.2024.2394955
32. McGahan, A.M., Bogers, M.L.A.M., Chesbrough, H., Holgersson, M.: Tackling societal challenges with open innovation. Calif. Manage. Rev. **63**, 49–61 (2021). https://doi.org/10.1177/0008125620973713
33. Agger, A.: Democratic innovations in municipal planning: potentials and challenges of place-based platforms for deliberation between politicians and citizens. Cities **117**, 103317 (2021). https://doi.org/10.1016/j.cities.2021.103317
34. Agger, A., Hedensted Lund, D.: Collaborative innovation in the public sector – new perspectives on the role of citizens? SJPA. **21**, 17–37 (2017). https://doi.org/10.58235/sjpa.v21i3.11557
35. Torfing, J.: Collaborative innovation in the public sector: the argument. Public Manag. Rev. **21**, 1–11 (2019). https://doi.org/10.1080/14719037.2018.1430248
36. Sengewald, T., Roth, A.: Actors' roles in citizen-driven innovation. In: Proceedings of ISPIM Innovation Symposium. The International Society for Professional Innovation Management (ISPIM), Osaka, Japan (2024)
37. Sengewald, T.: Heads or Tails? Two Sides of the. In: CO-CREATING SUSTAINABLE SOLUTIONS FOR FUTURE-PROOF SOCIETIES (2024). https://doi.org/10.1016/j.scs.2020.102301
38. King, S.F., Brown, P.: Fix my street or else: using the internet to voice local public service concerns. In: Proceedings of the 1st International Conference on Theory and Practice of Electronic Governance, pp. 72–80. ACM, Macao China (2007). https://doi.org/10.1145/1328057.1328076
39. Mergel, I., Desouza, K.C.: Implementing open innovation in the public sector: the case of challenge.gov. Public Admin Rev. **73**, 882–890 (2013). https://doi.org/10.1111/puar.12141
40. Schmidthuber, L., Piller, F., Bogers, M., Hilgers, D.: Citizen participation in public administration: investigating open government for social innovation. R&D Manag. **49**, 343–355 (2019)
41. Mann, M., Mitchell, P., Foth, M., Anastasiu, I.: #BlockSidewalk to Barcelona: technological sovereignty and the social license to operate smart cities. J. Am. Soc. Inf. Sci. **71**, 1103–1115 (2020). https://doi.org/10.1002/asi.24387

42. Lindgren, I., Melin, U., Sæbø, Ø.: What is E-Government? Introducing a work system framework for understanding e-government. CAIS **48**, 503–522 (2021). https://doi.org/10.17705/1CAIS.04842
43. Alter, S.: Work system theory: overview of core concepts, extensions, and challenges for the future. JAIS **14**, 72–121 (2013). https://doi.org/10.17705/1jais.00323
44. Alter, S.: A framework for describing theoretical perspectives: overview and application to the work system perspective. In: Proceedings of the 55th Hawaii International Conference on System Sciences (2022). https://doi.org/10.24251/HICSS.2022.795
45. Daiberl, C.F., Oks, S.J., Roth, A., Möslein, K.M., Alter, S.: Design principles for establishing a multi-sided open innovation platform: lessons learned from an action research study in the medical technology industry. Electron Markets **29**, 711–728 (2019). https://doi.org/10.1007/s12525-018-0325-2
46. Hevner, A.R., Chatterjee, S.: Design Research in Information Systems. Springer US, Boston, MA (2010). https://doi.org/10.1007/978-1-4419-5653-8
47. March, S.T., Smith, G.F.: Design and natural science research on information technology. Decis. Support Syst. **15**, 251–266 (1995). https://doi.org/10.1016/0167-9236(94)00041-2
48. Head, E.: The ethics and implications of paying participants in qualitative research. Int. J. Soc. Res. Methodol. **12**, 335–344 (2009). https://doi.org/10.1080/13645570802246724
49. Pater, J., Coupe, A., Pfafman, R., Phelan, C., Toscos, T., Jacobs, M.: Standardizing reporting of participant compensation in HCI: a systematic literature review and recommendations for the field. In: Proceedings of the 2021 CHI Conference on Human Factors in Computing Systems, pp. 1–16. ACM, Yokohama Japan (2021). https://doi.org/10.1145/3411764.3445734
50. Rao, P.S.B., et al.: Changes in Research Ethics, Openness, and Transparency in Empirical Studies between CHI 2017 and CHI 2022. Presented at the (2023). https://doi.org/10.17605/OSF.IO/N25D6
51. Masoumi, A.: "You Didn't Have to Pay Me": the meanings of monetary incentives in interview research. Int J Qual Methods **23**, 16094069241296210 (2024). https://doi.org/10.1177/16094069241296210
52. Fathullah, M.A., Subbarao, A., Ahmad, A., Muthaiyah, S.: Merging qualitative design methods with design science. Int J Qual Methods **24**, 16094069251337584 (2025). https://doi.org/10.1177/16094069251337585
53. Putnam, R.: Bowling alone: America's declining social capital. J. Democracy **6**, 65–78 (1995). https://doi.org/10.1353/jod.1995.0002
54. Gegenhuber, T., Mair, J.: Open social innovation: taking stock and moving forward. Ind. Innov. **31**, 130–157 (2024). https://doi.org/10.1080/13662716.2023.2271863
55. Sengewald, T., Riemer, M., Posselt, T.: A taxonomy of resident engagement barriers in public open innovation. In: Proceedings EGOV-CeDEM-ePart conference. , Ghent/ Leuven, Belgium (2024)
56. Dargentas, M.: Secondary analysis and culture of disputation in European qualitative research. Forum: Qual. Soc. Res. **7** (2006)
57. Ruggiano, N., Perry, T.E.: Conducting secondary analysis of qualitative data: should we, can we, and how? Qual. Soc. Work. **18**, 81–97 (2019). https://doi.org/10.1177/1473325017700701

58. Mauthner, N.S., Parry, O., Backett-Milburn, K.: The data are out there, or are they? Implications for archiving and revisiting qualitative data. Sociology **32**, 733–745 (1998). https://doi.org/10.1177/0038038598032004006
59. Kastelle, T., Steen, J.: Ideas are not innovations. Prometheus **29** (2011). https://doi.org/10.1080/08109028.2011.608554
60. Sonnenberg, C., Vom Brocke, J.: Evaluations in the science of the artificial - Reconsidering the build-evaluate pattern in design science research. In: International Conference on Design Science Research in Information Systems, pp. 381–397 (2012). https://doi.org/10.1007/978-3-642-29863-9_28

Value Perception Divergence in 6G Smart City Deployments: A Cross-Use-Case Analysis of Key Value Indicators

Imesha Wedikkara Gedara[1(✉)], Vishanth Weerakkody[1], Jing Li[1], Uthayasankar Sivarajah[2], Luis Cordeiro[3], Filipe Cabral Pinto[4], and Alexandre Moron[5]

[1] University of Bradford, Richmond Road, Bradford BD7 1DP, UK
imeshadevindi99@gmail.com
[2] Grove Crescent, Kingston University London, Kingston Upon Thames, Surrey KT1 2EE, UK
[3] OneSource, Consultoria Informática Lda, N 12, 3030-384 Coimbra, Portugal
[4] Altice Labs, Rua Eng. José Ferreira Pinto Basto, 3810-106 Aveiro, Portugal
[5] Airbus Defence and Space, ZI du Palays, 31 Rue Des Cosmonautes, 31402 Toulouse, France

Abstract. Sixth-generation (6G) telecommunications is increasingly framed as societal infrastructure whose success should be assessed not only by technical Key Performance Indicators (KPIs) but also by Key Value Indicators (KVIs) capturing economic, social, environmental, and service-quality outcomes. Against a common assumption that stakeholder value perception is broadly homogeneous within a given vertical, this paper presents mixed-methods evidence of sharp intra-vertical divergence within the Smart Cities vertical. Using Phase 1 field-trial results from a European 6G pilot, we compare KVI assessments across smart city use cases, focusing on UC-CITIES-1 (Connected and Sensing City) and UC-CITIES-3 (Security Coordination/Public Protection and Disaster Relief- PPDR). Despite largely adequate KPI attainment in UC-CITIES-3, stakeholder service-quality value perception is systematically negative, confirmed by complete stochastic dominance whilst UC-CITIES-1 exhibits strongly positive KVI perception across all four value dimensions. This KPI-KVI decoupling illustrates that technical capability alone does not translate into perceived value in mission-critical contexts. Triangulating survey results with semi-structured interviews and focus groups, we introduce Legacy Entrenchment, technical lock-in, regulatory embedding, identity anchoring, and risk aversion as a moderating construct explaining this pattern. We discuss methodological implications: vertical-level aggregation can mask use-case-level rejection, making disaggregated KVI reporting a prerequisite for valid evidence.

Keywords: 6G · KVIs · smart cities · Legacy Entrenchment · PPDR

Published by Springer Nature Switzerland 2027
G. Viale Pereira et al. (Eds.): EGOV 2026, LNCS 16933, pp. 182–198, 2027.
https://doi.org/10.1007/978-3-032-35747-2_12

1 Introduction

The telecommunication industry has long been acknowledged as a powerful driver of economic, social and institutional transformation. Introducing sixth generation (6G) into the industry is a multi-year global effort focused on transitioning from current fifth generation (5G) standards to a fundamentally different architecture. Hence, 6G, the next telecommunication revolution, reframes more as a societal infrastructure than merely a connectivity upgrade. Hence, it demands and takes evaluation far beyond Key Performance Indicators (KPIs) used in history, such as low latency and high-speed connectivity (Ziegler et al., 2020; Osman, Bradford and Mitchell, 2024). The standard bodies, including the European Union (EU) and the European Smart Networks and Services Joint Undertaking (SNS JU), have also stood with this transition and positioned Key Value Indicators (KVIs) as first-class artefacts that complement evaluation in addition to the KPIs (Wikström et al., 2024; Kerboeuf et al., 2024). This reflects a broader shift in evaluation logic, from what networks can technically deliver to what value they create for stakeholders.

This creates a practical evaluation problem for current 6G trials: KVI reporting is increasingly expected at programme scale, yet the unit of analysis that is convenient for reporting such as 'the Smart Cities vertical' may not be the unit at which value is actually perceived. Recent SNS JU work notes both the growing importance of KVIs and the ongoing difficulty of qualifying and quantifying them in a way that supports standardisation and consistent assessment across projects (SNS JU, 2025). If stakeholder value perceptions differ strongly across use cases inside a single vertical, then vertical-level aggregation becomes not merely a coarse summary but potentially misleading evidence. This paper tests that risk empirically and derives implications for how KVI frameworks should be applied in trials.

However, this evaluation shift is a critical challenge for the current real 6G trials. The reason is, although KVI reporting has become mandatory at programme scale, the unit of analysis, which is generally the vertical, as an example, 'smart city vertical', is not explicitly where value is perceived by stakeholders in the real world. Whilst prior research acknowledges that stakeholder value perceptions vary across deployment contexts, KVI evaluation frameworks and SNS JU reporting conventions default to vertical-level aggregation—which, as we demonstrate, can suppress use-case-level rejection of a magnitude sufficient to mislead policy and procurement decisions. This study aims to address the particular research problem by empirically testing the extent and implications of intra-vertical divergence in KVI perception among different stakeholders.

For this empirical test, the study will particularly employ the 6G-PATH project, a large ICT initiative, funded by the Smart Networks and Services Joint Undertaking (SNS JU) and co-funded by the European Union (EU). During the first trials and pilots' phase of the project, the smart city domain revealed a particularly relevant context for this investigation. It consists of three different use cases covering the contexts: connected and sensing city (CASC), industrial logistics (IL), and PPDR. Although all these test cases fall within one vertical, these contexts differ significantly in terms of stakeholder identity, regulatory constraints, risk exposure, and institutional history (Gohar & Nencioni, 2021; Fernandez-Anez et al., 2018).

The phase-1 trials' and pilots' data of the CASC use case of the 6G-PATH project generate strongly positive KVI perceptions across all four value dimensions: social, economic, environmental sustainability and user experience. Comparatively, the PPDR use case exhibits systematic non-acceptance. This divergence is confirmed by the complete stochastic dominance (Cliff's delta $\delta = 1.000$; $p < 0.001$) despite largely adequate technical KPI performance. Hence, this KVI-KPI gap emphasizes that stakeholder value perception is not something that technical capability can solely explain, and beyond that, it necessitates a broader socio-institutional explanation.

Although previous literature has established the significance of KVIs and highlighted the fact that value creation is context-dependent, to our knowledge, this is among the first studies to provide field-trial evidence demonstrating how value perception diverges across different contexts within the same vertical (Wikström et al., Wikström et al., 2024). Further, only a minimal number of studies have focused on proving the relationship between KPIs and KVIs (Wymeersch et al., 2025; Wikström et al., 2024). At last, the existing literature does not have clear evidence on why PPDR contexts especially fail to generate positive value perceptions when technological adoption is required where institutional constraints and operational risk play a central role (Wymeersch et al., 2025). This study aims to fill these empirical gaps by introducing legacy entrenchment as a construct to explain the observed dissociation between technical performance and perceived value by providing empirical field-trial evidence.

This paper aims to answer three research questions as follows:

- Research Question (RQ) RQ1 - How does stakeholder-perceived value (measured using KVIs) differ systematically across different use case contexts within the Smart Cities vertical?
- RQ2 -What construct accounts for the decoupling of adequate KPI performance from negative KVI perception in PPDR mission-critical deployment contexts?
- RQ3- What are the methodological implications of intra-vertical KVI divergence for 6G evaluation framework design and programme-level reporting?

Addressing these questions, this study aims to make contributions in three ways. First, this study will provide empirical evidence to prove intra-vertical divergence in stakeholder value perception. It challenges the assumption of homogeneous value creation across a vertical. Whilst prior research acknowledges heterogeneity in value perceptions, the implications for programme-level KVI evaluation reporting remain unaddressed (Dirsehan & van Zoonen, 2022; Hamamurad et al., 2022; Habib et al., 2019). Furthermore, the study will theoretically contribute by introducing the Legacy Entrenchment construct, which consists of technical lock-in, identity anchoring, regulatory embedding, and risk aversion to justify and explain reasons for stakeholders to systematically reject 6G value perceptions in the PPDR context despite adequate technical performance. It will propose four testable propositions. Finally, the study will empirically contribute to demonstrating that use-case-level KVI analysis is essential for credible evaluation supported by triangulated data and mixed methodology.

2 Literature Review

2.1 Values-Driven KVI Frameworks

Recent European 6G work increasingly distinguishes technical performance indicators (KPIs) from value-oriented measures that assess wider economic, social, and environmental outcomes. A key development is the emergence of structured, values-driven methods for defining and assessing Key Value Indicators (KVIs) across use cases. Wikström et al. (2024) propose a five-step KVI framework intended to operationalise value outcomes in next-generation ICT development, explicitly positioning KVIs as a complement to KPIs and illustrating application in smart city contexts; they also note that early piloting in major SNS JU projects has already led to methodological refinements including agreeing a Key Value set and introducing enabler-KVIs. Alongside this, the 6G-IA societal values white paper (Wikström et al., 2022) provides a roadmap connecting societal needs, key values, and KVIs, reinforcing that value assessment is a first-class design and evaluation concern. Hexa-X-II D1.4 (Kerboeuf et al., 2024) further documents how KVIs are operationalised across use cases in the flagship European 6G programme, noting ongoing context-dependence in KVI selection.

Xiang et al. (2024) propose a systematic framework to incorporate value propositions for ICT projects from a demand perspective. The paper explores values in both the vertical and horizontal dimensions, where horizontal dimensions include economic, social, ecological, cultural, and strategic values and vertical dimensions include nation, industry, enterprise, and individual. However, the researcher still finds that it is challenging to validate an evaluation framework. The SNS JU KVI survey white paper (SNS JU, 2025) confirms that qualifying and quantifying KVIs for standardisation and cross-project alignment remains an open challenge. It demonstrates intra-vertical heterogeneity as a challenge and states that if it is undetected, it can invalidate aggregate KVI claims. Although these types of previous literature have established the significance of KVIs and proposed frameworks to measure KVIs, there is still a dearth of empirical evidence. Addressing these gaps, this paper aims to provide field-trial evidence that remains still under-researched in the literature.

2.2 Technology Adoption in Mission-Critical Contexts

Traditional technology adoption models such as the Technology Acceptance Model (TAM) limit the adoption in tightly regulated institutional contexts such as PPDR mission-critical environments (Malatji et al., 2020; O'Dea, 2025). According to Kirk et al. (2016), structural and institutional barriers such as legacy systems, technical incompatibility, unreliable networks and poor integration strongly shape the practice in mission-critical environments. This is supported by Walle and Turoff (2008), which reveals that TAM does not model structural adoption barriers in PPDR which include mandatory interoperability standards, regulatory certification requirements, and asymmetric failure consequences in life-safety contexts. Therefore, in these contexts, technology adoption decisions are not solely driven by user perceptions. Beyond that, they are shaped by regulatory requirements, interoperability mandates, and the potentially severe consequences of system failure (Malatji et al., 2020). When analysed further, it can be observed that these dimensions closely align with the legacy entrenchment constructs developed in this study. They indicate resistance to new technologies in mission-critical contexts is multi-layered and deeply embedded. The study done by Savunen et al. (2023) analyses the business and operational risks faced by mobile network operators in delivering next-generation public safety services. They reveal procurement uncertainty and operational continuity requirements as primary barriers. Therefore, these factors highlight the tendency of public safety organisations to prioritise reliability and proven performance over innovation. Therefore, to sum up, previous literature suggests that technology adoption in PPDR contexts is shaped by a range of factors, including institutional, technical, and socio-cultural.

3 Conceptual Model and Propositions

3.1 The KV → KVI → KVE → KPI Framework

This study adopts an evaluation logic which follows a value-driven architecture. The evaluation flows from Key Values (KVs), which represent fundamental societal objectives, to measure them through KVIs and then enable them via KVEs to measure technical performance using KPIs. This directional sequence stresses that instead of the traditional focus of technical performance-driven metrics, the evaluation should reset mindsets to originate from stakeholder-defined value perceptions and proceed towards technical realisation. Therefore, this framework emphasises that technical success is assessed against what stakeholders actually value. In literature this is proposed by Wikström et al. (2024) and adopted and advanced by the SNS JU (2025) working group white paper. This framework structures a framework which enables a systematic linkage between societal/stakeholder values and technical performance, allowing it to expose any misalignments as well.

3.2 Legacy Entrenchment

Legacy entrenchment can be introduced as a multi-dimensional, structurally embedded condition that disrupts the relationship between technical capability and perceived stakeholder value. This is observable in contexts where incumbent systems are deeply integrated into technical infrastructures, regulatory frameworks, professional identities, and risk management practices. In this research, legacy entrenchment intervenes in the KVIàKVI pathway by producing the observed decoupling between technical attainment and stakeholder evaluation. Conceptually, it acts as a moderating variable. It does not make any negative influence for stakeholders over the identification of theoretical capabilities of 6G. However, it prevents those capabilities from generating positive value perception under current deployment conditions. Figure 1 presents the conceptual model. It illustrates the moderating effect of legacy entrenchment for the pathway from KVI to KPI.

Although previous literature brings forth different related constructs, legacy entrenchment is conceptually distinct from several related constructs such as path dependence proposed by Sydow et al. (2009) and institutional inertia proposed by DiMaggio & Powell (1983). Because path dependence primarily discusses how past decisions inhibit present choices. Comparatively, legacy entrenchment focuses on active, present-orientated conditions. It moderates how new technologies are evaluated and mitigated through targeted intervention. Furthermore, legacy entrenchment differs from institutional inertia (DiMaggio & Powell, 1983), which is typically conceptualised at the organisational level. Instead of institutional inertia, legacy entrenchment operates across multiple interacting domains and extends its resistant factors beyond resistance constructs derived from the TAM model. Hence, legacy entrenchment is a structurally embedded condition that shapes individual perceptions, rather than emerging from them.

Based on the above-described KV → KVI → KVE → KPI framework and legacy entrenchment, Fig. 1 illustrates the conceptual model of the study.

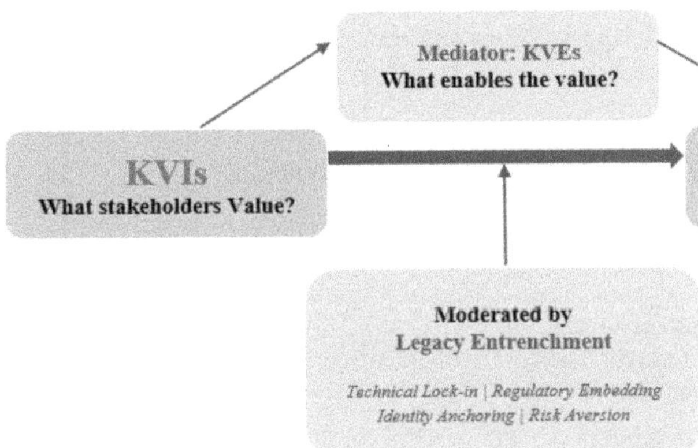

Fig. 1. Conceptual Model

The above conceptual model generates four propositions to test in this research, and they have derived from the conceptual model in Fig. 1.

- P1: Where Legacy Entrenchment is absent, adequate KPI attainment predicts positive KVI perception (Addresses RQ1)
- P2: Where Legacy Entrenchment is present, the KVI → KVE → KPI pathway is disrupted: adequate KPI attainment does not generate positive KVI perception (Addresses RQ2)
- P3: The four Legacy Entrenchment dimensions independently moderate the KVI → KPI pathway; single-dimension interventions are structurally insufficient to resolve adoption resistance (Addresses RQ2).
- P4: Intra-vertical KVI divergence can exceed inter-vertical variation, making use-case-level analysis the necessary unit for valid 6G value evaluation (Addresses RQ3)

4 Research Methodology

This study employs a mixed-methods design, combining quantitative survey data with qualitative data from semi-structured interviews and semi-structured focus group discussions (FGDs). The empirical basis is Phase 1 trial data from 6G-PATH, a Stream B SNS JU project co-funded by the EU, covering the smart cities vertical. Of its three smart city use cases, this study analyses the Connected and Sensing City (CASC) and PPDR use cases; the Automated Logistics use case lacked sufficient Phase 1 KVI data and is excluded.

Three instruments were deployed (Table 1). Surveys used a standardised structured questionnaire with a five-point Likert scale (1 = Strongly Disagree to 5 = Strongly Agree), organised under four KVI dimensions: Economic, Social, Environmental, and Service Quality. Semi-structured interviews (CASC: N = 9; PPDR: N = 5) followed a pre-defined guide covering perceived value, adoption barriers, institutional context, and technology trust, with probing permitted to follow participant-led narratives. Semi-structured FGDs (CASC: N = 2 groups; PPDR: N = 2 groups) used the same guide structure with open group dialogue. Both interviews and FGDs were conducted in person or online; notes were taken during sessions and transcribed into structured records immediately after each session.

Table 1. Summary of Primary Data Collection

Use case	Stakeholder Types	Number of Stakeholders	Data Collection Instruments
CASC use case	Urban tech professionals, city planners, Mayor, City council administrators	9	Semi-structured interviews
	Researchers, engineers, Urban tech professionals, city planners, City council administrators	47	Survey Questionnaires
	Researcher, Software Developer, Project Manager, Data Scientists, Senior Consultants	2	Semi-structured FGDs
PPDR use case	Operational firefighters, Security Coordinator	5	Semi-structured interviews
	Operational firefighters, industry professionals, data communication experts	2	Semi-structured FGDs
	Operational firefighters	63	Survey Questionnaires

PPDR participants were recruited across heterogeneous events, and dataset is therefore treated as a mixed-provenance sample. Qualitative sensitivity is applied by distinguishing operational PPDR respondents from non-operational participants where role metadata permits. Cross-method convergence; qualitative evidence from interviews and FGDs aligning directionally with survey patterns supports the primary inference of systematic non-acceptance. Sample heterogeneity is acknowledged as a key limitation.

For quantitative analysis, item means were computed identically from percentage distributions for both use cases. KPI–KVI gap robustness was confirmed under two normalisations: proportional (mean/5) and bounded ((mean − 1)/4), both yielding a stable gap of 0.32–0.47. Tests applied: Mann-Whitney U (one-tailed); Cliff's delta with 5,000-iteration bootstrap 95% CIs; Kruskal-Wallis H; Cronbach's alpha (at actual N: CASC N = 47; PPDR N = 63); and Spearman rank correlation. All computations used Stata. Qualitative data were analysed using manual thematic analysis (Braun & Clarke, 2006). Sessions were not audio-recorded to preserve operational confidentiality in PPDR contexts; notes taken during sessions were transcribed into structured records immediately after each interview and FGD. Coding was conducted manually by the lead researcher, with an initial codebook developed inductively from a first pass through all records. A second researcher independently cross-checked a sample of coded excerpts; disagreements were resolved by discussion. The codebook comprised five domains: trust and security, performance expectations, cost and procurement governance, professional identity and legacy systems, and adoption barriers. Qualitative themes were triangulated against survey distributions to confirm directional convergence.

All participants were informed of the study purpose and voluntary participation. Survey responses were anonymised and reported only in aggregate. Qualitative quotations were de-identified to remove personal identifiers. PPDR engagements followed host organisation protocols, and all data handling complied with 6G-PATH project General Data Protection Regulation (GDPR) obligations.

5 Results

5.1 KVI and KPI Analysis

The primary data analysis of this study arises from KVI data collection. Table 2 below summarises the dimension comparison of KVI data. It presents the mean sample standard deviation across the item means (± SD is between-item variability) and the gap. Further, they are supported by key percentage evidence for KVI items in the survey questionnaire. Based on the results, it is evident that all four dimensions present a large divergence between two use cases.

Table 2. KVI dimension comparison between two use cases

KVI Dimension	CASC Mean ± SD N = 47	PPDR Mean ± SD N = 63	Key Evidence (% distributions)	Gap
Economic	4.18 ± 0.23 (n = 13))	2.79 (n = 1)	CASC- 93.6% agree on accident/insurance cost reduction (mean 4.32) PPDR- 56% has identified cost as a critical adoption factor| only 12% agree 6G will positively impact dispatch costs	1.39
Social	4.05 ± 0.30 (n = 17)	2.96 ± 0.19 (n = 2)	CASC - 95.6% agree on emergency response enhancement as a social KV (mean 4.49, SD 0.65) | 91.5% agree on disaster preparedness as a KV (mean 4.30) PPDR- only 51% expect technology acceptance will be quick	1.08
Environmental	4.06 ± 0.27 (n = 6)	3.28 (n = 1)	CASC- 89.4% agree on Green House Gas (GHG) emission reduction (mean 4.17)| 91.5% agree on public transport quality improvement (mean 4.32) PPDR-91% neutral or disagree on environmental impact reduction of mission-critical communications	0.78

(*continued*)

Table 2. *(continued)*

KVI Dimension	CASC Mean ± SD N = 47	PPDR Mean ± SD N = 63	Key Evidence (% distributions)	Gap
Service Quality	4.19 ± 0.21 (n = 18)	2.13 ± 0.30 (n = 6)	CASC- 95.7% agree security measures are essential (mean 4.47, SD 0.58)| 65.96% strongly agreed on user privacy in data collection (mean 4.60-highest single-item score in dataset) PPDR-100% disagree or neutral on working better with 6G (mean 1.60, SD 0.49; no positive tail)| 74% dissatisfied (mean 2.01)	2.06

Based on the Table 2 results, there is a strong divergence in stakeholder value perceptions when compared with two different use cases. When the CASC use case exhibits higher scores across all value dimensions, PPDR remarkably presents lower values. The highest gap is observed in the service quality value dimension, and it indicates a fundamental difference in perceived system effectiveness. Compared to the PPDR use case, CASC reports high KVI scores supported by strong consensus among respondents. In contrast, PPDR deployment exhibits systematic non-acceptance.

The following Table 3 takes the highest divergent value category, service quality, out from the PPDR use case and analyses the item distribution as a percentage. It demonstrates a distribution with no positive tail. However, Cronbach's alpha for the particular use case is 0.941 (with 6 items, N = 63), and it confirms the non-acceptance pattern is internally coherent.

This study mainly focuses on KVIs, and KPI results will be utilised as supporting data for the primary analysis. Among the main four KPIs defined, the PPDR use case has achieved three targets in phase 1 trials: accordingly, DL throughput (>130 Mbps > target of 100 Mbps), latency (<20 ms), and application reliability (>99%). However, despite KPI target achievements, there is still a lack of positive value perceptions among stakeholders, which has led to a KPI-KVI paradox.

Table 3. UC-CITIES-3 Service Quality items

Survey Item	SA %	A %	N %	D %	SD %	Mean	SD
User satisfaction with 6G/5BG in mission-critical context	0%	3%	22%	49%	25%	2.01	0.77
Ease of use of 6G/B5G in mission-critical context	0%	2%	21%	65%	13%	2.14	0.64
Network reliability vs TETRA/TETRAPOL	0%	2%	40%	56%	3%	2.43	0.59
Data reliability vs legacy systems	0%	0%	32%	62%	6%	2.26	0.56
Overall trustworthiness of 6G vs legacy	0%	0%	38%	59%	3%	2.35	0.54
Will work better with this technology	0%	0%	0%	60%	40%	1.60	0.49
UC3 SQ subscale mean (6 items)						2.13	0.30

5.2 Statistical Evidence and the KPI-KVI Gap

Table 5 presents all statistical analyses to claim the magnitude and robustness of the observed divergence. The Mann-Whitney U test compares the service quality item means between the two use cases where $U = 108$ (theoretical maximum) and $n1 = 18$ and $n2 = 6$. This can be interpreted as every KV item in the CASC use case has been rated higher than every PPDR use case item. Further supporting this statistical analysis, effect size analysis identifies Cliff's delta is $\delta = 1.000$ (95% bootstrap CI [1.00, 1.00]). This indicates a complete non-overlap between the two distributions and reflects that there is at least a separation of 1.38 scale points between the lowest CASC item mean and the highest PPDR item mean.

Additional statistical tests such as Cronbach's alpha (CASC $\alpha = 0.989$ and PPDR $\alpha = 0.941$) confirm the internal validity of the findings. Further, according to the Kruskal-Wallis test, where $H = 168.60$ ($p < 0.001$), it reveals that within the PPDR deployment, negative perception varies across dimensions. In there, Service Quality (SQ) is being the most affected, and Environmental value is the least negative.

5.3 The KPI-KVI Gap

Based on the KPI analysis of the PPDR use case, KPI attainment was 0.75, as three out of four main KPIs were already achieved. When service quality KVIs are normalised in the PPDR use case, the mean/5 = 0.43, and the KPI-KVI gap is statistically 0.32. Further, when normalised as (mean-1)/4 = 0.28, the KPI-KVI gap is 0.47. Therefore, across both the normalisations, the gap is stable and evident to confirm that the KPI-KVI decoupling is not an artefact of scaling choice. Based on the Kruskal-Wallis test, H =

Table 4. Statistical Analysis

Type of Analysis	Method and Unit of Analysis	Statistic	p / CI	Sig
Inferential tests				
Mann-Whitney U Test (One tailed -Test (CASC SQ > PPDR SQ))	Unit: item-level means CASC - $n_1 = 18$, survey N = 47, PPDR - $n_2 = 6$, N = 63 H_0: UC1-SQ ≤ UC3-SQ H_1: UC1-SQ > UC3-SQ	U = 108 (max = 108)	p = 0.0002	p < 0.001 ***
Cliff's delta (δ) Effect size for Mann-Whitney	δ = (concordant − discordant)/total pairs = (108 − 0) / 108	δ = 1.000 (Maximum possible value)	N/A	Large |δ| > 0.474
Spearman rank correlation (ρ)	N/A	ρ = − 0.698	p < 0.001	p < 0.001 ***
Kruskal-Wallis H PPDR across KVI dimensions	Individual reconstructed scores pooled by dimension within UC3 (survey N = 63 per item). Groups: SQ (6 items × 63 = 378 scores, mean = 2.12), Economic (1 × 63 = 63, mean = 2.81), Social (2 × 63 = 126, mean = 2.96), Environmental (1 × 63 = 63, mean = 3.25). df = 3 (k − 1 = 4 − 1). Tests whether rejection is uniform or dimension specific	H = 168.60 df = 3	p < 0.001	p < 0.001 ***
Descriptive and reliability statistics				
KPI–KVI gap	Descriptive - no null hypothesis; KPI attainment = 0.75 (3/4 targets met)	Norm A: 0.324 Norm B: 0.467 *Range: 0.32–0.47*	N/A	Robust

(*continued*)

Table 4. (*continued*)

Type of Analysis	Method and Unit of Analysis	Statistic	p / CI	Sig
Cronbach's α - CASC	Descriptive reliability - no null hypothesis k = 18 items, N = 47	$\alpha = 0.989$	N/A	$\alpha \geq 0.90$
Cronbach's α - PPDR	Descriptive reliability - no null hypothesis k = 6 items, N = 63	$\alpha = 0.941$	N/A	$\alpha \geq 0.90$

168.60 ($p < 0.001$), and it states that rejection within the PPDR use case is not uniform. The most severely affected key value category is service quality, with a mean value of 2.13. Further, environmental value is least negative (mean 3.28).

5.4 The Legacy Entrenchment Construct and Proposition Assessment

Qualitative and quantitative evidence converge across five themes: trust and data security concerns (62% distrust 6G vs legacy in surveys; 'Our exchanges are precious and we don't want to be hacked'- Firefighter, FGD); performance expectations unmet ('Without reliability the solution will not be adopted' - Firefighter, FGD); cost and procurement governance (56% cite cost as critical; 'The decision level to buy or not is at a high level, far from end-users' - Fire Service Manager, interview); strong positive CASC convergence (95.6% agree emergency response enhancement; 'A quick reaction is increasingly important' -Mayor, interview; 95.7% agree security essential). This convergence of interview, FGD, and survey data confirms that value perception divergence is systematic, multi-dimensional, and context-dependent. Building on these findings, this section formalises Legacy Entrenchment as a multi-dimensional construct explaining the observed decoupling between KPIs and KVIs in PPDR contexts. Legacy Entrenchment comprises four interrelated dimensions: technical lock-in (Existing systems are so deeply embedded in physical infrastructure that replacing them requires rebuilding entire networks, making new technology adoption structurally impractical regardless of its technical advantages), regulatory embedding (Organisations are legally required to operate certified legacy systems, and no regulatory mandate yet exists for the emerging technology, leaving no compliant procurement pathway even when the technology is available), identity anchoring (Professional identity becomes bound to the technologies people routinely use and trust, causing new technologies to be perceived as foreign and threatening rather than superior, before any objective evaluation takes place), and risk aversion (Where the consequences of technology failure are severe and irreversible, the perceived cost of adopting an unproven system outweighs any anticipated benefit, producing systematic rejection independent of measured performance). These dimensions constrain the translation of technical capability into perceived value. None operate independently, they reinforce one another and therefore no single-dimension intervention is sufficient. Table 5 summarises the construct, linking each dimension to empirical evidence and theoretical grounding. The proposition assessment follows in Table 6.

Table 5. Legacy Entrenchment construct

Dimension	PPDR Use case Evidence	Distinction from Prior Constructs	Theoretical Anchor
Technical Lock-in	"*Going from narrowband to broadband implies changing our entire infrastructure*"- Fire Service Manager (At Interview)	Extends path dependence, not historical sunk cost but an active present-tense certification constraint that cannot be waived for procurement	Path dependence (Sydow et al., 2009)
Regulatory Embedding	PPDR agencies legally bound by ETSI TETRA mandates; MCX not mandated for PPDR procurement; *'The decision level to buy or not is at a high level, far from end-users'*- Fire Service Manager (interview, N = 5)	Extends institutional inertia, coercive isomorphism via regulatory mandate, not merely normative pressure	Institutional theory (DiMaggio & Powell, 1983)
Identity Anchoring	*"We only get TETRAPOL system today"* - Firefighter (FGD); professional self-identification with TETRA-based operations; 6G framed as alien rather than superior technology	Distinct from TAM ease-of-use, role-based identity attachment that precedes any assessment of 6G capability	Organisational identity Professional identity (Alvarez, 2008)
Risk Aversion	100% of UC3 survey respondents (N = 63) disagree/neutral on working better with 6G (mean 1.60, SD 0.49); "*Without reliability the solution will not be adopted*"- A Firefighter (FGD)	Distinct from TAM perceived usefulness, PPDR failure cost is life, an asymmetric calculus producing categorical rejection	Prospect theory (Ruggeri et al., 2020), Perceived risk from dread (Gregory & Mendelsohn, 1993)

The above results provide strong support for all four propositions and Table 6 presents a summary.

Table 6. Proposition Assessment

Proposition	Assessment against Phase 1 findings
P1:	Supported -CASC use case - (survey $N = 47$; interviews $N = 9$; FGDs $N = 2$) exhibits positive KVI perception across all four dimensions (means 4.05–4.19). Spearman $\rho = -0.698$ ($p < 0.001$, $n = 54$ items) confirms higher-performing items attract greater consensus
P2:	Supported. PPDR (survey $N = 63$; interviews $N = 5$; FGDs $N = 2$ groups): KPI attainment 0.75; SQ mean 2.13; KPI-KVI gap 0.32–0.47 (robust); Mann-Whitney $U = 108$ (max = 108); Cliff's $\delta = 1.000$
P3:	Supported by triangulation across survey ($N = 63$), interviews ($N = 5$), and FGDs ($N = 2$ groups). All four dimensions simultaneously evidenced
P4:	Supported. SQ gap $\Delta = 2.06$ (CASC = 4.19; PPDR = 2.13). Vertical aggregation $\approx$3.5 - masking complete distributional rejection in PPDR

6 Discussion and Implications

This study's findings provide methodological, theoretical, and policy insights for 6G evaluation in smart city contexts.

What we learned -Vertical-level aggregation can produce misleading evidence. A simple average of Service Quality scores across the two use cases CASC (4.19) and PPDR (2.13) yields approximately 3.5, classifying the Smart Cities vertical as moderate-positive whilst concealing complete rejection in one deployment. This directly addresses RQ3: use-case-level analysis is a prerequisite for valid KVI evaluation, not a methodological preference.

Why it matters -Theoretically, the study findings emphasised that the link between technical performance (KPIs) and perceived value (KVIs) is still context-dependent and not universal. Legacy Entrenchment explains this decoupling through the simultaneous operation of technical, regulatory, identity-based, and risk-related factors that reinforce one another systemically resistance therefore cannot be resolved by addressing any single dimension in isolation (Rinta-Kahila et al., 2023). The implication is not only methodological but organisational: where KVI reporting guides programme learning, standardisation inputs, or procurement narratives, the reporting unit must match the locus of value perception. In ecosystems where KVIs are still being refined (SNS JU, 2025), depicting intra-vertical heterogeneity accurately is itself a form of rigour aggregate scores risk masking acute rejection in safety-critical contexts.

Where it holds- Legacy Entrenchment is context-specific. CASC stakeholders operate where none of the four dimensions apply, and their perceptions remain strongly positive, confirming that the same technology can simultaneously generate acceptance and rejection within the same vertical depending on institutional and operational context.

From a policy perspective, effective intervention requires addressing all four dimensions simultaneously advancing 6G MCX regulatory certification for PPDR procurement, ensuring transparent data governance, enabling phased migration with legacy fallback, and engaging operational PPDR professionals from the earliest trial stages. These recommendations extend prior work on public safety adoption by providing an empirically grounded account of why structural barriers persist.

7 Concluding Remarks

This paper provides mixed-methods field-trial evidence that stakeholder-perceived 6G value can diverge sharply within a single Smart Cities vertical. In our Phase 1 comparison, UC-CITIES-1 exhibits consistently positive KVI assessments across economic, social, environmental, and service-quality dimensions, whereas UC-CITIES-3 (PPDR) exhibits systematic non-acceptance in service-quality perception despite meeting most reported technical KPI targets. This KPI–KVI decoupling confirmed by complete stochastic dominance indicates that technical competence is not, by itself, sufficient to generate perceived value in mission-critical contexts.

To explain this pattern, we introduce Legacy Entrenchment technical lock-in, regulatory embedding, identity anchoring, and risk aversion as a moderating construct that disrupts the KPI $\rightarrow$ KVI pathway in PPDR deployments. Methodologically, the findings imply that use-case-level KVI analysis is a prerequisite for valid evidence; vertical-level aggregation can mask both success and rejection and thus mislead evaluation and reporting. Limitations include incomplete KVI coverage for UC-CITIES-2 and heterogeneous sampling across UC-CITIES-3 engagement events. Future work will strengthen external validity through stratified sampling of operational PPDR roles, longitudinal Phase 2 comparisons, and explicit measurement of Legacy Entrenchment dimensions to test the proposed moderation mechanism more directly.

References

Alvarez, R.: Examining technology, structure and identity during an Enterprise System implementation. Inf. Syst. J. **18**(2), 203–224 (2008)

Chowdhury, M.Z., Shahjalal, M., Ahmed, S., Jang, Y.M.: 6G wireless communication systems: applications, requirements, technologies, challenges, and research directions. IEEE Open J. Commun. Soc. **1**(1), 1 (2020)

DiMaggio, P.J., Powell, W.W.: The iron cage revisited: institutional isomorphism and collective rationality in organizational fields. Am. Sociol. Rev. **48**(2), 147–160 (1983). https://doi.org/10.2307/2095101

Dirsehan, T., van Zoonen, L.: Smart city technologies from the perspective of technology acceptance. IET Smart Cities (2022). https://doi.org/10.1049/smc2.12040

Fernandez-Anez, V., Fernández-Güell, J.M., Giffinger, R.: Smart City implementation and discourses: an integrated conceptual model. The case of Vienna. Cities **78**, 4 (2018)

Gohar, A., Nencioni, G.: The role of 5G technologies in a smart city: the case for intelligent transportation system. Sustainability **13**(9), 5188 (2021)

Goldstein, J.E., Neimark, B., Garvey, B., Phelps, J.: Unlocking "lock-in" and path dependency: a review across disciplines and socio-environmental contexts. World Dev. **161**, 106116 (2023). https://doi.org/10.1016/j.worlddev.2022.106116

Gregory, R., Mendelsohn, R.: Perceived risk, dread, and benefits. Risk Anal. **13**(3), 259–264 (1993). https://doi.org/10.1111/j.1539-6924.1993.tb01077.x

Habib, A., Alsmadi, D., Prybutok, V.R.: Factors that determine residents' acceptance of smart city technologies. Behav. Inf. Technol. **39**(6), 610–623 (2019)

Hamamurad, Q.H., Jusoh, N.M., Ujang, U.: Factors affecting stakeholder acceptance of a Malaysian smart city. Smart Cities **5**(4), 1508–1535 (2022)

Imoize, A.L., Adedeji, O., Tandiya, N., Shetty, S.: 6G enabled smart infrastructure for sustainable society: opportunities, challenges, and research roadmap. Sensors **21**(5), 1709 (2021). https://doi.org/10.3390/s21051709

Kerboeuf, S., Porambage, P., Jain, A., et al.: Design methodology for 6G end-to-end system: Hexa-X-II perspective. IEEE Open J. Commun. Soc. 1–1 (2024). https://doi.org/10.1109/ojcoms.2024.3398504

Kirk, J.W., Sivertsen, D.M., Petersen, J., Nilsen, P., Petersen, H.V.: Barriers and facilitators for implementing a new screening tool in an emergency department: A qualitative study applying the Theoretical Domains Framework. Journal of Clinical Nursing (2016)

Malatji, W.R., Eck, R.V., Zuva, T.: Understanding the usage, modifications, limitations and criticisms of technology acceptance model (TAM). Adv. Sci. Technol. Eng. Syst. J. **5**(6), 113–117 (2020)

O'Dea, M.: Editorial: "Are technology acceptance models still fit for purpose?" J. Univ. Teach. Learn. Pract. **21**(08) (2025)

Osman, H., Bradford, J., Mitchell, S.: Bridging the gap between 6G technologies and societal values: a comprehensive analysis of key value indicators (KVIs) and business models. In: 2022 IEEE Wireless Communications and Networking Conference (WCNC) (2024)

Rinta-Kahila, T., Penttinen, E., Lyytinen, K.: Getting trapped in technical debt: sociotechnical analysis of a legacy system's replacement. MIS Q. **47**(1), 1–32 (2023)

Ruggeri, K., et al.: Replicating patterns of prospect theory for decision under risk (2020)

Savunen, T., Hämmäinen, H., Kilkki, K., Kekolahti, P.: The role of mobile network operators in next-generation public safety services. Telecommun. Policy **47**(3) (2023)

SNS JU. 6G KVIS -SNS PROJECTS INITIAL SURVEY RESULTS 2025 Smart Networks and Services Joint Undertaking (SNS JU) Test Measurements and Validation Working Group (2025)

Sydow, J., Schreyögg, G., Koch, J.: Organizational path dependence: opening the black box. Acad. Manag. Rev. **34**(4), 689–709 (2009)

Walle, de, B.V., Turoff, M.: Decision support for emergency situations. Inf. Syst. E-Bus. Manag. **6**(3), 295–316 (2008)

Wikström, G., et al.: Key value indicators: a framework for values-driven next-generation ICT solutions. Telecommun. Policy 102778–102778 (2024)

Wikström, G., et al.: What societal values will 6G address? Zenodo (CERN European Organization for Nuclear Research) (2022)

Wymeersch, H., et al.: 6G positioning and sensing through the lens of sustainability, inclusiveness, and trustworthiness. IEEE Wirel. Commun. **32**(1), 68–75 (2025)

Xiang, P., Wei, M., Liu, H., Wu, L., Qi, J.: How does technological value drive 6G development? Explanation from a systematic framework. Telecommunications Policy (2024)

Ziegler, V., Viswanathan, H., Flinck, H., Hoffmann, M., Raisanen, V., Hatonen, K.: 6G Architecture to connect the worlds. IEEE Access **8**, 173508–173520 (2020)

Human Judgment Risk in AI-Mediated Digital Government: A Configurational Perspective on Overconfidence and Institutional Controls

Youngmin Cho and HunYeong Kwon(✉)

School of Cyber Security, Korea University, Seoul, Korea
{ifman,khy0}@korea.ac.kr

Abstract. Generative AI is rapidly diffusing across digital government operations, reshaping how administrative judgments are formed and validated. While existing AI governance research has focused on algorithmic transparency, accountability, and regulatory design, far less attention has been paid to how reliance on AI alters the judgment processes of public sector users and produces new forms of vulnerability.

This study examines vulnerability in AI-mediated administrative environments not as the average effect of a single factor, but as patterns associated with the alignment of multiple conditions. We conceptualize Human Judgment Risk as the likelihood of inaccurate or insufficiently verified judgment under AI-mediated conditions, particularly when self-assessed capability diverges from observed task performance. The study focuses on three conditions: AI usage intensity, the Self–Actual Gap between self-assessed and observed performance, and institutional control environments. Using experimental data from 177 participants, we explore whether specific condition alignments are associated with concentrated risk patterns.

Approximately 28% of participants were classified as overconfident, rating their own performance higher than their observed task outcomes. AI usage intensity alone was not a strong independent predictor of security task performance. However, 13% of the sample combined high AI usage with overconfidence. Overconfidence rates were substantially higher among participants using non-certified devices. Within the high-AI-usage group, a 26.4 percentage-point difference was observed between certified and non-certified device environments.

These findings suggest that vulnerability in AI-mediated digital government does not stem primarily from lack of knowledge. Rather, risk appears to emerge when technological reliance and judgment miscalibration interact within institutional control environments. The study shifts AI governance discussions from a narrow focus on technical system oversight toward the role of human judgment structures in administrative settings, and proposes a configurational perspective for understanding AI-mediated judgment risk.

Keywords: Digital Government · Generative AI · Human Judgment Risk

Published by Springer Nature Switzerland 2027
G. Viale Pereira et al. (Eds.): EGOV 2026, LNCS 16933, pp. 199–213, 2027.
https://doi.org/10.1007/978-3-032-35747-2_13

1 Introduction

Generative AI is rapidly spreading across digital government operations. It is used to draft policy documents, summarize materials, prepare administrative reports, and generate responses to citizen inquiries. As these tools become embedded in routine workflows, they do more than increase efficiency. They reshape how administrative judgments are formed, framed, and validated. This shift raises a governance question: when AI systems structure the initial basis of decision-making, where does risk reside?

Existing research in digital government and AI governance has focused largely on algorithmic transparency, explainability, accountability, and institutional oversight. These concerns remain central. However, in generative AI environments, risk cannot be located solely within technical systems. When AI outputs provide the starting point for administrative reasoning, human actors often move into a reviewing or endorsing role. Under such conditions, vulnerability may emerge from the structure of human–AI interaction rather than from algorithmic malfunction alone.

Research on human–AI interaction has identified automation bias and overconfidence as recurring phenomena. At the same time, security awareness research has measured individual capability primarily in terms of knowledge and compliance behavior. Yet these strands of research tend to isolate single dimensions—technical safeguards, trust, or knowledge level—without examining how AI usage intensity, miscalibration between self-assessment and observed performance, and institutional control conditions combine to produce judgment vulnerability.

This study addresses that gap by asking:

How do AI usage intensity, the Self–Actual Gap between self-assessed and observed performance, and institutional control conditions combine to form Human Judgment Risk in digital government environments?

Rather than estimating the net causal effect of individual variables, the study examines how specific configurations of conditions are associated with elevated judgment risk. Risk is not treated as the outcome of AI use alone. It is understood as emerging when high AI reliance aligns with judgment miscalibration under particular control environments.

To explore this structure, we conducted an experimental study with 177 participants who completed survey instruments and judgment-based security tasks. Approximately 28% of participants were classified as overconfident, rating their performance higher than their observed outcomes. High AI usage alone was not a strong independent predictor of task performance. However, 13% of the sample combined high AI usage with overconfidence. Device certification conditions further differentiated risk patterns, with a substantial difference in overconfidence rates observed within the high-AI group.

The study makes three contributions. First, it reframes the introduction of generative AI in digital government as a question of human judgment risk rather than solely technical control. Second, it conceptualizes vulnerability as a configurational alignment of conditions, extending AI governance debates beyond single-factor explanations. Third, it provides empirical evidence that institutional controls can moderate specific risk configurations.

The remainder of the paper proceeds as follows. Section 2 reviews relevant literature and identifies the research gap. Section 3 presents the analytical framework. Section 4 reports the empirical findings. Section 5 discusses governance implications. Section 6 concludes.

2 Background and Related Work

2.1 AI Governance in Digital Government

Digital government has long relied on information technology to improve efficiency and transparency. The introduction of generative AI, however, alters not only administrative workflows but also how decision-relevant information is constructed. Reports document the rapid diffusion of generative AI in drafting policy documents, automating citizen responses, and summarizing official materials [1, 2]. In many cases, AI outputs now shape the starting point of administrative reasoning.

Governance frameworks such as the OECD AI Principles, the EU AI Act, and the NIST AI Risk Management Framework emphasize transparency, accountability, bias mitigation, and system-level oversight [3–6]. These approaches primarily conceptualize risk as residing in technical systems or regulatory gaps. Yet in AI-mediated settings, public officials interpret and validate AI-generated outputs. Under such conditions, vulnerability may emerge from the interaction between human judgment and AI outputs rather than from algorithmic malfunction alone [7, 8].

Cognitive research shows that discrepancies between self-assessed competence and observed performance increase error likelihood [9, 10]. Studies on automation bias similarly demonstrate that reliance on automated outputs can shape decision outcomes [11, 12]. If such miscalibration occurs in administrative contexts, its implications extend beyond individual mistakes to questions of public trust and institutional legitimacy [13, 14]. Empirical analyses that integrate these dimensions within digital government remain limited.

2.2 Human–AI Interaction and Judgment Miscalibration

Generative AI differs from earlier automation systems in that it produces linguistically structured outputs requiring interpretation rather than simple execution. Human–automation research has documented automation bias and algorithm aversion, with trust levels varying across contexts [11, 12, 15–17].

Most of this literature focuses on trust or attitudes toward AI. Less attention has been paid to how accurately users assess their own evaluative capacity. Overconfidence research demonstrates systematic gaps between subjective assessment and objective performance [9, 10]. In generative AI environments, such gaps may become consequential when users overestimate their ability to detect inaccuracies in AI-generated outputs.

Accordingly, vulnerability may arise not from AI use itself, but from the alignment of reliance and miscalibrated self-assessment.

2.3 Limitations of Security Awareness Research in AI-Mediated Contexts

Security awareness research traditionally emphasizes knowledge, attitudes, and compliance behavior as determinants of secure conduct [18–21]. While these models show that training can improve performance, they are primarily knowledge-centered and often treat vulnerability as the linear effect of individual variables.

In AI-mediated administrative settings, however, knowledge alone does not ensure accurate evaluation of AI outputs. Moreover, discrepancies between self-perception and actual performance are not consistently incorporated into awareness measures [22]. Existing models rarely examine how such discrepancies interact with technological reliance or institutional context.

This suggests the need to reconsider security awareness beyond knowledge acquisition, incorporating judgment calibration and condition alignment.

2.4 Research Gap and the Need for a Configurational Framework

AI governance research emphasizes regulatory and technical safeguards. Human–AI interaction studies focus on trust and bias. Security awareness research centers on knowledge and compliance. What remains underexplored is how AI usage intensity, calibration failure, and institutional control conditions jointly shape vulnerability in digital government.

Few empirical studies treat judgment miscalibration as a structured risk condition within administrative contexts, and even fewer examine how institutional controls moderate such configurations. To address this gap, the present study conceptualizes risk as the alignment of conditions rather than the effect of a single variable. By analyzing the configuration of AI usage intensity, Self–Actual Gap status, and institutional control environments, the study extends AI governance debates toward a framework that explicitly incorporates human judgment structures.

3 Analytical Framework

3.1 Conceptualizing Human Judgment Risk

The integration of generative AI into digital government reshapes the cognitive structure of public decision-making. AI systems increasingly perform tasks such as information retrieval, summarization, classification, and draft generation. In doing so, they influence how information is interpreted before final decisions are validated. Under these conditions, risk cannot be understood solely in terms of algorithmic malfunction or regulatory gaps. It may also emerge within the interaction structure between human users and AI-generated outputs.

This study conceptualizes this phenomenon as Human Judgment Risk. In this study, Human Judgment Risk refers to the increased likelihood of inaccurate or insufficiently verified judgment in AI-mediated administrative environments. Rather than simple calculation error, the concept refers to instability in judgment that may emerge when self-assessed capability diverges from observed task performance under particular organizational and technological conditions.

Existing literature has approached judgment risk from two main perspectives. Technology-centered approaches emphasize algorithmic bias, data limitations, or model performance constraints, while behavioral approaches focus on automation bias, trust calibration, and cognitive limitations of users. Although both perspectives identify important mechanisms, they primarily explain risk through the effects of individual variables.

In digital government settings, generative AI typically augments rather than replaces human decision-making. Public officials remain responsible for interpreting and approving AI-generated outputs. Under such conditions, vulnerability is unlikely to be explained by AI performance or user attitude alone. High AI usage, for example, does not necessarily imply greater risk if users accurately recognize the limits of their evaluative capability. Conversely, even moderate AI usage may become problematic when self-assessment substantially exceeds observed performance.

From this perspective, Human Judgment Risk is approached not as a linear outcome of single predictors, but as a pattern potentially associated with the alignment of multiple conditions. In particular, this study focuses on the relationship among AI usage intensity, judgment calibration status, and institutional control environments. This perspective differs from regression-oriented approaches that primarily estimate additive or independent variable effects.

Accordingly, this study adopts a configurational perspective to explore whether vulnerability patterns become concentrated under specific condition alignments in AI-mediated administrative environments. The concept of Human Judgment Risk provides the theoretical foundation for the exploratory analysis that follows.

3.2 Operational Definition of the Self–Actual Gap and the State of Judgment Calibration

One core condition associated with Human Judgment Risk is the discrepancy between self-assessed competence and observed task performance. This study conceptualizes that discrepancy as the Self–Actual Gap. It refers to the difference between how individuals perceive their own evaluative ability and how they perform on the same judgment task under measurable conditions.

Research on overconfidence has long examined the misalignment between subjective confidence and objective performance [9, 10]. Building on this tradition, the present study interprets such misalignment as a matter of judgment calibration. Calibration refers to the degree to which self-assessment corresponds to observed performance. When self-assessment closely matches observed outcomes, judgment is considered calibrated. When self-assessment consistently exceeds observed performance, calibration failure is assumed.

In the empirical design, participants reported their perceived competence before or alongside completing structured judgment tasks. Actual performance was measured using task accuracy scores. The Self–Actual Gap was calculated as the standardized difference between self-assessed score and observed performance score. Positive values indicate overestimation, reflecting overconfidence, whereas negative values indicate underestimation.

For analytical purposes, the Self–Actual Gap was initially measured as a continuous variable. To examine subgroup patterns, participants were subsequently categorized into OVER, ACCURATE, and UNDER groups using ± 0.5 standard deviation thresholds. Scores above $+0.5$ SD were classified as OVER, scores between -0.5 and $+0.5$

SD as ACCURATE, and scores below −0.5 SD as UNDER. The OVER category was interpreted as the form of judgment miscalibration most directly relevant to the present study's risk perspective.

Importantly, the Self–Actual Gap is not treated as a fixed psychological trait. In AI-mediated environments, calibration failure may function as a structural vulnerability condition. Users who substantially overestimate their evaluative capability under high AI usage conditions may be less likely to critically scrutinize AI-generated outputs. Under such circumstances, vulnerability may emerge not solely from algorithmic limitations, but from the alignment between perceived competence, technological reliance, and surrounding institutional conditions.

Although underestimation may also influence reliance on AI-generated outputs, the present study focuses primarily on overestimation because it more directly reflects the risk of insufficient verification under perceived competence.

Defined in this way, the Self–Actual Gap functions as one analytical condition within the broader framework of Human Judgment Risk. The study examines whether vulnerability patterns become concentrated when calibration failure aligns with high AI usage and weaker institutional control environments.

3.3 Conceptualization of AI Usage Intensity as a Risk Condition

In AI-mediated administrative environments, risk cannot be explained by the mere presence or absence of AI tools. Generative AI is gradually embedded in digital government workflows, and public officials engage with it at varying levels. For this reason, the study treats AI usage not as a binary variable, but as a continuous condition reflecting the degree to which AI intervenes in the judgment process.

AI usage intensity refers to the frequency and extent to which individuals rely on generative AI during task performance. It captures the degree of functional dependence on AI outputs in activities such as drafting, summarizing, or generating decision-relevant information. This construct differs from simple access to AI tools or attitudinal acceptance. Within the same organization, some officials may use AI as a supplementary reference, while others may depend on it to structure initial reasoning or produce core analytical content. These differences alter the cognitive architecture of decision-making.

Prior human–AI interaction research has often focused on trust, perceived usefulness, or acceptance. The present study shifts attention from attitude to reliance. As usage intensity increases, AI-generated outputs are more likely to shape the initial framing of administrative reasoning. Human actors then operate primarily in a reviewing or revising capacity. Under such conditions, the effectiveness of judgment calibration becomes critical. When evaluative capacity is overestimated, AI outputs may be adopted with insufficient scrutiny.

AI usage intensity, however, is not assumed to produce risk independently. High reliance does not automatically generate vulnerability if users accurately assess their own limits. Conversely, even moderate reliance may become problematic when calibration failure is present. The meaning of AI usage intensity therefore depends on its alignment with the Self–Actual Gap and with institutional control conditions.

Empirically, AI usage intensity is measured through self-reported frequency indicators. For configurational analysis, cases are categorized into higher and lower usage conditions based on defined thresholds. The purpose of this classification is not to estimate average marginal effects, but to identify whether particular combinations of conditions are associated with elevated Human Judgment Risk.

In this framework, AI usage intensity represents the degree of structural intervention of generative AI in the judgment process. It functions as a core condition whose implications vary depending on its interaction with calibration status and institutional controls.

3.4 Institutional Control as a Risk Mitigation Condition

Digital government operates within structured institutional control environments. Policies, procedural safeguards, technical standards, and audit mechanisms are designed to reduce the likelihood of administrative error and to preserve public accountability. In this study, institutional control is conceptualized as a condition that moderates the formation of Human Judgment Risk.

Institutional control encompasses formal and informal mechanisms established to manage organizational risk. It may be situated within broader Governance, Risk & Compliance (GRC) structures, where technical safeguards and policy-based oversight intersect. Traditionally, such controls include access management, authentication protocols, monitoring systems, and compliance review procedures. These mechanisms are intended to maintain operational integrity and regulatory conformity.

In AI-mediated environments, however, the function of institutional control extends beyond system protection. It may shape the context in which human actors interpret and validate AI-generated outputs. Controls such as certified device environments, standardized review procedures, and policy-based verification protocols can structure how AI outputs are scrutinized. In doing so, they may reduce the likelihood that calibration failure translates into decision distortion.

In the empirical analysis, device certification status is used as an observable proxy for institutional control. Certification indicates compliance with defined security standards and reflects the presence of structured oversight conditions. Such environments may signal stronger procedural discipline and heightened awareness of risk management practices. While certification does not eliminate cognitive bias, it may influence how AI tools are embedded within decision processes.

Institutional control is not assumed to exert uniform effects across all situations. When AI usage intensity is low and judgment calibration is accurate, its moderating role may be limited. By contrast, under conditions of high AI reliance combined with substantial Self–Actual Gap, institutional control may act as a constraining factor that mitigates risk escalation. For this reason, institutional control is treated not as an independent causal variable, but as a configurational condition whose relevance emerges in interaction with other factors.

This framing repositions AI governance in digital government. Rather than attributing vulnerability solely to technical flaws or individual cognitive limitations, it highlights how institutional design can shape the interaction between human judgment and AI outputs. The empirical analysis that follows examines whether institutional control moderates specific configurations associated with elevated Human Judgment Risk, thereby informing the design of governance mechanisms in AI-mediated administrative settings.

3.5 Configurational Perspective on Human Judgment Risk

This study approaches Human Judgment Risk from a configurational perspective rather than as the average effect of isolated variables. The approach differs from linear models that primarily estimate the independent contribution of each predictor to an outcome.

Regression-based methods are useful for identifying marginal effects. However, in AI-mediated decision environments, it is difficult to assume that risk increases in a linear or additive manner as any single factor rises. High AI usage intensity, for example, does not necessarily imply elevated judgment risk. The implications of AI reliance may vary depending on judgment calibration status and surrounding institutional control conditions. Under such circumstances, average-effect estimation alone may overlook structurally distinct vulnerability patterns.

A configurational perspective assumes that outcomes may become concentrated under particular alignments of conditions rather than emerging from a single cause [23]. In complex administrative environments, the relevance of one condition often depends on its relationship with others. This perspective is particularly relevant to AI-mediated governance, where technological reliance, human judgment, and institutional environments are closely connected.

Guided by this perspective, the present study compares combinations of three analytical conditions: AI usage intensity, Self–Actual Gap status, and institutional control environment. The objective is not to estimate precise causal magnitude or to establish a formal configurational causal model. Rather, the study explores whether Human Judgment Risk tends to become concentrated under specific condition alignments.

This perspective contributes to AI governance research in two ways. First, it reframes vulnerability not simply as a defect attributable to technical systems or individual bias, but as a condition associated with particular contextual alignments. Second, it enables examination of whether institutional controls are associated with reduced vulnerability under certain organizational and technological conditions.

The analysis does not employ formal configurational techniques such as fuzzy-set Qualitative Comparative Analysis (fsQCA), nor does it attempt to estimate comprehensive causal effects. Instead, the study adopts configurational logic as an exploratory analytical perspective for comparing subgroup patterns in AI-mediated digital government environments.

4 Empirical Analysis

4.1 Research Design and Sample Characteristics

To examine patterns associated with Human Judgment Risk in AI-mediated environments, the study employed a combined survey and judgment-task design. A total of 177 adult participants from diverse professional backgrounds were included in the final analysis. Participants were recruited online and completed the study anonymously.

The research consisted of two stages. In the first stage, participants responded to survey items measuring AI usage intensity, self-assessed competence, device environment, and occupational background. AI usage intensity was operationalized as the reported frequency of using generative AI tools in work- or task-related activities.

In the second stage, participants completed a structured judgment task composed of security-related identification items, including AI-generated content. Although the task does not directly replicate the full complexity of administrative decision-making, it was designed as an exploratory proxy for evaluative judgment under AI-mediated conditions. Task performance accuracy was recorded as an objective indicator of evaluative capability. Self-assessed competence was measured through survey items asking participants to rate their perceived ability to identify security-related issues.

The Self–Actual Gap was calculated as the standardized difference between self-assessed score and observed performance score. Positive values indicate overestimation and were interpreted as calibration failure. For subgroup comparison, the continuous gap measure was categorized into OVER, ACCURATE, and UNDER conditions using $\pm$ 0.5 standard deviation thresholds.

The sample included both IT and non-IT professionals. Occupational background was examined in baseline comparisons as a contextual factor potentially associated with performance variation. However, the primary analytical focus of the study is the alignment among AI usage intensity, calibration status, and institutional control conditions rather than occupational difference itself.

Institutional control was operationalized through device certification status. Specifically, the use of devices certified under the Common Criteria (CC), based on ISO/IEC 15408, was used as a proxy indicator of structured security control environments. While certification does not directly measure cognitive discipline or causally determine judgment quality, it reflects the presence of standardized compliance and oversight conditions within which AI tools are used.

The objective of the empirical analysis is not to estimate precise causal magnitudes or formal interaction effects, but to explore whether elevated Human Judgment Risk becomes concentrated under particular alignments of conditions. Accordingly, the analysis emphasizes subgroup patterns and proportional differences across contextual conditions.

Table 1. Distribution of Self–Actual Gap and Risk Configurations (N = 177).

Variable	Category	N	%
Total Sample	–	177	100
Self–Actual Gap	UNDER	71	40.1
	ACCURATE	57	32.2
	OVER (Overconfidence)	49	27.7
Core Risk (High-AI ∩ OVER)	–	23	13
Strict Risk (High-AI ∩ OVER ∩ No Certified Device)	–	21	12

4.2 Descriptive Statistics and Baseline Comparisons Across Groups

Task accuracy and self-assessed competence were first examined. On average, self-assessment exceeded observed performance, indicating the presence of calibration failure (Self–Actual Gap > 0) among a subset of participants.

IT professionals scored 13.1 points higher than non-IT participants on the judgment task ($p < .001$, $g \approx 0.50$), indicating an association between professional background and performance. However, occupational differences are not central to the configurational analysis.

High-AI users scored 2.4 points higher than low-AI users ($p = .007$, $g \approx 0.27$), suggesting that AI usage intensity alone does not uniformly degrade accuracy. GPT-generated items were identified more accurately than human-authored items (89.3% vs. 75.1%, $p = .027$), indicating variation in item difficulty.

Based on the Self–Actual Gap, 27.7% of participants were classified as overconfident. Among the full sample, 13% combined high AI usage with calibration failure. Under a stricter definition requiring both conditions, approximately 12% fell into the high-risk configuration.

Institutional control conditions further differentiated outcomes. Calibration failure occurred in 33.3% of non-certified device users compared to 5.6% of certified users. Within the high-AI group, the difference was more pronounced (29.8% vs. 3.4%), a 26.4 percentage-point gap.

Overall, these baseline comparisons suggest that elevated Human Judgment Risk aligns with specific combinations of reliance, calibration status, and control environment rather than with isolated variables.

Table 2. Baseline Group Comparisons on Security Awareness Performance

Comparison	Mean (Group 1)	Mean (Group 2)	Mean Difference	p-value	Hedges' g
IT vs Non-IT	84.9	71.8	+ 13.1	< .001	0.50
High-AI vs Low-AI	79.7	77.3	+ 2.4	.007	0.27
GPT vs Human Items	89.3	75.1	+ 14.2	.027	0.46

4.3 Configurational Analysis of Condition Combinations

The descriptive results presented above indicate variation across individual conditions. The central objective of this study, however, is to determine whether Human Judgment Risk concentrates in particular combinations of conditions rather than in isolated variables. To that end, AI usage intensity, calibration status (Self–Actual Gap), and institutional control environment were analyzed jointly.

The first comparison examined the alignment of AI usage intensity and calibration status. Participants characterized by both high AI usage and calibration failure accounted for approximately 13% of the total sample. While calibration failure alone was observed in 27.7% of participants, its concentration within the high-AI subgroup suggests that risk becomes more structurally defined when reliance and miscalibration coincide.

Applying a stricter classification—requiring simultaneous high AI usage and calibration failure—the "strict risk" configuration represented roughly 12% of the sample. This distribution indicates that judgment risk is not diffusely distributed across users but clustered within specific subgroups defined by condition alignment.

The inclusion of institutional control conditions further differentiated these patterns. When device certification status was incorporated, the concentration of calibration failure within high-AI users varied substantially by control environment. Among high-AI participants using non-certified devices, calibration failure was observed in 29.8% of cases. In contrast, within the high-AI group using certified devices, the rate declined to 3.4%. This 26.4 percentage-point difference indicates that institutional control conditions shape how reliance and miscalibration translate into risk.

A similar pattern was observed at the aggregate level. Calibration failure occurred in 33.3% of participants using non-certified devices, compared to 5.6% among those using certified devices. These differences do not imply that certification eliminates risk. Rather, they suggest that institutional environments structure the likelihood that other conditions culminate in judgment distortion.

Taken together, the results show that AI usage intensity alone does not generate elevated risk, nor does calibration failure uniformly produce adverse outcomes. Human Judgment Risk becomes most visible when high reliance, miscalibrated self-assessment, and weaker institutional control environments coincide. This configurational pattern is consistent with the analytical premise that vulnerability in AI-mediated digital government is structured rather than linear.

For governance design, the implication is not that AI adoption should be curtailed. Instead, risk mitigation requires attention to how reliance, calibration mechanisms, and institutional controls interact within administrative settings.

Table 3. Configurational Patterns of Human Judgment Risk and Device Certification Effects

Subgroup/Condition	Overconfidence Rate (%)
Full sample – Non-certified device	33.3
Full sample – Certified device	5.6
High-AI – Non-certified device	29.8
High-AI – Certified device	3.4
Non-IT + High-AI	43.5

4.4 Robustness Checks and Scope of Interpretation

The configurational analysis is intended to identify patterned alignments of conditions rather than to establish definitive causal effects. Several points therefore clarify the scope of interpretation.

First, AI usage intensity showed a small positive association with average task performance. This finding indicates that AI reliance does not inherently reduce judgment accuracy. The results should not be interpreted as evidence that AI usage is a direct source of risk. Elevated Human Judgment Risk was observed primarily when high usage coincided with calibration failure.

Second, occupational background (IT vs. non-IT) was associated with performance differences, but it did not substitute for the core configurational conditions. Professional expertise appears to influence average accuracy, yet it does not eliminate the relevance of the interaction between AI usage intensity and Self–Actual Gap status.

Third, device certification was used as a proxy for institutional control. While certification status differentiated risk concentrations across configurations, the findings do not establish a direct causal effect of certification itself. Certified environments may correlate with broader organizational characteristics, including compliance culture, procedural discipline, or resource allocation. The analysis identifies patterned associations rather than isolated institutional effects.

Fourth, the classification of calibration failure depends on threshold selection. Alternative threshold specifications were examined, and the concentration of elevated risk within high-AI and miscalibrated subgroups remained directionally consistent. This suggests that the observed patterns are not highly sensitive to minor adjustments in cutoff criteria.

Finally, the cross-sectional design limits inference about causal direction. It cannot be determined whether high AI usage contributes to calibration failure or whether individuals prone to overestimation are more likely to rely heavily on AI tools. The present analysis focuses on identifying structural alignments of conditions, leaving causal sequencing to future research.

Taken together, these considerations indicate that the findings should be understood as evidence of patterned vulnerability in AI-mediated digital government environments. They demonstrate how particular combinations of reliance, calibration status, and institutional context correspond to concentrated judgment risk, without asserting deterministic or universal effects.

5 Governance Implications and Contributions

This study extends AI governance debates by examining Human Judgment Risk in AI-mediated digital government from a configurational perspective. Rather than locating vulnerability solely in algorithmic opacity or regulatory gaps, it highlights how risk emerges within the interaction between technological reliance, judgment calibration, and institutional control environments.

Most AI governance frameworks emphasize transparency, accountability, explainability, and system-level oversight. These remain essential. However, when generative AI contributes directly to drafting, structuring, or framing administrative outputs, the locus of risk shifts. AI does not merely execute predefined rules; it shapes the informational starting point of administrative reasoning. Under such conditions, vulnerability may arise not only from technical error but from misalignment between perceived evaluative capacity and actual performance.

The findings demonstrate that elevated Human Judgment Risk concentrates in configurations where high AI usage coincides with calibration failure. Institutional control conditions further differentiate these configurations. Device certification, used here as a proxy for structured control environments, was associated with substantially lower concentrations of calibration failure within high-AI groups. This pattern suggests that institutional context shapes how technological reliance translates into risk.

These results carry three governance implications.

First, AI adoption policies should move beyond simple metrics of usage or access. The intensity of AI reliance interacts with users' calibration status. Public organizations may therefore need diagnostic mechanisms that monitor not only technical compliance but also patterns of evaluative misalignment. Measures such as the Self–Actual Gap are not proposed as tools for individual sanctioning, but as indicators of structural vulnerability within AI-mediated workflows.

Second, institutional control should be understood as a contextual design element rather than as a static technical safeguard. Within broader Governance, Risk & Compliance (GRC) architectures, control mechanisms shape how AI tools are embedded into administrative processes. The observed differences associated with certified device environments indicate that controls may mitigate risk under specific condition alignments. Governance design should therefore integrate human–AI interaction dynamics into compliance and oversight frameworks.

Third, strategies for expanding AI use in digital government should adopt a layered risk management approach. Restricting AI adoption may limit innovation and efficiency, while unstructured expansion may concentrate vulnerability within certain subgroups. Effective governance requires coordinated attention to reliance patterns, calibration capacity, and institutional safeguards.

From a scholarly perspective, the study contributes in three ways. It introduces judgment calibration as a systematic dimension within AI governance research. It connects human–AI interaction literature with security awareness research through the operationalization of the Self–Actual Gap. Finally, it applies a configurational logic to digital government analysis, demonstrating that risk in complex administrative environments is structured rather than additive.

In sum, the study reframes vulnerability in AI-mediated digital government as an outcome of interacting human and institutional conditions. By shifting attention from isolated technical controls to the architecture of judgment within governance systems, it offers a basis for rethinking how public institutions design and manage AI integration.

6 Conclusion

This study examined Human Judgment Risk in AI-mediated digital government through a configurational lens. While much of the existing AI governance literature concentrates on technical safeguards and regulatory design, the present analysis incorporated judgment calibration as a structural component of risk formation. The findings indicate that AI usage intensity alone does not consistently reduce or degrade task accuracy. Rather, elevated risk concentrates in configurations where high AI reliance coincides with calibration failure. Institutional control conditions, operationalized through device certification status, were associated with markedly lower concentrations of calibration failure within high-AI subgroups. These patterns suggest that vulnerability emerges from the alignment of conditions rather than from any single factor.

The results carry implications for digital government governance in the era of generative AI. Ensuring algorithmic transparency and system robustness remains essential, but it is insufficient. As AI tools increasingly shape the informational foundations of administrative reasoning, governance frameworks must account for the structure of human judgment within AI-mediated workflows. Risk mitigation strategies should therefore address not only technological design but also reliance patterns, calibration dynamics, and institutional control environments.

Several limitations warrant attention. The cross-sectional design does not allow determination of causal sequencing between AI reliance and calibration failure. The sample is bounded to a specific empirical context, which limits generalizability. Institutional control was measured through a single proxy indicator, and future research should examine more differentiated control architectures. Longitudinal and comparative studies across public sector settings would further clarify how judgment risk evolves as AI integration deepens.

Despite these constraints, the study contributes a structured account of how vulnerability may be patterned in AI-mediated digital government. Risk does not reside exclusively within technical systems. It emerges from the interaction between technological reliance, human self-assessment, and institutional design. Recognizing this interaction shifts AI governance from a narrow focus on system control toward a broader consideration of how administrative judgment is organized in the presence of generative AI.

Disclosure of Interests. The authors have no competing interests to declare that are relevant to the content of this article.

References

1. OECD: State of Implementation of the OECD AI Principles: Insights from National AI Policies. OECD Publishing, Paris (2021)
2. OECD: Global Trends in Government Innovation 2023. OECD Publishing, Paris (2023)
3. OECD: Recommendation of the Council on Artificial Intelligence. OECD Legal Instruments, OECD/LEGAL/0449 (2019)
4. European Commission: Proposal for a Regulation Laying Down Harmonised Rules on Artificial Intelligence (Artificial Intelligence Act). COM (2021) 206 final (2021)
5. European Union: Regulation (EU) 2024/1689 Laying Down Harmonised Rules on Artificial Intelligence (Artificial Intelligence Act). Official Journal of the European Union (2024)
6. National Institute of Standards and Technology (NIST): Artificial Intelligence Risk Management Framework (AI RMF 1.0). NIST AI 100–1 (2023)
7. Raji, I.D., et al.: Closing the AI accountability gap: defining an end-to-end framework for internal algorithmic auditing. In: Proceedings of the 2020 Conference on Fairness, Accountability, and Transparency (FAT*), pp. 33–44. ACM, New York (2020)
8. Veale, M., Borgesius, F.Z.: Demystifying the draft EU artificial intelligence act. Comput. Law Rev. Int. **22**(4), 97–112 (2021)

9. Kruger, J., Dunning, D.: Unskilled and unaware of it: how difficulties in recognizing one's own incompetence lead to inflated self-assessments. J. Pers. Soc. Psychol. **77**(6), 1121–1134 (1999)
10. Moore, D.A., Healy, P.J.: The trouble with overconfidence. Psychol. Rev. **115**(2), 502–517 (2008)
11. Parasuraman, R., Riley, V.: Humans and automation: use, misuse, disuse. Abuse. Human Factors **39**(2), 230–253 (1997)
12. Dietvorst, B.J., Simmons, J.P., Massey, C.: Algorithm aversion: people erroneously avoid algorithms after seeing them Err. J. Exp. Psychol. Gen. **144**(1), 114–126 (2015)
13. Cordella, A., Tempini, N.: E-government and organizational change: reappraising the role of ICT and bureaucracy in public service delivery. Gov. Inf. Q. **32**(3), 279–286 (2015)
14. Margetts, H., Dunleavy, P.: The second wave of digital-era governance: a quasi-paradigm for government on the web. Phil. Trans. R. Soc. A **371**(1987), 20120382 (2013)
15. Dzindolet, M.T., Peterson, S.A., Pomranky, R.A., Pierce, L.G., Beck, H.P.: The role of trust in automation reliance. Int. J. Hum. Comput. Stud. **58**(6), 697–718 (2003)
16. Lee, J.D., See, K.A.: Trust in automation: designing for appropriate reliance. Hum. Factors **46**(1), 50–80 (2004)
17. Logg, J.M., Minson, J.A., Moore, D.A.: Algorithm appreciation: people prefer algorithmic to human judgment. Organ. Behav. Hum. Decis. Process. **151**, 90–103 (2019)
18. Siponen, M.T.: A conceptual foundation for organizational information security awareness. Inf. Manag. Comput. Secur. **8**(1), 31–41 (2000)
19. Parsons, K., McCormac, A., Butavicius, M., Ferguson, L.: Human Factors and Information Security: Individual, Culture and Security Environment. DSTO Technical Report DSTO-TR-2484 (2010)
20. Parsons, K., McCormac, A., Butavicius, M., Pattinson, M., Jerram, C.: Determining employee awareness using the human aspects of information security questionnaire (HAIS-Q). Comput. Secur. **42**, 165–176 (2014)
21. Ifinedo, P.: Understanding information systems security policy compliance: an integration of the theory of planned behavior and the protection motivation theory. Comput. Secur. **31**(1), 83–95 (2012)
22. Acquisti, A., Brandimarte, L., Loewenstein, G.: Privacy and human behavior in the age of information. Science **347**(6221), 509–514 (2015)
23. Ragin, C.C.: Redesigning Social Inquiry: Fuzzy Sets and Beyond. University of Chicago Press, Chicago (2008)

Intelligent Ombudsman: An AI-Based Approach to Demand Classification

Ayrton Gomes(✉), Rafael Moura, Kellyton Brito, George Valença, and Ermeson Andrade

Department of Computing, Federal Rural University of Pernambuco (UFRPE), Recife, Brazil
{ayrton.gomes,rafael.mourasilva,kellyton.brito,george.valenca, ermeson.andrade}@ufrpe.br

Abstract. Public ombudsman offices play a central role in digital government by providing institutional channels through which citizens submit complaints, suggestions, and service requests to public authorities. The growing volume of textual submissions creates operational challenges for the triage process, which requires accurate identification and routing of citizen demands. In many public organizations, this task remains manual, making it time-consuming and difficult to scale, particularly when labeled data for training automated systems are scarce. This study examines the use of Natural Language Processing (NLP) and Machine Learning (ML) techniques to support the automated classification of ombudsman submissions under conditions of limited data availability. To mitigate data scarcity, a data augmentation strategy based on synthetic text generation using a large language model was adopted, enabling the construction of synthetic and hybrid datasets to complement real submissions. Five classification algorithms were evaluated across three experimental settings: real-only, synthetic-only, and hybrid datasets. Results suggest that hybrid configurations outperform real-only data, although category differences and possible synthetic-data bias limit this comparison. These findings indicate that synthetic data may support ombudsman triage when combined with validation and human review.

Keywords: Public Ombudsman Offices · Digital Government · Text Classification · Synthetic Data · Machine Learning

1 Introduction

Public ombudsman offices play an essential role in democratic governance by providing institutional channels through which citizens can submit complaints, suggestions, and service requests directly to public authorities. Through these mechanisms, citizens exercise participatory oversight over public administration, contributing to transparency, accountability, and the improvement of public services [4]. In Brazil, this role is formally reinforced by Law No. 13.460/2017 [3],

Published by Springer Nature Switzerland 2027
G. Viale Pereira et al. (Eds.): EGOV 2026, LNCS 16933, pp. 214–230, 2027.
https://doi.org/10.1007/978-3-032-35747-2_14

which regulates citizen participation in the evaluation and monitoring of public services. At the same time, ombudsman offices handle a growing volume of textual submissions each year. For instance, ombudsman units in the Executive Branch of Pernambuco, Brazil, registered 156,135 submissions in 2024, representing a 19.22% increase compared to the previous year [17], while the Office of the Comptroller General of the Union (CGU) recorded 10,177 submissions in the same period [7]. The increasing volume and linguistic diversity of these submissions create operational challenges for the triage process, which requires the correct identification and routing of citizen demands.

The analysis and triage stage constitutes a critical step in the workflow of ombudsman offices and, in many public institutions, is still performed manually. This process typically involves reading submissions in full, assessing their content and severity, and identifying the responsible internal unit [20]. Such activities require the evaluation of multiple criteria, including coherence, objectivity, and the possible need to split requests, making the process time-consuming, subjective, and prone to classification errors [5]. These limitations may lead to delays, inappropriate routing, and reduced reliability of consolidated information, ultimately limiting the strategic use of ombudsman data for institutional improvement.

In this context, the automation of submission triage has emerged as a relevant research problem within the scope of supervised text classification using Natural Language Processing (NLP) and Machine Learning (ML) techniques. Recent studies have explored the application of such methods to support tasks including the admissibility assessment of complaints [19], the classification of submissions for internal routing [6], and the identification of irregularities in public-sector oversight contexts [8]. However, the adoption of automated classification systems in public administration is often constrained by the scarcity of labeled real-world data and by class imbalance, conditions that are exacerbated by institutional restrictions, data sensitivity, and the high cost of manual annotation.

To mitigate these limitations, synthetic data generation has been investigated as a complementary strategy for increasing the availability of labeled examples through data augmentation techniques, including approaches based on large language models (LLMs) [16]. Nevertheless, empirical evidence indicates that models trained exclusively on synthetic data may produce overly optimistic performance estimates, since generated texts tend to be more homogeneous and semantically separable than authentic submissions, which are inherently noisy and heterogeneous [2,12]. These findings highlight the need for controlled experimental analyses that explicitly compare real, synthetic, and hybrid data configurations.

This study investigates the use of supervised text classification models to support the triage of submissions in public ombudsman offices under conditions of limited labeled data. An automatic classification pipeline is proposed in which different models are evaluated across three experimental scenarios: (i) a *Real* scenario based exclusively on authentic submissions, (ii) a *Synthetic* scenario relying only on generated data and analyzed as an upper-bound reference, and

(iii) a *Hybrid* scenario combining real and synthetic data to improve robustness under data scarcity. This study makes three empirical and application-oriented contributions. First, it evaluates classical and neural text classifiers for public ombudsman triage under limited availability of labeled real-world data. Second, it compares real-only, synthetic-only, and hybrid data configurations to analyze how LLM-generated synthetic submissions affect classification performance and stability. Third, it discusses methodological and operational risks associated with the use of synthetic data in this domain, including class imbalance, category differences, label leakage, synthetic-data validity, and the need for human oversight. Rather than introducing a new classifier or data augmentation method, the study provides empirical evidence on the use of existing NLP and ML techniques in a sensitive public-sector classification task.

The remainder of this paper is organized as follows. Section 2 reviews related work on automated classification of citizen demands and synthetic data augmentation. Section 3 describes the methodological approach. Section 4 presents the experimental setup. Section 5 reports and discusses the experimental results. Finally, Sect. 6 concludes the paper and outlines directions for future work.

2 Related Work

The automated classification of citizen demands has been explored in digital government as a way to support public agencies that process large volumes of textual submissions with limited human and technical resources. In ombudsman offices, classification may assist tasks such as identifying the type of manifestation, assessing admissibility, routing submissions to the responsible unit, or detecting irregularities. These tasks are commonly formulated as supervised text classification problems, but their performance depends on the taxonomy adopted, the availability of labeled data, class balance, and the degree of semantic overlap among categories.

In the Brazilian public-sector context, previous studies have applied NLP and machine learning to related problems. Cordeiro et al. [8] evaluated supervised classifiers for irregularity reports submitted to Courts of Accounts, considering both classical models and Transformer-based architectures. Caldeira et al. [6] addressed complaint classification in public administration using small and imbalanced datasets, adopting strategies such as class aggregation and back-translation. Paiva [19] presented a production-oriented study on complaint triage, highlighting the relevance of combining textual information with institutional context and structured metadata in real deployments. These studies show that automated triage is feasible, but remains affected by scarce labeled data, heterogeneous writing styles, institutional taxonomies, and class imbalance.

Data scarcity and imbalance are broader challenges in supervised text classification. Data augmentation techniques, including synonym replacement, noising, paraphrasing, back-translation, and sample generation, have been used to increase training data diversity in low-resource settings [9,13,21]. More recently, large language models have been used to generate synthetic examples for text classification. Such examples may improve model training when real examples are scarce, but may also introduce risks such as low diversity, distributional mismatch, and overly optimistic evaluation results [12,16,23].

This study builds on this literature by examining synthetic data augmentation in the specific context of public ombudsman triage. The goal is not to propose a new classifier or generation method, but to evaluate how classical and neural classifiers behave under real-only, synthetic-only, and hybrid data configurations. By using submissions associated with multiple Brazilian public institutions and by discussing risks such as label leakage, category differences, and synthetic-data validity, the study provides empirical evidence on the use of LLM-generated synthetic data in an e-government classification task.

3 Methodology

The methodological approach is summarized in Fig. 1. It comprises four stages: real-data acquisition and synthetic generation, synthetic-data validation and preprocessing, model training and optimization, and evaluation across experimental scenarios. This structure allows the analysis of how data availability and dataset composition affect model performance.

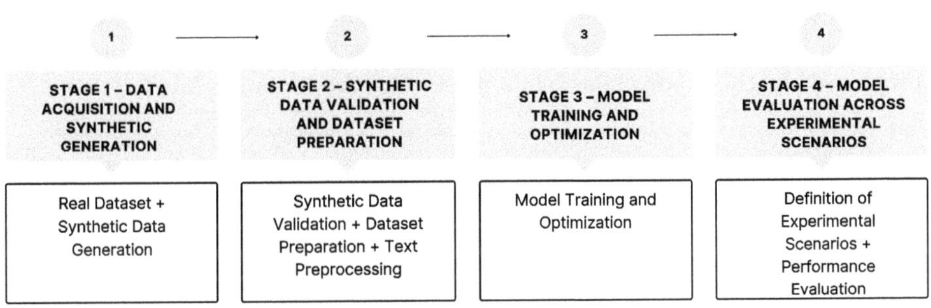

Fig. 1. Methodological pipeline adopted in this study, organized into four stages: data acquisition and synthetic generation, dataset preparation, model training, and evaluation across Real, Synthetic, and Hybrid scenarios.

3.1 Acquisition of Real Data and Complementary Synthetic Generation

The data acquisition process involved multiple Brazilian public institutions. All real datasets were obtained through formal institutional channels rather than public online sources or web scraping. The real-data scenario integrated 2,200 submissions from three institutions: 257 records from the Federal University of the São Francisco Valley (UNIVASF), 445 from the National Agency of Petroleum, Natural Gas and Biofuels (ANP), and 1,498 from the National Civil

Aviation Agency (ANAC). After cleaning, duplicate removal, encoding correction, and categorical-field standardization, 2,076 valid records remained. Categories with extremely low support were removed from the real-data configuration, resulting in 2,066 valid real submissions for the retained categories. Since the Real, Synthetic, and Hybrid scenarios differ in data sources and class support, their final category composition is described in Sect. 3.3.

Synthetic data generation relied on a small set of real submissions provided by the ombudsman office of the Pernambuco State Court of Accounts (TCE-PE) through a restricted data-sharing arrangement. Due to confidentiality constraints and the sensitive nature of ombudsman data, access was limited to two examples per category. Although insufficient for supervised training, these examples served as seed inputs for synthetic data generation, reflecting a realistic scenario of labeled data scarcity in public-sector environments.

To mitigate this limitation, a data augmentation strategy based on synthetic text generation was adopted following recent approaches [23]. Synthetic submissions were generated using the Gemini 2.5 Pro LLM, selected for its ability to follow prompts and produce plausible texts [23]. The generation process was conducted in two stages using standardized prompts. First, 20 base records were generated from each example using a structured prompt (Listing 1) specifying the target category, CSV format, and textual characteristics.

In the second stage, each base record was expanded through textual variation. Five additional variants were generated by rewriting only the "Submission Text" field while keeping all other attributes unchanged. This second prompt (Listing 2) increased linguistic diversity while preserving the semantic label.

```
Your task is to act as an AI assistant specialized in data augmentation for an ombudsman
     dataset.

Generate 20 new and distinct data entries for the category "[CATEGORY NAME]".

Each generated entry must be a data record in CSV format, using a semicolon (;) as a
     separator and containing 8 columns in the following order:
ID;Category;Submission Text;Submission Channel;Date;Response Status;Education
     Level;Location

For the columns, generate realistic and varied data. For "ID", use the placeholder [NEW
     ID]. The main text in 'Submission Text' must be new, detailed, and coherent with the
     category.

Follow EXACTLY the format and style of the examples below.

### FORMAT AND STYLE EXAMPLES

1;Report;Subject: Lack of transparency in the disclosure of public data by the new
     municipal administration. I hereby submit a formal report against the current
     administration of the Municipality of [Municipality]...;Online Form;08/15/2025;Under
     Review;Higher Education;[Municipality]
2;Compliment;Good evening! I have just read the study by the [Public Agency] on the
     panorama of inclusive education in the public education system of [Federative
     State]. I am a teacher and this topic greatly interests me. I would like to
     congratulate the team on the excellent
     work...;Email;08/17/2025;Answered;Postgraduate;[Municipality]

### GENERATE ONLY THE 20 DATA ENTRIES BELOW
```

Listing 1.1. Prompt for Generating Base Records.

```
Your task is to create 5 variations of a data entry for a data augmentation project.

Below is a line from a CSV file. Generate 5 new lines in which only the content of the
     "Submission Text" column is a rewritten version of the original. Keep the other
     information (ID, Category, etc.) exactly as it is, but replace the ID number with
     the placeholder [NEW ID].

### ORIGINAL LINE

[Complete Line of the Synthetic Submission with All Columns]

### GENERATE ONLY THE 5 REWRITTEN DATA LINES BELOW
```

Listing 1.2. Textual Variation Prompt.

This procedure resulted in 120 synthetic instances per category, yielding a final synthetic dataset of 720 records. Finally, the hybrid scenario was constructed by combining the real and synthetic datasets, resulting in a total of 2,786 submissions. This configuration allows the evaluation of the impact of incorporating synthetic data in classification tasks conducted under conditions characterized by limited availability of labeled real-world data.

To provide a qualitative illustration of the synthetic data generation process, Table 1 presents an anonymized real submission alongside a synthetic example generated from it. This example is illustrative only and does not, in isolation, constitute evidence of data quality. Synthetic data quality is assessed in the next subsection through automated diagnostics and human validation.

Table 1. Illustrative example of a real and a synthetic submission (Category: Criticism).

Type	Submission Text
Real	With reference to submission [Submission ID], the citizen contacted the Ombudsman Hotline because she did not agree with the response provided to her submission. She reported that there are deliberations issued by the [Public Authority] that address the facts described in complaint [Submission ID].
Synthetic	The management of the [Public Authority] of [Municipality] requires significant improvement. Service delivery is disorganized, there are insufficient service tickets for all users, and the staff appear to lack adequate training to provide accurate information, in addition to being overburdened.

3.2 Validation of Synthetic Data Quality

Given the risks associated with synthetic data generation, a validation stage was conducted before model training to assess semantic adequacy, textual plausibility, and label coherence. This stage combined automated analyses with qualitative human evaluation. The automated analysis used embedding-based semantic similarity and lexical diversity metrics, specifically the Type–Token Ratio and the Jaccard index, to compare real and synthetic vocabularies and assess thematic preservation.

Qualitative validation was performed on a stratified sample of synthetic submissions. Following finite population correction [15], $n = 48$ instances were selected across the generated categories and evaluated for label consistency, textual plausibility, absence of explicit label leakage, and argumentative complexity. Since synthetic submissions containing explicit category references were retained in the experimental dataset, performance estimates involving synthetic data may be partially inflated, particularly in the synthetic-only and hybrid scenarios. The following paragraphs describe the sampling procedure used for human validation and the annotation protocol adopted to assess the quality of the generated submissions.

Sample Size Determination. The sample size was estimated using finite population correction (FPC), following [15]. Considering the synthetic dataset population of $N = 720$, a confidence level of 90%, an admissible margin of error of approximately 12%, and maximum heterogeneity ($p = 0.5$), the procedure resulted in a final sample of $n = 48$ submissions. These parameters are consistent with recommendations for exploratory studies conducted under limited resources [10]. To ensure category coverage, stratified random sampling was applied, selecting eight instances from each of the six categories.

Annotation Protocol. Each sampled instance was subjected to human evaluation based on four questions to assess quality:

1. **Label Consistency**: Semantic alignment between the text and the assigned category.
2. **Plausibility**: Assessment of the naturalness and fluency of the generated text. A traditional five-point Likert scale was adopted [14], ranging from 1 (Completely Artificial) to 5 (Very Realistic). This metric captures human perception of textual quality, allowing for degrees of uncertainty (neutral point 3) regarding the synthetic or organic origin of the submission.
3. **Data Leakage**: Explicit presence of the category name within the text body, which could act as an artificial facilitator for machine learning models.
4. **Argumentative Complexity**: Whether the text presents structured reasoning or simple sentences.

The results of this validation are discussed in the Results section and serve as a basis for interpreting classifier performance.

3.3 Dataset Preparation and Textual Preprocessing

After the validation stage, the datasets were prepared for the classification experiments, and category distributions were analyzed separately for each experimental scenario.

The category sets differ across scenarios because real and synthetic data came from institutions with partially distinct taxonomies. The Synthetic scenario contains the categories available in the generated dataset after preprocessing, whereas the Real scenario contains only categories with sufficient support in the real datasets. The Hybrid scenario therefore reflects the combination of retained real categories and generated synthetic categories after applying minimum-support constraints.

Categories with insufficient support were removed only from scenarios that incorporated real submissions. In the Real scenario, multiple categories were excluded due to severe scarcity; in the Hybrid scenario, exclusion was applied only to categories that remained underrepresented after combining real and synthetic data. The Synthetic scenario preserved all categories available in the generated dataset after preprocessing. These decisions reflect practical constraints of public-sector datasets and support more stable comparative experiments. The texts were then processed through noise removal, lowercasing, lemmatization with the Portuguese spaCy model, short-token filtering, and stopword removal. The target variable was transformed through label encoding for compatibility with the supervised learning algorithms.

3.4 Model Training and Optimization

The five classifiers were selected to cover complementary modeling paradigms while remaining feasible under limited data and computational resources. Multinomial Naive Bayes was used as a probabilistic baseline, while Logistic Regression and Linear SVM were included as strong linear baselines for high-dimensional Term Frequency–Inverse Document Frequency (TF–IDF) representations, following prior public-sector text classification studies under data scarcity and class imbalance [6,8]. FastText was adopted as a lightweight neural model with subword representations [11], and BERTimbau as a Transformer-based model pretrained for Brazilian Portuguese [22]. This selection enables comparison across probabilistic, linear, lightweight neural, and Transformer-based approaches without assuming that higher model complexity necessarily improves performance.

Hyperparameter optimization followed model-specific strategies. Classical models were optimized through grid search with cross-validation, while neural models used Bayesian optimization with Optuna [1]. In all scenarios, optimization maximized macro F1-score, which was selected because of class imbalance and its ability to provide a more balanced evaluation across categories [18].

3.5 Model Evaluation and Definition of Experimental Scenarios

Performance evaluation was carried out using Repeated Stratified K-Fold Cross Validation, with five folds and ten repetitions, totaling fifty independent runs per model. Stratification ensured preservation of class proportions in each split.

To analyze the impact of dataset composition on model performance and stability, three experimental scenarios were defined: the Real scenario, in which models were trained and evaluated exclusively with authentic submissions, representing the most challenging operational condition under data scarcity; the Synthetic scenario, in which models were trained and evaluated exclusively with generated data, serving as a controlled and potentially optimistic upper-bound reference; and the Hybrid scenario, in which real and synthetic submissions were combined to assess whether synthetic data could improve robustness while preserving part of the semantic variability of authentic texts. For each scenario, the mean and standard deviation of Accuracy, Precision, Recall, and macro F1-score were computed across all runs.

4 Experimental Setup

This section describes the experimental setup used to implement and evaluate the classification pipeline, including the implementation environment, model configurations, and hyperparameter optimization procedures across the scenarios defined in Sect. 3.

4.1 Implementation Environment

The submission classification pipeline was implemented in Python using widely adopted libraries for data processing and natural language processing tasks. Data manipulation and organization were conducted using *Pandas*, a Python library for data analysis and manipulation, while textual preprocessing relied on *NLTK* (Natural Language Toolkit) and *spaCy*. These tools supported standard preprocessing procedures, including normalization, tokenization, and text preparation for vector representation and model training.

All experiments were executed under the same implementation pipeline across the three experimental scenarios in order to ensure comparability. Performance estimates were obtained through Repeated Stratified K-Fold Cross-Validation with five folds and ten repetitions, totaling fifty runs per model and scenario. The reported metrics correspond to the mean and standard deviation across these runs.

4.2 Model Configuration and Hyperparameter Optimization

The experimental evaluation included both classical machine learning models and neural approaches. Classical classifiers, namely LR, Multinomial NB, and Linear SVM, were trained using TF–IDF representations, a widely adopted approach for high-dimensional text classification tasks.

For TF–IDF-based models, hyperparameters were optimized through grid search over vectorizer and classifier settings. The search space included unigram and unigram–bigram representations, $C \in \{0.1, 1, 10\}$ for LR and Linear SVM, and $\alpha \in \{0.1, 0.5, 1.0\}$ for Multinomial NB.

Two neural approaches were also evaluated: FastText and BERTimbau, a transformer-based model pre-trained for Brazilian Portuguese. Hyperparameter optimization for neural models was conducted using the *Optuna* framework. For FastText, the search space included learning rate, embedding dimension, training epochs, and word n-grams. For BERTimbau, Optuna optimized learning rate, number of epochs, warmup ratio, and weight decay. The final model used the *neuralmind/bert-base-portuguese-cased* checkpoint with *AutoModelForSequence-Classification*, maximum sequence length of 128 tokens, batch size 8, three epochs, learning rate of 2.03×10^{-5}, warmup ratio of 0.054, weight decay of 0.023, and mixed precision when CUDA was available.

For BERTimbau, Optuna optimized learning rate, number of epochs, warmup ratio, and weight decay. The final model used the BERTimbau base checkpoint with a sequence-classification head, maximum sequence length of 128 tokens, batch size 8, three epochs, learning rate of 2.03×10^{-5}, warmup ratio of 0.054, weight decay of 0.023, and mixed precision when CUDA was available.

5 Results and Discussion

This section presents the experimental results across the different data scenarios, including synthetic data quality assessment, overall performance trends, category-level analysis, and a discussion of implications for public ombudsman contexts.

5.1 Synthetic Data Quality Assessment

Before presenting the classification results, the synthetic dataset was evaluated through human validation on a stratified sample ($n = 48$), as described in Sect. 3.2. The analysis assessed label consistency, textual plausibility, label leakage, and argumentative complexity. All sampled submissions were semantically consistent with their assigned categories (100% label consistency). Textual plausibility reached an average score of 4.17 on a five-point Likert scale, with 75% of the texts rated ≥ 4. However, explicit references to the target category were identified in 22.92% of the instances, indicating potential label leakage, while 58.33% of the texts exhibited argumentative structures beyond simple statements.

These characteristics help explain the high performance observed in the synthetic-only scenario. Because synthetic submissions tend to contain clearer lexical cues and fewer ambiguities than authentic messages, and because part of the sample contained explicit references to the target category, this configuration should be interpreted as an optimistic upper-bound reference rather than as an estimate of expected real-world performance. The same caution applies to the hybrid scenario, since synthetic examples may contribute artificial lexical cues during model training and evaluation.

5.2 Overall Results by Experimental Scenario

Table 2 reports the results obtained using exclusively real submissions. This scenario reflects the challenges of real-world ombudsman data, such as linguistic variability, semantic overlap, textual noise, and limited category support. Macro F1-scores ranged from 0.5159 to 0.5546, indicating moderate classification effectiveness under data scarcity.

Table 2. Model performance in the Real Scenario (mean ± standard deviation). Acc. = Accuracy, Prec. = Precision, Rec. = Recall.

Model	Acc.	F1 (macro)	Prec. (macro)	Rec. (macro)
Linear SVM	0.8288 ± 0.0147	0.5546 ± 0.0335	0.5829 ± 0.0393	0.5403 ± 0.0367
LR	0.8256 ± 0.0149	0.5501 ± 0.0310	0.5868 ± 0.0344	0.5305 ± 0.0332
Multinomial NB	0.8267 ± 0.0128	0.5501 ± 0.0331	0.5694 ± 0.0331	0.5424 ± 0.0348
FastText	0.8191 ± 0.0184	0.5509 ± 0.0318	0.5630 ± 0.0336	0.5447 ± 0.0342
BERTimbau	0.8400 ± 0.0062	0.5159 ± 0.0255	0.5334 ± 0.0369	0.5148 ± 0.0278

In the real data scenario, the evaluated models achieved similar Accuracy values, concentrated around 0.82–0.84. BERTimbau obtained the highest Accuracy (0.8400), but also the lowest macro F1-score (0.5159), indicating weaker balance across categories. In contrast, Linear SVM achieved the highest macro F1-score (0.5546), while FastText and Multinomial NB obtained the highest Recall values. These results suggest that, under data scarcity, model comparison depends not only on overall Accuracy but also on the ability to balance performance across minority and semantically overlapping categories.

Despite the preprocessing procedures described in the methodological section, the real dataset remained affected by class imbalance and limited category support. To ensure stable evaluation, the *Compliment* category was excluded from the real data experiments, resulting in a reduced set of operational categories consistent with common constraints in public-sector ombudsman data.

Table 3 presents the results obtained when models are trained and evaluated exclusively on synthetic data. In this controlled setting, all models achieved very high performance, with classical linear methods approaching ceiling values.

In the synthetic-only scenario, Linear SVM obtained the highest scores, followed by LR and Multinomial NB. FastText and BERTimbau also achieved high results, although they remained below the linear baselines.

These results should be interpreted cautiously. The synthetic-only configuration produces a much more regular classification setting, with clearer lexical patterns and lower semantic ambiguity than those observed in authentic ombudsman submissions. For this reason, the near-ceiling values obtained in this scenario are better understood as an optimistic upper bound associated with the internal structure of the generated dataset rather than as an estimate of expected behavior under operational conditions.

Table 3. Model performance in the Synthetic Scenario (mean ± standard deviation). Acc. = Accuracy, Prec. = Precision, Rec. = Recall.

Model	Acc.	F1 (macro)	Prec. (macro)	Rec. (macro)
Linear SVM	0.9977 ± 0.0051	0.9977 ± 0.0051	0.9978 ± 0.0047	0.9977 ± 0.0051
LR	0.9962 ± 0.0081	0.9962 ± 0.0081	0.9963 ± 0.0077	0.9962 ± 0.0081
Multinomial NB	0.9922 ± 0.0088	0.9922 ± 0.0088	0.9926 ± 0.0082	0.9922 ± 0.0088
FastText	0.9645 ± 0.0170	0.9644 ± 0.0169	0.9658 ± 0.0162	0.9645 ± 0.0170
BERTimbau	0.9492 ± 0.0259	0.9489 ± 0.0264	0.9505 ± 0.0255	0.9492 ± 0.0259

Table 4 presents the results of the hybrid scenario, in which synthetic data were combined with real data during training and evaluation. Relative to the real-only configuration, this scenario produced higher aggregate scores; however, these results should be interpreted cautiously because the hybrid configuration combines data sources and category distributions that are not strictly equivalent to those of the real-only scenario.

Table 4. Model performance in the Hybrid Scenario (mean ± standard deviation). Acc. = Accuracy, Prec. = Precision, Rec. = Recall.

Model	Acc.	F1 (macro)	Prec. (macro)	Rec. (macro)
Linear SVM	0.8591 ± 0.0132	0.8583 ± 0.0150	0.8884 ± 0.0140	0.8354 ± 0.0190
LR	0.8534 ± 0.0152	0.8497 ± 0.0185	0.8911 ± 0.0167	0.8181 ± 0.0213
Multinomial NB	0.8406 ± 0.0154	0.8319 ± 0.0189	0.8485 ± 0.0194	0.8235 ± 0.0216
BERTimbau	0.8559 ± 0.0131	0.8443 ± 0.0155	0.8635 ± 0.0236	0.8330 ± 0.0134
FastText	0.8226 ± 0.0133	0.7957 ± 0.0175	0.8159 ± 0.0175	0.7812 ± 0.0195

In the hybrid scenario, Linear SVM achieved the best overall performance, with the highest Accuracy (0.8591), macro F1-score (0.8583), and Recall (0.8354). LR and BERTimbau also produced strong results, while Multinomial NB benefited from synthetic enrichment but remained below the leading classifiers. FastText presented the lowest aggregate performance.

Compared with the real-only configuration, the hybrid scenario increased macro F1 from approximately 0.52–0.55 to 0.80–0.86, suggesting that synthetic data may improve class representation. However, this should not be read as a paired estimate of operational gain, since the hybrid setting differs in data composition and category coverage. Thus, the hybrid results provide exploratory evidence of the usefulness of synthetic data, rather than definitive evidence of deployment-ready performance.

5.3 Category-Level Performance and Integrated Analysis

Category-level analysis examines how classification performance varies across manifestation types. Recall and F1-score values are reported in Tables 5, 6, and 7. As described in Sect. 3.3, category sets differ across scenarios due to differences in data sources and minimum support constraints. Therefore, these results should be interpreted as scenario-specific evidence rather than as strictly paired category-by-category comparisons.

Results obtained using only real submissions (Table 5) show substantial variation across categories. *Service Request* achieved consistently high Recall and F1-score values, whereas *Communication* and *Complaint* presented more moderate performance. The most critical case is *Suggestion*, for which no model produced correct predictions due to the extremely limited number of training instances and its semantic proximity to adjacent categories. BERTimbau also showed low performance for *Communication* despite achieving the highest overall Accuracy in the real scenario, suggesting that correct predictions were concentrated in higher-frequency categories. Overall, the null Recall observed for *Suggestion* reflects structural data scarcity rather than limitations of the evaluated algorithms.

Table 5. Category-level Recall and F1-score for each model in the Real scenario.

Category	Linear SVM		LR		Multinomial NB		BERTimbau		FastText	
	Rec	F1	Rec	F1	Rec	F1	Rec	F1	Rec	F1
Communication	0.4212	0.4679	0.3904	0.4577	0.3981	0.4376	0.1462	0.2071	0.4327	0.4611
Report	0.7281	0.7489	0.7158	0.7461	0.7854	0.7701	0.8246	0.7779	0.7474	0.7504
Complaint	0.6109	0.6638	0.6042	0.6535	0.5911	0.6471	0.6645	0.6939	0.6228	0.6485
Service Request	0.9411	0.9039	0.9412	0.9022	0.9382	0.9052	0.9389	0.9156	0.9199	0.8987
Suggestion	0.0000	0.0000	0.0000	0.0000	0.0000	0.0000	0.0000	0.0000	0.0000	0.0000

By contrast, the synthetic-only scenario (Table 6) displays uniformly high category-level performance. All models achieved very high Recall and F1-score values across the evaluated classes, especially for *Compliment*, which reached perfect or near-perfect performance for most methods. Even the lowest-scoring model in this setting maintained high category-level results. This regularity confirms that the synthetic dataset is substantially easier to classify than the authentic data and reinforces the interpretation of this scenario as an optimistic benchmark rather than a realistic proxy for operational performance.

When synthetic data are incorporated alongside real submissions (Table 7), category-level performance improves across most classes, particularly those that were more difficult in the real-only setting. *Criticism*, *Compliment*, and *Service Request* achieved high results across nearly all models, while *Communication*, *Report*, and *Suggestion* also showed substantial gains. *Complaint* remained the

Table 6. Category-level Recall and F1-score for each model in the Synthetic scenario.

Category	Linear SVM		LR		Multinomial NB		BERTimbau		FastText	
	Rec	F1	Rec	F1	Rec	F1	Rec	F1	Rec	F1
Communication	0.9900	0.9946	0.9875	0.9912	0.9700	0.9839	0.9400	0.9141	0.9392	0.9447
Report	0.9983	0.9983	0.9975	0.9971	0.9908	0.9917	0.9517	0.9613	0.9617	0.9569
Compliment	1.0000	0.9996	1.0000	1.0000	1.0000	1.0000	1.0000	0.9917	0.9975	0.9934
Service Request	1.0000	0.9963	0.9958	0.9929	1.0000	0.9872	0.8717	0.8959	0.9367	0.9371
Suggestion	1.0000	0.9996	1.0000	0.9996	1.0000	0.9979	0.9825	0.9821	0.9875	0.9904

most difficult category, indicating persistent semantic overlap even after synthetic enrichment. Linear classifiers remained comparatively consistent across categories. Linear SVM combined strong aggregate performance with high category-level stability, followed closely by LR. BERTimbau also benefited from the hybrid configuration and produced competitive results, although it did not surpass the strongest linear baselines in overall balance. Overall, the hybrid scenario mitigates part of the instability observed in the real-only setting by increasing training data diversity while preserving the complexity of authentic submissions.

Table 7. Category-level Recall and F1-score for each model in the Hybrid scenario.

Category	Linear SVM		LR		Multinomial NB		BERTimbau		FastText	
	Rec	F1	Rec	F1	Rec	F1	Rec	F1	Rec	F1
Communication	0.7343	0.7850	0.6692	0.7484	0.7343	0.7507	0.6517	0.7006	0.6587	0.7020
Criticism	0.9533	0.9634	0.9150	0.9515	0.9167	0.9024	0.9642	0.9449	0.7767	0.8122
Report	0.8412	0.8404	0.8309	0.8377	0.8653	0.8117	0.8354	0.8170	0.8055	0.8008
Compliment	0.9233	0.9524	0.9233	0.9586	0.9194	0.9443	0.9543	0.9727	0.8798	0.8987
Complaint	0.6112	0.6634	0.6000	0.6531	0.5725	0.6385	0.6431	0.6771	0.6107	0.6296
Service Request	0.9397	0.9030	0.9449	0.8993	0.9156	0.8920	0.9302	0.9098	0.9063	0.8871
Suggestion	0.8451	0.9043	0.8437	0.9042	0.8408	0.8854	0.8535	0.8879	0.8310	0.8432

The category-level results suggest that the hybrid configuration may reduce instability observed in the real-only setting, especially for categories with limited support. However, because category sets differ across scenarios and synthetic examples may introduce more regular lexical patterns, these results should be interpreted as scenario-specific evidence rather than as a direct category-by-category operational comparison. Training exclusively on real data exposes the effects of data scarcity and semantic overlap, whereas relying solely on synthetic data produces results that are systematically inflated and potentially misleading. The hybrid approach therefore provides exploratory evidence on the possible contribution of synthetic data, but further validation with real-only test sets is needed before drawing stronger conclusions about practical deployment.

5.4 Discussion and Study Limitations

The results indicate that dataset composition and validation protocols strongly influence model performance. In the real-only scenario, data scarcity, class imbalance, and linguistic heterogeneity limited macro-level performance, even when Accuracy remained relatively high. The synthetic-only scenario produced near-ceiling results, suggesting internal consistency in the generated data but not operational realism. The hybrid scenario provided exploratory evidence that synthetic data may improve class representation when combined with real submissions, although this interpretation is limited by differences in category composition and by risks associated with synthetic data.

This study has limitations that should be considered when interpreting the results. The real datasets came from only three Brazilian public institutions, category sets differed across scenarios, no fixed global random seed was enforced across all libraries, and no formal statistical significance tests were conducted. In addition, explicit references to target categories were identified in part of the synthetic sample and retained in the experiments, which may have partially inflated results in the synthetic-only and hybrid scenarios. Future work should remove, mask, or regenerate such instances, evaluate hybrid strategies using real-only test sets, and assess the approach in operational workflows. In practice, the models should support human analysts by suggesting initial categories, confidence scores, or ranked alternatives, while sensitive and low-confidence cases remain subject to human review. Due to the sensitive nature of ombudsman submissions, full real-text datasets cannot be openly released, although prompts, notebooks, aggregate results, and anonymized or derived artifacts may be documented when institutional restrictions allow.

6 Conclusions

This study examined the use of NLP and machine learning to support the classification of citizen submissions in public-sector ombudsman offices under limited labeled data. The results indicate that classical linear models, particularly Linear SVM, provide strong baselines for this task, while more complex neural models do not necessarily outperform them under data scarcity. The comparison across real-only, synthetic-only, and hybrid configurations also shows that synthetic data should be interpreted with caution: synthetic-only results may represent an optimistic upper bound, whereas hybrid configurations are useful for examining whether generated data can complement authentic submissions.

The study also reinforces that automated classification should support, rather than replace, human analysts in ombudsman triage. The main limitations include the restricted number of participating institutions, differences in category composition across scenarios, possible label leakage in synthetic data, and the controlled nature of the experiments. Future work should evaluate the approach with additional institutions, remove or regenerate synthetic instances with explicit label cues, adopt real-only test protocols for hybrid evaluation, and assess the use of these models in operational ombudsman workflows.

Acknowledgments. This work was supported by the Foundation for the Support of Science and Technology of the State of Pernambuco (FACEPE).

Disclosure of Interests. The authors declare no conflicts of interest.

References

1. Akiba, T., Sano, S., Yanase, T., Ohta, T., Koyama, M.: Optuna: A next-generation hyperparameter optimization framework. In: Proceedings of the 25th ACM SIGKDD International Conference on Knowledge Discovery and Data Mining, pp. 2623–2631 (2019)
2. Alaa, A., van der Schaar, M.: How faithful is your synthetic data? In: Advances in Neural Information Processing Systems, vol. 35, pp. 21831–21845 (2022)
3. Brasil: Lei n.º 13.460, de 26 de junho de 2017 (2017)
4. Brasil, Controladoria-Geral da União, Ouvidoria-Geral da União: Manual de ouvidoria pública: rumo ao sistema participativo (2018)
5. Brasil, Ministério da Saúde: Manual das ouvidorias do sus (2014)
6. Caldeira, F., Nunes, L., Ribeiro, R.: Classification of public administration complaints. In: Proceedings of the 11th Symposium on Languages, Applications and Technologies (SLATE) (2022)
7. CGU: Relatório de gestão da ouvidoria setorial da cgu, p. 2024 (2025)
8. Cordeiro, F., Rabelo, R., Moura, R.: Classification of irregularity communications in public ombudsmen using supervised learning algorithms. In: Anais do XIX Encontro Nacional de Inteligência Artificial e Computacional, pp. 704–715 (2022)
9. Feng, S.Y., et al.: A survey of data augmentation approaches for nlp. arXiv preprint arXiv:2105.03075 (2021)
10. Israel, G.D.: Determining Sample Size, University of Florida (1992)
11. Joulin, A., Grave, E., Bojanowski, P., Mikolov, T.: Bag of tricks for efficient text classification. In: Proceedings of the 15th Conference of the European Chapter of the Association for Computational Linguistics, pp. 427–431 (2017)
12. Kuo, H.Y., Lin, C.Y., Chen, Y.N.: Not all llm-generated data are equal: Rethinking data weighting in text classification. arXiv:2410.21526 (2024)
13. Li, B., Hou, Y., Che, W.: Data augmentation approaches in natural language processing: A survey. arXiv preprint arXiv:2110.01852 (2021)
14. Likert, R.: A technique for the measurement of attitudes. Arch. Psychol. **22**(140), 5–55 (1932)
15. Lohr, S.L.: Sampling: Design and Analysis, Chapman and Hall/CRC (2021)
16. Long, L., Zhang, R., Zhao, Y., Li, L.: On llm-driven synthetic data generation, curation, and quality. In: Findings of the Association for Computational Linguistics, pp. 10452–10467 (2024)
17. OGE-PE: Relatório de gestão anual 2024 – versão 3.1.2 (2025)
18. Opitz, J., Burst, S.: Macro f1 and macro f1. arXiv preprint arXiv:1911.03347 (2019)
19. Paiva, E.S.d.: Classificação de denúncias: Utilização de processamento de linguagem natural para aprimorar atividades de ouvidoria (2023)
20. SGB/CPRM: Manual de procedimentos internos da ouvidoria-geral (2025)

21. Shorten, C., Khoshgoftaar, T.M., Furht, B.: Text data augmentation for deep learning. J. Big Data **8**(1), 101 (2021)
22. Souza, F., Nogueira, R., Lotufo, R.: Bertimbau: pretrained bert models for brazilian portuguese. In: Brazilian Conference on Intelligent Systems, pp. 403–417 (2020)
23. Zhao, H., Chen, H., Ruggles, T.A., Feng, Y., Singh, D., Yoon, H.J.: Improving text classification with large language model-based data augmentation. Electronics **13**(13), 2535 (2024)

The Emperor's New Digital Transformation? An LLM-Based Analysis of What Governments Actually Procure

Marcel Hofgesang(✉), Luca T. Bauer, Steffen Fock, and Björn Niehaves

Digital Public, University of Bremen, Bremen, Germany
hofgesang@uni-bremen.de

Abstract. European governments increasingly rely on GovTech markets to source modular digital components, yet it remains unclear whether public procurement actually delivers Digitization, process-focused Digitalization, or genuine Digital Transformation. This paper analyzes large-scale IT procurement data from Tenders Electronic Daily (TED), using LLM-as-a-judge classification to map awards onto these three types of digital change, enriched with firm-level supplier data. In the German TED award sample analyzed here, Digitalization dominates both award counts and contract value, while transformative projects remain rare and predominantly flow to established BigTech providers. GovTech firms mainly secure smaller Digitalization contracts, complementing rather than disrupting incumbent dominance. These findings provide evidence from a major European public IT procurement market and should not be read as EU-wide estimates. They instead speak to debates on digital sovereignty and strategic government Digitalization.

Keywords: Digital Transformation · Public procurement · GovTech · Digitalization · LLM-as-a-judge · Tenders Electronic Daily · Public-sector innovation

1 Introduction

Across Europe, public administrations are under pressure to renew how they source, build, and govern digital capabilities [4,23]. While decades of e-government reforms have relied on a mix of in-house development and large-scale contracting, current conditions increasingly tilt the balance toward "buying" digital capacity [32]: administrations face persistent constraints in specialist skills and delivery capacity, while market offerings–ranging from cloud platforms to modular "government components"–promise faster implementation and access to scarce expertise [19,20]. Yet this shift in sourcing is politically and strategically charged [11]. In the European context, procurement decisions intersect with concerns about dependency on dominant technology vendors, control over

Published by Springer Nature Switzerland 2027
G. Viale Pereira et al. (Eds.): EGOV 2026, LNCS 16933, pp. 231–247, 2027.
https://doi.org/10.1007/978-3-032-35747-2_15

critical digital infrastructures, and the safeguarding of public values–issues that recent GovTech research frames explicitly as risks to digital sovereignty when private providers leverage asymmetries in technical knowledge and platform power [4,6,23].

A key challenge for research and practice is that "digital change" is often invoked as a single umbrella term, despite important conceptual distinctions that imply different ambitions, risks, and governance requirements [19,26,30]. Digital innovation and transformation research commonly differentiates between (i) *Digitization* as converting analog information into digital form, (ii) *Digitalization* as using digital technologies to alter and optimize processes and interactions, and (iii) *Digital Transformation* as more pervasive reconfiguration that reshapes organizational logics, relationships, and value creation [2,19,30,31]. In the public sector, this ambiguity is particularly consequential: expert accounts show that administrations themselves use the labels inconsistently, even though the underlying change processes range from putting services online "1:1" to revising policies, processes, and citizen relationships in a continuous transformation journey. Complementing this lens, digital government scholarship has long modeled "stages" of evolution–moving from Digitization toward deeper transformation and engagement with stakeholders–highlighting that different forms of digital government differ in whether they transform internal operations, external relationships, and context-specific governance arrangements.

In parallel, the GovTech narrative has gained traction as a new market- and ecosystem-oriented framing of how governments modernize: digital public services increasingly integrate private-sector solution components (e.g., identity, signing, data validation, workflow tools) and depend on interoperability across actors [4,10,23]. GovTech can therefore be seen as extending classical "make-or-buy" sourcing choices by enabling governments to combine, replace, or "plug in" components around legacy systems–while simultaneously raising questions about lock-in, standards, and the long-term distribution of control and responsibility [13].

Despite these debates, we still know surprisingly little–systematically and at scale–about what European public administrations are actually procuring when they procure "digital" [8,32]. Strategy documents and GovTech narratives articulate ambitions for digital transformation, but procurement awards reveal which ambitions are translated into funded and contractually specified projects. Observed procurement behavior therefore complements these strategy narratives and may also challenge them when spending patterns point primarily to incremental Digitalization rather than more fundamental transformation. This gap matters because procurement is not merely an operational step. It is a policy instrument that shapes which reform aims become inscribed into technology choices and configurations. Prior public-sector IS research emphasizes that technologies are not neutral: design and selection embed specific reform logics and can produce durable, path-dependent effects through the installed base and through interoperability choices [1,2,30,31]. Yet most existing accounts of Digital Transformation in government focus on strategies, capabilities, or case narratives, with comparatively limited evidence that links procurement patterns to distinct types of digital change [19].

To address this gap, we analyze contract award notices from Tenders Electronic Daily (TED) [25] and classify the descriptions of these award notices to map each award to one of three types of digital change: Digitization, Digitalization, and Digital Transformation. We treat procurement as a trace of governments' enacted priorities and constraints, which leads to our research question:

RQ: *What types of digital change are procured in the German TED award sample analyzed here, and how does the provider landscape differ across these types?*

The remainder of the paper is structured as follows. Section 2 develops the conceptual background by connecting debates on Digital Transformation in the public sector, digital government evolution, and the emerging field of GovTech. Section 3 details our methodology, dataset construction from TED, and the LLM-based classification approach. Section 4 presents the results, first describing overall procurement patterns and then unpacking classification results across the three categories of digital change. Section 5 discusses implications for European public-sector digital sovereignty, interoperability, and the likely trajectory of administrative change. Section 6 concludes with contributions, limitations, and a research agenda for studying procurement as a mechanism of digital government evolution.

2 Conceptual Background

2.1 Digital Transformation in the Public Sector

Recent information systems and digital government research treats Digital Transformation as a broad organizational and institutional phenomenon rather than as the mere adoption of new technologies [2,19,28,30,31]. At the same time, Digital Transformation often is used encompassing its antecedents [19,26]. For this reason, a useful analytical starting point is the distinction between *Digitization*, *Digitalization*, and *Digital Transformation*, structured as follows [19,28].

Digitization refers to the conversion of analog information into digital form, aiming primarily at cost savings and more efficient use of existing resources. In the public sector this typically means a one-to-one transfer of existing administrative procedures into digital formats, like scanning paper files, digitizing patient records, or replacing paper forms with their online equivalents, without redesigning the underlying service logic.

Digitalization goes further by using digital technologies to improve and redesign existing processes and interactions, with the goal of raising process efficiency and service quality. Public-sector examples include online application workflows, e-prescription processes, and automated case routing, like initiatives that modernize service delivery through integrated workflows and back-office connectivity without fundamentally altering organizational structures or institutional relationships.

Digital Transformation, by contrast, denotes a holistic reconfiguration of organizational logics, structures, and relationships through digital technologies [19,28]. Rather than optimizing existing processes, it entails broader institutional change: redesigned relationships between administrations and citizens, life-event services spanning multiple agencies, and- integrated digital platforms that restructure how work is coordinated and delivered. Transformation is typically a continuous rather than finite process, unfolding through accumulated changes in architectures, roles, and governance [2,19,30].

Digital change is path dependent, technology choices do not merely support reform, they embed particular reform logics and create installed-base effects that shape future options [1,30,31]. Especially in government, where legacy systems, legal requirements, and interorganizational dependencies are pervasive, choices about architectures, standards, interfaces, and vendors can lock administrations into specific trajectories [18]. Procurement decisions are thus analytically relevant because they materialize these choices.

The public sector also differs from the private sector in what transformation is meant to achieve. Public administrations do not transform primarily to generate revenue or competitive advantage, but under conditions of democratic accountability, legality, transparency, fairness, and public value creation [7,19]. As a result, Digital Transformation in government is not only about efficiency gains, but also about how authority is exercised, how services are accessed, and how citizen-state relationships are configured.

What remains unclear, however, is where public administrations in the German TED award sample analyzed here currently stand on this spectrum. The literature offers many strategies, frameworks, and case accounts, but much less systematic evidence on whether procurement in this national setting is predominantly oriented toward simple Digitization, process-oriented Digitalization, or more 'transformative change' [8,32].

2.2 Public Procurement for Innovation

Research on public IT-sourcing and the acquisition side, what administrations concretely procure when they pursue digital change is still underexplored [13,21]. This is a significant blind spot because many of the practical hurdles of Digitization, Digitalization, and transformation can be grouped into two broad perspectives: an organizational one, illustrated by municipal digital change-agent initiatives [16], and an acquisition one. Even where administrations possess strategic intent, their ability to enact change depends on how they define needs, structure tenders, source capabilities, and allocate responsibilities to external providers.

Thus, procurement is a policy instrument through which administrations encode priorities, define acceptable solution spaces, and shape the direction of organizational change. Sourcing for scanning and archiving documents reflects a different orientation than one for service platforms, or shared digital identity.

This argument becomes more important as the classical public-sector make-or-buy decision becomes more unstable. Digital complexity has weakened the boundary between internally developed public IT and externally sourced solutions [27]. Governments increasingly rely on external cloud services, modular software, APIs, and specialized components that must be integrated into existing infrastructures [4,23]. As a result, procurement is no longer simply about buying a bounded system. It is increasingly about configuring evolving socio-technical arrangements across organizational and market boundaries.

Despite visible relevance, we still lack systematic evidence on what public administrations are procuring digitally and how such procurement maps onto different forms of digital change. This is where TED data become analytically useful. Tenders Electronic Daily provides a large-scale record of how European public buyers describe their needs and which providers receive contracts [25]. While such data do not capture implementation outcomes, they offer an underused window into enacted digital priorities. For our purposes, TED is valuable precisely because it allows us to move from abstract debates about Digital Transformation to observable procurement patterns.

2.3 Case in Point: Government Technology GovTech

GovTech adds an ecosystem perspective to these developments. Rather than viewing public digitalization primarily through the lens of large, monolithic IT contracts, the GovTech literature emphasizes a more modular landscape in which startups, scale-ups, and specialized providers offer reusable solution components for government [4,14,23]. This framing contrasts with legacy models of public IT dominated by large vendors and long-term system integration, and it suggests a more dynamic market for public digital capabilities. A key feature of GovTech is its component logic. Governments increasingly assemble digital services from pluggable parts such as identity, authentication, signing, payments, workflow, and data validation [11]. This can make digital service provision more flexible, but it also blurs the boundary between service delivery and platform dependency. Public services are no longer simply built or bought as single systems. They are composed through interdependent components whose interfaces, standards, and governance arrangements become strategically important.

This is why GovTech is closely tied to debates on digital sovereignty [3]. As governments rely more heavily on external providers, concerns grow around vendor dependency, asymmetric technical knowledge, proprietary lock-in, and control over core infrastructures [4,11,23]. These concerns do not only arise from direct contractor relationships: recent work on "clouded dependence" shows that supplier diversification at the contractor layer can coexist with concentrated dependence on underlying cloud platforms [9]. In the European context, these concerns are reinforced by the interoperability agenda [6]. Thus, through GovTech, we can locate one element of policy setting within the Digitization–Digitalization–Transformation continuum. Many GovTech offerings primarily enable Digitalization by improving workflows, service channels, and integration capacity–some support basic Digitization–and most of them market themselves as digital transformers [20,23]. Taken together, the three concepts point to a common empirical gap. We have conceptual distinctions between Digitization,

Digitalization, and Digital Transformation [19,28]. We understand procurement as a mechanism that materializes strategic priorities [8,21,27]. We know that GovTech is reshaping the supplier and component landscape of digital government [4,23]. What we do not yet have is systematic evidence linking procurement patterns to types of digital change and to the provider landscapes associated with them. This is the gap our study addresses.

3 Methodology and Data Collection

3.1 Dataset Construction

To address the empirical gap outlined above, this study relies on large-scale public procurement data as an observable record of governments' technological sourcing decisions. Procurement datasets provide structured information on contracts, suppliers, and contracting authorities and are increasingly used to analyze government spending patterns and procurement markets [24,29].

The dataset was constructed from procurement notices published on Tenders Electronic Daily (TED), the official online supplement to the Official Journal of the European Union for public procurement [12]. Monthly bulk downloads covering January 2024 to December 2025 yielded approximately 1.2 million records. The raw TED data were unzipped and converted into the eForms data structure. Due to changes in the TED publication format, efficient conversion was only possible for notices published from April 2024 onwards, leaving 1,018,300 procurement records after harmonization. To focus on IT-related procurements, the dataset was filtered using the Common Procurement Vocabulary (CPV). Only divisions 48 (Software package and information systems) and 72 (IT services: consulting, software development, internet and support) were retained, reducing the dataset to 46,256 records. Next, we restricted the dataset to procurement awards with identifiable contracting authorities and suppliers, removing records with unknown buyers or suppliers. This resulted in 28,385 procurement awards. For the final analysis, we retained only awards with both a German contracting authority and a German awarded supplier, an available LLM classification, and a positive normalized contract value in euros. This yielded the final analysis sample of 1,169 IT procurement awards.

3.2 LLM-as-a-Judge Classification

To categorize procurement awards by type of digital change, we employed a zero-shot, rubric-based LLM-as-a-judge classification setup [33]. While the CPV filter isolates IT procurement, distinctions between Digitization, Digitalization, and Digital Transformation require semantic coding of procurement intent from TED text fields. The model therefore received each award's title and description and assigned scores for all three dimensions following the conceptual framework by Verhoef et al. [28].

The prompt combined role framing, category definitions, and a fixed JSON schema, but no labeled examples. We therefore treat the procedure as a theory-guided coding protocol rather than as supervised training. Chain-of-thought prompting was not used, the reasoning field was retained only as a brief audit trace.

- Digitization: conversion of analog information into digital formats
- Digitalization: optimization or automation of processes using digital technologies
- Digital Transformation: strategic or business model changes enabled by digital technologies

Classification was performed using `gpt-4-turbo` (temperature 0.3), which returned JSON scores for digitization, digitalization, and digital_transformation, plus a short reasoning field. A single final class was assigned as the highest-scoring dimension. After currency normalization, we retained classified awards with positive contract value and both a German contracting authority and a German supplier, resulting in the final analysis sample of 1,169 awards.

For reproducibility, the underlying dataset (1,169 awards), award notice fields used in this study, award-level LLM classifications, coding protocol (including the full prompt), and data dictionary are publicly available (see [15]).

This operationalization is intentionally bounded: it relies on TED title and description fields rather than full tender documentation, implementation data, or ex post outcomes, and the three-category scheme abstracts from finer subtypes. The classification should therefore be interpreted as a transparent, model-specific coding protocol rather than as model-independent ground truth. Human-coder validation supports the plausibility of the category assignments, but no multi-model sensitivity analysis was conducted. Future research should compare alternative LLMs, prompting strategies, and multi-label coding schemes.

3.3 Firm-Level Data Enrichment

To analyze supplier characteristics, company-level data were added to the dataset. From the classified procurement awards, 646 unique supplier organizations were extracted. These organizations were matched against the Orbis company database [22], which provides standardized financial and organizational data for firms worldwide. Matching was primarily conducted using exact name matching. In cases of ambiguous matches, manual verification was performed to ensure correct firm identification.

A total of 65 organizations could not be matched. This was primarily due to suppliers not being present in the database (e.g., individual contractors or temporary consortium structures) or due to inconsistent naming in the procurement data (e.g., encoding errors or incomplete company names). Ultimately, 581 companies were successfully matched and enriched with firm-level data from Orbis, like year of founding and revenue in Euro.

To examine how award types are distributed across supplier categories, we classified companies into the three technology sectors GovTech, MediumTech and BigTech. GovTech companies include SMEs and startups younger than ten years. MediumTech companies are firms older than ten years with an annual revenue below €50 million. BigTech companies are firms older than ten years with an annual revenue exceeding €50 million.

4 Results

4.1 General Findings of Public IT Procurement

This section provides an overview of the distribution of IT procurement awards across the three types of digital change. In total, 1,169 procurement awards were classified using the LLM-as-a-Judge.

To examine how Digital Transformation manifests in public IT procurement, we analyze both the number of procurement awards and their associated contract values across the three categories. While the number of awards provides insight into how frequently certain types of digital solutions are procured, the contract values indicate where financial resources are concentrated. The following sections present these two perspectives.

4.2 Distribution of Awards Across Transformation Categories

The classification results indicate that the vast majority of IT procurement projects in the dataset relate to Digitalization efforts. Out of all classified awards, 83.0% awards were categorized as Digitalization initiatives. In comparison, 11.1% awards were classified as Digitization projects, while only 5.9% were identified as Digital Transformation initiatives.

A similar pattern emerges when considering the aggregated contract values. Procurement projects categorized as Digitalization account for the largest share of financial volume, totaling €2, 175, 422, 470. Digital Transformation projects represent a smaller, yet still substantial, share with a value of €252, 940, 504. In contrast, Digitization projects account for €83, 608, 474 of total procurement value. Results are summarized in Table 1.

The dominance of Digitalization awards indicates that public-sector IT procurement in the analyzed dataset primarily focuses on improving or extending existing digital processes. In contrast, comparatively few contracts explicitly target more fundamental Digital Transformation initiatives.

Table 1. Distribution of Procurement Awards and Contract Values Across Transformation Categories

Category	Awards	%	Contract Value (€)	%
Digitization	130	11.1	83,608,474	3.3
Digitalization	970	83.0	2,175,422,470	86.6
Digital Transformation	69	5.9	252,940,504	10.1
Total	1,169	100.0	2,511,971,448	100.0

4.3 Solutions Mapped on Provider Sizes

To examine how procurement awards are distributed across both the three types of digital change and the technological sectors of the suppliers, we analyzed the number of awards attributed to each supplier class and how these awards are distributed across the three digital transformation categories.

Figure 1 summarizes the proportional distribution of awards within each supplier sector. For example, within the BigTech sector a total of 642 awards were identified, of which 57 were classified as Digitization projects, 544 as Digitalization projects, and 41 as Digital Transformation initiatives.

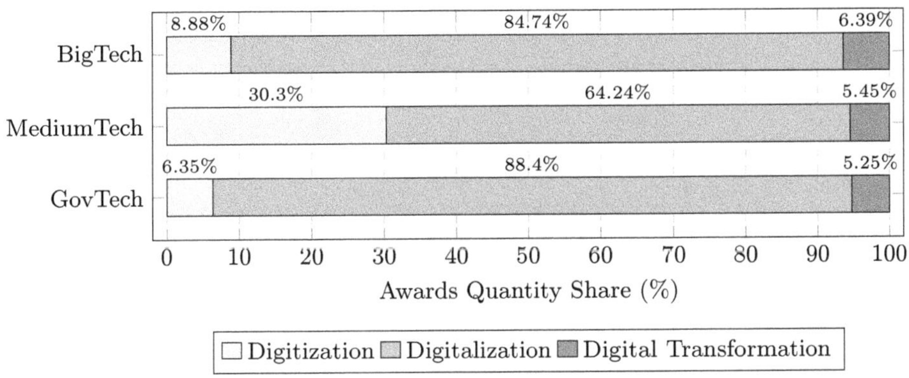

Fig. 1. Number of contracts per digital transformation stage and company size.

Overall, 54.92% of all procurement awards were adjudicated to BigTech firms, 30.97% to GovTech firms, and 14.11% to MediumTech firms, with Digitalization representing 82.98% of all awards, Digitization 11.12%, and Digital Transformation 5.9%.

Digital Transformation remains rare within each supplier class. Even among BigTech firms, only 41 of 642 awards (6.39%) were classified as Digital Transformation, while Digitalization clearly dominates their portfolio. When viewed from the opposite perspective, however, BigTech firms account for 41 of the 69 Digital Transformation awards in the dataset (59.4%), indicating that transformation-oriented awards are concentrated among large established providers.

Relative distributions differ markedly across supplier classes. MediumTech firms (165 awards) show the highest share of Digitization projects (30.30%), suggesting their focus on basic conversion of analog information. GovTech firms (362 awards) exhibit the strongest concentration in Digitalization projects (88.40%), indicating their role in process modernization. These patterns reflect a functional differentiation in the supplier landscape, with BigTech dominating transformation initiatives, MediumTech focused on digitization, and GovTech concentrated in digitalization.

4.4 Solutions Mapped on Award Values

To complement the analysis of award counts, we additionally examined the distribution of total contract values across suppliers technology sectors and types of digital change. In total, the analyzed dataset contains approximately €2.51 billion in awarded contract value. The vast majority of this financial volume was allocated to BigTech firms, which account for approximately €2.49 billion of the total value. In comparison, MediumTech firms received around €19.1 million in contract value, while GovTech firms account for less than €0.3 million. The relative shares of awards values will be discussed in the following and are summarized in Figure 2.

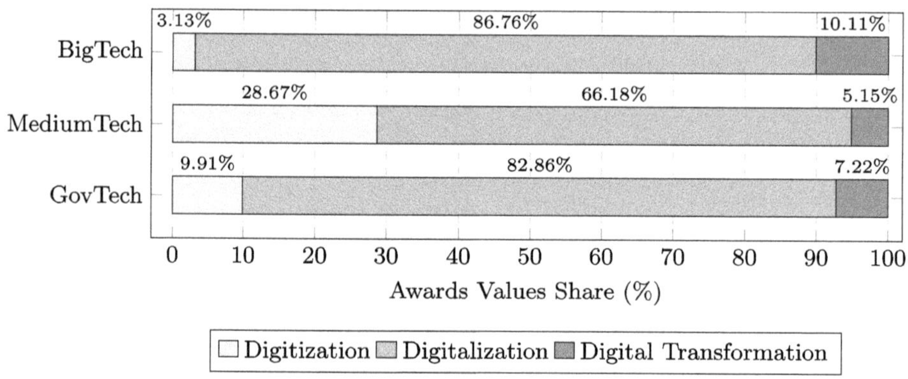

Fig. 2. Contract values by digitization class and company size.

The distribution of contract values within each supplier class reveals a pronounced stratification of financial resources. BigTech firms concentrate approximately €251.9 million on Digital Transformation but allocate 86.7% of their total contract value to Digitalization. MediumTech firms direct 66.2% of their value to Digitalization and 28.7% to Digitization, reflecting their focus on smaller-scale modernization. GovTech firms receive minimal overall volume, with 82.7% concentrated in Digitalization, 9.9% in Digitization, and 7.2% in Digital Transformation. Large-scale contracts, particularly for Digitalization and Digital Transformation, flow predominantly to BigTech firms, while smaller providers participate chiefly in incremental improvements to existing systems.

4.5 Human Validation of LLM Classification

To assess the reliability of the automated classification, a random subsample of 100 procurement awards was drawn and independently coded by a domain-informed human coder, without access to the LLM assignments. The human codes were then compared against the LLM classifications.

Most classifications fall into the category Digitalization, which represents the majority class in the dataset. Disagreements occur primarily between the conceptually adjacent categories Digitization and Digitalization, while classifications of Digital Transformation show comparatively high agreement. Table 2 summarizes the comparison in a confusion matrix.

Table 2. Validation of LLM-based digitization classification against examinee coding.

LLM	Human		
	Digitization	Digitalization	Digital Transformation
Digitization	5	5	1
Digitalization	1	79	1
Digital Transformation	1	1	6

A comparison of the LLM-based classifications with the human coding provides direct reliability evidence for the coding procedure. Percent agreement was high ($P_o = 0.90$), and Cohen's κ indicated substantial agreement after accounting for chance agreement ($P_e = 0.703$, $\kappa = 0.664$) [17]. These results support the reliability of the classification procedure, while indicating that disagreements occur primarily between the adjacent categories of Digitization and Digitalization. These results are summarized in Table 3.

Table 3. Interrater agreement between LLM and human examinee.

Metric	Value
Percent Agreement (P_o)	0.90
Expected Agreement (P_e)	0.703
Cohen's κ	0.664

5 Discussion

The findings of this study provide systematic evidence from the German TED procurement awards analyzed here on what types of digital change public administrations procure when acquiring IT capabilities. Digitalization projects clearly dominate, accounting for the vast majority of both contract numbers and procurement volume. In contrast, initiatives corresponding to Digitization and especially Digital Transformation remain comparatively rare. This pattern suggests that, in this single-country setting, public-sector IT procurement is primarily used to improve and extend existing administrative processes rather than to fundamentally reconfigure organizational structures or service models. By examining procurement as an empirical trace of digital reform priorities, the results offer a data-driven perspective on how digital change is operationalized in practice in a major European public IT procurement market.

Through applying Verhoef et al.'s (2021) [28] perspective, we strived to contribute to ongoing debates on Digital Transformation in the public sector [19]. While policy strategies and reform narratives frequently emphasize transformative change, the procurement patterns observed here complement these narratives as an empirical trace of funded priorities, and challenge them by showing that most investments are oriented toward incremental Digitalization rather than more fundamental transformation. Procurement decisions thus appear to reinforce existing administrative trajectories rather than acting as a primary driver of institutional transformation. This observation aligns with broader research highlighting the path-dependent and organizationally constrained nature of digital government development, where legacy infrastructures, regulatory constraints, unclear responsibilities, and organizational routines shape the scope of feasible reforms [16].

Our analysis also sheds light on the structure of the supplier landscape in public-sector IT procurement. While GovTech firms participate in a considerable number of procurement awards [32], their financial share of total contract value remains minimal compared to that of large technology providers. BigTech firms dominate the financial dimension of procurement in the German sample, particularly in large-scale Digitalization and Digital Transformation projects [11]. This distribution qualifies the often optimistic narrative of GovTech ecosystems as a disruptive force in public-sector innovation [4,23]. Rather than replacing established vendors, GovTech firms appear to complement existing provider structures by contributing primarily to smaller-scale Digitalization initiatives within this administrative setting.

The strong concentration of procurement value among major technology firms in the German sample indicates that key elements of public-sector digital infrastructures continue to depend on a relatively small group of established vendors. This finding should be interpreted as a direct-supplier view of dependency, since procurement data record awarded firms more reliably than the underlying platforms, resellers, or infrastructure layers on which digital services may ultimately depend [9]. As the Interoperable Europe Act and Digital Markets act imply [5,6], such dependencies may create long-term challenges related to vendor lock-in, asymmetric knowledge relationships, and reduced strategic autonomy for public administrations. This pattern is highly relevant for European policy debates because it speaks to open standards, interoperability, and a more diversified GovTech ecosystem [6].

Finally, our study demonstrates the analytical potential of combining large-scale procurement data with LLM-based text classification. By leveraging procurement descriptions as signals of governments' digital priorities, the approach provides a scalable method for linking digital government debates to observable sourcing practices. While procurement records cannot capture implementation outcomes, they offer a valuable empirical lens for examining how digital transformation agendas are translated into concrete technological acquisitions [24,29].

The human validation results provide additional evidence for the suitability of the LLM-as-a-Judge approach for classifying procurement descriptions. The observed substantial agreement between automated and human coding is consistent with recent cross-disciplinary benchmarks suggesting that zero-shot LLMs can achieve fair to good levels of agreement with human annotators on taxonomic labeling tasks [33]. Disagreements occurred primarily between the conceptually adjacent categories of Digitization and Digitalization, while classifications of Digital Transformation showed comparatively high consistency. This observation aligns with findings by Ziems et al. (2024), who noted that LLMs often face challenges with the subtle or non-conventional language of expert taxonomies, sometimes defaulting to more generic interpretations when categories are conceptually similar [33].

Given the conceptual proximity of the first two categories and the limited textual detail typically contained in procurement descriptions, this level of agreement supports a transparent and scalable approach to large-scale content classification that is strengthened by human validation. At the same time, future studies should complement automated classification with targeted manual validation samples, particularly when distinctions between closely related categories are analytically important. Overall, the results indicate that LLM-based classification can be applied effectively in similar research settings, especially when analyzing large procurement datasets where manual coding would be impractical.

5.1 Limitations and Further Research

This study is based on procurement awards associated with Germany. Germany is not treated as representative of Europe as a whole, but as a substantively important case for examining public IT procurement. It combines one of Europe's largest public IT procurement markets with complex federal administrative structures, persistent digitalization challenges, and direct exposure to European interoperability and digital sovereignty debates. The findings should therefore be interpreted as evidence from a major European public IT procurement market rather than as EU-wide estimates. Procurement practices, market structures, and Digitalization priorities may differ across countries, so future research should extend the analysis to comparative or EU-wide samples.

A second limitation relates to the conceptual abstraction used in the analysis. The classification relies on short TED descriptions, a coarse three-category taxonomy, and a single-model coding protocol without multi-model sensitivity testing. At the same time, the human validation on 100 randomly selected awards showed high percent agreement ($P_o = 0.90$) and substantial agreement overall ($\kappa = 0.664$), which supports the plausibility of the resulting classifications without turning them into model-independent ground truth. Future research could extend this large-scale, human-validated coding approach through larger manual validation samples, alternative LLMs, prompting strategies, and more fine-grained taxonomies of digital procurement.

A small subset of procurement records in the dataset contains extremely low reported contract values. Given that EU procurement notices published on TED typically concern contracts above established EU publication thresholds, these values likely reflect reporting artifacts, placeholder entries, or inconsistencies in the underlying procurement data rather than actual contract amounts. Since such cases represent only a small fraction of the dataset and occur predominantly outside the classified supplier groups, they do not materially affect the aggregated patterns observed in the analysis.

6 Conclusion

This study examined how public administrations in the German TED award sample procure digital technologies and what this reveals about the nature of digital change in the public sector. By analyzing procurement records and classifying them into the three stages of digital change (Digitization, Digitalization, and Digital Transformation), the study provides an empirical perspective on how public administrations translate digital reform agendas into concrete technological investments.

The findings show that public-sector IT procurement in the German sample is overwhelmingly oriented toward Digitalization, focusing on the improvement and extension of existing administrative processes. In contrast, procurement activities associated with more fundamental Digital Transformation remain comparatively rare. These results suggest that, despite ambitious policy narratives surrounding digital transformation, public administrations in this national setting continue to rely primarily on incremental modernization strategies when acquiring digital technologies.

The analysis also highlights important dynamics in the supplier landscape of public-sector IT markets. While GovTech firms participate in a notable number of procurement awards, the majority of procurement value remains concentrated among large technology providers in the German sample. This pattern suggests that GovTech ecosystems currently complement rather than fundamentally reshape existing procurement structures.

Beyond these substantive findings, the study demonstrates the potential of combining procurement data with LLM-based classification methods to analyze digital government developments at scale. Procurement records represent a valuable but underutilized empirical source for understanding how digital transformation agendas are operationalized through public-sector investments. Expanding such approaches to comparative country samples or EU-wide datasets offers promising opportunities for future research on the evolving relationship between digital transformation, public procurement, and technological sovereignty in government.

References

1. Baiyere, A., Grover, V., Lyytinen, K.J., Woerner, S., Gupta, A.: Digital "x"—charting a path for digital-themed research. Inf. Syst. Res. **34**, 463–486 (2023). https://doi.org/10.1287/isre.2022.1186
2. Baiyere, A., Salmela, H., Tapanainen, T.: Digital transformation and the new logics of business process management. Eur. J. Inf. Syst. **29**, 238–259 (2020). https://doi.org/10.1080/0960085X.2020.1718007
3. Bauer, L.T., Westermann, J., Degen, K., Niehaves, B.: European sociotechnical imaginaries of government technology between value proposition and tangible policymaking. In: EGOV-CeDEM-ePart-Ongoing 2025, pp. 1–12. CEUR Workshop Proceedings (2025)
4. Bharosa, N.: The rise of GovTech: Trojan horse or blessing in disguise? A research agenda. Gov. Inf. Q. **39**, 101692 (2022). https://doi.org/10.1016/j.giq.2022.101692
5. Commission of the European Union: Regulation (EU) 2022/1925 of the European parliament and of the council of 14 September 2022 on contestable and fair markets in the digital sector and amending directives (EU) 2019/1937 and (EU) 2020/1828 (digital markets act) (2022)
6. Commission of the European Union: Regulation (EU) 2024/903 of the European parliament and of the council of 13 march 2024 laying down measures for a high level of public sector interoperability across the union (interoperable Europe act) (2024). https://eur-lex.europa.eu/eli/reg/2024/903/oj
7. Cordella, A., Paletti, A.: ICTs and value creation in public sector: manufacturing logic vs service logic. Inf. Polity **23**, 125–141 (2018). https://doi.org/10.3233/IP-170061
8. Davies, N., McBride, K., Kleinaltenkamp, M.: Move fast and break things? barriers to GovTech procurement in the united kingdom. In: International Conference on Digital Government Research (dg.o 2025), vol. 1, pp. 1–15 (2025). https://doi.org/10.59490/dgo.2025.972
9. Davies, N., Rystrøm, J.: Clouded dependence: supplier diversity and hidden platform concentration in digital government. In: 27th Annual International Conference on Digital Government Research (dg.o 2026), pp. 1–15 (2026)
10. Daßler, L., Ruckstuhl, T., Hein, A., Krcmar, H.: From complexity to clarity - a taxonomy of GovTech startup business models for public sector innovation. In: International Conference on Digital Government Research (dg.o 2025), vol. 1, pp. 1–15 (2025). https://doi.org/10.59490/dgo.2025.971
11. Degen, K., Teubner, T.: Wallet wars or digital public infrastructure? Orchestrating a digital identity data ecosystem from a government perspective. Electron. Markets **34**, 50 (2024). https://doi.org/10.1007/s12525-024-00731-1
12. European Union: TED —- Bulk download of TED notices in XML format (2026). https://ted.europa.eu/en/simap/xml-bulk-download/-/xml-files/monthly/2024
13. Guggenberger, T., Schüll, M., Stoetzer, J.C., Urbach, N.: A resourcing perspective on public-private-sector collaborations for digital innovation. Inf. Organ. **36**, 100611 (2026). https://doi.org/10.1016/J.INFOANDORG.2026.100611
14. Hoekstra, M., Veenstra, A.F.V., Bharosa, N.: Success factors and barriers of GovTech ecosystems: a case study of GovTech ecosystems in the Netherlands and Lithuania. In: Proceedings of the 24th Annual International Conference on Digital Government Research, pp. 280–288. ACM (2023). https://doi.org/10.1145/3598469.3598500

15. Hofgesang, M.: LLM-classified European public it procurement awards: digitization, digitalization, and digital transformation in German ted notices, 2024–2025. https://doi.org/10.5281/zenodo.20184314
16. Jäger, I., Hein, A., Krcmar, H.: Wind of Change or Just Another Digitalization Breeze? Lessons from Municipal Digital Change Agent Initiatives 26. https://doi.org/10.59490/dgo.2025.1030
17. Landis, J.R., Koch, G.G.: The measurement of observer agreement for categorical data. Biometrics **33**(1), 159–174 (1977). https://doi.org/10.2307/2529310
18. Meijer, A., Thaens, M.: Path dependency of smart cities: how technological and social legacies condition smart city development, pp. 31–42. Springer International Publishing (2021). https://doi.org/10.1007/978-3-030-61033-3_2
19. Mergel, I., Edelmann, N., Haug, N.: Defining digital transformation: results from expert interviews. Gov. Inf. Q. **36**, 101385 [1–16] (2019).https://doi.org/10.1016/j.giq.2019.06.002
20. Mergel, I., Ulrich, P., Kuziemski, M., Martinez, A.: Scoping GovTech dynamics in the EU. Technical Report, Publications Office of the European Union (2022)
21. Moe, C.E.: Research on public procurement of information systems: the need for a process approach. Commun. Assoc. Inf. Syst. **34**, 1319–1335 (2014). https://doi.org/10.17705/1CAIS.03478
22. Moody's Corporation: Orbis Database: Global Private Company Data | Moody's. https://www.moodys.com/web/en/us/capabilities/company-reference-data/orbis.html
23. Niehaves, B., Klassen, G.: GovTech in Europe: influencing factors, common requirements and recommendations. Technical report, Publications Office of the European Union (2024)
24. Potin, L., Labatut, V., Morand, P.H., Largeron, C.: FOPPA: an open database of French public procurement award notices from 2010–2020. Sci. Data **10**(1), 303 (2023). https://doi.org/10.1038/s41597-023-02213-z
25. Publications Office of the European Union: Ted – EU tenders, the supplement to the official journal of the European union (2026). https://ted.europa.eu/en/
26. Scholta, H., Mertens, W., Kowalkiewicz, M., Becker, J.: From one-stop shop to no-stop shop: an e-government stage model. Gov. Inf. Q. **36**, 11–26 (2019). https://doi.org/10.1016/j.giq.2018.11.010
27. Thunes, J., Kempton, A.: Balancing insourcing and outsourcing towards digital government: establishing obligatory gateways as an approach for targeted insourcing. In: Proceedings of the 58th Hawaii International Conference on System Sciences, pp. 1–10. Schidler College (2025). https://doi.org/10.24251/HICSS.2025.240
28. Verhoef, P.C., et al.: Digital transformation: a multidisciplinary reflection and research agenda. J. Bus. Res. **122**(C), 889–901 (2021). https://doi.org/10.1016/j.jbusres.2019.09.022
29. Wachs, J., Fazekas, M., Kertész, J.: Corruption risk in contracting markets: a network science perspective. Int. J. Data Sci. Anal. **12**(1), 45–60 (2020). https://doi.org/10.1007/s41060-019-00204-1
30. Wessel, L., Baiyere, A., Ologeanu-Taddei, R., Cha, J., Jensen, T.B.: Unpacking the difference between digital transformation and it-enabled organizational transformation. J. Assoc. Inf. Syst. **22**, 102–129 (2021). https://doi.org/10.17705/1jais.00655
31. Wessel, L., Mosconi, E., Indulska, M., Baiyere, A.: Digital transformation: Quo vadit? Inf. Syst. J. **35**, 1294–1308 (2025). https://doi.org/10.1111/isj.12578

32. Westermann, J., Klassen, G., Bauer, L.T., Fritzsche, R.: Breaking tech monopolies: the role of public procurement in fostering SME-led innovation in Europe. In: International Conference on Digital Government Research (dg.o 2025). vol. 1, pp. 1–15 (2025). https://doi.org/10.59490/dgo.2025.973
33. Ziems, C., et al.: Can large language models transform computational social science? Comput. Linguist. **50**(1), 237–291 (2024). https://doi.org/10.1162/coli_a_00502

AI Adoption Despite Limited Readiness? Examining Early-Stage AI Adoption in Public Administration

Ina Jäger(✉) and Stephan Le

Technical University of Munich, Boltzmannstraße 3, 85748 Garching near Munich, Germany
{ina.jaeger,stephan.le}@tum.de

Abstract. Public administrations are increasingly adopting artificial intelligence (AI) to improve internal efficiency and service quality. This process has intensified with the launch of generative AI platforms, which have made AI more accessible for individuals. Yet many public administrations still lack full AI readiness in terms of data infrastructure, expertise, governance, or resources. Thus, it remains unclear what drives public administrations to adopt AI before establishing full AI readiness. To address this question, we conducted a qualitative study based on 38 semi-structured interviews with practitioners and experts across all federal levels in German public administration. Using an abductive coding approach and interpreting the findings through an institutional lens, we identify three mechanisms that drive and legitimize early-stage AI adoption before full readiness is established: external institutional pressure to maintain legitimacy, internal pressure to preserve functionality, and individual adoption of GenAI. Our findings suggest rethinking existing broad AI readiness frameworks as readiness requirements vary by AI type, task type, and adoption phase. The study contributes to AI adoption literature by conceptualizing adoption-before-readiness and explaining how public administration legitimizes early-stage AI adoption. It also informs practitioners who seek to leverage AI for their organization.

Keywords: Early-Stage AI Adoption · Public Administration · Artificial Intelligence · GenAI · AI Readiness

1 Introduction

Public administrations increasingly explore Artificial Intelligence (AI) to streamline operations, automate manual processes, and improve service delivery [1, 2]. The democratization of generative AI (GenAI) in 2022 has further accelerated governmental attention to AI adoption and lowered access barriers to AI-based applications, particularly for text- and language-heavy tasks such as drafting, translating, and conversational support [3–5]. Additionally, citizens increasingly expect digital public services that are responsive, efficient, and easy to use online [6].

However, the growing momentum around AI adoption creates a central tension for public administrations. A major challenge is the mismatch between rapid AI adoption and

Published by Springer Nature Switzerland 2027
G. Viale Pereira et al. (Eds.): EGOV 2026, LNCS 16933, pp. 248–263, 2027.
https://doi.org/10.1007/978-3-032-35747-2_16

the level of AI readiness, particularly in Germany [7, 8]. Although existing AI readiness frameworks identify technical, organizational, and managerial capabilities as critical preconditions for successful implementation [9, 10], many public administrations still lack adequate data, infrastructure, AI expertise, financial resources, and organizational capacity [7, 8]. As a result, AI readiness deficits increase the risk of wasted public funds, discriminatory outputs, and declining public trust [8, 9].

Beyond readiness deficits, AI includes a range of technologies with different readiness requirements, a distinction insufficiently reflected in existing frameworks. It thus remains unclear what drives early-stage AI adoption and how it can be justified in the context of public administration's accountability toward society [1, 11]. Understanding how and why AI enters administrative practice is therefore essential for ensuring that future adoption remains responsible, legitimate, and publicly accountable.

Prior research has mainly examined AI adoption in public administration through success factors, barriers, challenges, and technological, organizational, and environmental perspectives [2, 12–16]. This work offers valuable insights, including studies from Finland, the United States, and Switzerland [5, 13, 15], but it leaves several issues underexplored: the influence of institutional pressures and the role of individual actors in early-stage AI adoption, differences between AI technologies in their readiness requirements, and adoption-before-readiness as a distinct phenomenon [8–11]. Thus, researchers call for a more fine-grained examination of factors shaping different adoption stages [2, 11]. And although cultural context remains relevant in AI adoption research [17], the German public administration context is empirically absent in this literature. This leads to the guiding research question: *What rationales and mechanisms lead to early-stage AI adoption in public administrations before full AI readiness?*

To address this question, we conducted 38 interviews with practitioners and public sector experts across all federal levels of German public administration [18, 19]. This method allows us to gain in-depth insights into the rationales and mechanisms leading to early-stage AI adoption. We analyze the interviews using an abductive coding approach and interpret the findings through an institutional lens [19–22].

Our findings identify three mechanisms that drive and legitimize early-stage AI adoption: external institutional pressure, internal pressure to preserve functionality, and individual GenAI adoption. They also show that readiness requirements vary by AI type, task type, and adoption stage, allowing GenAI to begin before full AI readiness.

This study contributes to AI adoption literature in public administration by empirically examining why and how public administrations adopt AI before full AI readiness, thereby addressing empirical and theoretical gaps in the literature on AI adoption in public administration [2, 11, 13, 17]. It further suggests rethinking AI readiness frameworks to account for heterogeneous AI use cases that do not require full AI readiness. It also extends institutional theory by explaining how institutional pressures and informal GenAI use shape early-stage AI adoption, including reverse decoupling. Practitioners can use these findings for AI initiatives in their own organization.

2 Theoretical Background

2.1 AI Adoption in Public Administration

Artificial intelligence has received increasing attention in public administration. It is associated with the potential to improve service quality and administrative effectiveness through faster information processing and routine task automation [3, 4, 23, 24].

Although there is no unified definition for AI, it is commonly described as systems that perform tasks associated with human intelligence, such as learning, problem-solving, or decision support [23, 25]. Unlike conventional IT systems, which primarily follow predefined rules and produce stable, deterministic outputs, AI systems typically rely on large volumes of training data and evolve over time through learning feedback loops [25]. At the same time, public administrations must pursue such innovations under conditions of legality, accountability, fairness, transparency, and public legitimacy, which makes AI adoption both attractive and difficult [2, 23]. Within AI, practitioners and researchers distinguish between *traditional* AI and the newer branch of *generative* AI (GenAI). Traditional AI primarily analyzes existing data, recognizes patterns, classifies cases, and makes predictions or recommendations [26]. This also includes earlier (pre-ChatGPT-launch) versions of conversational AI, i.e., rule-based or retrieval-based chatbots. GenAI, by contrast, creates new outputs, such as text, images, or video, based on statistical inference [26]. It is usually provided as a ready-to-use, publicly available tool. It thus enables individual use, without prior model development, user training, or formal implementation.

The literature defines technology adoption as a process with several stages [2, 27]. For instance, Madan & Ashok [2] distinguish adoption, implementation, and diffusion as subsequent stages. They further point out that the literature still lacks a sufficiently contextual understanding of how AI enters public administration, namely the adoption decision [2]. Following this idea, this paper focuses on the early-stage adoption, before routinization and broad diffusion [2, 27]. We define early-stage adoption as the phase in which AI becomes organizationally relevant through exploration, testing, first pilots, or bottom-up individual use. It ranges from formal AI pilots to department-driven initial AI experiments to individual use. This focus captures the rationales and mechanisms through which AI enters administrative practice before full AI readiness, rather than formal procurement, scaled implementation, or diffusion.

A central concept in the AI adoption literature is AI readiness. AI readiness frameworks describe readiness as the organizational (pre)conditions and capabilities for successful AI adoption [9, 10, 16]. Common dimensions include skills and literacy, data and infrastructure, culture and leadership, governance, and financial and human resources [9, 10]. In public administration these dimensions are often only weakly developed [8]. Prior research repeatedly identifies skills gaps, data-related problems, resource constraints, and governance challenges as barriers to successful AI adoption [1, 12, 16]. This can lead to "adoption-before-readiness": the initiation of AI use, experimentation, piloting, or individual use under conditions in which not all readiness dimensions are yet fully established. Moreover, AI readiness frameworks (pre- and post-GenAI) treat AI as a uniform technology and adoption as a single event [9, 10].

2.2 Theoretical Lens

This study builds on Institutional Theory to examine early-stage AI adoption in public administrations. Institutional Theory explains how organizational behavior is shaped by the search for legitimacy within a broader institutional environment rather than by efficiency alone [20, 21]. The theory helps explain why organizations adopt structures, routines, and policies that are considered appropriate within their field. This perspective is especially relevant in public administration, where organizations operate under dense layers of legal expectations, professional norms, and public scrutiny.

One important concept, which describes the tendency of organizations facing similar environmental conditions to become alike over time, is *isomorphism* [20]. DiMaggio & Powell [20] distinguish three forms of pressure that lead to isomorphism. Coercive pressures arise from laws, mandates, and hierarchical directives. Mimetic pressures emerge when organizations imitate peers that appear successful under conditions of uncertainty. Normative pressures stem from professional standards, best practices and expert communities. Across these mechanisms, the core outcome is legitimacy, meaning that organizational actions are perceived as appropriate and desirable within socially constructed norms and expectations [20, 28]. The concept of institutional isomorphism can be applied as a lens to understanding AI adoption rationales in public administration. This lens has been used in similar contexts throughout the public sector AI literature [5, 29].

Another important concept is *decoupling*. Meyer & Rowan [21] argue that decoupling arises when organizations must comply with formal sometimes ceremonial rules and also meet efficiency demands. Ceremonial rules are institutionalized expectations and procedures that signal legitimacy and proper conduct to external audiences, such as extensive reporting processes. This creates conflict because these rules are often general and symbolic, while efficient work requires adaptation to specific local conditions and technical developments. For instance, a public administration may formally require detailed reporting for every case, while staff coordinate the information informally to efficiently deliver services. Decoupling resolves this by separating formal, ceremonial structures from daily activities. As a result, organizations maintain formal structures, while informal coordination allows work to continue in a practical and efficient way.

3 Method

To investigate rationales and mechanisms for early-stage AI adoption in public administrations, we applied a qualitative research approach [18]. We chose this approach because the phenomenon is relatively new and unaccounted for in the literature.

3.1 Data Collection

Public administrations at all levels are investing in AI although studies indicate insufficient AI readiness, particularly in Germany [6, 7]. Therefore, we used purposive sampling to recruit practitioners from German public administrations through personal networks and organizations' web presence, indicating at least some initial experience with AI to participate in interviews. Because our study focuses on early-stage AI adoption, we purposively included organizations characterized by incomplete AI readiness. For instance, we treated AI readiness as incomplete when interviewees described a weak organizational understanding of AI, including difficulties distinguishing AI from generative AI, or abandoned projects due to missing resources, or limited internal capabilities. To capture variation in AI implementation contexts, the sampling strategy covered all administrative levels, including federal, state, and municipal administrations in Germany. Table 1 summarizes the resulting distribution. Although response rates were lower among federal and state organizations, the stronger municipal representation is appropriate, as it reflects the German federal structures.

Table 1. Overview of interview sampling and technology instances.

Level of administration	Number of interviewees	AI Technology	Instances
Federal	9	GenAI	18
State	8	Trad. AI	5
Municipal	17	Multiple	3
Expert (E)	4	Other	8

We used semi-structured interviews with open-ended questions, providing flexibility by allowing follow-up questions and adaptation to topics that emerge during the interviews [18]. The interview guideline was structured into three sections: role and organizational readiness context, motivations and decision process surrounding AI project initiation, and questions on the current project status. In total, 34 practitioner interviews were conducted between June and October 2025 and four validating expert interviews were conducted at the beginning of 2026. Each interview lasted between 23 and 71 min with an average of 40 min. All interviews were conducted in German via the online conference tools Microsoft Teams or Zoom and translated to English when cited. The interviews were recorded and transcribed with the interviewees' consent. After 34 interviews, we stopped the data collection because no new themes appeared.

To validate the identified rationales, we conducted expert interviews with public sector consultants specializing in digital transformation and AI projects and practical researchers in this field. Having supported and investigated AI initiatives across multiple administrations, they offer a broader view of recurring patterns. We stopped after four interviews because all experts expressed that the list is sufficiently comprehensive.

3.2 Data Analysis

We first analyzed the practitioner interview data using a qualitative, interpretative coding approach [19, 22]. The analysis proceeded through three iterative steps [19]. First, we conducted open coding, assigning descriptive 1st order codes closely tied to practitioners' language and experiences [19, 22]. Second, we grouped conceptually related 1st codes into 2nd order themes based on similarity, co-occurrence, or conceptual affinity [19, 22].

Third, we aggregated the 2nd order themes into six aggregate dimensions, namely the rationale groups, and validated them through the expert interviews [19, 22]. Finally, we applied Institutional Theory as an interpretive lens to derive the three underlying mechanisms that lead to and legitimize early-stage AI adoption.

Throughout this process, we iteratively refined codes and categories through constant comparison until no new concepts emerged. We also stayed open to unexpected themes, by using an abductive coding approach and used peer debriefing to challenge our interpretations. Two researchers coded the data independently to strengthen validity and reduce interpretive bias. Discrepancies between coders were resolved through joint discussions until consensus was reached. To determine the success rate of the AI projects discussed, we labeled those that were implemented and in use as 'successful'.

4 Results

This section presents the findings of our study. Based on the experts' feedback, several refinements were made when backed with the initial interview data: (1) rationales were added (e.g., *Limited knowledge about (generative) AI*), (2) rationales were refined (e.g., *Vendor-driven initiation* into *Vendor-driven initiation and existing collaborations*), (3) overlapping rationales were refined through wording or removed (e.g., *Political will* and *Modernization* to *Reputation and "being seen to act and appear modern")*. The result of this iterative process is six rationale groups that lead to three mechanisms for early-stage AI adoption in German public administrations as illustrated in Fig. 1. Practitioner quotes are indicated with "P#" and expert quotes with "E#".

4.1 Legitimacy Seeking

The first rationale group in early-stage AI adoption is *Legitimacy Seeking*. It is primarily characterized by external influences and pressures that made AI, particularly GenAI, an increasingly relevant topic for public administrations. The global hype of generative AI, especially after the release of ChatGPT in 2022, intensified this dynamic by making AI appear both accessible and immediately relevant. As one interviewee recalled: *"So this whole AI topic really gained such hype due to ChatGPT and generative AI that it has also spilled over into public administration" (P29).* Coercively, one concrete motivation to explore AI in Germany stems mainly from the coalition agreement, which specifies AI as a topic that public administrations are expected to address. In addition, a substantial part of rationales in this group evolves around peer competition and reputation, particularly between states (e.g., P09, P14, P19, P20).

One interviewee described this as a strong competitive expectation with a quote from their superior: *"I don't want to see us trailing behind the other divisions, we need to be right out in front" (P16).* As a result, digital departments, AI units and officers were created, and AI was added to official strategy statements. This reflects public administrations' efforts to digitize and appear modern and not lagging behind in order to gain legitimacy.

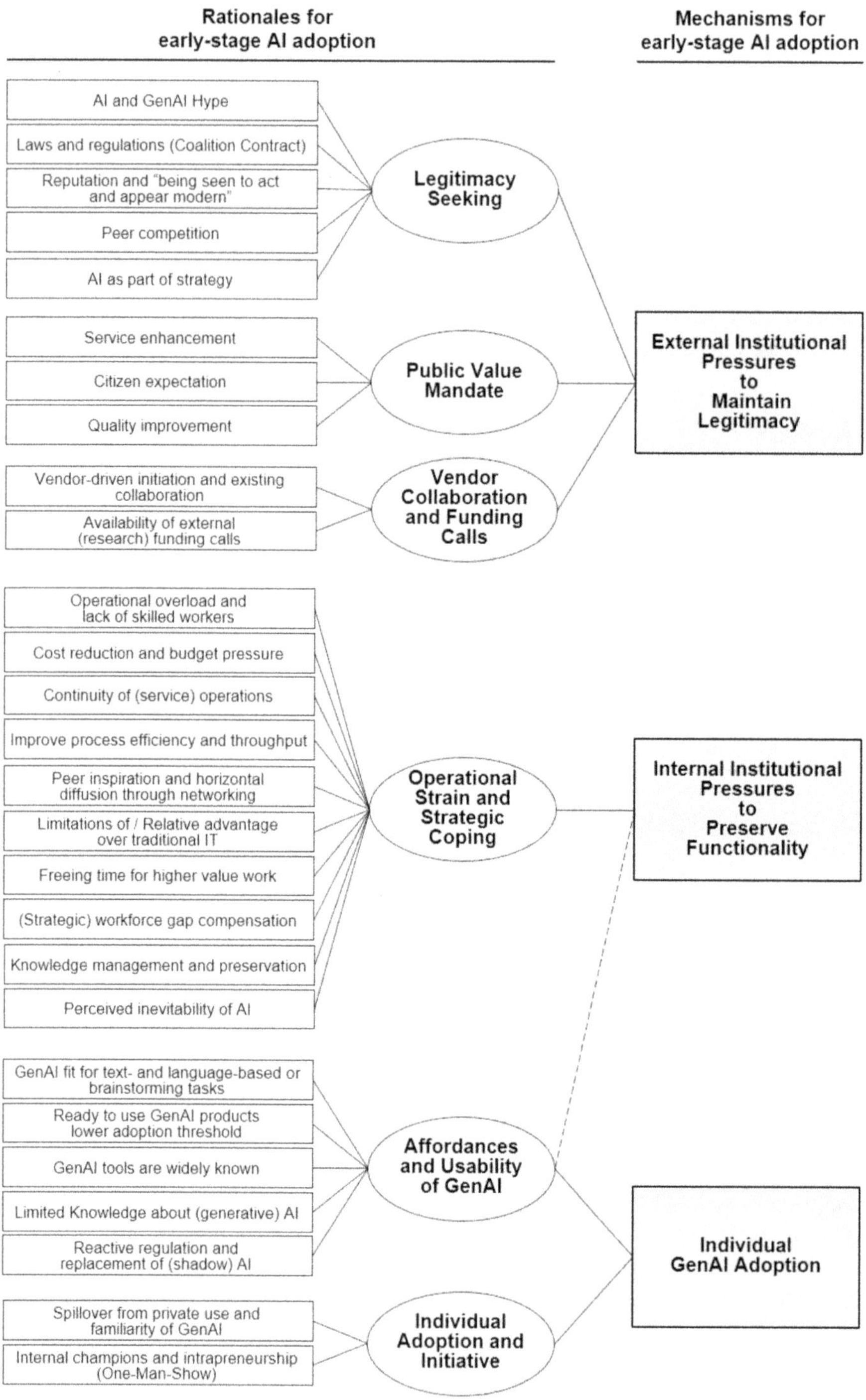

Fig. 1. Rationales & mechanisms for early-stage AI adoption in German public administrations.

Thus, reputational considerations shaped use case selection, as department heads prioritize highly visible and politically salient initiatives: *"Of course, all our department heads is, in a way, also a politician, wants to naturally wants to have something to showcase (...), you naturally always pick out something that can be presented as a lighthouse project (...)" (P10).* However, in the four top-down initiated AI projects discussed in the interviews, none was finally implemented.

4.2 Public Value Mandate

The rationale group *Public Value Mandate* summarizes rationales for early-stage adoption that are closely linked to public administration's purpose of creating value for citizens through faster, more reliable, and more accessible services. Public administrations use AI when they expect it to improve service quality, accessibility, and reliability, thereby enacting their public mandate to create public value. This need reflects recent studies reporting citizen satisfaction with German public services with 62% as limited and 64% describe interactions with authorities as exhausting [6]. Citizens expect seamless, fast and easy-to-use public services that require minimal to no effort (P25; P30). As one respondent put it, *"People expect to be able to shop with us like on Amazon. Yes, in the long run, we want to try to promote that, too" (P25).*

The rationale group is driven by both citizens and an internal sense of professional service identity. Public administrations implement AI because they are intrinsically motivated to improve weak services and reduce burdensome processes for citizens. They view AI as a practical means to make public services more accessible, user-friendly, and thus inclusive. Interviewees described AI applications such as real-time translation, easy language, chatbot support, and assistance with complex forms, implemented to ease citizen interactions with administration (P03; P11; P13). This service-oriented motivation also extends to internal quality improvement (P08).

4.3 Vendor Collaboration and Funding Opportunities

The rationale group *Vendor Collaboration and Funding Opportunities* captures rationales for early-stage AI adoption that arise when public administrations act on concrete external opportunities, such as vendor offers or funding calls. Interviewees described vendor-driven AI initiatives either based on existing relationships or persistent offerings. As one interviewee explained, *"All kinds of companies (...) come knocking on our door (...) the big tech corporations that everyone knows, and small startups. And everyone naturally wants a piece of the pie right now and to present their solutions" (P10).* They further described a more subtle pattern of the increasing appearance of AI add-on modules to existing IT systems: *"We are observing that AI modules are simply appearing in many specialized applications (...) you already have a specialist application, and then the provider says, here is an AI tool, do you want to use it, too?" (P30).*

Interviewees also linked early-stage AI adoption to external funding calls and special innovation funds. Several public administrations launched AI pilots only when grants or innovation budgets became available, and one respondent noted, *"We probably would not have done the project if there had not been a corresponding call" (P03).* While such opportunity exploitation rationale triggered early-stage AI adoption, they did not prove sustainable in the long run. Most AI initiatives (2/3) discussed in our study that were driven by this rationale did not progress to implementation because they ultimately lacked the financial, technical, or organizational readiness.

4.4 Operational Strain and Strategic Coping

The rationale group *Operational Strain and Strategic Coping* captures rationales for early-stage AI adoption that arise when public administrations respond to capacity shortages that already severely threaten service continuity. Thus, interviewees described AI adoption as an inevitable reaction to rising workload (e.g., P15, P28, P29) and persistent difficulty of hiring skilled staff (P22; P09; P33; P15). One interviewee summarized this pressure as: *"I see the burden of work in our departments, in the specialist departments. And if we have these kinds of technological tools at our disposal, there's simply no excuse for not using AI to take some of that pressure off our people" (P15).* Consequently, public administrations face pressure to maintain public service levels with fewer human resources, tighter budgets, and rising expectations for efficiency. Thus, AI is justified as a way to improve performance under resource constraints to maintain proper service provision (P09; P15; P28; P31).

To cope with the uncertainty about how to resolve this tension, most interviewees engage in cross-organizational networks to exchange with peers on best practices, find inspiration, or copy functioning AI solutions (P25; P28). Consequently, public administrations implement AI tools to automate routine, repetitive, and standardized tasks that do not require special expertise and thereby free scarce staff time for higher-value work (P22; P30). Thus, interviewees located AI use in repetitive checks, manual data entry, standard reporting requests, and pattern recognition in large data sets that absorbed capacity better spent on consultation and judgment-intensive casework (P33; P06; P10; P19; P32). For instance, *"In anti-money laundering, people still manually search Excel spreadsheets for patterns. AI can do that much better today, and it saves time and nerves" (P30).*

This strain extends beyond immediate workload relief to strategic compensation for demographic loss and knowledge drain. Interviewees emphasized that the retirement wave will cause a net workforce loss of about 30% until 2035 (P01; P25) which makes AI relevant as a strategic means to compensate this gap and preserve the often tacit knowledge (P25; P09; P32). One interviewee stated: *"We will face a substantial loss of knowledge in the coming years due to the shortage of skilled workers and the retirement of the baby boomer generation. For us, it is (…) a priority to preserve the knowledge of departing employees, store it, and pass it on appropriately to the next generations" (P25).* Public administrations therefore explore AI early to capture knowledge, enable chatbot-based knowledge management, and support on-, off-, and cross-boarding processes with AI (e.g., P06, P10, I25). Taken together, rationales for early-stage AI adoption often emerged as a coping response to already visible organizational strain. This phenomenon is further supported by the fact that the majority of AI initiatives (63%) discussed in the interviews were for internal use. Further, initiatives that were grounded in specific operational pain points tend to show a higher success rate (83%). For such projects, AI readiness was either not fully needed (e.g., GenAI) or built on the way.

4.5 Affordances and Familiarity of GenAI

The rationale group *Affordances and Familiarity of GenAI* summarizes rationales that enhance early-stage AI adoption because public administrations could apply the technology immediately to routine, text-heavy, or language-based work. Unlike traditional AI systems that required substantial training data and specialized expertise, GenAI lowered the entry barrier considerably: *"Five years ago, we only knew that you had to train AI models yourself, that you needed a lot of data to do that. (…) But [with] generative AI […] you simply have the chance to use it without having to train entire models" (P34).* Interviewees linked early-stage adoption to the close fit between GenAI and the text-heavy character of administrative work, like drafting emails, summarizing documents, brainstorming, translation, and knowledge management (e.g., P4, P12, P33). I12 captured this fit as follows: *"Public administration probably carries out about 80% of its routine work in Word or Excel, so it is very text-based. And this is exactly where AI tools, especially large language models, are of course extremely helpful" (P12).*

Familiarity reinforced this effect and mitigated skepticism because *"[AI adoption] has, of course, become much, much easier now because everyone has at least heard of generative AI, or everyone has used it at some point" (P11).* Digital departments of public administrations use this effect to leverage AI adoption by prioritizing the implementation of GenAI tools, either by acquiring licenses, whitelisting external models or developing proprietary models (e.g., P09, P11, P35). Yet this familiarity also produces misconceptions: several interviewees mentioned that employees and the organization equated "AI" with "GenAI", overestimating its functionalities and underestimating its limitations (P07; P16; P31). Interviewees described this as follows: *"When we talk about AI, everyone in the organization automatically thinks of generative AI. I always have to explain that AI is more than that. (…) That's why we almost exclusively use generative AI, because we're just not 'ready' for other systems" (P16).* One expert extended this observation to a broader adoption context: *"I think that [AI adoption without full readiness] is always the missing understanding. Many public administrations expect that they can simply work with what they currently have" (E3).* In order to balance this development and the potential risks associated with AI and GenAI use, almost all organizations interviewed are implementing guidelines or mandatory training programs pertaining to the use of AI and GenAI, though some question compliance to such rules in practice (e.g., P23, P34). In summary, GenAI's affordances, familiarity and misconceptions shape early-stage adoption despite incomplete AI readiness.

4.6 Individual Adoption and Initiative

The rationale group *Individual Adoption and Initiative* comprises rationales for early-stage AI adoption that emerges when public employees act on the curiosity, private experimentation, and persistence of a few individuals rather than on formal AI readiness. Across all cases, interviewees described GenAI use as spilling over from everyday private experience and media, especially after the launch of ChatGPT in 2022. One interviewee recalled, *"It actually started in my private life. Everyone knew about the ChatGPT hype from two or three years ago. I began exploring it and gradually realized that I could use it quite effectively in my work as well" (P31).* This private familiarity raised expectations inside administrations and yielded a strong bottom-up AI adoption momentum. Employees began to explore its use with concrete tasks and scenarios at work, like drafting an email, before rules or structures were established from above (P02; P03; P26). This early-stage adoption often gained momentum through intrapreneurial champions who pushed the integration of AI forward, beyond their formal mandate. As interviewees put it, *"The platform was built through the voluntary overtime of many dedicated employees" (P18)*, or *"the two of us brought the whole AI topic into the city" (P39)*. Although formally mandated AI officers or units are getting more established, they remain rare and AI is oftentimes still handled through the IT departments. The few AI leads in place often carry responsibility for the entire organization and tend to be highly enthusiastic champions of adoption. While formally mandated AI officers or units remain rare, the few individuals that took over responsibility for AI often drive adoption through their own enthusiasm: *"I am the only person in the ministry responsible for AI" (P16)*, and *"I love AI, I use AI tools exclusively" (P19)*.

5 Discussion

This study aimed to examine the rationales and mechanisms that lead to and justify early-stage AI adoption in public administrations before full AI readiness is in place. The findings suggest six rationale groups that cluster into three broader mechanisms to explain the phenomenon: External institutional pressures to maintain legitimacy, internal institutional pressures to preserve functionality, and individual GenAI adoption.

5.1 External Institutional Pressure to Maintain Legitimacy

The first mechanism shows that public administrations, especially administrative leaders and politicians, are pulled toward AI by external institutional pressures that make action appear legitimate, timely, and publicly appropriate. The included rationales show that early-stage AI adoption is often triggered less by AI readiness than by the need to be seen as modern, responsive, and future-oriented.

This mechanism shows strong evidence for institutional pressures. Coercive pressure appears when political agendas or public funding programs signal that AI is no longer optional, but a topic that public administrations are expected to address. This finding aligns with prior research [2, 15]. Mimetic pressure in this context displays when public leaders compare their organization with peers and initiate visible lighthouse projects to gain reputation. This can lead to decoupling: The ceremonial adoption of AI for the sake of appearing modern that might lead to employees not using it when functionality expectations are not met (e.g., P06). The stance of competition at the top level appeared particularly strong in the German federal context, compared to prior research [13–15]. Normative pressure appears when AI adoption becomes associated with competent and modern public administrations. Thus, using AI to fulfill the public value mandate seems to not only matter as a service logic, but also as a legitimacy claim [21, 28]. Public administrations justify AI by linking it to responsiveness or quality improvement, which makes adoption appear normatively appropriate. Taken together, these legitimacy pressures partly compensate for AI readiness in the adoption process. This also helps to explain why funding-driven and top-down projects showed lower success rates in our data. When reputation, visibility and funding calls drive AI use case selection despite limited readiness, long-term sustainability and implementation success suffered. Thus, the more AI adoption is driven by symbolic legitimacy alone, the more likely it is to remain symbolic and exhibit decoupling.

5.2 Internal Institutional Pressure to Preserve Functionality

This early-stage AI adoption mechanism shows that public administrations adopt AI because the internal pressure to preserve functionality becomes acute. In these cases, operational overload, staff shortages, budget pressure, and expected knowledge loss due to retirement created a situation in which AI was explored not as a visionary add-on, but as a practical means to maintain continuity of service. The interviewees unanimously perceive AI as a means to compensate for workforce gaps, rather than a replacement for current employees. This mechanism is currently underrepresented in the academic literature, which has focused more strongly on external pressure, readiness conditions, and implementation success factors [2, 13]. One possible explanation is that this mechanism is more relevant in aging societies like in Europe.

The uncertainty of how to resolve the tension of declining resources while preserving functionality displays in mimetic pressure. Public administrations heavily engage in networking around AI, best practices exchange, and trying to copy existing AI solutions. This mechanism shows that public administrations adopt AI when the pressure to act becomes stronger than the pressure to wait. Under these conditions, partial AI readiness is tolerated, worked around, or built along the way.

In public administration, functionality is itself an institutional demand. Administrations are coercively mandated and normatively expected to provide reliable, lawful, and continuous services despite worsening resource constraints. In this sense, institutional pressures only indirectly influence AI adoption. Therefore, using AI to preserve functionality becomes a way of preserving public value. AI initiatives that emerged from this mechanism were based on concrete operational pain points and thus more likely to become sustainable, while top-down initiatives with weak operational grounding struggled to move beyond symbolic commitment. The more early-stage AI adoption is tied to a concrete need, the more likely it is to be integrated into routine work, because AI readiness is built on the way to achieve the promised pain point relief.

5.3 Individual GenAI Adoption

The third mechanism that leads to early-stage AI adoption is driven by deliberate GenAI adoption especially by individual employees. Unlike the other two mechanisms, this one is not primarily driven by institutional pressures but by technology affordances and prior private experience. The launch of publicly available ready-to-use GenAI tools has democratized AI for the broad society, including public employees. They perceive GenAI tools as immediately useful for text- and language-heavy work found in knowledge- and service-intensive administrative environments. AI in the form of GenAI therefore enters public administrations not only for legitimacy reasons, but as a practical work tool. The literature on this mechanism in public administration is still nascent [4].

This mechanism also highlights the role of intrapreneurs, intrinsically motivated forerunners who pushed the topic forward beyond formal incentives. This stance is notable in the public administration context, which is known for hierarchy, limited innovation-incentive and -reward, and formal procurement procedures. Only recent studies explore the role of such intrapreneurs in this context [13, 15, 30]. Although the initial uptake was often linked to individuals, GenAI's strong fit with text- and language-heavy tasks and its familiarity led public administration to prioritize its integration as a lever for routine task automation. The dashed line in Fig. 1 displays this aspect. Based on our findings we argue that initial adoption of GenAI may support long-term adoption of (trad.) AI. As employees gain low-barrier practical experience with AI, skepticism tends to decline (e.g., P11) and they become more open-minded towards more complex AI systems which could ease AI implementation at scale.

The mechanism also inverts the concept of decoupling. In the classic formulation, organizations adopt formal structures ceremonially while actual operations remain unchanged (see 5.1). Within this mechanism, the inverse seems to occur. Formal structures persist on paper, while actual work practices change through informal GenAI adoption. Employees decouple from official workflows, manual routines, and lengthy procurement procedures in order to cope with everyday tasks more efficiently [4, 31].

Finally, this mechanism suggests that AI readiness is technology, task, and phase dependent. GenAI can compensate for some readiness deficits in early-stage adoption because it lowers technical, data, or cultural readiness requirements for suitable tasks. This indicates a *partial AI readiness compensation* and extends current generic readiness assumptions by showing that readiness varies by AI type, task type, and adoption stage. Still, while GenAI can lower some readiness requirements, it cannot replace them completely. It remains a basic readiness necessity for AI literacy and governance to balance GenAI risks (e.g., hallucinations) in the light of public administration's accountability. As the individual GenAI adoption preceded AI readiness, public administrations increasingly implement mandatory training programs and guidelines, to mitigate decoupling and restore legitimacy.

5.4 Contribution to Theory and Practice

This study has three theoretical contributions. First, it extends AI adoption literature in public administration by using an exploratory qualitative approach to shed light on the emerging phenomenon of adoption-before-readiness. Based on in-depth empirical evidence from German public administration, the study identifies the rationales and mechanisms that lead to and justify early-stage AI adoption, thereby addressing empirical and context-sensitive gaps of AI adoption in public administration in the literature [2, 11, 13, 17]. Second, the study highlights the need to rethink existing AI readiness frameworks. While prior frameworks treat AI readiness as uniform across technologies [2, 11], our empirical findings show that readiness requirements differ systematically by AI type, task type, and adoption stage. Rather than treating AI readiness as a uniform precondition, it shows that early-stage AI adoption can successfully occur before full AI readiness is in place as for GenAI technologies. Building on this insight, we suggest *partial AI readiness compensation* as a sensitizing concept that explains how GenAI can temporarily compensate for selected readiness deficits in early-stage AI adoption [32].

This extends conceptual development in IS and e-government research by differentiating readiness assumptions by AI type, task type, and adoption phase. Third, our study contributes to institutional theory literature by showing how institutional pressures shape distinct early-stage AI adoption mechanisms [11, 20, 21]. It also extends the explanatory power of decoupling by suggesting a reverse pattern in which employees begin using GenAI outside formal structures.

For practitioners, the findings suggest that public administrations can use GenAI despite partial AI readiness. However, such adoption still requires basic internal AI literacy and governance. Moreover, projects are more likely to progress when they address concrete operational pain points rather than symbolic visibility.

5.5 Limitations and Future Research

This study has limitations. First, qualitative interview analysis involves interpretive decisions. To reduce author bias and strengthen rigor, multiple researchers coded and regularly aligned their interpretations. Further, the scope could not cover an objective readiness audit. To approximate readiness levels, we coded readiness deficits when interviewees described limitations in AI readiness dimensions.

Second, the study focuses specifically on early-stage AI adoption in public administration. It does not address later stages of AI adoption, such as procurement, large-scale implementation, or diffusion that potentially show different rationales or mechanisms, a phenomenon that should be subject to future studies. Last, the empirical context is limited to Germany. Since cultural factors shape innovation adoption processes, future studies should verify and compare the findings in other cultural contexts.

6 Conclusion

This study examined the rationales and mechanisms for public administrations to adopt AI before full AI readiness. Based on a qualitative interview study in Germany, we identified six rationale groups and three mechanisms that drive early-stage AI adoption in public administration: external institutional pressure to maintain legitimacy, internal institutional pressure to preserve functionality, and individual GenAI adoption. We further found that GenAI requires lower levels of AI readiness than traditional AI.

The study contributes to AI adoption literature by conceptualizing adoption-before-readiness as an early-stage phenomenon and by showing that AI readiness is not a uniform prerequisite. Instead, readiness requirements vary by AI type, task type, and adoption stage. For instance, GenAI can lower AI readiness levels, while still requiring basic readiness in AI literacy and governance. For practice, the findings suggest that public administrations should prioritize concrete operational pain points to improve adoption outcomes.

Acknowledgments. We thank all advisors, colleagues, students, and reviewers for their valuable feedback and support.

Disclosure of Interests. The authors declare no competing interests.

References

1. Mergel, I., Dickinson, H., Stenvall, J., Gasco, M.: Implementing AI in the public sector. Public Manage. Rev. 1–14 (2023). https://doi.org/10.1080/14719037.2023.2231950
2. Madan, R., Ashok, M.: AI adoption and diffusion in public administration: a systematic literature review and future research agenda. Gov. Inf. Q. **40** (2023). https://doi.org/10.1007/s10796-024-10475-0
3. Mehr, H.: Artificial Intelligence for Citizen Services and Government (2017). https://ash.harvard.edu/files/ash/files/artificial_intelligence_for_citizen_services.pdf
4. Tangi, L., Rodriguez Müller, A.P., Combetto, M.: A silent partner: the shadow presence of generative artificial intelligence in public administrations. In: Hofmann, S., et al. (eds.) Electronic Participation. Lecture Notes in Computer Science, pp. 69–86. Springer, Cham (2026). https://doi.org/10.1007/978-3-032-02515-95
5. Chen, T., Gascó-Hernandez, M., Esteve, M.: The adoption and implementation of artificial intelligence chatbots in public organizations: evidence from U.S. state governments. Am. Rev. Public Adm. **54** (2024). https://doi.org/10.1177/02750740231200522
6. Jahn, S., et al.: eGovernment MONITOR 2024. Nutzung und Akzeptanz digitaler Verwaltungsleistungen aus Sicht der Bürger*innen. Die deutschen Bundesländer, Deutschland, Österreich und die Schweiz im Vergleich. (2024). https://initiatived21.de/publikationen/egovernment-monitor/2024
7. OECD: Artificial Intelligence Review of Germany. OECD Publishing (2024). https://doi.org/10.1787/609808d6-en
8. Kurhayadi, K.: Evaluating the readiness of public institutions for AI-Driven decision making: a framework for adaptive governance, pp. 2576–8484 (2025). https://doi.org/10.55214/25768484.v9i4.6335
9. Babšek, M., Murko, E., Aristovnik, A.: Organisational AI readiness for public administration: a comprehensive review and framework for conceptual modelling. Int. J. Econ. Bus. Adm. (2025). https://doi.org/10.35808/ijeba/894
10. Jöhnk, J., Weißert, M., Wyrtki, K.: Ready or not, AI comes—an interview study of organizational AI readiness factors. Bus. Inf. Syst. Eng. **63**, 5–20 (2021). https://doi.org/10.1007/s12599-020-00676-7
11. Rudko, I., Bashirpour Bonab, A., Fedele, M., Formisano, A.V.: New institutional theory and AI: toward rethinking of artificial intelligence in organizations. JMH **31** (2025). https://doi.org/10.1108/JMH-09-2023-0097
12. Sun, T.Q., Medaglia, R.: Mapping the challenges of Artificial Intelligence in the public sector: evidence from public healthcare. Gov. Inf. Q. (2019). https://doi.org/10.1016/j.giq.2018.09.008
13. Neumann, O., Guirguis, K., Steiner, R.: Exploring artificial intelligence adoption in public organizations: a comparative case study. Public Manage. Rev. **26** (2024). https://doi.org/10.1080/14719037.2022.2048685
14. Maragno, G., Tangi, L., Gastaldi, L., Benedetti, M.: Exploring the factors, affordances and constraints outlining the implementation of Artificial Intelligence in public sector organizations. Int. J. Inf. Manage. (2023). https://doi.org/10.1016/j.ijinfomgt.2023.102686
15. Heinisuo, E., Kuoppakangas, P., Stenvall, J.: Navigating AI implementation in local government: addressing dilemmas by fostering mutuality and meaningfulness. Inf. Syst. Front. (2025). https://doi.org/10.1007/s10796-025-10599-x
16. Alsheibani, S., Cheung, Y., Messom, C.: Artificial intelligence adoption: AI-readiness at firm-level. In: Twenty-Second Pacific Asia Conference on Information Systems (2018). https://aisel.aisnet.org/pacis2018/37

17. Barnes, A.J., Zhang, Y., Valenzuela, A.: AI and culture: culturally dependent responses to AI systems. Curr. Opin. Psychol. **58** (2024). https://doi.org/10.1016/j.copsyc.2024.101838
18. Myers, M.D., Newman, M.: The qualitative interview in IS research: examining the craft. Inf. Organ. **17**, 2–26 (2007). https://doi.org/10.1016/j.infoandorg.2006.11.001
19. Gioia, D.A., Corley, K.G., Hamilton, A.L.: Seeking qualitative rigor in inductive research. Organ. Res. Methods **16**, 15–31 (2013). https://doi.org/10.1177/1094428112452151
20. DiMaggio, P.J., Powell, W.W.: The iron cage revisited: institutional isomorphism and collective rationality in organizational fields. Am. Sociol. Rev. **48**, 147 (1983). https://doi.org/10.2307/2095101
21. Meyer, J.W., Rowan, B.: Institutionalized organizations - formal structure as myth and ceremony. Am. J. Sociol. **83**, 340–363 (1977). https://doi.org/10.1086/226550
22. Miles, M.B., Huberman, M.A., Saldaña, J.: Qualitative Data Analysis. A Methods Sourcebook. Del Rey/Ballentine Books, New York (2014)
23. Wirtz, B.W., Müller, W.M.: An integrated artificial intelligence framework for public management. Public Manag. Rev. **21**, 1076–1100 (2019). https://doi.org/10.1080/14719037.2018.1549268
24. Jäger, I., Weber, M.: Artificial intelligence's impact on public value: impact areas and future research. In: 27th Annual International Conference on Digital Government Research (2026)
25. Russell, S.J., Norvig, P.: Artificial Intelligence: A Modern Approach (2021)
26. Marr, B.: The Difference Between Generative AI and Traditional AI: An Easy Explanation for Anyone (2023). https://www.forbes.com/sites/bernardmarr/2023/07/24/the-difference-between-generative-ai-and-traditional-ai-an-easy-explanation-for-anyone/
27. Rogers, E.M.: The Diffusion of Innovation. New York (2003)
28. Suchman, M.C.: Managing legitimacy: strategic and institutional approaches. Acad. Manage. Rev. **20** (1995). https://doi.org/10.2307/258788
29. Nikiforova, A., et al.: Responsible AI adoption in the public sector: A data-centric taxonomy of AI adoption challenges. In: Proceedings of the 59th Hawaii International Conference on System Sciences (2026). https://doi.org/10.24251/HICSS.2026.289
30. Jäger, I., Hein, A., Krcmar, H.: Wind of change or just another digitalization breeze? In: 26th Annual International Conference on Digital Government Research (2025). https://doi.org/10.59490/dgo.2025.1030
31. Hofgesang, M., Fock, S., Westermann, J., Wyszynski, M.: Can we ProcureDat? - using open data procurement for digital government services. In: 27th Annual International Conference on Digital Government Research (2026)
32. Blumer, H.: What is wrong with social theory. Am. Sociol. Rev. **19** (1954). https://doi.org/10.2307/2088165

Neurosymbolic AI for Public Deliberation: Sentiment-Aware Knowledge Graphs and Multi-agent RAG for Natural Language Interaction

Gerasimos Papanikolaou-Ntais[1,2](✉), Dimitris Zeginis[3,4], Efthimios Tambouris[3,4], and Konstantinos Tarabanis[3,4]

[1] University of Piraeus, Piraeus, Greece
mpsp2540@unipi.gr
[2] Konnektable Technologies Ltd., Metamorfosi, Greece
[3] Information Technologies Institute, Center for Research and Technology Hellas, Thessaloniki, Greece
{zeginis,themis,kat}@iti.gr
[4] University of Macedonia, Thessaloniki, Greece

Abstract. Public forum deliberations are a key part of democracy nowadays, since they enable citizens to contribute to the formulation of public policies and legislation. However, implementing online deliberations at scale has many challenges, since the high volume and unstructured nature of citizen comments, make it difficult to understand the overall structure and comment sentiment of the debate. In Greece, deliberations conducted through opengov.gr generate thousands of comments on draft laws, forming a valuable but semantically opaque corpus of citizen input. This paper presents an approach that transforms these forum-like deliberation records into a sentiment-aware Knowledge Graph. A multilingual Natural Language Inference model is used to classify comments according to stance (support, oppose, neutral) enriching the Knowledge Graph. Building on this structured representation, we develop a multi-agent Retrieval-Augmented Generation system that allows non-expert users to explore deliberations through natural language and obtain insights that would otherwise be unavailable. The proposed approach is evaluated using deliberations from opengov.gr through Knowledge Graph coverage analysis, a human-annotated stance classification assessment, and an end-to-end evaluation of the RAG system. The results show how Knowledge Graphs and AI can support traceability, reduce information overload, and enhance the usability of large-scale public deliberation data.

Keywords: Neurosymbolic AI · e-Participation · Knowledge Graphs · Multi-Agent RAG · OpenGov

Published by Springer Nature Switzerland 2027
G. Viale Pereira et al. (Eds.): EGOV 2026, LNCS 16933, pp. 264–280, 2027.
https://doi.org/10.1007/978-3-032-35747-2_17

1 Introduction

Digital democracy platforms promise to democratize legislative processes by enabling large-scale citizen participation. However, this scale introduces a fundamental issue: as participation increases, the intelligibility of the discourse decreases. Public deliberation often fails not due to a lack of data, but due to its unstructured, forum-like, nature, which renders the reasoning behind citizen opinions inaccessible to both citizens and policymakers.

In Greece, OpenGov[1] is the official portal for national law consultations (consultations are similar in nature to deliberations, with the difference that deliberations lead to informed decisions, while consultations simply gather opinions). The consultations hosted on OpenGov collect a large amount of comments i.e., a single legislative article may collect thousands of comments during its public consultation period. This large amount of comments complicates the understanding of the overall structure of the debate.

To address this problem, Knowledge Graphs provide a suitable representation for domains involving heterogeneous entities and complex semantic relations. At the same time, recent advances in LLMs and agentic AI approaches enable natural language interactions with complex structured data such as Knowledge Graphs.

Building on these developments, this paper proposes a neurosymbolic AI approach for analysing and exploring public deliberations. The approach aims to: i) construct a Knowledge Graph based on deliberation data from OpenGov, ii) enrich the Knowledge graph by sentiment-aware information extracted from citizens' comments, iii) develop a multi-agent RAG system that enables the natural language interaction with the resulting Knowledge Graph.

The contribution of this paper is fourfold:

- It constructs a sentiment-aware Knowledge Graph for large-scale public consultation data, linking consultations, articles, citizen comments, users, ministries, and stance information.
- It applies and evaluates multilingual NLI-based stance classification for Greek deliberation comments, enriching the Knowledge Graph with Support, Oppose, and Neutral relations.
- It designs a governance-oriented Multi-Agent RAG architecture that separates natural-language translation, SPARQL validation, and answer narration, supporting read-only access and traceable responses.
- It evaluates the approach on real OpenGov data through Knowledge Graph coverage analysis, stance classification assessment, RAG query benchmarking, and validator security testing.

The rest of the paper is structured as follows. Section 2 presents background and related work, Sect. 3 describes the overall paper methodology, Sect. 4 describes the process of generating the sentiment-aware Knowledge Graph, Sect. 5 describes the multi-agent RAG for natural language interaction with the

[1] http://www.opengov.gr.

resulting Knowledge Graph, Sect. 6 presents the evaluation of both the Knowledge Graph and the multi-agent RAG, Sect. 7 includes a discussion of the finding and future work and Sect. 8 concludes the paper.

2 Background and Related Work

2.1 Neurosymbolic AI Architectures

Neurosymbolic AI has emerged as a solution to the limitations of purely neural and purely symbolic approaches [6]. Pure LLM approaches suffer from hallucinations and opacity, while purely symbolic approaches are not easily accessible to non-experts. The integration of Knowledge Graphs with LLMs has become an emerging research area aimed at enhancing transparency in AI-driven applications and environments [5]. Prominent taxonomies distinguish "Symbolic-to-Neural" pipelines from "Neural-to-Symbolic" ones [12], while Graph RAG represents a paradigm where knowledge graph information grounds generative model outputs [18].

Our architecture implements both directions: the Knowledge Graph generation ETL pipeline, which employs a "Neural-to-Symbolic" flow (NLI model populates the KG), while the RAG system employs a "Symbolic-to-Neural" flow (KG grounds LLM answers). This bidirectional integration is a distinguishing feature of our approach.

Our system also integrates symbolic and neural paradigms [6]: Symbolic AI (The Graph) provides deterministic, verifiable knowledge, for example when a query requests "Article 5," it retrieves exactly those triples, not a probabilistic approximation. Neural AI (LLMs and NLI Models) provides reasoning and interface, classifying stance during ETL and translating natural language into SPARQL queries. The neural components are constrained by the symbolic structure, reducing hallucination risk by grounding generated answers in explicit graph queries, while the symbolic components are made accessible by the neural components.

2.2 Knowledge Graphs for Public Policy

The SIOC ontology [11] provides concepts for describing online communities on the Semantic Web, widely adopted alongside FOAF for social networking information [3]. However, most SIOC implementations focus on static content representation rather than capturing the dynamic rhetorical relationships characterizing deliberative discourse. In public policy, knowledge graph approaches have primarily been applied to legal texts and parliamentary proceedings rather than citizen-generated deliberative content.

Our work extends the SIOC framework with a custom extension capturing rhetorical relationships, specifically support, objection, and topical relevance, between citizen comments and legislative provisions, transforming SIOC from a purely structural vocabulary into an argumentation-aware one.

2.3 Retrieval-Augmented Generation over Knowledge Graphs

Standard RAG systems rely on vector similarity search, which struggles with queries requiring precise structural navigation [9]. Graph RAG addresses this by using Knowledge Graphs as the retrieval source [18].

Recent work has explored natural language interfaces over Knowledge Graphs, including SparqLLM that demonstrated automating SPARQL generation from natural language [1], and multi-agent frameworks for Knowledge Graph Question Answering [14]. An approach that transforms natural language to SPARQL in the public administration domains is also proposed by [10].

Beyond query answering, the literature has identified the use of natural language interaction with mass deliberations data as a valuable add-on to enable the understanding of the discourse [16].

Our Multi-Agent RAG contributes a three-agent pipeline for the domain of public deliberations that enabled the natural language interaction with the deliberation Knowledge Graph. The system incorporates a Validator agent enforcing institutional trust constraints (read-only access) and a Narrator agent producing "glass box" summaries enabling traceability from AI conclusions to source data.

3 Approach

This section presents the approach used in the paper that consists of three main stages to transform the public consultation data to a multi-agent natural language interaction system. More specifically the paper follows these steps:

- **Step 1 - Knowledge Graph construction:** we construct a sentiment-aware Knowledge Graph from publicly available consultation data of OpenGov. This includes two main sub-steps: i) the generation of a Knowledge Graph based on the existing structure of the data (Consultation, Law article, Comment) and ii) enhance the Knowledge Graph with sentiment information by classifying the comments based on their stance (support, oppose, neutral) to the law article.
- **Step 2 - Multi-Agent RAG Development:** we develop three Agents to enable the natural language interaction with the Knowledge Graph. The Agents include: i) a Translator Agent that converts a natural language question to SPARQL, ii) a Validator Agent that performs safety checks on the produced SPARQL (e.g., to not include DELETE commands) and iii) a Narrator Agent that synthesizes the raw query results into a human readable summary
- **Step 3 - Evaluation:** we evaluated both the quality of the generated graph (including the accuracy of the comment stance classification) and the accuracy of the multi-agent RAG query.

4 Construction of the Sentiment-Aware Knowledge Graph

The transformation from unstructured deliberation data to a queryable Knowledge Graph is handled by our ETL pipeline, constituting the "Neural-to-Symbolic" part of our approach. The overall structure of the resulting sentiment-aware Knowledge Graph is illustrated in Fig. 1.

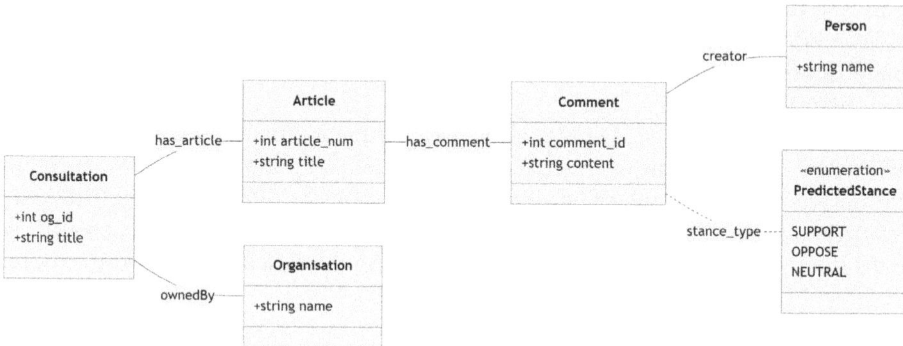

Fig. 1. UML Class Diagram for the Sentiment-Aware Knowledge Graph.

4.1 Data Extraction and Hierarchical Modelling

OpenGov data are publicly available in a downloadable relational database format[2]. The ETL pipeline connects to the relational database and constructs a hierarchical tree: **Consultations** (created by Ministries), contain **Articles**, which accumulate **Comments** (citizen contributions). This hierarchical extraction forms the backbone of the Knowledge Graph.

4.2 Comment Stance Classification via Natural Language Inference

The next step is determining whether a comment supports, opposes, or is neutral with respect to the legislative provision it addresses.

Model Selection and Comment Stance Classification. The system employs a multilingual NLI model based on XLM-roBERTa, fine-tuned on cross-lingual NLI datasets including XNLI and over 2.7 million hypothesis-premise pairs spanning 27 languages [8]. The model was selected because: (1) it supports comment **classification** by framing stance detection as an NLI problem, where the comment text serves as the premise, and hypotheses are constructed for each

[2] https://huggingface.co/datasets/glossAPI/opengov.gr-diaboyleuseis.

stance category (e.g., "This text expresses agreement with the article"), with the highest entailment probability determining the stance; (2) its multilingual pre-training on CC100 (100 languages) enables effective processing of Greek text via cross-lingual transfer; (3) the proposed approach eliminates the need for a manually annotated Greek deliberation corpus, improving scalability.

Fine Tuning. Initial experiments with the multilingual NLI model produced promising but insufficiently reliable results for the specific linguistic and rhetorical characteristics of Greek public consultation comments. To adapt the model to this domain, we manually annotated a subset of OpenGov comments using the three stance categories Support, Oppose, and Neutral. The annotated data were split into training, validation, and held-out test subsets (85/15 stratified split, random_state = 42), with the held-out test set excluded from model development and used only for the final evaluation reported in Sect. 6.

Table 1. Core Ontologies and Mappings used in the Knowledge Graph.

Prefix	Ontology	Usage
`sioc`	Semantically-Interlinked Online Communities	Forum structure: `Forum`, `Thread`, `post`. We extend (sub-class) these classes to define the Consultation, Article, Comment respectively
`foaf`	Friend of a Friend	Participants: `Person`, `Organization`
`dcterms`	Dublin Core	Metadata: `title`, `created`, `creator`
`og`	Our Custom Namespace	Domain: `Consultation`, `Article`, `Comment`

Fine-tuning was performed using `xlm-roberta-base` as the base model with the following configuration: maximum sequence length of 256 tokens, learning rate of 2e-5, batch size of 16 for both training and evaluation, weight decay of 0.01, warmup ratio of 0.1, and a maximum of 15 epochs. Early stopping with patience of 3 was applied, selecting the best checkpoint by macro-F1. Mixed precision (bf16) was enabled where GPU hardware supported it. This configuration improved the model's ability to recognize domain-specific expressions of agreement, disagreement, procedural remarks, and conditional positions in Greek deliberation comments, and provided the stance labels used to enrich the Knowledge Graph.

Batch Processing and Caching. The pipeline implements batch processing for efficient resource utilization and a caching mechanism that stores classification results keyed by cryptographic hashes of comment text. On re-execution, only unseen comments require inference, enabling efficient incremental updates, since the vast amount of comments present in the dataset can take several hours or even days to classify without a dedicated high-end GPU available.

Fallback Classification. A keyword-based fallback uses a curated Greek-language stance lexicon (e.g., "συμφωνώ"—"I agree"; "διαφωνώ"—"I disagree") for environments where the NLI model is unavailable, ensuring system resilience in degraded mode.

4.3 RDF Transformation and URI Minting

The representation of the Knowledge Graph employed RDF-based Semantic Web standards [2] for interoperability. The ontologies used to represent the Knowledge Graph are presented in Table 1.

The SIOC ontology provides the structural backbone of the deliberation data. The SIOC classes Forum, Thread and Post are similar to the Consultation, Article, Comment and thus we extend them (e.g., Consultation subClassOf Forum). FOAF was used to model Consultation participants as well as Organizations that initiate the Consultation. Dublin Core provides metadata attributes.

Each entity is assigned a persistent, deterministic URI through a dedicated minting component, ensuring stable logical connections across pipeline re-executions and compatibility with the Linked Data paradigm. For each comment, the transformation generates an og:Comment instance, a foaf:Person for the author, and a stance predicate linking the comment to its stance category. Triples are serialized in Turtle (.ttl) format for loading into the triple store.

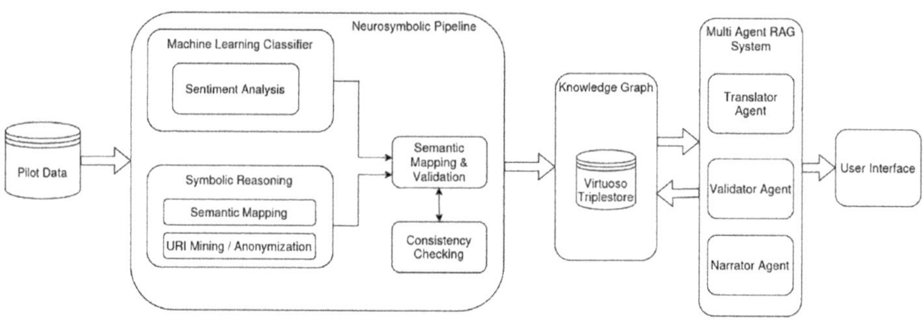

Fig. 2. Architecture of the proposed system.

5 The Multi-agent RAG System

Standard RAG systems relying on vector similarity search fail with queries requiring precise structural navigation through the KG based architecture (e.g., "What are the main objections to Article 3?"). We developed a **Multi-Agent RAG Architecture** comprising three specialized LLM agents exposed through a RESTful API endpoint, illustrated in Fig. 2. The architecture contains three

```
PREFIX og: <http://data.opengov.gr/ns/og#>
SELECT ?authorName ?stance ?text WHERE {
  ?article a og:Article ;
          og:title ?articleTitle .
  ?article og:has_comment ?comment .
  ?comment a og:Comment ;
          og:content ?text ;
          og:stance_type ?stance ;
          og:creator ?person .
  ?person og:name ?authorName .
  FILTER(CONTAINS(LCASE(?articleTitle), "article␣5"))}
```

Listing 1.1. SPARQL query generated by the Translator Agent to retrieve all the stances of a Comment.

agents with distinct roles. All three agents use Gemini 2.5 Flash-Lite as the underlying LLM.

The Translator Agent converts natural language questions into valid SPARQL 1.1 queries. It is implemented using a generative LLM with a system prompt encoding the complete ontological schema. Key capabilities include **schema-aware query generation** (e.g., mapping "objections" to `og:stance_type`), **REGEX-based entity matching** for approximate name lookup, and **cross-lingual query translation** for English queries targeting Greek text literals.

The Validator Agent receives every SPARQL query generated by the Translator and performs: **safety enforcement**, specifically rejecting any query containing `DELETE`, `INSERT`, `UPDATE`, `DROP`, or `CLEAR` commands, ensuring the AI cannot alter the public record, along with **syntax verification**, checking for structural errors and returning rejected queries to the Translator for regeneration. This agent addresses the trust deficit that impedes AI adoption in government by providing a verifiable guarantee stronger than policy-level access controls.

The Narrator Agent synthesizes raw query results into human-readable summaries using a "glass box" approach. A typical response might state: "Article 5 has received 47 comments: 18 supporting, 23 opposing, 6 neutral. Primary themes of opposition include concerns about accessibility." This enables users to trace every claim back to source data and educates them about the deliberation's argumentative structure.

The agents form a sequential pipeline: (1) the Translator generates a SPARQL query, (2) the Validator approves or rejects it (with rejected queries returned for regeneration), (3) the approved query executes against the Virtuoso endpoint and (4) the Narrator synthesizes results into a natural language response. The complete response includes the summary, the executed SPARQL query (for transparency), and relevant metadata. Thorough error handling is implemented at each stage. A screenshot of the resulting user interface is shown in Fig. 3.

6 Evaluation

We evaluate the system through three complementary studies: Knowledge Graph coverage statistics, human-annotated stance classification accuracy, and end-to-end RAG query assessment.

6.1 Experimental Setup

The system was deployed as the core technical component of the Greek national pilot within the AI4DELIBERATION project, targeting the OpenGov platform[3]. The dataset consisted of real-world deliberations from the Public Governance domain. The experimental infrastructure comprised: the Semantic ETL pipeline with the multilingual NLI model, an OpenLink Virtuoso triple store/endpoint, and the Multi-Agent RAG system deployed as a containerized service along with a web-based front-end user interface.

6.2 Study 1: Knowledge Graph Coverage

Graph Validation. A dedicated validation module acts as a semantic "linter," executing diagnostic SPARQL queries to detect: (1) **Orphan Comments**, meaning comments lacking `sioc:reply_of` or `foaf:maker` links, (2) **Disconnected Ministries**, consultations not linked to a fostering ministry. These records are quarantined rather than imported, preventing structural corruption.

Objective. To assess the structural and informational integrity of the Knowledge Graph, we report descriptive statistics obtained via SPARQL queries against the Virtuoso triple store.

Results. Table 2 summarizes the coverage of the Knowledge Graph.

Discussion. The validation module successfully yielded a fully connected graph with over one million RDF triples spanning 1,104 consultations across 37 ministries. The stance distribution provides a first quantitative overview of the landscape of Greek public deliberation. The dominance of negative comments (51.84%) is consistent with the well-documented negativity bias in public consultations: citizens are more likely to comment when they strongly disagree with a proposed legislation than when they approve of it. Pro-Comments account for 20.85% of comments, while the Neutral category (27.31%) captures comments such as questions, procedural remarks, and comments that don't express clear support nor opposition.

[3] http://www.opengov.gr.

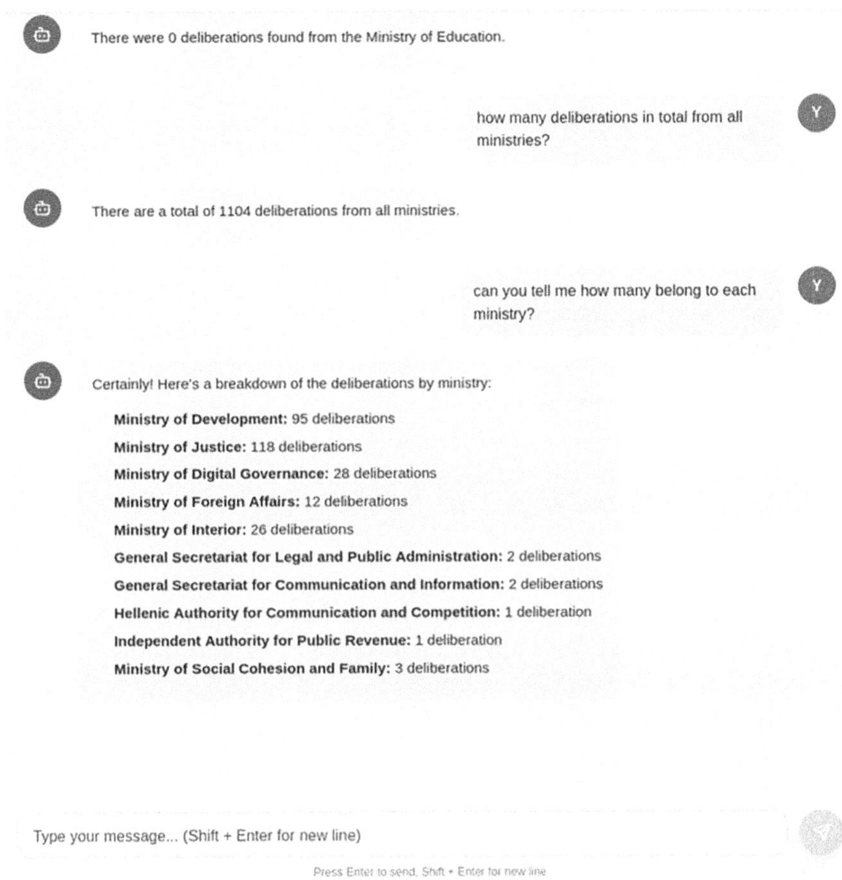

Fig. 3. Screenshot of the RAG system's user interface.

6.3 Study 2: Stance Classification Accuracy

Objective. To assess the accuracy of the NLI stance classifier against human judgement.

Annotation Protocol. We evaluated the stance classifier on a held-out human-annotated test set of 510 comments. The comments were sampled from the OpenGov dataset and labelled as *Support*, *Oppose*, or *Neutral* without access to the model's predictions. The ontology-level labels were mapped to these three stance categories as follows: `supports` to *Support*, `objectsTo` to *Oppose*, and `relatedTo` to *Neutral*. The final test set contained 161 Support comments, 203 Oppose comments, and 146 Neutral comments. We additionally computed Cohen's kappa between model predictions and the human gold labels, obtaining $\kappa = 0.797$, indicating substantial agreement.

Table 2. Knowledge Graph coverage statistics.

Metric	Value
Total Consultations processed	*1104*
Total Articles	*28942*
Total Comments	*115037*
Total RDF Triples generated	*1,095,083*
Unique Users (`foaf:Person`)	*46,564*
Ministries represented	*37*
Comments classified as Pro	*23,987 (20.85%)*
Comments classified as Con	*59,635 (51.84%)*
Comments classified as Neutral	*31,415 (27.31%)*
Orphan Comments detected (pre-validation)	*0 (0.0%)*
Orphan Comments post-validation	0
Avg. comments per Article	*3.97*

Classification Performance. We compare the fine-tuned NLI model against two baselines in Table 3: a keyword-based fallback and the same XLM-RoBERTa model in zero-shot mode (without any domain-specific fine-tuning).

Table 3. Stance classification performance against human gold standard (N = 510).

Method	Acc.	Macro-F1	F1-Sup.	F1-Opp.	F1-Neu.
Keyword baseline	*0.540*	*0.536*	*0.560*	*0.444*	*0.603*
XLM-RoBERTa (Zero-shot)	*0.629*	*0.511*	*0.822*	*0.671*	*0.039*
XLM-RoBERTa (Fine-tuned)	*0.865*	*0.864*	*0.899*	*0.853*	*0.840*

For the fine-tuned model, Cohen's kappa between model predictions and the human gold labels was $\kappa = 0.797$, indicating substantial agreement. The fine-tuned NLI model achieved 86.5% accuracy and 0.864 Macro-F1 on the held-out test set. The 95% confidence interval was [0.835, 0.894] for accuracy and [0.834, 0.893] for Macro-F1. Compared with the keyword-based fallback, the NLI model improves accuracy by approximately 32.5 percentage points and Macro-F1 by 0.328, demonstrating the value of contextual semantic classification over lexicon-based matching. The per-class results show balanced performance across the three stance categories, with F1-scores of 0.899 for Support, 0.853 for Oppose, and 0.840 for Neutral.

The zero-shot NLI model achieved 62.9% accuracy and 0.511 Macro-F1, demonstrating that cross-lingual transfer alone is insufficient for reliable Greek deliberation stance detection. Critically, the zero-shot model almost entirely fails to identify Neutral comments (F1 = 0.039), collapsing 121 of 146 Neutral comments into the Oppose category. This reflects the model's tendency to interpret any critical or procedural language as opposition in the absence of domain adaptation. Fine-tuning recovers this entirely, raising Neutral F1 from 0.039 to 0.840 and confirming that domain-specific annotation is essential for this task.

Error Analysis. Table 4 presents the confusion matrix for the fine-tuned NLI classifier.

Table 4. Confusion matrix for the XLM-RoBERTa (Fine-tuned) classifier (N = 510).

Gold	Predicted		
	Support	Oppose	Neutral
Support	*152*	*4*	*5*
Oppose	*16*	*160*	*27*
Neutral	*9*	*8*	*129*

The confusion matrix shows that the classifier performs well across all three classes, with particularly strong recall for Support comments (0.944). Most errors occur between Oppose and Neutral comments, where 27 Oppose comments were classified as Neutral and 8 Neutral comments were classified as Oppose. This is expected in deliberative settings, where citizen comments may contain criticism, procedural remarks, or conditional language without expressing an explicit stance. The Neutral class remains challenging because comments in this category often contain evaluative wording that may be interpreted as weak support or opposition. This finding is consistent with deliberation scholarship noting that citizens frequently adopt conditional or procedurally framed positions rather than explicit stances [7,13]. Nevertheless, the balanced Macro-F1 score and substantial Cohen's kappa indicate that the model provides a reliable stance classification layer for enriching the Knowledge Graph.

Table 5. Multi-Agent RAG end-to-end evaluation (N = 90).

Difficulty	N	Correct	Incorrect	Errors
Simple	30	28 (93.3%)	1	1
Medium	30	25 (83.3%)	1	4
Complex	30	22 (73.3%)	3	5
Total	**90**	**75 (83.3%)**	**5**	**10**

6.4 Study 3: Multi-agent RAG Query Accuracy

Objective. To evaluate the end-to-end performance of the RAG pipeline across queries of increasing structural and informational complexity.

Benchmark Design. We constructed a stratified benchmark of 90 natural language questions at three difficulty levels: 30 **Simple** questions, 30 **Medium** questions, and 30 **Complex** questions. Simple questions target single-hop factual retrieval, such as retrieving the number of consultations or comments in the database. Medium questions require Knowledge Graph traversal, filtering, or basic aggregation, such as identifying consultations with the highest number of opposing comments. Complex questions require multi-hop traversal, aggregation chaining, entity resolution, or arithmetic reasoning, such as comparing stance distributions across multiple consultations. The benchmark questions were constructed by the research team to systematically cover representative query types and difficulty levels; evaluating the system with queries collected from real policymakers or citizens is left for future work.

Assessment Criteria. For each question, we verified whether the agent's reported result matched the ground truth value obtained through manual SPARQL queries. A query was marked as successful if the agent returned the correct numerical count, entity name, or factual answer.

Results. Table 5 presents the RAG evaluation results by difficulty level.

The RAG system demonstrates strong overall end-to-end performance, achieving 83.3% accuracy across 90 natural language queries. As expected, performance decreases with increasing query complexity. The system achieved its highest accuracy on Simple queries (93.3%), followed by Medium queries (83.3%), while Complex queries achieved 73.3% accuracy.

The strong performance on Simple and Medium queries indicates that the Translator Agent can reliably map natural language questions to ontology-grounded SPARQL queries for factual retrieval, graph traversal, filtering, and aggregation operations. Complex queries remain more challenging due to the increased need for multi-hop reasoning, aggregation chaining, entity resolution, and computationally intensive SPARQL execution.

Failure Mode Analysis. The majority of failures were associated with execution and timeout-related issues rather than incorrect semantic interpretation. In particular, Complex queries involving nested aggregations, large-scale graph traversals, or multi-stage arithmetic operations frequently produced malformed or computationally expensive SPARQL queries exceeding the execution timeout threshold. Incorrect responses were comparatively rare, indicating that the ontology-grounded prompting strategy effectively constrains semantic interpretation and query generation. These findings suggest that the primary bottleneck of the architecture lies in SPARQL execution complexity and query optimization rather than natural language understanding.

Qualitative Examples. We present two representative end-to-end examples illustrating the pipeline's operation.

Example 1 (Medium, Successful). *User query:* "Which consultation has the most opposing arguments?"
Ground truth: "Ολοκλήρωση Δ.Δ" with 15,707 opposing arguments.
Agent response: "The consultation with the most opposing arguments is 'Ολοκλήρωση Δ.Δ' with 15,707 objections. This consultation exhibits significantly higher contention than the dataset average of 58.6 opposing arguments per consultation."
Status: **SUCCESS**—The agent correctly identified both the consultation title and the exact count, and provided contextual interpretation by comparing to the dataset average.

Example 2 (Complex, Partial Failure). *User query:* "Which article has the most objections?"
Ground truth: Article URI with 1,955 objections (title retrieval required).
Agent response: "The maximum number of opposing comments for a single article is 1,955. However, I am unable to retrieve the specific article's title or URI at this time."
Status: **PARTIAL FAILURE**—The agent correctly computed the aggregate maximum but failed to resolve the corresponding article entity. This indicates a gap in the SPARQL query structure: the aggregation operation (`MAX`) was performed without retaining the `GROUP BY` clause necessary to link the maximum value back to its source entity.

6.5 Validator Agent Security Assessment

To verify the Validator Agent's robustness, we submitted 50 adversarial inputs containing `DELETE`, `INSERT`, `DROP`, and `CLEAR` commands embedded within otherwise valid-looking queries. The Validator successfully identified and rejected all 50 malicious inputs (100% rejection rate), confirming its effectiveness as a security layer for the actual deployment.

7 Discussion and Future Work

7.1 Key Findings

The evaluation demonstrates three main findings. First, the ETL pipeline successfully transforms large-scale OpenGov consultation data into a connected sentiment-aware Knowledge Graph containing over one million RDF triples. Second, the fine-tuned multilingual NLI model provides a reliable stance classification layer, achieving 86.5% accuracy and 0.864 Macro-F1 on a held-out human-annotated test set. Third, the Multi-Agent RAG architecture can answer natural language queries over the deliberation Knowledge Graph with 83.3% overall accuracy across a stratified benchmark of 90 queries, with performance decreasing as query complexity increases. The Validator Agent additionally rejected all 50 adversarial write-oriented inputs, supporting the read-only safety design of the system.

7.2 Limitations

Argument Extraction. The current approach analyzes the sentiment of citizens' comments at the comment level. However, in practice a single comment may contain multiple positions as well as supporting and opposing arguments. As future work, we aim to develop AI components that analyze comments at this finer level of granularity in order to provide a more nuanced understanding of the debate. In this direction, we plan to adopt the IBIS (Issue-Based Information System) model to structure deliberations and capture the relationships between issues, positions, and arguments. LLMs have shown promising performance in extracting information from unstructured texts in the public administration domain [4,15,17]. We aim to explore such approaches also for argument extraction.

RAG Complexity Ceiling. The RAG pipeline's performance on Complex queries (73.3% success) indicates that multi-hop aggregation queries and entity resolution beyond simple counting remain significant challenges for LLM-based SPARQL generation. The agent demonstrates particular difficulty with queries requiring final-stage arithmetic operations, aggregation chaining, or queries where aggregate values must be linked back to specific entity identifiers. Future work should explore: (1) augmenting the Translator Agent with a dedicated post-processing module for arithmetic operations; (2) implementing explicit entity resolution heuristics that preserve entity bindings during aggregation; (3) few-shot prompting with curated query exemplars stratified by complexity; and (4) query decomposition strategies that break complex questions into sequential simpler sub-queries.

User-Based Evaluation. The current evaluation focuses on system-level performance, including stance classification accuracy, Knowledge Graph coverage, RAG query correctness, and validator robustness. It does not yet include a user study with policymakers, civil servants, or citizens. Future work should evaluate whether the system improves users' ability to understand consultation outcomes, identify recurring arguments, and navigate large-scale deliberation data in realistic institutional settings.

8 Conclusion

This paper presented a Neurosymbolic framework for structuring public deliberations. The architecture embodies bidirectional neurosymbolic integration: a multilingual NLI model classifies users' comments which populate a semantic Knowledge Graph (Neural-to-Symbolic), while a Multi-Agent RAG system enables natural language querying grounded in the graph (Symbolic-to-Neural). The Validator Agent's read-only enforcement and the Narrator's "glass box" summaries address the institutional trust prerequisites for government adoption.

Our three-part evaluation demonstrated the system's capacity to produce a structurally sound Knowledge Graph from real deliberation data, classify citizen stances with 86.5% accuracy and 0.864 Macro-F1 on a held-out human-annotated test set, and answer structural queries about the argumentative landscape with 83.3% overall accuracy across a benchmark of 90 natural language queries. The system achieved strong performance on Simple (93.3%) and Medium (83.3%) queries, while Complex queries involving aggregation-heavy reasoning and multi-hop graph traversal achieved 73.3% accuracy, demonstrating that ontology-grounded prompt engineering can effectively bridge natural language and formal semantic structures. This work demonstrates that AI can enhance institutional transparency by making collective deliberative output more structured, accessible, and understandable, transforming public discourse from a repository of unstructured opinions into a navigable landscape of reasoned argumentation.

Acknowledgements. Funded by the European Union under grant agreement No. 101178806. Views and opinions expressed are however those of the author(s) only and do not necessarily reflect those of the European Union or European Research Executive Agency. Neither the European Union nor the granting authority can be held responsible for them.

References

1. Arazzi, M., Ligari, D., Nicolazzo, S., Nocera, A.: Augmented Knowledge Graph Querying Leveraging LLMs. arXiv:2502.01298 (2025)
2. Berners-Lee, T., Hendler, J., Lassila, O.: The semantic web. Sci. Am. **284**(5), 34–43 (2001)
3. Bojārs, U., Breslin, J.G. (eds.): SIOC Core Ontology Specification. W3C Member Submission, 12 June 2007. World Wide Web Consortium (2007)
4. Bourmpoulias, S., Zeginis, D., Patsouras, C.F., Tarabanis, K.: Structuring information in government documents using model-driven zero-shot LLM prompting. In: Companion Proceedings of PoEM 2025. CEUR-WS, vol. 4171 (2026)
5. DeLong, L.N., Mir, R.F., Fleuriot, J.D.: Neurosymbolic AI for reasoning over knowledge graphs: a survey. IEEE Trans. Neural Netw. Learn. Syst. **36**(5), 7822–7842 (2024)
6. Garcez, A.D., Lamb, L.C.: Neurosymbolic AI: the 3rd wave. Artif. Intell. Rev. **56**, 12387–12406 (2023)
7. Janssen, D., Kies, R.: Online forums and deliberative democracy. Acta Politica **40**(3), 317–335 (2005)
8. Laurer, M., van Atteveldt, W., Casas, A., Welbers, K.: Less annotating, more classifying: addressing the data scarcity issue of supervised machine learning with deep transfer learning and BERT-NLI. Polit. Anal. **32**(1), 84–100 (2024)

9. Lewis, P., et al.: Retrieval-augmented generation for knowledge-intensive NLP tasks. Adv. Neural. Inf. Process. Syst. **33**, 9459–9474 (2020)
10. Maslaris, I., Karamanou, A., Kalampokis, E., Tarabanis, K.: Evaluating large language models in interaction with open government data. In: Proceedings of the 28th Pan-Hellenic Conference on Progress in Computing and Informatics, pp. 26–33. ACM (2024)
11. Passant, A., Bojārs, U., Breslin, J.G., Decker, S.: The SIOC Project: semantically-interlinked online communities, from humans to machines. In: Padget, J., et al. (eds.) COIN -2009. LNCS (LNAI), vol. 6069, pp. 179–194. Springer, Heidelberg (2010). https://doi.org/10.1007/978-3-642-14962-7_12
12. Rani, M., Mishra, B.K., Thakker, D.: Advancing Symbolic Integration in Large Language Models: Beyond Conventional Neurosymbolic AI. arXiv:2510.21425 (2025)
13. Strandberg, K.: public deliberation goes on-line? An analysis of citizens' political discussions on the internet prior to the finnish parliamentary elections in 2007. Javnost - Public **15**(1), 71–90 (2008)
14. Xu, J., Li, M., Tang, Y., Wang, P., Zhang, W.: Towards Open-World Retrieval-Augmented Generation on Knowledge Graph: A Multi-Agent Collaboration Framework. arXiv:2509.01238 (2025)
15. Zeginis, D., Kalampokis, E., Tarabanis, K.: Applying an ontology-aware zero-shot LLM prompting approach for information extraction in Greek: the case of DIAVGEIA.gov.gr. In: Proceedings of the 28th Pan-Hellenic Conference on Progress in Computing and Informatics, pp. 324–330. ACM (2024)
16. Zeginis, D., Patsouras, C.F., Promikyridis, R., Tambouris, E., Tarabanis, K.: Review of AI features to support mass deliberations. In: Lindgren, I. (ed.) Electronic Government. EGOV 2025. LNCS, vol. 15944. Springer, Cham (2026). https://doi.org/10.1007/978-3-032-01589-1_21
17. Zeginis, D., Tarabanis, K.: From document-centric to data-centric paradigm shift by employing event centric knowledge graphs: the Diavgeia.gov.gr case. In: Themistocleous, M., Bakas, N., Kokosalakis, G., Papadaki, M. (eds.) Information Systems. EMCIS 2024. LNBIP, vol. 535. Springer, Cham (2025). https://doi.org/10.1007/978-3-031-81322-1_27
18. Zhang, Q., et al.: A Survey of Graph Retrieval-Augmented Generation for Customized Large Language Models. arXiv:2501.13958 (2025)

Policy2Code: Comparing Approaches for Generating Web Application Code from SNAP Policy

Lisa Singh, Ariel Kennan, Mohamed Ahmed(✉), Alessandra Garcia Guevara, Avand Lakmazaheri, Sophia Dorr, and Ann Lian

Georgetown University, Washington D.C., USA
{lisa.singh,ariel.kennan,ma2323,al1844,amg476,smd317,al1698}@georgetown.edu

Abstract. We are in the early days of determining how to use large language models (LLMs) effectively to translate policy into code. This paper focuses on a specific use case: translating Supplemental Nutrition Assistance Program (SNAP) eligibility rules into web pages that help people determine whether they are eligible for SNAP benefits. We focus on categorical eligibility rules for four states and develop a methodology for rapid translation from policy to code. Our findings show that rapid translation of policy documents to code for our use case is straightforward using LLMs and is generally, fairly accurate. To support both research and application development, we share our prompts, pipeline, code, and application for others to use and replicate for other states.

Keywords: Rules as Code · computational law · LLMs · code generation · SNAP

Track: AI · Data Analytics and Automated Decision Making

1 Introduction

Government policies are often written in complex legal language that must be carefully interpreted and translated into software in order to build eligibility systems for public benefits. The process is time-consuming, error-prone, and typically repeated from scratch by different teams across agencies and jurisdictions [1]. It is also not unusual for the policy to be interpreted by software engineers who do not have expertise in the policy itself [2]. The Rules as Code (RaC) concept has proposed a new way of representing public policies as structured computational logic. The Organization for Economic Cooperation and Development (OECD) defines RaC as "an official version of rules (e.g., laws and regulations) in a machine-readable format that enables computer systems to understand and apply them consistently" [3]. This formal representation seeks to improve the

Published by Springer Nature Switzerland 2027
G. Viale Pereira et al. (Eds.): EGOV 2026, LNCS 16933, pp. 281–296, 2027.
https://doi.org/10.1007/978-3-032-35747-2_18

transparency, interoperability, and adaptability of systems that implement automated decisions based on public policies.

The intersection between generative artificial intelligence and Rules as Code presents significant opportunities to accelerate the necessary digital transformation. If generative AI tools can effectively translate official rules into code, this may accelerate the digitization of eligibility rules by translating them into machine-readable formats (e.g., YAML, JSON), enable humans to act as verifiers and editors of generated computational logic rather than developers generating code from scratch, facilitate the migration of rules between programming languages or technology platforms, and improve the integration of federal policy into state systems.

A number of success stories are emerging. Examples include generating application code that automates health insurance processes from text-based policies [4], turning infrastructure security requirements into specialized executable policy language [5], and generating declarative code based on statutory law [6].

Recently, a prototyping challenge, Policy2Code [7], brought together researchers, engineers, and practitioners to explore novel approaches in which generative AI, mainly LLMs, could facilitate the implementation of government policy into executable software. While LLMs are now widely used for code generation [8], applying them to sensitive domains such as determining eligibility rules for public benefits presents risks. For example, models may generate incorrect information with a confident tone, which can confuse users without specialized expertise [9].

This work investigates different approaches for using LLMs to translate Supplemental Nutrition Assistance Program (SNAP) eligibility rules into HTML (web pages) so that people can easily determine whether or not they are eligible for benefits. SNAP is a federal aid program in the United States designed to help low-income individuals and families purchase food. While there is a base set of federal SNAP policies, determining SNAP eligibility is complex. It varies by state, both in criteria and policy structure, making it difficult to build a reusable, state-agnostic code base. Previous work has shown that direct prompting is insufficient for directly translating policy to code for determining SNAP eligibility. However, when Retrieval Augmented Generation (RAG) was used for document retrieval and intermediate rules based on the policy were generated prior to the code, results were more promising [9].

In this paper, we present a larger scale study across four states. We share a framework that uses LLMs to extract and structure policy logic into an intermediate format that is then used to generate code. We apply our methodology to a simple form of eligibility, *categorical eligibility* across four states: Georgia, Oklahoma, Oregon, and Virginia, and generate HTML forms for people to determine their potential eligibility. We find that our approach leads to HTML pages that contain the correct policy logic for most cases. We share our prompts, pipeline, code, and application for both replicability and for others to use. This pilot lays the foundation for using LLMs to build scalable, transparent tools that help people better understand their potential SNAP eligibility.

2 Policy and Law to Logic

This section describes approaches for translating complicated policy and legal documents to formats containing embedded logic or code. These examples are meant to be representative of the space as opposed to exhaustive.

2.1 OpenFisca - A Policy Modeling Framework

In 2011, the French government advisory body France Stratégie developed OpenFisca,[1] a framework to model and simulate tax and social benefit policies as executable, open-source code. The framework enables contributors to write formulas in a python-based domain specific language (DSL) to model policy components (e.g., income tax) using user information (e.g., income and household size). In addition, its modular design allows countries or organizations to adapt the codebase to their own policy and administrative contexts. For example, PolicyEngine[2] originally used OpenFisca to model tax and benefit systems in the US and the UK. Although the framework does translate legal rules into computable code, the process is not fully automated and requires human experts to write and maintain formulas that are used in the framework.

2.2 Legal Documents to Logic

A series of studies investigated the use of LLMs to translate natural-language tax rules into formal logic statements that capture metamorphic relations. The goal was to determine whether tax software accurately placed similar individuals with a few key differences in the correct tax brackets. Srivinas et al. (2023) tested models with few-shot in-context learning, and manually evaluated the output. They found that, despite showing promise, the models were error prone [10].

Extending this research, Gogani-Khiabani et al. (2025) introduce a framework that modifies tax preparation software based on new or updated tax law. They sought to develop a scoring system to select the most accurate code candidate, ranking code produced by LLMs based on semantic similarity to the ground truth and similarity among candidates. Their study showed that including prior code substantially improved performance, highlighting the importance of providing context in automating tax law to software code translation [11].

2.3 Policy2Code Challenge - Previous Findings

Policy2Code emerged in June 2024 as a Prototyping Challenge hosted by the Beeck Center for Social Impact and Innovation and the Massive Data Institute (MDI), as part of the Rule as Code Community of Practice [12]. The challenge invited technologists, policy specialists, and practitioners to experiment with

---

1 https://openfisca.org/en/.

2 https://www.policyengine.org/us.

generative AI technology with the aim of translating government policies for US public benefit programs into plain language and software code.

Experiments by the Beeck Center and the MDI at Georgetown University revealed the following key findings: (1) LLMs can support the Rules as Code pipeline by extracting programmable rules using expert knowledge and well-crafted templates; (2) LLMs achieve better policy-to-code conversion when prompts are detailed and policy logic is simple; (3) state governments can facilitate the use of LLMs by making policies digitally accessible; and (4) humans should remain in the loop to review LLM outputs, with accuracy and fairness taking priority over efficiency in high-stakes benefit systems [9]. While an important first step, more robust experiments are needed to improve our understanding of the strengths and limitations of LLMs for translating policy to code.

3 SNAP Current Landscape

Several states and agencies provide online SNAP eligibility screeners. These tools, however, are often hard-coded, manually maintained, and narrowly tailored to a single state's policy.[3] Currently, translating benefits eligibility rules into software code relies on manual interpretation of federal and/or state legislative documents. This process is prone to inconsistency, as individuals may interpret eligibility rules differently. The absence of standardized interpretation also limits transparency, as users are typically unaware of how eligibility decisions are made. Administrators also struggle to quickly adapt screeners to policy changes, leading to delays or errors in benefit distribution for eligible individuals. States need the ability to rapidly create code that reflects policy in a cost-effective manner.

Experiments by the Beeck Center and MDI have shown that direct attempts to generate code from full policy documents produce inaccurate results, but suggest that guided approaches with detailed prompts can improve results. However, there is a gap in available structured approaches for consistently translating complex policies into code [1]. Our research seeks to address this gap by developing and empirically evaluating a framework for systematically translating SNAP policies into executable code that includes the use of LLMs.

4 Methodology

Our methodology can be divided into three core functions: variable extraction, logic generation, and code creation. Figure 1 presents an overview of the entire process. We describe each of these in the remainder of this section.

[3] For example, see the Mississippi State SNAP Screener: https://www.access.ms.gov/consumer/eligibility-questions.

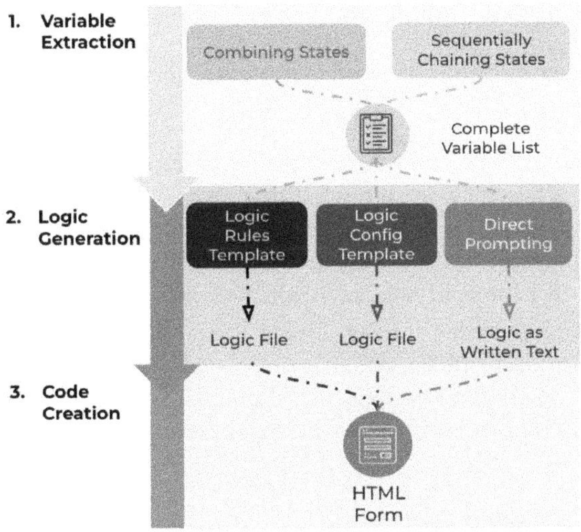

Fig. 1. Process flow diagram for experimenting with the translation of SNAP eligibility criteria policy to code.

4.1 Stage 1: Variable Extraction

One of the complex tasks associated with policy to code (Rules as Code) translation is the extraction of the components that will map to variables in the final code. In our case, we are interested in extracting eligibility related variables from each state's SNAP policy document by prompting an LLM. We test two different strategies for constructing the variable list: *extract-merge* and *sequential chaining*.

The process of *extract-merge* involves using an LLM to extract variables from the state of interest independently with a template and then merge the resulting state-specific variable lists into one structured file, e.g., YAML file, that contains all the variables across all the states. The template describes the expected format and specifications for the extracted variables to guide the generation and ensure consistency across different functions. Once all the variables are extracted, the LLM is further prompted to remove duplicate variables.

The process of *sequential chaining* begins with the same template. However, instead of prompting each state independently to extract the variables, the results from one state are used by the LLM to inform the results of the next state. This continues until all states have been added, producing a multi-state structured variable list (Fig. 2).

4.2 Stage 2: Logic Generation

Using the extracted variable list and a state's policy document, we experiment with three prompting strategies for generating eligibility logic[4]:

1. *Prompting with a logic rules template*: This approach prompts the LLM to complete a structured logic template that represents each eligibility criterion as a strict Boolean expression.
2. *Prompting with a logic configuration template*: This approach uses a more flexible structure to represent logical rules. Specifically, the LLM maps relevant information from the policy document into higher-level logical statements containing more descriptive language.
3. *Direct prompting without templates*: This omits the use of a template. The LLM is prompted to generate logic statements directly without a prespecified structure.

The first two strategies start with a structured template file, e.g. YAML or XML, that has been adapted to the format of interest. For our case study, we use a YAML file for the template. The third strategy has no initial template and results in writing statements directly in the LLM context window or a text file.

Fig. 2. Prompt compositions

4.3 Stage 3: Code Creation

In the final step, we prompt the LLM to use the state policy document and the logical statements to produce an HTML form that can be used to evaluate eligibility. The form presents a series of yes/no questions, where each question represents a variable used in the eligibility logic. The logic statements are encoded as a JavaScript function which takes the question responses as input and displays final eligibility.

4.4 Experimental Design

We initially experimented with three large language models: GPT4-o, Claude Sonnet 4.0, and Mistral 7B Instruct v0.3. Claude Sonnet 4.0 outperformed the others in our preliminary analysis of variable extraction (Stage 1), achieving an average score of 0.85 compared to 0.72 for GPT4-o, and therefore we used it for this study.

We selected four states for analysis (Virginia, Georgia, Oklahoma, and Oregon), chosen for their geographic distribution throughout the United States. We

[4] See Appendix B for the prompts used.

Table 1. Virginia-specific prompt and starter variable template used for variable extraction.

Prompt	Identify all variables required to determine categorical eligibility for SNAP in Virginia using the provided policy manual. Use the attached YAML file as a baseline template, and add any variables needed for determining categorical eligibility in Virginia that are not already present in the YAML file. Please only include the variables that are used to determine whether someone/a household is categorically eligible.

Variable Template	`tanf_receipt:`
	`  description: "Whether all household members are authorized to receive TANF cash assistance"`
	`  type: "boolean" |   states: ""`
	
	`ssi_receipt:`
	`  description: "Whether all household members are authorized to receive Supplemental Security Income"`
	`  type: "boolean" |   states: ""`
	
	`ipv_disqualified_member:`
	`  description: "Whether any household member is disqualified for intentional program violation"`
	`  type: "boolean" |   states: ""`
	
	`work_noncompliant_member:`
	`  description: "Whether any household member is failing to comply with work requirements"`
	`  type: "boolean" |   states: ""`

focused on categorical eligibility as it represents the most straightforward eligibility pathway in SNAP policy, allowing us to test the framework before expanding to more complex eligibility criteria.

Table 1 shows the Virginia-specific prompt and the starter template used for variable extraction. Additional examples of templates and prompts for all the steps in our process are provided in Appendices A and B, respectively.

5 Empirical Evaluation

To assess the effectiveness of our approach for translating policy to code for SNAP eligibility, we present our evaluation of each component of the methodology–variable extraction (Sect. 5.1), logic generation (Sect. 5.2), and code creation (Sect. 5.3).

5.1 Variable Extraction: Translating Policy to Variable YAML Files

We evaluate the two methods for variable extraction, extract-merge and sequential chaining, by comparing the variables generated by each method to a ground truth list manually curated by our research team from the policy documents.

We develop a system for scoring each generated variable list. The first step involves matching generated variables to those in the ground truth list. Since the variable names and descriptions generated by the LLM vary slightly each time, we quantify matches using semantic similarity between names and their descriptions. We begin with exact name matches for a variable, but if no exact match is available, we vectorize both the name and description of the variable using the all-MiniLM-L6-v2 sentence-transformer model[5] and compute cosine similarity to ground truth names and descriptions.

Each candidate variable pair is assigned a similarity score, computed as follows:

$$\text{score} = 0.3 \times \text{name\_similarity} + 0.7 \times \text{description\_similarity}$$

A generated variable is then matched to the most similar ground truth variable. A match occurs if the name and description similarities exceeded thresholds of 0.3 and 0.7, respectively[6] We then use variable recall as the metric for evaluating the generated variables. We choose recall because it is more important that the LLM identify relevant variables. Missing eligibility variables would compromise logic creation in later stages, whereas extra variables that are not part of the ground truth data set can simply be ignored without affecting subsequent processing. Recall is calculated as follows:

$$\text{recall} = \frac{\text{matched\_vars}}{\text{applicable\_ground\_truth\_vars}}$$

Here, *matched_vars* represents the number of matched variables, and *applicable_ground_truth_vars* refers to the number of ground truth variables relevant to the generated file. For example, if the generated file contained variables for GA, VA, and OR, then variables applicable only to OK in the ground truth list are not counted towards the recall score.

Table 2 shows the results of the evaluation. We see that sequential chaining has a recall of 87.2%, 6% higher than extract-merge (80.9%), suggesting that it is a more effective method for extracting eligibility variables. This difference in performance likely stems from how the LLM interprets state-specific policy language. Even when eligibility criteria are functionally similar across states, the model creates variables tailored to each state's unique wording, resulting in noticeably different names and descriptions even when the variables are similar. The subsequent merging step in the extract-merge approach then struggles to reconcile these differences, leaving variables that should be unified across states as separate entities that differ too much from the ground truth to be matched. In contrast, sequential chaining provides the model with previously extracted variables as context. When processing a new state, the LLM can reference existing variable names and definitions, making it more likely to group similar eligibil-

[5] https://huggingface.co/sentence-transformers/all-MiniLM-L6-v2.

[6] The thresholds were determined through empirical evaluation. We save a detailed sensitivity analysis for future work.

Table 2. Comparison of variable extraction method recall

Method			
Combining States		Chaining States	
States (in file)	Recall	States (in file)	Recall
GA, OK, OR, VA	0.809	GA, OK, OR, VA	0.872
GA	0.680	OK, VA, OR	0.850
OK	0.684	OK, VA	0.821
OR	0.500	OK	0.684
VA	0.720	–	–

ity criteria under shared variables, rather than creating redundant state-specific ones.

5.2 Logic Generation: Translating Policy to Logic Rules

Next, we evaluate the methods used for generating logic statements that capture policy eligibility criteria by analyzing the two logic templates introduced earlier.[7]

For each template, we compare the generated logic output of a state to that state's ground truth logic statement which we manually constructed based on policy manuals.[8] We first calculate the variable overlap between the generated and ground truth logic statements using the Jaccard coefficient, which quantifies the similarity between two sets. Next, we measure the logical correctness of the generated statements by verifying their truth value across all possible combinations of Boolean variable inputs. For instance, in the case of Oklahoma, which uses 12 variables, we tested all $2^{12} = 4096$ possible input combinations, comparing the outputs of the generated and ground truth logic for each combination. Results are shown in Table 3. We find that both template approaches lead to strong results, with the logic rules template slightly outperforming the logic configuration template (98% vs 97%).

Table 3. Performance of logic rules and logic configuration templates across states

	AVERAGE		GA		OK		OR		VA	
Template	Rules	Config	Rules	Config	Rules	Config	Rules	Config	Rules	Config
Jaccard Coefficient	0.93	0.88	0.93	0.93	1.00	0.75	0.895	0.895	0.89	0.95
Accuracy (%)	97.84	97.48	99.25	99.25	98.80	98.5	96.90	99.60	99.65	99.60

[7] Note , since there is no input template for the direct prompting method described in the methodology, this method is only evaluated in the next subsection.

[8] For examples of the logic template outputs and ground truth statement see the Appendix A.

Table 4. Proportion of correct eligibility determinations from the HTML form by method. Overall average is the mean of state percentages.

	Logic Rules Template	Logic Config Template	Logic as Written Text
GA	100%	100%	96%
OK	63%	98%	100%
OR	100%	100%	100%
VA	59%	25%	100%
Avg.	**81%**	**81%**	**99%**

5.3 Translating Logic Rules to Code

In the final component of the methodology, we evaluate methods for translating logic statements into HTML code (a questionnaire for SNAP categorical eligibility). We test three different approaches:

1. Logic Rules-Based Generation — Code is generated from the logic rules template output and the constructed variable list.
2. Logic Configuration-Based Generation — Code is generated from the logic configuration template output and the constructed variable list.
3. Direct Prompting — Code is generated by prompting the model to produce logic statements directly in the chat interface without a prespecified template structure. A second prompt then asks the LLM to create code based on the chat-generated logic statements, the original policy text, and the constructed variable list.

We evaluate the accuracy of each method using a process similar to the logic statement evaluation. For each state, we programmatically complete the HTML form using all possible combinations of Boolean input variables and compare the form output (i.e., the eligibility decision) to the expected output based on the ground truth logic statement for that state. Results are shown in Table 4. We find that the direct prompting method ("Logic as Written Text") had the highest accuracy, both on average and across individual states. It performs close to 20% better. However, if we use a weighted average based on the number of eligibility checks in each state, all the averages are very high (over 97%) and comparable.

6 Prototype Demonstration: Eligibility Form

We present the final HTML form output of our pipeline in Fig. 3. The form includes multiple sections (e.g., categorical eligibility factors, disqualification factors, and exemptions), each containing a set of yes/no questions. These questions are used to determine the user's SNAP categorical eligibility based on the

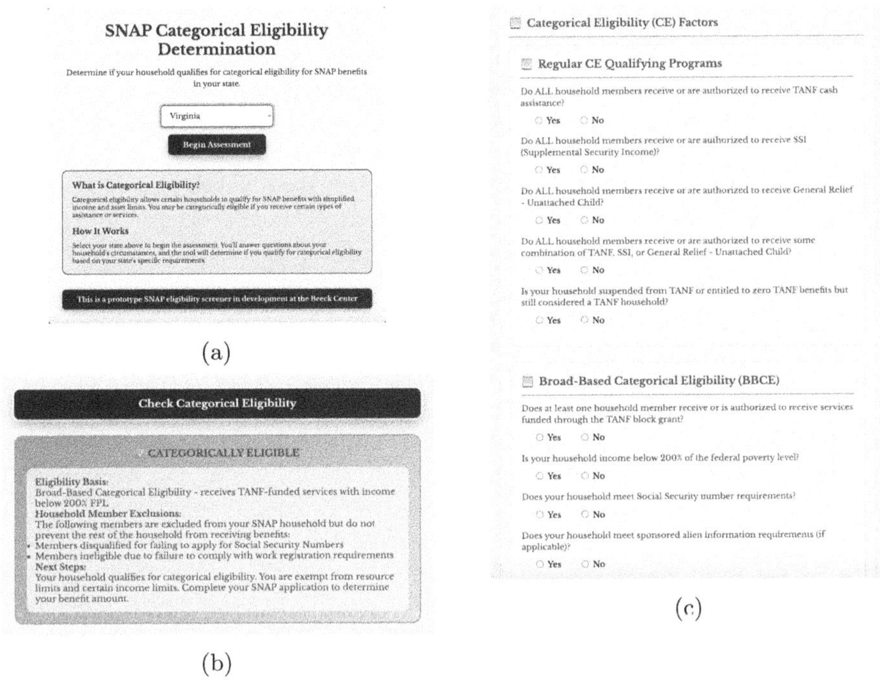

Fig. 3. Prototype SNAP categorical eligibility form. (a) Homepage overview, (b) Eligibility result summary, (c) Questions example: Categorical Eligibility Factors

automatically generated rules. At the end of the form, the eligibility result and decision explanation are displayed.[9]

We have created a step-by-step guide to generate this form for other states. It requires downloading the state's SNAP policy document and following the instructions in our GitHub repository.[10] All necessary files, including templates for each pipeline stage, and CSS for styling, are included.

7 Discussion

Overall, our results demonstrate that LLMs can accurately translate Categorical Eligibility SNAP policy documents into executable code when guided through a structured, multi-stage pipeline. In this study, we evaluated each stage of the methodology independently to better understand the strengths and weaknesses of each component.

For the variable extraction component, we find that the sequential chaining approach, in which policies from different states are processed within a sin-

[9] Our prototype is available at https://policy2code.georgetown.domains/snap-categorical-eligibility-determination/.

[10] https://github.com/georgetown-mdi/policy2code.

gle prompt sequentially, achieved a 6% higher variable recall than the extract-merge method. This suggests that incremental prompting, where each new state's extraction builds on the previous, helps the model maintain a coherent structure and reduces redundancy (the same variable with slightly different names) and/or omissions.

For the logic generation component, the full logic rules template slightly outperformed the configuration template in both variable overlap (Jaccard coefficient of 0.93 vs. 0.88) and correctness of logic (97.8% vs. 97.5%). Unlike the configuration template, which organizes policy information as descriptive eligibility criteria and thresholds, the rules template provides explicit variable definitions and formal logic expressions. This representation seems to be easier for the LLM to use when attempting to generate logically coherent and accurate rules.

Finally, for code creation, the direct prompting approach– where the LLM is asked to first generate an unstructured logic statement of the policy, then turn that statement into code– produced the most accurate and consistent results, outperforming both template logic-to-code approaches. This suggests that for policy to code task LLMs may perform best when given more flexibility in intermediate stages, as opposed to working from rigid template structures. We note that those other approaches did not perform poorly in most cases, just not as well. We hypothesize that because we are asking the LLM it generate code and that is a task it knows how to do well, it has strong internal logic for that task already. In other words, generating code directly from text is an easier task for an LLM for the simple policy than generating code from a template it has to create first.

7.1 Limitations

Although our framework and overall methodology performed well for the states in our case study, several limitations should be acknowledged. First, this study focuses exclusively on Categorical Eligibility, which is the most straightforward type of eligibility within SNAP. Expanding the pipeline to cover the full breadth of eligibility criteria would introduce significantly more complexity, particularly in logic modeling. This may mean that the templating approaches that were not necessary for the simpler categorical eligibility case, may be necessary to capture other, more complex cases. Second, our exhaustive evaluation of logic and code using all possible input combinations is manageable for Categorical Eligibility, but becomes impractical as the number of variables increases. This limits scalability of the current evaluation approach for analysis of the complete SNAP policy. One way to address this is to enhance the methodology to include evaluation of results by different LLMs to find cases that need more human evaluation.

Third, our analysis is limited to policies from only four states. Generalizing this workflow to other states, especially those with more ambiguous or loosely structured policy documents is needed to determine the overall viability of the approach for other policies. Fourth, our study evaluates the pipeline using policy documents from a single point in time. As SNAP policies are updated or amended, the logic and HTML code would need to be regenerated. While a key goal of this project is to create a pipeline that facilitates rapid encoding of policy updates, we have not yet tested how well the pipeline handles changes to a state's policy language. Finally, we have not yet conducted user testing with actual SNAP applicants or caseworkers. Even if automated evaluation is highly accurate, the tool is only valuable if end-users trust the information and are able to use it effectively.

8 Conclusions and Future Work

This study explored the potential of LLMs to automate the translation of SNAP policy into executable code, focusing specifically on categorical eligibility across four states. Through a three-stage methodology, consisting of variable extraction, logic generation, and code creation, we found that LLMs can perform this translation process with a high degree of accuracy. For variable extraction, sequentially chaining states yielded more complete and consistent variable lists compared to combining state policies all at once. In generating logic, a logic rule template that defines explicit variables and formal logical expressions slightly outperformed a configuration template, which presents eligibility criteria in a more descriptive and policy-focused format. However, when it came to code creation, direct prompting proved more effective than either template in producing accurate, usable code. These findings suggest that while structured guidance is important, allowing LLMs flexibility at key stages can enhance their performance, especially in cases where the logic is more straightforward.

Future work should focus on expanding the process along several dimensions: testing the pipeline on more states with varying SNAP policy formats, broadening the scope to cover the full spectrum of SNAP eligibility criteria beyond categorical eligibility, and applying the framework to other complex policy areas such as Medicaid. The ultimate goal is to develop interpretable tools that can help agencies modernize benefit systems, improve transparency, and better serve those in need.

All experimental code, prompts, and templates are publicly available in our GitHub repository,[11] including documentation for applying the pipeline to new states. The generated HTML eligibility questionnaires are hosted on our website.

Acknowledgments. We would like to acknowledge the Massive Data Institute (MDI) and the Beeck Center for supporting this work. We would also like to acknowledge the support of the MDI technical team and research manager, Rebecca Vanarsdall.

A Examples of Logic Template Outputs

Table 5 shows a sample of the logic template outputs using the rule-based and configuration-based templates in the case of Oklahoma SNAP, along with the ground-truth logic statement (manually produced by our research team).

[11] (https://github.com/georgetown-mdi/policy2code).

Table 5. Sample logic template outputs for Oklahoma SNAP

Logic Rules Template

```
eligibility_rules:

 meets_basic_categorical_criteria:
   description: "Meets a basic categorical criterion
"
   type: "boolean"
   formula: "tanf_receipt OR ssi_receipt
      OR ssi_tanf_combination
      OR two_one_one_services"

 has_disqualifying_factors:
   description: "Has factors preventing eligibility"
   type: "boolean"
   formula: "lottery_gambling_first_reapplication
      OR ipv_disqualified_member
      OR fleeing_felon_member
      OR post_2014_conviction_member
      OR head_of_household_work_noncompliant"

 meets_additional_req_for_211:
   description: "Meets extra requirements for 2-1-1"
   type: "boolean"
   formula: "NOT two_one_one_services
      OR (ssn_requirement_met
      AND sponsored_alien_requirements_met
      AND residency_requirements_met)"

 final_categorical_eligibility:
   description: "Categorically eligible for SNAP in
OK"
   type: "boolean"
   formula: "meets_basic_categorical_criteria
      AND NOT has_disqualifying_factors
      AND meets_additional_req_for_211"
```

Logic Config Template

```
categorical_eligibility:

 main_rule: "meets_basic_categorical_criteria
    AND NOT excluded_by_disqualification_factors"

 subrules:
   meets_basic_categorical_criteria:
      description: "Meets a qualifying criterion"
      logic: "(tanf_receipt = true)
        OR (ssi_receipt = true)
        OR (ssi_tanf_combination = true)
        OR (two_one_one_services = true)"

   excluded_by_disqualification_factors:
      description: "Excluded due to disqualifying
factors"
      logic: "(lottery_gambling_first_reapplication
= true)
        OR (ipv_disqualified_member = true)
        OR (fleeing_felon_member = true)
        OR (post_2014_conviction_member = true)
        OR (head_of_household_work_noncompliant =
true)"

 qualifying_conditions:
   two_one_one_services:
      description: "Services through 2-1-1 Oklahoma"
      income_requirement: "130% gross income
standard"
      additional_requirements:
        - ssn_requirement_met: true
        - sponsored_alien_requirements_met: true
        - residency_requirements_met: true
```

Ground-truth logic statement: `(tanf_receipt OR ssi_receipt OR ssi_tanf_combination OR (two_one_one_services AND ssn_requirement_met AND sponsored_alien_requirements_met AND residency_requirements_met)) AND NOT (ipv_disqualified_member OR fleeing_felon_member OR post_2014_conviction_member OR head_of_household_work_noncompliant OR lottery_gambling_first_reapplication)`

Key difference: The **Logic Rules Template** (left) defines each rule with a type and a strict Boolean formula that can be evaluated directly. The **Logic Config Template** (right) uses descriptive, hierarchically organized in-line logic blocks that retain richer policy context but require an additional translation step to produce executable logic.

B Prompts Used

Table 6 lists the prompts used at each pipeline stage. All prompts include the state policy manual and YAML variable file as attachments.[12]

[12] Some prompts are trimmed for brevity. Full prompts will be included in the project's repository upon publication.

Table 6. Prompts used at each pipeline stage.

Stage	Variant	Prompt
Variable Extraction	Single-state	Identify all variables required to determine categorical eligibility for SNAP in [STATE] using the policy manual. Use the attached YAML file as a baseline template, and update it with the full list of variables. Only include variables used to determine whether a household is categorically eligible.
	Extract-merge	Merge these variable files into one file, removing duplicates. Similar variables should be merged into one and the list of states should reflect the states in which that variable applies.
	Seq. chaining	Identify all variables required to determine categorical eligibility for SNAP in [STATE]. Use the attached YAML file as a baseline template, and add any variables needed for [STATE] that are not already present. Do not delete existing variables. Merge new variables into existing ones, or add them if they are new.
Logic Generation	Config template	Using the provided YAML template, variables, and policy manual, extract and organize the categorical eligibility rules for the [STATE] SNAP program. Use the template structure, but avoid filling in placeholder values with repetitive text. Structure the output as a YAML file useful for implementing these rules in code. Remove irrelevant sections and add new sections as needed.
HTML Form Creation	With templates	Using the attached CSS file, logic template, and state policy manual, create an HTML form that asks for the appropriate information and determines if the household is categorically eligible. Include section headings for state residency, categorical eligibility factors, broad-based categorical eligibility, disqualification factors, and member exclusions.
	Without templates (two-step)	*Step 1:* Using the [STATE] policy manual, write out the ways a household could be categorically eligible, and follow each with a logic statement combining the variables in the YAML file. *Step 2:* Create an HTML form using the attached CSS file and form template that determines if the household is categorically eligible for [STATE]. All questions are required except for member exclusions.

References

1. Kennan, A., Singh, L., Dammholz, B., Sengupta, K., Yi, J.: Exploring rules communication: Moving beyond static documents to standardized code for u.s. public benefits programs (2023). https://digitalgovernmenthub.org/publications/exploring-rules-communication-moving-beyond-static-documents-to-standardized-code-for-u-s-public-benefits-programs/
2. Lawsky, S.: Computational law and epistemic trespassing. J. Cross-Disc. Res. Comput. Law, **2**(2) (2024). https://journalcrcl.org/crcl/article/view/58
3. Mohun, J., Roberts, A.: Cracking the code: Rulemaking for humans and machines. OECD, OECD Working Papers on Public Governance 42 (2020). https://www.oecd.org/innovation/cracking-the-code-3afe6ba5-en.htm
4. Kang, I., Van Woensel, W., Seneviratne, O.: Using large language models for generating smart contracts for health insurance from textual policies (2024). https://doi.org/10.48550/arXiv.2407.07019
5. Romeo, F., Arena, L., Blefari, F., Pironti, F.A., Lupinacci, M., Furfaro, A.: Arpaccino: An agentic-rag for policy as code compliance (2025). https://doi.org/10.1007/978-3-032-05727-3_39

6. Merigoux, D., Chataing, N., Protzenko, J.: Catala: A programming language for the law (2021). https://doi.org/10.1145/3473582
7. Policy2code prototyping challenge. https://digitalgovernmenthub.org/get-involved/policy2code/, Accessed 25 July 2026
8. Jiang, J., Wang, F., Shen, J., Kim, S., Kim, S.: A survey on large language models for code generation. ACM Trans. Softw. Eng. Methodol. (2025). https://doi.org/10.1145/3747588
9. Kennan, A., Singh, L., Garcia Guevara, A., Ahmed, M., Goodman, J.: AI-powered rules as code: Experiments with public benefits policy. Beeck Center for Social Impact + Innovation and Massive Data Institute, Georgetown University, Tech. Rep. (2025). https://digitalgovernmenthub.org/publications/ai-powered-rules-as-code-experiments-with-public-benefits-policy/
10. Srinivas, D., Das, R., Tizpaz-Niari, S., Trivedi, A., Leonor Pacheco, M.: On the potential and limitations of few-shot in-context learning to generate metamorphic specifications for tax preparation software (2023)
11. Gogani-Khiabani, S., Dewangan, V., Olson, N., Trivedi, A., Tizpaz-Niari, S.: Technical challenges in maintaining tax prep software with large language models (2025)
12. Digital benefits network rules as code community of practice. https://digitalgovernmenthub.org/get-involved/rules-as-code-interest-area/, Accessed 15 June 2026

Large Language Models in Regulatory Impact Assessment: Evidence from the Greek Legislative Process

Fotios Fitsilis[1], Evangelos Kalampokis[2], Areti Karamanou[2](✉), Miltiadis Mourtias[2], Arsenios Chrysikopoulos[2], and Konstantinos Tarabanis[2]

[1] Universidad Austral, Buenos Aires, Argentina
ffitsilis@mail.austral.edu.ar

[2] Information Systems Lab, Department of Business Administration, University of Macedonia, Thessaloniki, Greece
{ekal,akarm,bad25018,bad25040,kat}@uom.edu.gr

Abstract. Regulatory Impact Assessment (RIA) is a key instrument of better regulation, yet in practice, RIA reports tend to be often overly simplistic, particularly in the use of data and evidence. This paper examines the use of Large Language Models (LLMs) in supporting RIA within the Greek legislative process. Following an exploratory case study, it evaluates two scenarios: a zero-shot approach and an LLM-augmented text-analytics workflow. The analysis employs the Mistral Large model, a sovereign European LLM, and evaluates AI-generated outputs against human-authored RIA fields from five legislative bills. The expert-led evaluation shows that zero-shot generation performs well in structuring RIA reports and ensuring procedural completeness, but falls short in providing detailed analysis and integrating evidence, frequently producing hallucinations. The LLM-augmented text-analytics workflow yields measurable score improvements in the consultation-related fields, which performed worst under zero-shot conditions.

Keywords: Regulatory Impact Assessment · legislative process · Better Regulation · GovTech · Digital Governance · Greece

1 Introduction

The continuous improvement of legislation constitutes a basic element of better regulation and is embedded, as a guiding principle, in virtually every stage of the legislative cycle [8]. The nature of improvement lies in the formulation of principles and mechanisms aimed at optimizing the legislative process, enhancing the quality of legislative measures and, ultimately, their effectiveness [25]. The general objective is to address the chronic pathologies of legislative output, such as over-regulation, overlap, and fragmentation of legislative provisions.

Published by Springer Nature Switzerland 2027
G. Viale Pereira et al. (Eds.): EGOV 2026, LNCS 16933, pp. 297–312, 2027.
https://doi.org/10.1007/978-3-032-35747-2_19

In Greece, a substantial turning point was brought about by the introduction of Law 4622/2019 on the Executive State, which incorporated domestic experience, best practices and the expertise of European Union member states and institutions [13]. Among other things, this law establishes the principles, the competent bodies and the instruments for improving the quality of legislation, and describes the law-making process. Furthermore, it contributes to the production of new legislative measures, taking into account the necessity of codifying existing ones, with a view to aligning the pre-existing legislative framework with contemporary practices, and to advancing the coherence and effectiveness of the domestic legal order. Digital technology, as well as legal informatics, may play a decisive role in the evolution of the legislative process. By harnessing cutting-edge technologies, approved standards and sophisticated digital tools, law-making can become more efficient and transparent, and legislative measures more readily accessible and comprehensible to the general public [24].

An efficient way to implement the above is through the creation of digital platforms that enable the active participation of stakeholders in the law-making process in real time and, where deemed appropriate, of citizens, for instance during public consultations [10]. Such platforms provide the technological backbone for the digitization and automation of selected legislative processes within the ever-evolving governance environment. In this context, it is noted that the Hellenic Republic does not possess an integrated digital law-making system, such as LEOS/EdiT, which is applied at the level of the European Union and in some of its Member States such as Spain [12]. This gap, however, is being addressed through the National Codification Portal [30].

Within this framework, Artificial Intelligence (AI) may be utilized across a multitude of processes throughout the full legislative cycle. Specifically, Large Language Models (LLMs) and their application in Agentic AI systems can be deployed to support traditional law-making workflows. These technologies offer the potential to enhance the precision, consistency, and accessibility of legislative instruments, without displacing the deliberative and democratic foundations upon which law-making depends [2].

Central to the better regulation agenda is the instrument of Regulatory Impact Assessment (RIA) [7]. Greece established a relevant framework with the adoption of Law 4622/2019, which mandates RIAs for all primary legislation and for subordinate regulations of major economic or social importance. Despite this robust *de jure* framework, the OECD Regulatory Policy Outlook (2025) notes that quantitative analysis in Greek RIAs remains largely confined to budgetary impacts, while broader economic, environmental, and social effects are typically assessed only qualitatively. According to the OECD Indicators of Regulatory Policy and Governance (iREG) survey [28], Greece scores 2.2 out of 4.0 for its RIA system, close to the OECD average of 2.3. This divergence between formal institutional design and practical analytical depth was the main motivation for conducting the present study.

This paper examines the use of LLMs in supporting RIA within the Greek legislative process. It focuses on exploring the potential of LLMs in drafting RIA reports following two approaches: a zero-shot approach and an LLM-augmented text-analytics workflow. The evaluation takes into account the analytical quality, the completeness and the use of evidence, while placing the findings within broader discussions on digital sovereignty, public sector innovation and the modernization of legislative drafting practices.

The paper begins with an overview of better regulation and the Greek RIA framework (Sect. 2), followed by a review of related work in GovTech and public sector AI (Sect. 3). It then presents the research approach (Sect. 4), including methodology and evaluation design. The results section (Sect. 5) provides empirical findings, which are then analyzed in the discussion (Sect. 6). The paper concludes by discussing the implications for hybrid AI–human workflows in legislative processes (Sect. 7).

2 Regulatory Impact Assessment

RIA is a structured, evidence-based tool that is internationally recognized and systematically used by OECD member states and EU institutions. RIA identifies, evaluates, and documents the expected effects of a proposed regulatory measure before it is enacted. Its principal function is to ensure that legislative and regulatory initiatives are empirically justified, that their objectives are specific, temporally defined, measurable, and practicable, and that no proposed regulation is introduced where equivalent policy objectives may be achieved by less burdensome means [27]. RIA serves as a major instrument of better regulation policy, having potential to increase transparency, accountability and the overall quality of the legislative process.

RIAs accompanying bills in the Hellenic legislative process are prepared in accordance with the relevant Manual (Completion Guide) and the Template for Regulatory Impact Analysis [15]. The Manual implements Article 62 of Law 4622/2019, which makes it mandatory to prepare a RIA for any bill, amendment or regulatory act with significant economic or social impact submitted to the Hellenic Parliament. It includes two parts: a Completion Guide, providing methodological instruction for each of the eight prescribed sections of the RIA, and a Template with the standardized format of the RIA report.

Those eight sections are the following: (a) The explanatory report (Fields 1–14); (b) The budgetary impact report (Fields 15–16); (c) The special fiscal report (Field 17); (d) The report on general consequences, covering economic, social, administrative, environmental, and regional effects (Fields 18–21); (e) The public consultation report (Fields 22–23); (f) The legality report, examining the compatibility of the proposed provisions with higher-order legal norms (Fields 24–28); (g) The table of amended or repealed provisions (Fields 29–30); and (h) The implementation report, identifying the competent authorities, and the timetable for issuing the requisite regulatory acts (Fields 31–40). The consolidation of these components into a single instrument reflects the European Commission's broader agenda for regulatory quality assurance within EU member states [9].

The Completion Guide and the Template represent a significant institutional reform that consolidates previously fragmented reporting requirements into a single coherent instrument and establishes the conditions for compliance with the principles of better regulation. However, the effectiveness of this instrument remains dependent upon the capacity and institutional culture of the civil servants responsible for its application [26]. This is exactly where the present work comes in: delivering and testing AI-driven tools to support law-making experts in preparing RIAs in a more systematic and efficient manner. By saving substantial time, both political and administrative, through workflow automation, these experts will have more capacity to concentrate on substantive qualitative and legal assessments, as well as the human oversight functions that such a process necessarily demands.

3 Related Work

In recent years, the integration of AI in public administration has attracted increasing scholarly attention. This reflects both the rapid advancement of the underlying technologies and ongoing digital government reforms worldwide. A detailed mapping of a decade of research shows that the dominant analytical focus is placed on algorithmic decision-making, with the main concerns centered on trust, bias, and accountability in automated systems [4]. Despite this broad coverage, an imbalance can be identified: research has mostly concentrated on policy frameworks rather than on their practical implementation. This again leaves substantial empirical gaps in the understanding of how AI tools are actually deployed and what consequences they produce within operational governance environments.

These concerns are particularly relevant in the context of GovTech, a term used to describe the application of emerging technologies to the modernization of public sector functions. The increasing number of GovTech solutions has resulted in scrutiny of the conditions under which they are introduced. One has to be aware that such tools may function as a Trojan horse, exploiting technical asymmetries between private providers and public agencies to shift effective decision-making authority away from government. This again may undermine digital sovereignty and compromise public values [3]. This observation makes the choice of AI infrastructure not merely a technical consideration, but a matter of democratic governance. At the European level, GovTech solutions exhibit considerable institutional variety: while mainly implemented at the national level, their design logic and governance arrangements offer transferable lessons applicable to regional and local contexts alike [20].

Moreover, AI adoption has increasingly been analyzed through the lens of organizational capability development. AI capability refers to the ability of organizations to mobilize data, technical expertise and governance structures in order to create value from AI applications [23]. In the public sector, these capabilities are influenced by institutional constraints and knowledge-intensive workflows, implying that AI tools typically complement rather than replace expert decision-making processes. The use of LLMs in RIA can therefore be interpreted as part of a broader capability-building process within legislative organizations.

Additionally, research on AI adoption in public administration emphasizes legal accountability, transparency requirements, and risk sensitivity as key implementation factors [31].

Studies of digital government transformation similarly highlight the role of AI in supporting evidence-based policy design while raising governance and legitimacy challenges [32]. Other reviews of AI in the public sector have examined the organizational and ethical challenges it brings [33]. While such early contributions provide a valuable baseline, technological progress has since made parts of these analyses outdated.

More recently, researchers have identified a substantial lag between practice and research, noting significant deficits in empirical evidence, theory and methodology, particularly regarding the organizational and managerial consequences of AI integration [22]. Their call for more interdisciplinary and evidence-based inquiry was also a direct motivation for the present study, which seeks to generate empirical knowledge in one of the most underexplored dimensions of public sector AI: the automation of distinct law-making processes. In this specific domain, the viability of AI-assisted drafting has been demonstrated within the European context, situating the findings within the broader Better Regulation agenda [6].

Complementing this, it can be argued that the future of work in knowledge-intensive environments is more appropriately characterized as *blended*, where human and machine contributions are deeply integrated at the level of task execution, rather than *hybrid* in the conventional organizational sense [5]. This distinction matters for LLM deployment in RIA workflows, where human judgment and AI-driven automation must be carefully balanced.

The present work also builds upon prior research conducted by our research team in the domain of LLM-based legal and governance applications. First, we developed an LLM-based legal assistant, augmented with retrieval-augmented generation and agent-based architectures, and applied it to EU GDPR legislation and case law [21]. The findings demonstrated that such systems are capable of producing generally accurate responses to legal queries, while also revealing that more complex questions lead to significantly lower accuracy. This is a pattern with direct implications for RIA production.

On top of that, we undertook a systematic comparative evaluation of nine large language models, spanning proprietary and open-source models, including GPT, Claude, Mistral, and Llama, with respect to their reliability in interpreting EU VAT Directive provisions of varying complexity [19]. That study identified significant inter-model variation in legal accuracy and derived practical recommendations for the safe deployment of LLMs in legal and public policy settings. Taken together, these contributions establish the empirical and methodological foundation upon which the present investigation is built and situate the current work within an evolving research agenda aimed at advancing the responsible integration of AI into legislative and governance processes.

4 Research Approach

This study follows an exploratory case study approach [34]. Given that the use of LLMs in legislative drafting and regulatory analysis is still in its early stages, there is limited empirical knowledge on how these tools perform in practice. An exploratory design is well suited to this situation, as it allows for a closer look at what LLMs can and cannot do within a real institutional setting. The Greek RIA process offers a good case for this purpose since it is formally structured yet analytically demanding, and provides a concrete context in which to test two different approaches, zero-shot report generation and an LLM-augmented text-analytics workflow. By examining LLM outputs across different RIA fields and types of legislation, the study aims to surface practical patterns and lessons that can guide both future research and policy application.

This study is organized around four main elements intended to produce findings that are transparent, relevant, and applicable to the question of how LLM-based tools can be integrated into the RIA preparation process. First, an AI model was selected on the basis of digital sovereignty considerations. Second, a set of five bills and their RIAs was identified as the empirical basis for the study. Third, an expert evaluation framework was developed to assess and compare human-authored and AI-generated RIA outputs in a consistent manner. Fourth, an LLM-augmented text-analytics workflow was created to enhance analytical quality, completeness, and the use of evidence.

4.1 Model Selection as Precursor of Digital Sovereignty

Digital sovereignty refers to the capacity of states, and by extension, democratic institutions such as parliaments, to develop, deploy and govern digital technologies in alignment with their own legal frameworks, societal values and strategic priorities. In the context of AI, this extends to control over infrastructure, models, and processes, thus maintaining meaningful autonomy in their adoption and operation [14].

Without sovereignty, there is a real risk of dependency on external providers and potential misalignment with democratic norms, due to reduced capacity for effective oversight and accountability. The necessity of ensuring digital sovereignty drove the methodological choices made in this study, and specifically the decision to use Mistral Large as the LLM infrastructure. Mistral Large is a European sovereign AI solution developed by Mistral AI, a French company.

The Greek AI Factory *Pharos*, developed within the EuroHPC Joint Initiative, is a key step toward strengthening national digital sovereignty by providing advanced computing, data and AI development capabilities. At its core, the *Daidalos* data center serves as the high-performance infrastructure for the training and deployment of large-scale AI models within national jurisdiction. This ecosystem is directly relevant to the Hellenic Parliament, as it creates the conditions for developing and operating legislative AI applications [11]. The Greek government's Memorandum of Understanding with Mistral AI additionally reflects a strategic orientation toward European-based AI solutions and constitutes a further consideration driving the present study's infrastructure choice [17].

4.2 Sample Selection

The empirical basis of this study consists of five bills enacted in 2026, selected to represent a diverse range of legislative types and policy domains. In the absence of an official bill numbering system, each bill is referred to by the number of the law it subsequently became upon publication in the Official Government Gazette. The five bills examined are the following:

- Provisions on the human resources of the public sector, Civil Society Organizations, the strengthening of Local Government, the National Register of Companion Animals, and other provisions (Bill 5270/2026).
- Protection of works of art and collectible items – Combating the production and trafficking of forged works of art and collectible items and the damage of works of art and collectible items – Criminal provisions – Establishment of a Register of Sworn Experts – Other provisions of the Ministry of Culture (Bill 5271/2026).
- Ratification of the Multilateral Competent Authorities Agreement on the Automatic Exchange of Information under the Crypto-Assets Reporting Framework and implementing provisions (Bill 5273/2026).
- National Social Agreement for the strengthening of Collective Labor Agreements (Bill 5278/2026).
- Establishment and operation of a Unified Digital Register for monitoring corruption cases, interventions in the Code of Civil Procedure, and other provisions (Bill 5282/2026).

These RIAs correspond to different types of legislation, classified according to a functional approach to legal taxonomy [29]. On this basis, Bill 5270/2026 is classified as an omnibus regulatory act, integrating multiple policy areas within a single instrument. Bill 5271/2026 constitutes sector-specific regulatory legislation with penal elements in the field of cultural heritage protection. Bill 5273/2026 is a ratification statute, serving to incorporate an international agreement into domestic law alongside implementing provisions. Bill 5278/2026 is a framework or policy-oriented law, establishing general principles and institutional mechanisms in labor relations. Finally, Bill 5282/2026 represents a mixed legislative act, combining institutional innovation with procedural law reform.

This functional classification reflects the diverse regulatory roles of the bills under examination. Sample diversity is a deliberate methodological choice: the bills cover different functional categories, ensuring that the corresponding RIAs span a broad legal spectrum, effectively testing the LLM.

4.3 Evaluation Framework

The evaluation framework is designed to assess the quality of the RIA reports for the five selected bills and to examine the capacity of a sovereign LLM to support their development. The framework allows for a systematic comparison between human-authored and AI-generated RIAs. The evaluation was conducted using a five-point Likert scale (Table 1) designed to capture the depth of analysis, completeness, and reasoning quality of human-generated vis-à-vis LLM-generated outputs.

Table 1. Expert evaluation Likert scale (1–5).

Score	Interpretation	General Meaning
1	Very Poor	No meaningful analysis or evidence
2	Poor	Limited explanation or weak evidence
3	Adequate	Covers basic requirements but lacks analytical depth
4	Good	Well developed and structured; minor gaps only
5	Excellent	Comprehensive, rigorous, and evidence-based

Assessment is conducted by a single senior domain expert, combining advanced legal and engineering competencies with extensive experience in parliamentary research, AI governance, and legislative technology. The selection criterion was demonstrated capacity for simultaneous judgment on both the substantive legal quality of RIA content and the technical performance of AI-generated outputs.

Evaluation is applied exclusively to fields that are populated in the original human-authored RIA; fields left blank in the original are not scored. Each of the 40 defined fields of the RIA template is assessed independently, where applicable. This approach ensures that scores reflect true analytical quality, rather than being affected by structural differences in how bills are completed. The reliance on expert judgment, rather than automated metrics, is intentional; given the interpretive and legal nature of RIA content, human assessment is considered the most appropriate and reliable means of evaluating validity and compliance with regulatory quality standards.

4.4 LLM-Augmented Text-Analytics Workflow

The evaluation of the zero-shot outputs revealed particularly weak performance in several RIA fields, including the public consultation report fields (Fields 22–23) (Sect. 5). To address this limitation, we developed a proof-of-concept LLM-augmented text-analytics workflow that integrates public consultation data directly into the analysis pipeline. The workflow comprises six steps and was applied to Bill 5282/2026, targeting specifically the public consultation report fields. The six steps, implemented in n8n[1], are:

[1] https://n8n.io/.

- **Article segmentation.** Both the consultation draft and the final bill are parsed into individual articles using regular-expression-based parsing tailored to Greek legal drafting conventions.
- **Article mapping and change detection.** Articles are aligned across versions through text normalization, tokenization and similarity-based matrix matching.
- **LLM-based change characterization.** Each changed article is submitted to an LLM via zero-shot prompting to classify the type of change and assign a binary substantiveness label. A change is considered substantive if it alters the meaning, scope or legal interpretation of the article.
- **Substantive filtering.** Programmatic filtering based on the LLM's classification retains only articles that underwent substantive modification or were newly introduced.
- **Comment mapping.** Consultation comments are linked to the retained articles through rule-based mapping using the chapter-level metadata provided in each comment. This produces candidate comment–article pairs representing potential relationships between citizen input and legislative amendments.
- **LLM-based adoption analysis.** Each comment–article pair is assessed through LLM-based semantic reasoning to determine whether the legislative change can plausibly be linked to the consultation comment.

The workflow operates on three data sources, namely the public consultation draft of the bill, the citizen-submitted comments collected from the OpenGov platform[2], the official Greek government portal for online public consultations, during the consultation period, and the final version of the bill, and proceeds through sequential steps combining rule-based text processing with LLM-driven semantic analysis. Its output was evaluated using expert judgment.

5 Results

5.1 Zero-Shot Report Generation

The evaluation of the AI-generated RIA reports provides empirical insights into both the quality of existing RIA practices and the performance of LLMs supporting their development. The evaluated outputs achieve average Likert scores ranging from 2.50 (Bill 5271) to 3.25 (Bill 5273), with an overall mean of 2.77. This places the outputs predominantly in the *Poor* to *Adequate* range of the scale, as summarized in Table 2.

The number of RIA fields evaluated per bill ranges from 16 to 27, corresponding to completion rates of between 39 and 66 per cent, with a mean of 20 fields, or 50 per cent of the full template. No bill in the sample achieves full completion. This variation in completion rates is itself a substantive finding: it reflects the condition of the human-authored RIAs against which the AI-generated outputs are assessed, and confirms that structural incompleteness is a common feature of RIA practice in Greece, independent of the LLM under evaluation.

[2] https://www.opengov.gr/.

Table 2. Per-bill evaluation results.

Bill	5270	5271	5273	5278	5282
Average Likert Score	2.67	2.50	3.25	2.60	2.81
Fields Covered (%)	51.2	43.9	39.0	48.8	65.9
RIA Fields Evaluated	21	18	16	20	27

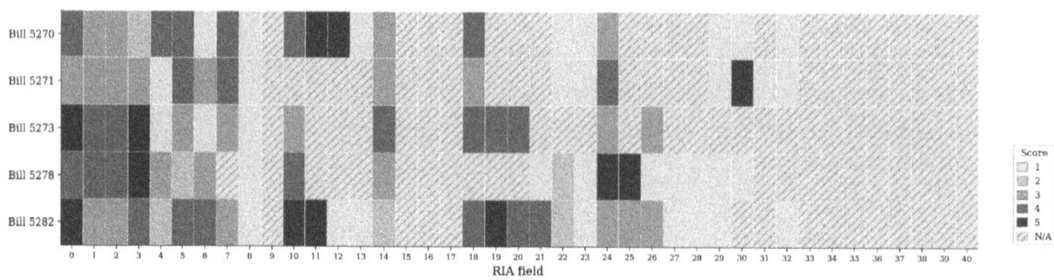

Fig. 1. Heatmap of per-field Likert scores across all five bills.

The per-field distribution of scores across all five bills is depicted in the heatmap presented in Fig. 1. The visual representation reveals a pattern of concentrated higher scores in the earlier, more structured sections of the RIA template, i.e., the explanatory report fields, alongside consistently low scores in the later sections concerned with public consultation, legality assessment and amended/repealed provisions.

Our evaluation highlights several cases where the model produces content that appears plausible but is unverifiable or factually incorrect, a phenomenon commonly referred to as *hallucinations* [18]. These outputs can be attributed to the absence of a direct connection to specific legislative repositories or official reports. Hallucinations are most evident in fields requiring references to external sources, including international good practices (Field 6), public consultation outcomes (Fields 22–23), and national and international case law (Fields 27–28).

5.2 LLM-Augmented Text-Analytics Workflow

The LLM-augmented text-analytics workflow was applied to Bill 5282/2026, selected on account of its comparatively high completion rate (65.9%) and mixed legislative character. During the public consultation period, the consultation draft of the bill received 299 citizen comments through OpenGov.

Article segmentation produced 72 articles from the consultation draft and 73 from the final bill. Similarity-based alignment between the two versions produced 75 mapped items, comprising matched article pairs, 3 additions and 2 removals. Of these, 25 involved content changes, while the remainder were unchanged or differed only through renumbering. Subsequent LLM-based assessment further narrowed the set to 8 articles that were either substantively modified or newly introduced.

The 299 consultation comments were then mapped to these 8 articles through chapter-level metadata, producing 124 comment–article pairs. The LLM-based adoption analysis did not identify direct one-to-one matches between specific comments and article-level amendments. These results did not correspond to the findings reported in the official RIA, which reports the incorporation of three consultation comments. However, these comment-based changes were, upon expert review, found to be minor legal adjustments, which accounts for the absence of matches in the workflow output.

Expert evaluation of the workflow output for Bill 5282/2026 showed a one-point improvement on the Likert scale in both Fields 22 and 23, with scores increasing from 2 to 3 and from 1 to 2, respectively. These findings have direct implications for the integration of task-specific pipelines into legislative workflows, as discussed in the following section.

6 Discussion

We determined that LLM-supported outputs perform well in terms of structural consistency and completeness. Across all cases, the generated reports successfully reproduce the standard architecture of RIAs, as provided by the reference template. The LLM shows a high degree of reliability in extracting and organizing metadata, including references to competent authorities and, to a large extent, relevant legal instruments.

There is a substantial variation in completion rates of the five RIAs examined, and no RIA in the sample achieves full completion. According to the RIA experts consulted, this is attributable primarily to two factors: insufficient time to conduct a thorough assessment within the designated margin of the legislative process, and inadequate access to relevant data sources. This again can be characterized as a major structural deficit and forms a practical argument for introducing LLM-based tools into the drafting process, which, by automating data retrieval and preliminary analysis, may address these constraints.

At the same time, the findings reveal further important limitations: while LLM-generated context adequately covers the required sections, it tends to provide more generic and less elaborated content compared to human-authored reports. In particular, the presentation of causal relationships and underlying national and international regulatory rationales is problematic. This affects core sections of the process in question:

- the identification of the existing regulatory framework (Field 4, per-bill scores: 4/1/1/3/2);
- international good practices and comparative references (Field 6, scores: 1/3/1/3/4), where evaluators spotted hallucinations in two of five cases;
- inter-ministerial consultation (Field 22, scores: 1/1/-/2/2); and
- the fields requiring identification of provisions amended or repealed by the bill (Fields 29–30), received the lowest scores—consistently 1—across most bills.

Furthermore, the analysis reveals a tendency of the LLM to simplify complex sections of the assessment. Multi-layered arguments, especially those involving legal interpretation or the interaction of economic and institutional factors, are reduced to more general statements. This might indicate a more general constraint in handling hierarchical and context-dependent reasoning, which again is a prerequisite for rigorous RIA development.

A related limitation is linked to the use of evidence. Our evaluation shows that LLM-generated outputs rarely incorporate specific data or quantitative analysis, relying instead on generalized claims or hallucinated content. This specific absence of empirical evidence is a core barrier to achieving high-quality outputs in several RIA fields, and importantly in RIA section (f): public consultation report (Fields 22–23).

The results also suggest that LLM performance is sensitive to the characteristics of the input material. Bills with clearer structure and more standardized content seem to yield higher-quality outputs (Bill 5273, average 3.25), compared to more complex ones (Bill 5271, average 2.50). Interestingly, the relatively lower completion rate of Bill 5273 (i.e., 39%), a ratification statute, suggests that structural simplicity in the source bill does not necessarily translate into higher template coverage, even where it correlates with higher average quality scores.

Based on the issues discussed above, the following set of technical limitations needs to be analyzed further:

- **Hallucinations.** The evaluation reveals several occasions where the model generates unverifiable or incorrect content. This is most evident in Field 6 (international good practices, Bills 5270 and 5273 scored 1 with explicit hallucinations mentioned by evaluators), Fields 22–23 (public consultation outcomes, all evaluated bills consistently scored 1 or—in a couple of occasions—2), and Fields 27–28 (national and international case law, a rapid verification check for Bills 5278 and 5282 indicated fabricated references).
- **Integration with external sources.** The model operates on the text of the bill, without being explicitly instructed to access external judicial databases, legislative repositories, or official publications. This seems to limit LLM performance on fields requiring verified citations. Several evaluator comments specifically recommend accessing ECLI-compliant judicial databases, OECD/ILO publications, and official UN/EU portals.
- **Agentic architecture.** As seen in the previous point, the current content generation approach does not allow the model to directly retrieve, verify or refine information. An agentic pipeline would significantly improve accuracy in evidence-intensive fields, for instance by enabling multi-step reasoning, use of external sources and verification loops.
- **OpenGov platform integration.** Fields 22–23 (public consultation) originally scored particularly low across all applicable bills. The evaluator noted that the model did not access public consultation reports from the official OpenGov platform (`opengov.gr`). Subsequently, the proof-of-concept workflow applied to Bill 5282/2026 produced measurable improvements: evaluation scores for Fields 22 and 23 increased by one Likert point each, from 2 to 3

and from 1 to 2, respectively. While modest, this improvement is substantively significant given the consistently low baseline scores recorded across all five bills in zero-shot conditions.

Beyond these technical limitations, the deployment of LLMs in legislative workflows raises broader organizational and governance concerns. One such concern is automation bias, described as the tendency of human reviewers to over-rely on automated outputs and reduce their critical scrutiny accordingly [16]. This risk could be particularly high in the legality and case-law fields (Fields 24–28), where fabricated references may pass undetected under time pressure. Meaningful human oversight therefore requires both domain expertise and quality control protocols to counteract these effects.

Automation can paradoxically increase the complexity and criticality of the human role rather than reduce it [1]. In the case of LLM-assisted drafting, it can reduce the time spent on pre-populating RIAs, while simultaneously generating new activities for users, such as output verification and source validation. This may necessitate Business Process Re-engineering (BPR), institutional safeguards, and expert training to be treated as prerequisites of LLM integration.

These results seem to confirm that poor LLM outputs in evidence-intensive RIA fields reflect the absence of structured access to reliable data sources, rather than an inherent technological limitation. The findings could also imply that LLMs could be most effective when integrated into hybrid and/or blended workflows [5,6]. In such human–machine configurations, AI can improve the efficiency of drafting and structuring RIA tasks, while human experts safeguard analytical validity, adapt outputs to context and ensure the reliability of the underlying evidence. Consequently, rather than substituting expert involvement, LLMs should be understood as complementary tools that augment, but do not replace, the core analytical functions of the RIA process.

7 Conclusion

This paper examined the capacity of a sovereign LLM to support RIA within the Greek legislative process. Following an exploratory case study approach, AI-generated outputs across diverse bills were evaluated against the original human-developed RIAs using two scenarios, namely a zero-shot approach and an LLM-augmented text-analytics workflow.

The findings highlight two major outcomes. First, LLMs perform well in structuring RIA reports and ensuring procedural consistency, demonstrating reliability in organizing metadata, identifying competent authorities, and referencing the main legal instruments. Hence, they may contribute to greater efficiency and standardization at the stage of the drafting process where the administrative burden is high. Second, the outputs reveal considerable limitations in the level of analysis, evidence integration, and legal reasoning. Hallucinations were identified across multiple fields, most consistently where references to external sources, comparative practices, public consultation outcomes or case law are required.

For this reason, an LLM-augmented text-analytics workflow incorporating public consultation data was developed and applied to one of the bills under examination. The results of this proof-of-concept are particularly encouraging and demonstrate that the integration of external information can substantially reduce the hallucination risk identified in the zero-shot evaluation.

Based on these findings, the group's future work will focus on integrating LLMs with authoritative data sources through agent-based architectures that allow the models to access and verify domain-specific information. The aim is to further strengthen reasoning capabilities, reduce hallucinations and improve performance in evidence-intensive tasks. Ultimately, the objective is to support the effective and responsible use of AI in complex, end-to-end law-making processes.

Disclosure of Interests. The authors have no competing interests to declare that are relevant to the content of this article.

References

1. Bainbridge, L.: Ironies of automation. In: Analysis, Design and Evaluation of Man-Machine Systems, pp. 129–135. Elsevier (1983)
2. Bar-Siman-Tov, I.: Legislatures and legislation in the age of artificial intelligence. Theory Pract. Legislat. **13**(3), 267–291 (2025). https://doi.org/10.1080/20508840.2025.2590971
3. Bharosa, N.: The rise of govtech: Trojan horse or blessing in disguise? A research agenda. Gov. Inf. Q. **39**(3), 101692 (2022). https://doi.org/10.1016/j.giq.2022.101692
4. Chandra, Y., Feng, N.: Algorithms for a new season? Mapping a decade of research on the artificial intelligence-driven digital transformation of public administration. Public Manag. Rev. **28**(3), 620–654 (2026). https://doi.org/10.1080/14719037.2025.2450680
5. Constantinides, M., Verma, H., Sadeghian, S., El Ali, A.: The future of work is blended, not hybrid. In: Proceedings of the 4th Annual Symposium on Human-Computer Interaction for Work, CHIWORK '25. Association for Computing Machinery, New York (2025). https://doi.org/10.1145/3729176.3729202
6. Corazza, M., Longo, G., Zilli, L., Di Sante, E., Sapienza, S., Palmirani, M.: Hybrid ai enhancing European drafting legislation for a better regulation. In: 2025 Eleventh International Conference on eDemocracy & eGovernment (ICEDEG), pp. 106–113 (2025). https://doi.org/10.1109/ICEDEG65568.2025.11081650
7. Dunlop, C.A., Radaelli, C.M.: Handbook of Regulatory Impact Assessment. Edward Elgar Publishing (2016)
8. European Commission: Better regulation guidelines. Commission Staff Working Document SWD(2021) 305 final, European Commission, Brussels (2021). https://commission.europa.eu/system/files/2021-11/swd2021_305_en.pdf
9. European Commission: Better regulation: Joining forces to make better laws. Communication from the Commission COM(2021) 219 final, European Commission, Brussels (2021). https://commission.europa.eu/system/files/2021-04/better_regulation_joining_forces_to_make_better_laws_en_0.pdf
10. Ferro, E., Loukis, E.N., Charalabidis, Y., Osella, M.: Policy making 2.0: from theory to practice. Gov. Inf. Q. **30**(4), 359–368 (2013). https://doi.org/10.1016/j.giq.2013.05.018

11. Fitsilis, F., Kamilaki, M., Gatos, B., Katsouros, V., Mikros, G.: The hellenic parliament's approach to digital sovereignty for the era of artificial intelligence. Int. J. Parliamentary Stud. 1–13 (2026). https://doi.org/10.1163/26668912-bja10127
12. Fitsilis, F., Mikros, G.: AI-based solutions for legislative drafting in the EU – Summary report. Publications Office of the European Union (2024). https://doi.org/10.2799/6892931
13. Fitsilis, F., Theodorakopoulos, G.: Better regulation and its evolution in the hellenic legislative and parliamentary system. Statute Law Rev. **45**(1), hmae003 (2024). https://doi.org/10.1093/slr/hmae003
14. Floridi, L.: The fight for digital sovereignty: what it is, and why it matters, especially for the EU. Phil. Technol. **33**(3), 369–378 (2020). https://doi.org/10.1007/s13347-020-00423-6
15. General Secretariat for Legal and Parliamentary Affairs, Presidency of the Government: Manual (completion guide) and template of regulatory impact analysis. Government manual, General Secretariat for Legal and Parliamentary Affairs, Presidency of the Government, Athens (2020). https://diavgeia.gov.gr/luminapi/api/decisions/6%CE%A8%CE%A3%CE%A846%CE%9C%CE%93%CE%A87-%CE%96%CE%A11/attachments/afaf12db-d6e5-4e33-8e78-d247e6b0109f/document
16. Goddard, K., Roudsari, A., Wyatt, J.C.: Automation bias: a systematic review of frequency, effect mediators, and mitigators. J. Am. Med. Inf. Assoc. **19**(1), 121–127 (2012)
17. Hellenic Republic: Prime minister Kyriakos Mitsotakis' meeting with the chief executive officer of Mistral AI Arthur Mensch. Official website of the Prime Minister of the Hellenic Republic (2025). https://www.primeminister.gr/en/2025/11/24/37447
18. Huang, L., et al.: A survey on hallucination in large language models: principles, taxonomy, challenges, and open questions. ACM Trans. Inf. Syst. **43**(2) (2025). https://doi.org/10.1145/3703155
19. Karamanou, A., Kalampokis, E., Fitsilis, F., Theodorakopoulos, G., Tarabanis, K.: Evaluating open and proprietary large language models in law interpretation: the case of the EU vat directive. In: Lindgren, I., et al. (eds.) Electronic Government, pp. 380–394. Springer, Cham (2026). https://doi.org/10.1007/978-3-032-01589-1_24
20. Kuziemski, M., Mergel, I., Ulrich, P., Martinez, A.: GovTech practices in the EU – A glimpse into the European GovTech ecosystem, its governance, and best practices. Publications Office of the European Union (2022). https://doi.org/10.2760/74735
21. Mamalis, M.E., Kalampokis, E., Fitsilis, F., Theodorakopoulos, G., Tarabanis, K.: A large language model agent based legal assistant for governance applications. In: International Conference on Electronic Government, pp. 286–301. Springer Heidelberg (2024). https://doi.org/10.1007/978-3-031-70274-7_18
22. Mergel, I., Dickinson, H., Stenvall, J., Gasco, M.: Implementing ai in the public sector. Public Manag. Rev. 1–14 (2023). https://doi.org/10.1080/14719037.2023.2231950
23. Mikalef, P., Gupta, M.: Artificial intelligence capability: conceptualization, measurement calibration, and empirical study on its impact on organizational creativity and firm performance. Inf. Manag. **58**(3), 103434 (2021). https://doi.org/10.1016/j.im.2021.103434
24. Mohun, J., Roberts, A.: Cracking the code: Rulemaking for humans and machines, OECD Working Papers on Public Governance (2020)

25. Mousmouti, M.: Effectiveness as an aspect of quality of EU legislation: is it feasible? Theory Pract. Legislat. **2**(3), 309–327 (2014). https://doi.org/10.5235/12050-8840.2.3.309
26. Mousmouti, M.: Designing Effective Legislation. Edward Elgar Publishing (2019)
27. OECD: Regulatory Impact Assessment. OECD Best Practice Principles for Regulatory Policy, OECD Publishing, Paris (2020). https://doi.org/10.1787/7a9638cb-en
28. OECD: Government at a glance 2025. Digital government index (2025). https://www.oecd.org/en/publications/government-at-a-glance-2025_0efd0bcd-en.html
29. Sherwin, E.: Legal taxonomy. Leg. Theory **15**(1), 25–54 (2009). https://doi.org/10.1017/S1352325209090041
30. Stasis, A., Dalakou, V., Karakatsanis, I., Demiri, L., Valatsou, G., Sarantis, D.: Better access to law by codification and consolidation of legal acts: the case of the hellenic law codification portal. In: Proceedings of the 13th International Conference on Theory and Practice of Electronic Governance, ICEGOV '20, pp. 696–704. Association for Computing Machinery, New York (2020). https://doi.org/10.1145/3428502.3428605
31. Sun, T.Q., Medaglia, R.: Mapping the challenges of artificial intelligence in the public sector: evidence from public healthcare. Gov. Inf. Q. **36**(2), 368–383 (2019). https://doi.org/10.1016/j.giq.2018.09.008
32. Valle-Cruz, D., Criado, J.I., Sandoval-Almazán, R., Ruvalcaba-Gomez, E.A.: Assessing the public policy-cycle framework in the age of artificial intelligence: from agenda-setting to policy evaluation. Gov. Inf. Q. **37**(4), 101509 (2020). https://doi.org/10.1016/j.giq.2020.101509
33. Wirtz, B.W., Weyerer, J.C., Geyer, C.: Artificial intelligence and the public sector–applications and challenges. Int. J. Public Adm. **42**(7), 596–615 (2019). https://doi.org/10.1080/01900692.2018.1498103
34. Yin, R.K.: Case Study Research: Design and Methods, Applied Social Research Methods Series, vol. 5, 4th edn. Sage Publications, Thousand Oaks (2009)

How Do Users Forage on OGD Portals? An Information Foraging Perspective Through Trace Data Analysis

Eudes Adiba[1(✉)], Antoine Clarinval[2], and Anthony Simonofski[1]

[1] Namur Digital Institute, University of Namur, Namur, Belgium
{eudes.adiba,anthony.simonofski}@unamur.be
[2] Swedish Center for Digital Innovation, Umeå University, Umeå, Sweden
antoine.clarinval@umu.se

Abstract. The documented benefits of Open Government Data (OGD) depend not only on data openness but also on users' ability to successfully forage: i.e. to actively search and navigate OGD portals in order to locate relevant datasets. Despite the importance of user foraging behaviors, this topic is underexplored and the few existing studies remain partial, as each focuses on an isolated aspect which fail to provide the full picture of the foraging behaviors. In this study: (1) we conceptualize OGD portals as information foraging environments following Information Foraging Theory; (2) and we leverage a fine-grained analysis of trace data to identify and explain distinct foraging behaviors within these foraging environments. Our computationally intensive analysis reveals three foraging behaviors: direct data extraction, data catalog browsing, and thematic exploration. These behaviors differ along several key dimensions such as: users' assumptions about the dataset location, their effort allocation, their navigation depth, and their stopping decisions. The identified behaviors offer a novel lens for evaluating OGD portals by assessing how effectively their design supports each behavior.

Keywords: Open Government Data · Open data portal · Human-data interaction · Information Foraging Theory · Trace data

1 Introduction

Open Government Data (OGD) portals represent a point of free access to verified public institutions data about a variety of domains (e.g., health, environment, mobility, economy). The abundance of information on OGD portals, combined with the limited temporal resources of users, leads them to forage, i.e. to actively search and navigate in order to find useful pieces of information. Information foraging refers to the pursuit of relevant information through the exploration of an information environment [32]. On OGD portals, the process of finding useful data for a particular task is cognitively demanding [21], as suitable datasets are

Published by Springer Nature Switzerland 2027
G. Viale Pereira et al. (Eds.): EGOV 2026, LNCS 16933, pp. 313–329, 2027.
https://doi.org/10.1007/978-3-032-35747-2_20

often embedded within dedicated portal structures or scattered between heterogeneous but related data resources [38]. Consequently, the well documented benefits of OGD are conditional not only on data openness, but also on whether users can effectively forage for data within the portal.

Understanding user foraging behaviors on OGD portals receives little attention from the literature, as the majority of OGD related work focuses on factors influencing users' intention to use OGD [27,31] or on the effect of data quality on OGD adoption [16]. Such understanding is essential to design OGD portals that not only attract users but also facilitate interaction, engagement and, in fine, unlock the benefits, as has been demonstrated for other types of information systems [29,37].

The few studies aimed at understanding user behaviors on OGD portals present several gaps. They adopt a conceptual view of user interactions based on experts feedback and little to no empirical evidence [5]. In some cases [11], the empirical evidence is based on a specific group of users and therefore do not represent the variety of user interactions. For works that are directly based on broad usage data to understand foraging behaviors, the analysis is rather partial: it focuses on specific aspects like portal entry points [34], query characteristics [10] or it leverages aggregate metrics such as dataset popularity or download counts [22], which do not offer a fine-grained understanding of foraging behaviors.

This study addresses these limitations by conceptualizing OGD portals as information foraging environments in which users continuously make decisions about where to navigate, whether to continue exploring, and when to stop. Rather than analyzing a specific group of users or relying on aggregate usage metrics, we leverage broad and detailed trace data analysis to uncover behavioral patterns that reflect distinct data foraging strategies. Trace data record a wide range of interactions between users and OGD portals; they are, in essence, the digital traces left behind by such interactions. The granularity and unobtrusive nature of these data enable fine-grained analysis of user behavior that is less prone to response biases [18]. Additionally, the computationally intensive analysis of trace data [3,15] aligns with the emerging calls for new research approaches to OGD portals that go beyond traditional descriptive statistics [7,28].

The entire process, from the conceptualization of OGD portals to the uncovering and description of foraging behaviors, is informed by Information Foraging Theory (IFT) [21] which defines information foraging as the pursuit of valuable information through the exploration of an information environment based on cues. IFT provides a suitable theoretical lens, particularly in the context of OGD portals [26] through its constructs and their interdependency. The theory is also aligned with the fine-grained behavioral perspective we are adopting. The following Sect. 2 introduces previous work about users behaviors on OGD portals, IFT and trace data analysis. Section 3 gives a clear overview of the methodology, while Sect. 4 presents the main foraging behaviors: direct data extraction, data catalog browsing, and thematic exploration. Section 5 concludes with a discussion of the results and future research directions.

2 Literature Review and Theoretical Background

2.1 User Behaviors on OGD Portals

The present work sits in the broader context of human-OGD interaction [33]. Early research in this area focused on conceptualizing the broader interaction process through which users discover, interpret, and use open government data. One of the first studies is the study by Koesten et al. [11] in which, leveraging interviews and logs analysis, the authors draw from participants' experience with OGD data to propose a framework for interacting with structured data. Although pioneering, their findings were further challenged and expanded by several other studies. Crusoe et al. [5] combined interviews and a literature review to design a data use process framework from identification to enrichment, which highlights the role of different stakeholders. More recently, Xiao at al. [33] have integrated the Koesten et al.'s framework [11] with Pirolli and Card's sense-making model [19] to conceptualize a model for human-OGD interaction. The model includes five stages: task preparation, data foraging, sense-making, use and sharing. While these studies have conceptualized how users interact with OGD, empirical evidence on how these interactions combine to form observable foraging strategies remains limited. Several subsequent studies have therefore focused more specifically on understanding users' behaviors during the data foraging stage.

Kacprzak et al. [10] analyzed the search logs of four national open data portals and examined data requests submitted by users to understand the characteristics of dataset search. Their analysis focuses primarily on query characteristics and information needs rather than the behaviors that emerge during the foraging stage. Xiao et al. [34] studied users' accessing behaviors on three local open data portals in the United States. The study highlights different accessing channels (organic search, referral and direct) that have a direct impact on the user chance of finding the needed data. It gives valuable insights on the portal entry points but limited overview of the subsequent behaviors on the portal. Recently, Ibáñez and Simperl [8] examined transaction logs from the European Data Portal to compare search sessions initiated directly on the portal with those originating from web search engines. Their results highlight important differences in the use of facets and keyword queries across these session types. However, the work focuses on how search behaviors vary according to the sessions, leaving open the question of broader end-to-end behavioral patterns that are not solely driven by facets or queries and that may generalize beyond the selected session types.

Although pioneering, these empirical investigations remain partial, as each focuses on an isolated aspect of user interaction without providing the full picture of user foraging behavior as we are doing in this work.

2.2 Information Foraging Theory

Information Foraging Theory (IFT) is derived from optimal foraging theory, which predicts that animals foraging for food in some environment structure maximize their net energy gain (i.e. energy gained from food - energy spent foraging). IFT rests on the idea that humans as "informavores" adopt a similar strategy when searching for information. The search process can be described as a cost-benefit optimization in which people adapt their strategies to maximize their rate of gaining valuable information while minimizing costs such as time spent [21].

The computational modeling of human foraging behaviors done by Pirolli [21] reveals that the key aspect guiding those strategies is the "information scent" which refers to the perceived usefulness of an information source inferred from available elements (e.g., name, tags, description, source) prior to access, much like the scent emanating from prey that guides a predator during foraging. Due to the specific characteristics of the world wide web, the theory was further tailored to information search on the web [20] and leveraged in different settings like mobile web [1], product search [12], social Q&A communities platforms [24] and also in cooperative and competitive settings [17].

However, it has not been used in data search situations on open data portals. As highlighted earlier, the fragmented focus of previous studies does not provide a full picture of user foraging behaviors on OGD portals, nor does it explain the mechanisms underlying them. IFT is suitable to provide an end-to-end analysis and can be useful for that through its constructs and their interdependency.

2.3 Trace Data Analysis

Digital trace data are event-based records of user's activities on digital systems [3]. Since 1999 [9], they served as a proxy for studying user behavior and have been useful in studies of human computer interaction [18,35,36] due to several key advantages. First, their granularity and volume allow one to extract detailed and far-reaching insights. The insights extracted are less prone to response biases and offer a broader view of all types of user behavior, capturing the often under-studied group of user behaviors unintentionally left by case study design research.

Few studies have used trace data to study the behaviors of OGD portal users in a way or another. Koesten et al. [11] have done so in combination with interviews in developing their framework. Other studies mentioned earlier [8,10,22,34], have also based their work on trace data analysis.

However, by limiting their analysis to isolated aspects of interaction or by focusing on aggregated metrics, these studies do not fully exploit the analytical potential of trace data. This fine-grained trace data can be used to reconstruct users' foraging behaviors through observable navigation actions. This reconstruction enables the operationalization of key IFT constructs that provide a theoretical basis for understanding the end-to-end behavioral patterns observed on open data portals.

3 Methodology

We used a data-driven computationally intensive approach aimed at generating theoretical insights [3,15]. This approach is efficient, as it introduces a dialogue between theory, empirical material, and an emergent understanding of OGD portal users' foraging behaviors. Figure 1 summarizes the approach and each part is described below.

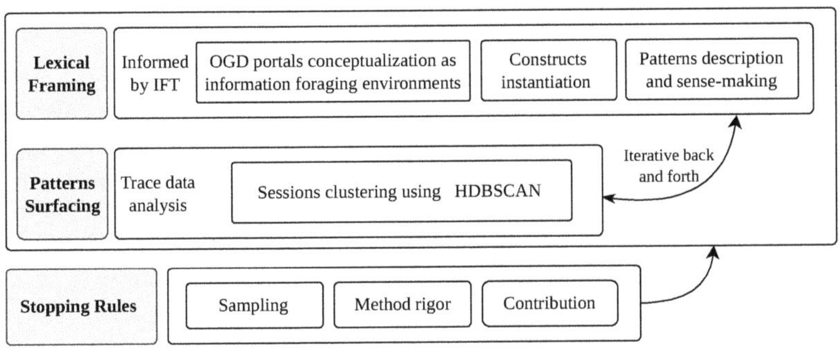

Fig. 1. Methodology.

The lexical framing part represents the language used as a lens to describe knowledge [6]. We focus on describing IFT as a novel theoretical lens for users foraging on OGD portals. The stress is put on theoretical framing because it is the one (in this work) influencing the others (methods and practice). As introduced earlier, IFT is about how people seek information analogous to how predators forage for preys in optimal foraging theory.

Pattern surfacing, on the other hand, is about extracting regularities from data. We identify groups of foraging behaviors on portals. The computational methods and data used to do so are described below by taking into account the lexical framing.

Lexical framing and pattern surfacing are iterative and intricate. When new patterns are discovered, their sense-making is shaped by lexical framing, and at the same time, the latter influences which patterns are seen and interpreted. Stopping rules help decide when it is appropriate to end this iterative process. We used three stopping rules [15]: sampling, method rigor, and contribution.

Sampling. We anchor the work in the analysis of a representative case by focusing on digital trace data from the OGD portal of the city of Namur (Belgium). The city has a portal with more than 290 datasets. We rely on an excerpt of trace data from the portal covering 6 weeks which contains 257,064 user actions. This data size is above the threshold used in previous studies [2], therefore, we consider it sufficient and did not engage in further data collection.

Method Rigor. Method rigor is about ensuring that observed patterns are not just artifacts of the methods used. We used a robustness check to do so, which is described in Sect. 3.2.

Contribution. We achieved two main contributions: the conceptualization of OGD portals as foraging environment (through lexical framing) and the derivation of usage behaviors embedded in IFT (through patterns surfacing). As we manage to do so, we deem it adequate to stop the iterative process.

3.1 Lexical Framing

The structure of the web has evolved to present regularities in how information is presented to users [20]. These regularities, such as the use of links accompanied by short textual hints and summaries, have also been adopted in portals. In the context of dataset search on portals, each link typically represents a dataset, and the associated textual hints correspond to metadata elements, such as the dataset title, data source, brief description, and tags. In IFT, these textual summaries are referred to as "cues". Cues are intended to provide users a clear and concise indication about a dataset and its content. Users base their navigation decisions on these cues by assessing their relevance to the dataset they are seeking. The perceived appropriateness of a dataset (to satisfy a user's information need), as inferred from available cues before accessing the dataset itself, is referred to as "information scent". Higher-quality and more accurate cues produce a stronger and more reliable information scent. Navigation is mediated through the information scent generated by those cues.

Beyond information scent, another key component of IFT is the structure of the information environment (in this case, the OGD portal). Prior research suggests that the web tends to evolve toward hierarchical structures [25]. Although, as websites, OGD portals typically adopt a hierarchical organization such as prestructured thematic pages that can smoothen data discovery, the organization of datasets within this hierarchical structure differs. Datasets are organized in a patchy (i.e., non-hierarchical) structure. A patch refers to a group of interconnected datasets that share one or more common metadata attributes. Datasets within a patch, or more specifically, their links and associated cues, are presented in a way that facilitates navigation within the patch compared to navigation between patches. Within a patch, users can access and navigate all related datasets guided by information scent. In contrast, navigating between patches requires additional effort, such as applying filters, making it more demanding than navigation within a patch. Figure 2 illustrates this and the IFT constructs are instantiated to the case of OGD portals in Table 1.

While information scent helps model navigation within patches, navigation between patches is explained by a complementary model: the information patch model. According to IFT, users are assumed to continuously seek to maximize their rate of valuable information gain. A user will decide to leave a given patch and move to another when the rate of information gain in the current patch falls below the average expected rate of gain across available patches as explained by Charnov's Marginal Value Theorem [4].

Table 1. IFT constructs instantiated to the case of OGD portals.

Construct	Definition	Example in OGD foraging
Predator	Person foraging for information	OGD Portal user
Prey	Information that the predator is seeking	Relevant dataset
Information environment	Environment where the foraging happens	OGD Portal
Patch	A cluster of prey	A thematic group of datasets
Link	A navigational element that connects patches	Hyperlinks based on similar topics, tags, or linked metadata
Cues	Small details that help the predator guess what they will find if they follow a link	Metadata
Information scent	Predator's perception of the value of a link based on cues	Perceived usefulness of a dataset

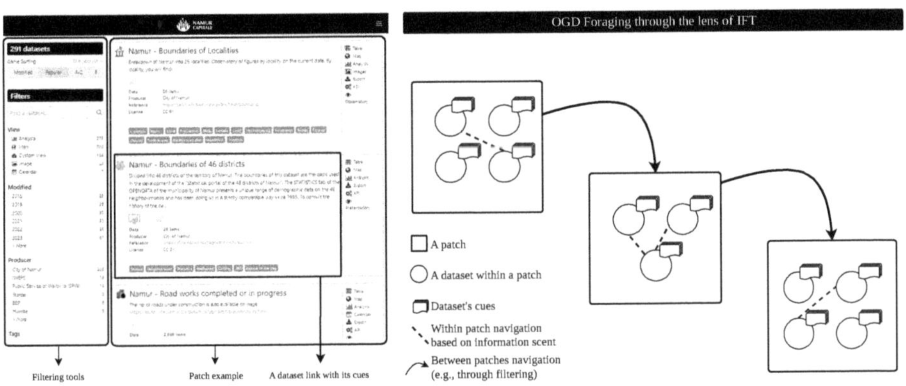

Fig. 2. OGD foraging through the lens of IFT.

3.2 Pattern Surfacing

Data. The trace data used for the analysis of foraging behaviors consists of 257,064 raw interaction logs collected from user activity on the Namur OGD portal (https://data.namur.be). Each log entry corresponds to a single user action and is stored as a structured record of key-value pairs describing the time of the action, the user and device context, the accessed resources, the request parameters, the interface module, and other technical execution details. Below is an example of the logs structure for an arbitrary selected set of keys.

{ "timestamp": "xxxx", "user_ip_addr": "xxx", "user_agent": "...", "dataset_id": ["id1"], "api_type": "...", "api": "...", "query_string": "...", "custom_attributes": "...", "referer": ".......", "action": ".....", "bot": "...", "mobile": "..." }

Data Preprocessing. User interaction logs were segmented into sessions using an inactivity threshold, such that consecutive actions from the same user were

Table 2. Sessions variables for clustering

Variable	Definition
refilter_ar	proportion of actions within a session involving any refiltering (facet or query based)
query_ar	proportion of actions within a session involving a query constraint It indicates reliance on query-based interaction rather than pure navigation or browsing
dataset_er	proportion of actions related to dataset pages or dataset-level operations It measures how central datasets are within the session, distinguishing catalog browsing from dataset-focused use
log_n_dataset	log-transformed number of distinct datasets accessed during the session It represents the scope of exploration while mitigating the influence of extreme values
explore_su	proportion of actions occurring in exploration interface like the data catalog
editorial_su	proportion of actions occurring in editorial/pre-built thematic pages
search_discov_sa	proportion of actions related to search and discovery operations It reflects navigation and discovery-oriented strategies
extraction_sa	proportion of actions involving data download or export or analysis It indicates exploitation-oriented behavior aimed at data reuse
log_n_action	log-transformed number of actions. It serves as engagement proxy
log_duration	log-transformed session duration It approximates user engagement while reducing the influence of extreme values

grouped unless a prolonged period of inactivity occurred. Each action was enriched to capture both the user interface context in which it took place and the type of operation performed. Interactions associated with administrative (publisher) interfaces were identified through the UI context and removed, as they reflect data management activities rather than public data use. Similarly, bot related actions were also discarded. Action-level information was then aggregated at the session level to characterize session scope, interaction intensity, use of constraints, and the distribution of activity across portal interfaces and action types. To account for large variations in session length, behavioral composition was expressed using proportions and rates rather than raw counts, and highly skewed variables were log-transformed. Sessions consisting of a single action were excluded from the clustering process. Variable selection focused on normalized, behaviorally distinct dimensions and avoided redundant or infrastructure-driven variables. The resulting set of session-level variables used for clustering is summarized in Table 2 and a full description of the entire process is provided as online supplementary material[1]. Before clustering, selected variables were standardized using z-score to avoid scale related distortion.

Session Clustering. Clustering was performed on scaled features using HDBSCAN, a density-based algorithm [13,14]. This clustering algorithm was chosen for several reasons: (i) it is suitable for data with heterogeneous densities, as we can expect for the sessions level data extracted; (ii) it does not require an initial number of cluster; (iii) it labels ambiguous data points as noise rather than forcing them into a particular cluster; and (iv) by construction, it allows robust cluster identification based on their stability across multiple neighborhood scales. Using a minimal cluster size of 150 and a minimal sample of 20 (number of data point need to estimate local density), we identified a total of 5 session clusters and a group of sessions labeled as noise. In the following result section, we only described the clusters as the noise was not of interest.

A robustness check based on cluster stability was done and the main cluster structures persisted across variations in minimal sample (10, 15, 20) and minimal cluster size (110, 120, 130, 140, 150, 160, 170, 180, 190, 200), with only minor changes affecting low-density boundary points and noise assignments. This consistency indicates that the identified clusters reflect stable structures rather than artifacts of a specific parameter configuration. Additionally, the silhouette score (excluding noise) is 0.70, which indicates good separation.

4 Results

4.1 Clusters

Table 3 shows the statistical description of the identified clusters. The first row indicates the number of sessions within each cluster. The following rows show the mean and standard deviation (std) of the number of actions per session, the session duration in seconds, and the number of different datasets visited, for each cluster. The remaining descriptive variables were introduced in Table 2. For variables which refer to a proportion, we provide the clusters' interquartile range (IQR). The main differentiating variables within each cluster are shaded in the table.

Sessions in Cluster C0 are exclusively centered on datasets (dataset_er [IQR] = [1.00-1.00]) and are specifically oriented toward value extraction activities, such as downloading, exporting, or analyzing data. These sessions consist of an

[1] https://zenodo.org/records/18699474.

Table 3. Clusters description

	C0	C1	C2	C3	C4
size	746	420	211	157	1218
actions mean (std)	2.21 (0.67)	13.86 (1.59)	28.17 (2.63)	5.92 (1.01)	6.33 (0.96)
duration mean (std)	148.04 (349)	3.16 (5.36)	74.52 (17.32)	35.65 (24.71)	0.50 (0.43)
unique dataset mean (std)	1.04 (0.24)	5 (0.12)	5.11 (0.37)	1 (0.00)	1 (0.00)
refilter_ar [IQR]	[0.00-0.00]	[0.21-0.23]	[0.21-0.25]	[0.00-0.00]	[0.00-0.00]
query_ar [IQR]	[0.00-0.00]	[0.00-0.00]	[0.00-0.00]	[0.00-0.00]	[0.00-0.00]
dataset_er [IQR]	[1.00-1.00]	[0.70-0.71]	[0.71-0.71]	[0.71-0.77]	[0.60-0.66]
explore_su [IQR]	[0.00-0.00]	[0.00-0.00]	[0.00-0.00]	[0.71-0.80]	[0.60-0.66]
editorial_su [IQR]	[0.00-0.00]	[1.00-1.00]	[1.00-1.00]	[0.00-0.00]	[0.00-0.00]
search_discov_sa [IQR]	[0.00-0.00]	[0.28-0.28]	[0.28-0.28]	[0.70-0.77]	[0.66-0.66]
extraction_sa [IQR]	[1.00-1.00]	[0.07-0.14]	[0.08-0.14]	[0.00-0.00]	[0.00-0.00]

average of 2 actions, corresponding to the minimal sequence required to directly access a dataset and retrieve its contents. They involve no exploration, search, or refinement activities. While the number of actions is stable, session duration exhibits greater variability, likely reflecting differences in download or processing. We label this behavior as **direct data extraction**. Below is a sequence of actions on the Namur OGD portal within a selected session of this cluster.

{ Direct access to city center parking location dataset -> Specific entry checking }

Cluster C1 is characterized by sessions that are not centered on a single dataset, with an average of 5 datasets accessed and approximately 14 actions per session. A defining feature of these sessions is their interaction context: all actions take place on pre-built thematic pages accessible through the hierarchical navigation menu of the portal (editorial_su [IQR] = [1.00-1.00]). Users enter this thematic area early and remain within it. Thematic pages aggregate multiple datasets around a shared topic. Within this confined space, users interact indirectly with several datasets and actively refine or adjust views (refilter_ar [IQR] = [0.21-0.23]). The sessions are short and clearly topic-oriented. We label this behavior as **short thematic exploration**, in which users focus on specific thematic interest and use available pre-defined thematic pages to gather information on the topic. Below is a session example:

{ Home -> Observatories -> Demographic observatories -> Zoom in on localities -> Filter for the locality of Erpent -> Interactions with the map }

Cluster C2 exhibits interaction patterns similar to those of C1 in terms of thematic focus, but is characterized by longer sessions, a higher number of actions, and slightly greater refinement effort. Unlike C1, where interactions tend to be short and targeted, sessions in C2 reflect a more sustained engagement with the topic, involving iterative exploration and comparison. We therefore label this behavior as **extended thematic exploration**.

Cluster C3 is characterized by sessions that ultimately focus on a single dataset, but are primarily dominated by the search and browsing process leading to it. With an average of 9 actions per session, most interactions occur prior to accessing the dataset and consist of search and navigation activities (search_discov_sa [IQR] = [0.70-0.77]) taking place almost exclusively within the data catalog (non-hierarchical) (explore_su [IQR] = [0.71-0.80]). Therefore, we label this behavior as **data catalog browsing**. Below is a session example:

{ Home –> Data Catalog –> Search in the search bar –> List of datasets –> Scanning –> Applying filters –> Exploring the dataset on planned road works }

Cluster C4 exhibits interaction patterns characterized by extremely short sessions (0.5 s on average) and an absence of refinement activity (refilter_ar [IQR] = [0.00-0.00], query_ar [IQR] = [0.00-0.00]). The sessions in this cluster correspond to shallow visits with minimal user commitment and are likely to reflect casual or accidental engagement. We therefore label them as **shallow exploration**.

4.2 Foraging Behaviors

The five identified clusters were consolidated into three foraging behaviors by merging Clusters C1 and C2, which reflect the same underlying foraging logic but differ in interaction intensity (short versus extended), and by excluding Cluster C4, which did not involve any foraging actions (search refinement, dataset discovery, or dataset access). The resulting foraging behaviors, presented in Fig. 3 can be interpreted as distinct foraging strategies shaped by the foraging environment (OGD portal structure) but also assumptions about prey (dataset) location, expected information value, and the cost of continued search within the portal environment.

Direct data extraction corresponds to a strategy in which the predator has reliable prior knowledge of prey location. The dataset (prey) is directly targeted. This suggests that the related information scent is highly qualitative. Patch selection is direct and interaction time is minimal. Effort allocation is concentrated on prey exploitation.

Data catalog browsing is a scent-driven evaluation strategy. In this specific case, the predator does not begin with a clearly identified prey but relies on cues such as titles, metadata, and categories to assess potential value. Navigation unfolds as a sequence of patch evaluations, with effort allocated to comparing alternatives before commitment. Patch switching is more frequent, and the predator likely stops when the prey is found.

Thematic exploration corresponds to an early commitment to a bounded (limited and pre-defined) thematic patch, which is made of multiple potential prey. Rather than evaluating patches broadly across the environment, the predator enters a pre-structured patch (mostly a thematic one) and allocates effort within that specific patch through refinement and comparison. Scent operates here, way before the patch selection, as the thematic grouping itself functions as a cue for relevance. Navigation occurs within the patch, and the predator likely stops when a broad satisfaction within the thematic patch is obtained.

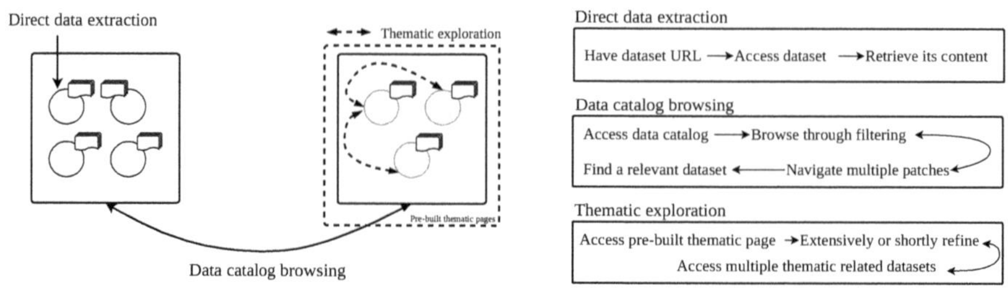

Fig. 3. Foraging behaviors.

Together, this forms a classification of OGD foraging behaviors, that differ according to foraging-related characteristics (see Table 4).

Table 4. Foraging behaviors characteristics

Foraging behavior	Prior knowledge of prey	Patch strategy	Effort allocation	Navigation depth	Stopping behavior
Direct data extraction	High	Immediate commitment to a specific dataset patch	Focused on exploitation, no search effort	Non-existent	After exploitation
Data catalog browsing	Low	Sequential evaluation of multiple patches	Effort distributed across cue evaluation and comparison	Moderate across-patch navigation	When a relevant prey is found
Thematic exploration	Moderate (topical)	Early commitment to a bounded thematic patch	Effort concentrated within a selected patch through refinement	Deep within-patch navigation	When goal satisfaction within the thematic patch is reached

5 Discussion

5.1 Contributions

The contributions of this study were crafted following the computational theory construction approach of Miranda et al. [15]. This involves analyzing empirical data with computational methods to surface patterns that are situated into a theoretical lexicon. Our work offers a contribution in terms of the patterns we identified, but also the theoretical lexicon we mobilized to characterize the patterns. The surfacing of patterns reveals that users forage on OGD portals by following three main strategies, namely direct data extraction, data catalog browsing, and thematic exploration. Each is characterized by different types of assumptions and expectations.

The proposed set of foraging behaviors has theoretical and research implications. It complements the work of Wang and Liu [30], who show that user expectations and perceived gains influence their search activities. More precisely the study reveals the behavioral structures that emerge from such influences on OGD portals. The work also extends the prior conceptual model of human interaction with open government data proposed by Xiao et al. [33]. Despite highlighting the importance of the data foraging stage, their model treats it as a uniform component of the interaction process. Our results zoom in and refine this perspective by showing that multiple distinct foraging strategies can exist within this stage. For researchers, the results provide an analytical lens that enables them to evaluate OGD portals not only in terms of OGD quality and general usability, but also in terms of how effectively their design supports different foraging behaviors.

The study also adds to the scarce body of work applying IFT to OGD users' behavior analysis as highlighted by Saxena et al. [23]. We conceptualize OGD portals as foraging environments and applied this newly defined lexicon to describe foraging behaviors. This lexicon offers a transferable lens to conduct other analyses on OGD portals or other data platforms such as statistics and transparency portals.

For public agencies managing OGD portals, the study points out the utility of thematic pages as topic related bounded patches that support goal-oriented exploration. This provides empirical support for investment in high-quality thematic pages, but most importantly with accurate thematic dataset grouping.

5.2 Limitations

Some limitations of the present work include the fact that the foraging behaviors are derived from patterns based on session-level features and in this sense, they emphasize dominant behavioral patterns. This choice, although relevant for the identification of general patterns, may mask hybrid behaviors that unfold within a session, but do not dominate it. The foraging strategies we identified therefore capture the dominant foraging behaviors, and our methodological choice prevents from diving into the granularity of those possible hybrid behaviors and behavioral transitions.

The analysis also relies on a single portal. The Namur OGD portal provides rich and realistic usage trace data and is built on one of the most widely adopted open data management systems, making it representative of a broad category of OGD portals. Nevertheless, behavioral patterns may differ across regional, national, or international portals, which vary in terms of dataset volume, metadata quality practices, and search functionalities. For instance, portals built on different data management systems (e.g., CKAN, DKAN, or custom implementations) may offer distinct navigation and discovery affordances that influence users' foraging strategies. Furthermore, the Namur portal can be considered small to medium-sized in terms of the number of available datasets. As the size of a data catalog increases, so does the effort required to manually explore it. Consequently, strategies such as data catalog browsing may become less attractive on larger portals. Therefore, the generalizability of the proposed behaviors remain to be assessed across portals that differ in their data management systems, administrative scope, and dataset volume.

Another limitation concerns Cluster C4. Although identified through the clustering process, this cluster was excluded from the final foraging behaviors because it neither led to dataset discovery nor involved dataset access or observable efforts to refine during the search process. As such, it could not be clearly associated with a foraging outcome and was not considered a foraging behavior. C4 was interpreted as reflecting casual or accidental visits to the portal. However, its extremely short average session duration (0.5 s) raises questions about the nature of the underlying activity. While known bots and automated requests were filtered out during preprocessing, the possibility of residual automated traffic cannot be entirely ruled out. Consequently, a more dedicated analysis of its sessions would help determine whether it reflects a form of user behavior or residual non-human traffic.

5.3 Future Works

Future research can expand this work along three main axes. First, the current trace data could be extended by including log data from a variety of OGD portals: different administrative levels, different sizes, and different data management systems. This would allow assessing the robustness and prevalence of the identified behaviors. This expanded dataset would also provide opportunities to investigate hybrid behaviors discussed in the limitations, especially through process mining approaches.

The second axis of improvement is related to a diachronic analysis [15] to complement the understanding of the behaviors. It would consist of behavior modeling and estimation by leveraging the important amount of trace data, already collected as part of the first axis. Within this second improvement step, for each foraging behavior, continuation probabilities would be estimated to capture satiation and marginal value constraints, as described by IFT. Such modeling will deepen the understanding of how users evaluate cues and how they decide whether to persist within patches or to leave them.

Trace data capture behaviors happening on the portal but do not fully explain how users arrive there or how their information need originates. For instance, direct data extraction may originate from users accessing datasets through external search engine results, AI generated links, or repetitive professional tasks where dataset links are reused. The third axis of improvement is about adopting an ecosystem perspective that connects information need emergence, external search mechanisms, portal entry channel, and subsequent foraging strategies. To do so, future research could plan on adopting a triangulation approach that will satisfy the need to "zoom out" from solely trace data analysis and give context. This third improvement step would build on previous trace data analysis complemented by new qualitative data.

6 Conclusion

The study analyzes fine-grained trace data from the OGD portal of the city of Namur (Belgium) to uncover three data foraging behaviors: direct data extraction, data catalog browsing, and thematic exploration. By conceptualizing OGD portals as foraging environments in which we situate the identified patterns, we form a classification of foraging behaviors on OGD portal. The identified behaviors differ in terms of users' assumptions about the location of datasets, how they allocate their efforts, the depth of their navigation on the portal, and how they decide to stop foraging.

Our findings advance current understanding of users' behaviors on OGD portals and constitute reusable analytical lenses for further design and evaluation studies of portals and similar platforms. They also offer useful insights to enable OGD portals to support distinct foraging behaviors by highlighting that users do not engage with an OGD portal in one unique way.

References

1. Adipat, B., Zhang, D., Zhou, L.: The effects of tree-view based presentation adaptation on mobile web browsing. Manag. Inf. Syst. Q. **35**(1), 99–122 (2011)
2. Azzopardi, L., Thomas, P., Craswell, N.: Measuring the utility of search engine result pages: an information foraging based measure. In: Proceedings of the 41st International ACM SIGIR Conference on Research & Development in Information Retrieval, pp. 605–614. Association for Computing Machinery, New York (2018)
3. Berente, N., Seidel, S., Safadi, H.: Data-driven computationally intensive theory development. Inf. Syst. Res. **30**(1), 50–64 (2019)
4. Charnov, E.L.: Optimal foraging, the marginal value theorem. Theor. Popul. Biol. **9**(2), 129–136 (1976)
5. Crusoe, J.R., Ahlin, K.: Users' activities for using open government data – a process framework. Transform. Gov. People Process Policy **13**(3/4), 213–236 (2019)
6. Gaskin, J., Berente, N., Lyytinen, K., Yoo, Y.: Toward generalizable sociomaterial inquiry: a computational approach for zooming in and out of sociomaterial routines. Manag. Inf. Syst. Q. **38**(3), 849–871 (2014)
7. Hossain, M.A., Dwivedi, Y.K., Rana, N.P.: State-of-the-art in open data research: insights from existing literature and a research agenda. J. Organ. Comput. Electron. Commer. **26**(1–2), 14–40 (2016)
8. Ibáñez, L.D., Simperl, E.: A comparison of dataset search behaviour of internal versus search engine referred sessions. In: Proceedings of the 2022 Conference on Human Information Interaction and Retrieval, pp. 158–168. Association for Computing Machinery, New York (2022)
9. Jiang, D., Pei, J., Li, H.: Mining search and browse logs for web search: a Survey. ACM Trans. Intell. Syst. Technol. **4**(4), 57:1–57:37 (2013)
10. Kacprzak, E., Koesten, L., Ibáñez, L.D., Blount, T., Tennison, J., Simperl, E.: Characterising dataset search—an analysis of search logs and data requests. J. Web Semant. **55**, 37–55 (2019)
11. Koesten, L., Emilia, M.K., Tennison, J., Simperl, E.: The trials and tribulations of working with structured data: a study on information seeking behaviour. In: CHI '17: Proceedings of the 2017 CHI Conference on Human Factors in Computing Systems. ACM (2017)

12. Liu, Z., Li, J., Wang, X., Guo, Y.: How search and evaluation cues influence consumers' continuous watching and purchase intentions: an investigation of live-stream shopping from an information foraging perspective. J. Bus. Res. **168**, 114233 (2023)
13. McInnes, L., Healy, J.: Accelerated hierarchical density based clustering. In: Proceedings of the 2017 IEEE International Conference on Data Mining Workshops (ICDMW), pp. 33–42 (2017). iSSN: 2375-9259
14. McInnes, L., Healy, J., Astels, S.: hdbscan: hierarchical density based clustering. J. Open Source Softw. **2**(11), 205 (2017)
15. Miranda, S., Berente, N., Seidel, S., Safadi, H., Burton-Jones, A.: Editor's comments: computationally intensive theory construction: a primer for authors and reviewers. Manag. Inf. Syst. Q. **46**(2), iii–xviii (2022)
16. Moradi, M., Mazoochi, M., Ahmadi, M.: A comprehensive method for improving the quality of open government data and increasing citizens' willingness to use data by analyzing the complex system of citizens and organizations. Complexity **2022**(1) (2022)
17. Nakayama, S., Richmond, S., Nov, O., Porfiri, M.: The gold miner's dilemma: use of information scent in cooperative and competitive information foraging. Comput. Hum. Behav. **109**, 106352 (2020)
18. Nam, D., Macvean, A., Myers, B.A., Vasilescu, B.: Understanding documentation use through log analysis: a case study of four cloud services. In: Proceedings of the 2024 CHI Conference on Human Factors in Computing Systems, pp. 1–17. Association for Computing Machinery, New York (2024)
19. Pirolli, P., Card, S.: The sensemaking process and leverage points for analyst technology as identified through cognitive task analysis. In: Proceedings of International Conference on Intelligence Analysis (2005)
20. Pirolli, P.: Rational analyses of information foraging on the web. Cogn. Sci. **29**(3), 343–373 (2005)
21. Pirolli, P., Card, S.: Information foraging. Psychol. Rev. **106**(4), 643–675 (1999)
22. Quarati, A., De Martino, M.: Open government data usage: a brief overview. In: Proceedings of the 23rd International Database Applications & Engineering Symposium, pp. 1–8. Association for Computing Machinery, New York (2019)
23. Saxena, S., Alexopoulos, C.: Assessing the quality and usability of open government data portals in the GCC constituents. In: Zafarullah, H., Siddiquee, N.A. (eds.) Open Government and Freedom of Information: Policy and Practice in Asia and the Middle East, pp. 353–376. Springer, Cham (2023)
24. Sedhain, A., Ragavan, S.S., McKinney, B., Leon, S., Kuttal, S.K.: Predicting information foraging on Q&A websites. In: Coman, A., Vasilache, S. (eds.) Social Computing and Social Media, pp. 322–342 (2025)
25. Simon, H.A.: The architecture of complexity. Proc. Am. Philos. Soc. **106**(6), 467–482 (1962)
26. Stuti, S., et al.: Information scent and open government data (OGD) engagement: research agenda. In: Proceedings of the 16th International Conference on Theory and Practice of Electronic Governance, pp. 235–241. Association for Computing Machinery, New York (2023)
27. Talukder, M.S., Shen, L., Hossain Talukder, M.F., Bao, Y.: Determinants of user acceptance and use of open government data (OGD): an empirical investigation in Bangladesh. Technol. Soc. **56**, 147–156 (2019)
28. Thorsby, J., Stowers, G.N.L., Wolslegel, K., Tumbuan, E.: Understanding the content and features of open data portals in American cities. Gov. Inf. Q. **34**(1), 53–61 (2017)

29. Tselios, N., Katsanos, C., Kahrimanis, G., Avouris, N.: Design and evaluation of web-based learning environments using information foraging models. In: Architecture Solutions for E-Learning Systems. IGI Global Scientific Publishing (2008)
30. Wang, B., Liu, J.: Understanding users' dynamic perceptions of search gain and cost in sessions: an expectation confirmation model. J. Am. Soc. Inf. Sci. **75**(9), 937–956 (2024)
31. Wang, F., Zhang, Z., Ma, X., Zhang, Y., Li, X., Zhang, X.: Paths to open government data reuse: a three-dimensional framework of information need, data and government preparation. Inf. Manag. **60**(8), 103879 (2023)
32. Wopereis, I.G.J.H., van Merriënboer, J.J.G.: Evaluating text-based information on the World Wide Web. Learn. Instr. **21**(2), 232–237 (2011)
33. Xiao, F., Chi, Y., He, D.: Promoting data use through understanding user behaviors: a model for human open government data interaction. J. Am. Soc. Inf. Sci. **74**(13) (2023)
34. Xiao, F., Wang, Z., He, D.: Understanding users' accessing behaviors to local Open Government Data via transaction log analysis. Proc. Assoc. Inf. Sci. Technol. **57**(1), e278 (2020)
35. Zhang, J., Liu, H.: Theory-based user search behaviour modelling and understanding through search log analysis. In: Proceedings of the 2025 ACM SIGIR Conference on Human Information Interaction and Retrieval, pp. 298–309. Association for Computing Machinery, New York (2025)
36. Zhang, W., Zhang, F., Chen, J., Lu, W.: Towards better evaluating multi-query sessions: a measure based on the theory of planned behavior. In: Proceedings of the 48th International ACM SIGIR Conference on Research and Development in Information Retrieval, pp. 148–158. Association for Computing Machinery, New York (2025)
37. Zhao, Y., Peñuela, A.M., Simperl, E.: User experience in dataset search. In: Plácido da Silva, H., Cipresso, P. (eds.) Computer-Human Interaction Research and Applications, pp. 113–130. Springer, Cham (2025)
38. Zuiderwijk, A., Reuver, M.d.: Why open government data initiatives fail to achieve their objectives: categorizing and prioritizing barriers through a global survey. Transform. Gov. People Process Policy **15**(4), 377–395 (2021)

The Social Dynamics of OGD-Based Application Development: A Case Study on Motivation and Networking

Eric Börner(✉)

TU Dresden, Helmholtzstraße 10, 01069 Dresden, Germany
eric.boerner1@tu-dresden.de

Abstract. Many OGD-based applications play a key role in making public data usable, yet most are short-lived because their sustainability hinges on the continued engagement and connections of independent developers. This study investigates how developer motivation and networking shape the long-term sustainability of such applications. Drawing on an exploratory case study of two mobile OGD-based applications that have been maintained for over a decade, we analyze the temporal evolution of motivational drivers and networking dynamics. Our findings show that sustainability depends not only on strong initial intrinsic motivation, but also on later obligation-based drivers, predictable maintenance demands, data-access conditions, and the changing strength of external ties. We derive six propositions that extend prior research by highlighting the temporal fragility of developer engagement and the conditional role of networking as a multiplier. Practically, the study offers insights for independent developers seeking to manage maintenance burdens and sustain long-term involvement in OGD-based initiatives.

Keywords: Open Government Data · Independent Developers · Motivation · Networking · Case Study

1 Introduction

Over the past two decades, open government data (OGD) has gained increasing prominence worldwide, accompanied by a rapid growth in datasets made publicly available [10, 23]. OGD refers to non-confidential public sector data that can be freely accessed, used, and shared [10]. OGD is widely recognized for its potential to foster transparency, accountability, citizen participation, as well as economic growth and innovation [10, 23]. However, meaningful value emerges primarily through data reuse rather than from the datasets themselves [1]. In this context, developers play a pivotal intermediary role in the OGD ecosystem [13], transforming raw datasets into applications accessible to citizens [2, 20], who often lack the technical skills and awareness necessary to engage directly with open data [6]. Alongside institutional and commercial initiatives, many OGD-based applications are created by independent developers in their spare time without financial compensation, or emerge from open data hackathons, frequently as open-source projects.

Published by Springer Nature Switzerland 2027
G. Viale Pereira et al. (Eds.): EGOV 2026, LNCS 16933, pp. 330–345, 2027.
https://doi.org/10.1007/978-3-032-35747-2_21

However, such applications are often short-lived: many fail to gain traction among users or are discontinued when developers cease to maintain them.

We argue that two factors are critical in explaining the long-term sustainability or failure of OGD-based applications: the trajectory of developer motivation and developer networking. While prior research has explored what motivates developers to engage with OGD and participate in hackathons [5, 11, 13, 14, 18], motivation is not static but dynamic, shifting over time. This temporal evolution may determine whether developers continue to operate an OGD-based application over the long term. Similarly, while prior studies have investigated how developers interact within OGD communities and with other stakeholders [12, 13, 19], the influence of networking dynamics over time on the sustainability of applications remains largely unexplored. Against this backdrop, this paper addresses the following research question: **How do developer motivation and networking shape the long-term sustainability of OGD-based applications?** To answer this question, we conducted an exploratory case study of two mobile OGD-based applications maintained for over ten years. We analyzed each case through two lenses: the evolution of developer motivation and networking dynamics over time. Based on our observations, we derived six propositions explaining how these trajectories shape the sustainability of OGD-based applications. This study contributes to understanding how motivation and networking shape the long-term sustainability of OGD-based applications and offers practical insights for developers and public institutions on sustaining engagement and managing maintenance challenges.

2 Conceptual Background

2.1 OGD-Based Applications and Independent Developers

OGD-based applications are web or mobile applications built on government-published open data to provide value-added services for private end users, such as citizens. By transforming raw datasets into accessible information, they enable non-technical users to benefit from open data without specialized analytical skills [2, 19]. Such applications are also referred to as *third-party applications* and *civic applications* [13, 20], which we subsume under the term OGD-based applications in this paper. Many OGD-based applications have a strong local focus, for example mobility planners or map-based tools that help users locate public facilities within a city or region. Following Smith & Sandberg [21], the evolution of OGD-based applications can be assed using the ITIL service lifecycle, comprising five phases: service strategy, service design, service transition, service operation, and continual service improvement. Numerous OGD-based applications emerge in the context of innovation contests, app competitions, or hackathons that stimulate open data experimentation [13]. Many OGD-based applications are created by independent developers who dedicate their time and expertise on a voluntary basis [12–14]. These actors are described as "*independent developers*" or "*tech-savvy citizens*" [13], "*external developers*" [21], "*civic developers*", or "*third-party developers*" [21]; we refer to them simply as developers. They play a key intermediary role in the OGD ecosystem by connecting public data providers with end users of open data services [13, 19]. Despite their pivotal role, their perspective remains underexplored in OGD research, which largely focuses on institutional and policy-level factors rather than on the experiences of the developers themselves [13]. Many OGD-based applications struggle to achieve long-term sustainability. As Kassen [13] notes, numerous civic initiatives initially attract attention and showcase the potential of OGD, but fail to remain active over time. To understand why some projects endure while others fade, this study adopts the developers' perspective on OGD-based application lifecycles.

2.2 Motivations of Independent Developers

Previous research identifies various motivations driving developers and tech-savvy citizens to create OGD-based applications or participate in hackathons, although most studies focus on the latter [5, 11, 18]. These motivations can be categorized as intrinsic or extrinsic, with some authors adding internalized extrinsic motivations [17]. Intrinsic motivations such as enjoyment, intellectual challenge and reputation are generally the most influential, with developers often describing participation as driven by fun, creativity, and the satisfaction of solving problems [5, 11, 13, 14, 18]. Social and civic motivations are also important, as many participants seek to contribute to their communities and generate public value through data-driven solutions [14]. Extrinsic motivations such as career advancement, skill development, and demonstrating expertise may also influence participation [11, 18], although financial rewards generally play a minor role compared to learning, enjoyment, and civic contribution [5, 11, 18]. While the development of OGD-based applications is rooted in the open data movement, it shares similarities with open source and open innovation practices. Research on open-source software (OSS) communities therefore provides a comparative perspective on developer engagement. Beyond intrinsic motivations, OSS developers are often motivated by pragmatic and internalized extrinsic factors, such as solving personal technical problems ('scratching a personal itch') or developing skills and career opportunities [9, 15, 17]. The literature further highlights social and ideological drivers, including reciprocity, collective identity and beliefs in openness and knowledge sharing [9, 15, 17].

Prior research has largely examined developer motivation as a static construct. However, motivation is inherently dynamic and evolves over time as individual circumstances, project contexts, and social environments change. Initial motivation therefore offers limited explanatory power for the long-term sustainability of OGD-based applications. In contrast, the temporal trajectory of developer motivation may determine whether initiatives persist or gradually fade out. Despite its potential, the evolution of developer motivation over time remains largely unexplored in the OGD literature.

2.3 Networks and Interactions of Independent Developers

Developer networking represents a second important perspective for understanding the longevity of OGD-based applications [12, 13, 19]. As Kassen [13] emphasizes, "networking among specialists [...] could be a core of the success in many independent civic projects" (p. 38). Developers act as technological bridges between key stakeholders in the open data ecosystem [2, 12]. The literature identifies six types of developer networking relationships: those with government agencies, citizens, businesses, NGOs, journalists/media, and other developers [12, 13, 19]. Interaction with government agencies is central because they serve as primary data providers. Through interactions, developers can communicate needs regarding data access, quality, and usability, helping align data provision with practical requirements [8, 13]. Governments can reduce innovation barriers through financial or technical support [8, 12, 14, 20], while hackathons and competitions stimulate innovation and engagement [8, 12, 13]. Citizens are the primary end users of many OGD-based applications [2, 13, 19], and contribute through usage and feedback that improves functionality and usability [2, 13, 21]. Businesses may provide financial or technical support [12, 13], although independent developers typically pursue civic rather than commercial goals [13]. NGOs often collaborate with developers by offering resources, infrastructure, and organizational support [12, 13]. Journalists and media increase the visibility of open data initiatives and data-driven applications, for example through coverage of hackathons and civic tech events [12, 13]. Relationships among developers themselves are characterized by collaboration and a division between commercially and altruistically motivated actors [13]. Those interactions foster knowledge exchange, and the diffusion of open data practices through venues such as hackathons, app competitions and informal peer networks [12, 13].

3 Research Method

The case study approach was chosen because it is well-suited to exploring multifaceted contemporary phenomena in their real-life contexts, especially when phenomenon and its context are not clearly separable [22]. Following Yin's [22] logic of literal replication, two comparable cases were selected to identify recurring patterns. Each case represents a long-term OGD-based mobile application developed by independent developers and maintained for over ten years. The selected cases differ in scope but share key characteristics enabling cross-case comparison: both are mobile applications developed by independent developers and maintained for over ten years - a parking occupancy app available in multiple cities (Case A) and a waste collection app for a single city (Case B). First, we conducted online research to gather background information on the cases, including news articles, project websites, and a podcast episode featuring the two main developers of Case A, which we included as an additional data source (see Table 1). Secondly, we conducted semi-structured interviews with the main developers, who served as key informants. The semi-structured interviews followed a common guide covering project development, motivation, networking, and maintenance, while allowing respondents to elaborate on emerging topics. Because the applications were developed and maintained by only a few individuals, all relevant developers were interviewed. Interviewees were recruited via email or Matrix direct messages. During these interviews, the developers pointed out additional case material to us (e.g., GitHub repositories, articles). These materials were used to reconstruct project histories, corroborate interview accounts, and triangulate key events and developments. In total, six semi-structured interviews were conducted, beginning in November 2024. All interviews were held online, lasted about 60 min, and were recorded and transcribed using the *aTrain* tool. Follow-up interviews conducted several months later clarified outstanding issues and reflected on preliminary findings.

Table 1. Overview of the collected data.

Source	Case A	Case B
Key informants	Podcast Developer 1,2 (P1) Developer 1, Interview 1 (A11) Developer 2, Interview 1 (A21) Developer 1, Interview 2 (A12) Developer 2, Interview 2 (A22)	Developer 1, Interview 1 (B11) Developer 1, Interview 2 (B12)
Other case material	2 News articles, 5 Websites, 1 Blog, 1 Document, 1 Github repository	3 News articles, 5 Websites

In parallel with data collection, we initiated analysis to take advantage of the iterative nature of qualitative case research [4]. We used an inductive coding approach, allowing categories and theoretical patterns to emerge from the data [7]. First, within-case analysis reconstructed the development trajectories of each application using timelines and narrative case histories capturing key events, motivational shifts, networking interactions, and outcomes. Following the idea of temporal bracketing [16], we used the ITIL service lifecycle as framework for structuring the temporal dynamics within each case. Building on the work of Smith & Sandberg [21], we mapped key events, decisions, motivational and networking developments onto the five phases of the service lifecycle, merging the operation and continual improvement phases because they occurred simultaneously in our cases. Building on the within-case insights, we conducted a cross-case analysis to compare patterns across cases, identify similarities and differences, and reveal explanatory mechanisms, moving from rich description to more abstract conceptual relationships [4]. This process led to the development of six theoretical propositions concerning the role of developer motivation and networking in sustaining OGD-based applications. Emerging insights were iteratively confronted with empirical evidence and checked against rival explanations to ensure logical coherence [3]. To strengthen rigor and mitigate interpretive bias, we triangulated interview data with public archival sources and conducted follow-up interviews with key informants to validate interpretations and ensure that our analysis reflected developer perspectives.

4 Results

4.1 Case A: From Student Project to Urban Mobility Tool

Context. The first case concerns a mobile application for Android and iOS with an additional web version. Launched in 2014 in a large German city, the app provides real-time information on parking availability. Because the data were not provided in structured formats, the developers initially scraped the city's website to make the information accessible through a mobile interface. Over time, the application expanded to approx. 20 cities in Germany and neighboring countries, supported by collaborations with research projects, open data communities, and municipal administrations. The app gained regional media attention and reached several thousand downloads. Over time, however, the development team shrank, leaving one developer responsible for maintaining the application. Today, the project continues in maintenance mode, with attempts to transfer it to external actors remaining unsuccessful.

Motivational Development. At the outset, the two core developers were highly motivated, reinforced by their engagement in communities such as the local Open Data Meetup and the Chaos Computer Club. Their reasons for initiating the project were multifaceted: they aimed to showcase the potential of open data, to experiment with new technologies, and to acquire software development skills. For example, one developer sought to learn how to build an Android application, while both shared a general enthusiasm for programming and creative experimentation. Their work was also driven by a strong belief in the emerging concept of open data, which at the time was still novel and lacked institutional support in their city, as no open data portal yet existed. Importantly, they were motivated by the idea of generating a tangible public benefit through their application, even though they did not directly benefit from it, as neither owned a car. As one developer stated: *"And if we [...] have enabled even just one person to drive less through the city to find a parking space and thus reduced the traffic congestion in the city a little, then that is already a success, albeit a very small one." (A11).*

In the early phase of the open data movement, the developers saw themselves as contributing to something new by building an application that had not previously existed. Visualizing parking availability provided a compelling use case that motivated them to develop a functional app. However, this initial enthusiasm was tempered by structural obstacles. From the outset, relevant data were unavailable in open or standardized formats and had to be scraped from municipal websites, causing recurring technical challenges. In addition, legal uncertainties, particularly concerns about liability without formal agreements, created difficulties and occasionally reduced motivation.

During the early development stages, the project progressed rapidly, as the developers translated the available data into a working prototype within a short time. Soon after, both iOS and Android versions were released. These quick achievements provided a strong motivational boost and reinforced their sense of progress. The collaborative nature of the work further enhanced this effect. Although the project was primarily driven by the two developers, additional contributors were occasionally involved in the design and implementation phases. One of the core developers highlighted the energizing effect of teamwork, comparing it to the motivation typically experienced at hackathons.

Over time, the technical challenges related to data access increasingly undermined this initial momentum. The developers were repeatedly confronted with unsuitable data formats that complicated implementation, especially as the application expanded to additional cities. In many cases, parking data could only be integrated through labor-intensive adjustments, such as developing custom scrapers. Changes by data providers frequently rendered these scrapers obsolete, forcing cities to be excluded or removed from the application. This dependency on unstable external data sources created persistent frustration and uncertainty about whether, and in what form the required data would remain available. Consequently, the developers' dependence on unreliable external data providers created a constant risk that changes or discontinuation of parking data would render their efforts meaningless, which they described as highly demotivating and harmful to the project's long-term sustainability.

Nevertheless, several experiences showed the developers that their work was not only noticed but also relied upon by external actors, which strengthened their motivation. For a brief period, the application even served as the official parking information source in their home city. Recognition from municipal administrations, local Open Data communities, and regional media further reinforced the sense that their efforts were valued. At one point, a local newspaper even expressed interest in purchasing the application, which the developers rejected because they saw the project primarily as a means of creating public value. Charging users for access to parking data was viewed as fundamentally incompatible with their goals. Additional motivation also stemmed from collaborations with external research projects, which temporarily granted the developers extended access to otherwise restricted data. Although initially perceived as strong recognition, this collaboration ended after about two years when the project concluded and data access was withdrawn, causing considerable frustration and incomprehension. As one developer commented: *"They evaluated it for two years and we were able to use the data [...]. And then they were done evaluating and said, yes, it works and then it was gone. [...] And I find that very disappointing." (A21).*

While the developers received recognition from various external actors, they experienced little support from the municipal administration of their home city, even though it provided the parking data. Attempts to establish contact, including requests for permission to scrape the data, were met with resistance and dismissal, leaving the developers feeling undervalued. The technical burden of maintaining the application further exacerbated this sense of frustration. Frequent, irregular changes to websites, data structures, and APIs on the side of data providers required constant adjustments to the scrapers and code base. This challenge intensified as more cities were added to the application, making maintenance increasingly time-consuming. The developers described this activity as demotivating and tedious, as it merely kept the service running without enabling improvements or new learning opportunities. A larger-scale architectural redesign was deemed infeasible, and thus never pursued, limiting the potential for future enhancements despite the availability of more modern technological options.

In parallel, the developers' personal circumstances changed. Initially students with flexible schedules and strong enthusiasm for open data, they later began full-time employment and their interests gradually shifted. For at least one of them, the initial excitement around open data diminished significantly. As their professional and personal responsibilities grew, the time and energy available for the project declined. Moreover, the developers bore all financial costs themselves, including hosting expenses of around €2000 over the project's lifetime. These costs became particularly demotivating in later years, when the application no longer provided enjoyment, recognition, or opportunities for personal growth. As one developer reflected: *"At the end of the day, a lot of energy, time, and partly money was invested so that a few people are happy they now have parking data. Apart from a bit of recognition, being invited somewhere or interviewed, you don't really get much out of it." (A21).*

As time went on, operating the application came to be perceived increasingly as a burden. Maintaining it alongside full-time work required significant effort, and responsibility eventually fell to a single remaining developer who now performs only the minimal tasks necessary to keep the service running. Maintenance has become an ongoing obligation, described as a weight that cannot be easily set aside. Yet despite these frustrations and the decline in personal motivation, the application continues to operate. Continued demand from its user base and the public value it provides remain the main reasons why developer keeps it alive: *"Besides work, I don't program that much anymore and the few things I do are just things I like doing and it's not the 15th time fixing the scraper [...]. I try to keep [the app] running as much as possible so that people who use it can continue to benefit from it. Otherwise, my interests have changed and it's no longer Open Data. And I don't have the energy to deal with it anymore." (A21).*

Networking Trajectories. At the beginning of the project, the developers were strongly embedded in communities such as the Chaos Computer Club and the local Open Data meetup. These networks supported idea generation and prototyping, and additional developers became involved through community discussions of the initial concept. This embeddedness in the Open Data community accelerated the early development. By contrast, networking with the key data provider - the municipal administration of their home city - proved much less fruitful. Attempts to engage the city, including requests to clarify data use, were largely unsuccessful, as officials appeared reluctant and provided neither formal support nor recognition. This lack of engagement contrasted sharply with the appreciation the developers received from other actors.

As the application expanded to additional cities, new contributors became involved, via GitHub. External developers provided parsers that enabled the integration of parking data from further cities. While these contributions acted as useful multipliers, they also required additional effort from the core developers, including adapting code, giving feedback, and ensuring quality. Although valuable during the transition phase, external participation later declined. In recent years, the remaining developer stopped integrating external code altogether, as it created more workload than it relieved.

The project also benefited temporarily from networking with academic institutions. A chance encounter at a university event led to a collaboration with a transport research project which granted the developers exclusive API access to an additional database. Although initially highly motivating, this partnership lasted only about two years and ended when the research project concluded. Over time, further connections emerged with municipal administrations in Germany and Switzerland, often facilitated through local Open Data communities. Some cities expressed interest in adapting the application, and developers were occasionally invited to present their work. Media exposure further expanded their network through interviews and newspaper coverage.

In later years, networking efforts became less successful. The remaining developer repeatedly expressed the desire to hand over the application to another actor who could maintain and further develop it, as he no longer considered himself able to carry this responsibility alone. Despite several attempts at transferring the project, all failed. As the developer reflected, once an application has reached a certain level of maturity and usage, it becomes very difficult to step away from it. Although there were various expressions of interest in contributing, none materialized once concrete commitments were required. In the last five years, the project has ultimately been maintained by only one developer, who has increasingly felt isolated and left without meaningful support. Figure 1 visualizes motivation and networking trajectories by mapping key events and drivers to the ITIL service lifecycle phases (arrows indicate increases ↑ or decreases ↓).

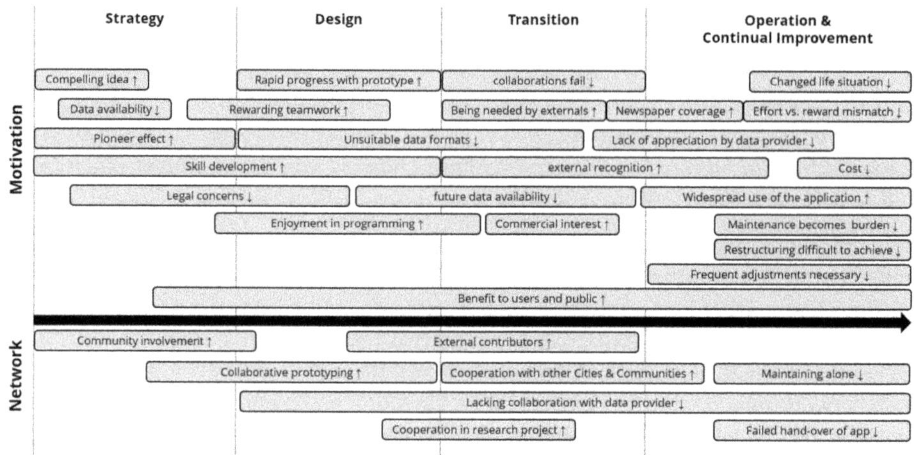

Fig. 1. Case A: Motivation and networking trajectory.

4.2 Case B: From Household Problem to Public Service Application

Context. The second case concerns an Android application with over 5,000 downloads. Developed in 2012 by a software engineer with initial support from his wife, the app aggregates municipal waste-management information of a Swiss city, including collection schedules and container locations, and provides reminders for collection dates. The first version was completed within a few weeks and gained early visibility through local newspaper coverage and a short radio interview. Since then, the developer has maintained the application alone. Over time, user numbers declined, particularly after the city introduced an official app with similar functionality. Today, the application still has 677 active users, and although the developer continues to maintain it, he has repeatedly questioned how long he will do so and is open to transferring it to another actor.

Motivational Development. The development of the second case application began in 2012. The project was initiated by a software developer with experience in mobile and Android development, who received initial support from his wife, who was professionally involved in municipal open data. Both saw the newly published datasets as an opportunity to experiment with open data and build a mobile application that combined personal learning with public value. The use case was anchored in their own everyday lives, as waste collection dates were frequently forgotten in their household. As no official application existed at the time for that purpose, they were among the first to transform newly available open data into a usable digital service. Due to the manageable complexity of the application, the developer's prior experience, and the division of tasks between the couple, the first version was completed within a few weeks. This rapid progress, combined with the sense of pioneering in a new field, generated a high level of motivation in the early stages. Following the release, however, the wife withdrew from active involvement, while the developer assumed full responsibility for the application's maintenance and further development. Thus, while the initial development phase was short, intense, and marked by high enthusiasm, the subsequent operational phase stretched across more than a decade, during which motivation fluctuated.

Several factors initially sustained motivation. The application quickly attracted more than 1,000 downloads and received positive feedback through emails, ratings, and reviews on the Google Play Store. This user appreciation, along with local newspaper articles and even a short radio interview, reinforced the sense of purpose and recognition for the developer, expressed as follows: *"So, what's nice is when feedback comes from people who use it and give praise or give good reviews. [...] It's also motivating and positive to see that over 1,000 people seem to need it." (B11).*

When the city later introduced an official waste management app, its poor technical execution and negative user reviews highlighted the value of the independent application, reinforcing the developer's motivation. Professional learning also played a role: while building the initial version barely expand his skills, long-term maintenance required keeping up with evolving Android versions, offering ongoing learning he valued. At the same time, these adjustments were a recurring source of frustration, as they were driven by external changes beyond his control and could require several days of work. Particularly challenging were operating system updates affecting the app's notification functions, which he considered the core feature. Routine maintenance tasks included the annual integration of new waste collection schedules, which the developer scheduled during the Christmas holidays, allowing him to minimize interference with his professional and personal life. Over time, the burden of this recurring work, combined with broader changes in his life, began to dampen motivation. After the couple had children and moved away from the city, the application was no longer directly relevant to their own household. At the same time, the official app improved and gradually drawing users away, reducing active users to 677 by the time of Interview B1. The developer noted a stark mismatch between the small effort required to build the application and the disproportionately high effort required to maintain it over more than ten years. This imbalance, combined with family members questioning why he continued, sometimes led him to doubt the project's sustainability. He stated: *"Well, I've often played with the idea that it's getting too much, I'll stop now. It's frustrating, especially when there's a lot of work. [...] It's actually also my vacation over Christmas. And [...] I also hear voices from the family, hey, why are you still doing this?" (B11).*

Nonetheless, the remaining user base continued to motivate the developer to keep the app running. He noted that he would consider discontinuing the project if user numbers fell to only a few hundred or if major architectural changes became necessary. Although motivation has declined in recent years, there were brief moments of renewed interest, for example when he added a new feature (a waste disposal truck schedule). Overall, however, he described his current motivation as far lower than at the beginning and now maintains the app mainly because it still provides value to users while requiring limited effort outside the annual update cycle. As he stated: *"So, for me, the main motivation is still to see that there are still people who need it" (B11).*

He also expressed a desire to hand over the application to another developer or organization, potentially by releasing the source code as open source, although this would require additional effort and no concrete interest has yet emerged.

Networking Trajectories. In contrast to Case A, networking in this case remained limited. The only significant collaboration occurred at the outset, when the developer worked with his wife, who handled the graphic design while he focused on technical implementation. Although she was professionally involved in Open Data within the city administration, this did not lead to direct interaction with the municipality regarding the app. The city, as data provider, never offered feedback or support, which the developer did not view as a major drawback. Beyond this initial phase, there was no notable involvement in the open data community or comparable networks. Instead, networking primarily took the form of sporadic interactions with end users, who provided bug reports, suggestions for improvement, and positive feedback through app store reviews and direct messages. These user interactions represented the main source of external engagement and recognition for the developer. Figure 2 visualizes the motivation and networking trajectories by mapping key events and drivers to the ITIL service lifecycle phases (arrows indicate increases ↑ or decreases ↓).

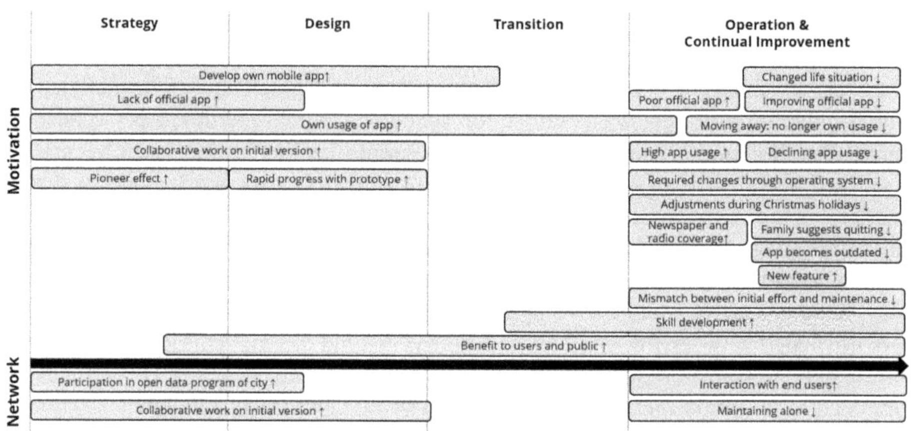

Fig. 2. Case B: Motivation and networking trajectory.

4.3 Cross-Case Analysis

Following Yin's [22] replication logic, we compare the cases to highlight patterns and differences in long-term developer dynamics. Both applications are long-lived, non-commercial mobile projects maintained for over a decade, yet they differ in scope and complexity. Case A evolved from a single-city initiative to a multi-city platform covering 20+ municipalities, increasing maintenance needs and reliance on multiple data sources. Case B remained limited to one city and a stable provider, reducing change requirements. Technical setups also diverged: Case A initially involved multiple developers across web, iOS, and Android before shrinking to one maintainer, whereas Case B was designed and sustained by a single Android specialist. Finally, Case A relied on real-time data integration, while Case B used static datasets, resulting in lower complexity and more predictable maintenance.

Across both cases, developers exhibited strong initial motivation characterized by enthusiasm, curiosity, and a pioneering spirit. Early phases involved rapid progress, experimentation, and exploration within the emerging open data movement. Intrinsic drivers - such as the joy of coding, learning new technologies, and creating innovative solutions - initially dominated. However, once prototypes were released, opportunities for experimentation declined and work increasingly shifted toward routine maintenance. Over time, motivation became tied to the perceived success and recognition of the applications. In both cases, high user adoption, positive feedback, and media attention provided important external reinforcement. Yet, as public interest declined and the applications became established, external appreciation faded. In the later stages, both developers described their motivation as being at a low point, with the maintenance of the applications perceived more as a burden than as a source of fulfillment. What persisted, however, was a sense of responsibility toward users and the public value the applications continued to provide. Thus, while initial intrinsic motivations faded over time, they were gradually replaced by a more duty-bound commitment to sustaining an existing, socially useful artifact. These patterns suggest the following proposition:

Proposition 1. *In OGD-based applications, developer motivation shifts from self-focused intrinsic drivers in early phases to other-focused, obligation-based motivations in later phases as novelty and external recognition decline.*

A further cross-case insight concerns the influence of maintenance intensity and predictability on developer engagement. In Case A, maintenance was technically complex and unpredictable, as data sources frequently changed and scrapers had to be rewritten. This unpredictability created a sense of burden and frustration, repeatedly undermining motivation and prompting considerations to discontinue the project. In contrast, Case B involved routine, predictable maintenance tasks, such as the annual integration of new datasets, which the developer could easily plan and integrate into his personal schedule. Thus, while high and unpredictable maintenance demands hinder sustained engagement, routine and predictable maintenance fosters persistence over time. These observations lead to the following proposition:

Proposition 2. *In OGD-based applications, the predictability and intensity of maintenance tasks shape the long-term sustainability: routine, manageable maintenance supports continued operation, whereas unpredictable and resource-intensive maintenance erodes motivation and threatens project longevity.*

Over time, both cases exhibited a growing mismatch between developer effort and the personal value derived from their work. While the initial development phase offered learning opportunities, experimentation with new technologies, and rapid early successes, these benefits were increasingly outweighed by the effort required for long-term maintenance. Routine updates, ongoing integration of new data, and operational costs increased, while opportunities for learning or creative engagement declined. Developers in both cases reflected on this imbalance, noting that the sustained effort no longer corresponded to the personal rewards they experienced, a dynamic that became particularly pronounced in Case A due to higher maintenance demands and hosting costs.

A key challenge for OGD-based applications is what we term the "*data-access paradox*": their value derives from facilitating data access for users, yet this dependency can undermine developer motivation in opposite ways. In Case A, heterogeneous and cumbersome data formats required constant adaptation and maintenance, imposing a high cognitive and technical burden on developers. Failure to manage these data pipelines risked rendering the application obsolete, which increasingly frustrated the developers and threatened their continued engagement. In contrast, Case B illustrates the opposite scenario: when the data provider itself improved accessibility - by offering an official mobile application - the independent app's unique value proposition weakened, user numbers declined, and the developer perceived the application as becoming obsolete. In both cases, despite different mechanisms, the looming or actual obsolescence of the application strongly undermined developer motivation and threatened the sustained operation of the service. These observations lead to two propositions:

Proposition 3a. *In OGD-based applications, reliance on heterogeneous or manually intensive data sources increases maintenance complexity, which can erode developer motivation over time and threaten the continued operation of the application.*

Proposition 3b. *In OGD-based applications, improvements in data accessibility by official data providers (e.g., through their own applications) can diminish the unique value proposition of existing independent applications, reducing developer motivation and jeopardizing their sustained operation.*

In both cases, networking activities declined over time. During the early stages, interactions with other stakeholders, such as fellow developers, community members, or interested parties, were frequent and productive, and supported ideation and prototyping. These collaborations provided technical and motivational support, fostering rapid progress. As the projects matured, however, opportunities and incentives for networking diminished, and engagement with external actors gradually decreased, leaving the remaining developers increasingly isolated. External relationships also varied in duration: some interactions, such as media coverage or exchanges with open data communities, were short-lived, while others, including collaborations with research projects or municipal administrations, lasted longer. Yet none persisted into the later maintenance phase, highlighting the transient nature of networking in OGD-based applications. These observations lead to the following proposition:

Proposition 4. *In OGD-based applications, networking intensity declines over time as initial connections fade and are rarely replaced, leading to increasing isolation of developers and reduced long-term sustainability.*

Although networking activities tend to decline over time, they can still shape the development of OGD-based applications. The cases illustrate contrasting pathways. In Case A, networking with developers and other stakeholders acted as a multiplier by providing access to additional skills, resources, and ideas, enabling expansion to multiple cities and platforms. By contrast, networking played little role in Case B, where the developer maintained the application independently. These contrasting cases suggest that networking is not required for continued operation but can amplify the scope, functionality, and impact of OGD applications. This leads to the following proposition:

Proposition 5. *In OGD-based applications, networking can serve as a multiplier that enhances scalability, functionality, and overall impact, even though it is not essential for continued operation.*

In both cases, transferring the application to an external party at a later stage proved difficult. In Case A, several attempts to hand over maintenance to other organizations or individuals failed. In Case B, while the developer was willing to transfer ownership, no suitable recipient emerged. These observations suggest that that once an OGD-based application becomes closely tied to a developer's technical and organizational processes, the likelihood of a successful handover diminishes significantly over time.

5 Discussion

This study examined how developer motivation and networking evolve over time and shape the long-term sustainability of OGD-based applications. Through an exploratory case study of two long-lived open data applications, we identified recurring mechanisms shaping their sustainability and synthesized them into six theoretical propositions. Our findings show that developer motivation gradually shifts from intrinsic drivers to obligation-based engagement. At the same time, maintenance demands and data dependencies influence continued operation, while networking activities tend to decline but can act as multipliers of success when present. Finally, transferring responsibility for OGD-based applications to new actors remains a persistent challenge. Our study contributes to the OGD literature in several ways. First, our findings confirm prior research on the independent OGD developers' motivations, emphasizing intrinsic and altruistic drivers such as enjoyment, experimentation, and skill development [11, 14, 18]. However, we extend this literature by showing that these motives do not remain stable over time. Instead, motivation gradually shifts toward obligation-based engagement as novelty and external recognition decline. This shift also highlights how seemingly individual motivations are closely intertwined with institutional factors such as public recognition, data provision practices, and support from public actors. In both cases, long-term survival of the apps depended on developers' residual motivation. Second, we advance the understanding of factors that sustain or diminish developer motivation over time. An OGD-specific finding concerns the role of public data infrastructures. Unlike many digital services, OGD-based applications depend on data providers outside developers' control. Our findings suggest that both limited data accessibility and increasing institutional provision can undermine long-term sustainability, albeit through different mechanisms. Third, our findings extend research on OGD ecosystems by highlighting the temporal dynamics of networking relationships. While prior studies highlight the importance of collaboration and community engagement [13], our results show that the degree and temporal dynamics of networking shape application trajectories. Networks can enable scaling, innovation, and resource access (as in Case A), but they are not essential for continued operation (as in Case B). We also demonstrate that networking ties tend to be short-lived and tend to weaken over time, implying that developers must actively maintain and renew connections to sustain collaborative benefits. Finally, our study provides an empirical extension to conceptual work on the transferability and governance of OGD-based initiatives. Despite calls in the literature to hand over applications to other stakeholders [13], we demonstrate that such transfers are often difficult in practice. This insight opens new avenues for future research into governance mechanisms and institutional arrangements to support the sustainable stewardship of OGD-based applications. Practically, our findings suggest that developers should anticipate long-term maintenance challenges and establish early collaborations to distribute workload and sustain motivation. Public institutions can support the sustainability of OGD-based applications by ensuring stable, machine-readable access to data and recognizing independent developers as important actors within OGD ecosystems. Additionally, our findings suggest that establishing lightweight governance or handover mechanisms, could prevent valuable applications from becoming obsolete.

This study has several limitations that suggest directions for future research. First, the number of key informants was limited due to the nature of open data applications. Second, the study examined two mobile applications from urban contexts in Central Europe, which may limit the generalizability of the findings. Future research should therefore examine OGD applications in other contexts, including non-urban settings, non-mobile platforms, and alternative national environments. Third, although both cases span more than a decade, the research design was not strictly longitudinal, as data were collected at two points in time. Future studies could adopt longitudinal or ethnographic approaches to better capture the evolution of OGD applications. Furthermore, future studies could empirically test the six theoretical propositions derived in this paper. Finally, subsequent work should aim to design and evaluate concrete measures and strategies for developers and institutional stakeholders to support the sustainable development and long-term operation of OGD-based applications. This includes exploring governance models, partnership frameworks, and mechanisms for transferring existing applications to new custodians to ensure their continued public value.

Acknowledgments. Financial support from the German Federal Ministry for Housing, Urban Development and Building (BMWSB) and the Kreditanstalt für Wiederaufbau (KfW) as part of the "Model Project Smart City (MPSC) Dresden" is gratefully acknowledged.

Disclosure of Interests. The authors have no competing interests to declare that are relevant to the content of this article.

References

1. Benmohamed, N., Shen, J., Vlahu-Gjorgievska, E.: Public value creation through the use of open government data in Australian public sector: a quantitative study from employees' perspective. Gov. Inf. Q. **41**(2), 101930 (2024)
2. Chokki, A.P., Simonofski, A., Clarinval, A., Frénay, B., Vanderose, B.: Fostering interaction between open government data stakeholders: an exchange platform for citizens, developers and publishers. In: Janssen, M. et al. (eds.) Electronic Government, pp. 228–243. Springer, Cham (2022)
3. Dubé, L., Paré, G.: Rigor in information systems positivist case research: current practices, trends, and recommendations. MIS Q. 597–636 (2003)

4. Eisenhardt, K.M.: Building theories from case study research. Acad. Manag. Rev. **14**(4), 532–550 (1989)
5. Gama, K.: Crowdsourced software development in civic apps - motivations of civic hackathons participants: In: Proceedings of the 19th International Conference on Enterprise Information Systems, pp. 550–555. SCITEPRESS (2017)
6. Gascó-Hernández, M., Martin, E.G., Reggi, L., Pyo, S., Luna-Reyes, L.F.: Promoting the use of open government data: cases of training and engagement. Gov. Inf. Q. **35**(2), 233–242 (2018)
7. Gioia, D.A., Corley, K.G., Hamilton, A.L.: Seeking qualitative rigor in inductive research: notes on the Gioia methodology. Organ. Res. Methods **16**(1), 15–31 (2013)
8. Harrison, T.M., Pardo, T.A., Cook, M.: Creating open government ecosystems: a research and development agenda. Future Internet **4**(4), 900–928 (2012)
9. Hertel, G., Niedner, S., Herrmann, S.: Motivation of software developers in Open Source projects: an Internet-based survey of contributors to the Linux kernel. Res. Policy **32**(7), 1159–1177 (2003)
10. Janssen, M., Charalabidis, Y., Zuiderwijk, A.: Benefits, adoption barriers and myths of open data and open government. Inf. Syst. Manag. **29**(4), 258–268 (2012)
11. Juell-Skielse, G., Hjalmarsson, A., Johannesson, P., Rudmark, D.: Is the public motivated to engage in open data innovation? In: Janssen, M. et al. (eds.) Electronic Government, pp. 277–288. Springer, Cham (2014)
12. Kassen, M.: Adopting and managing open data: stakeholder perspectives, challenges and policy recommendations. Aslib J. Inf. Manag. **70**(5), 518–537 (2018)
13. Kassen, M.: Open Data Governance and Its Actors: Theory and Practice. Springer, Cham (2022)
14. Kassen, M.: Understanding motivations of citizens to reuse open data: open government data as a philanthropic movement. Innovation **23**(1), 44–70 (2021)
15. Lakhani, K.R., Wolf, R.G.: Why hackers do what they do: understanding motivation and effort in free/open source software projects. Open Sour. Softw. Projects (2003)
16. Langley, A.: Strategies for theorizing from process data. Acad. Manag. Rev. **24**(4), 691–710 (1999)
17. O'Neil, M., Pentzold, C., Toupin, S. (eds.): The Handbook of Peer Production. Wiley (2021)
18. Purwanto, A., Zuiderwijk, A., Janssen, M.: Citizens' motivations for engaging in open data hackathons. In: Panagiotopoulos, P., et al. (eds.) Electronic Participation, pp. 130–141 Springer, Cham (2019)
19. Reggi, L., Dawes, S.S.: Creating Open Government Data ecosystems: network relations among governments, user communities, NGOs and the media. Gov. Inf. Q. **39**(2), 101675 (2022)
20. Rudmark, D., Lindgren, R., Schultze, U.: Open data platforms: design principles for embracing outlaw innovators. J. Strateg. Inf. Syst. **33**(3), 101850 (2024)
21. Smith, G., Sandberg, J.: Barriers to innovating with open government data: exploring experiences across service phases and user types. Inf. Polity **23**(3), 249–265 (2018)
22. Yin, R.K.: Case Study Research. Design and Methods, 5th edn. SAGE (2013)
23. Zuiderwijk, A., Janssen, M., Dwivedi, Y.: K: acceptance and use predictors of open data technologies: drawing upon the unified theory of acceptance and use of technology. Gov. Inf. Q. **32**(4), 429–440 (2015)

Citizens' Intention to (Re)Use Open Government Data: The Perspectives of Non-users and Users and the Moderating Role of Use Purposes

Richard Rau(✉), Martin Wiener, and Katja Bley

Dresden University of Technology, 01069 Dresden, Germany
richard.rau@tu-dresden.de

Abstract. Open Government Data (OGD) is promoted globally to enhance transparency, participation, and public value, yet citizen engagement remains limited. Existing research often examines OGD adoption using generic technology acceptance models and rarely differentiates between citizens who have previously used OGD and those who have not. This study investigates determinants of citizens' intention to (re)use OGD through a municipal survey (N = 621), explicitly distinguishing between users and non-users and examining how different use purposes moderate its use. The results show that hedonic motivation and social influence are the strongest predictors of use intention across both groups. However, important differences emerge; expected utility and data literacy significantly influence reuse among existing users, whereas awareness and transparency are more relevant for non-users. Furthermore, the use purposes transparency and participation exhibit targeted moderating effects on key adoption relationships. Overall, the model explains 42% of the variance in (re)use intention among users and 47% among non-users. By identifying differences in determinants between users and non-users and highlighting the role of civic use purposes, the study advances understanding of citizen engagement with OGD and provides insights for designing targeted digital government strategies for non-users and reusers that translate OGD availability into meaningful public use.

Keywords: open government data · open government data use · structured equation modeling

1 Introduction

Governments worldwide are pursuing improvements in service delivery, transparency, participatory governance, and civic engagement, increasingly utilizing open government data (OGD) as a tool to achieve these objectives [1–3]. OGD refers to data made publicly available by government bodies that can be freely accessed, used, and reused by anyone [4]. The two principal goals motivating the opening of government data are transparency and participation, which are described by Meijer et al. [5] as the connection between "vision" (citizens' capacity to see into government) and "voice" (their capability to act and participate). Both transparency ("vision") and participation ("voice")

Published by Springer Nature Switzerland 2027
G. Viale Pereira et al. (Eds.): EGOV 2026, LNCS 16933, pp. 346–362, 2027.
https://doi.org/10.1007/978-3-032-35747-2_22

are intended to create public value [6, 7]. In this context, transparency means that citizens are provided with the capability to access data and use it to hold their government to account, while participation describes the use of OGD by citizens to either "voice" their opinion and partake in the political process or generate personal or societal benefit [8]. Importantly, transparency and participation are normative goals articulated largely from the provider side; whether citizens themselves actually perceive and engage with OGD in these terms is far less established. Van Maanen [9] questions the philosophical assumptions underlying open government discourse and cautions against treating the link between data openness and democratic value as self-evident. This gap between the intended purposes of OGD and citizens' actual orientations is a key motivation for the differentiated, empirical examination of these use purposes in our study.

High-level political actions, such as President Obama's 2009 transparency initiative, along with significant economic projections, such as the European Union's 2011 estimate of OGD's potential value of 40 billion euros annually [10], have fueled the global momentum behind OGD. However, the anticipated benefits (e.g., improved public services, innovation, accountability, and greater trust in governance) are not automatic properties of data release but emerge only when citizens and other stakeholders actually access, interpret, and reuse the data [4, 6, 11]. Increasing citizen use is therefore critical for converting policy-driven transparency into public value and remains a core priority for administrations opening their data [12]. Despite the growing availability of OGD, the actual usage, especially among everyday citizens, remains limited [4, 13]. Prior literature has explored factors influencing OGD usage but often focuses on provider-side challenges, primarily those faced by governments [3, 14]. While some research has examined citizens' use of OGD, important shortcomings remain in understanding how different citizens engage with and reuse OGD.

Firstly, most existing studies do not distinguish between the initial use of OGD and its continued use [15, 16]. There is no distinction made between individuals who have never interacted with OGD before and others who have accessed OGD or even reused it. As a result, the unique motivations and barriers faced by non-users, such as lack of awareness, perceived complexity, or uncertainty about value, are mixed with those of existing users, who are more likely to evaluate continued use based on prior experiences, perceived usefulness, and portal usability [1, 4, 13]. This aggregation masks stage-specific determinants and limits our understanding of the different processes leading to initial adoption (acceptance) versus continued engagement [17, 18]. Differentiating between these groups is essential, as strategies to activate non-users (e.g., awareness campaigns or reducing entry barriers) may differ fundamentally from interventions needed to foster reuse, such as improving data quality or platform functionality [19, 20].

Secondly, the core purpose of opening government data lies in increasing transparency and participation [1]. However, prior studies rarely differentiate between distinct purposes of OGD use in their empirical analyses. Most existing research simplifies citizen engagement as a homogeneous phenomenon, without examining whether motivations and influencing factors vary depending on the citizen's perceived use purpose, such as employing OGD for holding governments accountable (transparency) versus actively engaging in policy-making or societal improvement (participation) [8, 12]. As a result, there remains a substantive gap in understanding how and why these purposes shape the behavioral pathways leading to OGD use. A nuanced, empirical examination of these different use purposes is essential, as it can uncover whether certain drivers (e.g., expected utility, social influence, or literacy) are more pronounced for transparency-oriented users versus those motivated by participation. Without such differentiation, the realization of OGD's intended value is ultimately limited.

Thirdly, extant research relies on basic applications of models like TAM (technology acceptance model) [21] and UTAUT (unified theory of acceptance and use of technology) [22], lacking refinement and contextual adaptation. Moreover, prior studies applying models such as UTAUT often remain at a basic level of analysis, testing only standard constructs and direct effects [20]. For example, facilitating conditions are rarely detailed and adapted to reflect the OGD context.

This study sets out to address these limitations by (1) distinguishing between OGD use factors of 'new' users – referred to as non-users – and prior users; (2) investigating both motivational and competency-related factors and how their influence is moderated by perceived use purposes; and (3) contextualizing the UTAUT2 for the OGD context. Accordingly, the following two research questions (RQs) are addressed:

RQ1: What factors influence citizens' intention to use or reuse OGD?
RQ2: How do distinct use purposes moderate the effects of these factors on the intention to (re)use OGD?

To answer these questions, the study draws on empirical data from a citizen survey (N = 621). On this basis, it provides new theoretical insights into citizen's use intentions in the OGD context, including the important moderating role of different use purposes. Additionally, it tests new determinants of OGD use intention by building on existing theory. For practitioners, the study results offer actionable insights into how the provision of OGD can be more effectively designed and managed to foster citizen engagement.

2 Theoretical Background

While frameworks of technology acceptance have been widely used to explain adoption decisions, they have been criticized for underrepresenting the broader context of digital government initiatives. In the context of OGD, citizen engagement is not only a matter of technology acceptance but also relates to democratic practices such as transparency and civic participation [12, 23].

Several studies have examined OGD adoption through the lens of acceptance models [1, 2, 16, 18, 20, 24]. From this broader body of research, three representative studies were selected to anchor our study in the prior literature: Saxena and Janssen [24], Zuiderwijk et al. [20], and Rasool et al. [2]. These studies were selected because they are widely cited, reflect a progressively expanding scope (from generic predictors to validated constructs and research opportunities), and collectively showcase the precise need for further research that the study at hand addresses (user group differentiation, analysis beyond direct effects, and insufficient skill operationalization).

Saxena and Janssen [24] present a generic application of UTAUT in a national context, focusing on direct effects only. They applied the UTAUT framework to explore OGD usage in India, examining predictors such as performance expectancy, effort expectancy, social influence, facilitating conditions, and voluntariness of use, and measuring their direct influence on usage intention. However, no context-specific adaptations of the model were included, nor were moderating factors such as user experience or purpose of use considered. Zuiderwijk et al. [20] exemplify early contextual extensions of UTAUT by integrating a trust-related construct to explain the adoption of OGD technologies in the Netherlands. Their approach highlighted the role of institutional trust and perceived risk alongside the standard variables but maintained a focus on direct influences, without exploring interaction effects such as moderating or mediating relationships. They explicitly recommended further research focusing on deeper contextualization of OGD and the investigation of additional constructs. Rasool et al. [2], in a systematic literature review, synthesize quantitative findings and highlight underexplored capability dimensions (e.g., data literacy) and contextual factors (e.g., awareness). Their review categorizes influences on OGD engagement into technical (e.g., accessibility), individual (e.g., motivation and skills), and contextual (e.g., trust and awareness) dimensions, emphasizing the need for deeper research into digital literacy and individual capabilities for OGD engagement. Together, these studies have laid a foundational understanding of OGD usage, primarily through the application or adaptation of the UTAUT framework. However, several gaps remain. Prior studies apply UTAUT without sufficient contextualization for OGD use. For instance, facilitating conditions are typically modeled generically, without operationalizing skills such as data or computer literacy, which are key enablers for finding and using complex datasets [2, 25, 26]. Additionally, existing models tend to focus on direct relationships and do not account for the possibility that factors may operate differently depending on the citizen's purpose (e.g., seeking transparency or participating in the political process) or level of experience with OGD (e.g., new users vs. reusers). Further analysis of moderation or mediation may therefore yield higher explanatory power. By integrating use purposes rooted in democratic and open governance into a behavioral adoption model, this study extends acceptance research toward a more governance-oriented perspective on OGD engagement.

3 Research Model and Hypotheses

Building on previous research, our study sets out to develop and empirically test a contextualized adaptation of the UTAUT2 model tailored to the OGD context, thereby differentiating between OGD users and non-users and considering their distinct use purposes. In this section, the underlying theoretic model is introduced, including the specific model constructs and their hypothesized interrelationships.

The UTAUT, developed by Venkatesh et al. [22], integrated eight prominent models of technology acceptance (e.g., including the theory of planned behavior and Social Cognitive Theory) and identified four core constructs: *performance expectancy, effort expectancy, social influence*, and *facilitating conditions* as predictors of behavioral intention and technology use behavior. While the first three constructs affect only the intention to use, facilitating conditions also impact actual usage directly. Additionally, the model includes moderating variables such as *gender, age*, and *experience*, which influence the strength of these relationships. The extended version, UTAUT2 [27], builds upon the original by adding three new constructs specifically relevant in consumer contexts:

hedonic motivation, price value, and habit. We build on UTAUT2 rather than UTAUT specifically for the merit of hedonic motivation. *Hedonic motivation* refers to the fun, pleasure, or intrinsic interest derived from using a technology [27], and it is particularly relevant for OGD, because citizen engagement with OGD is entirely voluntary and rarely tied to extrinsic rewards. Therefore, curiosity and the enjoyment of exploring data may be one of the decisive drivers of both initial and continued use. However, the fun, pleasure or interest citizens derive from OGD use does not depend on the individual alone; it can be plausibly shaped by the portal design, too (through interactive visualizations, intuitive layout or even gamified elements). Portal design may therefore condition how strongly hedonic motivation translates into use intention, a relationship we return to in the discussion.

The two remaining UTAUT2 constructs are not applicable in this context and are therefore not modeled: habit, which captures learned use based on prior experience, is not applicable because routine engagement with OGD has not yet been established among the general public. Price value is also not included, as OGD is freely accessible and thus lacks the cost-benefit considerations present in commercial technology adoption contexts [27]. Given that UTAUT2 also explains a greater proportion of variance than the original model and has proven relevance in e-government and public-sector contexts [1, 28], we adopt it as the foundation for studying citizens' intention to use OGD.

However, several constructs of the model require contextual adaptation or exclusion in the domain of OGD. First, *use behavior*, a central outcome variable in UTAUT2, cannot be meaningfully assessed in our study, as most citizens currently do not engage with OGD yet [3, 4, 28]. This lack of actual usage makes it unsuitable for measurement in a general population survey, so we treat behavioral *intention to use OGD* as the focal dependent variable.

Second, we replaced *performance expectancy*, which typically assumes prior experience with a technology and evaluates expected improvement in performance [22], with the construct of *expected utility*. The latter more accurately reflects the anticipated benefits of using OGD, even in the absence of prior interaction, and is thus more suitable for measuring citizens' perceptions. Accordingly, the first set of hypotheses regards all retained UTAUT2 constructs. These are expected to be directly influencing factors on the citizens' intention to use OGD (see RQ1) and are tested for both groups (users and non-users). As indicated above, prior OGD adoption studies using TAM/UTAUT (e.g., [20, 24]) show consistent relevance of performance (*expected utility*), hedonic motivation, social influence, and perceived effort, but typically apply them without group differentiation or contextual refinement. These are retained, which yields a parsimonious, theory-grounded base construct set (in particular: *expected utility, hedonic motivation, social influence,* and *effort expectancy*) tested for both users and non-users. Therefore, we hypothesize:

H1: Expected utility (EU) is positively associated with the intention to use OGD.
H2: Hedonic motivations (HM) are positively associated with the intention to use OGD.
H3: Social influence (SI) is positively associated with the intention to use OGD.
H4: Effort expectancy (EE) is negatively associated with the intention to use OGD.

The original UTAUT2 model conceptualizes facilitating conditions as users' perceptions of whether organizational and technical infrastructure exist to support system use

[27]. While suitable in workplace IT or consumer technology contexts, this construct is too generic for the OGD context, where institutional support structures are often lacking. Primary enabling factors for OGD are related to the individual's own skills in accessing, processing, and making sense of heterogeneous and oftentimes complex government datasets [19]. In this context, recent OGD studies highlight that skill deficits represent a significant barrier to broader OGD use [25]. In particular, two 'levels' of competence are assessed: *computer literacy*, covering basic digital skills necessary to access and navigate online data portals, and *data literacy*, encompassing higher-level abilities to search, interpret, and combine datasets, as well as drawing insights from OGD [4, 17, 29, 30]. From a behavioral perspective, individuals who possess higher levels of such competencies are more likely to perceive OGD engagement as manageable and beneficial, reducing cognitive barriers associated with interacting with complex datasets. In turn, these capabilities can increase individuals' confidence in their ability to successfully work with OGD, thereby strengthening their intention to engage with it [11, 25]. This suggests:

H5: Data Literacy (DL) is positively associated with the intention to use OGD.
H6: Computer Literacy (CL) is positively associated with the intention to use OGD.

In the UTAUT context, facilitating conditions refer to the user-perceived availability of necessary resources and technical infrastructure for technology use [27]. To retain these core aspects of facilitating conditions, *portal usability* is introduced as a user-specific construct replacing facilitating conditions. In this context, *portal usability* refers to the user experience and functional accessibility of OGD platforms through which data is discovered, browsed, and accessed. Unlike general constructs such as "ease of use" or "facilitating conditions" in classic technology acceptance models, *portal usability* in OGD specifically captures the ability of users to efficiently find datasets, navigate metadata, interpret file formats, and utilize search and filtering tools within often complex data repositories [4, 17, 31]. Empirical studies have shown that even motivated individuals and experienced data users may be discouraged from further engagement if the portal presents barriers such as poor structure, unclear labelling, or lacking metadata [13, 19]. Since *portal usability* can only be meaningfully rated by those who have actually used or attempted to use the platform, it is introduced as a direct influencing factor of OGD *use intention* and exclusively tested for the user group in the model. We thus propose:

H7: Portal Usability (PU) is positively associated with the intention to use OGD.

In the context of OGD, *awareness* refers to an individual's recognition of OGD as an available public resource, their understanding of its existence, and a basic comprehension of its potential relevance or utility. Awareness is a necessary antecedent to any consideration of adoption, as individuals cannot form intentions toward or perceive value in resources they do not know exist [4, 20]. Research on digital innovation and information systems similarly highlights awareness as a crucial initial stage in the technology adoption process, influencing whether individuals progress from non-adoption to active trial [1, 18]. As such, *awareness* is introduced as a distinct construct for non-users only, recognizing that a lack of awareness is a fundamental adoption barrier that does not apply to those who have already engaged with OGD. Therefore, we suggest:

H8: Awareness (AW) is positively associated with the intention to use OGD.

Finally, a key extension of our research is the integration of OGD use purposes, specifically *transparency* and *participation*, as distinct constructs. These constructs represent the core normative goals of OGD, mapping directly to established typologies that differentiate between 'monitorial' (transparency-focused) and participatory democratic processes [12]. By modeling *transparency* and *participation* as separate constructs, we can empirically test whether and how these specific purposes shape engagement with OGD. Accordingly, the two subsequent sets of hypotheses address their role as moderators (RQ2), exploring whether the influence of classical adoption factors (such as expected utility or social influence) on *use intention* changes depending on the use purpose. Since several constructs were newly adapted or introduced, we restricted the moderation analysis to the theoretically established core UTAUT2 pathways (hypotheses H1–H4). This approach ensures that the moderation effects are examined within well-established relationships, thereby reducing model complexity and avoiding the risk of overfitting when testing indirect effects. In general, we expect that *transparency* has a stronger moderating effect for the non-user group, as it aligns with the initial rationale for OGD provision by public administrations and acts as a primary motivator at the first point of contact. In contrast, individuals who have already used OGD may recognize that *transparency*-related goals can be achieved more efficiently through other channels (e.g., traditional news media). With growing familiarity, the passive consumption of information may change to active engagement, participation in co-creation processes, or influencing policy decisions. Thus, for experienced users, we expect *participation* to become a more meaningful use purpose, as it enables them to leverage OGD in ways that go beyond the original promise of governmental *transparency*. Nevertheless, we tested both moderating constructs for both non-users and users in order to empirically assess whether these theoretically expected differences hold across the two groups. On this basis, we hypothesize:

H9: Transparency (UT) strengthens the relationships between (a) expected utility, (b) hedonic motivations, and (c) social influence and the intention to use OGD, while weakening the relationship between (d) effort expectancy and this intention.
H10: Participation (UP) strengthens the relationship between (a) expected utility, (b) hedonic motivations, and (c) social influence and the intention to use OGD, while weakening the relationship between (d) effort expectancy and this intention.

The resulting research model is depicted in Fig. 1 below.

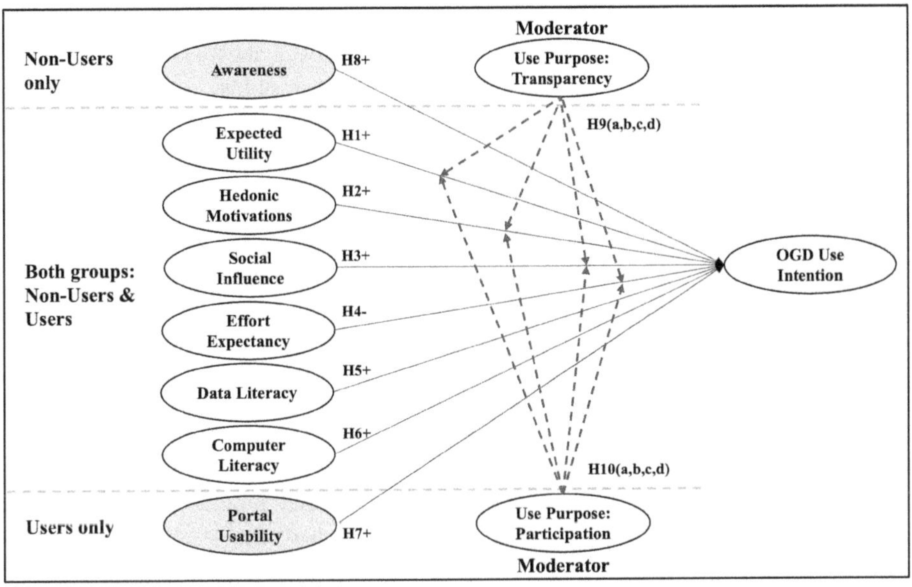

Fig. 1. Theoretical model and hypotheses.

4 Method

4.1 Operationalization of Variables

To measure the model constructs, we adapted existing scales from the literature. For the constructs borrowed from the UTAUT2 model, we contextualized the original items. These include the constructs *intention to use OGD*, *effort expectancy, hedonic motivations, social influence* [27], which were measured on 7-point Likert scales. *Expected utility* was adapted from the performance expectancy construct and operationalized by using semantic differential scales. These were utilized to counteract potential biases, including social desirability and a tendency toward overly positive responses [32]. The semantic differentials were also implemented with 7-point Likert scales.

Prior studies have shown that data literacy is a focal competence facilitating OGD use [2, 25]. In line with the results of these studies, facilitating conditions were contextualized through two constructs: *computer literacy* and *data literacy*. For both constructs, scales were adopted from earlier survey-based research on digital skills and information acquisition [33, 34].

The measurement scales for both use purposes of OGD (*transparency, participation*) were newly developed for this study. These constructs were informed by the normative goals of OGD in democratic contexts, as outlined by [12], who emphasize transparency and civic engagement as central pillars of open data initiatives. Furthermore, the operationalization of these use purposes was guided by a conceptual framework, which identifies transparency- and participation-oriented uses as key moderating factors in the relationship between OGD and its societal impact [14].

4.2 Data

The data was collected in a German municipality using an online questionnaire over a timespan of eight weeks. Citizens were contacted and asked to participate through multiple channels, including a news article on the city website, the local OGD portal and a city-wide newsletter. In total, we received 658 complete responses, of which 37 were removed due to failed attention checks. No respondents had to be excluded due to missing data, since all fields were marked as mandatory answers. The final sample comprised 621 responses, with 342 users and 279 non-users. Based on the inverse square-root method suggested by Hair et al. (2022) [35] the minimum sample size was estimated to be 619, calculating with the very conservatively set minimum path coefficient to be at 0.05–0.1 and a significance level of 5%. Since the inverse square-root method itself is expected to be relatively conservative, the method tends to slightly overestimate the required sample size [35]. Thus, our final sample size of 621 is considered sufficient.

In terms of gender, 48% of the survey respondents identified as male (n = 300), 44% as female (n = 273), and 8% as other (n = 48). The age distribution was slightly tilted towards younger participants: 39% were aged 29 years or younger, 23% were between 30 and 39 years, 21% between 40 and 49 years, 13% were 50 to 59, and 4% were 60 or older. Regarding education, participants reported a range of qualifications. While 18% held a high-school diploma or below and 7% had an associate's degree, 19% reported a bachelor's degree, 42% a master's degree, and 13% a doctoral degree. Thus, a considerable portion of the sample possessed higher educational qualifications. In terms of employment status, 49% of respondents were employed full-time, 20% worked part-time, and 2% were self-employed. Students made up 26.5% of the sample, while a very small proportion (0.5%) was seeking employment and 2% listed another status. Regarding place of residence, the majority (81%) reported living in urban areas, 12% in rural areas, and 7% in sub-urban locations.

4.3 Control Variables

Three factors were included as control variables based on suggestions from the literature: age, gender, and education [20, 27], while one additional control (residency) was included. A multigroup analysis was conducted for each of the controls. The results indicated that there were no significant differences between age, gender, education and residency groups. The tested control variables explained 7.4% of the observed variance ($R^2 = 0.074$). The tested effects did not change based on whether or not control variables were included in the model. For simplicity and clarity in the following analyses, control variables were therefore omitted from the model.

4.4 Measurement Model Assessment

PLS-SEM was used for the analysis within the SmartPLS 4 software [36]. PLS-SEM is particularly appropriate for maximizing explained variance and prediction of key constructs. It is also robust to violations of multivariate normality, which are common in survey data. A possible alternative, CB-SEM, was not deemed suitable as it assumes normally distributed indicators. Therefore, PLS-SEM was chosen for our study [35, 37].

The measurement model was assessed for reflective constructs according to established guidelines [35]. Firstly, indicator reliability was evaluated by examining the outer loadings of all indicators of each construct. Loadings 0.7 or higher are considered satisfactory, with item loadings between 0.4 and 0.7 being considered for removal. However, indicators should only be removed when the removal yields higher internal consistency reliability or convergent validity [35]. In both models, all indicators were above the 0.7 threshold, except for three indicators in the user group (DL3; UT3; HM4) and the non-user group (DL3; EE3; HM4). Ultimately, these four indicators were retained with the following rationale. The concerned constructs (DL, HM, EE and UT) meet the recommended thresholds for internal consistency reliability and convergent validity (see below) and the deletion of either indicator would not yield higher results for either internal consistency reliability or convergent validity. As well, the indicator loadings are reasonably close to the threshold of 0.7 (the lowest being HM4: 0.645).

Secondly, the internal consistency reliability is assessed by examining Composite Reliability (CR) and Cronbach's Alpha (CA). The values for both CR and CA are considered satisfactory, ranging from 0.7 to 0.95 [35].

Thirdly, convergent validity is assessed through the average variance extracted (AVE) of each construct. The AVE of each reflectively measured construct is clearly above the recommended threshold of 0.5 [35], with the lowest one being 0.615 (EE). Finally, discriminant validity is assessed for both group models through the Fornell-Larcker criterion and Heterotrait-Monotrait (HTMT) ratio. The Fornell-Larcker criterion shows that each construct explains more variance with its indicators ($\sqrt{AVE}$) than with any other construct, which can be confirmed for our constructs. Since the Fornell-Larcker criterion may perform poorly when indicator loadings differ only slightly [35], HTMT is proposed as a robust alternative to assess discriminant validity. It is deemed satisfactory when all HTMT ratios are significantly smaller than 1 (common threshold: 0.9), which is also true for our constructs. Thus, discriminant validity is established.

Finally, to assess the risk of common method bias, the Harman's one-factor test was conducted for both groups of users and non-users [38]. The results did not produce a single factor solution, as the maximum explained variance of a single factor was only 38.5%, which is clearly below the 50% threshold. In addition, we assessed our model for collinearity issues by examining the variance inflation factors (VIF). All VIF values were below the most conservative threshold of 3.3, with the highest one being 2.312 (HM). Thus, we conclude that collinearity is not an issue within the model.

5 Results: Structural Model Assessment

5.1 Direct Effects

Table 1 shows the path coefficients for the eight hypotheses concerning our study's first research question (H1-H8). Since all these hypotheses are predicting directional effects, a one-tailed test was used to test them. The t-statistics were obtained by conducting bootstrapping on 10,000 subsamples in SmartPLS 4 [35]. The test resulted in four of seven hypotheses being supported for the user group (H8 only applies to non-users). *Hedonic motivations* ($H2 : \beta = 0.308, t = 5.758, p < 0.001$) and *social influence* ($H3 : \beta = 0.203, t = 4.025, p < 0.001$) both have a significant positive effect on the *use intention.* Through comparison of the standardized path coefficients, a slightly higher effect on the OGD *use intention* can be attributed to *hedonic motivations*. Also, *data literacy* ($H5 : \beta = 0.215, t = 3.961, p < 0.001$) and *expected utility* ($H1 : \beta = 0.118, t = 2.192, p < 0.05$) both have a significant positive effect on the *use intention*, while *effort expectancy* (H4) did not have a significant negative effect on the *use intention.* Considering the absolute path coefficients, *data literacy* had a stronger effect on the dependent variable than *expected utility.* However, their effect is lower than the influence of *hedonic motivations* and *social influence.* The positive effect of *computer literacy* (H6) and *portal usability* (H7) on the *use intention* is not significant.

The structural model explains 42% of the variance of OGD use intention (R2 = 0.423), which is deemed as moderate-high explanatory power [35]. For the group of non-users, three out of seven hypotheses were supported by the results. Both *hedonic motivation* (H2) and *social influence* (H3) exhibited significant positive effects on *use intention*, mirroring the pattern observed in the user group. Similarly, *effort expectancy* (H4) and *computer literacy* (H6) did not show significant positive effects on use intention, which is consistent with findings for users. Notably, *expected utility* (H1) and *data literacy* (H5) did not have a significant impact on non-users' use intention. In contrast, the construct specific to non-users (*awareness*) demonstrated a significant positive effect ($H8 : \beta = 0.107, t = 1.705, p < 0.05$), although the strength of this effect was lower than that observed for *hedonic motivation* or *social influence*, as indicated by the relative path coefficients. The structural model for non-users explains 47% (R^2 =0.474) of the variance of OGD *use intention* [35].

Table 1. Hypothesis test results (direct effects).

Hypo	Path	Coefficient	t-value	Significance
User				
H1	Expected Utility → Use Intention	0.118	2.192	p < 0.05
H2	Hedonic Motivations → Use Intention	0.308	5.758	p < 0.001
H3	Social Influence → Use Intention	0.203	4.025	p < 0.001
H4	Effort Expectancy → Use Intention	0.055	0.803	n. s
H5	Data Literacy → Use Intention	0.215	3.961	p < 0.001
H6	Computer Literacy → Use Intention	−0.066	1.297	n. s
H7	Portal Usability → Use Intention	0.020	0.387	n. s
Non-User				
H1	Expected Utility → Use Intention	0.003	0.040	n. s
H2	Hedonic Motivations → Use Intention	0.294	4.103	p < 0.001
H3	Social Influence → Use Intention	0.176	3.070	p < 0.001
H4	Effort Expectancy → Use Intention	0.110	1.347	n. s
H5	Data Literacy → Use Intention	−0.080	1.257	n. s
H6	Computer Literacy → Use Intention	0.081	1.185	n. s
H8	Awareness → Use Intention	0.107	1.705	p < 0.05

5.2 Moderation Effects

The moderation analysis was also conducted in SmartPLS 4 [36] through bootstrapping on 10,000 subsamples. First, the direct relationships of the proposed moderators were included and tested in the model; otherwise, the moderating effect would be inflated [35, 37]. The significant results of the moderation analysis are shown in Table 2.

The evaluation of moderating effects is based on f-square values, with thresholds of 0.005, 0.010, and 0.025 representing small, medium, and large effects, respectively [35]. For the group of users, *participation* as a use purpose did not exert a significant direct effect on *use intention* ($\beta = 0.035$, $t = 0.491$, $p > 0.05$) but did moderate the relationship between *effort expectancy* and *use intention*. Specifically, *participation* significantly weakened the negative effect of *effort expectancy* on *use intention* (H10d: $\beta = -0.164$, $t = 1.889$, $p < 0.05$) with medium effect ($f^2 = 0.020$), indicating that when the purpose of *participation* becomes salient, the negative influence of effort required is less pronounced. No other significant moderating effects were observed for *participation* among users. *Transparency* did not have any significant direct or moderating effects for the group of users (H9a-d: all $p > 0.05$).

In contrast, for non-users, *transparency* as a use purpose exhibited a strong and significant direct effect on *use intention* ($\beta = 0.257$, $t = 3.318$, $p < 0.001$), underlining *transparency's* importance as a motivational driver in the early adoption phase. Furthermore, *transparency* significantly strengthened the effect of *hedonic motivation* on *use intention* (H9b: $\beta = 0.285$, $t = 3.224$, $p < 0.001$), suggesting that for non-users, the enjoyment or interest associated with accessing OGD is amplified when *transparency* is perceived as a salient use purpose. A large effect was observed ($f^2 = 0.044$). No direct or moderating effects were observed for the use purpose *participation* in the non-user group (H10a-d).

Table 2. Hypothesis test results (significant moderation effects).

Path	Coefficient	t-value	f^2	Significance
User				
Use Purpose Participation x *Effort Expectancy* → *Use Intention*	−0.164	1.889	0.020	$p < 0.05$
Non-User				
Use Purpose Transparency → *Use Intention*	0.257	3.318	0.044	$p < 0.001$
Use Purpose Transparency x *Hedonic Motivations* → *Use Intention*	0.285	3.224	0.043	$p < 0.001$

6 Discussion

This study set out to address three research shortcomings identified in prior work on citizen use of OGD; namely, the lack of differentiation between non-users and users; the insufficient consideration of distinct OGD use purposes (*transparency* vs. *participation*); and the limited contextualization of generic TAM/UTAUT constructs for the specific demands of OGD [2, 4, 15, 16, 20]. The results directly map onto these motivated gaps and show how a contextualized, multi-group, purpose-moderated adaptation of UTAUT2 advances explanation of citizens' intention to use OGD. Our findings also connect to the literature on open data ecosystems, which conceptualizes OGD value as co-produced through interactions among data providers, infrastructures, intermediaries, and users rather than through data release alone [39, 40]. While this stream has largely emphasized supply-side conditions and platform infrastructure, our results add a user-side perspective.

More specifically, a central contribution of our study relates to its focus on user group-specific motivations, which distinguishes it from prior research [15, 16]. Importantly, this study builds upon research directions outlined by earlier work. While prior studies predominantly applied generic models and focused on direct effects (e.g., [20, 24]), this paper introduces a contextualized extension by operationalizing facilitating conditions through the constructs *computer literacy* and *data literacy*. By separating non-users from users, we show empirically that predictors differ for non-users and users. For users, *expected utility* and *data literacy* are significant along with *hedonic motivation* and *social influence*. For non-users, *expected utility* and *data literacy* are not (yet) significant. Instead, *awareness* (a construct absent from prior models), *hedonic motivation* and *social influence* have a significant influence. This pattern validates the theoretical claim that the initial use of OGD depends more on activation levers (awareness, curiosity/enjoyment, peer cues) than on a preliminary evaluation of utility or user capabilities [18]. This also helps to clarify why earlier studies pooling users and non-users as respondents together reported weaker or inconsistent effects, as aggregating these groups masked differences in user-specific motivations and relevance [15, 16].

Three hypotheses were not supported. Effort expectancy was non-significant in both groups (H4), consistent with evidence that its deterrent effect fades in voluntary use and with greater digital experience [27]. Computer literacy was also non-significant (H6) while data literacy mattered for users but not for non-users, indicating that insufficient data literacy is a key barrier for continued use [26, 30], which can be overcome by some of the proposed group-specific interventions discussed shortly.

Another major contribution lies in showing how perceived use purposes moderate the relationships between key predictors and OGD use intention, adding explanatory depth that better reflects the diverse motivations of OGD users [12]. The moderation analysis confirmed the different hypothesized roles of use purposes for the user and non-user groups. *Transparency* has a strong direct effect for non-users and amplifies *hedonic motivation*, indicating that framing OGD as an engaging avenue into government accountability can convert curiosity into intention. *Participation*, meanwhile, weakens the negative relationship between *effort expectancy* and intention among users, suggesting that when reuse is framed as contribution or co-creation, perceived effort becomes less of a deterrent [41]. Based on our analysis and given the persistent gap between data availability and actual citizen engagement [11, 13], this framing matters and motivates several concrete recommendations for OGD providers:

The results can be translated into group-specific interventions that align OGD platforms better with citizens' motivations and overcome typical barriers [4, 17]. As *hedonic motivation* is the strongest predictor for both groups, portals should be designed for enjoyable exploration (e.g., with interactive visualizations, data previews and low-effort entry points) rather than for data provision only. The strong role of *social influence* suggests making community reuse visible through featured citizen "reuses" (e.g., apps) and sharing functions (e.g., community OGD app portals). For non-users, *awareness* and *transparency* are significant factors. Municipalities should pair outreach through existing channels with accountability-oriented framing of easy-to-understand datasets at the point of discovery (e.g., government spending data as featured datasets with explanations on the OGD landing page), thereby strengthening outreach efforts through accountability ("vision") framing [5, 7].

For users, where *expected utility* and *data literacy* drive reuse, the priority shifts to data quality, documentation, machine-readable formats, and embedded literacy support (e.g., dataset descriptions, explanations, AI tools). Since *participation* lowers the effort barrier for experienced users, providers should frame reuse as co-creation opportunities (e.g., by providing visibility for developers or through hackathons).

Across these interventions, framing materializes primarily through portal design at the citizen's OGD interaction points, which is where curiosity is either converted into use or lost.

7 Limitations and Future Research

While this study offers important insights into the motivational factors influencing citizens' intention to use OGD, some limitations must be acknowledged.

Firstly, the study relies on cross-sectional, self-reported survey data from a single municipality. Cross-sectional designs preclude inferences about temporal dynamics (e.g., how initial intention evolves into reuse) and self-reports may be subject to recall or social desirability biases and common method variance [42]. Mitigation steps were implemented (i.e., use of established scales, semantic differentials for expected utility, capability assessments instead of skill self-reports, attention checks, Harman's one-factor test indicating no dominant single factor), yet unmeasured method effects cannot be fully excluded. Future longitudinal or panel designs could trace transitions (non-user, first-time user, reuser) and strengthen causal interpretation.

Secondly, the focal outcome is behavioral intention rather than observed OGD use. This maintains the familiar knowing-doing gap [43] and limits conclusions about actual reuse, transformation, or participatory contribution. Although intention is a validated proximal predictor in technology acceptance frameworks [27], it may not translate linearly into use behavior. One of the reasons for focusing on intention was pragmatic: in a general municipal population we expected only a relatively small fraction of citizens to possess extensive knowledge or prior hands-on experience with OGD [4, 17], making reliable measurement of actual usage statistically difficult and potentially biased by a tiny subset of advanced users. Consequently, behavioral metrics would have produced floor effects and limited variance at this maturity stage of public OGD engagement. Future work should incorporate objective usage indicators and repeated measures to explore conditions translating intention to sustained, value-generating use behavior.

Thirdly, recruitment through official municipal digital channels (e.g., city website, OGD portal, newsletter) and voluntary participation yielded a sample with comparatively high formal education levels and a predominance of urban residents. While the multigroup checks for education and residency did not materially change core path relationships, self-selection may favor respondents already inclined toward digital public resources. Future studies should broaden sampling frames and test measurement invariance across municipalities and other regions to assess generalizability of our findings.

Additionally, our model treats hedonic motivation as an individual-level driver but does not capture the role of portal design in generating it. Because the enjoyment of using OGD is likely also determined by how data are presented and navigated, future research should test portal-design features as antecedents or moderators of hedonic motivation, analyzing whether well-designed portals amplify enjoyment that drives use.

Lastly, the findings should be interpreted considering the relatively mature digital government environment in which the study was conducted. In countries with lower levels of digital government maturity, citizens may face greater infrastructural barriers or lower digital literacy levels. Under such conditions, factors such as effort expectancy and computer/data literacy may play a stronger role than observed in this study.

In conclusion, drawing on a large-scale survey, this study demonstrates empirically that differentiated motivations, capabilities, and purpose salience jointly shape citizens' intention to use OGD. In doing so, it provides a solid foundation for future research, as well as for more targeted strategies to convert policy-driven OGD provision into sustained public engagement and, ultimately, public value.

Acknowledgements. Financial support from the German Federal Ministry for Housing, Urban Development and Building (BMWSB) and the Kreditanstalt für Wiederaufbau (KfW) as part of the "Model Project Smart City (MPSC) Dresden" is gratefully acknowledged.

Disclosure of Interests. The authors have no competing interests to declare that are relevant to the content of this article.

References

1. Jurisch, M.C., Kautz, M., Wolf, P., Krcmar, H.: An international survey of the factors influencing the intention to use open government. In: 48th HICSS, pp. 2188–2198 (2015)
2. Rasool, T., Sajid, M., War-Raich, N.F.: Factors influencing the citizens' satisfaction towards the use of open government data: a systematic literature review. eJournal eDemocracy Open Gov. (JeDEM) 167–196 (2022)
3. Sari, D., Gasco-Hernandez, M.: The use of open data: challenges and good practices from a user's perspective. In: 57th HICSS (2024)
4. Janssen, M., Charalabidis, Y., Zuiderwijk, A.: Benefits, adoption barriers and myths of open data and open government. Inf. Syst. Manag. **29**, 258–268 (2012)
5. Meijer, A.J., Curtin, D., Hillebrandt, M.: Open government: connecting vision and voice. Int. Rev. Adm. Sci. **78**, 10–29 (2012)
6. Attard, J., Orlandi, F., Auer, S.: Value creation on open government data. In: 2016 49th Hawaii International Conference on System Sciences (HICSS), pp. 2605–2614 (2016)
7. Scholl, H.J., Luna-Reyes, L.F.: Uncovering dynamics of open government, transparency, participation, and collaboration. In: 2011 44th HICSS, pp. 1–11 (2011)
8. Kassen, M.: Understanding motivations of citizens to reuse open data: open government data as a philanthropic movement. Innovation **23**, 44–70 (2021)

9. van Maanen, G.: What if? A short commentary on the philosophical bedrock of open government discourse. Inf. Polity **28**, 301–305 (2023)
10. European Commission: Open data An engine for innovation, growth and transparent governance. European Commission (2011)
11. Wang, F., Zhang, Z., Ma, X., Zhang, Y., Li, X., Zhang, X.: Paths to open government data reuse: A three-dimensional framework of information need, data and government preparation. Inf. Manage. **60**, 103879 (2023)
12. Ruijer, E., Grimmelikhuijsen, S., Meijer, A.: Open data for democracy: developing a theoretical framework for open data use. Gov. Inf. Q. **34**, 45–52 (2017)
13. Kawashita, I., Baptista, A.A., Soares, D.: Open government data use by the public sector - an overview of its benefits, barriers, drivers, and enablers. In: 55th HICSS (2022)
14. Rau, R., Glaser, K., Wiener, M.: Factors influencing the use of open government data: a scoping literature review. In: 58th HICSS, pp. 2152–2162 (2025)
15. Albano, C.S., Reinhard, N.: Open government data: facilitating and motivating factors for coping with potential barriers in the Brazilian context. In: Electronic Government, pp. 181–193. Springer, Heidelberg (2014)
16. Jiang, H., Duan, Y., Zhu, Y.: Citizens' continuous-use intention to open government data: empirical evidence from China. Big Data 62–76 (2021)
17. Smith, G., Sandberg, J.: Barriers to innovating with open government data: exploring experiences across service phases and user types. Inf. Polity **23**, 249–265 (2018)
18. Weerakkody, V., Kapoor, K., Balta, M.E., Irani, Z., Dwivedi, Y.K.: Factors influencing user acceptance of public sector big open data. Prod. Plan. Control (2017)
19. Crusoe, J., Simonofski, A., Clarinval, A., Gebka, E.: The impact of impediments on open government data use: insights from users. In: 2019 13th International Conference on Research Challenges in Information Science (RCIS), pp. 1–12 (2019)
20. Zuiderwijk, A., Janssen, M., Dwivedi, Y.K.: Acceptance and use predictors of open data technologies: drawing upon the unified theory of acceptance and use of technology. Gov. Inf. Q. **32**, 429–440 (2015)
21. Davis, F.D.: Perceived usefulness, perceived ease of use, and user acceptance of information technology. MIS Q. **13**, 319–340 (1989). https://doi.org/10.2307/249008
22. Venkatesh, V., Morris, M.G., Davis, G.B., Davis, F.D.: User acceptance of information technology: toward a unified view. MIS Q. **27**, 425–478 (2003)
23. Wirtz, B.W., Weyerer, J.C., Rösch, M.: Open government and citizen participation: an empirical analysis of citizen expectancy towards open government data. Int. Rev. Adm. Sci. **85**, 566–586 (2019)
24. Saxena, S., Janssen, M.: Examining open government data (OGD) usage in India through UTAUT framework. Foresight **19**, 421–436 (2017)
25. Boychuk, M., Cousins, M., Lloyd, A., MacKeigan, C.: Do we need data literacy? Public perceptions regarding Canada's open data initiative. Dalhousie J. Interdisc. Manage. **12** (2016). https://doi.org/10.5931/djim.v12i1.6449
26. Santos-Hermosa, G., Quarati, A., Loría-Soriano, E., Raffaghelli, J.E.: Why does open data get underused? A focus on the role of (open) data literacy. High. Educ. Dyn. **59**, 145–177 (2023)
27. Venkatesh, V., Thong, J.Y.L., Xu, X.: Consumer acceptance and use of information technology: extending the unified theory of acceptance and use of technology. MIS Q. **36**, 157–178 (2012). https://doi.org/10.2307/41410412
28. Natvig, M.K., Jiang, S., Stav, E.: Using open data for digital innovation: barriers for use and recommendations for publishers. JeDEM **13**, 28–57 (2021)
29. Purwanto, A., Zuiderwijk, A., Janssen, M.: Citizens' motivations for engaging in open data hackathons. LNCS, vol. 11686, pp. 130–141 (2019)

30. Wang, H.-J.: Adoption of open government data: perspectives of user innovators. Inf. Res. **25**, 849 (2020)
31. Krismawati, D., Hidayanto, A.N.: The user engagement of open data portal. In: 2021 International Conference on Advanced Computer Science and Information Systems (2021)
32. Podsakoff, P.M., Podsakoff, N.P., Williams, L.J., Huang, C., Yang, J.: Common method bias: it's bad, it's complex, it's widespread, and it's not easy to fix. Annu. Rev. Organ. Psych. Organ. Behav. **11**, 17–61 (2024)
33. Kourouthanassis, P.E., Mikalef, P., Pappas, I.O., Kostagiolas, P.: Explaining travellers online information satisfaction: a complexity theory approach on information needs, barriers, sources and personal characteristics. Inf. Manage. (2017)
34. Rubach, C., Lazarides, R.: Addressing 21st-century digital skills in schools – development and validation of an instrument to measure teachers' basic ICT competence beliefs. Comput. Hum. Behav. **118**, 106636 (2021). https://doi.org/10.1016/j.chb.2020.106636
35. Hair, J.F., Ringle, C.M., Sarstedt, M.: A Primer on PLS-SEM, 3rd edn. SAGE (2022)
36. Ringle, C.M., Wende, S., Becker, J.-M.: SmartPLS 4 (2024). https://www.smartpls.com/
37. Hair, J.F., Risher, J.J., Sarstedt, M., Ringle, C.M.: When to use and how to report the results of PLS-SEM. Eur. Bus. Rev. **31**, 2–24 (2019)
38. Harman, H.H.: Modern Factor Analysis. University of Chicago Press (1976)
39. van Loenen, B., et al.: Towards value-creating and sustainable open data ecosystems: a comparative case study and a research agenda. JeDEM **13**, 1–27 (2021)
40. Lnenicka, M., Nikiforova, A.: Transparency-by-design: what is the role of open data portals? Telematics Inform. **61**, 101605 (2021)
41. Wijnhoven, F., Ehrenhard, M., Kuhn, J.: Open government objectives and participation motivations. Gov. Inf. Q. **32**, 30–42 (2015)
42. Podsakoff, P.M., MacKenzie, S.B., Lee, J.-Y., Podsakoff, N.P.: Common method biases in behavioral research: a critical review of the literature and recommended remedies. J. Appl. Psychol. **88**, 879–903 (2003). https://doi.org/10.1037/0021-9010.88.5.879
43. Haamann, T., Basten, D.: The role of information technology in bridging the knowing-doing gap: an exploratory case study on knowledge application. J. Knowl. Manag. **23**, 705–741 (2018)

Shadows of Transparency: Signaling Transparency-Impeding Behavior Using Public Data

Jos Zuijderwijk[1,2](✉), Iris Beerepoot[1], Thomas Martens[1], Eva Knies[1], Tanja van der Lippe[1], and Hajo A. Reijers[1]

[1] Utrecht University, Princetonplein 5, 3584 CC Utrecht, The Netherlands
a.j.h.zuijderwijk@uu.nl

[2] Ministry of Infrastructure and Water Management, The Hague, The Netherlands

Abstract. Freedom of Information (FOI) laws aim to increase government transparency, yet existing assessments focus mainly on legal compliance and procedural outcomes, leaving organizational behavior underexamined. As FOI processes are increasingly mediated through digital information systems, public response data offer traces of how organizations handle requests and disclosures in practice. This paper develops and evaluates a pattern-based approach that uses such data to signal transparency-impeding behavior across government agencies and over time. Drawing on prior literature, we identify nine recurring behavioral patterns that undermine transparency. Using a dataset of 15,277 Dutch FOI dossiers comprising 139,449 documents, we operationalize and evaluate measurable indicators for six of these patterns, demonstrating that they enable systematic comparison of disclosure practices across agencies and over time. Expert interviews with researchers, journalists, and civil servants confirm the interpretability and practical usefulness of the indicators for investigative prioritization, comparative research, and transparency oversight.

Keywords: Freedom of Information · Government Transparency · Behavioral Patterns · Organizational Behavior · E-Government

1 Introduction

Government transparency is widely recognized as one of the pillars of democratic governance. It enables citizens to observe and evaluate their government by providing access to information about its decision-making process and, consequently, to hold their government accountable [16]. This principle has been institutionalized through Freedom of Information (FOI) legislation, which grants citizens the right to request government information and obliges public agencies to respond within defined timeframes. FOI laws, often described as the backbone of transparency [11], have been adopted in almost all democratic countries [8].

Published by Springer Nature Switzerland 2027
G. Viale Pereira et al. (Eds.): EGOV 2026, LNCS 16933, pp. 363–379, 2027.
https://doi.org/10.1007/978-3-032-35747-2_23

Yet the mere existence of FOI laws alone does not ensure transparency in practice (e.g., [35]). The performance of FOI legislation is typically assessed through field studies analyzing variables that influence request outcomes, such as approval rates or processing delays (e.g., [17,28,31,41]). FOI performance is usually assessed at a procedural level, for example, using response times and exemption rates (e.g., [12,39]), or at a legal level, considering the scope of exemptions or the presence of enforcement mechanisms (e.g., [1,24]). Such metrics capture formal FOI compliance but reveal little about how organizations behave when handling requests. This matters, because transparency is shaped in the day-to-day handling of records: e.g., how requests are interpreted or how searches are conducted, which exemptions are repeatedly invoked, how heavily documents are redacted, in what format information is released, and when disclosure is made. Consider, for example, the Dutch childcare benefits scandal, in which parents received government files so heavily redacted that they could not understand the basis for decisions affecting them [25]. The agency was formally compliant—it responded to requests and applied legal exemptions—yet the disclosed information was rendered meaningless. Prior work suggests that such transparency-impeding behavior occurs within government agencies [19,26], but is difficult to observe directly and systematically across organizations and over time. Existing FOI assessment approaches mainly measure compliance, but they offer limited means to make such recurring transparency-impeding behavior visible.

The rise of e-government has created new empirical opportunities to study this otherwise hidden behavior through digital data. Information systems are now central to all aspects of managing public information [10,18], and FOI procedures are no exception [32]. Governments worldwide have launched digital platforms for managing FOI requests and releasing the requested information[1]. As FOI requests are increasingly processed, logged, and published through information systems, they generate data that indirectly reflect disclosure practices. For instance, an agency that consistently releases documents as scanned images rather than searchable digital files makes information difficult to find and analyze. This would leave observable traces in public data as low machine-readability scores. Although FOI response data remain underused in empirical research, a few recent works have begun to explore them with regard to responsiveness, legislative differences, and the topics of citizen requests [30,35,36,43].

Building on this observation, this paper introduces a pattern-based approach for signaling transparency-impeding behavior in the FOI process using public response data. By identifying and operationalizing recurring behavioral patterns that impede transparency, we show how disclosure practices can be systematically compared through publicly available FOI data. A similar pattern-based approach has recently been used to study government transparency through logs of document management systems [44]. These internal logs, however, are usually not accessible to researchers. In contrast, our study applies the approach

[1] Examples include https://whatdotheyknow.com (UK), https://fragdenstaat.de (Germany), https://righttoknow.org.au (Australia), and https://asktheeu.org (EU). All accessed September 2025.

to publicly available FOI response data, thereby extending its applicability to large-scale transparency research.

Accordingly, our research question is: *How can recurring patterns in public FOI response data be operationalized into indicators of transparency-impeding behavior that allow for comparisons across government agencies and over time?*

We answer this question using a large dataset of Dutch FOI responses. We identify recurring behavioral patterns from existing literature, implement measurable indicators to examine technical feasibility and comparative outputs, and evaluate their interpretability and practical usefulness through expert interviews with researchers, journalists, and civil servants. In doing so, the paper contributes a pattern-based approach that complements compliance-oriented FOI assessment by enabling comparison of transparency-impeding behavior through publicly available data.

2 Research Background

This section establishes the elements necessary for our approach. We first examine how organizational behavior can impede transparency. We then discuss how the FOI process is mediated through information systems.

2.1 Transparency and Its Impediments

Transparency is a broad term. In general, it can be described as "looking through the window of an institution to see its inner workings" [3]. In terms of information relations, transparency can be defined as the availability of information about an actor that enables other actors to monitor the performance or inner workings of that actor [11,23]. Following this definition, one could infer that maximizing transparency means disclosing as much information as possible that is relevant to public decision-making. There are, however, legitimate reasons to constrain the release of government information, such as national security concerns, privacy protection, or commercial confidentiality [26].

Apart from legitimate reasons for withholding information, governments may be reluctant to disclose relevant information despite legal requirements for transparency [13]. It has been argued that governments can maintain FOI laws while loosening the constraints imposed by those laws through less visible administrative action, thereby creating the appearance of openness while limiting disclosure in practice [27].

Building on the concept of transparency as the availability of information that enables one actor to observe another's inner workings, we can distinguish between internal and external transparency [33]. *Internal* transparency refers to an organization's ability to know what information exists, where it is stored, and how it can be retrieved and interpreted. It reflects the quality of internal information management, i.e., how records are created, organized, and maintained within information systems. *External* transparency, by contrast, denotes

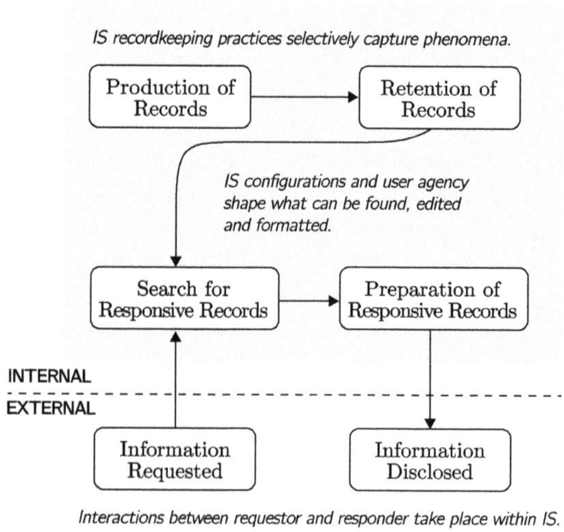

Fig. 1. FOI process through information systems (IS) from request to disclosure. Adapted from Carter and Stratton [4]. The internal/external boundary (dashed line) and minor wording adjustments have been added by the authors.

the degree to which internally available information is made visible to actors outside the organization, e.g., citizens or journalists.

For the present study, a further distinction is useful. Formal FOI compliance concerns whether agencies meet legal and procedural requirements, for example regarding timeliness or the formal use of exemptions. Disclosure behavior concerns recurring organizational practices in how requests are interpreted, how records are selected, how information is redacted, how documents are formatted, and when disclosures are made. The argument of this paper is that existing FOI assessment primarily captures formal compliance, while disclosure behavior remains comparatively difficult to observe even though it shapes transparency in practice.

In the age of e-government, external transparency increasingly takes the form of digital information disclosure. Whereas open data platforms have been widely studied as tools for proactive disclosure of data (e.g., [21]), FOI platforms supporting reactive disclosure have received comparatively little scholarly attention. The next section examines the FOI process and its implementation within information systems.

2.2 FOI Process Within Information Systems

FOI regimes generally combine two modes of disclosure: reactive and proactive. *Reactive* (or passive) disclosure refers to the FOI process in which individuals submit requests for information, agencies locate the relevant records, apply any necessary exemptions, and then release the material. In contrast, *proactive* (or active) disclosure requires public agencies to routinely publish certain categories of information on their own initiative, without waiting for a specific request [29]. This study focuses on reactive disclosure, as we are interested in request-response behavior. Throughout the paper, the term 'FOI process' refers to this reactive mode.

Information systems play a mediating role throughout the FOI process [4]. As shown in Fig. 1, they influence each step of the reactive FOI process, from the submission of a request to the disclosure of information. The process begins when information is requested by an external actor, triggering internal information system activities. Within the organization, records are first produced and subsequently retained according to recordkeeping practices, which determine what aspects of phenomena are captured in the first place. When an FOI request arrives, civil servants use information systems to search for responsive records, i.e., records within the scope of the request, relying on the system's structure and search capabilities to locate relevant material. The identified records are then prepared for release, a stage where system configurations and user agency influence how documents are redacted, edited, and formatted. Finally, information is disclosed externally, completing the process.

The internal and external dimensions are interdependent. Internal transparency is a prerequisite for external transparency: information that cannot be located or understood internally cannot be disclosed externally, regardless of legal requirements (cf. strained transparency [26]). Conversely, external transparency influences internal information management. Knowing that records might become public later, civil servants may document more, or less, carefully.

3 Research Approach

While data on internal information management, such as system logs or recordkeeping metadata, is rarely available to researchers, data from the external side of the FOI process is public by definition. Our study aims to complement existing transparency assessments using public data. As argued in Sect. 2, transparency is shaped by organizational disclosure behavior, i.e., the concrete actions and decisions of civil servants processing FOI requests. This behavior is mediated by information systems and can leave recurring traces in public response data.

To answer the research question, we identify recurring behavioral patterns from the literature, map them onto observable features in public FOI datasets, operationalize one or more indicators for each pattern, and apply them to a Dutch dataset to examine whether they enable comparison of disclosure practices across ministries and over time. We then evaluate the interpretability of these indicators and the practical usefulness of our method through expert interviews.

3.1 Behavioral Patterns

Transparency is a concept that is multi-faceted and inherently difficult to measure directly. We therefore construct proxies at the behavioral level of civil servants within organizations. Because it is more straightforward to identify behavioral patterns that signal impeded transparency than those that reflect its successful achievement, we focus on recurring organizational practices within the reactive FOI process that undermine transparency. We refer to behavioral patterns of transparency-impeding behavior as repeated but counterproductive routines. A similar approach to identifying recurring problematic behavior has been applied in the study of internal government information management [44]. Our study extends this logic to externally visible FOI disclosure data. For the present study, we scope such patterns to behavior within the FOI process as mediated through information systems and reflected in public response data. We derive behavioral patterns from prior literature and subsequently evaluate them with domain experts.

3.2 Public Data and Indicators

From the behavioral patterns, we move to the empirical level, where public data from FOI platforms are analyzed. An appropriate dataset for this purpose contains at least partial FOI dossiers, associated metadata such as request and response dates or file types, and sufficient organizational or temporal coverage to support comparison. FOI response platforms and datasets derived from them typically provide case-level data on the handling of requests, document-level metadata on the disclosed files, and content-level information from the documents themselves. Together, these elements capture both procedural and substantive aspects of disclosure. Where content-level data are not directly available, they can often be extracted from linked files through OCR. Building on the behavioral patterns and these data, we derive a set of indicators. These indicators do not prove the existence of transparency-impeding behavior; rather, they signal patterns that may warrant further scrutiny. Higher indicator values suggest a greater prevalence of the corresponding behavioral pattern. Once defined, the indicators can be computed per dossier and aggregated at appropriate analytical levels such as ministry or year, enabling longitudinal and cross-organizational comparison.

3.3 Evaluation

Because the indicators are proxies derived from metadata rather than direct observations of behavior, evaluation is needed to establish whether they are interpretable as signals of the behavioral patterns they are intended to capture. In this study, evaluation does not establish whether a ministry acted strategically in a particular case. Rather, it examines whether the indicators are technically feasible, interpretable, and practically useful as signals of transparency-impeding behavior. A key aspect of this evaluation is whether the indicators enable comparison across agencies and over time, as specified in our research question.

4 Case Study

We apply our approach to Dutch FOI responses to demonstrate how transparency-impeding behavior can be signaled and compared across ministries.

Table 1. Identified behavioral patterns of transparency-impeding behavior in the FOI process.

Behavioral Pattern	Description	Source
Obstructive Formatting	Releasing information in forms that hinder search and analysis, e.g., scanned printouts.	[19,22,34]
Excessive Redaction	Obscuring text so extensively that disclosed records lose meaning and context.	[19]
Catch-All Exemption	Repeated reliance on broad exemption grounds beyond their intended scope.	[2,19,42]
Narrow Reading	Interpreting requests restrictively to reduce what must be disclosed.	[19]
Overbroad Reading	Interpreting requests so expansively that key information is buried in volume.	[19]
Stale Release	Delaying disclosure long enough to reduce its value or impact.	[37]
Renamed Units	Relabeling terms or units after exposure so that subsequent requests yield no results.	[19]
Document Suppression	Reducing or ceasing production of certain records after prior exposure through FOI.	[19]
Reclassification	Shifting records into more restrictive categories to make them harder to access.	[9,26]

The goal of the case is not to make definitive claims about ministries' actual intent or misconduct, but to show how indicators derived from public FOI data can enable systematic comparison of disclosure practices within a single government.

4.1 Behavioral Patterns

For the purpose of our case study, we identified a set of behavioral patterns by drawing on existing literature. We scoped the analysis to recurring behavior within the reactive FOI process that may impede transparency and that can leave observable traces in public response data. We exclude internal information-management problems not observable through public responses and non-behavioral impediments such as high FOI fees [38] or broader infrastructural constraints [26]. The patterns were derived through a scoped review of literature on FOI administration and obstructive disclosure practices, using [19] as a starting point and extending through snowballing. Nine behavioral patterns were identified, summarized in Table 1.

Obstructive Formatting can be illustrated by releasing scanned printouts rather than machine-readable files, which limits not just readability but also analytical use of disclosed information (cf. [22] on informational vs. analytical transparency). Excessive Redaction concerns heavily redacted documents. For

Catch-All Exemptions, provisions such as ministerial secrecy may be stretched beyond their intended scope [2,42]. Narrow Reading and Overbroad Reading concern how requests are interpreted: one reduces the scope of disclosure, the other buries relevant information in volume. Stale Release concerns timing: delaying disclosure diminishes the value of the released information. Renamed Units, Reclassification, and Document Suppression all concern disappearance from the disclosure record, whether through relabeling, reclassifying sensitivity, or ceasing documentation.

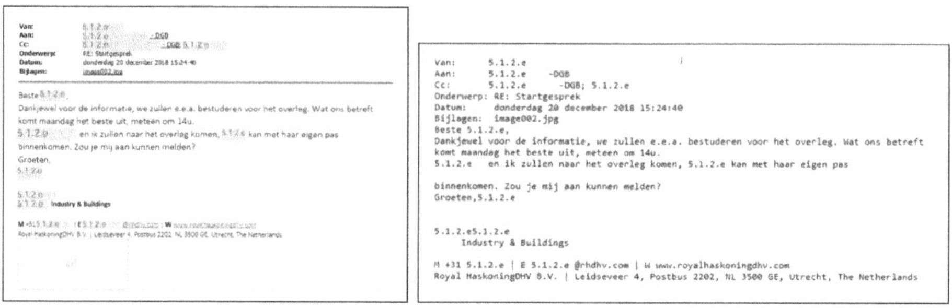

Van: 5.1.2.e
Aan: 5.1.2.e -DGB
Cc: 5.1.2.e -DGB; 5.1.2.e
Onderwerp: RE: Startgesprek
Datum: donderdag 20 december 2018 15:24:40
Bijlagen: image002.jpg
Beste 5.1.2.e,
Dankjewel voor de informatie, we zullen e.e.a. bestuderen voor het overleg. Wat ons betreft komt maandag het beste uit, meteen om 14u.
5.1.2.e en ik zullen naar het overleg komen, 5.1.2.e kan met haar eigen pas

binnenkomen. Zou je mij aan kunnen melden?
Groeten,5.1.2.e

5.1.2.e5.1.2.e
Industry & Buildings

M +31 5.1.2.e | E 5.1.2.e @rhdhv.com | W www.royalhaskoningdhv.com
Royal HaskoningDHV B.V. | Leidseveer 4, Postbus 2202, NL 3500 GE, Utrecht, The Netherlands

Fig. 2. Excerpt from an example FOI dossier: a released email and its corresponding OCR text. For reference: https://pid.wooverheid.nl/?pid=nl.mnre1130.2i.2023.14.

4.2 Public Data

We selected the Woogle[2] dataset [15] to operationalize the behavioral patterns identified above where feasible. The Woogle dataset was constructed through web scraping of Dutch government FOI platforms. The dataset contains responses from all Dutch ministries, provinces, and 31 of 342 municipalities, spanning the years 2001–2025. The dataset includes both reactively and proactively released files. For this study, we filtered the dataset on the reactively released documents to focus on behavior within the request-response process. The filtered dataset contains 15,277 dossiers, 139,449 documents, and 2,644,696 pages.

The dataset combines three interconnected data components: case-level data on request handling (request details, decision texts, organizational identifiers), document-level metadata on disclosed files (file characteristics, creation timestamps, format specifications), and page-level data (OCR results, redaction measurements, accessibility scores). An FOI dossier consists of a request, a response, an inventory list, and the disclosed documents themselves. Figure 2 shows an example of a released document from the dataset. Redacted portions are highlighted with yellow markers (though marker styles vary greatly across documents), with the legal basis[3] for each redaction noted inside the marked areas.

[2] Woogle is now called WooZM, see https://woozm.nl.

[3] Under the Dutch FOI Act (Wet open overheid), exemption grounds are specific legal provisions (e.g., Article 5.1.2.e for personal privacy) that justify withholding

4.3 Indicators and Results

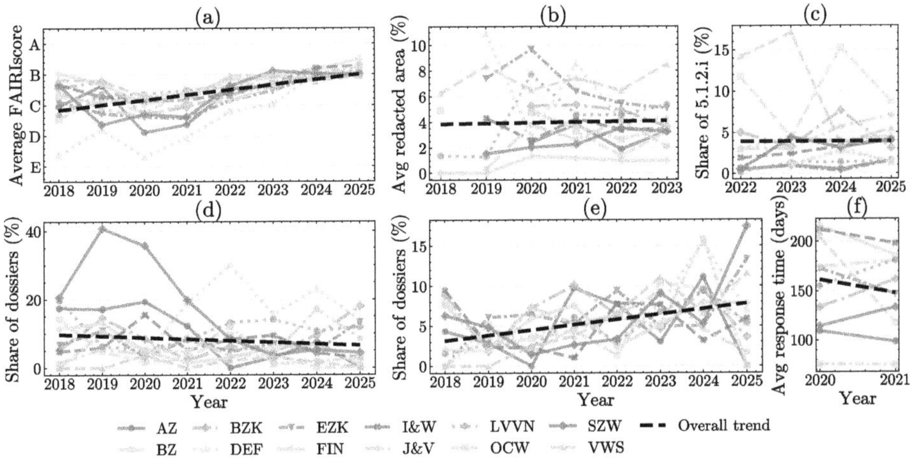

Fig. 3. Six indicators of transparency-impeding behavior per ministry over time. Top row: (a) Average FAIRIscore (Obstructive Formatting; A = best, E = worst); (b) Redaction rate (Excessive Redaction); (c) Catch-all exemption share (Catch-All Exemption; share of exemption ground 5.1.2.i). Bottom row: (d) Low-volume dossier rate (Narrow Reading); (e) High-volume dossier rate (Overbroad Reading); (f) Average response time in days (Stale Release). Dashed black line indicates the overall trend.

We expressed each of the nine behavioral patterns identified in Sect. 4.1 as measurable indicators based on observable characteristics in the Woogle dataset. As described in Sect. 3.2, indicators are continuous measurements that signal the presence of a behavioral pattern. Of the nine patterns, we could operationalize six using the metadata, redaction measurements, and accessibility scores available in the dataset: Obstructive Formatting, Excessive Redaction, Catch-All Exemption, Narrow Reading, Overbroad Reading, and Stale Release. The remaining three—Renamed Units, Document Suppression, and Reclassification—require semantic topic modeling over time, which exceeded the scope of the present study; they are discussed further in Sect. 5. We implemented the six indicators in Python. Data availability varies by indicator: Stale Release could be computed only for 2020âĂŞ2021 due to missing timestamps, Catch-All Exemption from 2022 onward following the new FOI Act, Excessive Redaction for 2018âĂŞ2023 based on available redaction measurements, and the remaining indicators for 2018âĂŞ2025. Three ministries established in 2024 were omitted from the figures. We refer to ministries by their official abbreviations.[4]

information. Some grounds are absolute (always block disclosure) while others are relative (require a balancing test).

[4] AZ (General Affairs), BZ (Foreign Affairs), BZK (Interior), DEF (Defence), EZK (Economic Affairs), FIN (Finance), I&W (Infrastructure), J&V (Justice), LVVN

Obstructive Formatting is operationalized as the *average FAIRIscore*, defined as the mean FAIRIscore [20] across all documents within an organization per year. The FAIRIscore grades machine readability and accessibility on a scale from A (best) to E (worst); scores closer to E capture formats that hinder text extraction, such as scans. Figure 3a shows the results. The overall trend improves clearly, moving from predominantly C- to D-level scores in 2018 toward B-level by 2024–2025, with the dashed overall trend line capturing this shift. DEF and AZ show the most pronounced early dips, with DEF recording the lowest formatting scores around 2019–2020 before both recover to B-level. Cross-ministerial differences persist throughout the period, but the convergence toward B-level suggests a broad shift in formatting practices, consistent with the 2022 Dutch FOI law's mandate for accessible document formats [5].

Excessive Redaction is operationalized as the *redaction rate*, defined as the average percentage of text area redacted, detected algorithmically [14]. Figure 3b shows the results, covering the period 2018–2023. EZK shows the most pronounced peaks, reaching approximately 9% in 2020, well above the overall average of approximately 4%. VWS also shows elevated rates. FIN and J&V remain consistently below the overall average throughout the period. The overall trend is relatively stable, suggesting neither a tightening nor loosening of redaction practices across ministries. The substantial cross-ministerial variation, with DEF showing notable year-to-year volatility, raises questions about whether redaction practices are proportionate to the sensitivity of the material disclosed.

Catch-All Exemption is operationalized as the *catch-all exemption share*, defined as the proportion of exemption ground 5.1.2.i ("proper functioning of the State") among all cited exemption grounds per ministry and year. Prior literature identifies this provision as one that can function as a catch-all in the Dutch FOI context due to its broad and discretionary applicability [6]. Exemption grounds were detected by matching each document's OCR text against a curated list of code variants (e.g., `5.1.2.i`, "5.1 lid 2 sub i") using regular expressions. Figure 3c shows the results, available from 2022 onward. While the overall average remains around 4–5%, VWS shows a pronounced peak exceeding 15% in 2023, and BZK and BZ show elevated use before declining.

Narrow Reading and Overbroad Reading are operationalized as two indicators using dossier size as a proxy for how broadly a request has been interpreted. The *low-volume dossier rate* is defined as the proportion of dossiers whose page count falls at or below the 5th percentile of the pooled dossier-size distribution across all ministries (two pages or fewer), signaling potential restrictive interpretation. The *high-volume dossier rate* is the proportion at or above the 95th percentile (636 pages or more), signaling potential overbroad interpretation. Global thresholds ensure comparability across ministries. Figure 3d–e show the results. The low-volume dossier rate shows SZW spiking around 2019–2020 before declining sharply. AZ shows consistently elevated rates in 2018–2019,

(Agriculture), OCW (Education), SZW (Social Affairs), VWS (Health). Full names and English translations are included in the repository (see Data and Code Availability).

remaining above 15%, and DEF spikes to roughly 30% in 2021. The high-volume dossier rate is comparatively rare across all ministries and shows no clear outliers, with values generally remaining below 15%. Both indicators differentiate ministries less consistently over time than the indicators discussed above.

Stale Release is operationalized as the *average response time*, defined as the mean number of days between the submission of a request and the publication of the corresponding dossier. Due to missing timestamps, this indicator could only be computed for 2020 and 2021. DEF is absent from panel (f) only, as it has no recorded 2020–2021 request dates. Figure 3f shows the results. Despite this limited window, the data reveal substantial cross-ministerial variation: average response times range from approximately 80 to over 200 days. FIN and I&W show the longest average response times, approaching or exceeding 200 days, while OCW shows among the shortest. The overall trend slightly decreases between the two years, though several ministries show an upward trend. When disclosure takes months, the information may lose its relevance for public debate, journalistic investigation, or policy scrutiny.

Taken together, the six indicators show that public FOI response data can surface cross-ministerial and temporal variation in transparency-impeding behavior. Catch-All Exemption, Excessive Redaction, Obstructive Formatting, and Stale Release generate the clearest comparative signals. The Narrow Reading and Overbroad Reading indicators reveal some outliers, e.g., SZW's spike in low-volume dossiers, but differentiate ministries less consistently over time. Notably, certain ministries (e.g., VWS) appear as outliers across multiple indicators simultaneously, suggesting that transparency-impeding patterns may cluster within particular organizations.

4.4 Evaluation

To evaluate our approach, we conducted six semi-structured expert interviews, each lasting approximately one hour. Participants were selected to capture different forms of expertise: two academic researchers (one full professor specializing in transparency, one PhD researcher involved with the dataset), two investigative journalists specializing in FOI, and two civil servants with an FOI-related function from a Dutch ministry. All participants were shown the set of behavioral patterns, the corresponding indicators, and the outputs from the Dutch case. The interview protocol combined a shared evaluative core with role-specific variants tailored to participants' expertise. Across versions, the protocol addressed three overarching dimensions: feasibility, quality and usability. Interviews were audio-recorded with consent and transcribed. The full protocol is provided in the repository. Responses were grouped thematically across participants along the three dimensions. The findings below were obtained by grouping recurring observations across the six transcripts along the three dimensions; we report points raised by multiple participants or flagged as particularly salient.

Implementation of the approach on Dutch FOI response data showed that several behavioral patterns can be operationalized and applied to a large dataset. Indicators such as dossier volume rates, redaction rates, and FAIRIscores were successfully implemented, demonstrating technical feasibility. Participants noted that the remaining patterns (Renamed Units, Document Suppression, and Reclassification) are inherently difficult to measure, because published FOI data provide visibility only into what is disclosed. While data quality is improving as more documents are digitally born and systematically published, one participant highlighted recurring sources of error such as OCR inconsistencies, divergent file structures, and incomplete metadata.

Participants widely recognized the conceptual plausibility of the identified behavioral patterns, judging them to reflect real practices in Dutch FOI processing. Catch-All Exemption and Excessive Redaction were identified as very common. Narrow Reading was described as a common but negotiated practice, whereas Renamed Units and Overbroad Reading were seen as rare or nonexistent in the Dutch context.

A central question in our evaluation was whether the indicators enable comparison across agencies and over time. When presented with the indicator outputs, participants were able to derive specific comparative interpretations. For instance, the high redaction rates at certain ministries were linked by participants to the sensitivity of policy domains those ministries cover, such as health or economic affairs, while the improving FAIRIscores were attributed to the 2022 legislative mandate for accessible document formats. The exemption concentration indicator prompted participants to distinguish between expected dominance of the privacy exemption (5.1.2.e), which they considered unremarkable, and the frequent use of the "proper functioning of the State" exemption (5.1.2.i), which several experts flagged as a potential marker of catch-all behavior (related to the frequency of other exemption grounds). Critically, participants emphasized that the indicators' value lies precisely in comparison: a single ministry's score is hard to interpret in isolation, but relative differences and temporal trends raise questions about why one ministry behaves differently from another.

Additionally, participants identified behavioral patterns not included in the current set, including the offshoring of records to private messaging channels (e.g., WhatsApp, Signal) and procedural discouragement tactics (e.g., characterizing requests as abusive or excessively burdensome). Related behaviors, such as avoiding documentation, simply declaring that records do not exist, and masking departments, were likewise reported as recurrent in practice. Each suggests potential measurable proxies, although participants stressed that such indicators remain highly context-dependent.

All participants agreed that the approach holds practical value for enabling systematic comparison. Journalists saw it as a means to support investigative prioritization by identifying which agencies warrant closer scrutiny. Civil servants viewed it as a diagnostic tool for internal comparison, noting that "dashboards could show why one ministry still does what another stopped doing". Researchers emphasized its potential for comparative, longitudinal analysis of transparency and its contribution to the empirical study of digital government. Participants agreed on two main guidelines for interpretation. First, indicators should serve as diagnostic signals, not definitive proof of intent: "they should raise questions, not point fingers". Second, indicators need to be considered alongside context to avoid misreading them. Several participants proposed combining quantitative indicators with qualitative follow-ups. For example, one participant noted a structural shift in recordkeeping: "there are many more documents now, and the types of documents have changed," with chat and messaging apps supplementing traditional memos and making disclosure "much more practically difficult".

5 Discussion

This study set out to examine how recurring patterns in public FOI response data can be operationalized into indicators of transparency-impeding behavior that allow for comparisons across government agencies and over time. The results suggest that this is feasible for several behavioral patterns. In particular, Catch-All Exemption, Excessive Redaction, Obstructive Formatting, and Stale Release produced indicators that enable cross-ministerial and temporal comparison. Expert interviews confirmed that these indicators are interpretable and practically useful as diagnostic signals: they reflect recognized practices, surface variation that experts could contextualize, and were seen as valuable for journalism, research, and internal oversight alike.

A consistent finding across indicators is that cross-ministerial variation is substantial, while temporal trends differ by indicator. The gradual improvement in FAIRIscores, for instance, suggests that legislative mandates can have observable effects on disclosure behavior, whereas redaction levels remain broadly stable, indicating neither a tightening nor loosening of disclosure boundaries. Not all indicators performed equally well, however. The Narrow Reading and Overbroad Reading indicators differentiated ministries less sharply, likely because dossier size is shaped by many factors beyond request interpretation, including the nature of the topic and the volume of relevant records. This suggests that proxy-based indicators work best when the observable feature is closely tied to the behavioral pattern, as with redaction rates or exemption shares, and less well when the mapping is indirect.

The paper contributes in two ways. First, it contributes conceptually by distinguishing between formal compliance, disclosure behavior, and transparency, and by arguing that disclosure behavior forms an analytically important but insufficiently visible layer between the first and the third. Second, it contributes methodologically by showing how public FOI response data can be used as a source for pattern-based analysis of recurring transparency-impeding behavior across organizations and over time. In this sense, the paper complements existing FOI assessments. The indicators should be interpreted as signals that help prioritize further investigation.

The proposed approach is expected to be applicable beyond the Dutch context. Several jurisdictions, including Germany, the United Kingdom, and Australia, maintain public FOI platforms capable of supporting comparable analyses. Cross-national comparisons could reveal whether behavioral patterns follow similar trajectories across administrative cultures or reflect country-specific disclosure norms. Moreover, linking behavioral indicators to established metrics of

FOI performance [12] or broader transparency assessments [40] may help validate the results further.

Our study also has limitations. Because we rely on publicly released FOI responses, our analyses are constrained by the quality and completeness of the available data. Some data, such as request dates, were incomplete. Three behavioral patterns—Renamed Units, Document Suppression, and Reclassification—remain unoperationalized. These patterns require content-level analysis to detect whether topics vanish and reappear under new names. Their implementation is left for future work. For the Obstructive Formatting indicator, the FAIRIscore is an ordinal measure (A–E), which constrains quantitative analysis, and it is subject to recalibration over time, meaning longitudinal comparisons may partly reflect changes in the scoring instrument; reporting the share of D- and E-rated documents is one alternative operationalization that may mitigate the latter issue. More broadly, the current implementation focuses on demonstrating that systematic comparison is achievable; alternative operationalizations, e.g., using medians instead of means to reduce sensitivity to outliers, may better reflect disclosure behavior in practice. Future work can extend the implementation with more advanced techniques such as topic modeling [7] and refined exemption detection, expand the catalogue of behavioral patterns, and examine the content of FOI requests in more detail, although original request texts are not always publicly available.

6 Conclusion

This study introduced a pattern-based approach for signaling transparency-impeding behavior in the FOI process using publicly available response data. Drawing on existing literature, we identified nine recurring behavioral patterns that undermine transparency and operationalized six of them as measurable indicators. Applying the approach to Dutch FOI dossiers revealed variation across ministries and over time: formatting practices improved following legislative change, redaction levels varied substantially across policy domains, reliance on broad exemption grounds proved unevenly distributed, and response times differed markedly between agencies.

Expert interviews with journalists, researchers, and civil servants confirmed the interpretability and practical usefulness of the indicators, and their comparative value, while highlighting the need for careful contextual interpretation. Intent is not captured in the data, and our approach does not replace legal or qualitative evaluation. Rather, it provides a scalable, data-driven mechanism to signal behavioral patterns that may warrant closer scrutiny.

Ultimately, the findings suggest that public FOI response data can serve to signal recurring disclosure behavior that may shape transparency. As governments continue to digitize the FOI process, this approach offers a foundation for comparative research, transparency monitoring, and informed oversight.

Data Availibility Statement. Our code and the interview protocol are available at https://edu.nl/dwbr3.

References

1. Ackerman, J.M., Sandoval-Ballesteros, I.E.: The global explosion of freedom of information laws. Admin. Law Rev. **58**(1), 85–130 (2006)
2. Arnold, J.R.: Secrecy in the Sunshine Era: The Promise and Failures of U.S. Open Government Laws. Univ. Press of Kansas (2014)
3. den Boer, M.: Steamy windows: transparency and openness in justice and home affairs. In: Deckmyn, V., Thomson, I. (eds.) Openness and Transparency in the EU, pp. 91–105. EIPA (1998)
4. Carter, D., Stratton, C.: Information systems as mediators of freedom of information requests. In: Toeppe, K., Yan, H., Chu, S.K.W. (eds.) iConference 2021. LNCS, vol. 12646, pp. 274–282. Springer, Cham (2021). https://doi.org/10.1007/978-3-030-71305-8_22
5. Drahmann, A.: De wet open overheid: een verbetering van de digitale informatiehuishouding van de overheid. Computerrecht **2021**(4), 321–329 (2021)
6. Drahmann, A.: Woo-verzoek over integriteitsschendingen door ambtenaren (2024). https://hdl.handle.net/1887/4082412
7. Eickhoff, M., Neuss, N.: Topic modeling methodology: Its use in information systems and other managerial disciplines. In: Proceedings of ECIS (2017)
8. Freedominfo.org: The global network of freedom of information advocates. https://freedominfo.org. Accessed 25 Sept 2025
9. Galison, P.: Removing knowledge. Crit. Inq. **31**(1), 229–243 (2004)
10. Gil-Garcia, J.R., Dawes, S.S., Pardo, T.A.: Digital government and public management research: finding the crossroads. Public Manag. Rev. **20**(5), 633–646 (2018)
11. Grimmelikhuijsen, S.: Transparency and Trust: An Experimental Study of Online Disclosure and Trust in Government, Utrecht Univ. Ph.D. thesis (2012)
12. Hazell, R., Worthy, B.: Assessing the performance of freedom of information. Gov. Inf. Q. **27**(4), 352–359 (2010)
13. Henninger, M.: Freedom of information and the right to know: tensions between openness and secrecy. Inf. Res. **22**(4) (2017)
14. van Heusden, R., de Ruijter, A., Majoor, R., Marx, M.: Detection of redacted text in legal documents. In: Proceedings of TPDL. LNCS, vol. 14241. Springer, Heidelberg (2023). https://doi.org/10.1007/978-3-031-43849-3_28
15. van Heusden, R., Larooij, M., Kamps, J., et al.: A collection of FAIR Dutch freedom of information act documents. Sci. Data **12**, 795 (2025)
16. Hood, C., Heald, D.: Transparency: The Key to Better Governance? Oxford Univ. Press, Cambridge (2006)
17. Jenkins, N.R., Landgrave, M., Martinez, G.E.: Do political donors have greater access to government officials? Evidence from a FOIA field experiment with U.S. municipalities. J. Behav. Public Admin **3**(2) (2020)
18. Kautto, T., Henttonen, P.: Records management as invisible work: a study of finnish municipalities. Gov. Inf. Q. **37**(4), 101460 (2020)
19. Luscombe, A., Walby, K.: Theorizing freedom of information: the live archive, obfuscation, and actor-network theory. Gov. Inf. Q. **34**(3), 379–387 (2017)

20. Marx, M., Larooij, M., Perasedillo, F., Kamps, J.: Enticing local governments to produce FAIR freedom of information act dossiers. In: Proceedings of ECIR. LNCS, vol. 13982. Springer, Heidelberg (2023). https://doi.org/10.1007/978-3-031-28241-6_25
21. Matheus, R., Faber, R., Ismagilova, E., Janssen, M.: Digital transparency and the usefulness for open government. Int. J. Inf. Manag. **73**, 102690 (2023)
22. Meijer, A.: De doorzichtige overheid, Erasmus Univ. Rotterdam. Ph.D. thesis (2002)
23. Meijer, A.: Understanding the complex dynamics of transparency. Public Adm. Rev. **73**(3), 429–439 (2013)
24. Mueller, C.E.: Evaluating freedom of information laws: objectives, approaches, and practical considerations. Int. J. Public Admin. **42**(12), 1020–1030 (2019)
25. NOS Nieuws: Ouders zwartgelakte dossiers: 'ik weet nog steeds niet wat ik fout heb gedaan' (2019). https://nos.nl/artikel/2314288. Accessed Sept 2025
26. Pasquier, M., Villeneuve, J.P.: Organizational barriers to transparency. Int. Rev. Admin. Sci. **73**(1), 111–130 (2007)
27. Roberts, A.S.: Blacked Out: Government Secrecy in the Information Age. Cambridge Univ. Press, Cambridge (2006)
28. Rodríguez, R.P., Rossel, C.: A field experiment on bureaucratic discretionary bias under FOI laws. Gov. Inf. Q. **35**(3), 418–427 (2018)
29. Ruijer, H.J.M.: Proactive transparency in the United States and the Netherlands: the role of government communication officials. Am. Rev. Public Admin. **47**(3), 354–375 (2017)
30. Ruohonen, J.: Empirical reasoning about FOI request delays in the EU. In: Proceedings of I3E, pp. 55–69. Springer, Heidelberg (2025). https://doi.org/10.1007/978-3-032-06164-5_5
31. Spáč, P., Pastarmadzhieva, D., Zagrapan, J.: Freedom of information and the volume of requested data: an experimental study. Gov. Inf. Q. **42**(2), 102030 (2025)
32. Stratton, C., Carter, D.: Locating information systems in the freedom of information process. Gov. Inf. Q. **40**(2), 101807 (2023)
33. Street, C.T., Meister, D.B.: Small business growth and internal transparency: the role of information systems. MIS Q. **28**(3), 473–506 (2004)
34. Tong, J.: Growing government secrecy: how and why information access has become increasingly restricted in the UK. Journal. Pract. 1–19 (2025)
35. Trautendorfer, J., Hohensinn, L., Hilgers, D.: From de jure to de facto transparency: analyzing the compliance gap in light of freedom of information laws. Regul. Gov. **19**(1), 253–283 (2025)
36. Trautendorfer, J., Schmidthuber, L., Hilgers, D.: Are the answers all out there? Investigating citizen information requests in the haze of bureaucratic responsiveness. Governance **37**(3), 845–865 (2024)
37. Treadwell, G.: FOI scholarship reflects a return to secrecy. Pac. Journal. Rev. **22**(2), 121–136 (2016)
38. Wagner, A.J., Cuillier, D.: To fee or not to fee: requester attitudes toward freedom of information charges. Gov. Inf. Q. **40**(4), 101879 (2023)
39. Wasike, B.: FOI in transition: a comparative analysis of the FOIA performance between the Obama and Trump administrations. Gov. Inf. Q. **37**(2), 101443 (2020)
40. Williams, A.: A global index of information transparency and accountability. J. Comput. Econ. **43**(3), 804–824 (2015)
41. Worthy, B., John, P., Vannoni, M.: Transparency at the parish pump: a field experiment to measure the effectiveness of freedom of information requests in England. J. Public Admin. Res. Theory **26**(4) (2016)

42. Žuffová, M.: Fit for purpose? Exploring the role of freedom of information laws and their application for watchdog journalism. Int. J. Press/Polit. **28**(1), 300–322 (2023)
43. Žuffová, M.: What the public wants to know: a text-as-data study of information requests to the UK government through the WhatDoTheyKnow platform. J. Quant. Descr.: Digit. Media **5** (2025)
44. Zuijderwijk, J., Beerepoot, I., Martens, T., Knies, E., van der Lippe, T., Reijers, H.A.: TAPAS: a pattern-based approach to assessing government transparency. In: Proceedings of EGOV. LNCS, vol. 15944. Springer, Heidelberg (2025). https://doi.org/10.1007/978-3-032-01589-1_22

Data Want to be Free: An Innovation Resistance Theory Model for Identifying Barriers to Government Data Sharing

Anastasija Nikiforova[1](✉), Antoine Clarinval[2], Anneke Zuiderwijk - van Eijk[3], Daniel Rudmark[4], Petar Milic[5], Charalampos Alexopoulos[6], and Katrin Rajamäe-Soosaar[7]

[1] University of Tartu, Tartu, Estonia
anastasija.nikiforova@ut.ee
[2] Umeå University, Umeå, Sweden
antoine.clarinval@umu.se
[3] Delft University of Technology, Delft, The Netherlands
a.m.g.zuiderwijk-vaneijk@tudelft.nl
[4] The Swedish National Road and Transport Research Institute, Linköping, Sweden
daniel.rudmark@vti.se
[5] University of Priština - Kosovska Mitrovica, Kosovska Mitrovica, Serbia
petar.milic@pr.ac.rs
[6] University of the Aegean, Samos, Greece
alexop@aegean.gr
[7] Association of Estonian Cities and Rural Municipalities, Tallinn, Estonia

Abstract. Data sharing is increasingly essential for digital government and data-driven innovation, yet many public organizations remain reluctant to make their data openly available. While prior research has examined factors influencing open data adoption, little theoretical work explores why resistance persists within public agencies. This study develops an Innovation Resistance Theory (IRT) model tailored to government data sharing to identify predictors of organizational resistance. An initial model was derived from literature and refined through interviews with 21 public organizations across six European countries. The resulting model - IRT4DS - identifies 39 barriers spanning usage, value, risk, tradition, and image dimensions, and 23 countermeasures mapped to the most critical barriers and the actors responsible for addressing them. By extending IRT into the context of governmental data sharing, the study advances theoretical understanding of why public data often remains closed and provides actionable guidance for policymakers seeking to design enabling data ecosystems and reduce structural and cultural barriers to OGD adoption.

Keywords: Data Sharing · Innovation Resistance Theory · Open Government Data · Public Sector Data · Technology Adoption

Published by Springer Nature Switzerland 2027
G. Viale Pereira et al. (Eds.): EGOV 2026, LNCS 16933, pp. 380–396, 2027.
https://doi.org/10.1007/978-3-032-35747-2_24

1 Introduction

Echoing the well-known maxim that "*information wants to be free*,"[1] government data are widely viewed as a foundational public resource. Open Government Data (OGD) have emerged as a catalyst for sustainability-oriented and inclusive data-driven innovation, enabling value creation for citizens, businesses, researchers, and public organizations [14, 37, 50]. As open data ecosystems evolve from basic transparency towards strategic and systemic reuse, OGD increasingly form the backbone of digital innovation. Companies develop new services using OGD [41], researchers combine datasets for scientific discovery and modelling, including crisis management [46], public agencies use each other's data to improve collaboration and service delivery [42]. Yet, despite their recognized value, many public organizations continue to resist (actively or passively) opening their data.

Prior research on OGD sharing has predominantly applied acceptance-oriented adoption theories such as Technology Acceptance Model (TAM) [45] and the Unified Theory of Acceptance and Use of Technology (UTAUT) [46, 51]. While these approaches illuminate motivational drivers, they pay limited attention to the *barriers* inhibiting openness. Existing studies identify issues such as low data quality, lack of technical skills, resource constraints, fears of misuse [2, 13, 42], yet insights remain fragmented. At the same time, e-government scholars increasingly call for renewal beyond repeatedly applied adoption models that offer diminishing explanatory value [1, 17]. This study fills these gaps by examining barriers to OGD sharing through Innovation Resistance Theory (IRT). IRT offers a theoretically rich framework by conceptualizing resistance as stemming from (a) functional barriers - usage difficulties, value of innovation, risk perceptions, and (b) psychological barriers - cultural misalignment, image concerns [36]. Viewing OGD as an innovation adopted by public agencies [14], IRT enables the integration of diverse barriers into a coherent explanation of resistance. Although widely applied in marketing and consumer innovation [10, 21], it remains underutilized in e-government.

The objective of this study is to develop and validate an IRT-based model tailored to OGD—IRT4DS (Innovation Resistance Theory for Data Sharing)—that identifies predictors of resistance among public agencies. We develop an initial model from literature and refine it through interviews with 21 agencies across six countries. The final model comprises 39 barriers across the five IRT categories and is complemented by 23 countermeasures mapped to the most relevant barriers. This theoretically grounded and practically actionable framework contributes to IS and digital government scholarships by serving as a diagnostic model explaining the mechanisms through which data become open or remain enclosed and offers insights essential for building resilient open data ecosystems and supporting digital transformation in the public sector.

Our empirical findings confirm known barriers but also reveal several underexplored or novel barriers, such as *format-specific capability gaps* (e.g., difficulty publishing in required GIS or RDF formats), *capacity mismatch* due to the absence of OGD-dedicated roles, *historical path dependence*, where openness conflicts with inherited mandates

[1] Expression that means that information naturally strives to become as freely available among people as possible (attributed to Stewart Brand, 1984 quote), later transformed to denote that all people should be able to access information freely.

and routines, the *ongoing maintenance burden, financial cannibalization risks* for agencies with legacy revenue models, and *difficulties prioritizing* under limited capacity. By surfacing these mechanisms, the study advances theoretical understanding of why public data remain closed and demonstrates the analytical value of IRT for OGD research, revealing barriers that have remained theoretically insufficiently visible but have practical implications.

2 Background and Related Work

2.1 Innovation Resistance Theory

Resistance to change has long been viewed as a natural response when established routines are challenged [35, 48]. Innovation resistance, in turn, was defined in [36] as a special version of resistance to change widely discussed in social psychology and behavioural science [15, 28] sharing a common opinion that individuals have an inherent / intrinsic desire for psychological balance called "*psychological equilibrium.*" This is because any change made to the individual's behaviour can disturb this balance, so the individuals often choose to resist change rather than go through the most likely disturbing and challenging process of readjustment. Therefore, it is believed that resistance is a normal response of individuals when faced with innovation [35]. IRT argues that adoption outcomes reflect the interplay of *functional* and *psychological* barriers. Functional barriers relate to *usage*, *value*, and *risk* perceptions, while psychological barriers derive from *traditions* and norms of individuals, and *image* concerns. Together, they explain why innovations are *rejected*, *adopted*, or selectively *modified* [35].

Although the IRT was developed over 30 years ago, it remains popular and has gained rapidly increasing popularity in the last 5 years. Most scholars used the IRT as the basis for the empirical evaluation of consumer resistance to innovations. Our literature analysis[2] suggests that existing research utilizing IRT can be classified into 5 high-level groups depending on their application domain: (1) digital financial services, e-commerce and online services [53]; (2) sustainable consumption, green innovations and organic food [44]; (3) cutting-edge technologies and emerging trends [10, 21]; (4) education and MOOC [25]; (5) e-government [30, 36]. We identified only two studies utilizing IRT in e-government. Prakash and Das [34] explored citizens' resistance to use digital contact tracing apps that governments worldwide used as a critical element in their COVID-19 pandemic lockdown exit strategy. Nikiforova and Zuiderwijk [30] presented the initial version of the IRT model tailored to OGD that we validate and extend in this study. IRT remains underutilized in e-government research, where its application could help uncover organizational, institutional, and operational mechanisms of resistance overlooked by traditional acceptance-oriented adoption theories. Viewing OGD as an innovation adopted by public agencies [14], IRT enables the integration of diverse barriers into a coherent explanation of resistance. Although IRT was originally developed to explain consumer resistance to innovations, its core mechanisms are equally relevant in organizational contexts where innovation adoption decisions are shaped by institutional routines, professional norms, and reputational considerations. In public

[2] See full analysis on ZENODO - https://doi.org/10.5281/zenodo.15291553.

sector organizations, these mechanisms often manifest collectively through managerial decisions, regulatory constraints, and organizational culture.

2.2 Barriers to Openly Sharing Government Data

Research on OGD consistently identifies barriers that impede data opening, ranging from technical constraints to institutional and cultural factors [2, 37]. Synthesizing prior work through the lens of IRT shows how these barriers map to its functional and psychological categories (Table 1): (1) usage barriers refer to data quality problems, complex publication processes, and low usability of portals or data formats; (2) value barriers - to unclear benefits, resource requirements, incomplete datasets, and concerns over lost revenue streams; (3) risk barriers involve fears of data misuse, misinterpretation, exposure of sensitive information, legal liability; (4) tradition barriers include risk-averse cultures, rigid routines, and limited skills; (5) image barriers stem from concerns that published data may lead to reputational harm if misused or if quality is questioned.

Table 1. Examples of barriers to sharing OGD (revisited [30]).

Resistance factors	Examples of barriers to openly sharing OGD leading to resistance
Usage barriers	OGD often suffer from quality issues [39;46] Openly sharing government data is a complicated process [2] OGD portals suffer from low ease of use [6;12] Insufficient user-friendliness of the data [26]
Value barriers	OGD do not always provide value to users [8;23;43] Datasets may be incomplete [29;52] Concerns about the quality of open data [3;26;29;46] Sharing government data requires resources, including time and costs [42] Impossible to sell the data when it is openly available [26;7] Data providers are usually the ones who invest the most effort in publishing data, while businesses and citizens profit the most [43;23]
Risk barriers	Fear that openly shared government data will be misused [43] Fear of open data users drawing false conclusions [2;7;46] Fear that (privacy) sensitive data will be shared openly [2;26;37;39] Fear of making mistakes when preparing data for publication [20;52] Fear of being liable for data quality [2]
Tradition barriers	Risk-averse culture avoids openly sharing the data [45] Reluctance to change organizational processes [7;42] Incompatible organizational routines and processes [24] Civil servants may lack the skills required for openly sharing data [23;24;42]
Image barriers	Fear that organizational reputation will be damaged due to the publication of low-quality data [6;9;52] Fear that the organization sharing the data will be associated with incorrect conclusions drawn from OGD analysis / misinterpreted [13;24]

While these studies offer valuable insights, they typically analyze individual barriers or isolated categories. What is missing is a coherent, theoretically grounded model integrating functional and psychological resistance factors. IRT provides such a structure, allowing diverse barriers to be systematically examined as part of a unified resistance mechanism rather than as disconnected obstacles.

3 Methodology

To develop an IRT-based model tailored to OGD (IRT4DS), we first conducted a literature review on both IRT and barriers to data sharing and used these insights to construct an initial model that has been outlined in [30] (summarized in Sect. 2). This model is now validated and refined through qualitative interviews with public organizations we favored to uncover context-specific mechanisms, identify unforeseen factors, and refine theoretical constructs, thereby contributing to the theory building [5].

3.1 Data Collection

We interviewed 21 public agencies across six European countries selected to reflect different administrative traditions [32], geographical areas, and unitary and federal states, and levels of open data maturity according to the Open Data Maturity Report 2022 (the most recent report at the time of sampling countries). Considering that IRT supposes consideration of non-adopters of innovation as those that potentially face actual barriers associated with adoption, we were interested in followers and beginners. The sample includes Latvia, Belgium, Greece, the Netherlands, Sweden, and Serbia. Following [4], a cross-country case study methodology has been developed to dive deeper into individual cases [27, 47] without losing sight of the bigger picture [22]. Within these contexts, public agencies operate with varying levels of engagement with and maturity in open data practices, ranging from highly specialized data governance units to organizations with more limited or emerging exposure to OGD initiatives.

Within each country, we used purposive sampling to recruit agencies with differing mandates and roles [33]. We selected public agencies based on their availability for interviews and aimed for diversity in the type of organization (e.g., thematic public service, statistical institute, etc.). A total of 21 interviews (i.e., one per public agency) were conducted with 25 interviewees, including directors, project managers, advisors, and data specialists. 17 interviews involved 1 respondent and 4 were done with 2 respondents. Within these contexts, the sample includes a diverse set of public sector roles and organizational domains, including data governance units, sectoral agency es (e.g., health, finance, agriculture, and energy), and public policy and advisory functions. This diversity in organizational roles and domains strengthens the exploratory nature of the study, it is important to note that levels of engagement with and maturity of open data practices vary across organizations and roles, ranging from highly specialized data and interoperability units to agencies with more limited or emerging exposure to OGD initiatives. Accordingly, the study does not aim to provide systematic comparisons across sectors or functional domains. Instead, it focuses on aggregated patterns of organizational resistance to OGD across heterogeneous institutional settings. Although country-level comparisons were not the objective of this study, instead, data were analysed at the aggregate level, with a comparable number of interviews in each country.

Interviews were conducted between May 2022 and April 2023. Table 2 shows the distribution of interviewees per role. The study purposefully targeted public organizations operating within OGD environments in countries classified as followers or beginners in terms of open data maturity according to the Open Data Maturity Report 2022.

Table 2. Distribution of interviewees per role.

Role	Number of interviewees	Interview ID
Project manager	8	I1, I4, I5, I8, I11, I12, I13, I18
Director	7	I2, I3, I9, I10, I17, I20, I21
Manager	4	I6, I15, I16
Advisor	4	I2, I7, I14, I19
Data analyst or scientist / researcher	2	I3, I5
Total	**25**	–

Interviews followed a semi-structured protocol derived from the initial model and its individual barriers (i.e., items)[3]. To ensure the reliability and validity, the items selected as constructs in our model were pre-tested by two researchers. Before the interviews took place, the items were checked for content validity and unambiguous wording. Protocol includes two major sections. The first section consists of 9 questions about the general profile of the organization that the respondent represents and their experience with OGD. The second section contains IRT model-related questions. Considering the explorative nature of the study and our intention to refine the model, each individual barrier was transformed into an open-ended question of the form "*To what extent do the following situations form a barrier to openly sharing your organization's data: …*" where each barrier was then addressed. Open-ended questions were given preference over closed-ended questions (yes/no) due to the exploratory nature of our study. Before the specific barriers within a category are addressed, the respondent is introduced with a definition of the barrier category (i.e., resistance sub-factor) and asked whether there is any situation that would pose a challenge in the scope of the category for the organization. Then, after going through each specific barrier within the category, the respondent is asked whether they can think of any other relevant barrier. This is repeated for the five barrier categories. Once all the barriers and their associated questions are asked, another general question enquires about other barriers not mandatorily related to the above categories. To avoid language barriers, the interview protocol was translated into the respondent's language. Before the interview, the purpose of the study was introduced, and informed consent was obtained for recording and further use of the collected data. Afterward, respondents were asked to confirm the transcription accuracy.

[3] Available in full at https://doi.org/10.5281/zenodo.15291553.

3.2 Data Analysis

The thematic analysis of the collected data and interpretation of the responses was carried out according to [11, 31]. Interview transcripts were reviewed and coded accordingly by two researchers to whether each barrier was perceived relevant, partly relevant, or irrelevant in the interviews. Coding discrepancies were discussed and resolved through iterative consensus-building sessions involving the full research team. Each barrier was ranked from low to very high (low/moderate/high/very high). If the number of respondents who consider the barrier relevant or partly relevant for them is below or equal to 10%, we consider the relevance of the individual barrier to be *low*, between 11 and 20% - *moderate*, between 21 and 50% - *high*, and over 50% - *very high*. Based on this, we formulated propositions to the initial model, such as reformulating, merging, adding, and removing barriers and reached consensus among the authors team (seven researchers in total) and refined the model accordingly.

4 IRT4DS - IRT Model Tailored to OGD

4.1 Experience with OGD and Barriers to Sharing

The interviewees demonstrated diverse experiences with data sharing, driven by legal obligations, mission mandates, internal efficiency goals, or societal expectations. All respondents reported challenges related to technical issues, legislative ambiguity, limited understanding of available data, or the absence of a formal mandate. Staffing and infrastructure constraints further complicate publication. Despite these obstacles, there is a growing acknowledgment of the importance of OGD and expressed efforts to improve their practices. Frequent mentions of resistance to change and innovation (I5, I7, I11, I12, I14-I19, I21) during the interviews support the relevance of IRT for explaining their experiences. Below, we summarize the insights obtained in the interviews across the five IRT barrier types, focusing on 10 barriers considered relevant by the most interviewees, complemented with most relevant (individual) insights. Figure 1 shows the distribution of relevance ratings, and Table 3 provides the full set of refined barriers.

Usage Barriers. Twelve (12) out of 21 respondents noted difficulties preparing data in line with OGD principles (UB2), although, as per I2, "*the complexity does not mean that the government does not open the data.*" The process tends to be recognized as challenging due to limited experience (I2, I8), organizational size and expertise (i.e., lack of expertise within smaller organizations) (I3), shortages of human resources (I3, I16, I21), and the technical demands of certain data types, i.e., opening geospatial data can require programming and additional security and data protection measures such as masking and anonymization (I14, I18).

Process automation (UB7) was frequently mentioned as desired but rarely available on portals (I1, I9, I14, I16, I17, I18). To this end, some organizations developed internal scripts for semi-automation (I3, I5). Although automation is often perceived as a technical barrier, the lack of a dedicated system to manage open data processes was found as not merely a functional barrier, but rather a cultural and motivational barrier (I14). Furthermore, I6 noted that they do not fully automate the process -although they could- because publication would outpace the data validation process. Respondent I5 also mentioned the *lack of willingness (low sense of priority) to open data,* and the *difficulty of the data prioritization process*, especially when an organization deals with large volumes of data, different data providers from whom data can be obtained, or data providers collecting similar data with implied difficulty to select the most appropriate provider with whom to collaborate, highlighting the strategic nature of this barrier.

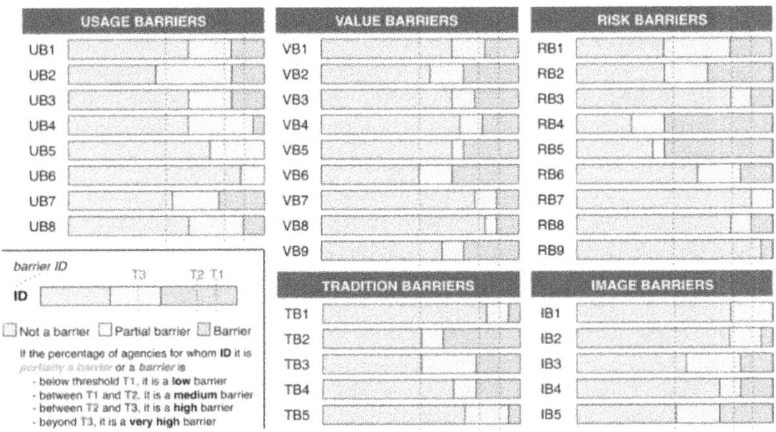

Fig. 1. Relevance assessment of the barriers by interviewees (for list of individual barriers, see Table 3).

Value Barriers. Eleven (11) respondents consider tasks associated with data preparation to be resource-consuming (VB6), with ten respondents, however, not considering this a major barrier that will prevent them from publishing data, rather mentioning delays in publication, manual processes, or legal obligations, manageable with the right means or expertise. Some respondents consider data preparation to be a major obstacle due to the substantial financial or staffing pressures (I4, I8, I10, I16, I17, I18). Over time these burdens were sometimes mitigated by process redesign (I13), accumulated experience, or better understanding of OGD's value.

Risk Barriers. Ten (10) respondents expressed concerns about data misuse (RB1), especially when data released in machine-readable formats could be exploited more easily than non-open formats - "*PDF is not dangerous, but an Excel table is*" (I5). This fear was particularly strong among agencies managing geospatial or national security-sensitive information, since, according to I7, "*you need a good map to win a war.*" I1, for whom this was a barrier at the beginning of data opening, explained that there was a lot of discussion about whether it is possible to open data about entrepreneurs, because there were fears that these data could be used for extortion.

Ten (10) respondents also fear misinterpretation (RB2), as some data "*could result in misconceptions, influencing erroneous political decisions or the creation of incorrect services*" (I14, I15, I18, I19). However, this rarely prevents data opening and is rather a risk publishers coexist with. I1 indicates that they do not experience the barrier because they "*accompany datasets with the well-developed documentation.*"

Data protection concerns (RB4) were among the most prominent issues - 13 out of 18 respondents who were able to comment on this are concerned about violating data protection legislation when sharing data. For some organizations "*this is the decisive factor to understand whether the data will be published" (I1) "because it entails unwanted responsibilities*" (I11, I12). For others, this does not prevent data publishing, but is a problem that they "*try to combat*" (I3, I14) by turning to relevant bodies (e.g., special committees) (I1-I4, I21) to discuss issues arising from unclear laws (I4, I6, I10), including "*lack of basic knowledge such as GDPR*" (I10) or lack of clarity regarding "*what anonymous data really are*" (I4). Some organizations do not find this a barrier, which they justify by the nature of the data, which do not contain personal data (I9, I18) or are provided in an anonymous or aggregated manner (I9).

Most respondents (11) reported fear of unintentionally exposing sensitive data (RB5), with the reasons largely overlapping with those associated with RB4. Organizations lacking advisory bodies or privacy expertise (including GDPR) were especially affected (I10), while those handling non-sensitive datasets reported minimal concern (I2).

Tradition Barriers. Responses vary regarding the reluctance of organizations to implement the cultural change required for openly sharing government data (TB2). While many organizations (15) express no strong reluctance, indicating an openness-driven approach or an established culture of publication to some extent (e.g., I2, I3, I4, I9), others highlighted limited time, training, and resources (I8, I10) or a lack of understanding of OGD's value (I16, I17). For half of respondents, skills shortages (TB3) were generally not perceived as outright barriers, although still seen as a certain challenge. More critical obstacles are attributed to (1) resource constraints (including human resources and the fear of losing skilled staff) (I1, I2) or (2) specific format requirements.

Overall, while some organizations embrace a culture of openness, many acknowledge the challenges of transitioning from traditional approaches to a more sharing-oriented culture, especially since most public sector organizations' system development traditions prioritize internal use ("*long tradition of developing in-house, and being self-contained*" (I14)), "*making it challenging to adapt these systems for broader information access and sharing*" (I13).

Image Barriers. Fear of published data being associated with incorrect conclusions drawn from OGD analysis by users with consequent damage to the reputation of an organization (IB5) was common and found severity, although it also does not become a decisive factor not to publish data. However, organizations dealing with more sensitive data or data on a topical issue concerning users (e.g., mobility or crisis-related data) tend to experience criticism (I3, I6). As such, I3 strongly agrees that associating with incorrect conclusions from OGD analysis could damage their reputation, citing examples of crises and increased interest to stay informed regarding their management (I15).

Countermeasures to the Barriers. The qualitative approach allowed participants to provide rich insights into why certain barriers were not experienced and which strategies they used to alleviate those that were. Based on these accounts, we identified 23 countermeasures that can help public agencies address the ten most widely experienced and severe barriers described in the previous section.

These countermeasures span *internal actions* (e.g., process redesign, improved data validation, enhanced documentation), *collaborative approaches* involving OGD portal providers or government bodies (e.g., publishing workflow support, infrastructure improvements, policy and compliance guidance), and *engagement with external expertise* (e.g., anonymization, quality auditing). The distribution of responsibilities highlights that overcoming OGD resistance is not the task of a single stakeholder but requires coordinated interventions across the open data ecosystem, where public agencies address internal process challenges, portal providers support publication through automation and usability improvements, government bodies shape the enabling environment through policy, legal clarity, funding, and capacity building, and external experts offer specialized capabilities that many agencies lack in-house. Figure 2 presents the identified countermeasures, mapping them to the main barriers within each category and to the stakeholder(s) responsible for implementing them.

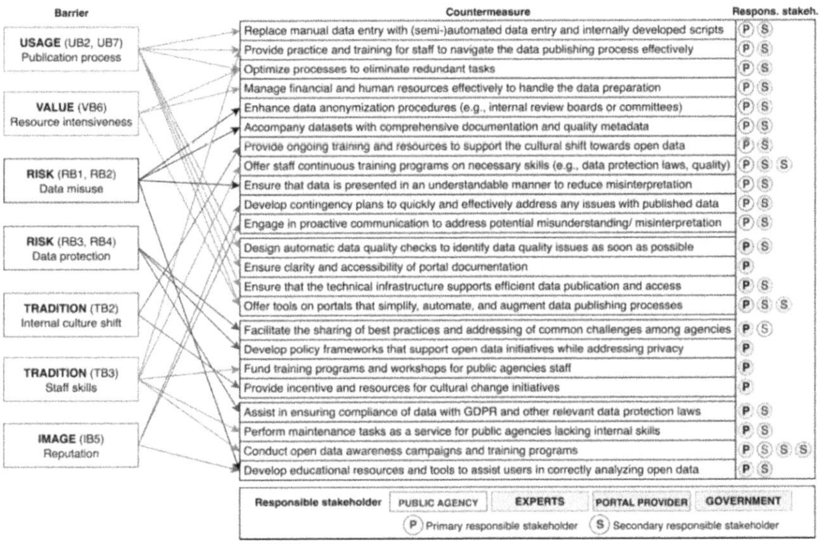

Fig. 2. Countermeasures mapped to the most severe barriers to OGD sharing.

4.2 Revised IRT Model Tailored to OGD

The assessment of construct relevance showed broad agreement on the overall structure of the proposed model, with most barriers, especially within the image, tradition, value, and risk categories, considered meaningful (Fig. 1). Nine barriers were viewed at least partly relevant by more than half of respondents.

Based on the relevance scores and subsequent author discussions, we refined the model to a final set of 39 items (Table 3). Several barriers were clarified to ensure clearer

Table 3. Final set of barriers in the IRT4DS model.

	Barrier
Usage	UB1: It is difficult to attain the appropriate quality level for data to be shared openly UB2: It is difficult to prepare data for publication so that they comply with OGD principles UB3: It is difficult to prepare data for publication so that they become appropriate for reuse UB4: Data are difficult to publish on the OGD portal due to the complexity of the process UB5: Data are difficult to publish on the OGD portal due to the unclear (poorly defined) process UB6: Data are difficult to publish on the OGD portal due to their limited functionality UB7: OGD portals often do not allow for semi-automation of the publishing process UB8: It is difficult to maintain openly shared government data (keep data and metadata made openly available on the OGD portal updated) ***UB9:*** *It is difficult to prepare, publish and/or maintain data due to lack of human resources* ***UB10:*** *It is difficult to prepare and publish data in required formats (i.e., those that differ from those stored in the organization, as well as in "advanced" formats, including GIS data or RDF)* ***UB11:*** *It is difficult to prioritize data for publication (i.e., understand what data to publish, prioritize data to be published first, as well as what data can or cannot be published)*
Value	VB1: My organization believes that openly sharing data is often not valuable for the public VB2: Open government datasets are not appropriate for reuse VB3: Many open government datasets suffer from data quality issues (completeness, accuracy, uniqueness, consistency etc.) VB4: The public gains of openly sharing government data are often lower than the costs VB5: Organizations' gains of openly sharing government data are often lower than the costs VB6: Data preparation is too resource-consuming for my organization VB7: Open government data do not provide any value to my organization *[VB8: Open data that my organization can openly share will not provide value to users – removed from the model, it is covered as part of IB2]* VB8: The amount of resources to be spent to prepare, publish and maintain open government data outweigh the benefit my organization gains from it

(*continued*)

Table 3. (*continued*)

	Barrier
Risk	RB1: My organization fears the misuse of openly shared government data RB2: My organization fears the misinterpretation of openly shared government data RB3: My organization fears that openly shared government data will not be reused RB4: My organization fears violating data protection legislation when openly sharing data RB5: My organization fears that sensitive data will be exposed as a result of opening its data RB6: My organization fears making mistakes when preparing data for publication RB7: My organization fears that users will find existing errors in the data RB8: My organization fears that openly sharing its data will reduce its gains (otherwise the organization could sell the data or use it in another beneficial way) RB9: My organization fears openly sharing data will allow its competitors to benefit from it
Tradition	TB1: Freedom of information requests are sufficient for the public to obtain government data TB2: My organization is reluctant to implement the culture change required for openly sharing government data TB3: Employees in my organization lack the skills required for openly sharing government data TB4: Employees in my organization lack the skills required for maintaining openly shared data TB5: My organization is reluctant to radically change the organizational processes that would enable openly sharing government data ***TB6***: *My organization is not actively sharing government data because data opening is not part of the culture from the very beginning*
Image	IB1: My organization has a negative image of open government data IB2: My organization believes that open government data is not valuable for users IB3: My organization fears that openly sharing government data will damage its reputation IB4: My organization fears that the accidental publication of low-quality data will damage its reputation IB5: My organization fears that associating it to incorrect conclusions drawn from OGD analysis by OGD users will damage its reputation

distinctions, particularly between initial data publication and ongoing maintenance (e.g., UB2, UB4–UB6, UB8, VB5, VB7, IB2). VB8 and IB2 were merged due to their overlap. Three additional usage barriers emerged from the interviews, namely (1) lack of human resources, (2) lack of resources to publish in the required formats, and (3) difficulty in prioritizing data (UB9–UB11). A new tradition-related barrier ("*data opening not being part of the organization's culture*") was added as TB6. Although some barriers appeared conceptually close (e.g., VB5 with VB7, UB4 with UB5), we retained them for analytical granularity, providing clearer definitions where needed. We also distinguished more explicitly between barriers affecting publication and those affecting post-publication maintenance. In cases of strong overlap, such as IB2 and VB8, we kept only the former. UB2 was retained despite initial suggestions to remove it, given divergent interpretations of OGD principles among respondents.

5 Discussion

This study introduces a novel theoretical model that shifts attention from factors supporting the *acceptance* of OGD [38, 51] to the *resistance* that prevents public agencies from sharing their data. By applying IRT, we offer a more nuanced understanding of the interplay between functional and psychological mechanisms that shape decisions about openness. In contrast to widely used adoption theories such as TAM or UTAUT, centred on positive determinants of intention, IRT enables the systematic identification of inhibiting factors that remain obscured in acceptance-oriented perspectives. This helps explain why OGD initiatives often stall despite supportive regulatory frameworks, infrastructures, and strategic commitments.

Our findings confirm several well-documented challenges, such as data protection concerns, fear of exposing sensitive information, and the complexity of preparing data for publication [19, 39, 49]. However, this study identifies multiple barriers that are underexplored or absent in prior OGD literature, thereby extending theoretical understanding of why public data remains closed. These include (a) **format-specific capability gaps**, where agencies struggle to convert data into advanced or mandated formats (e.g., GIS, RDF); (b) **capacity mismatch**, reflecting the absence of dedicated OGD-specific staffing rather than general resource scarcity, pointing to structural, not merely quantitative, constraints; (c) **historical-path-dependence barrier**, where openness conflicts with inherited organizational mandates and routines, extending traditional accounts of "*risk-averse culture*"; (d) **ongoing maintenance burden** distinct from initial publication; (e) **financial cannibalization risks** for agencies relying on revenue-generating data services; (f) **difficulty prioritizing datasets** with agencies often facing uncertainty not only of *whether* but also of *which* data to release first when capacity is limited. Together, these barriers illustrate how IRT uncovers deeper organizational, operational, and institutional dynamics that traditional adoption frameworks overlook.

As a practical contribution, validating the model across 21 agencies in six European countries enables governments, open data coordinators, and policymakers to diagnose resistance more precisely and design targeted interventions. The model can support readiness assessments for national and regional data initiatives, including those arising from the European Data Act and emerging cross-sectoral data spaces. Beyond national OGD programs, the model can inform analyses in business-to-government (B2G) data sharing [41] and support efforts to strengthen local data ecosystems, where many barriers -capacity, skills, culture- are even more pronounced [40].

Complementing the diagnostic model, we identify 23 countermeasures mapped to the strongest barriers and the stakeholders responsible for acting upon them. These include **process automation**, **metadata quality practices**, **targeted training**, **cultural change initiatives**, **data protection safeguards**, and **communication strategies**. Rather than general recommendations, this mapping provides a concrete, actor-specific blueprint for addressing resistance in real OGD ecosystems and highlights that many barriers demand coordinated multi-stakeholder action, not merely technical fixes.

5.1 Limitations and Future Work

This study has several limitations, most of which outline directions for future research. First, the qualitative approach, though essential for developing and refining the model, limits generalizability. However, qualitative methods are well suited for uncovering context-specific mechanisms of innovation resistance [5] and align with recommendations in IRT research, which suggests qualitative inquiry as a precursor to quantitative validation [16]. Future work should test the IRT4DS model quantitatively across a larger sample of public organizations. Second, IRT is often most powerful when applied to contexts where reluctance to adopt is pronounced [18]. Although we selected countries positioned as "*beginners*" or "*followers*" in the Open Data Maturity index, it remains possible that interviewees were relatively advanced OGD practitioners within their national contexts. This could mean that some barriers were under-reported. Expanding the sample to include less mature organizations or those explicitly struggling with OGD would help capture a fuller range of resistance mechanisms.

6 Conclusions

This study presents an IRT-based model for OGD -IRT4DS- to explain why public agencies resist sharing their data. Drawing on literature review and interviews with 21 public organizations across six European countries, we refine the model to 39 barriers organized across five IRT categories, providing a coherent and theoretically grounded view of OGD resistance. The results confirm established challenges but also reveal several new or underexamined barriers, e.g., format-specific capability gaps, absence of OGD-dedicated staff (capacity mismatch), historical path dependence, the ongoing maintenance burden of datasets, financial cannibalization concerns, and difficulties prioritizing data for publication. These insights extend OGD research by uncovering mechanisms of resistance rarely captured by technology acceptance–oriented models and demonstrate the value of IRT for studying organizational openness. Complementing the model, we identify 23 countermeasures mapped to responsible stakeholders, illustrating that overcoming OGD resistance requires coordinated technological, organizational, and cultural interventions. Together, the model and countermeasures provide actionable guidance for practitioners and strategic insights for policymakers seeking to strengthen open data ecosystems. Overall, the IRT4DS model advances scholarship by offering a structured explanation of why public data often remains closed and by highlighting critical levers for enabling sustainable, innovation-oriented OGD initiatives.

Acknowledgments. We want to thank all interviewees for sharing their insights providing empirical foundation for this study. DR thanks Lina Andersson, Li Sjölund, and Andreas Kalin Winkler whose original interview work provided the empirical foundation for parts of this study. PM thanks the Ministry of Science, Technological Development and Innovation of the Republic of Serbia for funding his scientific research work (contract no. 451-03-34/2026-03/200155, realized by the Faculty of Technical Sciences in Kosovska Mitrovica, University of Pristina).

Disclosure of Interests. The authors have no competing interests to declare that are relevant to the content of this article.

GenAI Use Disclosure. During the preparation of this work the authors used ChatGPT-4o in order to improve readability and language. After using this tool/service, the authors reviewed and edited the content as needed, and take full responsibility for the content of the publication.

References

1. Bannister, F.: Beyond the box: reflections on the need for more blue sky thinking in research. Gov. Inf. Q. **40**(3), 101831 (2023)
2. Barry, E., Bannister, F.: Barriers to open data release: a view from the top. Inf. Polity **19**(1–2), 129–152 (2014)
3. Beno, M., Figl, K., Umbrich, J., Polleres, A.: Perception of key barriers in using and publishing open data. JeDEM-eJournal eDemocracy Open Gov. **9**(2), 134–165 (2017)
4. Breaugh, J., Rackwitz, M., Hammerschmid, G.: Leadership and institutional design in collaborative government digitalisation: evidence from Belgium, Denmark, Estonia, Germany, and the UK. Gov. Inf. Q. **40**(2), 101788 (2023)
5. Bryman, A.: Social Research Methods. Oxford University Press, New York, USA (2016)
6. Chokki, A.P.: Open Government data: empowering reuse through collaboration, data quality, and data storytelling. Doctoral dissertation, University of Namur (2023)
7. Conradie, P., Choenni, S.: On the barriers for local government releasing open data. Gov. Inf. Q. **31**, S10–S17 (2014)
8. Crusoe, J., Simonofski, A., Clarinval, A., Gebka, E.: The impact of impediments on open government data use: insights from users. In: Proceedings 13th International Conference on Research Challenges in Information Science (RCIS), pp. 1–12. IEEE (2019)
9. de Souza, A.A.C., d'Angelo, M.J., Lima Filho, R.N.: Effects of predictors of citizens' attitudes and intention to use open government data and government 2.0. Gov. Inf. Q. **39**(2), 101663 (2022)
10. Dwivedi, Y.K., Balakrishnan, J., Das, R., Dutot, V.: Resistance to innovation: a dynamic capability model based enquiry into retailers' resistance to blockchain adaptation. J. Bus. Res. **157**, 113–632 (2023)
11. Eriksson, N., Gökhan, A., Stenius, M.: A qualitative study of consumer resistance to mobile payments for in-store purchases. Procedia Comput. Sci. **181**, 634–641 (2021)
12. Francey, A., Mettler, T.: Satisfaction with open government data portals: a user-centric configurational perspective. In: ICIS 2022 Proceedings, p. 2 (2022)
13. Garcia, L.V.: Civil servants on open data: perceptions of Azorean civil servants before an imminent open government data initiative. In: Proceedings of the 15th International Conference on Theory and Practice of Electronic Governance, Guimarães, Portugal, October 4 – 7, 2022, pp. 591–593. ACM (2022)
14. Haberer, B.: Implications of open government data for the digital economy. In: Proceedings of the 28th European Conference on Information Systems (ECIS), An Online AIS Conference, June 15–17, 2020 (2020)
15. Heider, F.: The Psychology of Interpersonal Relations (1958)
16. Huang, D., Jin, X., Coghlan, A.: Advances in consumer innovation resistance research: a review and research agenda. Technol. Forecast. Soc. Chang. **166**, 120594 (2021)
17. Janssen, M., et al.: Reflections on the nature of digital government research: marking the 50th anniversary of government information quarterly. Gov. Inf. Q. **42**(4), 102086 (2025)
18. Kaur, P., Dhir, A., Singh, N., Sahu, G., Almotairi, M.: An innovation resistance theory perspective on mobile payment solutions. J. Retail. Consum. Serv. **55**, 102059 (2020)

19. Kleiman, F., Meijer, S., Janssen, M.: Behavioral factors influencing the opening of government data by civil servants: initial findings from the literature. In: Proceedings of the 13th International Conference on Theory and Practice of Electronic Governance, pp. 529–534 (2020)
20. Kubler, S., Robert, J., Neumaier, S., Umbrich, J., Le Traon, Y.: Comparison of metadata quality in open data portals using the analytic hierarchy process. Gov. Inf. Q. **35**(1), 13–29 (2018)
21. Leong, L.Y., Hew, T.S., Ooi, K.B., Wei, J.: Predicting mobile wallet resistance: a two-staged structural equation modeling-artificial neural network approach. Int. J. Inf. Manage. **51**, 102047 (2020)
22. Lijphart, A.: Comparative politics and the comparative method. Am. Polit. Sci. Rev. **65**(3), 682–693 (1971)
23. Lnenicka, M., et al.: Identifying patterns and recommendations of and for sustainable open data initiatives: a benchmarking-driven analysis of open government data initiatives among European countries. Gov. Inf. Q. **41**(1), 101898 (2024)
24. Martin, S., Foulonneau, M., Turki, S., Ihadjadene, M.: Open data: barriers, risks and opportunities. In: Proceedings of the 13th European Conference on eGovernment: ECEG, Como, Italy, June 13–14, 2013, pp. 301–309. ACPI (2013)
25. Ma, L., Lee, C.S.: Understanding the barriers to the use of MOOCs in a developing country: an innovation resistance perspective. J. Educ. Comput. Res. **57**(3), 571–590 (2019)
26. Ma, R., Lam, P.T.: Investigating the barriers faced by stakeholders in open data development: a study on Hong Kong as a "smart city." Cities **92**, 36–46 (2019)
27. Mergel, I., Edelmann, N., Haug, N.: Defining digital transformation: results from expert interviews. Gov. Inf. Q. **36**(4), 101385 (2019)
28. Newcomb, T.M.: An approach to the study of communicative acts. Psychol. Rev. **60**(6), 393 (1953)
29. Nikiforova, A.: Timeliness of open data in open government data portals through pandemic-related data: a long data way from the publisher to the user. In: Proceedings of the 4th International Conference on Multimedia Computing, Networking and Applications (MCNA), Valencia, Spain, October 19–22, 2020, pp. 131–138. IEEE (2020)
30. Nikiforova, A., Zuiderwijk, A.: Barriers to openly sharing government data: towards an open data-adapted innovation resistance theory. In: Proceedings of the 15th International Conference on Theory and Practice of Electronic Governance, pp. 215–220 (2022)
31. Ose, S.O.: Using excel and word to structure qualitative data. J. Appl. Soc. Sci. **10**(2), 147–162 (2016)
32. Painter, M., Peters, B.G.: Administrative traditions in comparative perspective: families, groups and hybrids. In: Painter, M., Peters, B.G. (eds.) Tradition and Public Administration, pp. 19–30. Palgrave Macmillan, London (2010)
33. Palys, T.: Purposive sampling. Sage Encycl. Qual. Res. Methods **2**(1), 697–698 (2008)
34. Prakash, A.V., Das, S.: Explaining citizens' resistance to use digital contact tracing apps: a mixed-methods study. Int. J. Inf. Manage. **63**, 102468 (2022)
35. Ram, S.: A model of innovation resistance. Adv. Consum. Res. **14**(1) (1987)
36. Ram, S., Sheth, J.N.: Consumer resistance to innovations: the marketing problem and its solutions. J. Consum. Mark. **6**(2), 5–14 (1989)
37. Ruijer, E., Détienne, F., Baker, M., Groff, J., Meijer, A.J.: The politics of open government data: understanding organizational responses to pressure for more transparency. Am. Rev. Public Adm. **50**(3), 260–274 (2020)
38. Shao, D.: Empirical analysis of open government data usage in Tanzania. Inf. Discov. Deliv. **52**(1), 73–84 (2024)
39. Shepherd, E., et al.: Open government data: critical information management perspectives. Rec. Manag. J. **29**(1/2), 152–167 (2019)

40. Soosaar, K.R., Nikiforova, A.: Bridging the gap: unravelling local government data sharing barriers in Estonia and beyond. Comput. Law Secur. Rev. **56**, 106099 (2025)
41. Susha, I., Schiele, J., Frenken, K.: Business-to-government data sharing for public interests in the European union: results of a public consultation. In: Proceedings of the 15th IFIP WG 8.5 International Conference, EGOV 2016, Guimarães, Portugal, September 5–8, 2016, pp. 515–529. Springer, Cham (2022). https://doi.org/10.1007/978-3-031-15086-9_33
42. Toots, M., Mcbride, K., Kalvet, T., Krimmer, R.: Open data as enabler of public service co-creation: exploring the drivers and barriers. In: 2017 Conference for E-Democracy and Open Government (CeDEM), pp. 102–112. IEEE (2017)
43. Van Loenen, B., et al.: Towards value-creating and sustainable open data ecosystems: a comparative case study and a research agenda. JeDEM-eJournal eDemocracy Open Gov. **13**(2), 1–27 (2021)
44. Verma, A., Chakraborty, D., Verma, M.: Barriers of food delivery applications: a perspective from innovation resistance theory using mixed method. J. Retail. Consum. Serv. **73**, 103369 (2023)
45. Wirtz, B.W., Piehler, R., Thomas, M.J., Daiser, P.: Resistance of public personnel to open government: a cognitive theory view of implementation barriers towards open government data. Public Manag. Rev. **18**(9), 1335–1364 (2016)
46. Yiannakoulias, N., Slavik, C.E., Sturrock, S.L., Darlington, J.C.: Open government data, uncertainty and coronavirus: an infodemiological case study. Soc Sci Med **265**, 113549 (2020)
47. Yin, R.K.: Case Study Research and Applications. Sage (2018)
48. Zaltman, G., Wallendorf, M.: Consumer Behavior, Basic Findings and Management Implications. Wiley (1979)
49. Zhao, Y., Fan, B.: Effect of an agency's resources on the implementation of open government data. Inf. Manag. **58**(4), 103465 (2021)
50. Zhenbin, Y., Kankanhalli, A., Ha, S., Tayic, G.K.: What drives public agencies to participate in open government data initiatives? An innovation resource perspective. Inf. Manag. **57**(3), 103179 (2020)
51. Zuiderwijk, A., Janssen, M., Dwivedi, Y.K.: Acceptance and use predictors of open data technologies: drawing upon the unified theory of acceptance and use of technology. Gov. Inf. Q. **32**(4), 429–440 (2015)
52. Zuiderwijk, A., Janssen, M., Meijer, R., Choenni, S., Charalabidis, Y., Jeffery, K.: Issues and guiding principles for opening governmental judicial research data. In: 11th IFIP WG 8.5 International Conference, EGOV 2012, Kristiansand, Norway, September 3–6, 2012, pp. 90–101). Springer, Berlin Heidelberg (2012). https://doi.org/10.1007/978-3-642-33489-4_8
53. Talwar, S., Dhir, A., Kaur, P., Mäntymäki, M.: Barriers toward purchasing from online travel agencies. Int. J. Hosp. Manag. **89**, 102593 (2020)

Enabling Innovation Capability Through Collaborative Digital Innovation in the Public Sector

Katrin Jonsson(✉), Ulrika H. Westergren, and Alexandra G. Brauns

Department of Informatics, Umeå University, Umeå, Sweden
katrin.jonsson@umu.se

Abstract. This study investigates how collaborative digital innovation arrangements can enhance innovation capability in the public sector. While prior research has primarily emphasized realized value in terms of project outcomes, our findings reveal that innovation projects also create value during the collaboration process itself. We conceptualize these emergent benefits as innovation capabilities, the collaboration, learning, and experimentation that enable actors to participate in and conduct innovation more effectively. Through our study of 14 public sector collaborative IoT innovation projects in Sweden, five key catalysts for building innovation capability are identified: orchestrating collaboration and contextual expertise, leveraging complementary partner skills, capturing knowledge, temporal awareness, and contextualizing technology. Together, these strengthen participating actors' ability to sustain and develop innovation over time.

Keywords: Collaborative Projects · Digital Innovation · Public Sector · Internet of Things (IoT)

1 Introduction

Digital innovation in the public sector is rarely conducted in isolation; rather, it occurs in various collaborative settings involving multiple government agencies as well as actors from the private sector, such as in public–private partnerships [1], living labs [2], or public data ecosystems [3]. Research suggests that strategic investments in such collaborative projects, that bring together public authorities, private actors, and research institutions, can strengthen innovation capacity and help address the complexities and uncertainties associated with public sector digitalization [4]. Further research is however needed to better understand how public sector organizations develop the capabilities required for innovation [5]. Although prior studies have highlighted the importance of innovation capabilities in the public sector, there remains limited knowledge about how such capabilities emerge and can be built during collaborative innovation processes. This study contributes to addressing this gap by providing new insights into the processes through which organizations develop their innovation capabilities while participating in innovation projects aimed at contributing to societal good [6, 7].

Published by Springer Nature Switzerland 2027
G. Viale Pereira et al. (Eds.): EGOV 2026, LNCS 16933, pp. 397–413, 2027.
https://doi.org/10.1007/978-3-032-35747-2_25

While much of the existing research has focused on understanding the outcomes of innovation projects, such as value co-creation resulting in value-in-use [8] or collaborative innovation leading to public value creation [6], this study seeks to provide a deeper understanding of the mechanisms that underpin collaborative digital innovation and therefore adopts a process-oriented perspective rather than an outcome-oriented perspective. By exploring the following research question: "*How can collaborative digital innovation arrangements enable increased innovation capability in the public sector?*", we examine the collaboration, learning, and experimentation that enable actors to participate in and conduct innovation more effectively, thereby contributing to the discourse on digital government literature. More specifically, we investigated 14 Swedish collaborative innovation projects that aim to create societal value through the use of Internet of Things (IoT). Through a thematic analysis we identified five catalysts for building innovation capabilities within these collaborative innovation arrangements and while they were ongoing: orchestrating collaboration and contextual expertise, leveraging complementary partner skills, capturing knowledge, temporal awareness, and contextualizing technology. Together, these catalysts strengthen participating actors' ability to sustain and develop innovation over time.

2 Digital Innovation in the Public Sector

Digital government research shows that public sector innovation is increasingly collaborative and ecosystem-based, involving actors across the public, private, and civic sectors who jointly negotiate purposes, share resources, and co-produce outcomes [4]. Studies have found that public-private partnerships are popular but difficult to evaluate [9], co-creation with citizens can enhance legitimacy and creativity [10], platform ecosystems may decentralize innovation participation [11], and cross-sector networks can support system-wide innovation [12]. Despite its potential, collaborative innovation can also pose challenges, such as increased complexity due to multiple actors with conflicting interests [13] and power asymmetries influencing decision-making [14]. Additionally, collaborative initiatives often struggle to move beyond experimentation, revealing an implementation gap between the development of innovations and their actual use [15]. These challenges highlight the need to better understand how collaboration enables innovation in practice.

Emerging technologies have become a central and increasingly expected feature of public sector digital innovation [16]. Their adoption opens substantial opportunities for new ways of organizing, delivering, and transforming public services and governance [17]. One example is IoT, a term for everyday objects with embedded technology and connectivity that allows data exchange or remote control [18]. By generating detailed real-time data through sensors, IoT supports "smart" public services, enabling organizations to make more responsive decisions and allocate resources more effectively [18, 19].

The outcomes of public sector digital innovation can take many forms, including innovations in products and services, processes, organizational arrangements, and policies [20]. Innovations may be incremental or radical [21], and their scope can range from a single organization to multiple organizations and policy domains. Since public administration has traditionally been characterized by static, rule-bound processes emphasizing correctness over experimentation, a key challenge lies in balancing bureaucratic rigidity with the dynamic nature of collaborative innovation involving emerging technologies [5, 22]. Organizational inertia, limited agile practices, and inflexible routines can hinder digital initiatives and reduce the benefits of new technologies [22].

A unique feature of public sector innovation is its focus on addressing societal challenges and creating public value [23]. Emerging technologies can foster co-creation of public services and public value, leveraging their collaborative, social, and horizontal nature [24]. This applies to IoT, which relies on interconnected networks of sensors, digital platforms, and data analysis tools operating across organizational boundaries [16, 18]. To fund experimentation, public organizations often turn to external agencies, framing technological development within a collaborative innovation narrative to qualify for national innovation programs [19, 25]. Indeed, research shows that 60% of projects submitted to a U.S. national innovation award program involved interorganizational collaboration [26].

In this paper, we adopt the concept of collaborative innovation to describe how an organization promotes innovation by leveraging internal knowledge and resources while deliberately incorporating external ideas and partners [14, 27].

2.1 Innovation Capabilities

For digital innovation to be sustainable in the long-term, public sector organizations need to build a culture that is both collaborative and receptive to change [28]. It is thus crucial to develop innovation capabilities that make it easy to maintain an innovative culture and adopt digital technologies, and at the same time balance that with the traditional public sector landscape. In this paper, we draw on previous research [29–31] and use the term 'innovation capability' to denote an organization's ability to purposefully generate, integrate, and apply knowledge and resources to create and implement new ideas, products, services, or processes. The concept of innovation capability originates from the literature on dynamic capabilities [32] which explores how firms approach technological change and uncertain market conditions by developing sensing, seizing and transforming capabilities that allow them to continuously adapt, learn and evolve. In the same manner, digital innovation requires sensing, analytic-driven, digital platform, and orchestration capabilities to leverage digital technologies for competitive advantage [33]. Such capabilities are not static but can evolve and change over time. Mendoza-Silva [30] lists three innovation capability determinants with a range of dimensions: managerial (management style & leadership and corporate strategy), intraorganizational (resources, work climate, ideation and organizational structure, technology, know-how development, and individual activity), and interorganizational (external relations and network characteristics) and posits that further research regarding the relationship between the different dimensions is needed to understand how they impact a firm's capacity to innovate.

While much of the literature on innovation capabilities originates in the private sector, the concept has increasingly been adapted to the public sector, where innovation is often motivated by the pursuit of public value [5–7, 34, 35]. Gullmark [5] finds that public sector innovation depends on both managerial and organizational dynamic capabilities. When innovation is driven by individual leadership and entrepreneurial skills (dynamic managerial capabilities), it tends to be less routinized. In contrast, when it is embedded in organizational structures, processes, and routines (dynamic organizational capabilities), innovation becomes more systematic and routinized. Additionally, Joukhadar et al. [36] show that public sector organizations must address both core rigidities and innovation capabilities in response to the disruptive changes caused by digital innovation. Although these recent insights shed some light on different forms of innovation capability and how public sector organizations strive to continuously develop and implement innovations together with others [37], additional explorations into how collaborative digital innovation projects within the public sector develop the capabilities that make them innovative are needed.

3 Method

This study examines projects conducted within a Swedish national strategic innovation program running between 2014–2023. The program was selected because it provided a structured setting and similar conditions among different projects for the study. The program explicitly aimed to strengthen Sweden's international competitiveness by funding collaborative innovation projects designed to identify solutions to global societal challenges using IoT as the enabling technology. In addition, funded projects needed to demonstrate a clear objective related to the development of new (or prototypes of new) services, products, and/or processes for the public sector using IoT. Projects were also expected to contribute to broader public value objectives, including increased quality, sustainability, and efficiency for residents in Sweden, while emphasizing knowledge sharing and dissemination across participating actors. The program was particularly relevant for this study because funded projects were required to involve collaboration among actors from the public sector, industry, and/or academia, thereby offering empirically rich cases of cross-sector digital innovation. Rather than evaluating the success of individual projects, the study focuses on how participants described their collaboration processes and how capability-building dynamics were emerging during project work.

3.1 Data Collection

Data was collected through semi-structured interviews with stakeholders from selected projects participating in the strategic innovation program. A purposive sampling strategy was used to capture variation in scope, size, geographic location and application area, while maintaining similar conditions through the shared program context. The aim was to include projects involving a diverse constellation of actors across public, private and research organizations. This resulted in the selection of 14 projects, out of a total 53 funded projects. Respondents were identified through project documentation, with the aim of including representatives from municipalities, regions, private organizations, and research institutions. In total, we interviewed 26 respondents (see Table 1).

Data collection was conducted in two phases. The first phase consisted of semi-structured online interviews with primarily public sector actors from the selected projects. Each interview lasted approximately 45–60 min and followed an interview guide focusing on the participants' experiences of the collaboration process, perceived project outcomes, value creation, and potential barriers related to the innovation work.

The second phase consisted of follow-up interviews with participants from six of the 14 projects selected for further exploration based on their ability to provide richer insights into collaborative digital innovation. In this phase, additional interviews were conducted with both public and private sector project partners. A revised interview guide was used to allow for more in-depth conversations regarding collaboration processes, perceived value of the project format, investment considerations, and experiences related to the IoT solutions developed within the projects. In addition to the interview material, project plans and selected project documentation were reviewed to provide understanding of the projects and support the interpretation of interview data.

Table 1. Projects and respondents, PU = public sector, PR = private sector.

Projects	Respondents
Project A: IoT-Infrastructure	R1PU: Project leader; R2PU: Project leader from energy company; R3PR: IoT expert
Project B: School and education	R4PU: Project leader; R5PR: Innovation manager; R6PR: Project member
Project C: Climate and environment	R7PU: Project leader
Project D: Infrastructure	R8PU: Project member
Project E: Healthcare and welfare	R9PU: Project member
Project F: Healthcare and welfare	R10PU: Project leader; R11PU: Unit manager
Project G: Healthcare and welfare	R12PU: Project leader; R13PU: Project leader and researcher; R14PR: Platform-provider
Project H: Healthcare and welfare	R15PU: Project leader
Project I: Healthcare and welfare	R16PU: Project member
Project J: Infrastructure	R17PU: CEO IT Cluster and Digital Innovation Hub
Project K: School and education	R18PU: Researcher; R19PU: Researcher
Project L: Climate and environment	R20PU: Project leader; R21PU: Project leader; R22PU: Project leader and researcher; R23PU: Technical and scaling responsibility
Project M: Climate and environment	R24PU: Team leader
Project N: Climate and environment	R25PU: Project member; R26PU: Project leader from energy company

3.2 Data Analysis

The collected data material was analyzed using an inductive thematical analysis approach [38]. All interviews were first transcribed and then carefully read through to support familiarization with the material. In the first stage of the analysis, first-order codes were developed through open coding, where segments related to collaboration experiences, learning processes, perceived value creation, and organizational challenges were identified and annotated [39]. In the second stage, the authors iteratively compared and discussed emerging codes, patterns and interpretations across the empirical material. Related first order codes were grouped into broader themes capturing recurring mechanisms and conditions associated with innovation capability-building in collaborative digital innovation processes. Through this process, five themes, conceptualized as catalysts for innovation capability-building, were identified and refined: 1) Orchestrating collaboration and contextual expertise, 2) Leveraging complementary partner skills, 3) Capturing knowledge, 4) Temporal awareness, and 5) Contextualizing technology. In the final stage, the themes were further refined through ongoing comparison between empirical material and related literature and developed into a coherent analytical narrative supported by relevant quotes from the interviews.

4 Results

The analysis identified five recurring catalysts for innovation capability-building, understood as conditions perceived by participants as supporting collaborative digital innovation processes in the studied projects.

4.1 Orchestrating Collaboration and Contextual Expertise

The first identified innovation capability catalyst centers on the role of the national innovation program and their associated program office in enabling and facilitating innovation and developing innovation capabilities. Besides allocating funds to the different projects, the innovation program actively orchestrated the network of funded IoT projects, with their program office acting as an overarching project coordinator. R17PU from project J stated:

> *"For us [the program office] has been absolutely crucial. It has been incredibly important, both financially, as it allowed us to drive projects, but also in terms of networking and connecting our regional innovation environment to a national level."*

The quote above shows how the innovation program aimed to be more than just a financial support mechanism, routing funds to receivers. Through its program office it provided access to technology-, innovation- and contextual expertise and served as a trigger for wider regional integration and collaboration. This helped smaller projects stay updated with emerging technologies and enabled local authorities to engage in innovation they might not have been able to pursue otherwise. R17PU further explains:

> *"[...] it's also been really valuable to discuss ideas with those who have been involved...especially in terms of market monitoring. They [the program office] have been instrumental in helping us stay informed about new projects, technologies, and current challenges that we don't have the resources to track ourselves."*

In addition, innovation projects in the public sector must handle the numerous requirements and rules that come from bureaucracy and public procurement, which was something that several respondents considered a major challenge. Besides turning to the program office for advice and mentorship, several projects formed strategic partnerships outside of their immediate project constellation to handle this particular challenge. Thus, by partnering with contextual experts such as lawyers and public procurement experts, some projects claimed to avoid the pitfalls of public sector politics and instead were able to focus on their innovation objectives.

> *"[...] that is also something we have learned in all these projects, that you should have lawyers with you from the beginning." (Project B, R6PR)*

4.2 Leveraging Complementary Partner Skills

It was emphasized, in most interviews, how municipalities, research institutions, and private sector actors had strengthened their innovation capabilities by coming together and collaborating to create innovative digital solutions. This collaborative culture facilitated overcoming challenges, sharing knowledge, and further contributing to the development of new technologies and solutions. R17PU who was involved in Project J claimed that the blend of *"[...] municipal squares, fluffy researchers, and driven entrepreneurs"* - government, academia, and private industry - has been a "*good mix*" for the success of an environment of cross-sectoral collaboration. This indicates that cooperation between diverse stakeholders was seen as an important influence on innovation capability, while at the same time appearing as something practical and further scalable. Project B's respondent R4PU claimed that the mix of competencies, such as tech, healthcare, universities, and education was proven to be very beneficial as well, stating that ideas for certain organizational solutions emerged from the tech industry and would never have been considered if it weren't for this cross-sector collaboration. R23PU from Project F praised the equality mindset that was present within their project group:

> *"Everyone got to talk and we were able to challenge ourselves in this way that it doesn't matter if you're technically super-skilled or operationally super-skilled or not good at anything, you listen anyway and it became a good dialogue, so cross-functionality is key. And we became a tight-knit group because of that, and it turned out well, plus the agile way of working."*

R12PU from Project G, operating in the health care area, expressed that having an academic partner in the process and their support with needs assessments and provision of expert knowledge in the technical and application area was invaluable. This shows that collaborating with research institutions and experts can be vital, especially if the participants' core competencies lie elsewhere. However, academic experts may have a different language than the rest of the group and R25PU from Project N claimed that this was the biggest obstacle for their project's collaboration, although it seems to have been a learning experience:

> *"The researchers who were involved from the beginning had a really hard time communicating when not speaking in hexadecimal terms. There were huge contrasts between our field personnel and getting a collaboration where we could communicate understandably with each other—it was really complicated [...]*

Like, I'm not a data expert and don't understand all the data conversion stuff, or how to program—that's not my thing. However, we need to be able to explain to each other what's important for you and what's important for me, so that we can achieve a good result together. That was a tough challenge, and we carry that experience with us."

Project L seemed to have had similar challenges in the beginning of getting all parties to *"speak the same language."* However, it was stated that this was overcome through their structured, agile, and cross-functional working methods. Not only did it foster partnership, but they were also able to overcome obstacles effectively and the respondent stated that this was crucial for the project's overall success. Further, by connecting this project to their neighboring municipalities in a jointly owned company, the innovation project was not only possible but also extended and developed. R20PU stated:

"So, together with other municipalities—our neighboring municipalities—we have a jointly owned company that handles finance, payroll, and IT. And then we knocked on the door of X, and started a discussion: 'Here we have something—couldn't we build this here on X so that more municipalities could benefit from the same capabilities and platforms?' And that's how it happened, and then we received some extra funding to make it happen. [...] The goal was to find a long-term solution so that we could manage this and continue developing it if the project turned out to be successful."

This strategic decision portrays how networking and collaborating strengthened innovation initiatives. In this case, it created not only knowledge sharing but also operational efficiency and is a good example of the value of regional and municipal partnerships. It also demonstrates that strong cooperative networking efforts can aid financial support and innovation scaling.

R4PU claimed that one of the biggest outcomes of the project was the creation of lasting relationships between the project actors and discussed how it already had created new collaborative opportunities among them:

"For starters, it meant that we developed a habit of collaborating in projects and thinking beyond our own boundaries. And now, we have actually just received approval for a new project where the partners are [municipality], us, and other municipalities, [region], [university], and [private organization]. I don't think this would have happened if we hadn't gained experience from this project. Because now we have these points of contact, we know the people, we know where to turn, and we know who we can trust and who we can't."

4.3 Capturing Knowledge

Several respondents claimed that while the initial focus was to develop and implement applicable solutions, the most valued outcome turned out to be the enhancement of, and ability to capture new knowledge. R8PU from Project D stated that the knowledge-increase from their project was very beneficial to participating individuals by strengthening roles and competencies. In a similar vein R4PU from Project B stated that:

> *"[...] innovation in itself as a phenomenon is a knowledge value that has been created. [...] I thought it would be a more targeted technical project, more IoT, but the knowledge formation that was around everything was beyond expectations from my perspective."*

Furthermore, knowledge capture was pursued both within and outside of the participating organizations through presentations and information-sharing events, such as the funding agency's own events. Knowledge capture was, within this investment, extended to other stakeholders and interested parties as well. R5PR from project B shared:

> *"My main responsibility, I believe, is to constantly talk about previous projects we have been involved in—to never forget them or put them away in a drawer but to always bring them along, compare them, or even reach out in some cases if there are certain stakeholders where we need to investigate something. It's about discussing how we thought and what we did. One tends to forget over time."*

Another statement underscores knowledge capture as a structured process where the organization first developed a digital solution and secondly established a way of preserving that knowledge within the department. R25PU from project N stated:

> *"We have made manuals for what we have created. And these will form a major foundation, and then the training is planned to include training days for those who are intended to be the technicians for this, who will inherit the knowledge. Once they've become comfortable with it, they will be the ones to drive this forward."*

These cases manifest that systematic documentation works as a method of preventing knowledge from falling through and instead using it as an organizational advantage which future innovation projects can build upon.

4.4 Temporal Awareness

The fourth innovation capability catalyst highlights developing the ability to navigate the reality of operating within time constrained short-term innovation projects in slow-moving organizations that want to create long-term impact. That is, while initial financial support normally concerned a shorter pilot project with set parameters, there was no guarantee that additional funding would be obtained or that project results would be further implemented in the organizations, regardless of the whether the pilot was deemed successful or not. R18PU from Project K expressed:

> *"You initiate processes, and the [public organization] is a large and a rather slow-moving organization. This slowness means that persistence is required to achieve significant long-term value. In a project like this, you start to see benefits, and just as things begin to gain momentum, the funding is cut because the project's period ends. It simply takes a long time to make real progress, and I see that as a major problem."*

Furthermore, time constraints were a hindrance to collaboration efforts. R17PU from Project J stated:

"It's a bit harsh with two-year projects—they are a bit too short for the project itself to build much collaboration. Instead, it's more the project environment that fosters collaboration. Looking at [organization], we have fantastic collaboration platform nationally and are also starting to establish them at the European level, partly through this type of project."

This quote demonstrates the importance of fostering a broader collaborative environment to help sustain long-term collaborative efforts, instead of only focusing on short-term individual project collaboration which can be difficult regarding time constraints.

It can be inferred that some projects dealt with time constraint more than others and in different ways, specifically relating to R4PU from Project B, who emphasized that implementing sensors was one thing, but to collect and analyze the data from the sensors took time and time which they didn't have in the end. This highlights a challenge with value capturing regarding short-term projects. R4PU stated:

"We didn't have time to collect data because the project ended. Then we received equipment from a company to set up for measuring different movements, but we didn't have time for that either since it couldn't be installed before the project ended. And that was because the first year just disappeared. But we really wanted to continue, we had such a clear plan. But yeah, I just realized I suddenly got a bit bitter now."

4.5 Contextualizing Technology

The use and the integration of IoT seems to have led to unexpected outcomes for many projects, for example Project N's platform could be used as a proactive problem-solver and with a bigger scope than they originally thought when they were creating the solution. R25PU stated:

"Our environmental unit realized we had more groundwater meters than X, which could be used to dimension individual sewage systems—an unexpected benefit. Similarly, when building flood barriers around our low-lying city, we used groundwater meters to monitor water levels. This was an unforeseen development that turned out to be very positive, benefiting multiple departments."

Another aspect that Project N aimed to facilitate was opening up the platform for public use to access environmental data, which was not only a technological upgrade but also displayed transparency and public inclusion.

Respondent R9PU from Project E highlighted that while their project was developed and implemented successfully, obstacles about getting the intended users to use the solution arose. R9PU stated:

"A challenge that will remain regardless of the technology is user handling - getting the end users, those who are supposed to utilize the system, to actually do

so. That is also one of the reasons we are somewhat cautious. If we make a large investment and it is not fully utilized, we won't achieve the benefits we aim for. It is an important lesson to understand how users would actually adopt and make use of the system."

This stresses the importance of ensuring the use context within digital innovation projects, it requires more than just technology upgrades, it must also embrace user engagement and long-term support.

Challenges of this kind are prominent in other projects as well. R14PR from Project G, delivering platforms, underscored the need to align their digital solutions with operational changes to ensure effectiveness for the intended users:

"Digitalization is great, but without implementing a new way of working and supporting an organization in changing its processes, it won't be effective. As a provider, when we take on these projects, we must set clear requirements for how they should operate. Otherwise, it wouldn't make much sense for us to engage, as our business model rewards us based on the number of patients. If they fail to attract many patients or users, our revenue decreases."

Challenges with technical integration were also brought up and especially one project had troubles with that already from the start. R24PU stating:

"Implementing new technologies, even those already available on the market, can be extremely challenging. This project has faced significant challenges in determining whether we achieve the desired results, if we can trust the product enough, and when to decide on scaling up or terminating the project."

These innovation projects were foremost about experimenting with IoT. However, a great amount of money was invested in the innovation process. A solid lesson from the projects was that the ability to contextualize digital innovation and situate the digital solutions within real use situations was a major benefit from this type of collaborative arrangements and thus an important catalyst for building innovation capability.

5 Discussion

This study set out to answer the research question: *How can collaborative digital innovation arrangements enable increased innovation capability in the public sector?* The analysis identified five recurring catalysts for innovation building in collaborative digital innovation projects. In this section, we discuss these findings in relation to research on collaborative innovation and innovation capability in the public sector.

5.1 Increased Innovation Capability in the Public Sector

Creating public value through collaborative innovation is a complex endeavor, and many initiatives fail to realize the innovativeness they set out to achieve [37]. By adopting a process-oriented perspective rather than an outcome-oriented perspective this study identified and explored catalysts for building innovation capability within a collaborative context, pointing to the importance of stakeholder complementarity and contextual awareness. By orchestrating collaboration and providing access to contextual expertise the national innovation program boosted the ability of individual organizations to undertake and manage innovation projects, for example by suggesting potential partners, providing access to expert advice, and helping to address regulatory challenges specific to the public sector context. Acting as an interorganizational orchestrator [30] it tackled funding, mentorship, expertise, knowledge transfer, and network access so that actors who might lack internal capacity could engage in innovation projects.

The cross-sectoral nature of the projects, where public actors collaborated with academia, private companies, and research institutions, thereby *leveraging complementary partner skills,* was described by many respondents as key to their success. This reflects Osborne et al. [28], who argue that public value is most effectively created through ecosystem-based collaboration, where diverse actors contribute distinct but interdependent resources and capabilities. In this sense, collaborative arrangements can act as arenas for learning and capability development, where participants gain access to new competencies and perspectives that would be difficult to develop in isolation. However, as Torfing et al. [13] show, the involvement of multiple actors can also lead to increased complexity and conflicting interests. In our study, we observed how differing institutional logics resulted in misaligned goals, while communication barriers also arose between actors with different professional backgrounds. These findings illustrate that collaborative settings require significant coordination efforts and the development of joint understanding, including a shared vocabulary and mutual trust to function effectively.

Beyond technical insights, the projects generated knowledge relevant at both individual and organizational levels, and as input for policy and decision-making. In this regard, *capturing knowledge,* understood as the ability to recognize, articulate, and retain the diverse forms of knowledge and learning generated through innovation activities and transform them into capability for innovation, emerged as an important catalyst. This finding resonates with research on dynamic capabilities, which emphasizes sensing, seizing, and reconfiguring knowledge resources to sustain innovation [40]. Participants described the outcomes of the projects as learning across multiple dimensions such as collaboration, cross-functional work, experimentation, and a deeper understanding of innovation as a phenomenon. This broader take on value emphasizes how innovation projects can create knowledge that persists beyond the project's timeframe and contributes to strengthening the organization's overall innovation capability.

The projects that, over time, developed temporal awareness and agility in managing the pace and sequencing of their innovation processes were more satisfied with their overall project outcome and more likely to ensure that resulting products, services or changed processes were implemented beyond the duration of the project. This finding points to the importance of *temporal awareness* which resonates with the ability to adapt, reconfigure, and align activities in response to changing activities [40]. In this study, temporal awareness can be understood as balancing short-term project demands with longer-term objectives related to learning and sustained innovation.

Finally, the process of situating technological development and innovation in real user- and environmental settings emerged as a key catalyst for building innovation capability. Through substantial efforts to *contextualize technology* by engaging early with end-users and focusing explicitly on contextual needs, participants described how they gained insights not only into the technology's functionality but also its potential applications across different domains. This aligns with research on co-creative approaches in public sector innovation, which emphasizes that involving users in real-world contexts enhances both the relevance and legitimacy of innovations [10] Testing IoT technologies in real public environments rather than in laboratories revealed practical and contextual limitations that would not have emerged otherwise, highlighting the importance of experimentation under authentic conditions. At the same time, these contextualized experiments generated insights for alternative applications in other domains, demonstrating how contextualizing technology serves as a crucial catalyst for building innovation capability, fostering both practical learning and adaptive understanding of how technologies perform across contexts.

5.2 Collaborative Digital Innovation Projects in the Public Sector

Collaborative digital innovation in the public sector is primarily driven by societal needs and collective goals, with a focus on public value and legitimacy [14], rather than on profit or market positioning. However, private organizations participating in public collaborative innovation projects may still pursue profit-oriented objectives, seeking value creation through the commercialization of their solutions. For the projects to succeed, it is therefore crucial to identify the diverse motivations of participating actors, as this forms the foundation for effectively leveraging partner skills. In line with Klassen et al. [41], who emphasize the importance of long-term strategic thinking in innovation processes, this study demonstrates that the collaborative digital innovation projects laid the groundwork for future partnerships and innovation initiatives. The resulting effects can be understood as a form of long-term value, where the initial investment continues to generate benefits over time through captured knowledge. Moreover, we observed an increase in self-confidence among public sector actors, who reported a strengthened belief in their own capacity to drive digital innovation.

Many of the projects demonstrated that even limited initiatives can have a long-lasting impact when knowledge is systematically documented and shared. Manuals, training programs, and follow-up projects all served as examples of how knowledge was captured and preserved for future use. In some cases, the projects even inspired other municipalities, which, in turn, can generate an innovative "snowball effect" in knowledge transfer and the adoption of new ideas. These cases highlight that innovation capability in collaborative digital innovation is not only created for the benefit of individual organizations but also contributes to the wider public service ecosystem [28].

While the projects had predefined time limits, many respondents envisioned outcomes extending into the future, which sometimes led to frustration when the projects concluded. If organizations are unable to navigate these temporal constraints, there is a risk of a "sparkler effect," meaning that the project simply ends without creating a basis for continuation. This underscores the importance of long-term strategies to facilitate scaling. The sparkler effect represents a potential risk and reflects a broader challenge associated with this type of innovation funding, where conducting innovation projects can become an end in itself, potentially prioritizing the activity of running projects over the actual outcomes. On the other hand, without such an innovation program, many public sector organizations would never be able to pursue innovation projects due to a lack of resources. Moreover, public sector organizations may require external motivation to innovate and be encouraged to address the challenge of running short-term innovation projects within slow-moving organizations, where procedures and decision-making processes often take considerable time.

The collaborative nature of these projects provided significant opportunities for digital innovation and knowledge creation and exchange, but it also revealed multiple layers of complexity. Managing these complexities requires strategic planning, shared understanding, and long-term organizational commitment. The findings suggest that developing catalysts for innovation capability is central to digital innovation in the public sector, and that it is not simply about upgrading or investing in technology, but foremost about people, processes, and partnerships working together to create lasting value [22].

6 Conclusions

This study explored how collaborative digital innovation arrangements can enhance innovation capability in the public sector. While existing literature on collaborative digital innovation often emphasizes realized value in terms of project outcomes, our findings suggest that collaborative innovation processes may also generate capability-building effects during the collaboration process itself.

The analysis identified five recurring catalysts perceived by participants as supporting innovation capability-building in the studied projects: orchestrating collaboration and conceptual expertise, leveraging complementary partner skills, capturing knowledge, temporal awareness, and contextualizing technology. Together, these findings suggest that collaborative digital innovation arrangements may contribute not only to the development of new services, products, or processes, but also strengthened collaborative and organizational capacities for future innovation work. This suggests that actors engaged in public sector digital innovation must strike a balance between maintaining the tangible results of innovation and sustaining the capabilities developed through the collaborative innovation process itself.

The study contributes to research on collaborative digital innovation by highlighting how capability-building may emerge through ongoing collaboration, learning, and experimentation during innovation processes. At the same time, the findings should be interpreted in relation to the empirical context, as the analysis is based on interview data from IoT-related projects within a single Swedish national innovation program. The study is also limited to the participants' experiences and perceptions of collaborative innovation processes in the studied projects.

Future research could benefit from longitudinal studies that follow individual projects over time to better understand if and how innovation capabilities evolve. Such studies could examine how the knowledge generated during projects is captured, institutionalized, and leveraged for future innovation, particularly once external funding ends. It would also be highly informative to explore initiatives initiated and fully funded by public organizations, to assess how digital innovation in the public sector can occur without external facilitators.

Disclosure of Interests. The authors have no competing interests to declare that are relevant to the content of this article.

References

1. Liu, L.X., Clegg, S., Pollack, J.: The effect of public–private partnerships on innovation in infrastructure delivery. Proj. Manag. J. **55**(1), 31–49 (2024)
2. Gascó, M.: Living labs: implementing open innovation in the public sector. Gov. Inf. Q. **34**(1), 90–98 (2017)
3. Nikiforova, A., Lnenicka, M., Luterek, M., Milic, P., Rodríguez, M.P.B.: Theorizing the evolution of public data ecosystems: an empirically grounded multi-generational model and future research agenda. Gov. Inf. Q. **42**(3) (2025)
4. Barrutia, J.M., Echebarria, C.: Drivers of exploitative and explorative innovation in a collaborative public-sector context. Public Manag. Rev. **21**(3), 446–472 (2019)
5. Gullmark, P.: Do all roads lead to innovativeness? A study of public sector organizations' innovation capabilities. Am. Rev. Public Adm. **51**(7), 509–525 (2021)
6. Crosby, B.C., 't Hart, P., Torfing, J.: Public value creation through collaborative innovation. Public Manag. Rev. **19**(5), 655–669 (2017)
7. Pardo, T.A., Gil-Garcia, J.R., Gascó-Hernández, M., Cook, M.E., Choi, I.: Creating public value in cities: a call for focus on context and capability. In: Smart Cities and Smart Governance: Towards the 22nd Century Sustainable City, pp. 119–139. Springer, Cham (2021). https://doi.org/10.1007/978-3-030-61033-3_6
8. Scutella, M., Plewa, C., Reaiche, C.: Virtual agents in the public service: examining citizens' value-in-use. Public Manag. Rev. **26**(1), 73–88 (2024)
9. Hodge, G.A., Greve, C.: On public–private partnership performance: a contemporary review. Public Works Manag. Policy **22**(1), 55–78 (2017)
10. Khan, A., Krishnan, S.: Citizen engagement in co-creation of e-government services: a process theory view from a meta-synthesis approach. Internet Res. **31**(4), 1318–1375 (2021)
11. Gong, Y., Li, X.: Designing boundary resources in digital government platforms for collaborative service innovation. Gov. Inf. Q. **40**(1) (2023)
12. Zhang, S., Yang, Y., Gan, H.: Can cross-sector collaboration contribute to boundaries reshaping of digital government platforms? Empirical evidence based on machine learning and text analysis. Public Adm. **103**(3), 756–772 (2025)
13. Torfing, J., Sørensen, E., Røiseland, A.: Transforming the public sector into an arena for co-creation: barriers, drivers, benefits, and ways forward. Adm. Soc. **51**(5), 795–825 (2019)
14. Sørensen, E., Torfing, J.: Enhancing collaborative innovation in the public sector. Adm. Soc. **43**(8), 842–868 (2011)
15. Kurtmollaiev, S., Pedersen, P.E., Lie, T.: A bird in the hand: empirically grounded archetypes of collaborative innovation in the public sector. Public Manag. Rev. **26**(5), 1266–1298 (2024)
16. Hong, S., Kim, S.H., Kwon, M.: Determinants of digital innovation in the public sector. Gov. Inf. Q. **39** (2022)
17. Gil-Garcia, J.R., Helbig, N., Ojo, A.: Being smart: emerging technologies and innovation in the public sector. Gov. Inf. Q. **31**, 11–18 (2014)

18. Velsberg, O., Westergren, U.H., Jonsson, K.: Exploring smartness in public sector innovation – creating smart services with the internet of things. Eur. J. Inf. Syst. **29**(4), 350–368 (2020)
19. Velsberg, O., Jonsson, K., Westergren, U.H.: IoT triggers: how municipalities are transforming to smarter cities through IoT use. Scand. J. Inf. Syst. **33**(1), 17–64 (2021)
20. Hartley, J.: Innovation in governance and public services: past and present. Public Money Manag. **25**(1), 27–34 (2005)
21. Roberts, N.C., Bradley, R.T.: Stakeholder collaboration and innovation: a study of public policy initiation at the state level. J. Appl. Behav. Sci. **27**(2), 209–227 (1991)
22. De Vries, H., Bekkers, V., Tummers, L.: Innovation in the public sector: a systematic review and future research agenda. Public Adm. **94**(1), 146–166 (2015)
23. Bekkers, V., Edelenbos, J., Steijn, B.: Linking innovation to the public sector: contexts, concepts and challenges. In: Innovation in the Public Sector: Linking Capacity and Leadership, pp. 3–32. Palgrave Macmillan, London (2011)
24. Criado, J.I., Gil-Garcia, J.R.: Creating public value through smart technologies and strategies: from digital services to artificial intelligence and beyond. Int. J. Public Sect. Manag. **32**(5), 438–450 (2019)
25. Newman, J., Raine, J., Skelcher, C.: Transforming local government: Innovation and modernization. Public Money Manag. **21**(2), 61–68 (2001)
26. Borins, S.: Encouraging innovation in the public sector. J. Intellect. Cap. **2**(3), 310–319 (2001)
27. Vivona, R., Demircioglu, M.A., Audretsch, D.B.: The costs of collaborative innovation. J. Technol. Transf. **48**, 873–899 (2022)
28. Osborne, S.P., Radnor, Z., Kinder, T., Vidal, I.: Value creation in the public service ecosystem: an integrative framework. Public Adm. Rev. **82**(2), 202–213 (2022)
29. Lawson, B., Samson, D.: Developing innovation capability in organisations: a dynamic capabilities approach. Int. J. Innov. Manag. **5**(3), 377–400 (2001)
30. Mendoza-Silva, A.: Innovation capability: a systematic literature review. Eur. J. Innov. Manag. **24**(3), 707–734 (2021)
31. Tavares, M.S., Gohr, C.F., Morioka, S., da Cunha, T.R.: Systematic literature review on innovation capabilities in clusters. Innov. Manag. Rev. **18**(2), 192–220 (2020)
32. Teece, D.J.: Towards a capability theory of (innovating) firms: implications for management and policy. Camb. J. Econ. **41**(3), 693–720 (2017)
33. Motamedimoghadam, M., Mira da Silva, M., Amaral, M.: Organizational capabilities for digital innovation: a systematic literature review. Eur. J. Innov. Manage. **28**(7), 3024–3048 (2025)
34. Gullmark, P., Clausen, T.H.: In search of innovation capability and its sources in local government organizations: a critical interpretative synthesis of the literature. Int. Public Manag. J. **26**(2), 258–280 (2023)
35. Sørensen, E., Torfing, J.: Metagoverning collaborative innovation in governance networks. Am. Rev. Public Adm. **47**(7), 826–839 (2017)
36. Joukhadar, G., Jiang, R., Harrington, K., Thorogood, A.: Promoting digital innovation for sustainability in the public sector. Commun. Assoc. Inf. Syst. **53**(1), 240–277 (2023)
37. Neumann, O., Matt, C., Hitz-Gamper, B.S., Schmidthuber, L., Stürmer, M.: Joining forces for public value creation? Exploring collaborative innovation in smart city initiatives. Gov. Inf. Q. **36**(4), 101411 (2019)
38. Naeem, M., Ozuem, W., Howell, K., Ranfagni, S.: A step-by-step process of thematic analysis to develop a conceptual model in qualitative research. Int. J. Qual. Methods **22**(1) (2023)
39. Miles, M.B., Huberman, A.M., Saldaña, J.: Qualitative Data Analysis: A Methods Sourcebook, 3rd edn. SAGE Publications, Thousand Oaks, CA (2014)

40. Piening, E.P.: Dynamic capabilities in public organizations: a literature review and research agenda. Public Manag. Rev. **15**(2), 209–245 (2013)
41. Klassen, M., Wilson, G.A., Dobni, C.B.: The long game of innovation and value creation. J. Bus. Strategy (2022)

Mitigating Cost Overruns in Public Works Procurement: Design Objectives for GenAI-Based Assistant Systems

Cedric Pauken[1,2](✉), Matthias Hartmann[1,2], and Maria A. Wimmer[1]

[1] University of Koblenz, Universitätsstraße 1, 56070 Koblenz, Germany
{cpauken,mhartmann,wimmer}@uni-koblenz.de

[2] Landesbetrieb Mobilität Rheinland-Pfalz, Friedrich-Ebert-Ring 14-20, 56068 Koblenz, Germany

Abstract. Cost overruns remain a persistent challenge in public works procurement. Although extensive research has already examined potential causes and mitigation strategies, only modest improvements have been achieved thus far. Concurrently, Generative AI (GenAI) has been discussed as a key technology for digital transformation, with scholars anticipating GenAI to reduce workloads and costs, increase process efficiency, and strengthen quality control mechanisms. Hence, in this study, we explore how GenAI-based assistant systems can be designed to help experts in mitigating cost overruns in the domain of public works procurement. By applying Echeloned Design Science Research (eDSR), we combine findings from a systematic literature review with insights from on-site project workshops in a large federal state construction authority in Germany. We derive six validated design objectives that aim to strengthen quality assurance mechanisms during early procurement planning stages. Our findings suggest that GenAI-based systems can mitigate cost overruns in public works procurement by enabling change order risk predictions, legal compliance checks, document coherency checks, bidder question simulations, multi-level quality assessments and semantic standardization of free text into standardized items. Anticipated implementation constraints include a lack of AI-ready data, poor procurement document management, and high levels of change resistance within the organization.

Keywords: Public Works Procurement · Cost Overruns · Generative Artificial Intelligence · Echeloned Design Science Research

1 Introduction

Public procurement constitutes almost one third of government expenditure worldwide [1]. In Germany, public procurement accounted for over 18% of GDP and 37% of government expenditures in 2024 [1]. In literature, we note a long-standing discussion on how to reduce procurement costs, ranging from the late 2000s [2] to the present days [3]. Despite the substantial research already undertaken in this field, public procurement

Published by Springer Nature Switzerland 2027
G. Viale Pereira et al. (Eds.): EGOV 2026, LNCS 16933, pp. 414–429, 2027.
https://doi.org/10.1007/978-3-032-35747-2_26

is still considered to be inefficient even today [4, 5]. In particular, public procurement of construction and civil engineering works is regarded as highly susceptible to errors, delays, and cost overruns in literature [6, 7]. In practice, infrastructure project costs commonly exceed initial estimates by up to 45%, with 86% of large transportation infrastructure projects being affected by cost overruns [7, 8]. Despite this relevance and persistent scholarly attention, only modest progress has been achieved in reducing time and cost overruns thus far, if any at all [9, 10]. Due to the inherent complexity and interdependence of large-scale construction projects, even simple planning oversights and errors may snowball into serious cost overruns over time [11, 12]. Several scholars argue that fixing such errors and thereby ensuring a high quality of initial planning documents leads to significant reductions in construction delays and cost overruns [13–15]. Nevertheless, doing so requires overcoming fragmented responsibilities, a complex regulatory landscape, and providing adequate digital support [16, 17].

Academic discussions frequently argue the role of disruptive technologies such as Artificial Intelligence (AI) as a catalyst for successful digital transformation in the public sector [18, 19]. Notably, the use of AI may contribute to reducing workloads [20] and automating processes [21]. In the German public sector, studies estimate that GenAI can generate up to 23, 9 billion Euro in productivity gains while simultaneously reducing overall workloads for 82% of public employees [22]. Consequently, GenAI is increasingly expected to enhance operational performance and reduce process-related costs in public procurement [23, 24]. Despite these expectations, Andersson et al. evidence that the maturity of overall AI implementations in public procurement remains low [25]. Also, actual implementations of GenAI in public procurement are limited to just a few studies [26–29]. This gap is particularly pronounced in public works procurement [24, 30], where cost overruns frequently impair infrastructure projects even today [10].

Prior research demonstrates that rigorous quality assurance during early planning and specification stages can significantly reduce downstream overruns [13, 15]. Scholars also indicate GenAI to be suitable for assisting experts in performing such quality control checks [31, 32]. Thus, we recognize GenAI to bear significant potential to mitigate cost overruns in public works procurement by strengthening quality control mechanisms. Consequently, our research goal is to investigate how GenAI-based assistant systems should be designed to help experts in mitigating cost overruns in the domain of public works procurement. Two research questions guide our research: **RQ 1:** Which influencing factors contribute to downstream cost overruns in public works procurement? **RQ 2:** Which design objectives and requirements should guide the development of a GenAI-based assistant system to address these factors?

Using Echeloned Design Science Research (eDSR) [33], this study combines empirical research within a large federal state construction authority in Germany with a systematic literature review to answer these research questions (cf. Research design in Sect. 2). In Sect. 3, we elaborate the foundational understanding. Subsequently, we provide three key contributions to the field: First, in the context of **RQ 1**, Sect. 4 synthesizes influencing factors of cost overruns from both literature and practice into an empirically validated problem statement. Second, Sect. 5 builds upon these foundations to discuss **RQ 2**, which yields consolidated design objectives and requirements that guide researchers and practitioners alike in designing and integrating GenAI-based assistant systems to mitigate cost overruns in public works procurement. Third, Sect. 6 discusses further implementation challenges for the system from the perspective of the federal state construction authority. Section 7 concludes with a summary of key contributions, limitations of the work and future research needs.

2 Research Design

This research combines rigorous findings from literature with relevant insights from practice to produce consolidated design knowledge on the integration of GenAI-based assistant systems in public works procurement. We identify Design Science Research (DSR) [34, 35] as a suitable approach, and we adopt the Echeloned Design Science Research Methodology (eDSR) of Tuunanen et al. [33] to address the complexity of the real-world setting. The eDSR partitions Design Science Research into several self-contained parts, the so-called 'echelons', along real-world projects. Similar to the DSRM [34], the core eDSR process consists of 1) Problem Analysis, 2) Objectives and Requirements Definition, 3) Design and Development, 4) Demonstration, and 5) Evaluation [33]. Furthermore, eDSR accounts for macro and micro-level iterations as well as coherency validations to handle complexity of constantly evolving DSR projects. Each process phase contains at least one self-contained echelon that is developed, demonstrated and validated independently before serving as input for subsequent echelons [33]. A systematic literature review (SLR), based on the approaches of Webster and Watson [36] and Carrera-Rivera et al. [37], grounds the research in rigorous foundations, whereas a series of project workshops rooted in the guidelines of Thoring et al. [38] ensure relevant grounding within the application domain of public works procurement. This study addresses the first two phases of eDSR, 1) Problem Analysis and 2) Objectives and Requirements Definition, by analyzing underlying causes of cost overruns (cf. Section 4) and providing adequate design objectives and requirements for GenAI-based systems in addressing these issues (cf. Section 5).

The SLR consists of two cycles. The first cycle follows Webster and Watson [36] to identify and synthesize concept-related knowledge from literature. Keywords such as *"Public Procurement"*, *"Digital Transformation"*, and *"Generative AI"* are derived from the scope of this research and combined in various formats to query SCOPUS and Google Scholar. Thereafter, the relevance of each retrieved article is evaluated by subsequently screening its title, abstract, conclusion, and full text. Once an article is deemed relevant to the scope of our research, it is mapped to the applicable concept area and included in this paper. As a result of the first cycle, a total of 34 articles were included in this paper. Furthermore, an additional four gray literature sources were included in this study due to their practical relevance.

Following the established foundational understanding of the first SLR cycle, the second cycle adheres to guidelines of Carrera-Rivera et al. [37] to perform a systematic evaluation of the problem statement (**RQ 1**) as well as possible design objectives (**RQ 2**). The following search string is derived from the research objective to understand influencing factors of cost overruns in public works procurement: *(("procurement") AND ("public" OR "government") AND ("construction" OR "infrastructure" OR "works") AND (("budget" OR "cost") AND ("overrun" OR "escalation" OR "deviation" OR "discrepancy" OR "growth")))*. Furthermore, a list of preliminary inclusion and exclusion criteria is defined alongside a quality assessment checklist to rigorously assess potentially relevant literature. For an article's preliminary inclusion, both title and abstract must be relevant to the scope of this research, it must be peer-reviewed, and it must be written in English. For every preliminarily included article, the full text is evaluated against the following quality assessment criteria: 1) *Do the authors clearly define research objectives or research questions for their research?* 2) *Does the paper explicitly address public procurement rather than other contexts?* 3) *Does the paper explicitly focus on the construction of public infrastructure rather than private-sector contexts?* 4) *Does the paper clearly describe challenges related to cost overruns?* 5) *Do the authors present empirical or analytical evidence for these challenges?* 6) *Do the authors discuss limitations in regard to the validity of the paper's results?* SCOPUS and the ASCE Library are queried with slight adjustments of the search string to match the expected query syntax for each database. After querying the databases, 255 articles were exported for further evaluation. Subsequent application of the above criteria yields 80 articles. After application of the quality assessment criteria, 24 articles remained for inclusion in this paper.

In parallel to the SLR, we follow guidelines of Thoring et al. [38] to conduct five project workshops from December of 2025 to March of 2026 within a large public construction authority in Germany as part of a larger case study. The public authority currently has over 3000 employees and is responsible for procuring the construction and maintenance of public infrastructure, including roads, bridges, tunnels, and other civil engineering works within a federal state in Germany. Each workshop was assigned a research scope as well as guiding questions for the participants to ensure purposeful results. Participants of the workshops carried heterogenous roles, knowledge and responsibilities within the public authority, including procurement officers, legal experts, civil engineers, and procurement system experts. Due to the embedded nature of the research, confidentiality constraints, and to avoid future trust issues in the project, audio recordings and verbatim transcripts were not produced during the workshops. Instead, detailed researcher notes were taken from joint discussions, illustrated during the session, and consolidated immediately after each workshop. Afterwards, collected data was iteratively analyzed, validated, and corrected through member checking with the participating experts until final approval was given.

By synthesizing the results of the SLR and project workshops, we developed design knowledge via a validated problem statement echelon and a validated design objectives and requirements echelon (cf. [33]).

3 Foundational Understanding

Public procurement refers to the acquisition of goods, works and services by public sector organizations [39] and can be conducted electronically through the utilization of digital technologies and systems [40]. As defined in annex II of directive 2014/24/EU [41], public works procurement encompasses activities related to construction site preparation, building of complete constructions or parts thereof, building installation, building completion, and renting of construction or demolition equipment. In public works procurement, cost overruns, referring to "*the amount by which actual cost exceeds estimated cost, with cost measured in the local currency, constant prices, and against a consistent baseline*" [14, p. 175], have been researched for decades [42], yet hardly improved over time [10]. We consider digital public procurement a focus area of e-government research, where the term e-government encompasses the use of innovative information and communication technologies within the government sector to transform and improve public processes and services [43, 44]. In e-government research, the concept of digital transformation has gained increasing attention over the past years [45]. While digital transformation has no uniform definition in literature [46], scholars characterize digital transformation as a continuous process that triggers significant organizational and societal changes alongside disruptive technological advancements [19, 47]. The public sector is particularly affected by these dynamics [48] and requires systemic approaches to overcome fragmented skills, responsibilities, and IT infrastructures [49]. In the past years, artificial intelligence (AI) has emerged as a key enabler of digital transformation in the public sector, with potential to reduce workloads [20], automate processes [21], and support quality control checks [31, 32]. Following Wang, we understand AI as one or more information systems that are able to adapt to their environment while operating under insufficient knowledge and resources [50]. Furthermore, we consider GenAI as a subset of AI that is rooted in (multi-)modality, interaction, flexibility, and productivity [51] and able to generate content in the form of text, images, and videos through the use of probabilistic models [52] such as transformers and diffusers. The above understanding builds the foundation of the subsequent research contribution.

4 Understanding Underlying Causes of Cost Overruns in Public Works Procurement

This section answers RQ 1 in the form of a validated problem statement echelon. The results presented are retrieved from the second literature cycle (see Sect. 2). In the following, the nature and cause of cost overruns in public works procurement are discussed from scholarly (Sect. 4.1) and practitioner (Sect. 4.2) perspectives.

4.1 Findings from Literature

Cost overruns are a persistent and integral challenge of public works procurement. Forty years of research has been conducted on the nature and cause of cost overruns in public works procurement, ranging from early studies of Arditi et al. [42] to recent studies such as those of Naseem et al. [6]. Surprisingly, actual progress in mitigating cost overruns is estimated to be modest [10], with Park even finding that project performance has not improved at all since 1999 from a schedule perspective [9]. For instance, Chong and Hopkins find that the mean increase between authorized funding and final costs of road construction projects lies at 135%, often overrunning by as much as 200% [53]. Flyvbjerg et al. present that 86% of large transportation infrastructure projects face cost overruns. Such findings become increasingly striking when considering the similarity of identified causes that lead to cost overruns [7]. Chong and Hopkins argue that insufficient due diligence, inexperience with cost estimation, and poor contract management are the main causes of road related cost overruns [53]. Asiedu and Adaku find that four factors lead to 61% of all cost overruns in Ghanaian public works procurement: poor contract planning and supervision, change orders, a weak institutional and economic environment of projects, and a lack of effective coordination among contracting parties [54]. Ali et al. identify inadequate investigation, unclear work scope, high project complexity and incomplete design and specifications to be key contributing factors of downstream cost overruns [55]. Idrees and Shafiq add upon this discussion and find technical errors, reworks, poor project management and legal issues as major causes for time and cost overruns in Pakistan [56]. Similarly, Xie et al. discuss insufficient design and design changes to be significant yet avoidable causes of cost overruns in China [12]. A risk analysis of Alshihri et al. confirms such observations for Saudi Arabia, highlighting that apart from financial risk factors, change orders and ineffective project planning are some of the most significant issues for cost overruns [57]. Similarly, in the United Arabian Emirates, design changes are identified as the most influential cause of cost overruns [58]. Given such findings, Love et al. provide an in-depth analysis of design changes and change orders in public sector infrastructure projects, finding that the mere existence of change orders cause an average cost overrun of 23,75% [59].

Although not all country- and case-specific findings can be generalized, we conclude that the initial planning stage of public works procurement is crucial for mitigating cost overruns. Incomplete, erroneous or ambiguous specification documents commonly lead to downstream issues such as design changes and change orders that ultimately cause significant cost overruns. Consequently, Hanak et al. [13] and Odeck et al. [14, 15] research the potential of quality control mechanisms during the planning stage of such procedures to mitigate downstream cost overruns. The scholars identify that ensuring high quality specifications through early quality assurance and control mechanisms has a significant positive impact on reducing downstream cost overruns [13–15]. Nevertheless, attempting to mitigate cost overruns is shown to require overcoming fragmented responsibilities, navigating a complex regulatory landscape, and providing adequate digital support [16, 17].

4.2 Findings from Project Workshops with the German Construction Authority

During project workshops with a large public construction authority in Germany, most of the underlying causes could be confirmed in practice. From the organization's perspective, causes and effects of cost overruns vary greatly depending on the procurement scope. On the one hand, workshop participants find certain kinds of cost overruns to be entirely unavoidable, thus being a natural part of the public construction process. Such cost overruns cannot be attributed to individual errors or mistakes; rather, they occur naturally due to events of higher power, such as unexpected archaeological or paleontological discoveries, or natural disasters during construction work. Furthermore, due to the use of standardized pricing functions and historical data, workshop participants agreed that accurate cost estimations of procurement projects were no major concern in current organizational practice. However, on the other hand, participants agreed that several significant cost overruns are a result of small oversights during the preparation of service specifications at the beginning of procurement procedures in line with § 7b of the German VOB/A[1]. Such specifications break down detailed information about the planned construction project into standardized positional items with unit prices. They allow for a precise and structured description of works that potential economic operators may easily evaluate, calculate, and subsequently submit a bid on. Hence, these service specifications are considered to be the standard model by both the state authority as well as potential contractors from the construction industry. However, complex works are difficult to capture in such service specifications. Extensive construction descriptions and plans must be manually translated into predefined positions and compared against a multitude of documents, including historical projects, soil analyses and a variety of legal regulations. Hence, quality inspectors must be familiar with all relevant regulations and projects for each procurement. However, a shortage of such skilled experts and limited internal capacities often prevent holistic breakdowns in advance. Since quality reviews involve enormous amounts of work by understaffed and overworked public sector departments, small oversights and errors such as mixed-up quantities or regulations being unadhered to may find their way into the final service specification, which commonly lead to downstream issues that ultimately spiral into change orders and thus cost overruns during construction. Notably, since the contractor has already won the award when executing the construction work, change orders and addenda may be billed for particularly high prices at this point, leading to even higher cost overruns. The relevance and impact of change orders on cost overruns have been confirmed in [59].

In summary, the majority of avoidable cost overruns within the public construction authority occur due to change orders that result from oversights and errors in the initial procurement documents. Common causes of change orders include: undetected high-risk areas for addenda, legal complexity and lack of regulatory compliance, project complexity and lack of coherence between planning and procurement documents, procurement specification ambiguities, insufficient quality control mechanisms, semantic specification mismatches between free-text and standardized catalog positions.

5 Design Objectives and Requirements for GenAI-Based Mitigation of Cost Overruns in Public Works Procurement

To effectively counteract the problems identified in Sect. 4, integrating quality control mechanisms during the planning stage to ensure high quality documents and thus mitigate change orders has been identified as a central solution component in both literature [13–15] and in practice. In particular, workshop participants consider high quality service specification as the single most important mitigator of cost overruns in practice. The higher the quality of initial specifications, the lower the predicted risk of additional downstream issues that lead to change orders and thus cost overruns. Participants define high quality service specifications as fully compliant with all applicable regulations and case laws, rooted in comprehensive historical data of similar projects, and fully consistent with all related construction documents. However, as established in Sect. 4.2, the manual quality assurance of service specifications is a time-consuming undertaking, as it

[1] https://www.verwaltungsvorschriften-im-internet.de/bsvwvbund_31012019_BWI781063060120180001604634.htm.

requires tremendous legal expertise, experience with similar projects from the past, and comparisons to a multitude of planning and analysis documents. Due to limited resources of the authority, performing such comprehensive checks is considered to become even more challenging in the future. Hence, the public authority would benefit greatly from digital support in such quality control checks.

In literature, GenAI has been identified as a key success factor in transforming public procurement [23, 24] and enabling such effective quality control mechanisms [31, 32]. In particular, GenAI is capable of utilizing expert knowledge and historic data [24] to perform legal compliance analyses [60] and coherency checks [61], simulate bidding scenarios [62], and indicate textual improvements [63]. Hence, we consider GenAI to be particularly suitable for performing quality control measures on service specifications in public works procurement. By synthesizing these insights, we establish an overview of design objectives, design requirements, and addressed cost overrun factors in Table 1, which have been validated by the participating domain experts. Thereafter, each design objective, its corresponding design requirements and cost overrun factors are discussed in more detail.

Predictive Risk Mitigation of Change Orders and Addenda. Based on historical data from similar projects, the system must be able to make predictions on where change orders and addenda would be most likely to occur in the current project. Given such information, procurement officers can place a particular emphasis on analyzing the most relevant documents related to the identified risk factors. For example, when procuring the construction of a street in a certain region, the system may indicate that past change orders and addenda have been related to certain kinds of undesirable soil materials. Based on this information, experts can ensure comprehensive checking of the soil analyses to ensure an accurate representation of such risks in the service specification. Furthermore, they can preemptively notify construction supervisors to be wary about certain types of groundwork claims during the downstream construction process. Consequently, the risk of change orders and addenda that cause cost overruns can be mitigated in advance. GenAI is considered to be particularly suitable for implementing the discussed requirements due to its capability to utilize historical data and expert knowledge via fine-tuning and Retrieval Augmented Generation to predict likely future trends [24, 64].

Regulatory and Legal Alignment. The system must be able to perform automated comparisons of the service specification against all relevant legal statutes, case laws, DIN standards and similar legal specifications to identify potential violations or ambiguities. In doing so, the system must provide accurate references to all relevant passages of the law or standard that must be evaluated for potential applicability. Furthermore, the service specification should be checked for common legal terms to identify discrepancies between individually intended meaning and legally regulated meaning. The purpose of this second check is to provide experts with the information they need to decide whether or not to adjust such positions. Related work in literature indicates that GenAI is suitable for performing such legal compliance checks [60, 65], for instance through the utilization of RAG [66].

Coherence and Plausibility Verification with Related Project Documents. The system must be able to carry out automated comparisons of the service specification against

Table 1. Design Objectives and Requirements

ID	Design Objective	Design Requirement	Addressed factor
DO-1	Predictive risk mitigation	The system must analyze historical procurement data to indicate high-risk areas for change orders and addenda (e.g., groundwork)	Undetected high-risk areas
DO-2	Regulatory and legal alignment	The system must perform compliance checks with direct references against relevant legal statutes, case law and technical DIN-Standards to indicate legal discrepancies	Legal complexity and regulatory compliance
DO-3	Coherence and plausibility verification	The system must perform coherence and plausibility checks against project related documents (e.g., construction plans, soil analyses) to indicate domain related discrepancies	Project complexity and procurement plausibility
DO-4	Simulation capabilities	The system must be able to simulate bidder questions to help identify uncertainties and ambiguities in the services specification	Specification ambiguity
DO-5	Multi-level quality assessment	The system must provide both item-by-item auditing and audit report summaries alongside a graded warning hierarchy (Fatal, Error, Warning, Information) and suggestions for text improvement to minimize potential errors	Insufficient quality control mechanisms
DO-6	Semantic standardization	The system must map unstructured free-text descriptions into standardized service catalog unit price items to minimize manual translation errors	Semantic specification mismatches

other relevant documents of the project, such as building specifications, construction plans, and soil analyses. This ensures coherent information for potential contractors and mitigates careless oversights such as simple material or quantity errors. Furthermore, sample specifications should be developed to provide a ground-truth for various types of public works procurements. Such sample specifications would subsequently serve as an additional point of comparison for individual service specifications. The capability of GenAI to perform such coherence checks has been presented by Yang et al. [61] in the context of highway construction projects.

Simulation Capabilities for Bidder Questions. In order to gain a better understanding of how potential contractors perceive the service specifications, the system must be able to simulate potential bidder questions about the current service specifications. The aim of this simulation would not be to answer the fictitious questions, but to better understand potential ambiguities for contractors that can be mitigated by improving the service specifications accordingly. While the significance of this module is perceived as polarizing in the workshop due to a lack of consolidated data on bidder questions, participants agree that contractor ambiguities should be avoided, nonetheless. The ability of GenAI-based agents to simulate such construction bidding environments has been demonstrated by Heo et al. [62].

Multi-level Quality Assessment of Service Specifications. The system must be able to indicate the identified problems on both a per-item basis as well as a consolidated quality report summary. This enables experts to evaluate potential problems at the item-specific and the consolidated summary levels. Also, potential problems or errors should be indicated using a graded warning concept (e.g., fatal, error, warning, information) and be accompanied by suggestions for improvement. While suggestions for improvement could be generated via GenAI [63], all problem indications and summaries themselves should follow clear deterministic scripts rather than be subject to probabilistic GenAI behavior as discussed by Carrera and Maldonado-Ruiz [67].

Semantic Standardization of Free Text into Catalog Items. The system must be able to transform unstructured free texts into standardized unit price catalog positions to avoid ambiguities in the service specification. Since procurement officers are often unable to cleanly translate complex information into such standardized positions, contractors would deal with more concise specifications and thus be faced with less complexity and less speculative freedom for the tendering process. As a result, the risk of change orders, addenda and entailing cost overruns could potentially be reduced. At present, the exact role of GenAI in fulfilling these requirements is undecided upon. However, in line with Carrera and Maldonado-Ruiz [67], it would be advisable to keep core transformations as deterministic scripts while letting GenAI reason on which semantic mapping is most suitable for the provided free-text from the user.

6 Challenges and Implementation Constraints of the Design Objectives Along GenAI Use in Procurement Cost Overruns

While implementing the identified design objectives and requirements would significantly improve the status quo according to the participating experts, several challenges must be addressed in doing so. First, a variety of data must be utilized by the GenAI-based system for effective output. Historical data such as past service specifications, bidder questions and change orders must be extracted from the authority's procurement management system for each procedure and grouped into relevant types of procurements, such as road repairs, construction of bypass roads, or construction of bridges. Furthermore, such procedures must be evaluated through relevant metrics and labels to distinguish between good and bad procurement documents. In this context, the current lack of standardized procurement processes and data within the organization is considered to be a particular barrier. To enable effective quality control checks, relevant technical standards, legal documents, and project-related data such as construction descriptions and soil analyses must be readily available to the system. In order to incorporate further nuances of relevant domain knowledge, normative reference data such as sample service specifications and business rules must be defined beforehand. Due to the sensitive information contained in many such files, as well as the need for a customized system, the public authority estimates the use of publicly available GenAI tools to be inappropriate for most parts of the quality control checks. Hence, the system is intended to be built as an on-premise solution that operates within the organization's intranet. However, system architecture, pre- and post-processing pipelines, utilized weights, and other non-sensitive information will be made publicly available to encourage cross-organizational understanding and learning of GenAI implementation in public works procurement.

Overall, developing the required knowledge base for the GenAI-based system is considered challenging. The experts estimate that the database has entries for only three to four thousand procurement procedures so far; experts are uncertain whether openly available procurement documents from other German construction authorities would foster or impair the system's domain accuracy. Matching past service specifications to downstream documentations of change orders is also considered to be challenging, since some change orders have only been documented on paper and are sometimes missing procurement procedure identifiers. Another overarching challenge is the lack of AI-ready data. While effective GenAI use is facilitated by machine-readable and semantically rich data [68], the organization mostly relies on scanned PDFs so far. Hence, building a robust pre-processing pipeline for these documents will be crucial. Apart from these considerations, organizational resistance is also identified as a potential challenge. Workshop participants consider the organizational culture to not be AI-ready, with several experts estimating that individual fears and concerns will hinder the digital transformation of the GenAI-based system in practice. Participants therefore urge that the development and introduction of such a system must be carefully planned and carried out. This should involve the introduction of effective countermeasures, such as active stakeholder involvement, clear communication strategies, and openly available training courses for all potential users.

7 Conclusion

In this study, we employed Echeloned Design Science Research (eDSR) to derive design objectives and requirements for a GenAI-based assistant system capable of mitigating cost overruns in public works procurement. Two research questions have been discussed to achieve this objective. RQ1 explores underlying causes of cost overruns in public works procurement by conducting a systematic literature review [36, 37] alongside multiple project workshops within a large federal state construction authority in Germany. Findings from literature suggest that incomplete, erroneous or ambiguous planning documents cause downstream issues such as change orders that ultimately lead to cost overruns [12, 54, 57], averaging at 23,75% [59]. Independent on-site project workshops with the German construction authority confirm these findings, with experts estimating that most cost overruns stem from small oversights and errors in the service specifications, which capture detailed information about the planned construction project in standardized positional items. Such oversights happen frequently due to the sheer amount of work required to perform quality control measures from commonly understaffed and overworked project teams.

Along RQ2, findings of the SLR and project workshops suggest that thorough quality control checks on initial procurement documents could significantly mitigate downstream change orders and cost overruns [13–15]. To perform such comprehensive quality checks, service specifications must be checked against comparable historical procurement documents, relevant construction documents and analyses, and all potentially applicable legal and technical regulations, including case law. Due to the limited resources of the public construction authority to perform such comprehensive assessments, and due to the potential of GenAI to support experts in conducting quality control checks [13–15], the use of GenAI has been identified as a key solution component for mitigating cost overruns in public works procurement.

Through further investigation with the federal state construction authority and confirmation with literature, we derive six design objectives that may guide researchers and practitioners alike. GenAI-based assistant systems are expected to mitigate cost overruns by enabling change order risk predictions, legal compliance checks, document coherence checks, bidder question simulations, multi-level quality assessments and semantic standardization of free text into standardized items. To achieve these design objectives, multiple design requirements must be adhered to. In particular, the system requires a diverse knowledge base consisting of historical procurement documents, relevant legal documents, relevant construction project documents, and normative reference data to predict change orders and indicate potential oversights in the service specification. However, constructing such a knowledge base for GenAI integration is considered challenging in practice. Potential implementation constraints include poor procurement document management in the past, a lack of AI-ready data, and potentially high change resistance within the organization. Furthermore, although this study explicitly investigated GenAI as a key technology for mitigating cost overruns in public works procurement, it should be noted that other technologies may be equally or more appropriate depending on the organizational scope and context.

Besides these contributions, three limitations arise from the scope of this research. First, empirical grounding is limited to the case of a single public construction authority in Germany. Hence, only contextual insights are provided, which are further limited to the procurement of roads, bridges, tunnels, and other civil engineering works. Future research may validate our findings across different organizational settings. Second, to maintain trust and confidentiality within the project, workshops were documented via researcher notes rather than verbatim transcripts. This approach, while necessary for the long-term project setting, may introduce biases during the member-checking process. Consequently, future research may validate these findings in further expert interviews. Third, this research has focused on the problem statement and design objectives and requirements echelons of the eDSR process. As such, future research will explore how a GenAI-based system can implement the specified design objectives in its implementation architecture, and whether it is actually able to achieve significant impact in reducing cost overruns in practice or be yet another failed attempt at mitigating cost overruns in public works procurement [10].

Acknowledgments. This study was funded by a joint research cooperation project between the University of Koblenz and the Landesbetrieb Mobilität Rheinland-Pfalz.

Disclosure of Interests. The authors have no competing interests to declare that are relevant to the content of this article.

References

1. OECD: Size of public procurement - Government at a Glance (2025). https://www.oecd.org/content/dam/oecd/en/publications/reports/2025/06/government-at-a-glance-2025_70e14c6c/0efd0bcd-en.pdf. Accessed 17 Nov 2025
2. Singer, M., Konstantinidis, G., Roubik, E., Beffermann, E.: Does e-procurement save the state money? J. of Public Proc **9**(1), 58–78 (2009). https://doi.org/10.1108/JOPP-09-01-2009-B002
3. Gorgun, M.K., Kutlu, M., Tas, B.K.O.: Information is essential for competitive and cost-effective public procurement. J. Inf. Sci. **51**(2), 445–454 (2025)
4. Siapera, M., Schmitz, A., Wimmer, M. A., Prentza, A.: Closing the gap: leveraging data for seamless integration between pre-award and post-award in public procurement. In: 57th Hawaii International Conference on System Sciences (2024). https://doi.org/10.24251/HICSS.2024.270J
5. Gallego, J., Rivero, G., Martínez, J.: Preventing rather than punishing: an early warning model of malfeasance in public procurement. Int. J. Forecast. **37**(1), 360–377 (2021)
6. Naseem, A., Ayyaz, M., Khan, M. S., Ahmad, Y., Naseem, F.: Analyzing and mitigating critical factors of delay and cost overrun in public procurement process using relative importance method and interpretive structural modelling technique. In: International Conference on Information Management, pp. 347–355. Springer, Cham (2025). https://doi.org/10.1007/978-3-031-99353-4_30
7. Flyvbjerg, B., et al.: Five things you should know about cost overrun. Transp. Res. Part A Policy Pract. **118**, 174–190 (2018)
8. Flyvbjerg, B., Skamris Holm, M.K., Buhl, S.L.: How common and how large are cost overruns in transport infrastructure projects? Transp. Rev. **23**(1), 71–88 (2003)
9. Park, J.E.: Schedule delays of major projects: what should we do about it? Transp. Rev. **41**(6), 814–832 (2021)

10. Abdelalim, A.M., Salem, M., Salem, M., Al-Adwani, M., Tantawy, M.: An analysis of factors contributing to cost overruns in the global construction industry. Buildings **15**(1), 18 (2024)
11. Lafhaj, Z., Rebai, S., AlBalkhy, W., Hamdi, O., Mossman, A., Alves Da Costa, A.: Complexity in construction projects: a literature review. Buildings **14**(3), 680 (2024)
12. Xie, W., Deng, B., Yin, Y., Lv, X., Deng, Z.: Critical factors influencing cost overrun in construction projects: a fuzzy synthetic evaluation. Buildings **12**(11), 2028 (2022)
13. Hanak, T., Mikulik, M., Soniewicki, M.: Impact of the quality of technical specifications of the tender documentation on the construction projects' success. Int. J. Manag. Projects Bus. **18**(8), 79–99 (2025)
14. Odeck, J.: Measuring cost and time overruns: median-based metrics, reform effect, and simultaneous estimation. Transp. Res. Part A Policy Pract. **199**, 104587 (2025)
15. Odeck, J., Welde, M., Volden, G.H.: The impact of external quality assurance of costs estimates on cost overruns: empirical evidence from the Norwegian road sector. Eur. J. Transp. Infrastruct. Res. **15**(3) (2015)
16. Flyvbjerg, B.: What you should know about megaprojects and why: an overview. Proj. Manag. J. **45**(2), 6–19 (2014)
17. Beach, T.H., Hippolyte, J.-L., Rezgui, Y.: Towards the adoption of automated regulatory compliance checking in the built environment. Autom. Constr. **118**, 103285 (2020)
18. Ahn, M.J., Chen, Y.-C.: Digital transformation toward AI-augmented public administration: the perception of government employees and the willingness to use AI in government. Gov. Inf. Q. **39**(2), 101664 (2022)
19. Wimmer, M. A., Pereira, G. V., Ronzhyn, A., Spitzer, V.: Transforming government by leveraging disruptive technologies: Identification of research and training needs. eJournal of eDemocracy and Open Gov **12**(1), 87–114 (2020). https://doi.org/10.29379/jedem.v12i1.594
20. Alhosani, K., Alhashmi, S.M.: Opportunities, challenges, and benefits of AI innovation in government services: a review. Discov. Artif. Intell. **4**(1), 18 (2024)
21. Madan, R., Ashok, M.: AI adoption and diffusion in public administration: a systematic literature review and future research agenda. Gov. Inf. Q. **40**(1), 101774 (2023)
22. IWConsult p.p. Google: Der digitale Faktor - Potenziale künstlicher Intelligenz in der öffentlichen Verwaltung (2024). https://der-digitale-faktor.de/download/IW_Google-Studie_DeepDive_PublicSector_DE.pdf. Accessed 17 Nov 2025
23. Nai, R., Sulis, E., Fatima, I., Meo, R.: Large language models and recommendation systems: a proof-of-concept study on public procurements. In: International Conference on Applications of Natural Language to Information Systems, pp. 280–290. Springer, Cham (2024). https://doi.org/10.1007/978-3-031-70242-6_27
24. Ghimire, P., Kim, K., Acharya, M.: Opportunities and challenges of generative AI in construction industry: focusing on adoption of text-based models. Buildings **14**(1), 220 (2024)
25. Andersson, P.E., Arbin, K., Rosenqvist, C.: Assessing the value of artificial intelligence (AI) in governmental public procurement. J. Public Procurement **25**(1), 120–139 (2025). https://doi.org/10.1108/JOPP-05-2024-0057
26. Wibowo, A. R., Fauziati, S., Hartanto, R.: Government product recommendation systems in e-katalog: leveraging large language models with retrieval-augmented generation. In: IET Conference Proceedings, pp. 603–610. Institution of Engineering and Technology (2024). https://doi.org/10.1049/icp.2025.0317
27. Sofat, A., Sodhi, B.: Speeding up government procurement workflows with LLMs. In: Kö, A., Kotsis, G., Tjoa, A.M., Khalil, I. (eds.) Electronic Government and the Information Systems Perspective. EGOVIS 2024. Lecture Notes in Computer Science, vol. 14913, pp. 27–33. Springer, Cham (2024). https://doi.org/10.1007/978-3-031-68211-7_3

28. Alozie, M.: Generative AI in procurement: rethinking bid evaluation, fairness and transparency in engineering and construction contracts. World J. Adv. Res. Rev. **24**(3), 3551–3567 (2024)
29. Liu, C.-Y., Chou, J.-S.: Automated legal consulting in construction procurement using metaheuristically optimized large language models. Autom. Constr. **170** (2025). https://doi.org/10.1016/j.autcon.2024.105891
30. Regona, M., Yigitcanlar, T., Xia, B., Li, R.Y.M.: Opportunities and adoption challenges of AI in the construction industry: a PRISMA review. J. Open Innov. Technol. Market Complex. **8**(1), 45 (2022)
31. Carrasco, M., et al.: Generative AI for the Public Sector: From Opportunities to Value. Boston Consulting Group, Boston, MA (2023)
32. Kim, E.: Generative AI in public administration: a quasi-experimental analysis of bureaucratic productivity. Gov. Inf. Q. **43**(1), 102108 (2026)
33. Tuunanen, T., Winter, R., vom Brocke, J.: Dealing with complexity in design science research: a methodology using design echelons. MIS Q. **48**(2), 427–458 (2024)
34. Bichler, M.: Design science in information systems research. Wirtschaftsinformatik **48**(2), 133–135 (2006). https://doi.org/10.1007/s11576-006-0028-8
35. Peffers, K., Tuunanen, T., Rothenberger, M.A., Chatterjee, S.: A design science research methodology for information systems research. J. Manag. Inf. Syst. **24**(3), 45–77 (2007)
36. Webster, J., Watson, R.T.: Analyzing the past to prepare for the future: writing a literature review. MIS Q. **26**(2), xiii–xxiii (2002). https://doi.org/10.1.1.104.6570
37. Carrera-Rivera, A., Ochoa, W., Larrinaga, F., Lasa, G.: How-to conduct a systematic literature review: a quick guide for computer science research. MethodsX **9**, 101895 (2022). https://doi.org/10.1016/j.mex.2022.101895
38. Thoring, K., Mueller, R., Badke-Schaub, P.: Workshops as a research method: guidelines for designing and evaluating artifacts through workshops. In: 53rd Hawaii International Conference on System Sciences (2020). https://doi.org/10.24251/HICSS.2020.620
39. Uyarra, E., Flanagan, K.: Understanding the innovation impacts of public procurement. Eur. Plan. Stud. **18**(1), 123–143 (2010)
40. European Parliament: Directive 2014/24/EU of the European Parliament and of the Council of 26 February 2014 on public procurement and repealing Directive 2004/18/EC. Official Journal of the European Union (2014)
41. Mavidis, A., Folinas, D.: From public e-procurement 3.0 to e-procurement 4.0: a critical literature review. Sustainability **14**(18) (2022). https://doi.org/10.3390/su141811252
42. Arditi, D., Akan, G.T., Gurdamar, S.: Cost overruns in public projects. Int. J. Project Manage. **3**(4), 218–224 (1985)
43. Fang, Z.: E-government in digital era: concept, practice, and development. Int. J. Comput. Internet Manag. **10**(2), 1–22 (2002)
44. Traunmüller, R., Wimmer, M.: E-government: the challenges ahead. In: International Conference on Electronic Government, pp. 1–6. Springer (2004). https://doi.org/10.1007/978-3-540-30078-6_1
45. Janssen, M., et al.: Reflections on the nature of digital government research: marking the 50th anniversary of government information quarterly. Gov. Inf. Q. **42**(4), 102086 (2025)
46. Gong, Y., Yang, J., Shi, X.: Towards a comprehensive understanding of digital transformation in government: analysis of flexibility and enterprise architecture. Gov. Inf. Q. **37**(3), 101487 (2020)
47. Vial, G.: Understanding digital transformation: a review and a research agenda. Manag. Digit. Transform. **28**(2), 118–144 (2019)
48. Kutzner, K., Schoormann, T., Knackstedt, R.: Digital transformation in information systems research: a taxonomy-based approach to structure the field. In: Proceedings of the 26th European Conference on Information Systems (ECIS) (2018)

49. Brunetti, F., Matt, D.T., Bonfanti, A., De Longhi, A., Pedrini, G., Orzes, G.: Digital transformation challenges: strategies emerging from a multi-stakeholder approach. TQM J. **32**(4), 697–724 (2020)
50. Wang, P.: On defining artificial intelligence. J. Artif. Gen. Intell. **10**(2), 1–37 (2019)
51. Ronge, R., Maier, M., Rathgeber, B.: Towards a definition of generative artificial intelligence. Philos. Technol. **38**(1), 1–25 (2025)
52. Goodfellow, I., Bengio, Y., Courville, A., Bengio, Y.: Deep Learning. MIT Press, Cambridge (2016)
53. Chong, U., Hopkins, O.: An international experience on the evolution of road costs during the project life cycle. Transp. Policy (Oxf.) **48**, 60–66 (2016)
54. Asiedu, R.O., Adaku, E.: Cost overruns of public sector construction projects: a developing country perspective. Int. J. Manag. Projects Bus. **13**(1), 66–84 (2020)
55. Ali, Z., Ahmad, I., Hussain, Z.: Analysis of critical causes of transaction cost escalation in public sector construction projects. Pak. J. Comm. Soc. Sci. **14**(4), 838–865 (2020)
56. Idrees, S., Shafiq, M.T.: Factors for time and cost overrun in public projects. J. Eng. Proj. Prod. Manag. **11**(3) (2021)
57. Alshihri, S., Al-Gahtani, K., Almohsen, A.: Risk factors that lead to time and cost overruns of building projects in Saudi Arabia. Buildings **12**(7), 902 (2022)
58. Johnson, R.M., Babu, R.I.I.: Time and cost overruns in the UAE construction industry: a critical analysis. Int. J. Constr. Manag. **20**(5), 402–411 (2020)
59. Love, P.E.D., Irani, Z., Smith, J., Regan, M., Liu, J.: Cost performance of public infrastructure projects: the nemesis and nirvana of change-orders. Prod. Plann. Control **28**(13), 1081–1092 (2017)
60. Hassani, S.: Enhancing legal compliance and regulation analysis with large language models. In: 2024 IEEE 32nd International Requirements Engineering Conference (RE), pp. 507–511. IEEE (2024)
61. Yang, Y., Jing, X., Liu, Y.-M.: Automated checking of highway bridge BIM models based on large language models. Buildings **15**(19), 3465 (2025)
62. Heo, C., Ahn, C.R., Park, M.: Tacit collusion by LLM agents in construction bidding: evidence from a simulated bidding environment. J. Manag. Eng. **42**(2), 04025063 (2026)
63. Ray, P.P.: ChatGPT: a comprehensive review on background, applications, key challenges, bias, ethics, limitations and future scope. Internet Things Cyber-Physical Syst. **3**, 121–154 (2023)
64. Fan, W., et al.: A survey on RAG meeting LLMs: towards retrieval-augmented large language models. In: Proceedings of the 30th ACM SIGKDD Conference on Knowledge Discovery and Data Mining, pp. 6491–6501 (2024)
65. Ioannidis, J., Harper, J., Quah, M.S., Hunter, D.: Gracenote.AI: legal generative AI for regulatory compliance. In: Third International Workshop on Artificial Intelligence and Intelligent Assistance for Legal Professionals in the Digital Workplace (2023)
66. Das, S., Deb, N., Chaki, N., Cortesi, A.: A multi-agent RAG framework for regulatory compliance checking of software requirements. ACM Trans. Softw. Eng. Methodol. (2025). https://doi.org/10.1145/3785472
67. Carrera, I., Maldonado-Ruiz, D.: The plausibility trap: using probabilistic engines for deterministic tasks. arXiv preprint arXiv:2601.15130 (2026)
68. Yeasmin, S., Alshemaimri, B.: Bridging machine-readable code of regulations and its application on generative AI: a survey. Int. J. Adv. Comput. Sci. Appl. **16**(10), 2025

When Proactivity Means Everything and Nothing: Interpretive Drift and Governance of EU Proactive Public Services

Anastasija Nikiforova[1(✉)], A. Paula Rodriguez Müller[2(✉)], and Luca Tangi[3]

[1] University of Tartu, Tartu, Estonia
Anastasija.Nikiforova@ut.ee
[2] Joint Research Centre, European Commission, Seville, Spain
Paula.Rodriguez-muller@ec.europa.eu
[3] Joint Research Centre, European Commission, Ispra, Italy
Luca.Tangi@ec.europa.eu

Abstract. Proactive public services (PPS) - services initiated by public authorities without prior request - are increasingly promoted as a cornerstone of human-centric digital government in Europe. Yet what "proactivity" means in practice remains conceptually unstable. Drawing on 20 semi-structured interviews across 12 EU Member States, this study examines how practitioners interpret PPS and the governance consequences of conceptual ambiguity. Findings show that conceptual ambiguity is not merely semantic but operationally consequential. Across interviews, most respondents demonstrated uncertainty in distinguishing between digitization and proactivity, automation and proactivity, and personalization and proactivity, leading to three recurring patterns: under-recognition of existing proactive practices, over-classification of digitized services as proactive, and the equation of proactivity with full automation. These divergent interpretations affect service prioritization, funding, and comparability across jurisdictions. We argue that proactivity should be understood as a service initiation logic - authority-initiated delivery - rather than as a technology, delivery channel, or automation level. Failing to make this distinction risks reinforcing technology-first reform logic, overlooking existing innovations, and distorting governance decisions. By introducing the proactivity interpretation gap, the study contributes to digital government research by highlighting how conceptual ambiguity shapes service classification, governance decisions, and public sector innovation trajectories.

Keywords: Digital Government · Governance · Proactivity · Proactive Public Service · Digitization · Public Service · Public Administration

Published by Springer Nature Switzerland 2027
G. Viale Pereira et al. (Eds.): EGOV 2026, LNCS 16933, pp. 430–448, 2027.
https://doi.org/10.1007/978-3-032-35747-2_27

1 Introduction

In an era characterized by rapid technological advancement and evolving societal expectations, traditional bureaucratic governance structures face increasing criticism. Public administrations across Europe are under growing pressure to deliver services that are efficient, equitable, and user-centred[1]. Citizens and businesses frequently encounter complex procedures, unclear responsibilities, and fragmented service delivery. In response, governments are exploring proactive public services (PPS) - services initiated by public authorities without a prior request - designed to anticipate user needs and trigger service delivery at critical life or business events (Scholta & Lindgren, 2019; Nikiforova et al., 2023). In essence, by preventing non-take-up of entitlements and shifting navigational responsibility to the state, PPS represent a significant reorientation of service logic.

European Union (EU) frameworks, from the *eGovernment Action Plan* to the *GDPR*, the *Data Act*, and the *Interoperable Europe Act*, reinforce a human-centric vision of digital governance and provide the regulatory and infrastructural foundations for PPS.

Proactive public services promise multiple benefits. They can reduce administrative complexity for users, enhance equity by ensuring that eligible citizens or businesses do not miss out on rights or fail to meet obligations, improve efficiency, reduce bureaucratic burden and costs, and improve trust in government by demonstrating responsiveness and competence (Bharosa et al., 2021; Nikiforova et al., 2023, 2026; OECD, 2020; Scholta & Lindgren, 2019; Lindgren & Scholta, 2023). Technological developments, including digital identity systems, cross-agency data sharing, and predictive analytics, have expanded the feasibility of such services at scale, making them a central focus of ongoing digital government transformation (Gil-Garcia et al., 2018; Desouza & Jacob, 2017). However, the transition from reactive to proactive service delivery is far from straightforward. Authority-initiated service provision introduces new governance challenges, including lawful service initiation without explicit request, cross-domain data reuse, accountability for automated decisions, and heightened expectations of trust and legitimacy (Nikiforova et al., 2025). Moreover, the operational meaning of proactivity remains insufficiently stabilized across policy and administrative contexts. As a result, PPS are often developed in an ad hoc manner, with limited shared understanding of what constitutes proactivity, which services are suitable for proactive delivery, and how such transformations should be implemented and evaluated (e.g., Pawlowski & Scholta, 2023; Nikiforova et al., 2025; OECD, 2020).

Despite growing policy attention and technological experimentation, PPS remain conceptually unsettled. In digital government research, proactivity is often associated with related but distinct phenomena, including *digitization*, *automation*, *personalization*, life-event integration, or AI-enabled prediction. Existing studies have explored taxonomies of proactive services (Pawlowski & Scholta, 2023), levels of proactivity (Bharosa et al., 2021), automation within "no-stop government" models (Lindgren & Scholta, 2023), key benefits and barriers towards their implementation (Nikiforova et al., 2025, 2026); yet these perspectives rarely converge on a consistent conceptual foundation. As a result, proactivity increasingly functions as a broad reform narrative rather

[1] Decision (EU) 2022/2481 of the European Parliament and of the Council of 14 December 2022 establishing the Digital Decade Policy Programme 2030 (OJ L 323, 19.12.2022, p. 4).

than a clearly defined governance concept. Such interpretive drift[2] in digital government reforms is common in periods of administrative transformation (Mergel et al., 2019; Gil-Garcia et al., 2018; Janssen & Estevez, 2013; Pollitt & Hupe, 2011; Cordella & Paletti, 2019; Margetts & Dunleavy, 2013; OECD, 2020).

Without clear conceptual boundaries, several risks emerge: (a) misaligned policy expectations, where technological sophistication alone is assumed to deliver proactivity, (b) ineffective governance prioritization, with resources flowing toward high-tech solutions while simpler, incremental proactive measures remain underdeveloped, (c) fragmented evaluation and comparability, as ambiguous definitions impede cross-agency and cross-national learning, maturity assessments, and evidence-based policy design. In short, clarifying proactivity is essential to ensure that ambitions for human-centric, anticipatory services translate into consistent, implementable, and measurable public service innovations. Importantly, conceptual clarity also underpins trust and legitimacy as citizens need to understand *when and why governments act on their behalf*, especially when services are automatically triggered without an explicit request from the citizen.

To address this conceptual challenge, the study investigates how the idea of proactive public services is interpreted and operationalized within administrative practice. Specifically, it asks: *How is the concept of proactivity interpreted and operationalized within EU public administrations, and what governance consequences emerge from divergent interpretations of proactive public services?*

To answer this question, we conducted 20 semi-structured interviews with 21 public sector practitioners from 12 EU Member States, exploring their conceptual understanding of proactivity, examples of proactive service initiatives, governance, organizational and legal considerations, and perspectives on the future evolution of PPS. The interviews were complemented by two expert workshops used for validation and triangulation. By analysing how practitioners interpret and operationalize proactivity across diverse institutional contexts, including variations within individual countries, this study contributes to digital government research in three ways. First, it introduces the concept of the **proactivity interpretation gap**, describing how policy ambitions for proactive government are translated into administrative practice through existing technological and organizational frames. Second, it provides empirical evidence on how practitioners across EU public administrations understand and classify proactive public services in practice, revealing substantial variation in interpretations of the concept. Third, it demonstrates that conceptual ambiguity generates divergent implementation trajectories, leading both to the under-recognition of existing proactive practices and to the over-classification of digitized services as proactive. Building on these findings, we argue that proactivity should be understood primarily as a **service initiation logic**, in which public authorities anticipate needs or eligibility and initiate service delivery on behalf of citizens or businesses. Proactivity therefore concerns who initiates the service interaction rather than the technology, delivery channel, or level of automation used. Clarifying this distinction is essential for enabling more consistent evaluation of proactive initiatives, supporting cross-jurisdictional learning, and strengthening evidence-based policymaking.

[2] We use interpretive drift not to denote temporal change from a single original definition, but to describe the gradual expansion of meanings attached to PPS across policy and administrative contexts.

By grounding the analysis in governance, institutional interpretation, and conceptual clarity, the paper advances a more rigorous analytical foundation for proactive service research and practice in EU digital government.

The study forms part of a broader European Commission Joint Research Centre (JRC) study on proactive public services in the EU, reported in Nikiforova et al. (2026), which examined readiness, maturity, implementation pathways, and governance considerations across Member States. The present paper focuses specifically on the conceptual interpretation of proactivity and the governance consequences of conceptual ambiguity.

2 Conceptual Background: What is Proactivity?

2.1 Proactivity in Literature

The concept of PPS has gained increasing attention in both policy discourse and academic research on digital government. In its simplest formulation, PPS refers to public services initiated by public authorities without a prior request from citizens or businesses (Bharosa et al., 2021; Linders et al., 2018; Lindgren & Scholta, 2023). Rather than requiring users to navigate administrative procedures and submit formal requests, proactive service provision relies on administrative data and institutional knowledge to anticipate eligibility or obligations and trigger service delivery or service-related actions. Proactive services are frequently associated with broader transformations in digital government. For example, research on "*no-stop government*" envisions a model in which services are delivered automatically and seamlessly without explicit user interaction, enabled by integrated data infrastructures and advanced analytics (Scholta & Lindgren, 2019). Similarly, the digital government transformation literature highlights a shift from digitizing existing services towards redesigning governance models around data integration, interoperability, and user needs rather than institutional structures (Bharosa et al., 2021; Janssen & Estevez, 2013; Janowski, 2015; Mergel et al., 2019). Within these perspectives, proactivity is often positioned as a progression toward increasingly automated and anticipatory service provision.

However, the literature reveals considerable variation in how proactivity is conceptualized and operationalized. A central source of ambiguity lies in its overlap with related concepts. *Digitization* does not imply proactivity, as online services may still require user initiation. *Automation*, while often enabling proactive services, may operate within reactive processes if triggered by user requests (Lindgren & Scholta, 2023). Similarly, *personalization* enhances user experience but does not inherently involve authority-initiated service delivery (Bertot et al., 2016). These distinctions suggest that proactivity cannot be reduced to technological sophistication or user interface design. Rather than focusing on how services are delivered, proactivity concerns *who initiates the service interaction*. Proactive public services are thus characterized by authority-initiated service delivery, where government actors assume responsibility for triggering services on behalf of citizens or businesses, making proactivity less a technical specification than a governance logic, one that, as the following section discusses, has proved vulnerable to interpretive drift as it diffuses across administrative contexts.

This perspective aligns with broader discussions on data-driven and anticipatory governance, where public administrations use data infrastructures and analytics to detect needs and intervene earlier in administrative processes (Desouza & Jacob, 2017; Janssen et al., 2017; Valle-Cruz et al., 2020; Guston, 2014). However, despite these developments, the literature remains fragmented. Existing studies have explored taxonomies of proactive services (Pawlowski & Scholta, 2023), levels of proactivity (Bharosa et al., 2021), and the role of automation in anticipatory service delivery (Lindgren & Scholta, 2023). Yet these approaches often focus on specific technological or organizational dimensions rather than offering a unified conceptual foundation for proactivity as a governance paradigm.

While some prior research has conceptually distinguished proactive service delivery from related phenomena such as digitization, automation, and personalization (Bertot et al., 2016; Bharosa et al., 2021; Lindgren & Scholta, 2023), these distinctions remain fragmented and are not consistently operationalized across policy and administrative contexts.

2.2 Interpretive Drift and Its Governance Consequences

Interpretive drift is a common phenomenon in emerging governance and innovation domains. As new reform ideas gain prominence, they are often adopted across diverse institutional contexts before their analytical boundaries are fully stabilized. Different actors may therefore attach varying meanings to the same concept depending on organizational roles, technological capabilities, and policy priorities. In digital government research, concepts such as e-government, digital transformation, and platform government have exhibited similar patterns of expansion and reinterpretation (Pollitt & Hupe, 2011; Margetts & Dunleavy, 2013; Gil-Garcia et al., 2018; Mergel et al., 2019).

PPS illustrate this dynamic. While widely referenced in policy frameworks, the concept is used to describe a broad range of practices, including automated service delivery, predictive analytics, personalized services, and life-event-based integration. This diversity reflects the experimental nature of digital government innovation, but it also risks obscuring what proactivity requires in terms of service logic and governance arrangements. Interpretive drift has tangible governance consequences. If digitized services are labelled as proactive, administrations may appear to achieve reform objectives without transforming service logic. Conversely, if proactivity is equated exclusively with fully automated or AI-driven systems, simpler forms of authority-initiated service delivery may be overlooked. In both cases, ambiguity undermines comparability, measurement, and policy learning across jurisdictions, weakening the analytical value of the concept itself.

While prior research has examined the technological enablers, typologies, maturity levels, and potential benefits of PPS, comparatively little attention has been paid to how the concept itself is understood and operationalized within public administrations. Existing studies largely define proactivity normatively or conceptually, while empirical evidence on how practitioners interpret the concept in day-to-day administrative settings remains limited. In particular, no study has systematically examined how practitioners across multiple EU jurisdictions interpret PPS in practice or explored the governance consequences of divergent interpretations. As a result, it remains unclear whether administrations share a common understanding of what constitutes a proactive service and how conceptual variation influences implementation, evaluation, and policy priorities. This study addresses this gap by empirically examining how proactivity is interpreted across EU public administrations and by analysing the governance consequences that emerge from conceptual ambiguity.

3 Research Design and Methodology

To investigate how PPS are understood and operationalized in practice, this study adopts a qualitative research design based on semi-structured interviews with practitioners involved in digital public service design, policy development, and implementation across the EU. A qualitative approach is particularly suitable for examining emerging governance concepts characterized by interpretive flexibility and institutional experimentation, as it enables researchers to capture how policy actors understand, interpret, and apply reform concepts within their organizational and institutional contexts (Merriam, 2009).

The study was conducted in two stages. First, the interview protocol was piloted with academic experts specializing in PPS to refine the research instrument. Second, the revised protocol was applied in interviews with public sector practitioners across the EU, which constitute the primary analytical dataset of this study.

3.1 Pilot Phase with Academic Experts

The interview protocol explored several thematic areas related to proactive public services, including (a) conceptual understandings of proactivity in public services, (b) examples of proactive service initiatives, (c) enabling conditions and barriers to implementation, (d) governance, organizational, and legal considerations, (e) perspectives on the future evolution of proactive public services.

To ensure conceptual clarity, topical relevance, and practical applicability, the interview protocol was pretested with four academic experts specializing in PPS, whose experience ranged from 11 to 40 years in digital government research. These exploratory interviews followed the practitioner protocol but included additional open-ended questions aimed at probing conceptual challenges, cross-national differences, and potential future developments of proactive public services. Participants were also asked to comment on the structure and clarity of the interview guide.

The pilot interviews were used exclusively for instrument refinement and are not included in the analytical sample reported in this paper. Feedback from this pilot stage informed several refinements to the protocol, including the rephrasing and reordering of questions, the consolidation of overlapping themes, and the removal of items considered too context-specific or conceptually ambiguous, thereby ensuring stronger alignment between the protocol and the realities of PPS research and practice.

3.2 Main Data Collection

The finalized protocol was then applied in interviews with public sector practitioners across the EU. Participants were selected using purposive sampling to ensure (a) subject-matter expertise in digital public services, (b) representation of different institutional roles, (c) geographical diversity across EU Member States and administrative traditions.

The study aimed to obtain perspectives from a wide range of administrative contexts, including national ministries, digital government agencies, innovation labs, and regional administrations. While the study sought representation from all EU Member States, 21 practitioners from 20 institutions across 12 EU Member States accepted the invitation and participated in 20 interviews. The sample reflects a balanced mix in terms of country, level of government, expertise, and gender (Table 1), and includes experts working at national, regional, and multi-level governance structures, reflecting the institutional diversity of digital government implementation in Europe.

The 20 interviews were conducted remotely via Microsoft Teams between July and December 2025 and lasted between 50 and 84 min (average: 66 min). Following informed consent, interviews were recorded and transcribed verbatim.

Table 1. Interview participants' general profiles – public sector practitioners.

Country	Organization / entity	Governmental level	Code	Interview duration
Austria	Federal government administration	National (operates also regionally)	I1	55 min
Denmark	National tax administration	National	I2	65 min
Estonia	Central government ministries	National	I3, I4, I5	62 min, 56 min, 79 min
Germany	Digital innovation hub / government digitalization bodies	Regional / state / national	I6, I7, I20	78 min, 58 min, 59 min
Greece	Regional administration units	Regional	I8, I9	83 min, 50 min
Hungary	National digital government agency	National	I10, I11	79 min
Netherlands	Ministry / public research organization	National	I12, I21	59 min, 57 min
Poland	Government IT centre	National	I13	66 min
Portugal	Public sector innovation lab	National	I14	58 min
Spain	Digital administration consortium / EU representation	National / Regional	I15, I16	62 min, 54 min
Sweden	Digital government agency	Regional	I17	84 min
Belgium	Digital government support organizations	Regional / federal	I18, I19	55 min, 63 min

I10 and I11 participated jointly in one interview.

3.3 Data Analysis

The interview transcripts were subsequently analysed using qualitative thematic analysis (Braun & Clarke, 2012). The analysis followed a primarily inductive approach, allowing categories to emerge from the interview data through iterative coding and comparison across transcripts. At the same time, concepts identified in prior digital government research, including digitization, automation, and personalization, served as analytical anchors that informed interpretation without imposing predetermined categories.

The coding process focused on identifying patterns in how respondents (a) defined and conceptualized proactivity, (b) distinguished proactive services from related concepts such as automation, digitization, and personalization, (c) described governance and implementation challenges, and (d) reflected on the future development and transformation of public services towards proactive models within their organizations and broader administrative ecosystems. Codes were subsequently grouped into higher-order themes capturing recurring patterns across administrative contexts.

Thematic analysis was conducted iteratively, allowing themes to be refined through repeated comparison across interviews while remaining grounded in the empirical material. This approach enabled the study to capture both current interpretations of proactive public services and emerging expectations regarding their future evolution in EU public administrations (Braun & Clarke, 2012). Two expert workshops involving practitioners and researchers working on proactive public services were conducted following the interview phase. The workshops were not treated as a primary data source and were therefore not formally coded. Instead, they were used to validate and contextualize emerging interpretations from the interviews, discuss areas of convergence and divergence, and reflect on possible future developments of proactive public services. Together with the literature analysis, they provided a form of analytical validation, strengthening the credibility and transferability of the interpretations.

4 Results: Proactivity as a Floating Signifier in Digital Government

The analysis of interview data reveals that PPS remain conceptually unstable in administrative practice. While the concept is widely referenced in policy discourse, practitioners interpret proactivity in diverse and sometimes contradictory ways. As such, proactivity functions less as a stable administrative concept than as an interpretive category through which practitioners make sense of digital service innovation.

Across interviews, respondents frequently associated proactivity with technological characteristics such as *digitization*, *automation*, or *service personalization* rather than with the underlying service logic of authority-initiated service delivery. This diversity of interpretations suggests that proactivity currently functions as a **floating signifier in digital government** - a concept that symbolizes innovation but lacks a shared operational meaning across administrative contexts.

Five recurring themes emerged inductively from the analysis: (1) conceptual confusion between proactivity and related digital government concepts; (2) systematic under-recognition and over-classification of PPS; (3) the equation of automation with proactivity; (4) the channel-agnostic character of proactive services; and (5) governance challenges associated with consent, trust, and institutional legitimacy. These themes reveal that conceptual ambiguity operates not only at the level of definition, but also through classification practices, technological assumptions, and governance interpretations (Table 2).

Table 2. Empirical themes identified in the interviews.

Theme	Description	Illustrative examples
Conceptual ambiguity	frequent conflation of proactivity with digitization, automation, or personalization	Online portals or personalized dashboards described as "proactive"
Misclassification of proactive services	both under-recognition of existing authority-initiated services and over-classification of digitized services as proactive	Eligibility notifications, pre-filled forms, digital service catalogues
Automation as proxy for proactivity	proactivity often equated with full automation or "invisible government"	Automated tax systems seen as an archetype
Channel-agnostic proactivity	PPS exist independently of digital channels	Paper-based notifications, scheduled appointments
Governance and legitimacy challenges	issues related to consent, trust, data governance, and institutional legitimacy; includes variation in opt-out expectations and service types	Opt-out debates; "surveillance state" concerns; differences across duties, entitlements, discretionary services

4.1 Proactivity as a Contested Concept in Practice

Across interviews, a significant share of respondents demonstrated uncertainty in distinguishing proactivity from closely related concepts, particularly digitization, automation, and personalization.

Digitized services were frequently described as proactive simply because they were available *online* or *integrated with administrative data.* For instance, one respondent equated proactive public services with digital self-service solutions:

"With regards to proactive public services for our agency, it's digital self-service solutions" (I2; I3 expressed similar views). In other cases, respondents associated proactivity primarily with *advanced automation.* However, when discussing concrete service examples, these interpretations often diverged from the analytical definition of PPS as authority-initiated service delivery. For example, one respondent explained PPS as digital services that guide users and trigger automated processes: "*Something they can click on…it triggers some automatic task, or at least semi-automatic. So, citizens don't have to figure something out from scratch*" (I2). One respondent cited a recommender system, suggesting services for which citizens are eligible, as an example of proactive service delivery (I5). This interpretation reflects a view of proactivity grounded in user interaction rather than service initiation.

Overall, the results indicate that in practice technological features, such as automation, interaction design, or anticipation, often serve as proxies for conceptual understanding. As a result, proactivity is often interpreted through the technological lens of digital transformation rather than through the service logic that defines it. This leads to inconsistent classification of services across administrations and complicates cross-country and even within-country comparisons of proactive government initiatives.

4.2 Under-Recognition and Over-Classification of Proactive Services

The interviews revealed two opposing but closely related classification patterns. The first pattern concerns the **systematic under-recognition** of existing proactive practices. Eight respondents stated that their organizations *did not yet provide proactive public services,* yet subsequently described examples such as (a) proactive eligibility notifications, (b) pre-filled administrative forms, (c) automated reminders for legal obligations, (d) scheduled appointments triggered by administrative data. These services correspond to moderate forms of proactivity, in which the administration initiates interaction while still requiring citizen confirmation. However, several respondents dismissed these practices as "*not proactive enough*" because they did not operate invisibly or fully automatically in the background. This finding suggests that prevailing narratives of "**no-stop government**" or "**invisible government**" shape practitioners' expectations of what constitutes true proactivity. While such visions represent an important future trajectory for digital government, their dominance in policy discourse may inadvertently obscure incremental forms of proactivity already implemented in many administrations.

Conversely, five respondents **over-classified digitized services** as proactive even when service recipients were still required to initiate the process. Examples included (a) online application portals, (b) personalized service dashboards, (c) digital service catalogues with tailored recommendations. In these cases, digitization or interface personalization was interpreted as evidence of proactivity, even though the underlying service logic remained reactive.

Importantly, this pattern also highlights the **channel-agnostic nature of PPS**. Although contemporary discussions frequently associate proactivity with digital infrastructures, respondents highlighted several examples delivered through **non-digital or hybrid channels**, including (a) mailed eligibility notifications, (b) proactive outreach by social services, (c) pre-scheduled administrative appointments, (d) targeted information campaigns triggered by administrative records. These examples illustrate that **digitization enables scale and efficiency but is not a defining condition of proactivity**. Public administrations have historically implemented proactive practices even in paper-based administrative environments. Nevertheless, interviewees widely agreed that large-scale, cross-agency proactive services increasingly depend on digital infrastructures, particularly where automated eligibility checks or real-time data exchange are required.

4.3 Automation as a Proxy for Proactivity

A third recurring pattern concerned the equation of proactivity with full automation. Five interviewees defined PPS as services that operate *fully automatically*, without requiring any form of service recipient interaction or confirmation. Under this interpretation, services requiring confirmation, even when initiated by authorities, were considered insufficiently proactive. For instance, when discussing tax services, one respondent noted: "*It's very much automated... but then you have to validate it and maybe correct what is put there*" *(I1)*. Such examples illustrate that many proactive services operate through **hybrid models**, combining automated data processing with human confirmation.

However, the dominance of automation-centric interpretations risks narrowing the conceptual scope of PPS and overlooking incremental forms of proactivity that already exist in practice. These findings reinforce the analytical distinction between **proactivity as service logic and automation as enabling technology**.

Looking ahead, many participants anticipated growing integration of AI and automation in PPS, particularly for real-time eligibility assessments and predictive notifications. However, they also raised significant concerns about institutional readiness, emphasizing that AI adoption must remain coupled with strong oversight, transparency, and consent mechanisms.

4.4 Consent, Control, and the Role of Opt-Out Mechanisms

PPS raise critical questions regarding **consent, autonomy, and democratic legitimacy**, as administrations initiate services without explicit requests from citizens or businesses.

Interviewees emphasized that proactive government action may require safeguards such as **confirmation steps, transparency mechanisms, or opt-out options**. At the same time, views diverged significantly regarding when such mechanisms are appropriate.

For services related to **statutory duties**, such as tax registration or mandatory reporting, respondents *generally opposed opt-out mechanisms*. In these cases, legal obligations exist independently of service delivery mechanisms. For **entitlement-based services**, such as pensions or child benefits, *views were more mixed*. Some practitioners supported opt-out to preserve user autonomy, while others argued that automatic service delivery can reduce non-take-up and improve equality. For **discretionary or data-driven services**, respondents broadly supported *stronger safeguards, including confirmation steps, opt-out mechanisms, or human oversight*.

Concerns about potential **"surveillance state" dynamics** emerged particularly in discussions of highly personalized or data-driven services. Interviewees emphasized that such services require transparency, explainability, and human oversight. Table 3 synthesizes interview positions across different categories of proactive public services.

Importantly, the interviews revealed that the acceptability of PPS varies significantly across national contexts. **Cultural attitudes** toward state intervention, **levels of institutional trust**, and **legal traditions** shape how authority-initiated services are perceived. This suggests that **proactive governance models cannot be implemented uniformly across jurisdictions**, even within the European administrative space. Instead, administrations appear to adopt differentiated models depending on the nature of the legal obligation, the degree of data sensitivity, and the level of discretion involved.

Table 3. Service categories and their implications for opt-out mechanisms.

Service category	Typical examples	Dominant positions	Opt-out implications	Key considerations
Duties / obligations	Tax registration, mandatory reporting, compulsory social security contributions	Strong opposition to opt-out	Opt-out generally inappropriate	Legal obligation exists independently of service delivery; opt-out may be meaningless or misleading
Rights / entitlements	Child benefits, pensions, allowances, subsidies	Mixed views; contested	Opt-out often expected, but not universal	In some legal systems, automatic delivery ensures equality and prevents non-take-up; user agency may shift from accepting the benefit to deciding whether to use it

(continued)

Table 3. (*continued*)

Service category	Typical examples	Dominant positions	Opt-out implications	Key considerations
Discretionary or conditional services	Targeted support, social assistance, vulnerability-based interventions	Strong support for opt-out	Opt-out and confirmation strongly recommended	Higher trust, legitimacy, and ethical risks; discretion and profiling increase need for user control
Highly personalized or data-driven PPS	Life-event services using cross-domain data, AI-supported targeting	Broad consensus on safeguards	Opt-out or human intervention essential	GDPR and AI Act requirements; heightened expectations for transparency, explainability, and reversibility
Moderately proactive services	Pre-filled forms, proactive notifications, reminders	Broad acceptance	Soft opt-out or confirmation preferred	Maintains efficiency while preserving autonomy

5 Conceptual Synthesis: The Proactivity Interpretation Gap

Synthesizing the findings reveals a persistent **gap between policy ambitions for PPS and administrative interpretations of the concept**. When the concept of PPS lacks a shared operational definition, public administrations tend to interpret proactivity through **existing technological or organizational frames**, such as digitization, automation, or personalization.

We refer to this phenomenon as the ***proactivity interpretation gap*** (Fig. 1). The gap illustrates how policy narratives of anticipatory or AI-enabled government are translated into practice through existing administrative frames, leading to divergent implementation pathways and inconsistent assessments of PPS maturity.

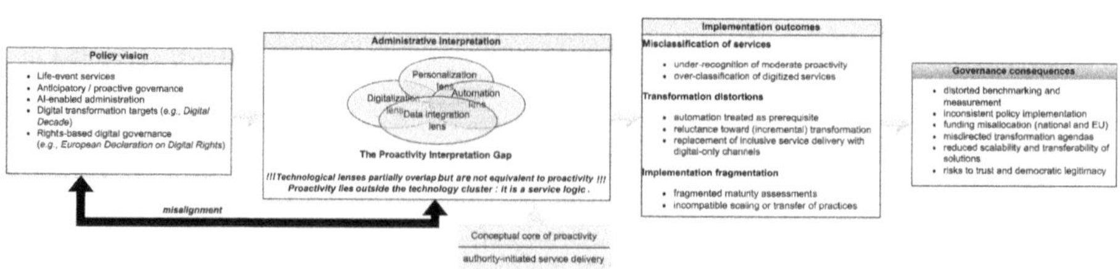

Fig. 1. Proactivity Interpretation Gap.

At the **policy level**, proactivity is typically associated with transformative narratives such as *life-event services*, *anticipatory governance*, *AI-enabled administration*, and broader *digital transformation agendas* embedded in European policy frameworks. However, the interview evidence suggests that **public administrations** frequently interpret proactivity through more familiar technological categories, particularly *digitization*, *automation*, *personalization*, and *data integration*. While these lenses are conceptually overlapping, they are also analytically distinct.

This interpretive shift, however, produces a range of **implementation outcomes**. Administrations may under-*recognize existing moderate forms of proactivity*, *over-classify digitized services as proactive*, or *assume that full automation is a necessary prerequisite*. In addition, divergent interpretations lead to *fragmented maturity assessments* and *limit the scalability or transferability* of PPS across institutional contexts. These dynamics generate broader **governance consequences**. Conceptual ambiguity can *distort benchmarking and policy evaluation*, *complicate cross-country comparisons*, and *influence funding allocation* decisions. It may also contribute to *misdirected transformation agendas,* in which technologically visible solutions receive priority over simpler authority-initiated service models that could deliver immediate public value. Ultimately, the proactivity interpretation gap illustrates *how conceptual ambiguity can shape innovation trajectories in digital government, affecting not only service design but also administrative coordination, policy implementation, and citizen trust.*

The following discussion develops the implications of these findings for digital government research and practice.

6 Discussion

The findings suggest that the primary challenge of proactive public services is not technological feasibility but conceptual stabilization. PPS should be understood primarily as a governance logic of service initiation—one that reallocates responsibility for initiating services from citizens or businesses to the state—rather than as a technological feature of digital government.

While the literature commonly defines proactivity as authority-initiated service delivery, practitioners frequently associate the concept with technological characteristics such as digitization, automation, or interface personalization. This divergence suggests that proactivity currently functions less as a stable analytical category and more as a **contested governance concept** whose meaning evolves alongside digital transformation, acquiring **multiple operational meanings as it diffuses across administrative contexts** (Pollitt & Hupe, 2011; Gil-Garcia et al., 2018; Mergel et al., 2019).

Conceptual ambiguity has important implications for the governance of digital transformation. **When proactivity lacks a shared operational definition, public administrations interpret it through existing institutional and technological frames**. As the results demonstrate, this leads to over-classification of digitized services as proactive, under-recognition of moderate proactive practices, and the conflation of automation with proactivity itself. These patterns directly impede cross-country comparability and consistent scaling of PPS.

Based on the empirical findings and the conceptual analysis, we understand proactive public services as *services in which public authorities anticipate eligibility or need and initiate service delivery or service-related action on behalf of citizens or businesses without requiring a prior request from the recipient.*

This definition highlights several essential characteristics often overlooked or misunderstood by public administrations, namely, authority-initiated service delivery; coverage of both citizens and businesses; channel-agnostic implementation; and a clear distinction from digitization, automation, and personalization. Conceptualizing proactivity as a **governance logic** rather than a technological feature helps clarify its analytical boundaries, supports more consistent cross-country benchmarking, and provides a firmer foundation for empirical research on PPS maturity.

6.1 Governance Tensions in Proactive Public Services

While the primary contribution of this study concerns conceptual ambiguity and the proactivity interpretation gap, the interviews also revealed several recurring **governance tensions** associated with proactive service design and implementation. These tensions do not represent contradictions that can be fully resolved but rather competing objectives that administrations must continuously balance.

Tension 1: Equity - Justification and Risk. Proactive services are often justified as mechanisms for improving equity by reducing non-take-up of public benefits. However, targeting mechanisms based on administrative data may simultaneously reproduce or amplify existing inequalities if data coverage is incomplete or biased.

Tension 2: Trust - Motivator and Constraint. Proactive services are often perceived as potential facilitators of trust. However, they also require a high level of institutional trust, as governments act on behalf of citizens or businesses without explicit requests. Moreover, the same mechanisms may also undermine trust if they are perceived as intrusive or as forms of excessive state surveillance.

Tension 3: Data and Digital Infrastructure - Enabler and Exclusion Mechanism. While integrated administrative data and digital channels are prerequisites for enabling PPS at scale, particularly those relying on eligibility detection or cross-agency coordination, individuals who are less visible in administrative datasets or lack digital access or capabilities may be excluded.

Tension 4: Automation – Enabler and Over-Standardization Risk. Automation allows PPS to operate at scale and with greater efficiency, particularly by streamlining routine processes. However, excessive reliance on automated workflows can obscure moderate forms of proactive service, reduce discretionary flexibility, and risk over-standardization, potentially neglecting context-specific needs of users.

Tension 5: AI - Enabler and Risk Amplifier. AI and advanced analytics may enhance the targeting and efficiency of proactive services. At the same time, algorithmic decision-making introduces new risks related to bias, transparency, and accountability.

These reflect a broader **digitization–inclusion dilemma in digital government**, where technological progress may simultaneously expand and restrict access to public services (Helbig et al., 2009; Cordella & Paletti, 2018; Weigl et al., 2024).

6.2 Implications for Research and Practice

For digital government research, the study highlights the importance of distinguishing between **digital maturity and proactive service maturity**. Indicators such as service digitization, automation, or platform integration do not necessarily capture whether services are initiated by administrations or by users. Proactivity is a distinct institutional logic of service delivery, not a technological attribute of digital services. Future research may therefore benefit from developing analytical frameworks capable of measuring degrees of proactivity in public service delivery.

The findings point to the risks associated with **innovation rhetoric in digital governance**. Concepts such as proactive services, anticipatory governance, or AI-enabled administration often gain prominence in policy discourse before their operational meaning stabilizes. While such concepts can mobilize reform efforts, insufficient definitional clarity may lead to inconsistent implementation and limit the comparability of empirical studies. Continued research is therefore needed to refine conceptual frameworks and identify measurable characteristics of proactive service delivery.

For policymakers and practitioners, the results highlight the importance of **establishing a shared operational understanding of PPS**. Without conceptual clarity, administrations may classify services inconsistently, complicating benchmarking and policy evaluation. Practitioners consistently emphasized the importance of gradual, context-sensitive expansion of proactivity, carefully aligned with trust, legitimacy, and citizen acceptance. Practical guidance instruments, such as reference architectures, design templates, and curated case repositories, were identified as key enablers for supporting administrations at different levels of PPS maturity.

Policymakers could **avoid equating proactivity exclusively with advanced technologies such as artificial intelligence**. Although AI and data analytics can enable proactive services, many forms of proactivity rely on simpler mechanisms such as administrative data sharing, automated notifications, or pre-filled applications. Recognizing these incremental forms of proactivity may allow administrations to expand proactive service delivery without waiting for complex technological solutions.

This study has several limitations. First, although the sample covers 12 EU Member States, it does not represent all administrative contexts within the EU. Second, the findings reflect practitioner perceptions rather than direct observation of PPS implementation. Third, workshop insights were used primarily for contextualization and validation rather than systematic data collection. Future studies could complement interview-based evidence with comparative case studies and quantitative assessments of proactive service maturity.

7 Conclusion

This study examined how proactive public services are interpreted and operationalized across European public administrations. While proactive services are increasingly promoted as a cornerstone of user-centred digital government, the findings demonstrate that the concept remains interpretively unstable in practice. This instability is not merely semantic: it carries concrete governance consequences, shaping how services are designed, evaluated, and compared across jurisdictions.

The empirical evidence demonstrates that proactivity functions as a floating signifier in EU public administrations. The proactivity interpretation gap, as introduced and illustrated here, offers a conceptual tool for understanding how reform ambitions are filtered through existing technological and institutional frames, producing divergent and often inconsistent implementation trajectories. This perspective distinguishes proactivity from related but analytically distinct phenomena—digitization, automation, and personalization—and clarifies it as a governance logic of service initiation rather than a technological attribute.

The findings further suggest that progress toward proactive public services does not require fully automated or AI-driven solutions. Moderately proactive services, such as notifications, pre-filled forms, and authority-initiated triggers, represent immediately scalable steps that administrations can take without waiting for full technological maturity.

From a practical perspective, clearer conceptual foundations are essential for developing consistent policy frameworks, evaluation criteria, and maturity models for proactive public services. Structured approaches to assessing PPS readiness across legal, organizational, societal, and technological dimensions could support administrations in identifying implementation barriers and designing context-sensitive pathways toward proactive service delivery.

More broadly, proactive public services provide an important lens for understanding the evolving relationship between citizens, businesses, and the state in the context of digital transformation. As governments increasingly rely on data-driven decision-making and anticipatory governance mechanisms, ensuring that proactive services remain lawful, legitimate, transparent, and trusted will be critical for sustaining public trust and democratic accountability.

The findings also open several avenues for future research. First, comparative studies could further investigate how institutional, legal, and cultural contexts shape interpretations and implementation pathways of proactive public services across countries. Second, future work may explore how citizens and businesses perceive authority-initiated service delivery, particularly regarding issues of consent, transparency, and trust in data-driven governance. Third, further research is needed to develop and empirically validate maturity models or evaluation frameworks that distinguish between digitization, automation, personalization, and proactivity in public service delivery. Fourth, future work could examine how institutionalized knowledge-sharing mechanisms accelerate PPS maturity across administrations at different readiness levels. Addressing these questions would advance a more rigorous and empirically grounded understanding of PPS as an emerging institutional governance practice across the EU.

Disclosure of Interests. The authors have no competing interests to declare that are relevant to the content of this article.

References

Bertot, J., Estevez, E., Janowski, T.: Universal and contextualized public services: digital public service innovation framework. Gov. Inf. Q. **33**(2), 211–222 (2016)

Bharosa, N., Oude Luttighuis, B., Spoelstra, F., Van Der Voort, H., Janssen, M.: Inclusion through proactive public services: findings from the Netherlands: classifying and designing proactivity through understanding service eligibility and delivery processes. In: Proceedings of the 22nd Annual International Conference on Digital Government Research, pp. 242–251 (2021)

Braun, V., Clarke, V.: Thematic analysis. In: Cooper, H., Camic, P.M., Long, D.L., Panter, A.T., Rindskopf, D., Sher, K.J. (eds.) APA Handbook of Research Methods in Psychology, vol. 2, pp. 57–71. American Psychological Association, Washington, DC (2012). https://doi.org/10.1037/13620-004

Cordella, A., Paletti, A.: ICTs and value creation in public sector: manufacturing logic vs service logic. Inf. Polity **23**(2), 125–141 (2018)

Cordella, A., Paletti, A.: Government as a platform, orchestration, and public value creation: the Italian case. Gov. Inf. Q. **36**(4), 101409 (2019). https://doi.org/10.1016/j.giq.2019.101409

Desouza, K.C., Jacob, B.: Big data in the public sector: lessons for practitioners and scholars. Adm. Soc. **49**(7), 1043–1064 (2017)

Gil-Garcia, J.R., Dawes, S.S., Pardo, T.A.: Digital government and public management research: finding the crossroads. Public Manag. Rev. **20**(5), 633–646 (2018)

Guston, D.H.: Understanding 'anticipatory governance.' Soc. Stud. Sci. **44**(2), 218–242 (2014)

Helbig, N., Gil-García, J.R., Ferro, E.: Understanding the complexity of electronic government: implications from the digital divide literature. Gov. Inf. Q. **26**(1), 89–97 (2009)

Janssen, M., Estevez, E.: Lean government and platform-based governance—doing more with less. Gov. Inf. Q. **30**, S1–S8 (2013)

Janssen, M., Van Der Voort, H., Wahyudi, A.: Factors influencing big data decision-making quality. J. Bus. Res. **70**, 338–345 (2017)

Janowski, T.: Digital government evolution: from transformation to contextualization. Gov. Inf. Q. **32**(3), 221–236 (2015)

Linders, D., Liao, C.Z.P., Wang, C.M.: Proactive e-Governance: flipping the service delivery model from pull to push in Taiwan. Gov. Inf. Q. **35**(4), S68–S76 (2018)

Lindgren, I., Scholta, H.: Untangling the relationship between public service automation and no-stop government. In: International Conference on Electronic Government, pp. 83–94. Springer Nature Switzerland, Cham (2023). https://doi.org/10.1007/978-3-031-41138-0_6

Margetts, H. and Dunleavy, P.: The second wave of digital-era governance: a quasi-paradigm for government on the web. Philos. Trans. R. Soc. A: Math. Phys. Eng. Sci. **371**(1987) (2013)

Mergel, I., Edelmann, N., Haug, N.: Defining digital transformation: results from expert interviews. Gov. Inf. Q. **36**(4), 101385 (2019)

Nikiforova, A., Bharosa, N., Draheim, D., Taveter, K.: PPPS'2023-proactive and personalised public services: searching for meaningful human control in algorithmic government. In: CEUR workshop proceedings, vol. 3449. CEUR-WS (2023)

Nikiforova, A., Rodriguez Müller, A.P., Tangi, L.: Proactive Public Services in the EU: Readiness, maturity, and pathways to implementation. Publications Office of the European Union, Luxembourg (2026). https://data.europa.eu/doi/10.2760/4554259, JRC146641

Nikiforova, A., Rodriguez Müller, A.P., Tangi, L., Martin-Bosch, J.: Proactive public services in the age of artificial intelligence: towards post-bureaucratic governance. In: International Conference on Electronic Government, pp. 395–413. Springer Nature Switzerland, Cham (2025). https://doi.org/10.1007/978-3-032-01589-1_25

OECD: The E-Leaders Handbook on the Governance of Digital Government. OECD Publishing (2020)

Pawlowski, C., Scholta, H.: A taxonomy for proactive public services. Gov. Inf. Q. **40**(1), 101780 (2023)

Pollitt, C., Hupe, P.: Talking about government: the role of magic concepts. Public Manag. Rev. **13**(5), 641–658 (2011)

Scholta, H., Lindgren, I.: The long and winding road of digital public services—one next step: proactivity. In: ICIS 2019 Proceedings, p. 7 (2019). https://aisel.aisnet.org/icis2019/digital_government/digital_government/7
Merriam, S.B.: Qualitative Research: A Guide to Design and Implementation. Jossey-Bass, San Francisco (2009)
Valle-Cruz, D., Criado, J.I., Sandoval-Almazán, R., Ruvalcaba-Gomez, E.A.: Assessing the public policy-cycle framework in the age of artificial intelligence: from agenda-setting to policy evaluation. Gov. Inf. Q. **37**(4), 101509 (2020)
Weigl, L., Roth, T., Amard, A., Zavolokina, L.: When public values and user-centricity in e-government collide–a systematic review. Gov. Inf. Q. **41**(3), 101956 (2024)

Author Index

Published by Springer Nature Switzerland 2027
G. Viale Pereira et al. (Eds.): EGOV 2026, LNCS 16933, pp. 449–450, 2027.
https://doi.org/10.1007/978-3-032-35747-2

GPSR Compliance
The European Union's (EU) General Product Safety Regulation (GPSR) is a set of rules that requires consumer products to be safe and our obligations to ensure this.

If you have any concerns about our products, you can contact us on

ProductSafety@springernature.com

In case Publisher is established outside the EU, the EU authorized representative is:

Springer Nature Customer Service Center GmbH
Europaplatz 3
69115 Heidelberg, Germany

www.ingramcontent.com/pod-product-compliance
Ingram Content Group UK Ltd.
Pitfield, Milton Keynes, MK11 3LW, UK
UKHW022110180926
475695UK00001B/81
9783032357465